A Century of Wrong and Injustice
Annotated and Illustrated

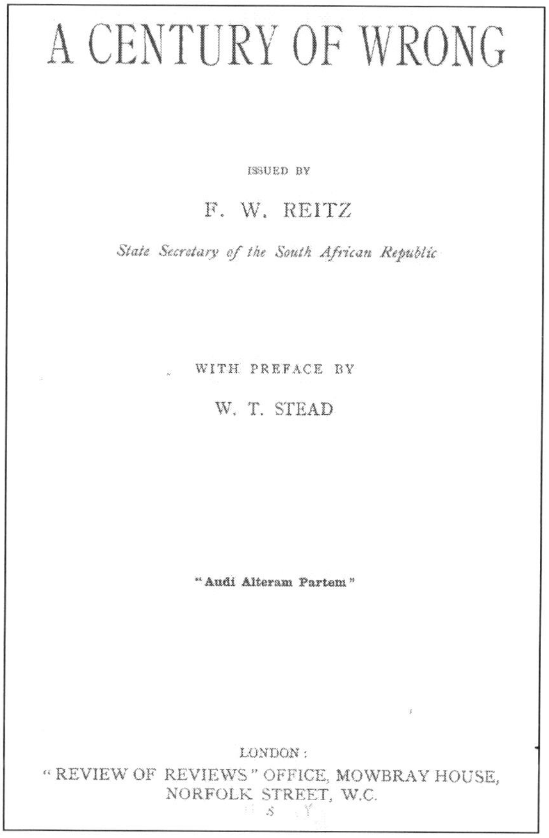
A CENTURY OF WRONG

ISSUED BY

F. W. REITZ

State Secretary of the South African Republic

WITH PREFACE BY

W. T. STEAD

"Audi Alteram Partem"

LONDON:
"REVIEW OF REVIEWS" OFFICE, MOWBRAY HOUSE,
NORFOLK STREET, W.C.

Issued By: Francis W. Reitz, State Secretary of the South African Republic

With Preface by: William Thomas Stead

"Audi Alteram Partem"[1]

Published by: "Review Of Reviews" London, Mowbray House, Norfolk Street, W.C. First published anonymously, in Dutch, under title: Een eeuw van onrecht. (A Century of Injustice)

Volume 9 of the series; The Last Horse War.

Series compiled, annotated, illustrated and expanded by Payton Fireman, JD.

ISBN: 978-1-7320124-7-9

Front Cover Photo Credits: Francis Reitz Circa 1890.[1] Jan Smuts Circa 1902.[2]

Back Cover Photo Credits: South African Railway System 1901.[3]

Title Page Photo Credit: [4]

[1] "Hear The Other Side."

[2] Please see the Bibliography for license links and other information regarding the material in this volume.

Contents

PF Preface

This work is a compilation of primarily four publications; 'A Century of Wrong,'[3] 'A Century of Injustice,'[4] 'The Story of the Boers,'[5] and 'The war in South Africa, its Cause & Conduct.'[6] Each of these originally published works included material that was duplicative of that in other volumes along with valuable original material.

This work contains only the original material assembled from each of the four publications. I've assembled the material in what I consider the most informative order. For the most part, the articles and tracts have been grouped together by topic rather than in three blocks of material devoted to each work. Each has been individually cited as to which of the three works it originated from. The Table of Contents provides the order of the material. I've also been forced to be more of an editor by excising out material that is not primary source or is simply commentary. The original works are accessible and can be referred to by those who want to refer to them.

I wish that I had been able to more fully integrate material with cross references. The disparate timelines, correspondence and despatches could be re-ordered to conform to one timeline but at the cost of breaking up each. I have erred on the side of keeping each, all of a piece.

History

A Century of Wrong, was published in the Review of Reviews with a preface by Mr. W. T. Stead dated January 1st, 1900.

In November of 1899 Cornelius Van Der Hoogt organized the publication of a synopsis of 'A Century of Wrong' for the American audience under the title of 'A Century of Injustice.'

Subsequently, in March of 1900, Mr. Van Der Hoogt published a second work titled 'The Story of the Boers;' with additional articles and government despatches.

By this point in the series I am assuming that the reader is familiar with many of the more prominent and famous individuals who are mentioned in the text. I am closing in on three years for this project and by now it is apparent that most individuals, even individuals that appear in passing, all have interesting journeys that can be followed with a little effort. Space limitations in this volume have required that I be more selective in my annotation and confine myself to those persons, usually minor characters who pique my interest rather than the shotgun approach in previous volumes where virtually everyone was researched. The same ease of research can also be applied to some of the arcane nomenclature and foreign language phrases that I may not have defined.

Sidenotes were used in the original text to describe the topic under discussion. I have simply bolded the text at the beginning of the paragraph rather than at the side. It makes for a lot of bold in the text but is less interrupting than identifying each instance as a 'Sidenote.' Original footnotes are enclosed in brackets [ ].

I'm not sure why some quotes are opened but then not closed but then continue with opening and sometimes closing quote marks in the next paragraph. It was so unedifying and confusing that in many cases where it is clear that the person or newspaper is the 'speaker' I have omitted them. In some cases it was so confusing I could not figure out where to close them at all.

These individuals believed in their government and its right to occupy its territory. They were willing to oppose the most powerful empire of the time to preserve their autonomy.

This tract, as dense and particular as it is, is their justification for their subsequent actions. I realize that some of this material is fairly arcane. The prose is dense and the arguments closely reasoned. I simply felt that it was important enough to put all of it together, as much as I could find, into one volume where it would be more easily accessible.

[3] Francis William Reitz, A century of wrong. Issued by F. W. Reitz, state secretary of the South African Republic. With pref. by W. T. Stead. 1900. Jan Smuts co-author. https://babel.hathitrust.org/cgi/pt?id=coo1.ark:/13960/t2d79wr7w&view=1up&seq=1&skin=2021

[4] Cornelius W. Van der Hoogt, A century of injustice; synopsis of a message to the people of South-Africa, sent by the government of the South-African republic. Baltimore Md. November 1899. https://babel.hathitrust.org/cgi/pt?id=wu.89100085885&seq=5

[5] The Story of the Boers, C. W. Van der Hoogt, March, 1900. Harper Ed. https://archive.org/details/storyboersnarra00whitgoog

[6] Doyle, Arthur Conan, 1859-1930 The war in South Africa, its cause & conduct; 1902 McClure, Phillips & Co. U. Cal. Copy: https://archive.org/details/warinsouthafrica00doylrich

The volume in total comprises ~217k words and by draconian measures to excise blank space it is still a manageable ~365 numbered pages. This does result in a somewhat disjointed transition from one topic to another. It is my opinion that the substance is more important than the layout.

By comparison London to Ladysmith, a jam-packed volume of 391 pages only contains 147k words. This is mostly to do with illustration which this volume is deficient in.

Maps

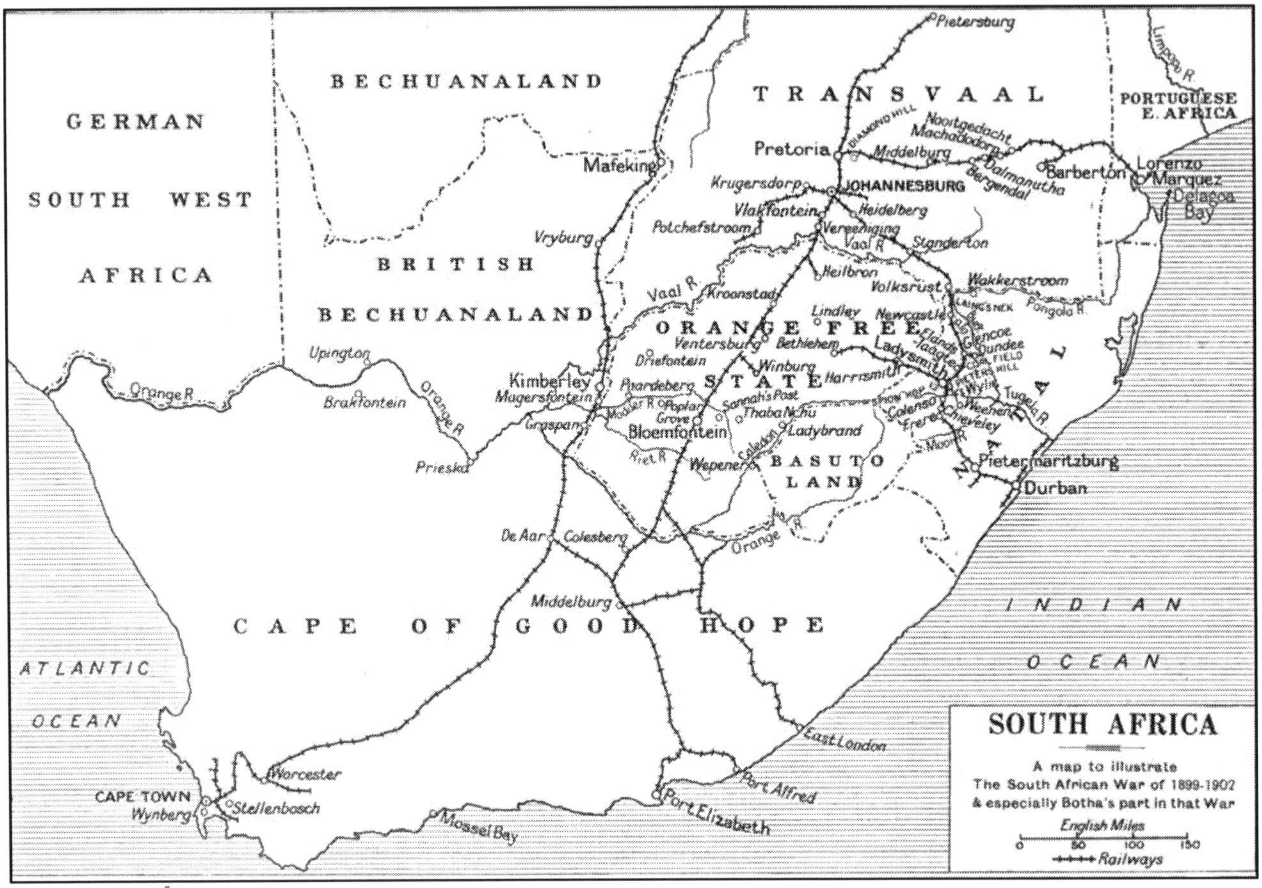

South Africa.[5]

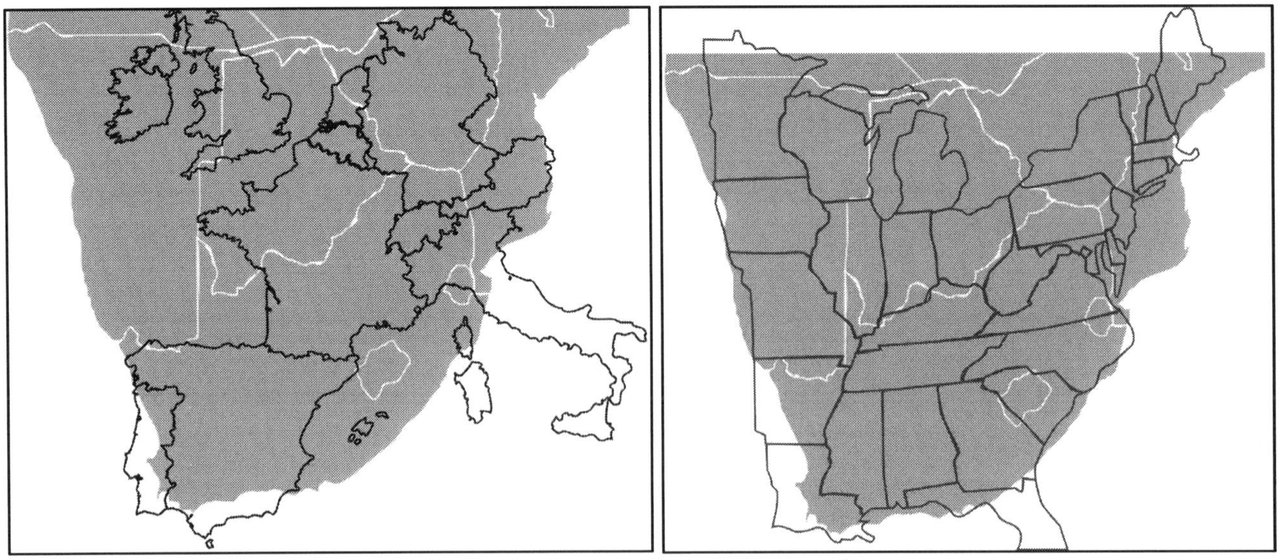

Relative size of Southern Africa compared to Europe and North America.[6]

South & Central Africa.[7]

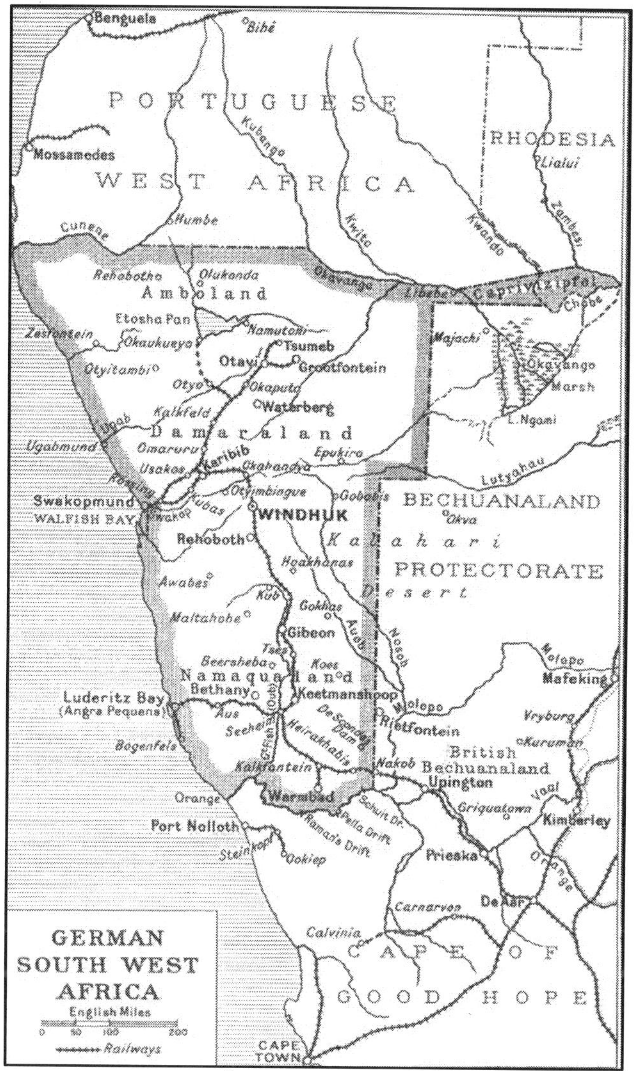

South West Africa.[8]

Colonies & Conflicts

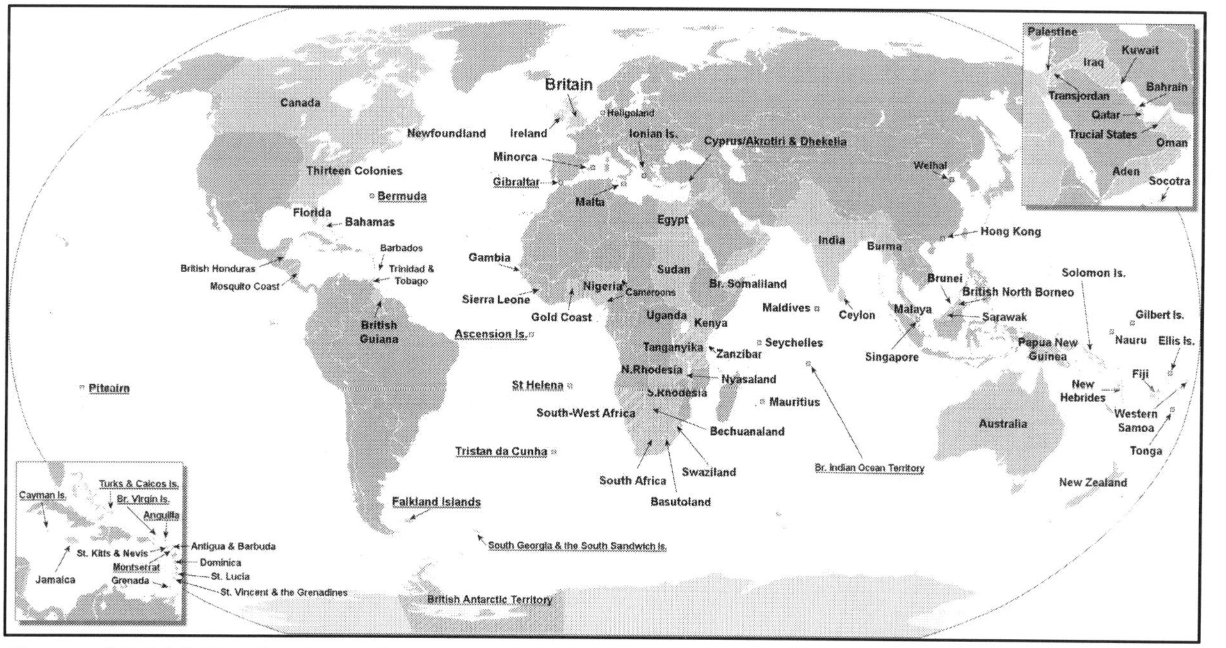

Extent of British Empire Over Time. Not all territories were under British sovereignty at the same time.[9]

Crown Colonies	From	Responsible Govt. Colonies	From	To	
The Bahamas	1718	Canadian Confederation		1973	Became an independent Commonwealth Realm.
Basutoland (Lesotho)	1884	United Province of Canada	1848	1964	Became British protectorate in 1964
Bermuda	1684	New Brunswick	1848	1981	Became British Dependent Territory in 1981.
British Bechuanaland	1885	Prince Edward Island	1851	1895	Became part of British Cape Colony in 1895.
British Guiana	1831	Newfoundland	1855	1966	Became independent as Guyana in 1966.
British Honduras (Belize)	1884			1981	Became independent (as Belize) in 1981.
Ceylon (Siri Lanka)	1815	Australia		1948	Became independent as Dominion of Ceylon in 1948.
Falkland Islands	1841	New South Wales	1856	1981	Became a British Dependent Territory in 1981.
Gambia	1888	Victoria	1855	1965	Became independent as The Gambia in 1965.
Gibraltar	1713	South Australia	1857	1981	Became British Dependent Territory in 1981.
Gold Coast (Ghana)	1821	Queensland	1859	1957	Became independent in 1957 as Ghana.
Hong Kong	1842	Western Australia	1890	1997	Reverted to China.
Jamaica	1655	New Zealand	1856	1962	Became independent in 1962 as Jamaica.
Malta	1813	Tasmania	1856	1964	Became independent in 1964 as the State of Malta.
Mauritius	1903			1968	Became independent as Mauritius in 1968.
St. Helena	1834	South Africa		1981	
Saint Christopher-Nevis	1882	Cape Colony	1872	1981	Became Independent in 1983.
Sierra Leone	1808	Natal	1893	1961	Became independent as Sierra Leone in 1961.
Malaya Strts. Settlements	1786	Transvaal	1906	1946	re-organised as the Federation of Malaya in 1948
Province of Nova Scotia	1848	Orange River	1907		
Australia Commonwealth	1901			1901	Became part of the Commonwealth of Australia in 1901.
New South Wales	1788			1901	Became part of the Commonwealth of Australia in 1901.
Queensland	1859			1901	Became part of the Commonwealth of Australia in 1901.
South Australia	1834			1901	Van Diemen's Land from to 1856; Joined f Australia in 1901.
Tasmania	1803			1901	Became part of the Commonwealth of Australia in 1901.
Victoria	1851			1901	Formerly Swan River Colony. Joined Australia in 1901.
Western Australia	1829				
United Province of Canada	1841			1867	Became part of Canada in 1867.
		Malta	1921		Malta (suspended from 1936 to 1947, and from 1959 to 1962)
		Southern Rhodesia	1923		Southern Rhodesia
		India	1947		India
		Pakistan	1947		Pakistan
		Israel	1948		Israel (independence from the British Mandate)

Adapted from article on Responsible Government.[7] Not included are the 13 American Colonies.

British Wars During Queen Victoria's Reign (1837–1901)

Queen Victoria's 64-year reign coincided with rapid imperial expansion. British forces engaged in over 230 conflicts, ranging from major wars against European powers to "little wars" and frontier expeditions in Asia and Africa. Below is a representative sampling, organized by scale and theatre.

The Queen, in 1860.[10]

The Empress during her Golden Jubilee, (1887).[11]

[7] https://en.wikipedia.org/wiki/Responsible_government

List of Wars Involving The United Kingdom.

Queen Victoria's 64-year reign (1837-1901) coincided with rapid imperial expansion. British forces engaged in over two hundred conflicts, large and small during her reign. Most resulting in British victories. Below is a representative sampling, organized by scale and theatre.[8]

Major Conflicts.[9]

Conflict	Years	Region / Opponent
First Opium War	1839–1842	Qing China
First Anglo-Afghan War	1839–1842	Durrani Afghanistan
First Anglo-Sikh War	1845–1846	Sikh Empire (Punjab)
Second Anglo-Sikh War	1848–1849	Sikh Empire (Punjab)
Second Opium War	1856–1860	Qing China
Crimean War	1853–1856	Russia (allied with France & Ottoman)
Indian Rebellion	1857–1858	Indian sepoys & princely states
Second Anglo-Afghan War	1878–1880	Emirate of Afghanistan
Zulu War	1879	Zulu Kingdom (Southern Africa)
Anglo-Egyptian War	1882	Urabi revolt in Egypt
Third Anglo-Burmese War	1885	Konbaung Burma
Mahdist War	1884–1899	Mahdist Sudan
Second Boer War	1899–1902	Boer republics (Transvaal & Orange Free)

Selected Colonial "Little Wars" and Expeditions.[10]

Abyssinian Expedition (1867–1868)—punitive campaign in Ethiopia
Second Asante War (1873–1874)—Ashanti Empire (modern Ghana)
Anglo-Transvaal War (First Boer War) (1880–1881)—Transvaal Republic uprising
Reconquest of the Sudan (1896–1898)—defeating the Mahdists to restore Anglo-Egyptian rule
Anglo-Persian War (1856–1857)—Persia's attempt on Afghanistan repulsed
Third Ashanti Expedition (1900)—Ashanti uprising quelled; Ghana became Crown Colony.

Frontier Campaigns on the Northwest Indian Frontier.[11]

Between 1868 and 1908 the British undertook dozens of border expeditions against tribal groups in today's Pakistan and Afghanistan. A few key examples:
Umbeyla Campaign (1863)
Hazara Expedition (1868)
Jowaki Expedition (1877–1878)
Miranzai Expedition (1891)
Tirah Campaign (1897–1898)

The Second Boer War was one of the last of her reign along with the Boxer Rebellion which was an international coalition.

[8] Microsoft Copilot Query and reply. July 2025: https://copilot.microsoft.com/chats/NPxRZGDu5jbSqJosUB6CL

[9] See List of wars involving the United Kingdom: https://en.wikipedia.org/wiki/List_of_wars_involving_the_United_Kingdom#

[10] Sources: Bond, Victorian Military Campaigns; Miller, Queen Victoria's Wars; The Highlanders' Museum. https://www.thehighlandersmuseum.com/?p=29363

[11] Oxford Bibliographies: https://www.oxfordbibliographies.com/abstract/document/obo-9780199791279/obo-9780199791279-0214.xml

President Kruger's Prediction[12]

"Instead of rejoicing you would do better to weep, for this gold will cause our country to be soaked in blood."
Paul Kruger.[13]

Biographical Summaries

Francis Reitz Summary

Before we begin the main text, I think it is worthwhile to survey the biographies of the two principal authors of the tract(s).

Francis William Reitz, 1890.[12]

Francis William Reitz (1844–1934) Was a South African lawyer, politician, statesman, publicist and poet; member of parliament of the Cape Colony; Chief Justice and fifth State President of the Orange Free State; State Secretary of the South African Republic at the time of the Second Boer War; and the first president of the Senate of the Union of South Africa.[14]

Reitz had a very diverse political and legal career that spanned more than forty years and played out in four different political entities: the Cape Colony, the Orange Free State, the South African Republic and the Union of South Africa. Reitz was trained as an attorney in Cape Town and London and started out as an attorney and diamond prospector before being appointed Chief Justice of the Orange Free State. Reitz played an important role in the modernisation of the judicial system and the state's administrative organisation in the Orange Free State. At the same time, he was also a prominent public figure and was involved in Afrikaans and Afrikaner cultural movements and cultural life as a whole.

Reitz was a popular figure because of his political activities and his openness. When State President Brand died suddenly in 1888, Reitz won the presidential election unopposed. After being re-elected in 1895 and making a trip to Europe, he became very ill and had to retire. In 1898, after recovering, he was appointed State Secretary of the South African Republic and became a leading political figure during the Anglo-Boer War. After the war, he voluntarily went into exile because he was unwilling to show allegiance to the British. Several years later, he returned to South Africa and opened another law firm in Pretoria. In the early 1900s he became involved in politics again and with the declaration of the Union of South Africa in 1910 he was elected the first President of the Senate.

Reitz was an important figure in the cultural life of the Afrikaner throughout his life, especially through his poems and other publications.

[12] A short invocation for help, blessing and guidance from God.

[13] Byron Farwell, The Great Anglo-Boer War. New York: Harper & Row, 1976. (page 21)

[14] Francis William Reitz - Wikipedia and Francis William Reitz - Wikisource, the free online library

Jan Smuts Summary

Jan Christian Smuts,[15] (24 May 1870–11 September 1950) was a South African statesman, military leader and philosopher. In addition to holding various military and cabinet posts, he served as prime minister of the Union of South Africa from 1919 to 1924 and 1939 to 1948.

He was educated at Victoria College, Stellenbosch before reading law at Christ's College, Cambridge on a scholarship. He was called to the bar at the Middle Temple in 1894 but returned home the following year. In the lead up to the Second Boer War, Smuts practised law in Pretoria, the capital of the South African Republic. He led the republic's delegation to the Bloemfontein Conference and served as an officer in a commando unit following the outbreak of war in 1899.

In 1902, he played a key role in negotiating the Treaty of Vereeniging, which ended the war and resulted in the annexation of the South African Republic and Orange Free State into the British Empire. He subsequently helped negotiate self-government for the Transvaal Colony, becoming a cabinet minister under Louis Botha.

Jan Smuts' college graduation portrait in 1891.[13] "Mr. Smuts, State Attorney of the Transvaal."[14] Field Marshall Smuts, circa 1942.[15]

Smuts' Commando in April of 1902.[16] Jan Smuts is seated. Viewer left standing is General Jaap van Deventer and standing viewer right with his leg up is General Manie Maritz.

[15] See: Jan Smuts - Wikipedia Jan Smuts and the Old Boers - Wikipedia Jan Smuts in the South African Republic - Wikipedia Jan Smuts and a British Transvaal - Wikipedia Jan Smuts in the Boer War - Wikipedia

Rompel Character Sketch.

This character sketch of Jan Smuts is useful to document the circumstances by which he was appointed to the position of State Attorney and also the political situation in the Transvaal at the time. Recall that the constitutional crisis with the Supreme Court is occurring at this time and it is one thing the British are objecting to. Also there is turnover in the Hollander influence including Dr. Leijds [Leyds] himself.[16]

Dr. Willem Johannes Leyds.[17] Abraham Fischer, of The Orange Free State. [18 17]

J. C. Smuts.[19]

It was after Dr. Leijds retired as State Secretary and departed for Europe as Envoy Extraordinary and Minister Plenipotentiary of the South African Republic. The Volksraad and Government were at their wits' end. A new State Secretary had to be appointed by the First Volksraad; but those best fitted for this position refused. Abraham Fischer, of Bloemfontein, was the favourite. The Transvaal people did their utmost to induce Fischer to accept the candidature, and he would certainly have been elected:

"If he had any conditions, they could be granted; and, if any objections, they could be removed."

The Free State people looked upon all this with regret and persuaded Fischer to remain. And he remained where he was, for the Free State and his position there were, in fact, too dear to him that he should care to charge himself with the ungrateful and difficult office of State Secretary of the South African Republic. When Fischer refused, the Transvaal Government really not did know whom to approach. Should they ask Dr. H. J. Coster,[18] who had been State Attorney in '96' They went to see him. He would not think of it. Some suggested Danie Wolmarans,[19] and the Opposition immediately agreed to this suggestion; for then, at least, Danie, with his prodigious influence, would disappear from the Volksraad. But Danie was no lawyer and this was an essential qualification. A few clever minds then turned to Jan Smuts.

"Who is Jan Smuts?" most men asked.

[16] Willem Johannes Leyds (Magelang, Dutch East Indies, 1 May 1859–The Hague, Netherlands, 14 May 1940) was a Dutch lawyer and statesman, who pursued a career as a lawyer (1884–1889) and State Secretary (1889–1898) in the Zuid-Afrikaansche Republiek. From 1899 to 1902, during the critical period of the Second Boer War, he was a Special Envoy of the Republic and Fully Authorized Minister in Brussels, accredited to various European countries. He was State Secretary of the South African Republic Tenure 10 January 1889–31 May 1898 Succeeded by Francis William Reitz. William Johannes Leyds - Wikipedia

[17] Abraham Fischer (9 April 1850–16 November 1913) was a South African statesman. He was the sole Prime Minister of the Orange River Colony in South Africa, and when that ceased to exist joined the cabinet of the newly formed Union of South Africa. A. Fischer

[18] Dr. Hermanus Jacob Coster was born in the Netherlands in 1866 and arrived shortly after had obtained his doctorate in law in Leiden, and moved to Pretoria, where he worked as a professor established a lawyer. See Military Officer Album for picture and bio.

[19] A.D.W. Wolmarans - Wikipedia W was the grandson of F.G. Wolmarans of George who accompanied the Great Trek to the Transvaal, one of the signatories to the Sand River Convention in January 1852 and an avid supporter of kmdt. A.W.J. Pretorius.

Well, Jan Smuts was a young lawyer from Cape Colony, who was writing brilliant articles in Ons Land on the crisis in the Supreme Court in the South African Republic, when Chief Justice Kotze had been relieved from his duties.

Jan Smuts was a true young Africander, (sic) extraordinarily clever, who had finished his legal training in England brilliantly. He had set up as a lawyer in Johannesburg, but, in spite of his cleverness, the Rand capitalists disliked him: he was too much of a patriot for their taste. As for his candidature for the position of State Secretary, his friends did what they could; but his youth was an insuperable objection. He was only twenty-eight years old, and the constitution of the South African Republic required a State Secretary to be thirty at least. Eventually, the Transvaal had the good fortune to secure Judge Reitz, the former President of the Sister Republic of the Orange Free State, to fill that position; and Smuts became State Attorney. ....

Smuts performed his work with all the activity appertaining to his youth. The careers of the different State Attorneys of the South African Republic have been rich in interesting experiences; but that of the last State Attorney has excelled all others in this respect.

He accompanied President Kruger on his journey to Bloemfontein, in June 1899, and took part in the conferences with Sir Alfred Milner. It was he who had the well-known conference with Mr. William. Conyngham Greene,[20] the British Agent at Pretoria. from which Smuts, on his side, understood that the British Government would be satisfied if the Outlanders were granted full burgher rights after five years' residence: an assurance that raised expectations in official circles in the Transvaal which were never realized.

William Conyngham Greene.[20]

Smuts drew up the famous memorandum in which he sketched, in the form of a report to his Government, the points of the conversation between himself and the British Agent and the course which it had assumed.

He advised immediate publication so soon as the evasive answer of the British Government reached Pretoria, on the 28th of August 1898. The President however, who had grown old in diplomacy, warned the young functionary to remain calm and drew his attention to the fact that the proposed publication might possibly induce the British Government to break off all negotiations. ....

The last English Blue-book[21] that appeared before the war suddenly put an end to the confidence which Smuts had hitherto entertained in the British Agent. The young State Attorney was at least able to read, in this Blue-book, that even Mr. Conyngham Greene was not always to be relied upon to give a faithful rendering of a conversation, and, from that moment, he firmly refused to be present at any of the many visits which the British Representative paid to Government Buildings at Pretoria. ....

[20] Sir William Conyngham Greene, (29 October 1854–30 June 1934) was a British diplomat who served as minister to Switzerland, Romania and Denmark, and as ambassador to Japan. Conyngham Greene - Wikipedia

[21] There are several types. He is probably referring to the diplomatic Blue Book but may there is also a set of Colonial Blue Books. Neither are very accessible online. Blue book - Wikipedia

His lack of official severity, which latter is the characteristic of riper statesmen, appears in a Century of Wrong, both in his chapter on the Cape of Good Hope and in his vigorous assertion that Dingaan[22] was instigated by the English, in 1838, to murder Piet Retief and his men: an assertion which is contradicted by historians of standing, such as Theal[23] and Van Oordt,[24] and which must naturally diminish the value of Smuts' arguments throughout the book in the eyes of those who are enemies of his country. But patriotism und indignation seethed within him. What he lacked, as yet, was quiet earnestness. He had not yet learnt how to retain his equanimity in all circumstances nor how to work on quietly when wrath filled his heart.

As State Attorney, it was also his business to draft projects of laws and to defend and explain those projects in the Volksraad. One of these laws, the so-called Law against Prostitution, bears witness to his lack of practice.

By this law, the accused had to prove his innocence, while the prosecution was called upon to bring forward hardly any proof of the offence. Even landlords were held responsible for the acts of their tenants. Smuts drafted this law the doubtful honour belongs for the most part to him.

It cannot, however, be denied that the evil had assumed such proportions at Johannesburg that a rigorous intervention had become a matter of urgent necessity. And the State Attorney of the South African Republic was certainly not the first man to fail in finding the means by which this social evil was to be fought.

But, apart from all this, Smuts showed himself, in his official career, to be a young Africander of promising talents. His intentions and endeavours were all of the most sacred character. ....

But, even though Smuts the lawyer was, for a time, dissolved in Smuts the soldier, his incisive pen was not doomed to inefficiency. His reports to Presidents Steijn and Kruger concerning the misery endured and the results inflicted by this painful war proved in a marked manner that that pen could still move the whole world to rage against the execrable actions committed during the war. Jan Smuts taught us that a new Century of Wrong had commenced for the Africanders; but, from behind the heavy wall of the British army, he shouted to us, with austere emphasis:

"We will endeavour to realize a peace for the whole of South Africa which will be worthy of the precious sacrifices that have been made".

Truly, those were the words of a young patriot. of a young hero of Young Africa. Such language, in such desperate circumstances. marked the resolution of his character and marked the man he was. ....

Jan Smuts who, in August 1901, passed with 200 Boers from the Potchefstroom District in the Transvaal across the block-house lines of the British military posts, who pushed forward to the centre of Cape Colony and there maintained himself. There were other reasons that convinced Jan Smuts, and these are to be found in the resolution in which the representatives of the commandoes at Vereeniging explain why they were compelled to put an end to the war.

Jan Smuts, however, is too energetic, too diligent and assiduous a man to remain inactive. His destiny, his influence amongst the Africanders, his thorough knowledge of persons and affairs have increased: Jan Smuts has been through a hard school, through which the ancestors of the Africanders passed before him. I have no doubt but that he will make the best use of his knowledge for the sake of his people and his country.

[22] Dingane ka Senzangakhona Zulu (c. 1795–29 January 1840), commonly referred to as Dingane or Dingaan, was a Zulu prince who became king of the Zulu Kingdom in 1828, after assassinating his half-brother Shaka Zulu. Dingane - Wikipedia

[23] George McCall Theal (11 April 1837, Saint John, New Brunswick–17 April 1919, Wynberg, Cape Town), was the most prolific and influential South African historian, archivist and genealogist of the late nineteenth and early twentieth century. George McCall Theal - Wikipedia

[24] Dr. Jan Willem Gerbrand van Oordt (1826–1904), editor of De Zuid Afrikaan, father of D'Arbez, pseudonym of Johan Frederik van Oordt (1856–1918). JWG van Oordt was a member of the University of the Cape of Good Hope Council (ca. 1895). Works 'History of the Eastern Cape Frontier, 1834-37'. MS consisting of 6 parts. https://www.nationalarchives.gov.za/node/3810589 .

Secretary Reitz's Exhortation

F. W. Reitz, Secretary of State of the South-African Republic; Ex-President of the Orange Free State.[25]

The catastrophe with which we have so long been threatened has at last overtaken us and our country is to be bathed in blood.

And why?

Let the murderers, the peace and treaty breakers who are attacking us answer the question.

With their usual unblushing effrontery they will now declare that not they, but we, are the aggressors.

We the aggressors!

Who is it that has answered all our attempts for a peaceful settlement with contempt and even threats?

Who is it that for months past has been mobilizing troops on our border from all parts of the world to enforce their friendly advice?

Who is it that has for years past accused us of being oppressors and tyrants?

Who is it that, while hypocritically declaring that they did not wish to impair our independence, yet continually attempted to interfere in the internal affairs of our country? That also entrapped us, and even their own representative, in a mean and despicable manner into making certain proposals which they would be willing to consider on their merits even while they were ready as soon as these proposals, made undeniably at their own suggestion, were formulated to reject them as an insult to the British nation put forward with the object of making mischief?

Who is it that under the pretext of obtaining the redress of the supposed Uitlander grievances have ranged themselves with the capitalists and rebels with the object of possessing themselves of Naboth's vineyard?

Who is it that have supported and aided that traitorous and rebellious organization, so-called the League, notwithstanding the warnings of their Own Acting High Commissioner, Sir William Butler,[26] an honorable, famous and highly respected general, and of: Mr. Schreiner, [27] the premier of the only South African colony of any standing?

[25] This clarion call to arms was issued by Secretary Reitz at the beginning of the War. It is as fine an articulation of the justifications relied upon by the Boer Republics as will be found in the remainder of this work. Reproduced from John Bull's Crime by Webster Davis which is extensively cited and discussed in this book. Pages 172–177.

[26] General Sir William Francis Butler, (31 October 1838–7 June 1910), was an Irish 19th-century British Army officer, writer, and adventurer. ...... In 1898 he succeeded General Sir William Howley Goodenough as commander-in-chief in South Africa, with the local rank of lieutenant-general. For a short period (December 1898–February 1899), during the absence of Sir Alfred Milner in England, he acted as High Commissioner, and as such, and subsequently in his military capacity, he expressed views on the subject of the probabilities of war which were not approved by the home government; he was consequently ordered home to command the Western District, and held this post until 1905. William Butler (British Army officer) - Wikipedia

[27] William Philip Schreiner (30 August 1857–28 June 1919) was a barrister, politician, statesman and Prime Minister of the Cape Colony during the Second Boer War. William Schreiner - Wikipedia He is also the brother of Olive Schreiner.

Who is it that openly accepted a false petition filled with thousands of forged signatures and others obtained by fraud without attempting to prove any of those signatures?

Who is it that not only let the instigators of the shameful Jameson raid practically go unpunished, but even condoned the raid and allowed the prime movers, with the aid of Her Majesty's High Commissioner and Her Majesty's Colonial Secretary, to insult, defraud and libel the Afrikander nation in every possible way, backed by all the influence which cannon can subvert and control to the undying disgrace of our times? Who are these people?

Is it Sir Alfred Milner, Her Majesty's High Commissioner in South Africa?

Is it Mr. Joseph Chamberlain, the Colonial Secretary?

Is it Lord Salisbury and the rest of the British cabinet?

Is it Her Majesty, the Queen of England?

Is it the British nation?

Alas, we had hoped to be able to answer the last two questions in the negative, but we cannot!

The British cabinet-the British nation-the noble, peace-loving and aged sovereign, honored and respected by us an till now, they have all either condoned the injustice which is being done to us or they have allowed themselves to be misled by a man like Chamberlain in a manner that a just God will not allow to pass unpunished.

If nations must be punished like individuals for condoning an offense as well as for committing one, then this Prime Minister, this nation, this sovereign, will not be able to defend themselves at the bar of the Great Judge for their unrighteous and unjust deeds.

The nation that has encouraged race-hatred, their prime minister and their anointed queen who have allowed such a disgrace, have made themselves equally guilty with the evil-doers, and if it should happen in South Africa, as was the case in North America a hundred years ago, that 'Ichabod' become the password of the British Empire, on whom will the blame rest?

If the blind lead the blind they will both fall into the pit, and we shall be able, who knows how soon, to declare of our enemies, that whom God wishes to destroy He will first make insane.

The statesmen of England. the warriors, the press, aye, even the preachers, have so often declared to us and the whole world that the British Empire is a mighty empire, but we know that whosoever may be mighty the Lord our God is Almighty.

Brother Afrikanders, the great day is at hand! The God of our fathers will be with us in our struggle, the Lord whose arm has not been shortened so that He cannot help those who call to Him in their time of trouble. Let us lay aside our trust in princes and raise our eyes in supplication to God, our Banner. By His help we will do great deeds.

Even as the mighty Spain with her bloodthirsty Alva [sic][28] and her invincible armada had to swallow the bitterness of defeat, so too will God give our enemies into our hands. Who are we that the mighty England should send her thousands of mercenary troops against us? A young and weak nation, small in numbers and insignificant in military strength.

Tempted by the wealth of our mines, the enemy have cast about for an excuse to attack us. Let them deny that if they are able. Who in South Africa will believe them? The cry is the Uitlanders in South Africa are oppressed, and they are debarred political rights!

Only after seven long years of waiting can they obtain the longed-for franchise and not after five years-what an unheard of injustice!

[28] Fernando Álvarez de Toledo y Pimentel, 3rd Duke of Alba (29 October 1507–11 December 1582), known as the Grand Duke of Alba (Spanish: Gran Duque de Alba, Portuguese: Grão Duque de Alba) in Spain and Portugal and as the Iron Duke (Dutch: IJzeren Hertog) or shortly 'Alva' in the Netherlands, was a Spanish nobleman, general and statesman. He has often been considered the most effective general of his generation, as well as one of the greatest in history. Fernando Álvarez de Toledo, 3rd Duke of Alba - Wikipedia
The Spanish Armada, 1588 was captained by Alonso de Guzmán y Sotomayor, 7th Duke of Medina Sidonia - Wikipedia
Spanish Armada - Wikipedia

They are eager to forget that there are thousands of the so-called oppressed ones for whom it is possible on account of the retroactive force of the seven-years franchise law to obtain the franchise at once, but decline to take it.

In England-that free England-the new comer must wait twelve years before he can vote for the House of Commons.

Of the House of Lords they will prefer to say nothing, because are not the members of that body rulers by birth? But in our republic it must be five years or-war!

According to their Colonial Secretary, England has constituted herself champion of all the Uitlanders. And what do we find?

On the borders, side by side with our burghers, we find these same Uitlanders in hundreds-Hollanders, Americans, Irishmen-ready to lay down their lives in order to rid themselves of these self-constituted champions.

Verily, a fine champion of the oppressed is that nation which has ever since the birth of our nation been the oppressor of the Afrikander and the native alike.

From Slaghter's Nek to Lang's Nek, from the Pretoria convention to the Bloemfontein conference, they have ever been the treaty-breakers and robbers. The diamond fields of Kimberley and the beautiful land of Natal were robbed from us, and now they want the gold fields of the Witwatersrand.

Where is Waterboer to-day? He who had to be defended against the Free State is to-day without an inch of ground.[29]

Where lies Lobengula?[30] In his unknown grave to-day, and what filibusters and fortune hunters are possessors of his country?

Where are the native chiefs of Bechuanaland now, and who owns their land?[31]

Read the history of South Africa and ask yourselves, Has the British government been a blessing or a curse to the subcontinent?

Brother Afrikanders, I repeat, the day is at hand on which great deeds are expected of us! War has broken out! What is it to be? A wasted and enslaved South Africa or a free, united South Africa?

Come, let us stand shoulder to shoulder and do our holy duty! The Lord of Hosts will be our Leader!

Be of good cheer!

(Signed) F. W. Reitz.

[29] Griqualand West - Wikipedia

[30] Lobengula Khumalo (c. 1845–presumed January 1894) was the second and last official king of the Northern Ndebele people (historically called Matabele in English). Both names in the Ndebele language mean "the men of the long shields," a reference to the Ndebele warriors' use of the Nguni shield. Lobengula - Wikipedia

[31] The Bechuanaland Protectorate was technically a protectorate rather than a colony. Originally the local Tswana rulers were left in power, and British administration was limited to the police force to protect Bechuanaland's borders against other European colonial ventures. But on 9 May 1891 the British Government gave the administration of the protectorate to the High Commissioner for Southern Africa, who started to appoint officials in Bechuanaland, and the de facto independence of Bechuanaland ended. Bechuanaland Protectorate - Wikipedia

President Steyn's Proclamation

M. J. Stein, (sic) President of the Orange Free State.[32]
Martinus Theunis Steyn.[33]

A Proclamation to the Orange Free State Burghers

Burghers of the Orange Free State by President M. J. Stein:

The time which we had so much desired to avoid, the moment when we as a nation are compelled with arms to oppose injustice and shameless violence, is at hand. Our sister Republic to the north of the Vaal River is about to be attacked by an unscrupulous enemy, who for many years has prepared himself, and sought pretexts for the violence of which he is now guilty, whose purpose it is to destroy the existence of the Afrikander race.

Bound by Many Ties.

With our sister Republic we are not only bound by ties of blood, of sympathy and of common interest, but also by formal treaty, which has been necessitated by circumstances. This treaty demands of us that we assist her if she should be unjustly attacked, which we, unfortunately, for a long time have had too much reason to expect. We, therefore, cannot passively look on while injustice is done her, and while also our own dearly bought freedom is endangered, but are called as men to resist, trusting the Almighty, firmly believing that He will never permit injustice and unrighteousness to triumph.

Now that we thus resist a powerful enemy, with whom it has always been our honest desire to live in friendship, notwithstanding injustice and wrong done by him to us in the past, we solemnly declare, in the presence of the Almighty God, that we are compelled thereto by the injustice done to our kinsmen, and by the consciousness that the end of their independence will make our existence as an independent State of no significance, and that their fate, should they be obliged to bend under an overwhelming power, will also soon after be our own fate.

Solemn treaties have not protected our sister Republic against annexation; against conspiracy; against the claim of an abolished suzerainty; against the continuous oppression and interference, and now against a renewed attack, which aims only at her downfall.

Our own unfortunate experiences in the past have also made it sufficiently clear to us that we cannot rely on the most solemn promises and agreements of Great Britain, when she has at her helm a Government prepared to

[32] A century of injustice; synopsis of a message to the people of South-Africa, sent by the government of the South-African republic. Baltimore Md. November 1899. https://babel.hathitrust.org/cgi/pt?id=wu.89100085885&seq=5

[33] Martinus (or Marthinus) Theunis Steyn; 2 October 1857–28 November 1916) was a South African lawyer, politician, and statesman. He was the sixth and last president of the independent Orange Free State from 1896 to 1902. Martinus Theunis Steyn - Wikipedia

trample on treaties, to look for feigned pretexts for every violation of good faith by her committed. This is proved among other things by the unjust and unlawful British intervention, after we had overcome an armed and barbarous black tribe on our eastern frontier, as also by the forcible appropriation of the dominion over part of our territory where the discovery of diamonds had caused the desire for this appropriation, although contrary to existing treaties.

The desire and intention to trample on our rights as an independent and sovereign nation, notwithstanding a solemn convention existing between this State and Great Britain, have also been more than once, and are now again, shown by the present Government by giving expression in public documents to an unfounded claim of paramountcy over the whole of South Africa, and, therefore, also over this State.

With regard to the South Africa Republic, Great Britain has, moreover, refused until the present to allow her to regain her original position in respect to foreign affairs, a position which she had lost in no sense by her own faults. The original intention of conventions, to which the Republic has consented under pressure of circumstances, has been perverted and continually been used by the present British administration as a means for the practice of tyranny and of injustice, and, among other things, for the support of a revolutionary propaganda within the Republic in favor of Great Britain.

And while no redress has been offered, as justice demands, for injustice done to the South Africa Republic on the part of the British Government, and while no gratitude is exhibited for the magnanimity shown at the request of the British Government to British subjects who had forfeited under the laws of the Republic their lives and property, yet no feeling of shame has prevented the British Government, now that the gold mines of immense value have been discovered in the country, to make claims of the Republic, the consequence of which, if allowed, will be that those who, or whose forefathers have saved the country from barbarism and have won it for civilization with their blood and their tears, will lose their control over the interests of the country, to which they are justly entitled according to divine and human laws.

The consequence of these claims would be, moreover, that the greater part of the power will be placed in the hands of those who, foreigners by birth, enjoy the privilege of depriving the country of its chief treasure, while they have never shown any loyalty to a foreign government.

Besides, the inevitable consequence of the acceptance of these claims would be that the independence of the country as a self-governing, independent sovereign republic would be irreparably lost. For years past British troops in great numbers have been placed on the frontiers of our sister republic in order to compel her by fear to accede to the demand which would be pressed upon her, and in order to encourage revolutionary disturbances and the cunning plans of those whose greed for gold is the cause of their shameless undertakings.

Those plans have now reached their climax in the open violence to which the present British Government now resorts. While we readily acknowledge the honorable character of thousands of Englishmen, who loathe such deeds of robbery and wrong, we cannot but abhor the shameless breaking of treaties, the feigned pretexts for the transgression of law, the violation of international law and of justice, and the numerous right-rending deeds of the British statesmen, who will now force a war upon the South African Republic. On their heads be the guilt of blood, and may a just Providence reward all as they deserve.

Burghers of the Orange Free State, rise as one man against the oppressor and the violator of right.

In the strife, to which we are now driven, have a care to commit no act unworthy of a Christian and of a Burgher of the Orange Free State. Let us look forward with confidence to a fortunate end of this conflict, trusting to that Higher Power, without whose help human weapons are of no avail.

May He bless our arms. Under His banner we advance to battle for liberty and for Fatherland.

M. J. Stein, (sic) State President.

A Century of Injustice

Synopsis of a Message to the People of South-Africa, sent by the Government of the South-African Republic.
An Earnest Representation and Historical Reminder to
Her Majesty Queen Victoria of Great Britain and Ireland, Empress of India, etc.
In View of The Prevailing Crisis.

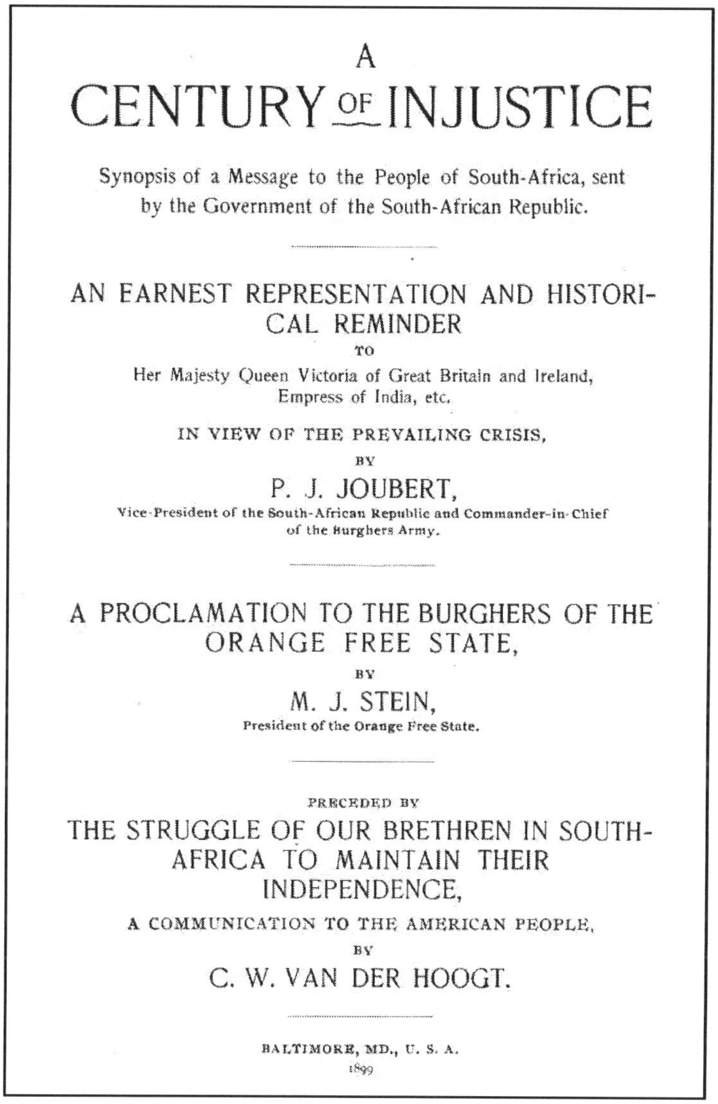

A

CENTURY OF INJUSTICE

Synopsis of a Message to the People of South-Africa, sent by the Government of the South-African Republic.

AN EARNEST REPRESENTATION AND HISTORICAL REMINDER

TO

Her Majesty Queen Victoria of Great Britain and Ireland, Empress of India, etc.

IN VIEW OF THE PREVAILING CRISIS,

BY

P. J. JOUBERT,

Vice-President of the South-African Republic and Commander-in-Chief of the Burghers Army.

A PROCLAMATION TO THE BURGHERS OF THE ORANGE FREE STATE,

BY

M. J. STEIN,

President of the Orange Free State.

PRECEDED BY

THE STRUGGLE OF OUR BRETHREN IN SOUTH-AFRICA TO MAINTAIN THEIR INDEPENDENCE,

A COMMUNICATION TO THE AMERICAN PEOPLE,

BY

C. W. VAN DER HOOGT.

BALTIMORE, MD., U. S. A.

1899

Frontispiece, Century of Injustice, 1899.[34]

[34] Cornelius W. Van Der Hoogt, A century of injustice; synopsis of a message to the people of South-Africa, sent by the government of the South-African republic. Baltimore Md. November 1899. https://babel.hathitrust.org/cgi/pt?id=wu.89100085885&seq=5

November 1899 Van Der Hoogt Preface,

My Fellow Citizens: I offer to you a true story of the struggle of the Boers in South-Africa. It will be sent to everyone who makes application for it. If you feel after reading the story that it is worth something to learn the real grievances, not of the "Uitlanders," but of the "Inlanders" on South African soil, I shall feel highly rewarded if you will send a little contribution to one of the local committees, which I hope will soon be organized all over the country, to receive money for the wounded.

We will probably not be so fortunate as to send a hospital ship to South-Africa. If we could, I should like to see it named "Oom Paul," but I do not dare to entertain such expectations. It will be well to inform you that the committees have opened communication with the Red-Cross Society at the Hague, in the Netherlands, and all amounts, small or large, will be thankfully received.

I hope the editors of newspapers will kindly assist in this effort to help the relief fund for our wounded brethren in far South Africa. The generosity of the American people is too well-known, and a call to that effect has never remained unanswered. I express my gratitude for the sympathy the press has shown to the Boers' cause, and especially for its friendly attitude toward them in my home city, convinced as I am that it will continue the good work.

I thank my friend H. H. de Vos, in New York, ex-Vice Consul of the Netherlands in Constantinople and Hamburg, for his assistance in the translation of documents, and my friends in the East and West for their encouragement, their enthusiasm and devotion to the Boers' cause, and finally, I ask consideration for the literary shortcomings of the work, not for my own sake, but for that of the Boers.

Sincerely yours,

Cornelius W. Van Der Hoogt.

Baltimore, Md., November 27, 1899.

Paul Kruger.[35]

[35] Story of Boers U. Cal Copy, Bradley Co.: https://archive.org/details/storyofboersnarr00vand/page/n9/mode/2up

Reitz Synopsis of A Century of Injustice

A Century of Injustice.
Synopsis of A Message to the People of South Africa,
Sent by the Government of the South-African Republic.

By: F. W. Reitz, Secretary of State of the South-African Republic; Ex-President of the Orange Free State.

The history of South-Africa during the last century is written in blood, in the blood of a race closely related to the British or so-called Anglo-Saxon race, and animated with the same love for liberty and independence. The first Dutch and French Huguenot settlers landed in Cape Colony in the middle of the seventeenth century, under the auspices of the Dutch East India Company. It cannot be truthfully claimed that the administration of the Dutch East India Company was a liberal one, nor was it calculated to promote the interests of the settlers. As a matter of fact, the Company only cared for the Colony in connection with its possessions in the East Indies. Notwithstanding these unfavorable conditions the Colony flourished and was in a prosperous state at the time it was taken by the British in 1806.

The original Dutch and Huguenot settlers had assimilated to one nation-one in religion, one in quiet respect for the law and with a passionate love of liberty. From the very start the British Government bent all its energies to the suppression of this proud race, and treated the settlers with contempt.

Under the pretext of protecting the poor oppressed native against the cruel Boer, the latter was deprived of the means to protect his property by the confiscation of his arms and ammunition. The Government even went so far as to organize a police force of Hottentots, the lowest class of the African tribes. An attempt at insurrection in 1815 was smothered in blood by the execution of six Boers at Slachtersnek on March 9, 1816, women and children being compelled to attend the horrible spectacle.

As to the cruel treatment of the slaves by the Boers, we may refer to the opinion of the British Historian Froude, who says that the scandals of the East Indian plantations were unknown in South Africa, and that because the Dutchmen were a slow people and did not show any high enthusiasm for the new ideas of emancipation they were called inhuman. Accusations of cruel treatment of slaves and natives were continually trumped up, and although by far the greater part of these accusations were shown to be false before the Cape Colony courts, still it was published throughout the world that the Boers were the most cruel race.

It is a fact that the Boers, as a whole, did not oppose the principle of the emancipation of the slaves, but it is also a fact that they had every reason to object to the methods chosen by the British Government to carry this laudable purpose into effect.

Notwithstanding the value of the slaves was estimated at three millions by British officials, only one and three-quarter millions were set apart for compensation to be paid to the Boers, and this money was only payable at London. A great many of the Boers sold their certificates for little more than nothing to speculators and others, unknown with the formalities, entirely relinquished their claims.

Little or no protection was afforded by the British Government against the continual raids of Kaffir tribes, always accompanied by awful atrocities, and if ever the Boers attempted to defend their property and to recapture the cattle, stolen by the natives, the British Government would interfere, seize the cattle and sell it at public auction.

Another grief of the Boers was the suppression of their language, for notwithstanding the use of their language was guaranteed to the Boers in 1806, the Government, in 1825, ordered that henceforth all official documents should be written in the English language. Petitions in the Dutch language were ignored. The Boers were not admitted as jurors owing to their deficient knowledge of English, and they were brought before English juries and tried in a language which they did not understand.

No wonder, that under such circumstances, the Boers decided to leave their native country and to seek shelter elsewhere, but before doing so they desired to ascertain that in their new settlement, wherever it might be, they would be no further molested by the British Government and be allowed to make their own laws.

Lieutenant-Governor Stockenstroom, consulted in the matter, stated that there was no statute forbidding them to leave the Colony and to settle elsewhere, and that if such law should exist it would be a tyrannical law, that could not be enforced. Attorney-General Oliphant gave a similar advice, stating that the Boers evidently proposed to go elsewhere and not to consider themselves any longer as British subjects, which was of daily occurrence in England in regard to the United States of America, and that the Government had no power and could not obtain any power to prevent this. Consequently the Boers started on their "trek" as free men, no subjects to any prince on earth, but from the very start they were persecuted by the British Colonial Office.

The first two parties were under the leadership of Trichardt and Van Rensburg. The former reached, after the most atrocious suffering, Delagoa Bay, where nearly all of them died of fever, and the latter was entirely wiped out by the Kaffirs.

The second party, under the leadership of Pieter Retief, met with no better result. Although the Boers had contracted with the Kaffir chief, Dingan, for the cession of a parcel of land, the present Natal, they were treacherously attacked by the Kaffirs, instigated by England, and a large number of them, among them Pieter Retief, were murdered. The same chief took the principal Boer laager (camp) by surprise and murdered there more than 500 people, mostly women and children. In a subsequent battle, on December 16, 1838, however, about 500 Boers defeated Dingan's army of 10,000 men and then founded a free Republic in the present Colony of Natal.

But this Republic was not to last for any length of time. The free Republic would of course draw a large migration from the Cape Colony, and the British Government would not tolerate this. The first step was a military occupation of Natal, with the purpose of preventing the Boers of securing the needed arms and ammunition, and thus to stop the further migration. They were warned that they would be treated as rebels, and that the British Government would assist the natives against them.

Although the Boers succeeded twice in repulsing the British invaders, they could not prevent the annexation of their country, but the protest issued at this occasion by the President of the Volksraad, Joachim Prinsloo, will remain for ever famous. In his letter to the Governor, Prinsloo said:

> "We know that there is a God, the Lord of heaven and earth, and who has the power and is willing to protect the weak against their oppressors. We rely upon Him and the justice of our cause. If it should be His will that we, our wives and children should be totally wiped out, we will humbly submit to His will. We will not defy England's power, but we cannot tolerate that might should conquer right without having fought with all our forces."

Of course it was not to be expected that this protest would stay the hand of the British, and the Boers thereupon decided to leave Natal and to march back into the interior. This trek was accompanied with such suffering and misery, that even the British Governor, Sir Harry Smith, declared that it was "a scene of misery as he had never seen before."

Part of the Boers thereupon settled in the present Orange Free State and others went further and crossed the Vaal River, settling in the present Transvaal.

Although the English Government first intended also to annex the Free State, this plan was abandoned because the possession of the land did not warrant the trouble and expense and it was deemed best to recognize the independence of both Republics, hoping that the Boers would go under in their continual fights with the overwhelming numbers of the surrounding native tribes.

Such were the "noble" sentiments that animated the British Government at the time of the conclusion of the Convention of the Zand River in 1852. In this convention the independence of the two Republics was recognized and the British Government also agreed not to interfere with the native tribes north of the Orange River.

In regard to the Orange Free State, this convention was flagrantly violated by the English at the first occasion, viz.: the war between the Republic and the Basutos. During this war the Basutos were supplied by England with arms and ammunition, and the supplies for the Orange Free State Boers were seized and detained. After the defeat of the Basutos, the English interfered in their favor and prevented the Republic from securing the well-earned benefits of the victory.

Again, with the discovery of the diamond fields near Kimberly, the British Government stepped in and claimed the territory, which claim is characterized by Froude as "perhaps the most discreditable page in British Colonial history."

Later on, the British Government apparently admitted the justice of the Free State protest and thereupon, with its "usual generosity," paid the "enormous" sum of £90,000 as damage to the Free State Government! £90,000 for the Kimberly diamond fields! Is it a wonder that the Boers claim that old, blunt John Bull had the best of the bargain?

After the conclusion of the Zand River Convention, the Transvaal Republic was also recognized by the United States, Holland, France, Germany and Belgium. The United States Secretary of State, writing to President Pretorius, on November 19, 1870, that the United States Government gladly recognizing the sovereignty of the Transvaal Republic, would be willing to take any steps necessary in the premises.

The first flagrant violation of the 1852 convention in regard to the Transvaal was coincident with the annexation of the Free State diamond fields. Part of the territory desired by England belonged to the Transvaal, and was simply taken by the great civilizer of South Africa. Shortly afterwards the Transvaal Government was compelled to lodge a strong protest against the selling of enormous quantities of firearms to the Kaffirs, but the protest was simply ignored.

The climax came when, in 1877, the Transvaal was annexed to England by proclamation of Sir Theophile Shepstone. The British Government claimed that this step was necessary for the civilization of South-Africa, and the protest of President Burgers, the Volksraad and the Burghers passed unheeded.

Bishop Colenso declared that "the sly, underhand way in which the Transvaal has been annexed appears to me unworthy of the British name." Gladstone did not like it, but yet he stated that he could not advise the Queen to withdraw her sovereignty from the Transvaal.

The great Zulu War was one of the direct consequences of Transvaal annexation, England claiming a certain territory on the Transvaal border, which she had formerly admitted to belong to the Zulus.

Finally, when the Burghers were satisfied that protests were in vain, they decided to take up arms to reconquer their independence, and it will remain Gladstone's eternal glory, that notwithstanding the clamor for revenge after the British defeats at Lainsneck and Majuba Hill, he concluded the Pretoria convention of 1881, whereby the independence of the Transvaal was restored.

To the unprejudiced mind it would appear logical that if the British Government had made up its mind to admit that the annexation was unjustified, it would wipe out its former action by a "restitutio in integrum." But even the great Gladstone could not be prevailed upon to go that far, and it is safe to say that if he had been willing to do this such magnanimity would have been entirely beyond the possibilities of the British Colonial Office.

It certainly did not require a large amount of perspicacity to predict that in its practical application the Pretoria convention was doomed to be a failure, and it may be safe to assume that it was never considered to be a final settlement of the difficulties.

Its dual character was born to cause no end of difficulties between the two Governments, and it was, therefore, absolutely necessary, in the interest of the peace in South Africa, that it should be superseded by another convention. For these reasons the London convention of 1884 was concluded, whereby the South African Republic was granted absolute independence, and the British Government agreed not to interfere in any way in its domestic affairs. The word suzerainty was eliminated, and England only reserved the right of approval of any treaty concluded by the South African Republic with nations other than the Orange Free State.

The history of recent years has shown how Great Britain has lived up to her "promises," and how, through its continual intrigues since the discovery of the gold fields in the Rand, it has compelled the Boers to take up arms once more for the preservation of freedom and independence.

The history of these recent years is already given in the preceding pages, and a great many salient features are also stated in the last part of this book, and no further reference is therefore necessary at this place. But the concluding part of the message to the people of South Africa certainly deserves to be placed in full before the American public and is as follows:

I have now given the facts of a Century of Oppression and Persecution. They are not air-born assumptions, but are taken from the mouth of the most trustworthy historical witnesses, nearly all of them of British nationality; they are facts admitted as incontestable before the court of history. As to the more recent events, since 1898, I have personal knowledge of all negotiations and differences described, and I can state that I have confined myself to facts, that will be more clearly elucidated in coming years, when the curtain will rise and the events of the last two years in this deeply-stricken country will be fully published.

Arrived at this terrible turning point in the history of South-Africa, at the eve of a struggle, wherein our people are threatened with total extinction, it behooves us to speak-with what may, perhaps, be our last word to the world-the truth, so that even if we should perish, truth may triumph through us over our victors, and may continue to eat like a cancer in his public life, until it will be his turn to sink down into the night of oblivion.

Hitherto our people have kept silent, the enemy has calumniated, slandered and struck our people, and treated us with contempt and hatred. But with dignity that may remind the world of a suffering still greater and deeper, our people have borne the insult and contempt of the enemy, and impelled by the conscientiousness of its duty, has tried to remove the errors and abuses that might have been committed by its State Government in moments of less watchfulness. Even this was called weakness and cowardice.

Upon hundreds of platforms in Great Britain and by the most prominent statesmen our people has been, of late, called incompetent, uncivilized, faithless, corrupt, bloodthirsty, void of honor, treacherous, and the like, until not only the British public, but nearly the entire civilized world, has commenced to believe that we are well-nigh the equals of wild beasts. Those insults, those defiance's, we have passed them in silence.

From the official blue books of Her Majesty's Government, from the despatches of Her Majesty's High Commissioner in South Africa, we were compelled to hear that our corrupt State Government and our unjust, unprincipled and disorderly administration were running sores, putrefying like a pestilence the moral and political atmosphere of South-Africa. And we have kept silent.

In numerous newspapers we have been accused of all possible crimes against civilization and humanity, crimes have been laid at our door, the mere mentioning of which make the heart shudder. If the reading public believed only one-hundredth part of the enormities told about our people and Government, it must have come to the conclusion that this Republic was a den of murderers and brigands; that we were a people, the mere existence of which was a blot upon humanity.

Nobody has seen any effects of the enormous sums which we were alleged to spend from the secret fund in order to buy the public opinion of the world, but the slander went its course like an all destroying hurricane. But our people kept silent, partly from ignorance and partly from a feeling of despairing helplessness; partly because, as a simple agricultural people, it does not read newspapers, and thus could not realize how the feelings of the entire world were aroused against us with malignant rage. The practical result was that our cause was lost by default before the tribunal of public opinion.

For these reasons I have now deemed it my duty to state the facts that have characterized the British policy toward our people during the nineteenth century. Naboth's title upon his vineyard was to be annulled and, according to the hypocritical British policy, that result could be best attained by showing him up as a scoundrel and Achab as an angel. I have elucidated the facts of Achab's career and will now proceed to draw my conclusions-conclusions that must irresistibly appeal to the mind of every just and unbiased man.

During this century there are three periods, each of them characteristic of the policy of the British Government toward us. The first period commenced in 1806 and lasted until the second half of this century. During this period contempt, pure and simple, constitutes the essential feature of the British policy. The stupid and dirty Dutch was, during that time, the prevailing opinion of the Britisher toward our poor people.

But the hypocritical nature of the British policy found ways to express this contempt in terms of most sublime ideas then ruling the civilized world. A sentimental philanthropy ruled over the civilized world and was used by the British Government to show up the Boers to the world as the oppressors of the poor, peaceful natives, which were susceptible of religion and civilization, and who were likewise our brethren. If it should appear inconceivable that the power who, under the treaty of Utrecht, acted as the shameless champion of slavery, should show a sickly affection for the natives in South Africa, it is to be borne in mind that in this case its action was not so much dictated by love for the native than by its hatred and contempt for the Boer, which was the distinguishing characteristic of its policy.

As a consequence of this hatred for the Boer, concealed under the pretext of love for the native, the natives were used as police against us, they were provided with arms and ammunition against us, they were incited to fight us and wherever possible to murder and rob us. It was compelled by this hatred that we had to leave the Cape Colony and all that was dear to us and to seek a shelter in the unknown wilderness in the North, and as a consequence of that hatred we had to continue our martyr's crusade through South Africa, until every part of the country was dyed red with blood, not so much of men capable of bearing arms, but of women and children.

The second period runs up to 1881. During this period the foundation of the British policy toward our people was not in the first place the hatred of the Afrikander. The result had already shown that this hatred was powerless to subject the Afrikander; on the contrary, it had caused the Afrikanders to spread over the whole of South-Africa as the reigning people. In a moment of despondency and thoughtless disinterestedness England had concluded a treaty with the Boers (1852 and 1854) whereby they were given full possession of certain wild and apparently valueless parts of the country. The main feature of the policy during the second period was a feeling of spite on account of this mistake and the deliberate purpose to neutralize its consequences.

The wild and valueless territory ceded to the Boers appeared to be very valuable after the Boers had saved it and opened it to civilization; these territories had again to shine as pearls in Her Majesty's crown, notwithstanding the treaties concluded with the Boers. This was the secret purpose, as regards the ways to attain it, in harmony with the inherent hypocrisy of the British policy, they were partly concealed and partly open, and there was a very wide difference between the two kinds.

The concealed way was to arm the Kaffir tribes against us and to incite them to attack us in violation of the solemn treaties and promises. If successful in this, England could conceal its true purpose and means, and could openly interfere for the preservation of peace and order and to protect civilization in this part of the world, and under these pretexts the Republics could be annexed. With regard to the Orange Free State this policy was not successful, as notwithstanding the unlawful detention of their firearms and ammunition by the British Government, the brave Burghers of our neighboring Republic, after a hard struggle, succeeded in defeating Moshesh. In this case, England was compelled to confine itself to the protection of its Basuto instruments, to prevent the Boers from attaining any benefit from their victories, and to the unlawful annexation of the diamond fields.

As to the South-African Republic, unfortunately, its citizens were not careful enough to guard against the shrewd policy of the enemy. The Transvaal Boers had vanquished the most powerful Kaffir tribes and did not realize for a moment that the small Kaffir wars, which had been brought about by English intrigues, and which they did not prosecute with all possible energy, could ever be used as a pretext to annex their country to the British empire. Thus the wars with Magato and Sekoekoeni were prolonged to the greatest satisfaction of Sir Theophile Shepstone and his principals. And thus came the annexation with the extension to the South-African Republic of Her Majesty's authority and protection, by which means only the unity of purpose and action could be assured, and a happy prospect of peace and prosperity could be opened for the future.

These words of the Shepstone proclamation reveal in all its horrible nakedness the hypocrisy which secretly plunges the dagger into the Boer Republic and openly played the part of the disinterested and merciful Samaritan.

The third period of our history is characterized by the combination of the old well-known policy of deceit with the new power of capitalism, born from the mineral treasures of the South-African Republic. Both our national and our political independence are now threatened by an unrivalled complication of powers and influences. We are now confronted by the numbers, the British public opinion seeking blood and vengeance, the capital of the world and all powers that can only be called together under the banner of rapaciousness and cupidity. During the last year our situation has become gradually more precarious. The cordon of beasts and birds of prey has, during the last ten years, been gradually tightened around our poor doomed people.

Like the wounded goat feeling the approach of the lion, the fox or the buzzard, our people all over South Africa are surrounded by the intrigues, vindictiveness, hatred and cupidity of its enemies. Every ocean carries the vessels laden with British troops from all parts of the world to crush this handful of people.

Even Xerxes, with his millions moving against little Greece, does not furnish a more unnatural spectacle to the surprised world than this sweet mother of nations, holding the sharpened knife in her hands and using all her power, all her treasures, all her high traditions to kill this poor baby crawling in the dust. This is no war, but an attempt at infanticide.

And when the thought of the spectator is struck by horror and his brain refuses to work, then rises before him, as a dream in the near future, the scene of Bantu children playing in the gardens and the ruins of the sunny South, over the graves wherein the children of the heroes of faith and liberty of all Europe are slumbering. And the Bantu bands of brigands and murderers again roam where the dwelling of the white European used to stand. And if he asks why all this has happened; why, the heroic children of a heroic race, to which civilization owes its highest possessions, were murdered in this remote part of the world, an invisible satyr will answer:

Civilization is a failure, the Caucasian has gone under, and then he will make up with the screeching of the word: Gold! Gold! Gold! in his ears.

The orchids of Birmingham are yellow, the traditions of the greatest empire of the world have faded and become yellow. The laurels fought for by the British legions in South-Africa are yellow. But the heaven over South-Africa will always remain blue. And justice invoked by Piet Retief when our fathers left the Cape Colony; invoked by Joachim Prinsloo in the Volksraad of Natal, at the time of the annexation by England, and to which the Burghers of the Transvaal devoted their cause at Paardekraal, in 1880, remains unchanged and is like a rock, against which the rushing waves of British diplomacy will break.

It works according to eternal laws, unaffected by human pride or change. As the old Greek poet said, it allows the tyrant and his brutal bride to climb higher and higher, to increase his honor and power until he reached the zenith allotted to him, and then he plunges down into the bottomless precipice. Africans, I call upon you! Act as Leonidas and his 300 men, who faced Xerxes and his followers at the Thermopylae, and do not fear men like Milner, Rhodes and Chamberlain, and not even the British Empire, but rely upon the God of our fathers and that justice, which sometimes acts slowly but never slumbers or forgets. Our fathers did not pale before the Spanish Inquisition, but commenced the great struggle for freedom and right, even with the mighty Philipp, regardless of any consequences. Neither torture, nor the murderous bands of Louis XIV could break the spirit of our fathers.

No Alva, no Richelieu succeeded in rendering tyranny victorious over the spirit of freedom and independence of our forefathers, nor will a Chamberlain make the power of capitalism triumph in our lands.

If it is so disposed that we, no matter how small we may be, must be the first of all nations to take up the struggle with the new world tyrant of capitalism, we will be found ready, even if this tyrant is supported by all the power of Jingoism.

May the hope that animated us in our struggle of 1880 be also indelibly engraved upon our hearts in the present supreme moment. May that hope be a beacon of light on our path, wading through blood and tears, that will guide us to a truly United South Africa. And like in 1880 we now confidently lay our cause before the whole world. Whether we conquer, whether we die, liberty will rise in South Africa like the sun rises from the morning clouds, and like it rose in the United States of America, and then it will be from the Zambesi to Simons Bay.

"Africa For The Afrikander."

A Century of Wrong, January 1900, W. T. Stead's Preface

William Thomas Stead.[36] Photo portrait by E. H. Mills, 1905.[21]

In this awful turning point of the history of South Africa, on the eve of the conflict which threatens to exterminate our people, it behoves us to speak the truth in what may be, perchance, our last message to the world."

Such is the raison d'etre[37] of this book. It is issued by State Secretary Reitz as the official exposition of the case of the Boer against the Briton. I regard it as not merely a duty but an honour to be permitted to bring it before the attention of my countrymen.

Rightly or wrongly the British Government has sat in judgment upon the South African Republic, rightly or wrongly it has condemned it to death. And now, before the executioner can carry out the sentence, the accused is entitled to claim the right to speak freely - it may be for the last time - to say why, in his opinion, the sentence should not be executed. A liberty which the English law accords as an unquestioned right to the foulest murderer cannot be denied to the South African Republic. It is on that ground that I have felt bound to afford the spokesman of our Dutch brethren in South Africa the opportunity of stating their case in his own way in the hearing of the Empire.

Despite the diligently propagated legend of a Reptile press fed by Dr. Leyds for the purpose of perverting public opinion, it is indisputable that so far as this country is concerned Mr. Reitz is quite correct in saying that the case of the Transvaal "has been lost by default before the tribunal of public opinion." ....

For nearly a quarter of a century it might almost have been contended that I was one of the leading counsel for the prosecution. First as the friend and advocate of the Rev. John Mackenzie,[38] then as the friend and supporter

[36] William Thomas Stead (5 July 1849–15 April 1912) was a British newspaper editor who, as a pioneer of investigative journalism, became a controversial figure of the Victorian era. Stead published a series of hugely influential campaigns whilst editor of The Pall Mall Gazette, and he is best known for his 1885 series of articles, The Maiden Tribute of Modern Babylon. These were written in support of a bill, later dubbed the "Stead Act", that raised the age of consent from 13 to 16.
Stead's "new journalism" paved the way for the modern tabloid in Great Britain. He has been described as "the most famous journalist in the British Empire." He is considered to have influenced how the press could be used to influence public opinion and government policy and advocated "Government by Journalism". He was known for his reportage on child welfare, social legislation and reformation of England's criminal codes. Stead died in the sinking of the RMS Titanic. W. T. Stead - Wikipedia

[37] The reason for being. (More specifically, the most important reason or purpose for someone or something's existence.)

[38] John Mackenzie (30 August 1835–23 March 1899) was a Scottish Christian missionary who worked in Southern Africa, and who argued for the rights of the native Africans. John Mackenzie (missionary) - Wikipedia

of Mr. Cecil Rhodes,[39] and latterly as the former colleague and upholder of Sir Alfred Milner,[40] it had been my lot constantly, in season and out of season, to defend the cause of the progressive Briton against the Conservative Boer, and especially to advocate the Cause of the Reformers and Uitlanders against the old Tory Administration of President Kruger.

By agitation, by pressure, and even, if need be, in the last resort by legitimate insurrection, I had always been ready to seek the establishment of a progressive Liberal Administration in Pretoria.[41] And I have at least the small consolation of knowing that if any of the movements which I defended had succeeded, the present crisis would never have arisen, and the independence of the South African Republic would have been established on an unassailable basis. But with such a record it is obvious that I was almost the last man in the Empire who could be regarded as an authorised exponent of the case of the Boers.

That in these last months I have been forced to protest against the attempt to stifle their independence is due to a very simple cause. To seek to reform the Transvaal, even by the rough and ready means of a legitimate revolution, is one thing. To conspire to stifle the Republic in order to add its territory to the Empire is a very different thing.

The difference may be illustrated by an instance in our own history. Several years ago I wrote a popular history of the House of Lords, in which I showed, at least to my own satisfaction, that for fifty years our "pig-headed oligarchs" - to borrow a phrase much in favour with the War Party - had inflicted infinite mischief upon the United Kingdom by the way in which they had abused their power to thwart the will of the elected representatives of the people. I am firmly of opinion that our hereditary Chamber has done a thousand times more injury to the subjects of the Queen than President Kruger has ever inflicted upon the aggrieved Uitlanders.

I look forward with a certain grim satisfaction to assisting, in the near future, in a semi-revolutionary agitation against the Peers, in which some of our most potent arguments will be those which the War Party has employed to inflame public sentiment against the Boers.[42]

But, notwithstanding all this, if a conspiracy of Invincibles were to be formed for the purpose of ending the House of Lords by assassinating its members, or by blowing up the Gilded Chamber and all its occupants with dynamite, I should protest against such an outrage as vehemently as I have protested against the more heinous crime that is now in course of perpetration in South Africa. ....

In introducing *A Century of Wrong* to the British public, I carefully disassociate myself from assuming any responsibility for all or any of the statements which it contains. My imprimatur was not sought, nor is it extended to the history contained in *A Century of Wrong*, excepting in so far as relates to its authenticity as an exposition of what our brothers the Boers think of the way in which we have dealt with them for the last hundred years.

That is much more important than the endorsement by any Englishman as to the historical accuracy of the statements which it contains. For what every judicial tribunal desires, first of all, is to hear witnesses at first hand. Hitherto the British public has chiefly been condemned to second-hand testimony. In the pages of A Century of Wrong it will, at least, have an opportunity of hearing the Dutch of South Africa speak for themselves.

There is no question as to the qualifications of Mr. F. W. Reitz to speak on behalf of the Dutch Africander. Although at this moment State Secretary for President Kruger, he was for nearly ten years Chief Justice and then President of the Orange Free State, and he began his life in the Cape Colony. The family is of German origin, but his ancestors migrated to Holland in the seventeenth century and became Dutch. His grandfather emigrated from Holland to the Cape, and founded one of the Africander families. His father was a sheep farmer; one of his uncles was a lieutenant in the British Navy.

[39] Cecil John Rhodes (5 July 1853–26 March 1902) was a British mining magnate and politician in southern Africa who served as Prime Minister of the Cape Colony from 1890 to 1896. Cecil Rhodes - Wikipedia

[40] See: Alfred Milner, 1st Viscount Milner - Wikipedia And generally: High Commissioner for Southern Africa - Wikipedia And, List of governors of British South African colonies - Wikipedia

[41] He is referring to the Jameson Raid. Jameson Raid - Wikipedia

[42] See Winston Churchill's tract 'The People's Rights': selected from his Lancashire and other recent speeches.-London: Hodder & Stoughton, [1909] Catalog Record: Catalog Record: The people's rights : selected from his... | HathiTrust Digital Library

Mr. Reitz is now in his fifty-sixth year, and received a good English education. After graduating at the South African College he came to the United Kingdom, and finished his studies at Edinburgh University, and afterwards at the Inner Temple, where he was called to the Bar in 1868. He then returned to the Cape, and, after practising as a barrister in the Cape courts for six years, was appointed Chief Justice of the Orange Free State, a post which he held for fifteen years. He was then elected and re-elected as President of the Orange Free State. In 1893 he paid a lengthy visit to Europe and to the United Kingdom. After Dr. Leyds was appointed to his present post as foreign representative of the South African Republic, Mr. Reitz was appointed State Secretary, and all the negotiations between the Transvaal and Great Britain passed through his hands.

Mr. Reitz's narrative is not one calculated to minister to our national self-conceit, but it is none the worse on that account. Of those who minister to our vanity we have enough and to spare, with results not altogether desirable. In the long controversy between the Boers and the missionaries Mr. Reitz takes, as might be expected, the view of his own people.

An English lady in South Africa writing to the British Weekly of December 21st, in reply to the statement of the Rev. Dr. Stewart,[43] makes some observations on this feud between the Boers and the missionaries, which it may be well to bear in mind in discussing this question. The lady ("I.M.") says: -

> Dr. Stewart naturally starts from the mission question. I speak as the daughter of one of the greatest mission supporters that South Africa has ever known when I say that the earliest missionaries who came to this country were to a very large extent themselves the cause of all the Boer opposition which they may have had to encounter. When they arrived, they found the Boers at about the same stage of enlightenment with regard to missions as the English themselves had been in the time of Carey.[44] And yet, in spite of prejudice and ignorance, every Boer of any standing was practically doing mission work himself, for when, according to unfailing custom, the "Books" were brought out morning and evening for family worship, the slaves were never allowed to be absent, but had to come and receive instruction with the rest of the family.

But the tone and methods which the missionaries adopted were such as could not fail to arouse the aversion of the farmers, their great idea being that the coloured races, utter savages as yet, should be placed upon complete equality with their superiors. At Earl's Court[45] we have recently seen something of how easily the natives are spoilt, and they were certainly not better in those days. When, however, the Boers showed that they disapproved of all this, the natives were immediately taught to regard them as their oppressors, and were encouraged to insubordination to their masters, and the ill-effects of this policy on the part of the missionaries has reached further than can be told.

May I ask was this the tone that St. Paul adopted in his mission work among the oppressed slaves of his day? It is not those who do not know the Boers, like Dr. Stewart, but those who know them best, like Dr. Andrew Murray,[46] who are not only enamoured of their simple lives, but who know also that with all their disadvantages and their positive faults they are still a people whose rule of life is the Bible, whose God is the God of Israel, and who as a nation have never swerved from the covenant with that God entered into by their fathers, the Huguenots of France and the heroes of the Netherlands.

Upon this phase of the controversy there is no necessity to dwell at present, beyond remarking that those who are at present most disposed to take up what may be regarded as the missionary side should not forget that they are preparing a rod for their own backs. The Aborigines Protection Society[47] has long had a quarrel with the

[43] Unable to identify this individual.

[44] Unable to identify this term.

[45] Earl's Court is a district of Kensington in West London. It lent its name to the now defunct eponymous pleasure grounds opened in 1887 Earl's Court - Wikipedia

[46] Unable to identify this individual.

[47] The Aborigines' Protection Society (APS) was an international human rights organisation founded in 1837, to ensure the health and well-being and the sovereign, legal and religious rights of the indigenous peoples while also promoting the civilisation of the indigenous people who were subjected under colonial powers, in particular the British Empire. In 1909 it merged with the British and Foreign Anti-Slavery Society to form the Anti-Slavery and Aborigines' Protection Society (now Anti-Slavery International). Aborigines' Protection Society - Wikipedia

Boers, but if our Imperialists are going to adopt the platform of Exeter Hall[48] they will very soon find themselves in serious disagreement with Mr. Cecil Rhodes and other Imperialist heroes of the hour.

That the Dutch in South Africa have treated the blacks as the English in other colonies have treated the aborigines is probably true, despite all that Mr. Reitz can say on their behalf. But, whereas in Tasmania and the Australian Colonies the black fellows are exterminated by the advancing Briton, the immediate result of the advent of the Dutch into the Transvaal has been to increase the number of natives from 70,000 to 700,000, without including those who were attracted by the gold mines.

In dealing with native races all white men have the pride of their colour and the arrogance of power. The Boers, no doubt, have many sins lying at their door, but it does not do for the pot to call the kettle black, and so far as South Africa is concerned, the difference between the Dutch and British attitudes toward the native races is more due to the influence of Exeter Hall and the sentiment which it represents than to any practical difference between English and Dutch Colonists as to the status of the coloured man. The English under Exeter Hall have undoubtedly a higher ideal as to the theoretical equality of men of all races; but on the spot the arrogance of colour is often asserted as offensively by the Briton as by the Boer.

The difference between the two is, in short, that the Boer has adjusted his practice to his belief, whereas we believe what we do not practice.

That the black population of the Transvaal is conscious of being treated with exceeding brutality by the Boers is disproved by the fact that for months past all the women and children of the two Republics have been left at the absolute mercy of the natives in the midst of whom they live.

The English reader will naturally turn with more interest to Mr. Reitz's narrative of recent negotiations than to his observations upon the hundred years of history which he says have taught the Dutch that there is no justice to be looked for at the hands of a British Government.

The advocates of the war will be delighted to find that Mr. Reitz asserts in the most uncompromising terms the right of the Transvaal to be regarded as an Independent Sovereign International State. However unpleasant this may be to Downing Street, the war has compelled the Government to recognise the fact. When it began we were haughtily told that there would be no declaration of war, nor would the Republics be recognised as belligerents. The war had not lasted a month before this vainglorious boast was falsified, and we were compelled to recognise the Transvaal as a belligerent State.

It is almost incredible that even Sir William Harcourt[49] should have fallen into the snare set for him by Mr. Chamberlain[50] in this matter. The contention that the Transvaal cannot be an Independent Sovereign State because Article 4 of the Convention of 1884 required that all treaties with foreign Powers should be submitted for assent to England may afford a technical plea for assuming that it was not an Independent Sovereign International State. But, as Mr. Reitz points out, no one questions the fact that Belgium is an International Independent Sovereign State, although the exercise of her sovereignty is limited by an international obligation to maintain neutrality.

A still stronger instance as proving the fact that the status of a sovereign State is not affected by the limitation of the exercise of its sovereignty is afforded by the limitation imposed by the Treaty of Paris on the sovereign right of the Russian Empire to maintain a fleet in the Black Sea. To forbid the Tsar to put an ironclad on the sea which washes his southern coast was a far more drastic limitation of the inalienable rights of an Independent International Sovereign State than the provision that treaties affecting the interests of another Power should be subject to the veto of that Power, but no one has protested that Russia has lost her international status on account of the limitation imposed by the Treaty of Paris.

[48] Exeter Hall was a large public meeting place on the north side of the Strand in central London, opposite where the Savoy Hotel now stands. From 1831 until 1907 Exeter Hall was the venue for many great gatherings by promoters of human betterment, most notably the anti-slavery movement. Exeter Hall - Wikipedia

[49] Sir William George Granville Venables Vernon Harcourt KC (14 October 1827–1 October 1904) was a British lawyer, journalist and Liberal statesman. He served as Member of Parliament for Oxford, Derby then West Monmouthshire and held the offices of Home Secretary and Chancellor of the Exchequer under William Ewart Gladstone before becoming Leader of the Opposition. William Harcourt (politician) - Wikipedia

[50] Joseph Chamberlain (8 July 1836–2 July 1914) was a British statesman who was first a radical Liberal, then, after opposing home rule for Ireland, a Liberal Unionist, and eventually served as a leading imperialist in coalition with the Conservatives. He split both major British parties in the course of his career. Joseph Chamberlain - Wikipedia

In like manner Mr. Reitz argues that the Transvaal, being free to conduct its diplomacy, and to make war, can fairly claim to be a Sovereign International State. The assertion of this fact serves as an Ithuriel's spear[51] to bring into clear relief the significance of the revival by Mr. Chamberlain of the Suzerainty of 1881. Upon this point Mr. Reitz gives us a plain straightforward narrative, the justice and accuracy of which will not be denied by anyone who, like Sir Edward Clarke,[52] takes the trouble to read the official dispatches.

I turn with more interest to Mr. Reitz's narrative of the precise differences of opinion which led to the breaking-off of negotiations between the two Governments. Mr. Chamberlain, it will be remembered, said in his dispatch he had accepted nine-tenths of the conditions laid down by the Boers if the five years' franchise was to be conceded. What the tenth was which was not accepted Mr. Chamberlain has never told us, excepting that it was "a matter of form" which was "not worth a war." Readers of Mr. Reitz's narrative will see that in the opinion of the Boers the sticking point was the question of suzerainty.

If Mr. Chamberlain would have endorsed Sir Alfred Milner's declaration, and have said, as his High Commissioner did, that the question about suzerainty was etymological rather than political, and that he would say no more about it, following Lord Derby's[53] policy and abstaining from using a word which was liable to be misunderstood, there would have been no war. So far as Mr. Reitz's authority goes we are justified in saying that the war was brought about by the persistence of Mr. Chamberlain in reviving the claim of suzerainty which had been expressly surrendered in 1884, and which from 1884 to 1897 had never been asserted by any British Government.

Another point of great importance is the reference which Mr. Reitz makes to the [Jameson] Raid. On this point he speaks with much greater moderation than many English critics of the Government. Lord Loch[54] will be interested in reading Mr. Reitz's account of the way in which his visit to Pretoria was regarded by the Transvaal Government. It shows that it was his visit which first alarmed the Boers, and compelled them to contemplate the possibility of having to defend their independence with arms. But it was not until after the Jameson Raid that

[51] Ithuriel is an angel mentioned in John Milton's epic poem Paradise Lost. In Paradise Lost, Ithuriel is charged to go in search of Satan, who is loose in the Garden of Eden. They find him lurking, in the shape of a toad, close to the ear of the sleeping Eve, attempting to corrupt her thoughts. Ithuriel touches Satan with his spear, causing him to instantly resume his true form. Ithuriel - Wikipedia

[52] Sir Edward Clarence Kerrison, 2nd Baronet (2 January 1821, Brighton–11 July 1886) was a British Conservative Party politician and the Member of Parliament for the borough of Eye. Sir Edward Kerrison, 2nd Baronet - Wikipedia

[53] Edward George Geoffrey Smith-Stanley, 14th Earl of Derby, (29 March 1799–23 October 1869, was a British statesman, three-time Prime Minister of the United Kingdom and, to date, the longest-serving leader of the Conservative Party. He was scion of one of Britain's oldest, wealthiest and most powerful families. He is one of only four British prime ministers to have three or more separate periods in office. However, his ministries each lasted less than two years and totaled three years and 280 days. Derby introduced the state education system in Ireland, and reformed Parliament Edward Smith-Stanley, 14th Earl of Derby - Wikipedia

[54] Henry Brougham Loch, 1st Baron Loch in June 1889 he succeeded Sir Hercules Robinson as Governor of Cape Colony and High Commissioner for Southern Africa. Henry Loch, 1st Baron Loch - Wikipedia

As High Commissioner his duties called for the exercise of great judgment and firmness. The Boers were at the same time striving to frustrate Cecil Rhodes's schemes of northern expansion and planning to occupy Mashonaland, to secure control of Swaziland and Zululand and to acquire the adjacent lands up to the ocean. Loch firmly supported Rhodes, and, by informing President Paul Kruger that troops would be sent to prevent any invasion of territory under British protection, he effectually crushed the Banyailand trek across the Limpopo River (1890–1891). Loch, however, with the approval of the imperial government, concluded in July–August 1890 a convention with President Kruger respecting Swaziland, by which, while the Boers withdrew all claims to territory north of the Transvaal, they were granted an outlet to the sea at Kosi Bay [Near the coast in northern Natal Kosi Bay - Wikipedia]on condition that the republic entered the South African Customs Union. This convention was concluded after negotiations conducted with President Kruger by Jan Hendrik Hofmeyr on behalf of the high commissioner, and was made at a time when the British and Bond parties in Cape Colony were working in harmony.

The Transvaal did not fulfil the necessary conditions, and in view of an increasingly hostile attitude from Pretoria administration Loch became a strong advocate of annexation of the territory east of Swaziland, through which the Boer railway would have to pass to the sea. At length he induced the British government to adopt his view; and on 15 March 1895 it was announced that these territories (Amatongaland, etc.), would be annexed by Britain, an announcement received by Kruger with the greatest astonishment and regret.

Meanwhile, Loch had been forced to intervene in another matter. When the commandeering difficulty of 1894 had roused the Uitlanders in the Transvaal to a dangerous pitch of excitement, he travelled to Pretoria to use his personal influence with President Kruger, and obtained the withdrawal of the obnoxious commandeering regulations. In the following year he entered a strong protest against the new Transvaal franchise law. Nonetheless the general situation in South Africa was assuming year by year a more threatening aspect. Cecil Rhodes, then prime minister of Cape Colony, was strongly in favor of a more energetic policy than was supported by the Imperial government. At the end of March 1895 the high commissioner, finding himself, it is believed, out of touch with his ministers, returned home embarrassed, a few months before the expiry of his term of office. When the Second Boer War broke out in 1899 Loch took a leading part in raising and equipping a body of mounted men, named after him Loch's Horse. Henry Loch, 1st Baron Loch - Wikipedia

they began arming in earnest. As there is so much controversy upon this subject, it may be well to quote here the figures from the Budget of the Transvaal Government, showing the expenditure before and after the Raid.

	Military.	Public Works.	Special Payments.	Sundry Services.	Total.
	£	£	£	£	£
1889	75,523	300,071	58,737	171,088	605,419
1890	42,999	507,579	58,160	133,701	742,439
1891	117,927	492,094	52,486	76,494	739,001
1892	29,739	361,670	40,276	93,410	528,095
1893	19,340	200,106	148,981	132,132	500,559
1894*	28,158	260,962	75,859	163,547	521,526
1895†	87,308	353,724	205,335	838,877	1,485,244
1896	495,618	701,022	682,008	128,724	2,007,372
1897	396,384	1,012,686	248,864	135,345	1,793,279
1898‡	163,451	383,033	157,519	100,874	804,877

*1894.—Year of Lord Loch's visit (in June) to Pretoria.
†1895.—Conspiracy, culminating in the Raid.
‡1898.—First nine months.

Of the Raid itself Mr. Reitz speaks as follows: -

The secret conspiracy of the Capitalists and Jingoes to overthrow the South African Republic began now to gain ground with great rapidity, for just at this critical period Mr. Chamberlain became Secretary of State for the Colonies. In the secret correspondence of the conspirators, reference is continually made to the Colonial Office in a manner which, taken in connection with later revelations and with a successful suppression of the truth, has deepened the impression over the whole world that the Colonial Office was privy to, if not an accomplice in, the villainous attack on the South African Republic.

Nor has the world forgotten how, at the urgent instance of the Africander party in the Cape Colony, an investigation into the causes of the conflict was held in Westminster; how that investigation degenerated into a low attack upon the Government of the deeply maligned and deeply injured South African Republic, and how at the last moment, when the truth was on the point of being revealed, and the conspiracy traced to its fountain head in the British Cabinet, the Commission decided all of a sudden not to make certain compromising documents public.

Here we see to what a depth the old great traditions of British Constitutionalism had sunk under the influence of the ever-increasing and all-absorbing lust of gold, and in the hands of a sharp-witted wholesale dealer, who, like Cleon of old, has constituted himself a statesman.

When Mr. Reitz wrote his book he did not know that immediately after the Raid the British Government began to accumulate information, and to prepare for the war with the Republic which is now in progress. The reason why Mr. Reitz did not refer to this in A Century of Wrong was because documents proving its existence had not fallen into the hands of the Transvaal Government until after the retreat from Glencoe.

Major White and his brother officers who were concerned in the Raid were much chaffed for the incredible simplicity with which he allowed a private memorandum as to preparations for the Raid to fall into the hands of the Boers. His indiscretion has been thrown entirely into the shade by the simplicity which allowed War Office documents of the most secret and compromising nature to fall into the hands of the Boers, showing that preparations for the present war began immediately after the defeat of the Raid. The special correspondent of Reuter with the Boers telegraphed from Glencoe on October 28th as follows: -

The papers captured at Dundee Camp from the British unveil a thoroughly worked out scheme to attack the independence of both Republics as far back as 1896, notwithstanding constant assurances of amity towards the Free State.

Among these papers there are portfolios of military sketches of various routes of invasion from Natal into the Transvaal and Free State, prepared by Major Grant, Captain Melvill, and Captain Gale immediately after the Jameson Raid.

A further portfolio marked secret styled "Reconnaissance Reports of Lines of Advance through the Free State" was prepared by Captain Wolley, on the Intelligence Division of the War Office, in 1897, and is accompanied by a special memorandum, signed by Sir Redvers Buller,[55] to keep it secret.

Besides these there are specially executed maps of the Transvaal and Free State, showing all the natural features, also a further secret Report of Communications in Natal north of Ladysmith, including a memorandum of the road controlling Lang's Nek position.

Further, there is a short Military Report on the Transvaal, printed in India in August last, which was found most interesting. The white population is given at 288,000, of whom the Outlanders number 80,000, and of the Outlanders 30,000 are given as of British descent - which figures the authorities regard as much nearer the truth than Mr. Chamberlain's statements made in the House of Commons.

One report estimates that 4,000 Cape and Natal Colonists would side with the Republics in case of war, and that the small armament of the Transvaal consists of 62,950 rifles, and that the Boers would prove not so mobile or such good marksmen as in the War of Independence.

Further, the British did not think much of the Johannesburg and Pretoria forts.

A further secret Report styled "Military Notes on the Dutch Republics of South Africa," and numbers of other papers, not yet examined, were also found, and are to be forwarded to Pretoria. ....

The concluding chapter of Mr. Reitz's eloquent impeachment of the conduct of Great Britain in South Africa is devoted to a delineation of what he calls Capitalistic Jingoism. It is probable that a great many who will read with scant sympathy his narrative of the grievances of his countrymen in the earlier part, of the century will revel in the invective which he hurls against Mr. Rhodes and the Capitalists of the Rand.[56] If happier times return to South Africa, Mr. Reitz may yet find the mistake he has made in confounding Mr. Rhodes with the mere dividend-earning crew, who brought about this war in order to diminish the cost of crushing gold by five or six shillings a ton. In the realisation of the ideal of Africa for the Africanders Mr. Rhodes might be more helpful to Mr. Reitz and the Dutch of South Africa than any other living man. Whether it is possible for them to forget and forgive the future alone will show. But at present it seems rather as if Mr. Reitz sees nothing between Africanderism and Capitalistic Jingoism but war to the death.

Mr. Reitz breaks off his narrative at the point immediately before the Ultimatum. Those curious politicians who begin their survey of the war from the launching of that declaration will, therefore, find nothing in *A Century of Wrong* to interest them. But those who take a fresh and intelligent view of a long and complicated historical controversy will welcome the authoritative exposition of the causes which, in the opinion of the authors of the Ultimatum, justified, and, indeed, necessitated that decisive step. To what Mr. Reitz has said it is only necessary to add one fact.

The Ultimatum was dated October 9th, 1899. It was the natural response to the menace with which the British Government had favoured them three days previous, when on October 6th they issued the formal notice calling out the Reserves for the avowed object of making war upon the South African Republic.

[55] General Sir Redvers Henry Buller, VC, (7 December 1839–2 June 1908) was a British Army officer and a recipient of the Victoria Cross. He served as Commander-in-Chief of British Forces in South Africa during the early months of the Second Boer War and subsequently commanded the army in Natal until his return to England in November 1900. Redvers Buller - Wikipedia

[56] The location of the gold finds: Witwatersrand - Wikipedia And: Randlord - Wikipedia Randlords were the capitalists who controlled the diamond and gold mining industries in South Africa in its pioneer phase from the 1870s up to World War I. A small number of European financiers, largely of the same generation, gained control of the diamond mining industry at Kimberley, Northern Cape. They set up an infrastructure of financing and industrial consolidation which they then applied to exploit the discoveries of gold from 1886 in Transvaal at Witwatersrand—the "Rand".

Whether they were right or wrong, it is impossible to withhold a tribute of admiration and sympathy for the little States which confront the onslaughts of their Imperial foe with such heroic fortitude and serene courage. As Dr. Max Nordau [57] remarks in the North American Review for December: -

> The fact that a tiny people faces death without hesitation to defend its independence against an enemy fabulously superior in number, or to die in the attempt, presents an aspect of moral beauty which no soul, attuned to higher things, will disregard. Even friends and admirers of England - yea, even the English themselves - strongly sense the pathos in the situation of the Dutch Boers, who feel convinced that they are fighting for their national existence, and agree that it equals the pathos of Leonidas, William Tell, and Kosciusko.[58]

Over and above all else the note in the State Secretary's appeal which will vibrate most loudly in the British heart is that in which he appeals to his countrymen to cling fast to the God of their forefathers, and to the righteousness which is sometimes slow in acting, but which never slumbers or forgets. "It proceeds according to eternal laws, unmoved by human pride and ambition. As the Greek poet of old said, it permits the tyrant, in his boundless self-esteem, to climb higher and higher, and to gain greater honour and might, until he arrives at the appointed height, and then falls down into the infinite depths."

Who is there who remembers the boastings of the British press at the outbreak of the war can read without awe the denunciations of the Hebrew seers against the nations and empires who in arrogance and pride forgot the Lord their God?

"Behold, I am against thee, O thou most proud, saith the Lord God of Hosts: for thy day is come, the time that I will visit thee. And the most proud shall stumble and fall, and none shall raise him up."

This, after all, is the great issue which underlies everything. Is there or is there not in the affairs of men a Providence which the ancients pictured as the slow-footed Nemesis, but which we moderns have somewhat learned to disregard? "If right and wrong, in this God's world of ours, are linked with higher Powers," is the great question which the devout soul, whether warrior or saint, has ever answered in one way. When in this country a leading exponent of popular Liberalism declares that "morally we can never win, but that physically we must and shall," we begin to realise how necessary is the chastisement which has fallen upon us for our sins. If this interpretation of the situation be even approximately correct, the further we go the worse we shall fare. It is vain for us to kick against the pricks.

W.T. Stead. January 1st, 1900.

[57] Max Simon Nordau (born Simon Maximilian Südfeld; July 29, 1849–January 23, 1923) was a Zionist leader, physician, author, and social critic. He was a co-founder of the Zionist Organization together with Theodor Herzl, and president or vice president of several Zionist congresses. Max Nordau - Wikipedia

[58] Andrzej Tadeusz Bonawentura Kościuszko (English: Andrew Thaddeus Bonaventure Kosciuszko; 12 February 1746–15 October 1817) was a Polish military engineer, statesman, and military leader who became a national hero in Poland, Lithuania, Belarus, France and the United States. He fought in the Polish–Lithuanian Commonwealth's struggles against Russia and Prussia, and on the US side in the American Revolutionary War. Tadeusz Kościuszko - Wikipedia

The Executive Council of the Transvaal Boer Government at the start of the war.[22]

Orange Free State Government and Commandants.

Left: Dickson (State Aty.) Swanpoel, Steenkamp, Ferreira, Fick, Poigieter, Wessels Du Toit, Van der Mewe.
Middle: Albrecht, Du Plessis, Nel, Pres. Steyn, Olivier, Prinsloo, De Villiers.
Lower: Prinsloo, Van zyl, Du Plooy, Lubbe, Naudi.[23] Identifications from this copy.[24]

Final Exchanges & Ultimatums

Timeline

1. Friday, September 8th, 1899 British Despatch to Transvaal, setting forth demands for immediate acceptance.
2. Saturday, September 16th, 1899 Unsatisfactory reply by Transvaal Government.
3. Monday, October 9th, 1899 Boer Ultimatum, making war inevitable. Orange Free State joins with the Transvaal.
4. Wednesday, October 11th, 1899 Boer Ultimatum time-limit expired. Great Britain commenced to be at war with Transvaal and Orange Free State.

Adapted from Harold Brown Summary of Final Negotiations.[59] And Boer Politics: Chapter XVII.[60] The Boer Ultimatum.

The Convention of 1884 did not contain any and specific mention of the rights of foreigners to a vote.

Mr. Brown asserts that since 1882 a five year residency for the franchise and citizenship was in effect. He does not say in which Republic but I'm assuming it is the Transvaal.

As the immigrant population continued to increase, in 1887 the qualifying period was raised from five to fifteen years.[61]

In 1897 it was officially estimated that the Boer population of the Transvaal and Orange Free State combined was 70,861.

While resident within the same two territories were 62,509 British subjects, and 15,558 foreigners of other nationalities. [Total 78,067]

Yet there were only 18,126 registered as voters on the voter Rolls. [23.2%][62]

In 1890 a Second Volksraad was convened to address several important legislative subjects.

Dr. Leyds published at Brussels a fairly accurate summary of the subjects discussed by this body.

These were: the franchise, the dynamite monopoly, Swaziland, indemnity for the Raid, and arbitration.

Only the first and last were seriously discussed. President Kruger postponed Swaziland; Sir Alfred Milner postponed the dynamite grievance; and by mutual consent the question of the indemnity was to be left in abeyance till further documents arrived from England.

The British demand as regards the franchise was that everyone who had resided in the country for five years, and anyone who, in future, put in five years' residence, should be entitled to vote.

Further, that the oath of allegiance to the Boer Government should be modified, that the Uitlanders should be guaranteed a certain fixed minimum of representation, and that those properly qualified to vote should be allowed to do so at once.

The Boer reply was an insistence on seven years as the minimum period to qualify for a vote, and numerous restrictions were added. Such as giving up British Citizenship 5 years prior.

[59] War with the Boers, H. Brown, London [1902?] Vol 1 p. 243–248.
Harold Brown, War with the Boers: an account of the past and present troubles with the South African republics London : H. Virtue, [1902?] Catalog Record: War with the Boers : an account of the past... | HathiTrust Digital Library
Five scans, all of University of Wisconsin–Madison origin. Volume 1: #1 - War with the Boers : an account of the past and present ... 1. - Full View | HathiTrust Digital Library

[60] This text from: Boer Politics, By Yves Guyot Translated from the French John Murray, Albemarle Street London 1900. Boer Politics by Yves Guyot - Free Ebook (gutenberg.org) https://gutenberg.org/ebooks/17968 p. 108.

[61] This is what is printed in the book. Some sources state 14 years.

[62] Since half the population were women (18,126) who had not yet been granted the franchise, this figure of 23% doubles to 46%. Also probably 1/4 of the remaining were children and 1/2 male, we would subtract 1/8 (4,879) for an eligible population of 34,154. So, 18,126/34,154 equals 53% of the eligible voters were registered. This is respectable for any democracy. At this time the vote in the UK was similarly restricted by sex and age. It would be interesting to identify what their percentage of population was eligible to vote.

There was also a request that "That all proposals by the President [Kruger] should be subject to the acceptance by the British Government of the principle of arbitration on the differences between the two countries."

In Mr. Brown's view this request, to renounce warfare as a means of resolving differences was a diminution if not abolition of the suzerainty that the British had reserved in the Convention 1884.

There is no doubt that the Boer Republics would like to be recognized as "Sovereign International State."

Between July 10-19 [1899] the Raad passed what they called the new Franchise Bill, putting the period of qualification at seven years.

At the end of the same month our Government proposed another conference, to reconsider the whole matter.

On August 19th this proposal was rejected by the Boer Government, which again gave prominence to its demand that Great Britain should pledge itself never again to intervene in Transvaal affairs, should cease to assert its Suzerainty, and should agree to arbitration.

On these terms they spoke of thinking about considering the five years' franchise.

On August 28th the Boers were told that their terms were impossible.

On September 2nd they withdrew their franchise proposal and insisted anew on their claim to be regarded as a Sovereign International State.

On September 2nd, the Government of Pretoria withdrew its proposal to reduce the delay in granting the franchise to five years; the British Government not having accepted the conditions imposed: (1) Refusal of all enquiry into the condition of the Franchise Law by a Joint Commission; (2) Abrogation of Suzerainty in conformity with the note of the Government of Pretoria, of April 16th, 1898; (3) Refusal to submit questions under discussion to Arbitration.

Despatches of the 8th and 22nd September.

Mr. Chamberlain replied in his despatch of September 8th. He was unable to accept the terms of the Note of April 16th, 1898, which he had formally refused.

He maintained that the Franchise Law was insufficient to guarantee an immediate and effective representation of the Uitlanders.

He demanded that a joint, or unilateral, Commission should be instituted to examine whether the law on the Franchise were not rendered inoperative by the conditions which would make such representations impossible.

The acceptance of these propositions by the South African Republic would put an end to the tension existing between the two Governments, and, in all probability, would render ulterior intervention on the part of Her Majesty's Government to ensure redress of the Uitlanders' grievances unnecessary, as they themselves would thenceforth be entitled to bring them directly to the cognizance of the Executive and the Raad.

Mr. Chamberlain adds that the British Government is prepared to authorise a fresh Conference between the President of the South African Republic and the High Commissioner in order to settle all details of a Tribunal of Arbitration, and the questions capable of being submitted to it on the basis of the Note of August 30th.

This very moderately worded despatch, embodying equally moderate propositions, ended as follows:

"Should, however—which Her Majesty's Government earnestly trusts may not be the case—the reply of the South African Government be negative, or dilatory, it reserves to itself the right to consider the situation de novo, and to formulate its own propositions for a final settlement."

The Government of Pretoria replied on September 16th, by referring to its Note of September 2nd. It devotes an entire paragraph to the statement that the English language will not be admitted in the Volksraad. It refuses to consider at that juncture the appointment of a fresh Conference; it accepts, however, the proposed Joint Commission.

On September 13th the British announced that they would want to discuss the Boer offer of August 19th as to a five years' franchise, but added that Suzerainty would not be waived, and that the Uitlanders must be allowed to use English in the Volksraad.

On September 19th the Boers withdrew all their former offers, and halfheartedly assented to the appointment of a joint committee of inquiry.

On September 22nd, Mr. Chamberlain sent this message effectively breaking off the negotiations.

"Her Majesty's Government are now compelled to consider the matter afresh, and to formulate their own proposals for the settlement of the issues which have been created in South Africa by the policy constantly followed during many years by the Government of the South African Republic."

Mr. Chamberlain replied in his despatch of September 22nd, in which he clearly states the attitude of the British Government. It has no desire to interfere in any way with the independence of the South African Republic. It has not asserted any other rights of interference in the internal affairs of the South African Republic than those derived from the Conventions, or "which belong to every neighbouring Government for the protection of its subjects and of its adjoining possessions. But, by the action of the Government of the South African Republic, who have in their Note of May 9th, asserted the right of the Republic to be a Sovereign International State, it has been compelled to repudiate any such claim."

He repeats that the Franchise would enable the Uitlanders to procure just treatment for themselves, and concludes by saying: "the refusal of the South African Republic to entertain the offer thus made coming, as it does, at the end of nearly four months of negotiations, and of five years of agitation, makes it useless to further pursue a discussion on the lines hitherto followed, and Her Majesty's Government are now compelled to consider the situation afresh and to formulate their own proposals for a final settlement."

The Transvaal Government has accused Sir Alfred Milner of not keeping his word. Two despatches, one from Mr. Chamberlain, September 16th, the other from Sir Alfred Milner, September 20th, refute this allegation.

On September 28th, the Volksraad of the Orange Free State proclaimed that it would "faithfully and honorably fulfil its obligations towards the South African Republic, in accordance with the alliance between the two States, whatever might be the consequences." …..

The Cape presented a petition drawn up by fifty-eight members of the Cape Parliament, five of whom were Ministers and had adopted Mr. Steyn's view; on the other side, fifty-three members of both Chambers passed a resolution approving the policy of the British Government.

On September 29th, the Netherlands Railway stated that communication with Natal was interrupted. The telegraph wires were cut.

On October 2nd, President Kruger, in adjourning the Volksraad sine die, stated that "War is inevitable,"

On October 9th President Kruger, threw aside all semblance of submitting to a convention... handed an Ultimatum to the British Agent at Pretoria.

The Ultimatum demanded Arbitration on all subjects; the withdrawal of British troops; the re-embarkation of British troops landed after June 1st; troops on the high seas not be landed.

"The Transvaal Government requires an immediate and affirmative reply on these four points, before five o'clock, p.m. on Wednesday, October 11th, and it is added that should a satisfactory reply not have reached within that period, it will, to its great regret, be compelled to consider the action of Her Majesty's Government as a formal declaration of War."

Next day [October 10th] Mr. Chamberlain naturally replied that "henceforth all discussion was impossible." Notification was made on the 11th of October. Englishmen and suspected foreigners were expelled.

Ultimatum of October 9th, 1899

Ultimatum of South African Republic, 9th October, 1899.[63] [64] And[65]

Ministry of Foreign Affairs,

Pretoria, 9th October, 1899.

Sir,—

The Government of the South African Republic feels itself compelled to refer the Government of Her Majesty the Queen of Great Britain and Ireland once more to the Convention of London, 1884, concluded between this Republic and the United Kingdom and which in its XIVth Article secures certain specified rights to the white population of this Republic, namely, that "All persons, other than natives, conforming themselves to the laws of the South African Republic

(a) will have full liberty, with their families, to enter, travel, or reside in any part of the South African Republic;
(b) they will be entitled to hire or possess houses, manufactories, warehouses, shops, and premises;

(c) they may carry on their commerce either in person or by any agents whom they may think fit to employ;

(d) they will not be subject, in respect of their persons or property, or in respect of their commerce or industry, to any taxes, whether general or local, other than those which are or may be imposed upon citizens of the said Republic."

This Government wishes further to observe that the above are only rights which Her Majesty's Government have reserved in the above Convention with regard to the Uitlander population of this Republic and that the violation only of those rights could give that Government a right to diplomatic representations or intervention while, moreover, the regulation of all other questions affecting the position or the rights of the Uitlander population under the above-mentioned Convention is handed over to the Government and the representatives of the people of the South African Republic.

Amongst the questions the regulation of which falls exclusively within the competence of the Government and of the Volksraad, are included those of the franchise and representation of the people in this Republic, and although thus the exclusive right of this Government and of the Volksraad for the regulation of that franchise and representation is indisputable, yet this Government has found occasion to discuss in a friendly fashion the franchise and the representation of the people with Her Majesty's Government, without, however, recognizing any rights thereto on the part of Her Majesty's Government.

This Government has also, by the formulation of the now existing Franchise Law and the Resolution with regard to representation, constantly held these friendly discussions before its eyes.

On the part of Her Majesty's Government, however, the friendly nature of these discussions has assumed a more and more threatening tone, and the minds of the people in this Republic and in the whole of South Africa have been excited and a condition of extreme tension has been created, while Her Majesty's Government could no longer agree to the legislation respecting franchise and the Resolution respecting representation in this Republic, and finally, by your note of 25th September, 1899, broke off all friendly correspondence on the subject, and intimated that they must now proceed to formulate their own proposals for a final settlement, and this Government can only see in the above intimation from Her Majesty's Government a new violation of the Convention of London, 1884, which does not reserve to Her Majesty's Government the right to a unilateral settlement of a question which is exclusively a domestic one for this Government and has already been regulated by it.

On account of the strained situation and the consequent serious loss in and interruption of trade in general which the correspondence respecting the franchise and representation in this Republic carried in its train, Her Majesty's Government have recently pressed for an early settlement and finally pressed, by your intervention,

[63] Selected Official Documents of The South African Republic and Great Britain. Hugh Williams and Frederick Hicks, Editors, Library of Congress. 1900 Chapter IV. https://gutenberg.org/ebooks/17136

[64] This document is also in De Wet's book, Three Years' War: By: Christiaan Rudolf De Wet. Charles Scribner's Sons, (1902) Trow Directory Printing and Bookbinding Company New York. Harvard Copy: https://archive.org/details/threeyearswar00wetgoog/mode/2up Project Gutenberg Copy: https://gutenberg.org/ebooks/18794 [EBook #18794] prepared by Marilynda Fraser-Cunliffe, Taavi Kalju.

[65] Three Years' War By: Christiaan Rudolf De Wet. Charles Scribner's Sons, (1902) Trow Directory Printing And Bookbinding Company New York. Harvard Copy: https://archive.org/details/threeyearswar00wetgoog/mode/2up

for an answer within forty-eight hours (subsequently somewhat modified) to your note of the 12th September, replied to by the note of this Government of the 15th September, and your note of the 25th September, 1899, and thereafter further friendly negotiations broke off and this Government received the intimation that the proposal for a final settlement would shortly be made, but although this promise was once more repeated no proposal has up to now reached this Government.

Even while friendly correspondence was still going on an increase of troops on a large scale was introduced by Her Majesty's Government, and stationed in the neighborhood of the borders of this Republic. Having regard to occurrences in the history of this Republic which it is unnecessary here to call to mind, this Government felt obliged to regard this military force in the neighborhood of its borders as a threat against the independence of the South African Republic, since it was aware of no circumstances which could justify the presence of such military force in South Africa and in the neighborhood of its borders.

In answer to an inquiry with respect thereto, addressed to His Excellency the High Commissioner, this Government received, to its great astonishment, in answer, a veiled insinuation that from the side of the Republic (van Republikeinsche zyde) an attack was being made on Her Majesty's Colonies and at the same time a mysterious reference to possibilities whereby it was strengthened in its suspicion that the independence of this Republic was being threatened.

As a defensive measure it was therefore obliged to send a portion of the burghers of this Republic in order to offer the requisite resistance to similar possibilities.

Her Majesty's unlawful intervention in the internal affairs of this Republic in conflict with the Convention of London, 1884, caused by the extraordinary strengthening of troops in the neighborhood of the borders of this Republic, has thus caused an intolerable condition of things to arise whereto this Government feels itself obliged, in the interest not only of this Republic but also of all South Africa, to make an end as soon as possible, and feels itself called upon and obliged to press earnestly and with emphasis for an immediate termination of this state of things and to request Her Majesty's Government to give it the assurance

(a) That all points of mutual difference shall be regulated by the friendly course of arbitration or by whatever amicable way may be agreed upon by this Government with Her Majesty's Government.

(b) That the troops on the borders of this Republic shall be instantly withdrawn.

(c) That all reinforcements of troops which have arrived in South Africa since the 1st June, 1899, shall be removed from South Africa within a reasonable time, to be agreed upon with this Government, and with a mutual assurance and guarantee on the part of this Government that no attack upon or hostilities against any portion of the possessions of the British Government shall be made by the Republic during further negotiations within a period of time to be subsequently agreed upon between the Governments, and this Government will, on compliance therewith, be prepared to withdraw the armed burghers of this Republic from the borders.

(d) That Her Majesty's troops which are now on the high seas shall not be landed in any port of South Africa.

This Government must press for an immediate and affirmative answer to these four questions, and earnestly requests Her Majesty's Government to return such an answer before or upon Wednesday the 11th October, 1899, not later than 5 o'clock p.m., and it desires further to add that in the event of unexpectedly no satisfactory answer being received by it within that interval it will with great regret be compelled to regard the action of Her Majesty's Government as a formal declaration of war, and will not hold itself responsible for the consequences thereof, and that in the event of any further movements of troops taking place within the above-mentioned time in the nearer directions of our borders this Government will be compelled to regard that also as a formal declaration of war.[66]

I have the honour to be, etc.,

F.W. Reitz,

State-Secretary.

[66] Quote of Winston Churchill from 'My Early Life' Chapter XVIII "An ultimatum requiring the withdrawal of the British forces from the neighbourhood of the Republican frontiers, and the arrest of further reinforcements, was telegraphed from Pretoria on the 9th [October]. The notice allowed before its expiry was limited to three days. And from that moment war was certain."

Reply of Great Britain.

Reply of Great Britain, October 10, 1899.[67]

Her Majesty's Government have received with great regret the peremptory demands of the Government of the South African Republic conveyed in your telegram of 9th October, No. 3.

You will inform the Government of the South African Republic, in reply, that the conditions demanded by the Government of the South African Republic are such as Her Majesty's Government deem it impossible to discuss.

Second Version of Reply(s)

Mr. Chamberlain's Telegrams:—[68]

From Mr. Chamberlain to the High Commissioner, Sir Alfred Milner.

(Sent 7.30 p.m. 10th October, 1899)

"10th October, No. 7. The British Agent [Probably William Conyngham Greene] has, in answering the demands of the Government of the South African Republic, to say that, as the Government of the South African Republic have declared in their dispatch, that they will look upon a refusal to consent to their demands as a formal declaration of war, he has received orders to demand his passport." [Presumably, his passport was being held by the Transvaal Govt. while he was in residence]

From Mr. Chamberlain to the High Commissioner, Sir Alfred Milner.

(Sent 10.45 p.m. 10th October, 1899)

"10th October, No. 8. The Government of Her Majesty has received with great sorrow the determined demands of the Government of the South African Republic contained in your telegram of the 9th of October, No. 3. You will, as an answer to the Government of the South African Republic, communicate to them that the conditions put forward by the Government of the South African Republic are of such a nature that the Government of Her Majesty cannot possibly think of taking them into consideration."

67 Selected Official Documents of The South African Republic and Great Britain. Hugh Williams and Frederick Hicks, Editors, Library of Congress. 1900 Chapter IV. https://gutenberg.org/ebooks/17136

68 From the Correspondence Appendix of 'Three Years' War' By: Christiaan Rudolf De Wet. Charles Scribner's Sons, (1902) Trow Directory Printing And Bookbinding Company New York. Harvard Copy: https://archive.org/details/threeyearswar00wetgoog/mode/2up

Century of Wrong Introduction

Brother Afrikanders!

Once more in the annals of our bloodstained history has the day dawned when we are forced to grasp our weapons in order to resume the struggle for liberty and existence, entrusting our national cause to that Providence which has guided our people throughout South Africa in such a miraculous way.

The struggle of now nearly a century, which began when a foreign rule was forced upon the people of the Cape of Good Hope, hastens to an end; we are approaching the last act in that great drama which is so momentous for all South Africa; we have reached a stage when it will be decided whether the sacrifices which both our fathers and we ourselves have made in the cause of freedom have been offered in vain; whether the blood of our race, with which every part of South Africa has been, as it were, consecrated, has been shed in vain; and whether, by the grace of God, the last stone will now be built into the edifice which our fathers began with so much toil and so much sorrow.

The hour has struck which will decide whether South Africa, in jealously guarding its liberty, will enter upon a new phase of its history, or whether our existence as a people will come to an end,

whether we shall be exterminated in the deadly struggle for that liberty which we have prized above all earthly treasures, and whether South Africa will be dominated by Capitalists without conscience, acting in the name and under the protection of an unjust and hated Government 7,000 miles away from here.

In this hour it behooves us to cast a glance back at the history of this great struggle. We do so not to justify ourselves, because liberty, for which we have sacrificed everything, has justified us and screened our faults and failings, but we do so in order that we may be, as it were, sanctified and prepared for the conflict which lies before us, bearing in mind what our people have done and suffered by the help of God. In this way we may be enabled to continue the work of our fathers, and possibly to complete it. Their deeds of heroism in adventures with Bantu and Briton shine forth like guiding stars through the history of the past, in order to point out the way for posterity to reach that goal for which our sorely tried people have made such great sacrifices, and for which they have undergone so many vicissitudes.

The historical survey will, moreover, aid in bringing into stronger relief those naked truths to which the tribunal of impartial history will assuredly testify hereafter, in adjudging the case between ourselves and our enemy. And the questions which present themselves for solution in the approaching conflict have their origin deep in the history of the past; it is only by the light of that history that it becomes possible to discern and appreciate the drifting straws which float on the currents of to-day. By its light we are more clearly enabled to comprehend the truth, to which our people appeal as a final justification for embarking upon the war now so close at hand.

History will show convincingly that the pleas of humanity, civilization, and equal rights, upon which the British Government bases its actions, are nothing else but the recrudescence of that spirit of annexation and plunder which has at all times characterized its dealings with our people.

The Cape of Good Hope

The cause for which we are about to take up arms is the same, though in somewhat different form, as that for which so many of our forefathers underwent the most painful experiences centuries ago, when they abandoned house and fatherland to settle at the Cape of Good Hope, to enjoy there that freedom of conscience which was denied them in the land of their birth. In the beautiful valleys lying between the blue mountains of the Cape of Good Hope they planted the seed-germ of liberty, which sprang up and has since developed with such startling rapidity into the giant tree of to-day - a tree which not only covers a considerable area in this part of the world, but will yet, in God's good time, we feel convinced, stretch out its leafy branches over the whole of South Africa. In spite of the oppressive bonds of the East India Company, the young settlement, containing the noblest blood of old Europe as well as its most exalted aspirations, grew so powerfully that in 1806, [69] when the Colony passed into the hands of England, a strong national sentiment and a spirit of liberty had already been developed.

The Africander Spirit of Liberty

As is forcibly expressed in an old document dating from the most renowned period of our history, there grew out of the two stocks of Hollanders and French Huguenots "a united people, one in religion, united in peaceful reverence for the law, but with a feeling of liberty and independence equal to the wide expanse of territory which they had rescued as a labour of love from the wilderness of nature, or from its still wilder aboriginal inhabitants." When the Dutch Government made way for that of Great Britain in 1806, and, still more, when that change was sealed in 1814 by a transaction in which the Prince of Orange sold the Cape to Great Britain for £6,000,000 against the wish and will of the inhabitants, the little settlement entered upon a new phase of its history, a phase, indeed, in which its people were destined by their heroic struggle for justice, to enlist a world-wide sympathy on their behalf.

England's Native Policy.

Notwithstanding the wild surroundings and the innumerable savage tribes in the background, the young Africander nation had been welded into a white aristocracy, proudly conscious of having maintained its superiority notwithstanding its arduous struggles. It was this sentiment of just pride which the British Government well understood how to wound in its most sensitive part by favouring the natives as against the Africanders. So, for example, the Africander Boers were forced to look with pained eyes on the scenes of their farms and property devastated by the natives without being in a position to defend themselves, because the British Government had even deprived them of their ammunition. In the same way the liberty-loving Africander burgher was coerced by a police composed of Hottentots, the lowest and most despicable class of the aborigines, whom the Africanders justly placed on a far lower social level than that of their own Malay slaves.

Slachter's Nek.

No wonder that in 1815 a number of the Boers were driven into rebellion, a rebellion which found an awful ending in the horrible occurrence of the 9th of March, 1816, when six of the Boers were half hung up in the most inhuman way in the compulsory presence of their wives and children. Their death was truly horrible, for the gallows broke down before the end came; but they were again hoisted up in the agony of dying, and strangled to death in the murderous tragedy of Slachter's Nek. Whatever opinions have been formed of this

[69] When in 1795, France occupied the Dutch Republic, the mother country of the Dutch United East India Company [VOC]. This prompted Great Britain to occupy the Cape Colony in 1795 as a way to better control the seas in order to stop any potential French attempt to reach India. The British sent a fleet of warships which anchored at Simon's Town and, following the defeat of the VOC militia at the Battle of Muizenberg, took control of the territory. The United East India Company transferred its territories and claims to the Batavian Republic (the Revolutionary period Dutch state) in 1798. Improving relations between Britain and Napoleonic France, and its vassal state the Batavian Republic, led the British to hand the Cape of Good Hope over to the Batavian Republic in 1803, under the terms of the Treaty of Amiens.
In 1806, the Cape, now nominally controlled by the Batavian Republic, was occupied again by the British after their victory in the Battle of Blaauwberg. The temporary peace between the UK and Napoleonic France had crumbled into open hostilities. The British, set up a colony on 8 January 1806, to keep Napoleon out of the Cape, and to control the Far East trade routes.

occurrence in other respects, it was at Slachter's Nek[70] that the first bloodstained beacon was erected which marks the boundary between Boer and Briton in South Africa, and the eyes of posterity still glance back shudderingly through the long vista of years at that tragedy of horror.

The Missionaries.

This was, however, but the beginning. Under the cloak of religion British administration continued to display its hate against our people and nationality, and to conceal its self-seeking aims under cover of the most exalted principles. The aid of religion was invoked to reinforce the policy of oppression in order to deal a deeper and more fatal blow to our self-respect.

Emissaries of the London Missionary Society[71] slandered the Boers, and accused them of the most inhuman cruelties to the natives. These libellous stories, endorsed as they were by the British Government, found a ready ear amongst the English, and the result was that under the pressure of powerful philanthropic opinion in England our unfortunate people were more bitterly persecuted than ever, and were finally compelled to defend themselves in courts of law against the coarsest accusations and insults. But they emerged from the ordeal triumphantly, and the records of the criminal courts of the Cape Colony bear indisputable witness to the fact that there were no people amongst the slave-owning classes of the world more humane than the Africander Boers. Their treatment of the natives was based on the theory that natives ought not to be considered as mature and fully developed people, but that they were in reality children who had to be won over to civilisation by just and rigid discipline; they hold the same convictions on this subject to-day, and the enlightened opinion of the civilised world is inclining more and more to the same conclusion. But the fact that their case was a good one, and that it was triumphantly decided in their favour in the law courts, did not serve to diminish, but rather tended to sharpen, the feeling of injustice with which they had been treated.

Emancipation of the Slaves.

A livelier sense of wrong was quickened by the way in which the emancipation of the slaves - in itself an excellent measure - was carried out in the case of the Boers.[72]

Our forefathers had become owners of slaves chiefly imported in English ships and sold to us by Englishmen. The British Government decided to abolish slavery. We had no objection to this, provided we received adequate compensation.[73] Our slaves had been valued by British officials at three millions, but of the twenty millions voted by the Imperial Government for compensation, only one and a quarter millions was destined for South Africa; and this sum was payable in London. It was impossible for us to go there, so we were forced to sell our rights to middlemen and agents for a mere song; and many of our people were so overwhelmed by the difficulties placed in their way that they took no steps whatever to receive their share of the compensation.

Greyheads and widows who had lived in ease and comfort went down poverty-stricken to the grave, and gradually the hard fact was borne in upon us that there was no such thing as Justice for us in England.

[70] The Slachter's Nek Rebellion was an uprising by Boers in 1815 on the eastern border of the Cape Colony Slachter's Nek Rebellion - Wikipedia

[71] The London Missionary Society was an interdenominational evangelical missionary society formed in England in 1795 at the instigation of Welsh Congregationalist minister Edward Williams. It was largely Reformed in outlook, with Congregational missions in Oceania, Africa, and the Americas, although there were also Presbyterians (notable for their work in China), Methodists, Baptists, and various other Protestants involved. It now forms part of the Council for World Mission. London Missionary Society - Wikipedia

[72] The Slavery Abolition Act 1833 (3 & 4 Will. IV c. 73) provided for the gradual abolition of slavery in most parts of the British Empire. This Act of the Parliament of the United Kingdom was passed by Earl Grey's reforming administration and expanded the jurisdiction of the Slave Trade Act 1807 and made the purchase or ownership of slaves illegal within the British Empire except for some areas controlled by the East India Company. Slavery Abolition Act 1833 - Wikipedia

[73] [Theal, History of the Boers, page 64.] See: George McCall Theal - Wikipedia

Slavery at the Cape.

Froude,[74] the English historian, hits the right nail on the head when he says: -

"Slavery at the Cape had been rather domestic than predial;[75] the scandals of the West India plantations were unknown among them.[76]

Because the Dutch are a deliberate and slow people, not given to enthusiasm for new ideas, they fell into disgrace with us, where they have ever since remained. The unfavourable impression of them became a tradition of the English Press, and, unfortunately, of the Colonial Office. We had treated them unfairly as well as unwisely, and we never forgive those whom we have injured."

The Glenelg Policy.

But this was not all. When the English obtained possession of the Cape Colony by convention, the Fish River formed the eastern boundary.[77] The Kaffirs [78] raided the Colony from time to time, but especially in 1834, when they murdered, plundered, and outraged the helpless Colonists in an awful and almost indescribable manner. The Governor was ultimately prevailed upon to free the strip of territory beyond the **Fish River** from the raids of the Kaffirs, and this was done by the aid of the Boers.

But Lord Glenelg,[79] the Colonial Secretary, reversed this policy and restored the whole territory to the natives. He maligned the Boers in even more forcible terms than the emissaries of the London Missionary Society, and openly favoured the Kaffirs, placing them on a higher pedestal than the Boers. The latter had succeeded in rescuing their cattle from the Kaffirs, but were forced to look on passively while the very same cattle, with the owner's brand marks plainly visible, were sold by public auction to defray the cost of the commando. It was useless to hope for justice from Englishmen. There was no security for life and property under the flag of a Government which openly elected to uphold Wrong. The high-minded descendants of the proudest and most stubborn peoples of Europe had to bend the knee before a Government which united a commercial policy of crying injustice with a veneer of simulated philanthropy.

The Dutch Language.

But it was not only in regard to the Natives that the Boers were oppressed and their rights violated. When the Cape was transferred to England in 1806, their language was guaranteed to the Dutch inhabitants. This guarantee was, however, soon to meet the same fate as the treaties and conventions which were concluded by England with our people at later periods.

The violator of treaties fulfilled its obligation by decreeing in 1825 that all documents were for the future to be written in English. Petitions in the language of the country and complaints about bitter grievances were not even acknowledged. The Boers were excluded from the juries because their knowledge of English was too faulty, and their causes and actions had to be determined by Englishmen, with whom they had nothing in common.

[74] James Anthony Froude - Wikipedia

[75] Praedial from Medieval Latin praediālis, from Latin praedium ("farm, estate, land").

[76] [James Anthony Froude, Oceana, page 34.]

[77] [William IV., ch. 57.]

[78] During the Dutch and English Colonial Period the word Kaffir was used to describe monotheistic peoples (Nguni ethnic groups in particular) of South Africa, who were not of a Christian or of an Islamic religious background, without derogatory connotations, until the early twentieth century. It appears in many historical accounts by anthropologists, missionaries and other observers, as well as in academic writings. See Also: Kaffraria and British Kaffraria (Queen Adelaide's Province) were historical regions along the coast north or Port Elizabeth. See: File:Eastern Frontier, Cape of Good Hope, ca 1835.png - Wikimedia Commons Subsequently it became a racial slur. Kaffir (racial term) - Wikipedia See also the British military unit Kaffrarian rifles which were white and black units which were still organized as late as 1947. East London, 1 March 1947. King George VI inspecting 'Kaffrarian Rifles' guard of honour. - Atom site for DRISA And: Kaffrarian Rifles AKA: Buffalo Volunteer Rifles Buffalo Volunteer Rifles - Wikipedia Also: a historical region in Afghanistan and the setting of most of Rudyard Kipling's famous 1888 novella "The Man Who Would Be King." Kafiristan - Wikipedia And: an Arabic and Islamic term which, in the Islamic tradition, refers to a person who disbelieves in God as per Islam. Kafir - Wikipedia PF Note: I have no authority to change the wording used by original authors. There are instances where a pejorative or admiring modifier is used. While this is racist in and of itself, to identify someone by their complexion, in this narrative, identifiers such as Dutch, Boer, English, Uitlander, Indian, and many others are used as means of identification sometimes with pejorative or admiring modifiers.

[79] Charles Grant, 1st Baron Glenelg - Wikipedia

The Great Trek.

After twenty years' experience of British administration it had become abundantly clear to the Boers that there was no prospect of peace and prosperity before them, for their elementary rights had been violated, and they could only expect oppression. They were without adequate guarantees of protection, and their position had become intolerable in the Cape Colony.

They decided to sell home, farm, and all that remained over from the depredations of the Kaffirs, and to trek away from British rule. The Colony was at this time bounded on the north by the Orange River. [80]

Legality of the Trek.

At first, Lieutenant-Governor Stockenstrom[81] was consulted; but he was of opinion that there was no law which could prevent the Boers from leaving the Colony and settling elsewhere. Even if such a statute existed, it would be tyrannical, as well as impossible, to enforce it.[82]

The Cape Attorney-General, Mr. Oliphant,[83] expressed the same opinion, adding that it was clear that the emigrants were determined to go into another country, and not to consider themselves British subjects any longer. The same thing was happening daily in the emigration from England to North America, and the British Government was and would remain powerless to stop the evil.

The territory to the north of the Orange River and to the east of the Drakensberg lay outside the sphere of British influence or authority, and was, as far as was then known, inhabited by savages; but the Boers decided to brave the perils of the wilderness and to negotiate with the savages for the possession of a tract of country, and so form an independent community rather than remain any longer under British rule.

The Manifesto of Piet Retief

In the words of Piet Retief, [84] when he left Grahamstown: -

We despair of saving the Colony from those evils which threaten it by the turbulent and dishonest conduct of vagrants who are allowed to infest the country in every part; nor do we see any prospect of peace or happiness for our children in a country thus distracted by internal commotions.

We complain of the severe losses which we have been forced to sustain by the emancipation of our slaves, and the vexatious laws which have been enacted respecting them.

We complain of the continual system of plunder which we have for years endured from the Kaffirs and other coloured classes, and particularly by the last invasion of the Colony, which has desolated the frontier district and ruined most of the inhabitants.

We complain of the unjustifiable odium which has been cast upon us by interested and dishonest persons, under the name of religion, whose testimony is believed in England to the exclusion of all evidence in our favour; and we can foresee, as the result of this prejudice, nothing but the total ruin of the country.

[80] Great Trek - Wikipedia Good Map to use!

[81] Stockenström family - Wikipedia

[82] [William IV., ch. 57.]

[83] Sir Anthony Oliphant (17 November 1793–9 March 1859) was a Scottish lawyer who was the eighth Chief Justice of Ceylon. In 1827, Oliphant was offered the post of attorney general in the Cape Colony. This was the year when the judicial system in Cape Colony was being reformed. Oliphant was also appointed King's Advocate in the Vice-Admiralty Court. His salary for the two positions amounted to £1,500 per annum. Anthony Oliphant - Wikipedia

[84] Pieter Mauritz Retief (12 November 1780–6 February 1838) was a Voortrekker leader. Settling in 1814 in the frontier region of the Cape Colony, he assumed command of punitive expeditions in response to raiding parties from the adjacent Xhosa territory. He became a spokesperson for the frontier farmers who voiced their discontent, and wrote the Voortrekkers' declaration at their departure from the colony.

He was a leading figure during their Great Trek, and at one stage their elected governor. He proposed Natal as the final destination of their migration and selected a location for its future capital, later named Pietermaritzburg in his honour. The massacre of Retief and his delegation by the Zulu King Dingane and the extermination of several Voortrekker laager camps in the area of the present town of Weenen led to the Battle of Blood River on the Ncome River. The short-lived Boer republic Natalia suffered from ineffective government and was eventually annexed to the British Cape Colony. Piet Retief - Wikipedia

We quit this Colony under the full assurance that the English Government has nothing more to require of us, and will allow us to govern ourselves without its interference in future.

We are now leaving the fruitful land of our birth, in which we have suffered enormous losses and continual vexation, and are about to enter a strange and dangerous territory; but we go with a firm reliance on an all-seeing, just, and merciful God, whom we shall always fear and humbly endeavour to obey.

In the name of all who leave this Colony with me. [Signed] P. Retief.

The English in Pursuit.

We journeyed then with our fathers beyond the Orange River into the unknown north, as free men and subjects of no sovereign upon earth. Then began what the English Member of Parliament, Sir William Molesworth,[85] termed a strange sort of pursuit. The trekking Boer followed by the British Colonial Office was indeed the strangest pursuit ever witnessed on earth.[86] The British Parliament even passed a law in 1836 to impose punishments beyond their jurisdiction up to the 25th degree south, and when we trekked further north, Lord Grey[87] threatened to extend this unrighteous law to the Equator. It may be remarked that in this law it was specially enacted that no sovereignty or overlordship was to be considered as established thereby over the territory in question.

[85] PF: There are several possibilities but believed to be: Sir William Molesworth, 8th Baronet, PC (23 May 1810–22 October 1855) was a Radical British politician, who served in the coalition cabinet of The Earl of Aberdeen from 1853 until his death in 1855 as First Commissioner of Works and then Secretary of State for the Colonies. Sir William Molesworth, 8th Baronet - Wikipedia

[86] [William IV., ch. 57.]

[87] Charles Grey, 2nd Earl Grey (13 March 1764–17 July 1845), known as Viscount Howick between 1806 and 1807, was a British Whig politician who was Prime Minister of the United Kingdom from 1830 to 1834. He was a descendant of the House of Grey and the namesake of Earl Grey tea. Grey was a long-time leader of multiple reform movements. During his time as prime minister, his government brought about two notable reforms. The Reform Act 1832 enacted parliamentary reform, greatly increasing the electorate of the House of Commons.

The Slavery Abolition Act 1833 led to the abolition of slavery in most of the British Empire via a programme of compensated emancipation. Grey was a strong opponent of the foreign and domestic policies of William Pitt the Younger in the 1790s. In 1807, he resigned as foreign secretary to protest against George III's uncompromising rejection of Catholic emancipation. Grey finally resigned as prime minister in 1834 over disagreements in his cabinet regarding Ireland, and retired from politics. Scholars rank him highly among British prime ministers, believing that he averted much civil strife and enabled Victorian progress. Charles Grey, 2nd Earl Grey - Wikipedia

The Trichardt Trek.

The first trek was that of Trichardt[88] and the Van Rensburgs.[89] They went to the north, but the Van Rensburgs were massacred in the most horrible way by the Kaffirs, and Trichardt's party reached Delagoa Bay after indescribable sufferings in a poverty-stricken condition, only to die there of malarial fever.

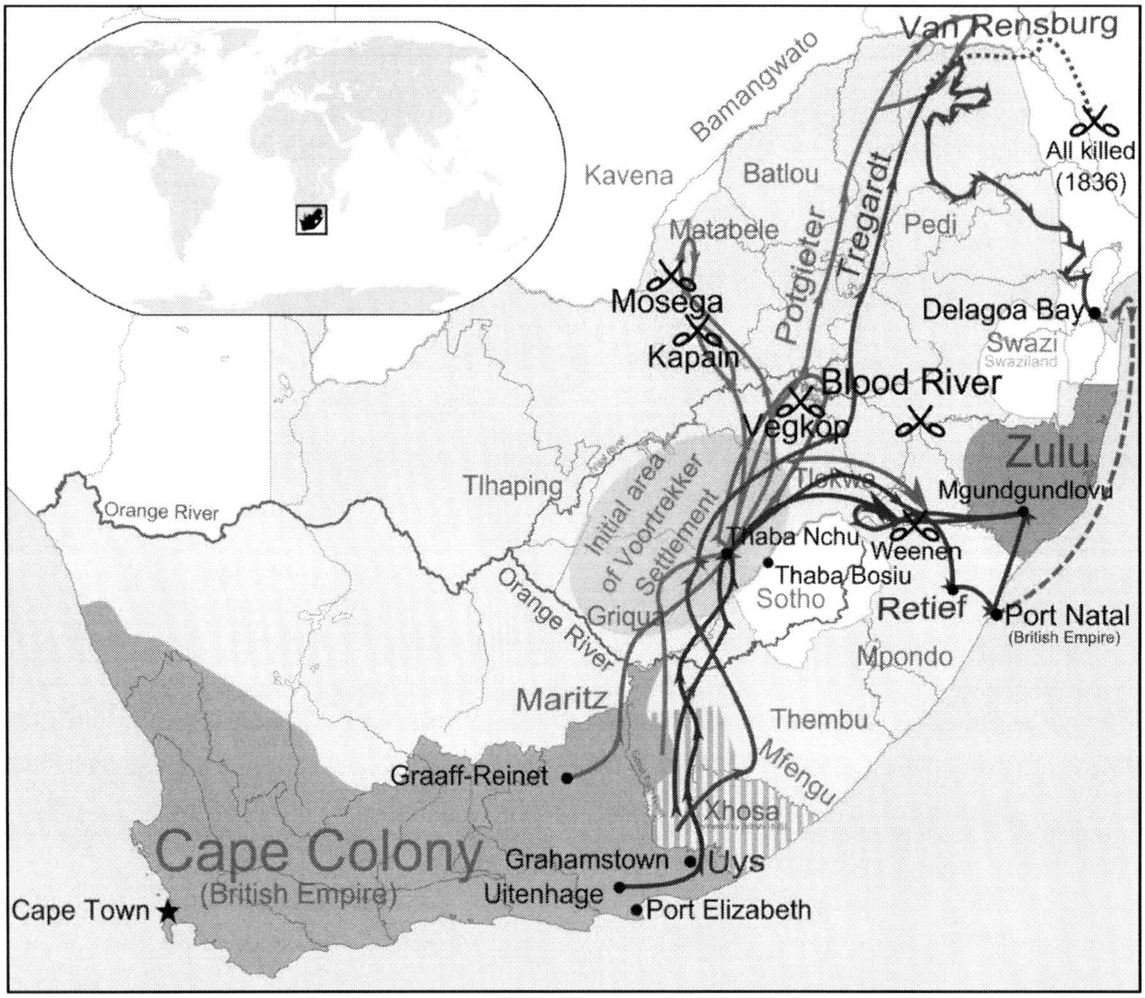

Great Trek Migrations.[25]

[88] Louis Johannes Tregardt, commonly spelled Trichardt (10 August 1783–25 October 1838) was a farmer from the Cape Colony's eastern frontier, who became an early voortrekker leader. Shunning colonial authority, he emigrated in 1834 to live among the Xhosa across the native reserve frontier, before he crossed the Orange River into northern territory. His northward trek, along with fellow trekker Johannes (Hans) van Rensburg, was commenced in early 1836. He led his small party of emigrants, composed of seven Boer farmers, with their wives and thirty-four children & native servants, into the uncharted interior of South Africa, and settled for a year at the base of the Zoutpansberg. At this most northerly point of their trek, unhealthy conditions began to take a toll on man and animal. Seemingly abandoned by a follow-up trek, and distant from supplies and buyers for their ivory, Tregardt abandoned the settlement, and led the party southeastwards to the Portuguese outpost at Delagoa bay that would later become Maputo (the capital city of Mozambique). The oceanward route proved arduous and included the challenge of traversing a section of the northern Drakensberg. Though reaching the fort at Delagoa bay, a number of their party contracted malaria en route. Tregardt's wife perished at the fort in May 1838, followed by Tregardt six months afterward. Louis Tregardt - Wikipedia

[89] Johannes Jacobus (Lang Hans) Janse van Rensburg (12 August 1779–July 1836) was a leader of one of the early Voortrekker groups. His entire group of 51 people was massacred by an 'impi' of Manukosi near Inhambane. Only his two children were spared, as a result of an intervention by another Zulu warrior. Included in the party was Nicholaas Balthasar Prinsloo, who was a Slagtersnek rebel, his wife, Petronella Maria Krugel/Kruger and their family. Lang Hans van Rensburg - Wikipedia See Also African Wikipedia: Schoemansdal - Wikipedia The settlement originated when the Voortrekker leaders Louis Trichardt and Hans van Rensburg reached the Soutpansberg during 1836. After an argument between the two leaders, Van Rensburg continued east towards Maputo but his trek was massacred on the way. Trichart and its people stayed here for over a year. After doing reconnaissance work as far as Zimbabwe and also further east to find van Rensburg, they decided to reach Maputo, away from British control. The epic trek began in September 1837 and they reached their destination seven months later. However, the price was high; 27 of 53 people died of fever, Trichardt too. It took them two and a half months to slide down the Drakensberg Plateau with their nine wagons; The rear wheels of the wagons had to be removed to allow them to slide down the mountain.

The Founding of Natal

Murder of Piet Retief.

The second trek was equally unfortunate. Piet Retief had duly paid for and obtained possession from Dingaan,[90] chief of the Zulus, of that tract of territory now known as Natal, the latter, incited by some Englishmen, treacherously murdered him and his party on the 6th February, 1838;[91] 66 Boers and 30 of their followers perished. The Great Trek thus lost its most courageous and noble-minded leader.[92] Dingaan then sent two of his armies, and they overcame the women and children and the aged at Boesmans River[93] (Blaauw-krantz), where the village of Weenen now stands; 282 white people and 252 servants were massacred.

Towards the end of the year we entered the land of this criminal with a small commando of 464 men, and on the 16th December, 1838 [94]- since known as "Dingaan's Day," the proudest in our history - we overthrew the military might of the Zulus, consisting of 10,000 warriors, and burnt Dingaan's chief kraal.

No Extension of British Territory.

After that we settled down peaceably in Natal, and established a new Republic.[95] [96]The territory had been purchased with our money and baptised with our blood. But the Republic was not permitted to remain in peace for long. The Colonial Office was in pursuit. The Government first of all decided upon a military occupation of Natal, for, as Governor Napier[97] wrote to Lord Russell[98] on the 22nd June, 1840, "it was apparently the fixed determination of Her Majesty's Government not to extend Her Colonial possessions in this quarter of the Globe." The only object of the military occupation was to crush the Boers, as the Governor, Sir George Napier, undisguisedly admitted in his despatch to Lord Glenelg, of the 16th January, 1838. The Boers were to be prevented from obtaining ammunition, and to be forbidden to establish an independent Republic. By these means he hoped to put a stop to the emigration. Lord Stanley[99] instructed Governor Napier on the 10th April, 1842, to cut the emigrant Boers off from all communication, and to inform them that the British Government would assist the savages against them, and would treat them as rebels.

[90] Dingane ka Senzangakhona Zulu (c. 1795–29 January 1840), commonly referred to as Dingane or Dingaan, was a Zulu chief who became king of the Zulu Kingdom in 1828, after assassinating his brother Shaka. He set up his royal capital, uMgungundlovu, and one of numerous military encampments, or kraals, in the Emakhosini Valley just south of the White Umfolozi River, on the slope of Lion Hill (Singonyama). Dingane - Wikipedia And Zulu Kingdom - Wikipedia

[91] The Piet Retief Delegation massacre was the 1838 killing of 100 Voortrekkers by the Zulu king Dingane in what is now KwaZulu-Natal, South Africa. The Voortrekkers, led by Piet Retief, migrated into Natal in 1837 and negotiated a land treaty in February 1838 with Dingane. Upon realizing the ramifications of the imposed contract, Dingane betrayed the Voortrekkers, killing the delegation including Retief on 6 February 1838. The land treaty was later found in Retief's possession. It gave the Voortrekkers the land between the Tugela River and Port St. Johns. This event eventually led to the Battle of Blood River and the eventual defeat of Dingane. Piet Retief Delegation massacre - Wikipedia

[92] [Theal, pages 104–130.]

[93] The Weenen massacre (Afrikaans: Bloukransmoorde) was the massacre of Khoikhoi, Basuto and Voortrekkers by the Zulu Kingdom on 17 February 1838. The massacres occurred at Doringkop, Bloukrans River, Moordspruit, Rensburgspruit and other sites around the present day town of Weenen in South Africa's KwaZulu-Natal province.
After killing Piet Retief and about 100 people of his delegation, the Zulu King Dingane sent his impis to kill the remaining voortrekkers who were camped at Doringkop, Bloukrans (Blaauwekrans), Moordspruit, Rensburgspruit and other sites along the Bushman River (Zulu: Mtshezi), in the present province of KwaZulu-Natal, South Africa, near the town of Weenen. Weenen massacre - Wikipedia

[94] The Battle of Blood River (16 December 1838) was fought on the bank of the Ncome River, in what is today KwaZulu-Natal, South Africa between 464 Voortrekkers ("Pioneers"), led by Andries Pretorius, and an estimated 10,000 to 15,000 Zulu. Estimations of casualties amounted to over 3,000 of King Dingane's soldiers dead, including two Zulu princes competing with Prince Mpande for the Zulu throne. Three Voortrekker commando members were lightly wounded, including Pretorius. Battle of Blood River - Wikipedia

[95] [Theal, 169.]

[96] The Natalia Republic was a short-lived Boer republic founded in 1839 after a Voortrekker victory against the Zulus at the Battle of Blood River. The area was previously named Natália by Portuguese sailors, due to its discovery on Christmas ('Natal' is the Portuguese word for Christmas). The republic came to an end in 1843 when British forces annexed it to form the Colony of Natal. After the British annexation of the Natalia Republic, most local Voortrekkers trekked northwest into Transorangia, later known as the Orange Free State, and the South African Republic. Natalia Republic - Wikipedia

[97] [Theal, 155.]

[98] While he was serving as Secretary of State for the Colonies. John Russell, 1st Earl Russell - Wikipedia

[99] Lord Russell's successor as Secretary of State for the Colonies. Edward Smith-Stanley, 14th Earl of Derby - Wikipedia

Twice we successfully withstood the military[100] occupation; more English perished while in flight from drowning than fell by our bullets.

Commissioner Cloete[101] was sent later to annex the young Republic as a reward for having redeemed it for civilisation.

Protest of Natal

Annexation, however, only took place under strong protest. On the 21st February, 1842, the Volksraad[102] of Maritzburg, under the chairmanship of Joachim Prinsloo,[103] addressed the following letter to Governor Napier: - We know that there is a God, who is the Ruler of heaven and earth, and who has power, and is willing to protect the injured, though weaker, against oppressors. In Him we put our trust, and in the justice of our cause; and should it be His will that total destruction be brought upon us, our wives and children, and everything we possess, we will with due submission acknowledge to have deserved from Him, but not from men. We are aware of the power of Great Britain, and it is not our object to defy that power; but at the same time we cannot allow that might instead of right shall triumph, without having employed all our means to oppose it.[104]

The Boer Women

The Boer women of Maritzburg[105] informed the British Commissioner that, sooner than subject themselves again to British sway, they would walk barefoot over the Drakensberg to freedom or to death.[106] And they were true to their word, as the following incident proves. Andries Pretorius,[107] our brave leader, had ridden through to

[100] The Battle of Congella, beginning 23 May 1842, was between the British of the Cape colony and Voortrekkers or the Boer forces of the Natalia Republic. The Republic of Natalia sought an independent port of entry, free from British control and thus sought to conquer the Port Natal trading settlement which had been settled by mostly British merchants in modern-day KwaZulu-Natal. The battle ended in a British victory due to the heroic ride of Dick King for reinforcements. Battle of Congella - Wikipedia Thirty one days after Captain Smith recruited King, the reinforcements arrived at Port Natal by ship, aboard the Conch and the South Hampton. The reinforcements relieved Captain Smith and the surrounding Boers soon dispersed.

[101] Henry Cloete (a brother of Colonel Josias Cloete) had been Special Commissioner in the Colony of Natal. Cited from: Stuart Cloete - Wikipedia

[102] The Volksraad (English: "People's Council") was the parliament of several of the former South African Republics Volksraad - Wikipedia

[103] Only present reference found: Rietfontein is a peaceful neighbourhood situated in the Pretoria area. Joachim Petrus Prinsloo was well-off and owned several farms in the area, among them Wildebeesfontein, Elandsvlei, Rietfontein,.... Rietfontein, Pretoria - Wikipedia

[104] Annexation: Finally, in deference to the strongly urged views of Sir George Napier, Lord Stanley, in a despatch of 13 December, received in Cape Town on 23 April 1843, consented to Natal becoming a British colony. The institutions adopted were to be as far as possible in accordance with the wishes of the people, but it was a fundamental condition "that there should not be in the eye of the law any distinction or disqualification whatever, founded on mere difference of colour, origin, language or creed."

Sir George then appointed Mr. Henry Cloete (a brother of Colonel Josias Cloete) a special commissioner to explain to the Natal Volksraad the decision of the government. There was a considerable party of Natal Boers still strongly opposed to the British, and they were reinforced by numerous bands of Boers who came over the Drakensberg from Winburg and Potchefstroom. Commandant Jan Mocke of Winburg (who had helped to besiege Captain Smith at Durban) and others of the "war party" attempted to induce the Volksraad not to submit, and a plan was formed to murder Pretorius, Boshoff and other leaders, who were now convinced that the only chance of ending the state of complete anarchy into which the country had fallen was by accepting British sovereignty.

Extent of the colony: On 8 August 1843 the Natal Volksraad unanimously agreed to the terms proposed by Lord Stanley, setting Drakensberg as the northern limit of Natal. Many of the Boers who would not acknowledge British rule trekked once more over the mountains into what became the Orange Free State and Transvaal provinces to seek their freedom and independence. At the end of 1843 there were not more than 500 Dutch families left in Natal.

Cloete, before returning to the Cape, visited Mpande and obtained from him a valuable concession. Hitherto the Tugela River from source to mouth had been the recognized frontier between Natal and Zululand. Mpande gave up to Natal all the territory between the Buffalo and Tugela rivers, which later formed Klip River county. Natalia Republic - Wikipedia

[105] [Theal, 179.]

[106] [Theal, 244.]

[107] Andries Wilhelmus Jacobus Pretorius (27 November 1798–23 July 1853) was a leader of the Boers who was instrumental in the creation of the South African Republic, as well as the earlier but short-lived Natalia Republic, in present-day South Africa. The large city of Pretoria, executive capital of South Africa, is named after him. Andries Pretorius - Wikipedia

Grahamstown, hundreds of miles distant, in order to represent the true facts of our case to Governor Pottinger.[108] He was unsuccessful, for he was obliged to return without a hearing from the Governor, who excused himself under the pretext that he had no time to receive Pretorius. When the latter reached the Drakensberg, on his return, he found nearly the whole population trekking over the mountains away from Natal and away from British sway. His wife was lying ill in the waggon, and his daughter had been severely hurt by the oxen which she was forced to lead.

Suffering in Natal

Sir Harry Smith,[109] who succeeded Pottinger, thus described the condition of the emigrant Boers: -

"They were exposed to a state of misery which he had never before seen equalled, except in Massena's[110] invasion of Portugal. [During the Peninsular War of 1810] The scene was truly heart-rending."

This is what we had to suffer at the hands of the British Government in connection with Natal.

We trekked back over the Drakensberg to the Free State, where some remained, but others wandered northwards over the Vaal River.

The Orange Free State

Boomplaats

Giving effect to Law 6 and 7, William IV[111]., ch. 57, the English appointed a Resident in the Free State. Pretorius, however, gave him 48 hours' notice to quit the Republic.[112] Thereupon Sir Harry Smith mobilised an army, chiefly consisting of blacks, against us white people, and fought us at Boomplaats,[113] on the 29th August, 1848. After an obstinate struggle a Boer named Thomas Dreyer[114] was caught by the blacks of Smith's army, and to the shame of English reputation, was killed by the English Governor for no other crime than that he was once, though years before, a British subject, and had now dared to fight against Her Majesty's Flag. Another murder and deed of shame in South Africa's account with England!

108 Sir Henry Pottinger was governor of the Cape of Good Hope from 1846 to 1847. Born in 1789, he became the first governor of the new colony of Hong Kong. He spent about two years as governor of the Cape mostly on the Eastern Frontier. After his dismissal in 1847 he retired to Malta, where he died in 1856. https://af.wikipedia.org/wiki/Henry_Pottinger

109 Lieutenant-General Sir Henry George Wakelyn Smith, 1st Baronet, GCB (28 June 1787–12 October 1860) was a notable English soldier and military commander in the British Army of the early 19th century. A veteran of the Napoleonic Wars, he is also particularly remembered for his role in the Battle of Aliwal, India in 1846, his subsequent governorship of the Cape Colony, and as the husband of Lady Smith. Ladysmith, KwaZulu-Natal - Wikipedia

In 1847 he returned to South Africa as Governor of Cape Colony and high commissioner, with the local rank of Lieutenant-General, to grapple with the difficulties he had foreseen eleven years before. He took command of an expedition to deal with the disaffected Boers in the Orange River Sovereignty, and fought the Battle of Boomplaats on 29 August 1848. Sir Harry Smith, 1st Baronet - Wikipedia

110 André Masséna, (born; 6 May 1758–4 April 1817) was a French military commander during the French Revolutionary Wars and the Napoleonic Wars. He was one of the original 18 Marshals of the Empire created by Napoleon I. André Masséna - Wikipedia

111 William IV (William Henry; 21 August 1765–20 June 1837) was King of the United Kingdom and King of Hanover from 26 June 1830 until his death in 1837. The third son of George III, William succeeded his elder brother George IV, becoming the last king and penultimate monarch of Britain's House of Hanover.

112 [Theal, 256–64. Hofstede.]

113 The Battle of Boomplaats is a battle that took place on 29 August 1848 near Jagersfontein between Voortrekkers under Andries Pretorius and British forces of Harry Smith. Pretorius was in command of about 300 men against Smith's 1,200 men. Although the British won the battle and Pretorius' force had to go on the run, he suffered only seven casualties compared to the twenty-two (sixteen according to some sources) on the British side. The battle was the first armed struggle of the Boers against British occupation of the area between the Orange and Vaal rivers. Its aftermath also led to the first execution of a Cape Rebel by British authorities in the Cape. Battle of Boomplaats - Wikipedia

114 PF: Not this individual who lived until 1889, but perhaps related: Thomas Dreyer - Wikipedia

Annexation of the Orange Free State

In the meantime Sir Harry Smith had annexed the Free State as the "Orange River Sovereignty,"[115] on the pretext that four-fifths of the inhabitants favoured British dominion, and were only intimidated by the power of Pretorius from manifesting their wishes.

Moshesh

But the British Resident soon came into collision with Moshesh,[116] the great and crafty head chieftain of the Basutos.[117] The Boers were called up to assist, but only 75 responded out of the 1,000 who were called up. The English had then to eat the leek.[118] The Resident informed his Government that the fate of the Orange River Sovereignty depended upon Andries Pretorius, the very man on whose head Sir Harry Smith had put a price of £2,000. Earl Grey[119] censured and abandoned both Sir Harry Smith and the Resident, Major Warden, saying in his despatch to the Governor dated 15th December, 1851, that the British Government had annexed the country on the understanding that the inhabitants had generally desired it. But if they would not support the British Government, which had only been established in their interests, and if they wished to be freed from that authority, there was no longer any use in continuing it.

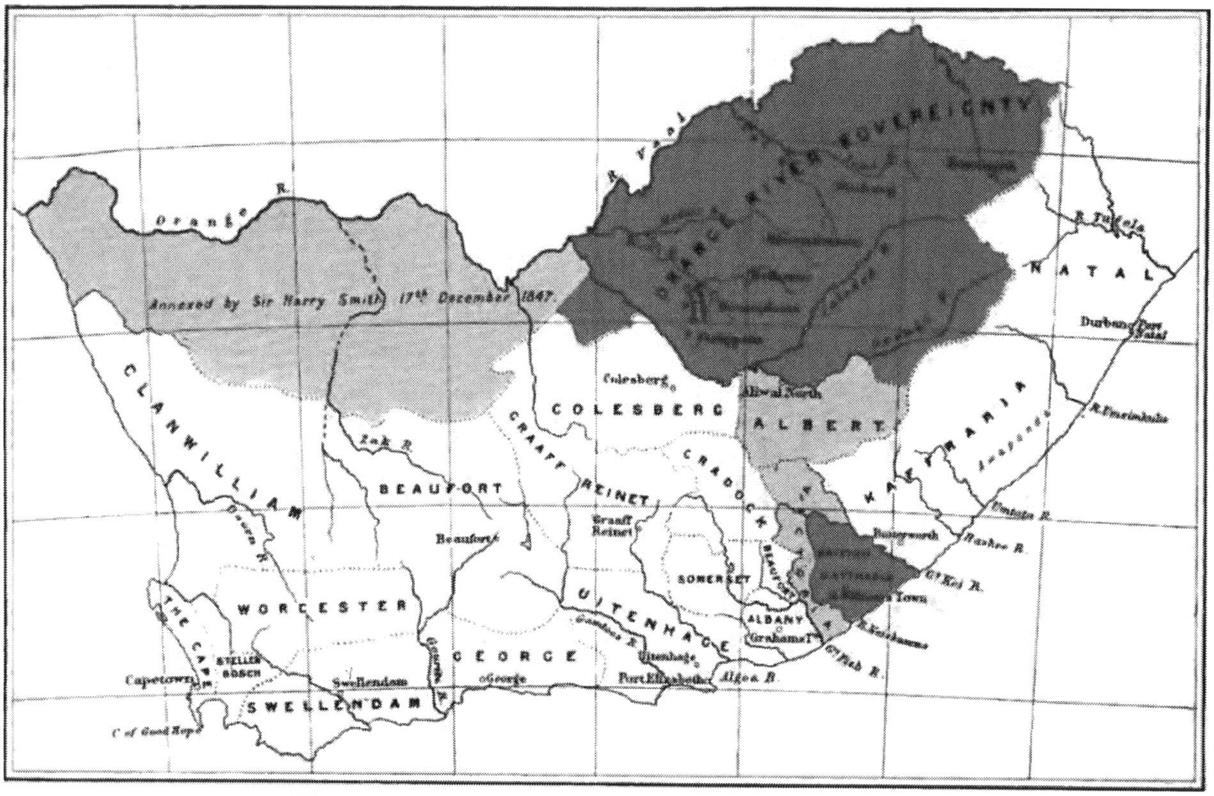

South Africa 1847–1854.[120]

[115] The Orange River Sovereignty (1848–1854) was a short-lived political entity between the Orange and Vaal rivers in Southern Africa, a region known informally as Transorangia. In 1854, it became the Orange Free State. Orange River Sovereignty - Wikipedia

[116] Moshoeshoe I (c. 1776–11 March 1870) At the age of 34 Moshoeshoe formed his own clan and became a chief. He subsequently successfully established Lesotho as a country and became its first ruler from 1822 to 1870. Moshoeshoe I - Wikipedia and Lesotho - Wikipedia An almost unique accomplishment.

[117] Sotho people - Wikipedia , Basuto Gun War - Wikipedia Basutoland - Wikipedia , Lesotho - Wikipedia

[118] Eat the leek - to be compelled to take back one's words or put up with insulting treatment -from the scene between Fluellen and Pistol in Henry V.

[119] Henry George Grey, 3rd Earl Grey 28 December 1802–9 October 1894), known as Viscount Howick from 1807 until 1845, was an English statesman. He was Secretary of State for War and the Colonies from 1846 until 1852. Henry Grey, 3rd Earl Grey - Wikipedia

[120] File:Harry Smith's Annexations, South Africa 1847-1854.jpg - Wikimedia Commons

The Orange Sovereignty once more a Republic.

The Governor was clearly given to understand by the British Government that there was in future to be no interference in any of the wars which might take place between the different tribes and the inhabitants of independent states beyond the Colonial boundaries, no matter how sanguinary such wars might happen to be.

In other words, as Froude says,[121] "In 1852 we had discovered that wars with the Natives and wars with the Dutch were expensive and useless, that sending troops out and killing thousands of Natives was an odd way of protecting them. We resolved then to keep within our own territories, to meddle no more beyond the Orange River, and to leave the Dutch and the Natives to settle their differences among themselves."

And again:[122] "Grown sick at last of enterprises which led neither to honour nor peace, we resolved, in 1852, to leave Boers, Kaffirs, Basutos, and Zulus to themselves, and make the Orange River the boundary of British responsibilities. We made formal treaties with the two Dutch States,[123] [124] binding ourselves to interfere no more between them and the Natives, and to leave them either to establish themselves as a barrier between ourselves and the interior of Africa, or to sink, as was considered most likely, in an unequal struggle with warlike tribes, by whom they were infinitely outnumbered."

The administration of the Free State cost the British taxpayer too much. There was an idea, too, that if enough rope were given to the Boer he would hang himself.

A new Governor, Sir George Cathcart,[125] was sent out with two Special Commissioners to give effect to the new policy. A new Treaty between England and the Free State was signed, by which full independence was guaranteed to the Republic, the British Government undertaking at the same time not to interfere with any of the Native tribes north of the Orange River.[126] [127]

As Cathcart remarked in his letters - the Sovereignty bubble had burst, and the silly Sovereignty farce was played out.

[121] [James Anthony Froude, Oceana, page 31.]

[122] [James Anthony Froude, Oceana, page 36.]

[123] The Sand River Convention with the Boers north of the Vaal River. (Transvaal) South African Republic (SAR) Sand River Convention - Wikipedia and the Orange River Convention with the Orange Free State. Orange River Convention - Wikipedia

[124] See Appendix E for the full text: Also, Sand River Convention - Wikipedia The convention was signed on 17 January 1852, by Commandant-General Andries Pretorius and others, on behalf of the new country, and Major William Samuel Hogge and Charles Mostyn Owen, clerk to the Civil Commissioner of Winburg, duly authorised to, and on behalf of, the British government. The treaty was signed on the farm called Sand River belonging to P. A. Venter, near Ventersburg.

The treaty contained the following provisions:

1. The British government guarantees and grants the emigrant farmers across the Vaal river the right to govern themselves, according to their own laws free from any and all British interference and that the British Government wishes to promote peace, free trade and friendly intercourse with the new country.
2. Britain disclaims any and all alliances with coloured nations to the North of the Vaal river.
3. No slavery be practised in the country to the North of the Vaal river.
4. Ammunition and arms crossing over the border from the South of the Vaal river shall require a certificate from a British Magistrate, and that no arms or munitions be supplied to the natives by either the British or by the people of the new country
5. Criminals will be exchanged between the British and the new country and that summonses for witnesses from both sides of the river be backed up by the magistrates at both sides of the river.
6. It is agreed that certificates of marriages will be recognised on both sides of the river.

7 It is agreed that any and all people now residing in British land but being in possession of land in the new country shall have the free right to sell the property and to move freely over the Vaal river.

[125] Major-General Sir George Cathcart GCB (12 May 1794–5 November 1854) was a British general and diplomat. In 1852 to 1853, as Governor of the Cape of Good Hope, he granted the first constitution to the colony, ending the 8th Cape Frontier War. Coming to terms after the Battle of Berea. George Cathcart - Wikipedia See Also: Battle of Berea - Wikipedia

[126] [James Anthony Froude, Oceana. Hofstede.]

[127] The Orange River Convention signed February 23rd 1854 (sometimes also called the Bloemfontein Convention) was a convention whereby the British formally recognised the independence of the Boers in the area between the Orange and Vaal rivers, which had previously been known as the Orange River Sovereignty. This resulted in the formation of the independent Boer Republic of the Orange Free State. Orange River Convention - Wikipedia

The Diamond Fields

It must not be forgotten that as long as the Free State was English territory it was supposed to include that strip of ground now known as Kimberley[128] and the Diamond Fields; English title deeds had been issued during the Orange River Sovereignty in respect of the ground in question, which was considered to belong to the Sovereignty, [The Orange River Sovereignty] and to be under the jurisdiction of one of the Sovereignty Magistrates. At the reestablishment of the Free State it consequently became a part of the Orange Free State.

The Basutos.

Not fifteen years had elapsed since the Convention between England and the Free State before it was broken by the English. It had been solemnly stipulated that England would not interfere in Native affairs north of the Orange River.

The Basutos had murdered the Freestaters, plundered them, ravished their wives, and committed endless acts of violence. After a bitter struggle of three years, the Freestaters had succeeded in inflicting a well-merited chastisement on the Basutos, when the British intervened in 1869 in favour of the Natives,[129] notwithstanding the fact that they had reiterated their declaration of non-interference in the Aliwal Convention.[130]

The Diamond Fields.

To return to the Diamond Fields, as Froude remarks:[131] "The ink on the Treaty of Aliwal [1869] was scarcely dry when diamonds were discovered in large quantities in a district which we had ourselves treated as part of the Orange Territory." Instead of honestly saying that the British Government relied on its superior strength, and on this ground demanded the territory in question, which contained the richest diamond fields in the world, it hypocritically pretended that the real reason of its depriving the Free State of the Diamond Fields was that they belonged to a Native,[132] notwithstanding the fact that this contention was falsified by the judgment of the

[128] Kimberley is the capital and largest city of the Northern Cape province of South Africa. It is located approximately 110 km east of the confluence of the Vaal and Orange Rivers. The city has considerable historical significance due to its diamond mining past and the siege during the Second Anglo-Boer war. British businessmen Cecil Rhodes and Barney Barnato made their fortunes in Kimberley, and Rhodes established the De Beers diamond company in the early days of the mining town. Kimberley, Northern Cape - Wikipedia

[129] In 1858, hostilities broke out between the Basuto and the Orange Free State. The Basuto suffered a series of defeats in the ensuing three wars that lasted until 1868. In 1866, the two sides signed the Treaty of Thaba Bosiu, whereby Moshoeshoe ceded most of his kingdom's arable land to the Boers. Hostilities resumed soon afterwards and the Boers began employing a scorched earth policy, leading to starvation among the Basuto. Fearing that the destruction of the Basuto people was imminent, Moshoeshoe, his sons and local missionaries began appealing to British High Commissioner for Southern Africa Sir Philip Edmond Wodehouse and the Colony of Natal for protection. Although, initially reluctant to intervene, the British were worried by the disruption in trade caused by the war and the possibility of Boer expansion to the Pondoland coast. In December 1867, the Colonial Office approved Basutoland's annexation by Natal. Distrusting the Natal administration and believing that the Cape Colony was not yet ready to absorb the new territory, Wodehouse disregarded those instructions. He blocked the supply of ammunition to the Free State and on 12 March 1868 proclaimed Basutoland to be a royal dominion. Moshoeshoe died in 1870 and was succeeded by his oldest son Letsie I. Moshoeshoe I - Wikipedia

[130] Intervention of the Governor of Cape Colony led to the conclusion of the treaty of Aliwal North (12 February 1869), which defined the borders between the Orange Free State. Orange Free State - Wikipedia

[131] [James Anthony Froude, Oceana, page 41.]

[132] Nic(h)olaas Waterboer (1819 - 17 September 1896) was a leader ("Kaptijn") of the Griqua people. He ruled during the tumultuous era that followed the discovery of diamonds on his land in the 1860s. As enormous numbers of "diggers" arrived and the population of the diamond fields exploded, tensions grew between the different groups - including the Griquas, the indigenous Tswana people, the Boers and the white English diggers. Disagreements ensued on exactly what the borders of the semi-nomadic Griquas' land was, and a range of regional states, including the Transvaal Republic and the Orange Free State vied for ownership of the land. The Cape Colony meanwhile, the largest and most powerful state in the region, was uniquely uninterested in any form of union with the territory, in spite of strong pressure from the British to enact a form of union.

Against the backdrop of the land tensions, the diggers, led by the eccentric Stafford Parker, proclaimed the independent "Diggers/Klipdrift Republic" in 1870, but it was swiftly annexed to the British Empire as the separate colony of Griqualand West. After briefly moving to Griqualand East, Waterboer moved back to his official residence in Griekwastad in 1874 to reassume his traditional rulership.

With his agent, David Arnot, Waterboer launched a lawsuit over his land rights, which led to him losing significant portions of his territory, but which in the end he won. Waterboer was a famously eloquent orator, and enormously persuasive in his speech. He was fluent in English and Dutch, as well as the native languages of his people - Afrikaans and Griqua. He briefly led a revolt against the British Empire in 1878, which led to his arrest and brief exile to Hopetown. He returned in 1880 though. He died in Griekwastad on 17 September 1896. Nicolaas Waterboer - Wikipedia See Also: Griqua people - Wikipedia

English Courts.[133] "There was a notion also," says Froude, "that the finest diamond mine in the world ought not to be lost to the British Empire."[134] [135]

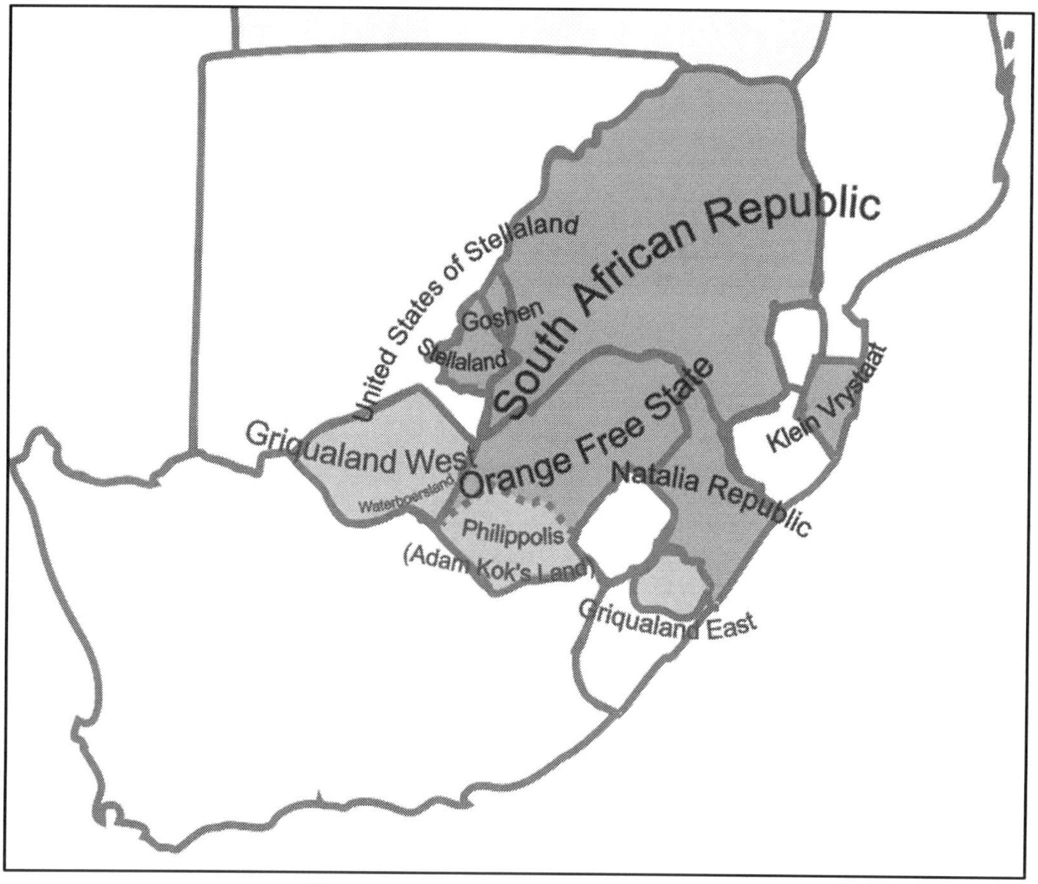

Griqualand West and East.[26]

[133] [James Anthony Froude, Oceana, page 40.]

[134] In the years 1870–1871 a large number of foreign diggers had settled on the diamond fields near the junction of the Vaal and Orange rivers, which were situated in part on land claimed by the Griqua chief Nicholas Waterboer and by the Orange Free State.
The Free State established a temporary government over the diamond fields, but the administration of this body was satisfactory neither to the Free State nor to the diggers. At this juncture Waterboer offered to place the territory under the administration of Queen Victoria. The offer was accepted, and on 27 October 1871 the district, together with some adjacent territory to which the Transvaal had laid claim, was proclaimed, under the name of Griqualand West, British territory.
It was then disposed of by Henry Herbert, 4th Earl of Carnarvon, at that time Secretary of State for the Colonies, who granted to the Free State a £90,000 payment "in full satisfaction of all claims which it considers it may possess to Griqualand West." In the opinion of historian George McCall Theal, the annexation of Griqualand West was probably in the best interests of the Free State. "There was," he stated, "no alternative from British sovereignty other than an independent diamond field republic."
At this time, the Free State Boers, like their Transvaal neighbors, had drifted into financial straits. A paper currency had been instituted, and the notes, known as "bluebacks", soon dropped to less than half their nominal value. Commerce was largely carried on by barter, and many cases of bankruptcy occurred in the state. The influx of British and other immigrants to the diamond fields, in the early 1870s, restored public credit and individual prosperity to the Boers of the Free State. The diamond fields offered a ready market for stock and other agricultural produce. Money flowed into the pockets of the farmers. Public credit was restored. "Bluebacks" recovered par value, and were called in and redeemed by the government. Valuable diamond mines were also discovered within the Free State, of which the one at Jagersfontein was the richest. Capital from Kimberley and London was soon provided with which to work them. Orange Free State - Wikipedia See also: Griqualand West Annexation Act - Wikipedia

[135] Colonial Commissioners arrived in New Rush on 17 November 1871 to exercise authority over the territory on behalf of the Cape Governor. Digger objections and minor riots led to Governor Barkly's visit to New Rush in September the following year, when he revealed a plan instead to have Griqualand West proclaimed a Crown Colony. Richard Southey would arrive as Lieutenant-Governor of the intended Crown Colony in January 1873.
New Rush became Kimberley, by Proclamation dated 5 July 1873. Digger sentiment was expressed in an editorial in the Diamond Field newspaper when it stated "we went to sleep in New Rush and waked up in Kimberley, and so our dream was gone."
Following agreement by the British government on compensation to the Orange Free State for its competing land claims, Griqualand West was annexed to the Cape Colony in 1877. The Cape Prime Minister John Molteno initially had serious doubts about annexing the heavily indebted region, but, after striking a deal with the Home Government and receiving assurances that the local population would be consulted in the process, he passed the Griqualand West Annexation Act on 27 July 1877. Kimberley, Northern Cape - Wikipedia

The ground was thereupon taken from the Boers, and "from that day no Boer in South Africa has been able to trust to English promises."

Later, when Brand [136] went to England, the British Government acknowledged its guilt and paid £90,000 for the richest diamond fields in the world, a sum which scarcely represents the daily output of the mines.

But notwithstanding the Free State Convention, notwithstanding the renewed promises of the Aliwal Convention[137]- the Free State was forced to suffer a third breach of the Convention at the hands of the English. Ten thousand rifles were imported into Kimberley through the Cape Colony, and sold there to the natives who encircled and menaced the two Dutch Republics.[138] General Sir Arthur Cunynghame,[139] the British Commander-in-Chief in South Africa, admits that 400,000 guns were sold to Kaffirs during his term of office. Protests from the Transvaal and the Free State were of no avail.[140] And when the Free State in the exercise of its just rights stopped waggons laden with guns on their way through its territory, it was forced to pay compensation to the British Government.

"The Free State," says the historian Froude, "paid the money, but paid it under protest, with an old-fashioned appeal to the God of Righteousness, whom, strange to say, they believed to be a reality."

It seems thus that there is no place for the God of Righteousness in English policy.

So far we have considered our Exodus from the Cape Colony, and the way in which we were deprived of Natal and the Free State by England. Now for the case of the Transvaal.

The South African Republic

The disastrous fate of the Trichardt Trek has already been told. The Trichardts found the Transvaal overrun by the warriors of Moselikatse,[141] the King of the Matabele and father of Lobengula.[142] The other tribes of the Transvaal were his "dogs," according to the Kaffir term.

Moselikatse.

As soon as he heard of the approach of the emigrant Boers he sent out an army to exterminate them. This army succeeded in cutting off and murdering one or two stragglers, but it was defeated at Vechtkop[143] by the small laager of Sarel Celliers,[144] where the Boer women distinguished themselves by deeds of striking heroism.

[136] Sir Johannes Henricus Brand, GCMG (commonly known as Jan Brand and sometimes as John Henry Brand) (6 December 1823, Cape Town–14 July 1888, Bloemfontein) was a South African lawyer and politician and the fourth State President of the Orange Free State, from 2 February 1864 until his death in 1888. His motto was "Everything will be all right if everyone does his duty". Jan Brand - Wikipedia Also English Wikipedia: Johannes Brand - Wikipedia

[137] [James Anthony Froude Oceana, page 42.]

[138] [Cunynghame, page XI.] My command in South Africa, 1874-1878 : comprising experiences of travel in the colonies of South Africa and the independent states : Cunynghame, Arthur Augustus Thurlow, Sir, 1812-1884 : Free Download, Borrow, and Streaming : Internet Archive

[139] General Sir Arthur Augustus Thurlow Cunynghame (3 August 1812–10 March 1884) was a British Army commander and memoirist. From 1873–78, he commanded the forces at the Cape of Good Hope, serving through the Xhosa Wars in 1877, when he was appointed Lieutenant-Governor of the Colony Arthur Cunynghame - Wikipedia

[140] [James Anthony Froude Oceana, page 42.]

[141] Mzilikazi(c. 1790–9 September 1868) was a Southern African king who founded the Mthwakazi Kingdom now known as Matebeleland, in Zimbabwe. His name means "the great river of blood". Many consider him to be the greatest Southern African military leader after the Zulu king, Shaka. In his autobiography, David Livingstone referred to Mzilikazi as the second most impressive leader he encountered on the African continent. Mzilikazi - Wikipedia

[142] Lobengula Khumalo (c. 1845–presumed January 1894) was the second and last official king of the Northern Ndebele people (historically called Matabele in English). Both names in the Ndebele language mean "the men of the long shields", a reference to the Ndebele warriors' use of the Nguni shield. Lobengula - Wikipedia

[143] The Battle of Vegkop, took place on 16 October 1836 near the present-day town of Heilbron, Free State, South Africa. After an impi of about 600 Matebele murdered 15 to 17 Afrikaner voortrekkers on the Vaal River, abducting three children, King Mzilikazi (c. 1790–9 September 1868; also known as Mzilikazi, Oemsiligasi or Moselekatse; Afrikaans: Silkaats) ordered another attack. The voortrekkers, under the command of Andries Potgieter, repulsed them, but at the cost of abandoning their livestock. Battle of Vegkop - Wikipedia

Shortly afterwards the emigrant Boers journeyed across the Vaal River,[145] and after two battles drove Moselikatse and his hordes across the Limpopo [River][146] right into what is now Matabeleland.[147] Andries Pretorius[148] had come into the Transvaal after the Annexation of Natal, and lived there quietly, notwithstanding the price which had been put on his head after Boomplaats.[149] The British Resident in the Free State, which at this time still belonged to England, was compelled to admit in a letter to the English Governor that the fate of the Free State depended upon the self-same Pretorius. It was owing to his influence that Moshesh had not killed off the English soldiers. People had decided in England - to quote Froude once more - to abandon the Africanders and the Kaffirs beyond the borders to their fate, in the hope that the Kaffirs would exterminate the Africanders.

The Sand River Convention.

According to Molesworth, the English member of Parliament, the Colonial Office was delighted when the Governor received a letter in 1851 from Andries Pretorius, Commandant-General of the Transvaal Boers, in which he offered on behalf of his people to enter into negotiations with the British Government for a Treaty of Peace and Friendship.[150] The price put on his head was promptly cancelled, and when Sir Harry Smith was recalled in disgrace, Governor Cathcart was sent out to recognise the independence of the Boers. The Aberdeen Ministry[151] declared through its representative in the House of Commons that they regretted having crossed the Orange River, as the Boers were hostile to British rule, and that Lord Grey had permitted it out of deference to the views of Sir Harry Smith, against his own better judgment and convictions. This policy was almost unanimously endorsed by the House of Commons.

The proposal of Pretorius was then accepted, and two Assistant Commissioners, Hogge[152] and Owen,[153] were sent out with Governor Cathcart, and met the Boer representatives at Sand River, a meeting which resulted in the Sand River Convention,[154] respectively signed by both the contracting parties.

In this Convention, as in the later Free State Treaty, the Transvaal Boers were guaranteed in the fullest way against interference or hindrance on the part of Great Britain, either in regard to themselves or the natives, to whom it was mutually agreed that the sale of firearms and ammunition should be strictly forbidden. The British Commissioners reported that the recognition of the independence of the Transvaal Boers would secure great advantages, as it would ensure their friendship and prevent any union with Moshesh. It would also be a guarantee against slavery, and would provide for the extradition of criminals.[155] On the 13th May, 1852, great satisfaction was expressed by the Governor, Sir George Cathcart, in his proclamation that one of the first acts of his administration was to approve and fully confirm the Sand River Convention. On the 24th June, 1852, the Colonial Secretary also signified his approval of the Convention.

144 Charl (Sarel) Arnoldus Cilliers (7 September 1801–4 October 1871) was a Voortrekker leader and a preacher. With Andries Pretorius, he led the Boers to a huge victory over the Zulus at the Battle of Blood River in 1838. In particular, Cilliers lead the Voortrekkers in a vow which promised that if God would protect them and deliver the enemy into their hands, they would build a church and commemorate the day of their victory as if it were an annual Sabbath day, which their descendants would also be instructed to honour. Sarel Cilliers - Wikipedia

145 Vaal River - Wikipedia

146 Limpopo River - Wikipedia

147 Matabeleland is a region located in southwestern Zimbabwe. Matabeleland - Wikipedia

148 Andries Wilhelmus Jacobus Pretorius (27 November 1798–23 July 1853) was a leader of the Boers who was instrumental in the creation of the South African Republic, as well as the earlier but short-lived Natalia Republic, in present-day South Africa. The large city of Pretoria, executive capital of South Africa, is named after him. Andries Pretorius - Wikipedia

149 Unknown Reference.

150 [Molesworth.]

151 After the collapse of Lord Derby's minority government, the Whigs and Peelites formed a coalition under the Peelite leader Lord Aberdeen. The government resigned in early 1855 after a large parliamentary majority voted for a select committee to enquire into the incompetent management of the Crimean War. The former Home Secretary, Lord Palmerston, then formed his first government. Aberdeen ministry - Wikipedia

152 Major William Samuel Hogge.

153 Charles Mostyn Owen.

154 See Citation Supra and Appendix E for full text.

155 [Theal, 305.]

Recognition of the South African Republic by Foreign Powers.

The Republic was now in possession of a Convention, which from the nature of its provisions seemed to promise a peaceful future. In addition to Great Britain it was recognised in Holland, France, Germany, Belgium, and especially in the United States of America. The American Secretary of State at Washington,[156] writing to President Pretorius on the 19th November, 1870, said: -

"That his Government, while heartily acknowledging the Sovereignty of the Transvaal Republic, would be ready to take any steps which might be deemed necessary for that purpose."

But no reliance could be placed on England's word, even though it was embodied in a Convention duly signed and ratified, for when the Diamond Fields were discovered, barely seventeen years later, England claimed a portion of Transvaal territory next to that part which had already been wrested from the Free State. Arbitration was decided upon. As the Arbitrators could not agree, the Umpire, Governor Keate,[157] gave judgment against the Transvaal.[158] Thereupon it appeared that the English Arbitrator had bought 12,000 morgen[159] (of the ground in dispute) from the Native Chief Waterboer for a mere song, and also that Governor Keate had accepted Waterboer as a British subject, which was contrary to the Convention. Even Dr. Moffat, who was no friend of the Boers, entered a protest in a letter to the Times, on the ground that the territory in question had all along been the property of the Transvaal.

Sale of guns to Natives.

But this was only one of the breaches of the Convention. When the 400,000 guns, about which Cunynghame and Moodie[160] testify, were sold to the Kaffirs, the Transvaal lodged a strong protest in 1872 with the Cape High Commissioner. Their only satisfaction was an insolent reply from Sir Henry Barkly. [161]

Annexation of the Transvaal.

As a crowning act in these deeds of shame came the Annexation of the Transvaal by Shepstone[162] on the 12th April, 1877. Sir Bartle Frere[163] was sent out as Governor to Cape Town by Lord Carnarvon[164] to carry out the

[156] Hamilton Fish (August 3, 1808–September 7, 1893) was an American politician who served as the 16th Governor of New York from 1849 to 1850, a United States Senator from New York from 1851 to 1857 and the 26th United States Secretary of State from 1869 to 1877. Fish is recognized as the "pillar" of the presidency of Ulysses S. Grant and considered one of the best U.S. Secretaries of State by scholars, known for his judiciousness and efforts towards reform and diplomatic moderation. Fish settled the controversial Alabama Claims with Great Britain through his development of the concept of international arbitration. Hamilton Fish - Wikipedia

[157] Robert William Keate (16 June 1814–17 March 1873) was a career British colonial governor, serving as Lieutenant-governor of the Colony of Natal from 1867 to 1872. Robert William Keate - Wikipedia

[158] The Keate ruling was arbitration on the property rights of the Griqualand West diamond field carried out by Lieutenant General Robert Keate of Natal. In 1870 he ruled in favour of the South African Republic in its border dispute with the Orange Free State. When he was summoned a year later as final arbiter in a similar difference between the South African Republic and the Griqua chief, Nicolaas Waterboer, Keate gave his verdict against the republic. Keate pronunciation - Wikipedikia (wikipedia.org)

[159] A morgen was a unit of measurement of land area in Germany, the Netherlands, Poland, Lithuania and the Dutch colonies, including South Africa and Taiwan. The size of a morgen varies from 1⁄2 to 2+1⁄2 acres (2,000 to 10,100 m2). Morgen - Wikipedia

[160] Thomas Moodie (29 November 1839 - 30 April 1894) was a pioneer who in 1892 led a party of mostly Afrikaner farmers from the Orange Free State to settle in Rhodesia. Moodie, known as "Groot Tom", left Bethlehem on 5 May 1892 with his party, and settled on 4 January 1893, establishing the town of Melsetter, named after the Moodie ancestral home in the Orkney Islands Thomas Moodie (Rhodesian settler) - Wikipedia

[161] Sir Henry Barkly (24 February 1815–20 October 1898) was a British politician, colonial governor and patron of the sciences. Henry Barkly - Wikipedia

[162] Sir Theophilus Shepstone KCMG (8 January 1817–23 June 1893) was a British South African statesman who was responsible for the annexation of the Transvaal to Britain in 1877.

For over thirty years, he was the director of native policy in Natal. A man of strong will and pronounced views he gained a great influence over the indigenous people, by whom he was called "father," The main line of his policy was to maintain tribal customs as far as consistent with principles of humanity, and not to attempt to force the civilisation. The result of his policy remained traceable for some time in the condition and status of the Natal peoples. While he remained in charge there was but one serious revolt—that of Langalibalele in 1873 against a demand that guns be registered.

confederation policy of the latter. Shepstone was also sent to the Transvaal to annex that State, in case the consent of the Volksraad or that of the majority of the inhabitants could be obtained. The Volksraad protested against the Annexation. The President protested. Out of a possible 8,000 burghers, 6,800 protested. But all in vain.

Bishop Colenso[165] declared that:[166] "The sly and underhand way in which the Transvaal has been annexed appears to be unworthy of the English name."

The Free State recorded its deepest regret at the Annexation.

Even Gladstone, [167] in expressing his regret, admitted that England had in the Transvaal acted in such a way as to use the free subjects of a kingdom to oppress the free subjects of a Republic, and to compel them to accept a citizenship which they did not wish to have.

But it was all of no avail.

Sir Garnet Wolseley[168] declared: "As long as the sun shines the Transvaal will remain British Territory." He also stated that the Vaal River would flow backwards to its source over the Drakensberg before England would give up the Transvaal.

Pretexts for the Annexation.

Shepstone's chief pretexts for the Annexation were that the Transvaal could not subdue Secoecoeni,[169] and that the Zulus threatened to overpower the Transvaal. As far as Secoecoeni is concerned, he had shortly before sued for peace, and the Transvaal Republic had fined him 2,000 head of cattle. With regard to the Zulus, the threatened danger was never felt by the Republic. Four hundred burghers had crushed the Zulu power in 1838, and the burghers had crowned Panda, Cetewayo's[170] father, in 1840.

Sir Bartle Frere acknowledged in a letter to Sir Robert Herbert[171] dated 12th January, 1879, that he could not understand how it was that the Zulus had left Natal unmolested for so long, until he found out that the Zulus had

Shepstone went to Pretoria in January 1877, and on 12 April issued a proclamation announcing the establishment of British authority over the Transvaal. Shepstone's force consisted of twenty-five men of the Natal Mounted Police only, but no overt opposition was made to the annexation; the republic at the time was in a condition bordering on anarchy. "Nothing but annexation," wrote Sir Theophilus to the Colonial Office, "will or can save the state, and nothing else can save South Africa from the direst consequences. All the thinking and intelligent people know this, and will be thankful to be delivered from the thraldom of petty factions by which they are perpetually kept in a state of excitement and unrest because the government and everything connected with it is a thorough sham" Theophilus Shepstone - Wikipedia

[163] Sir Henry Bartle Edward Frere, (29 March 1815–29 May 1884) was a Welsh British colonial administrator. He had a successful career in India, rising to become Governor of Bombay (1862–1867). However, as High Commissioner for Southern Africa (1877–1880), he implemented a set of policies which attempted to impose a British confederation on the region and which led to the overthrow of the Cape's first elected government in 1878 and to a string of regional wars, culminating in the invasion of Zululand (1879) and the First Boer War (1880–1881). The British Prime Minister, Gladstone, recalled Frere to London to face charges of misconduct; Whitehall officially censured Frere for acting recklessly. Henry Bartle Frere - Wikipedia

[164] Henry Howard Molyneux Herbert, 4th Earl of Carnarvon, (24 June 1831–29 June 1890), was a British politician and a leading member of the Conservative Party. He was twice Secretary of State for the Colonies and also served as Lord Lieutenant of Ireland. Henry Herbert, 4th Earl of Carnarvon - Wikipedia

[165] John William Colenso (24 January 1814–20 June 1883) was a Cornish cleric and mathematician, defender of the Zulu and biblical scholar, who served as the first Bishop of Natal. He was a scholar of the Zulu language. In his role as an Anglican theologian, Colenso is now remembered for views of the Bible that set off intense controversy. John Colenso - Wikipedia

[166] [30th April, 1877, Letter to the Rev. La Touche.]

[167] William Ewart Gladstone - Wikipedia

[168] Field Marshal Garnet Joseph Wolseley, 1st Viscount Wolseley, (4 June 1833–25 March 1913), was an Anglo-Irish officer in the British Army. He became one of the most influential and admired British generals after a series of successes in Canada, West Africa and Egypt, followed by a central role in modernizing the British Army in promoting efficiency. He served in Burma, the Crimean War, the Indian Mutiny, China, Canada and widely throughout Africa—including his Ashanti campaign (1873–1874) and the Nile Expedition against Mahdist Sudan in 1884–85. Wolseley served as Commander-in-Chief of the Forces from 1895 to 1900. His reputation for efficiency led to the late 19th century English phrase "everything's all Sir Garnet", meaning, "All is in order." Garnet Wolseley, 1st Viscount Wolseley - Wikipedia

[169] PF: Unable to identify this reference.

[170] Cetshwayo - Wikipedia and: Zulu Kingdom - Wikipedia

[171] Sir Robert George Wyndham Herbert, GCB (12 June 1831–6 May 1905), was the first Premier of Queensland, Australia. At 28 years and 181 days of age, he was the youngest person ever to be elected premier of an Australian state. Robert Herbert - Wikipedia

been thoroughly subdued by the Boers during Dingaan's time. Just before the Annexation a small patrol of Boers had pursued the Chief Umbeline[172] into the very heart of Zululand. But Bishop Colenso points out clearly what a fraudulent stalking horse the Zulu difficulty was. There had been a dispute of some years standing between the Transvaal and the Zulus about a strip of territory along the border, which had been claimed and occupied by the Boers since 1869. The question was referred to Shepstone before the Annexation, while he was still in Natal, and he gave a direct decision against the Boers, and in favour of the Zulus.

There was thus no cause on that account for the fear of a Zulu attack upon the Transvaal. But scarcely had Shepstone become administrator of the Transvaal when he declared the ground in dispute to be British territory, and discovered that there was the strongest evidence for the contention of the Boers that the Zulus had no right to the ground. Bulwer,[173] the Governor of Natal, appointed a Boundary Commission, which decided in favour of the Zulus, but Shepstone vehemently opposed their verdict, and Bartle Frere and the High Commissioner (Wolseley) followed him blindly.[174] The result was that England sent an ultimatum to the Zulus, and the Zulu War took place, which lowered the prestige of England among the Natives of South Africa.

It will thus be seen that Shepstone's two chief reasons for the Annexation were devoid of foundation.

It was naturally difficult for the Secretary of State to justify his instructions that the Annexation of the Transvaal was only to take place in case a majority of the inhabitants favoured such a course, in face of the fact that 6,800 out of 8,000 burghers had protested against it.

But both Shepstone and Lord Carnarvon declared without a shadow of proof that the signatures of the protesting petitions were obtained under threats of violence. The case, indeed, was exactly the reverse. When the meeting was held at Pretoria to sign this petition, Shepstone caused the cannons to be pointed at the assemblage. As if this were not enough, he issued a menacing proclamation against the signing of the petition.

When these pretexts were thus disposed of, they relied on the fact that the Annexation was a fait accompli.

Delegates were sent to England to protest against the Annexation, but Lord Carnarvon told them that he would only be misleading them if he held out any hope of restitution. Gladstone afterwards endorsed this by saying that he could not advise the Queen to withdraw her Sovereignty from the Transvaal.

When it was represented that the Annexation was a deliberate breach of the Sand River Convention, Sir Bartle Frere replied, in 1879, that if they wished to go back to the Sand River Convention, they might just as well go back to the Creation!

It is necessary here not to lose sight of the fact that the ground, which according to the Keate award in 1870 had been declared to lie beyond the borders of the Republic, was now included by Shepstone as being a part of the Transvaal.

There were, however, other matters which under Republican administration were branded as wrong, but which under English rule were perfectly right. In the Secoecoeni War under the Republic the British High Commissioner had protested against the use of the Swazies[175] and Volunteers by the Republic in conducting the campaign.

Under British administration the war was carried on at first by regulars only, but when these were defeated by the Kaffirs, an army of Swazies, as well as Volunteers, was collected. The number of the former can be gathered from the fact that 500 Swazies were killed. The atrocities committed by these Swazi allies of the English on the people of Secoecoeni's tribe were truly awful.

Bishop Colenso, who condemned this incident, said, with regard to the results of the Annexation of the Republic, that the Zululand difficulty, as well as that with Secoecoeni, was the direct consequence of the unfortunate Annexation of the Transvaal, which would not have happened if we had not taken possession of the

[172] PF: Unable to identify this reference.

[173] Sir Henry Ernest Gascoyne Bulwer, GCMG (11 December 1836–30 September 1914), the nephew of Sir Henry Lytton Bulwer and brother to Edward Earle Gascoyne Bulwer, was a British colonial administrator and diplomat. Henry Ernest Gascoyne Bulwer - Wikipedia

[174] [Martineau, The Transvaal Trouble, page 76.]

[175] The Swazi or Swati (Swati: Emaswati, singular Liswati) are a Bantu ethnic group in Southern Africa, inhabiting Eswatini, a sovereign kingdom in Southern Africa.

The Swati people and the Kingdom of Eswatini today are named after Mswati II, who became king in 1839 after the death of his father King Sobhuza who strategically defeated the British who occupied Eswatini. Swazi people - Wikipedia And: Eswatini - Wikipedia

country like a lot of freebooters, partly by "trickery," partly by "bullying." Elsewhere he said: "And in this way we annexed the Transvaal, and that act brought as its Nemesis the Zulu difficulty."

That the British Government had all along considered the Zulus as a means of annihilating the Transvaal when a favourable opportunity occurred, is clear from a letter which the High Commissioner, Sir Bartle Frere, wrote to General Ponsonby,[176] in which he says: -

"That while the Boer Republic was a rival and semi-hostile power, it was a Natal weakness rather to pet the Zulus as one might a tame wolf who only devoured one's neighbours' sheep. We always remonstrated, but rather feebly, and now that both flocks belong to us, we are rather embarrassed in stopping the wolf's ravages."[177]

And again in a letter to Sir Robert Herbert: -

"The Boers were aggressive, the English were not; and were well inclined to help the Zulus against the Boers. I have been shocked to find how very close to the wind the predecessors of the present Government here have sailed in supporting the Zulus against Boer aggression. Mr. John Dunn, still a salaried official of this Government, thinking himself bound to explain his own share in supplying rifles to the Zulus in consequence of the revelations in a late trial of a Durban gun-runner, avows that he did so with the knowledge, if not the consent, and at the suggestion of (naming a high Colonial official) in Natal. There can be no doubt that Natal sympathy was strongly with the Zulus as against the Boers, and, what is worse, is so still."[178]

Under such circumstances did the Annexation take place. The English did not scruple to make use of Kaffir aid against the Boers, as at Boomplaats, and it was brought home in every possible way to the British Nation that a great wrong had been committed here; but even the High Commissioner, though he heard the words issue from our bleeding hearts, wished that he had brought some artillery in order to disperse us, and misrepresented us beyond measure.

Full of hope we said to ourselves if only the Queen of England and the English people knew that in the Transvaal a people were being oppressed, they would never suffer it.

The War of Freedom.

But we had now to admit that it was of no use appealing to England, because there was no one to hear us. Trusting in the Almighty God of righteousness and justice, we armed ourselves for an apparently hopeless struggle in the firm conviction that whether we conquered or whether we died, the sun of freedom in South Africa would arise out of the morning mists. With God's all-powerful aid we gained the victory, and for a time at least it seemed as if our liberty was secure.

At Bronkorst Spruit,[179] at Laing's Nek,[180] at Ingogo,[181] and at Majuba,[182] God gave us victory, although in each case the British troopers outnumbered us, and were more powerfully armed than ourselves.[183]

After these victories had given new force to our arguments, the British Government, under the leadership of Gladstone, a man whom we shall never forget, decided to cancel the Annexation, and to restore to us our violated rights.

[176] Major-General Sir Henry Frederick Ponsonby (10 December 1825–21 November 1895) was a British soldier and royal court official who served as Queen Victoria's Private Secretary. Henry Ponsonby - Wikipedia

[177] [Martineau, The Transvaal Trouble, page 69.]

[178] [The Transvaal Trouble, page 76.]

[179] The Battle of Bronkhorstspruit was the first major engagement of the First Boer War. It took place by the Bronkhorst Spruit (river), a few kilometres east of the town of Bronkhorstspruit, Transvaal on 20 December 1880 Battle of Bronkhorstspruit - Wikipedia

[180] The Battle of Laing's Nek was a major battle fought at Laing's Nek during the First Boer War on 28 January 1881. Battle of Laing's Nek - Wikipedia

[181] Battle of Schuinshoogte, also known as Battle of Ingogo, was fought north of Newcastle, KwaZulu-Natal, on 8 February 1881 Battle of Schuinshoogte - Wikipedia

[182] The Battle of Majuba Hill on 27 February 1881 was the final and decisive battle of the First Boer War that was a resounding victory for the Boers. Battle of Majuba Hill - Wikipedia

[183] The First Boer War was a war fought from 16 December 1880 until 23 March 1881 between the United Kingdom and Boers of the Transvaal. The war resulted in a Boer victory and eventual independence of the South African Republic See: First Boer War - Wikipedia

Conventions of 1881 and 1884

Pretoria Convention.

An ordinary person would have thought that the only upright way of carrying a policy of restitution into effect would have been for the British Government to have returned to the provisions of the Sand River Convention. If the Annexation was wrong in itself - without taking the Boer victories into consideration - then it ought to have been abolished with all its consequences, and there ought to have been a **restitutio in integrum**[184] of that Republic; that is to say, the Boers ought to have been placed in exactly the same position as they were in before the Annexation. But what happened?

With a magnanimity which the English press and English orators are never tired of vaunting, they gave us back our country, but the violation of the Sand River Convention remained unredressed. Instead of a sovereign freedom, we obtained free internal administration, subject to the suzerain power of Her Majesty over the Republic. This occurred by virtue of the Convention of Pretoria, [Convention of 1881, see Appendix A.] the preamble of which bestowed self-government on the Transvaal State with the express reservation of suzerainty. The articles of that Convention endeavoured to establish a modus vivendi[185] between such self-government and the aforesaid suzerainty. Under this bilateral arrangement the Republic was governed for three years by two heterogeneous principles - that of representative self-government, and that represented by the British Agent. This system was naturally unworkable; it was also clear that the arrangement of 1881 was not to be considered as final.

The London Convention.

The suzerainty was above all an absurdity which was not possible to reconcile with practical efficacy. So with the approval of the British Government a Deputation went to London in 1883, in order to get the status of the Republic altered, and to substitute a new Convention for that of Pretoria. The Deputation proposed to return to the position as laid down by the Sand River Convention, and that was in fact the only upright and statesmanlike arrangement possible. But according to the evidence of one of the witnesses on the British side, the Rev. D.P. Faure, [186] the Ministry suffered from a very unwholesome dread of Parliament; so it would not agree to this, and submitted a counter proposal (see Appendix A.), which eventually was accepted by the Deputation, and the conditions of which are to-day of the greatest importance to us.

This Draft was constructed out of the Pretoria Convention with such alterations as were designed to make it acceptable to the Deputation. The preamble under which complete self-government, subject to the suzerainty, was granted to the Republic was deliberately erased by Lord Derby, then Secretary of State for the Colonies, so that the suzerainty naturally lapsed when the Draft was eventually accepted. In order to make it perfectly clear that the status of the Republic was put upon another basis, the title "Transvaal State" was altered to that of the "South African Republic." All articles in the Pretoria Convention which gave the British Government any authority in the internal affairs of this Republic were done away with. As far as foreign affairs were concerned, a great and far-reaching change was made. It was stipulated in Article 2 of the Pretoria Convention that "Her Majesty reserves to herself, her heirs and successors (a), the right from time to time to appoint a British Resident in and for the said State, with such duties and functions as are hereinafter defined; (b), the right to move troops through the said State in time of war or in case of the apprehension of immediate war between the Suzerain Power and any Foreign State or Native tribe in South Africa; and (c) the control of the external relations of the said State, including the conclusion of treaties and the conduct of diplomatic intercourse with Foreign Powers, such intercourse to be carried on through Her Majesty's diplomatic and consular officers abroad."

This was superseded by Article 4 of the Convention of London, which was to the following effect: -

[184] A Latin term that means "restoration to original condition."

[185] A Latin phrase that means "mode of living" or "way of life". It often is used to mean an arrangement or agreement that allows conflicting parties to coexist in peace.

[186] David Pieter Faure was the founder of the Unitarian Church in South Africa, an interpreter and a Grand Master of the Freemasons in South Africa. David Faure - Wikipedia

"The South African Republic will conclude no treaty or engagement with any State or Nation other than the Orange Free State, nor with any Native tribe to the eastward or westward of the Republic, until the same has been approved by Her Majesty the Queen.

"Such approval shall be considered to have been granted if Her Majesty's Government shall not, within six months after receiving a copy of such treaty (which shall be delivered to them immediately upon its completion), have notified that the conclusion of such treaty is in conflict with the interests of Great Britain, or any of Her Majesty's possessions in South Africa."

The right of the British Government to exercise control over all our foreign relations, and to conduct all our diplomatic negotiations through its own Agent, was thus replaced by the far more slender right of approving or disapproving of our treaties and conventions after they were completed, and then only when it affected the interests of Great Britain or Her Majesty's possessions in South Africa.

Status of the Republic.

It was this Article 4 which gave an appearance of truth (and an appearance only) to Lord Derby's declaration in the House of Lords that although he had omitted the term of suzerainty, the substance thereof remained. It would have been more correct to have said that owing to the lapse of suzerainty the South African Republic no longer fell under the head of a semi-suzerain State, but that it had become a free, independent, sovereign international State, the sovereignty of which was only limited by the restriction contained in Article 4 of the Convention. Sovereignty need not of necessity be absolute. Belgium is a sovereign international State, although it is bound to observe a condition of permanent neutrality. The South African Republic falls undoubtedly under this category of States, the sovereignty of which is limited in one or other defined direction. But the fact of its sovereignty is nevertheless irrefutable. It will be pointed out later how this position, which is undoubtedly the correct one, has been consistently upheld by the Government of the South African Republic, but it is necessary now to revert to the historical development.

Capitalistic Jingoism—First Period

The Gold Fields.

In 1886 gold was discovered in great quantities and in different parts of the South African Republic, and with that discovery our people entered upon a new phase of their history.[187] The South African Republic was to develop within a few years from a condition of great poverty into a rich and prosperous State, a country calculated in every respect to awaken and inflame the greed of the Capitalistic speculator. Within a few years the South African Republic was ranked among the first gold-producing countries of the world.

The bare veldt of hitherto was overspread with large townships inhabited by a speculative and bustling class brought together from all corners of the earth. The Boers, who had hitherto followed pastoral and hunting pursuits, were now called upon to fulfil one of the most difficult tasks in the world, namely, the management of a complicated administration, and the government of a large digging population, which had sprung up suddenly under the most extraordinary circumstances. And how have they acquitted themselves of the task? We quote the following from a brilliant pamphlet by Olive Schreiner,[188] who possesses a deeper insight into the true condition of affairs in South Africa than has been vouchsafed to any other writer on the same subject: -

"We put it to all generous and just spirits, whether of statesmen or thinkers, whether the little Republic does not deserve our sympathy, which wise minds give to all who have to deal with new and complex problems, where the past experience of humanity has not marked out a path - and whether, if we touch the subject at all, it is not

[187] Witwatersrand Gold Rush - Wikipedia

[188] Olive Schreiner (24 March 1855–11 December 1920) was a South African author, anti-war campaigner and intellectual. She is best remembered today for her novel The Story of an African Farm (1883), which has been highly acclaimed. It deals boldly with such contemporary issues as agnosticism, existential independence, individualism, the professional aspirations of women, and the elemental nature of life on the colonial frontier. Olive Schreiner - Wikipedia

necessary that it should be in that large impartial, truth-seeking spirit in which humanity demands we should approach all great social difficulties and questions?"[189]

"It is sometimes said that when one stands looking down from the edge of this hill at the great mining camp of Johannesburg stretching beneath, with its heaps of white sand and debris mountain high, its mining chimneys belching forth smoke, with its seventy thousand Kaffirs and its eighty thousand men and women, white or coloured, of all nationalities, gathered here in the space of a few years on the spot where, fifteen years ago, the Boer's son guided his sheep to the water and the Boer's wife sat alone at evening at the house door to watch the sunset, we are looking upon one of the most wonderful spectacles on earth. And it is wonderful; but as we look at it the thought always arises within us of something more wonderful yet - the marvellous manner in which a little nation of simple folk, living in peace in the land they loved, far from the rush of cities and the concourse of men, have risen to the difficulties of their condition; how they, without instruction in statecraft or traditionary rules of policy, have risen to face their great difficulties, and have sincerely endeavoured to meet them in a large spirit, and have largely succeeded.

Nothing but that curious and wonderful instinct for statecraft and the organisation and arrangement of new social conditions which seem inherent as a gift of the blood to all those peoples who took their rise in the little deltas on the north-east of the Continent of Europe where the English and Dutch peoples alike took their rise could have made it possible. We do not say that the Transvaal Republic has among its guides and rulers a Solon[190] or a Lycurgus,[191] but it has to-day, among the men guiding its destiny, men of brave and earnest spirit, who are seeking manfully and profoundly to deal with the great problems before them in a wide spirit of humanity and justice. And we do again repeat that the strong sympathy of all earnest and thoughtful minds, not only in Africa, but in England, should be with them."

If one compares the gold fields of the Witwatersrand with those of other countries, it is certain that the former can claim to be the best governed mining area in the world. This is the almost unanimous verdict of people who have had a lengthy experience of the gold fields of California, Australia, and [the Alaskan] Klondike.

As far as South Africa is concerned, it is only necessary to instance the diamond fields of Griqualand West when they were directly administered by the British Government. They then afforded a continual spectacle of rebellion, rioting, and indescribable uncertainty of, and danger to, life and property.

In Appendix B. are certain extracts from the evidence of eye witnesses as to the chaos which characterised the condition of the diamond fields when under British rule - a condition which differs from that of the Witwatersrand gold fields as night from day. Reference will be made later on to the administration of the gold fields of the South African Republic. For the present it is necessary to glance at certain forces which had been developed on the diamond fields of the Cape Colony, and which have introduced a new factor of overwhelming importance into the South African situation.

Capitalism.

The development of British policy in South Africa had hitherto been influenced at different times, and in a greater or less degree, by the spirit of Jingoism,[192] and by that zeal for Annexation which is so characteristic of the trading instincts of the race. It was, however, a policy that had been conducted in other respects on continuous lines, and it might be justified by the argument that it was necessary in the interests of the Empire. But Capitalism was the new factor which was about to play such an important role in the history of South

[189] [Olive Schreiner, Words in Season, page 62.]

[190] Solon (630–c. 560 BC) was an Athenian statesman, constitutional lawmaker and poet. He is remembered particularly for his efforts to legislate against political, economic and moral decline in Archaic Athens. His reforms failed in the short term, yet Solon is credited with having laid the foundations for Athenian democracy His constitutional reform also succeeded in overturning most laws established by Draco. Solon - Wikipedia

[191] Lycurgus (c. 820 BC) was the quasi-legendary lawgiver of Sparta who established the military-oriented reformation of Spartan society in accordance with the Oracle of Apollo at Delphi. All his reforms promoted the three Spartan virtues: equality (among citizens), military fitness, and austerity. Lycurgus (lawgiver) - Wikipedia

[192] Jingoism is nationalism in the form of aggressive and proactive foreign policy, such as a country's advocacy for the use of threats or actual force, as opposed to peaceful relations, in efforts to safeguard what it perceives as its national interests. Colloquially, jingoism is excessive bias in judging one's own country as superior to others–an extreme type of nationalism Jingoism - Wikipedia

Africa. The natural differences in men find their highest expression in the varieties of influence which one man exercises over another; this influence can either be of a religious, moral, political, or purely material nature.

Material influence generally takes the form of money, or the financial nexus, as an English writer has termed it. An unusual combination of this form of influence leads to Capitalism just as an unusual combination of political influence leads to tyranny, and an unusual combination of religious influence to hierarchical despotism. Capitalism is the modern peril which threatens to become as dangerous to mankind as the political tyranny of the old Eastern world and the religious despotism of the Middle Ages were in their respective eras.

In a part of the world so rich in minerals of all descriptions as the Transvaal, it is natural that Capitalism should play a considerable role. Unfortunately, in South Africa it has from the very first attempted to go far beyond its legitimate scope; it has endeavoured to gain political power, and to make all other forms of government and influence subservient to its own ends. The measure of its success can be clearly gauged by the fact that all South Africa is standing to-day on the brink of a great precipice, and may be hurled into the abyss before the ink on these pages is dry.

Mr. Cecil Rhodes

The spirit of Capitalism found its incarnation in Mr. Cecil Rhodes, who was able to amalgamate the pressing and conflicting interests of the Diamond Fields into the one great Corporation of which he is the head.

Although he probably had no exceptional aptitude for politics, he was irresistibly drawn towards them by the stress of his interests. By means of his financial influence, together with a double allowance of elasticity of conscience, he succeeded so far as to become Prime Minister of the Cape Colony, and was powerfully and solidly supported by the Africander party.[193] The Africanders believed in him because they were really and deeply imbued with the necessity of the co-operation and fusion of the two white races in South Africa, and he, as a loyal Englishman, but fully possessing the confidence of Colonial Africanderdom, seemed to them just the very person to realise their ideal.

To a careful observer the alliance between Africanderdom and Capitalism was bound to lead to a rupture sooner or later. Deeply rooted and pure national sentiment as well as burning conviction form the basis of Africander Policy, and it was obvious that in the long run it would be discovered that this policy could never be made subservient to purely financial interests.

Jingoism.

But there was another factor. There was that debased form of patriotism called Jingoism. It is a form of party politics without solid convictions or real beliefs, which puffs itself out with big words, and with the froth of high-sounding ideas and principles. It is a policy, nevertheless, which appeals most strongly to the instincts of self-interest and to the illegal appropriation of other people's property. It revels in the lust of boasting, so deeply ingrained in human nature. In a word, it is a policy which is in direct opposition to the true spirit of religion, to the altruistic ideals of humanity, and to that sentiment of humility and moderation which is the natural basis of all morality.

Alliance Between Capitalism and Jingoism.

Here, indeed, were the elements of an enduring alliance - an alliance between Capitalism, with its great material influence, but barren of any one single exalted idea or principle on the one hand, and Jingoism, sterile, empty, soulless, but with a rich stock-in-trade of bombastic ideas and principles, prompted by the most selfish aspirations, on the other hand.

The one was eminently calculated to form the complement of the other, thus creating a natural alliance which is rapidly becoming a menace, all the world over, to the best and most enduring interests of humanity.

[193] The Afrikanerbond was an important Cape political party in the last quarter of the 19th century and up to the formation of the Union in 1910. Between 1881 and 1882, however, it grew very rapidly as a result of the First Boer War. By the end of 1883, the Afrikanerbond was the largest political party in South Africa. The objective of the Afrikanerbond was the "United States of South Africa." Afrikanerbond (party) - Wikipedia

This Capitalistic Jingoism is the tree from which it is the lot of our unfortunate South Africa to gather such bitter fruit to-day.

Mr. Rhodes, with that treacherous duplicity which is an enduring characteristic of British policy in South Africa, co-operated publicly, and in the closest relationship, with the Colonial Africanders, while he was secretly fomenting a conspiracy with Jingoism against the Cape Africanders and the South African Republics. He already had the Africanders in the Cape Colony under his sway; his aim was now to gain the same influence in the South African Republic, with its rich gold mines - not so much, perhaps, for himself personally as for Capitalism, with which his interests were so closely identified. In case of success, he would obtain his personal aim, and Capitalism would be absolutely despotic in South Africa. With an eye to this end he, with other Capitalists, began in 1892 to foment a political agitation in Johannesburg against the Republic. In a place like Johannesburg, where drink is consumed in great quantities, and where the high altitude and the stress of business all tend to keep people's spirits in a constant state of excitability, it was easy enough, with the aid of money, to bring about a state of political ferment in a very short time, especially as just that measure of grievances existed to give a colour of truth to the imaginary ones.

The National Union.

Under these conditions the National Union movement[194] originated in 1892. Its adherents were entirely composed of the creatures and parasites of the Capitalists, with a few honest fools and enthusiasts who naturally did not think deeply enough to discern the aim and the trend of this hypocritical movement.

The Capitalists at this time certainly kept well in the background, in order that the movement might have the appearance of being a popular one. The Capitalists of Johannesburg were, however, a theatrical lot, and the desire to play a prominent role was too intense to be suppressed for any length of time, so that after the lapse of a couple of years they naturally took the leading part in the opera bouffe agitation which followed.

Corruption of the Capitalists.

They began, by means of the lowest and most repulsive methods, to undermine the Boer policy in order to gain the mastery of the mining legislation and administration. They had persuaded themselves and the rest of the world that the Boers were as a body corrupt and tainted, so they armed themselves, with the power of money in order to overthrow them.

Lionel Phillips[195] wrote in this spirit on the 16th June, 1894, to Beit in London: -

"I may here say that, as you of course know, I have no desire for political rights, and believe as a whole that the community is not ambitious in this respect. The bewaarplaatsen[196] question will, I think, be settled in our favour, but at a cost of about £25,000. It is proposed to spend a good deal of money in order to secure a better Raad, but it must be remembered that the spending of money on elections has, by recent legislation, been made a criminal offence, and the matter will have to be carefully handled."[197]

On the 15th July, 1894, he wrote again to the same correspondent: - "Our trump card is a fund of £10 - 15,000 to improve the Raad. Unfortunately the companies have no secret service fund. I must divine away. We don't want to shell out ourselves."[198]

Here we catch a glimpse behind the scenes, and we observe how the Capitalists in 1894 had already endeavoured to lower and vitiate our public life by methods which did not even recoil before the criminal law of the land, to say nothing of elementary morality.

And did they succeed? Were the people and the Volksraad as corrupt as they thought, and as they still endeavour to make the world believe? Their failure is the best and most complete answer to this calumny.

194 PF: Unable to identify this political party.

195 Sir Lionel Phillips, (6 August 1855–2 July 1936) was a British-born South African financier, mining magnate and politician. Lionel Phillips - Wikipedia

196 Dutch for "repository."

197 [Transvaal Green Book No. 1 of 1896.]

198 [Transvaal Green Book No. 1 of 1896.]

If corruption on a large scale, however, failed to ensure the triumph of Capitalism over the community, the other trump card of Jingoism still remained. The pulse of the High Commissioner was felt by Mr. Lionel Phillips, and what was the answer of Sir Henry Loch, Her Majesty's representative in South Africa? We extract from the same secret letter book from which we have already quoted the following letter, dated 1st July, addressed to Wernher, a member of the influential firm of Wernher,[199] Beit & Co.: -

(Sir) Henry Loch's indiscretion.

"Sir Henry Loch (with whom I had two long private interviews alone) asked me some very pointed questions, such as what arms we had in Johannesburg, whether the population could hold the place for six days until help could arrive, etc., etc., and stated plainly that if there had been three thousand rifles and ammunition here he would certainly have come over."[200]

And so on in the same strain. Sir Henry Loch endorsed the truth of these statements two years later by boasting openly in the House of Lords about his plans for organising a raid into the South African Republic.

And all this happened while he (Sir Henry Loch) was the guest of our Government, and engaged in friendly negotiations about the interests of British subjects. To what a depth had British Policy in South Africa already degenerated. Within two years, however, a deeper abyss was to open.

The Conspiracy.

The secret conspiracy of the Capitalists and Jingoes to overthrow the South African Republic began now to gain ground with great rapidity, for just at this critical period Mr. Chamberlain became Secretary of State for the Colonies. In the secret correspondence of the conspirators, reference is continually made to the Colonial Office in a manner which, taken in connection with later revelations and with a successful suppression of the truth, has deepened the impression over the whole world that the Colonial Office was privy to, if not an accomplice in, the villainous attack on the South African Republic.

The Jameson Raid

It is unnecessary to dwell at length on the Jameson Raid; the world has not yet forgotten how the Administrators of a British province, carrying out a conspiracy headed by the Prime Minister of the Cape Colony [Cecil Rhodes],[201] [202] attacked the South African Republic with an armed band in order to assist the Capitalist

[199] Sir Julius Charles Wernher, 1st Baronet (9 April 1850–21 May 1912) was a German-born Randlord and art collector who became part of the English establishment. Julius Wernher - Wikipedia

[200] [Transvaal Green Book No. 1 of 1896.]

[201] The prequel to this raid is the Drifts Crisis and the conflict between the Cape Railway and Transvaal Rail Company.
Cecil Rhodes and Co. had loaned the Transvaal the money to finish the Transvaal and Delagoa Bay (West to East) line in exchange for permission to build a (North South) line for the Cape Railway to access Johannesburg.

Once the Cape Colony had finished building its railway, it attempted to get as much of the railway traffic of the Transvaal as possible by reducing its rates. The Transvaal government increased the rates on the part of the railway that ran through the Transvaal, once it had crossed the Vaal River. In answer to this, goods were taken to the Vaal River by train and then taken further by wagon to avoid paying the higher prices in the Transvaal. Kruger reacted by blocking access to the Transvaal, closing the drifts on the Transvaal side.

Afrikaners as well as the British wanted access to the markets of the Transvaal and to share in the wealth being generated by the gold mining; the Transvaal government wanted to preserve markets for its own farmers, build up manufacturing to help employ its landless white burghers, and make itself as free as possible from influence by the British.

The British government demanded that Kruger open the drifts which Kruger was forced to comply. Subsequently, Rhodes planned direct action by instigating plans for an uprising of Uitlanders in Johannesburg to be timed with the commencement of the Jameson Raid. See: Drifts Crisis - Wikipedia

[202] The Jameson Raid (29 December 1895–2 January 1896) was a botched raid against the South African Republic (commonly known as the Transvaal) carried out by British colonial administrator Leander Starr Jameson, under the employment of Cecil Rhodes. It involved 500 British South Africa Company police launched from Rhodesia over the New Year weekend of 1895–96.

The raid was intended to trigger an uprising by the primarily British expatriate workers (known as Uitlanders) in the Transvaal but failed to do so. The workers were called the Johannesburg conspirators. They were expected to recruit an army and prepare for an insurrection; however, the raid was ineffective, and no uprising took place.

revolution of Johannesburg in overthrowing the Boer Government; how this raid and this revolution were upset by the vigilance of the Boers; how Jameson and his filibusters[203] were handed over to England to stand their trial; although the Boers had the power and the right to shoot them down as robbers; how the whole gang of Johannesburg Capitalists pleaded guilty to treason and sedition; how, instead of confiscating all their property, and thus dealing a death blow to Capitalistic influence in South Africa, the Government dealt most leniently with them (an act of magnanimity which was rewarded by their aiding and abetting a still more dangerous agitation three years later).

The Parliamentary Commission.

Nor has the world forgotten how, at the urgent instance of the Africander party in the Cape Colony, an investigation into the causes of the conflict was held in Westminster; how that investigation degenerated into a low attack upon the Government of the sorely maligned and deeply injured South African Republic, and how at the last moment, when the truth was on the point of being revealed, and the conspiracy traced to its fountain head in the British Cabinet, the Commission decided all of a sudden not to make certain compromising documents public.

"Constitutional Means."

Here we see to what a depth the old great traditions of British Constitutionalism had sunk under the influence of the ever-increasing and all-absorbing lust of gold, and in the hands of a sharp-witted wholesale dealer, who, like Cleon of old, has constituted himself a statesman. Treachery and violence not having been able to attain their objects, "Constitutional means" were to be invoked (as Mr. Rhodes openly boasted before the aforesaid Commission), so as to make Capitalistic Jingoism master of the situation in South Africa.

Rhodes-Kruger and the Lion

Paul Kruger came to loath Cecil Rhodes.

Rather prominently, almost famously, Kruger had a pair of marble lions on the front portico of his cottage home.

President Kruger at his home with the two marble lions on pedestals.[204] Central Hall of the State Museum at Pretoria.[205]

The results included embarrassment of the British government; the replacement of Cecil Rhodes as prime minister of the Cape Colony; and the strengthening of Boer dominance of the Transvaal and its gold mines. Jameson Raid - Wikipedia

203 A filibuster (from the Spanish filibustero), also known as a freebooter, is someone who engages in an unauthorized military expedition into a foreign country or territory to foster or support a political revolution or secession. The term is usually applied to United States citizens who incited insurrections across Latin America, particularly in the mid-19th century, usually with the goal of establishing an American-loyal regime that may later be annexed into the United States Filibuster (military) - Wikipedia

204 Richard Harding Davis With Both Armies in South Africa. Charles Scribner's Sons, New York 1900.

205 Heroes of the Boer War. Review of Reviews, 1903. Note what appear to be Coelacanths among the displays. Coelacanth - Wikipedia

At some point in their dealings Cecil, perhaps as a peace offering, arranged to give a live lion to the Transvaal Zoological Garden and Dr. Gunning,[206] its director, accepted the gift without fully informing Kruger about it. With respect to live lions in Southern Africa, it is not like there were not enough actual lions roaming around the Transvaal or its outskirts that one might be obtained fairly easily. When Kruger found out that the Zoological Garden had accepted this gift he was so angry that he demanded that the animal be returned. An alternative was found whereby the animal was shot and stuffed and put into the State Museum.

Stuffed Lion at Staats Museum.[207]

Kruger & Marble Lion at his house.[27]

Capitalistic Jingoism—Second Period

National Sentiment in South Africa Kindled by the Jameson Raid.

The foregoing sketch has shown how deeply our people felt and resented the wrong that was done to them. It was to be expected that such a treacherous attack on the Republics, emanating from their own leader, would awaken the Africanders even in the remotest districts, and would bring fresh energy into the arena of politics. To give an instance of the measure of the feeling which had been quickened by the raid, a short extract is given below from an article published in the organ of the Africander party, Our Land, a few months after the Raid, an article which undoubtedly expressed the feeling of Africanders: -

"Has not Providence over-ruled and guided the painful course of events in South Africa since the beginning of this year (1896)? Who can doubt it?

"The stab which was intended to paralyse Africanderdom once and for all in the Republics has sent an electric thrill direct to the national heart. Africanderdom has awakened to a sense of earnestness and consciousness which we have not observed since the heroic war for Liberty in 1881. From the Limpopo as far as Cape Town the Second Majuba has given birth to a new inspiration and a new movement amongst our people in South Africa.

A new feeling has rushed in huge billows over South Africa. The flaccid and cowardly Imperialism, that had already begun to dilute and weaken our national blood, gradually turned aside before the new current which permeated our people. Many who, tired of the slow development of the national idea, had resigned themselves to Imperialism now paused and asked themselves what Imperialism had produced in South Africa? Bitterness and race hatred[208] it is true!

[206] Dr. J. W. B. Gunning is the administrator and the censor at the State Model School where Captain Haldane is detained. Dr. J. W. B. Gunning, per Brian Davis, Churchills in Africa p. 201.

[207] The Boer "Tower of London." A Visit To The Staats Museum, Pretoria. By Rev. John C. Harris, Of Johannesburg. The Strand Magazine, Volume XIX April 1900 No. 112 p. 46. Cecil Rhodes gave a lion to the Zoological Garden and Dr. Gunning accepted it. Kruger was so angry that he demanded that the animal be returned. An alternative was found whereby the animal was shot and stuffed.

[208] In this and most subsequent references this term refers to antipathy between Boer and English residents in South Africa.

Since the days of Sir Harry Smith and Theophilus Shepstone and Bartle Frere to the days of Leander Jameson and Cecil Rhodes, Imperialism in South Africa has gone hand in hand with bloodshed and fraud. However wholesome the effects of Imperialism may be elsewhere, its continual tendency in this country during all these years has been nothing else but an attempt to force our national life and national character into foreign grooves; and to seal this pressure with blood and tears.... This is truly a critical moment in the existence of Africanderdom all over South Africa. Now or never! Now or never the foundation of a wide-embracing nationalism must be laid. The Iron is red hot, and the time for forging is at hand....

... The partition wall has disappeared. Let us stand manfully by one another. The danger has not yet disappeared; on the contrary, never has the necessity for a policy of a Colonial and Republican Union been greater; now the psychological moment has arrived; now our people have awakened all over South Africa; a new glow illuminates our hearts; let us now lay the foundation stone of a real United South Africa on the soil of a pure and all-comprehensive national sentiment."

Such language caused the Jingoes to shudder - not because it was disloyal, because that it certainly was not, but because it proved that the Jameson Raid had suddenly awakened the Africanders, and that owing to this defeat of the Jingoes a vista of further and greater defeats widened out in the future. The Colonial Africanders would certainly have to be reckoned with, in case an annexation policy were followed with regard to the Republics.

Victory of the Africander Party in the Cape Parliament.

For some time the Jingoes cherished the hope that they would gain the majority in the Cape Parliament under an amended Redistribution Act. The General Election of 1898 took place, with the result that the Africander party obtained a small majority, and later, under a Redistribution Act forced upon them by the Jingoes, the majority of the former was considerably increased.

The Cry of Disloyalty

Instead of honestly admitting that the Africander victory was the natural result of the Jameson Raid, the Jingoes began, not only in South Africa, but also in England, to shout that the rule and supremacy of England in South Africa was menaced.

The Transvaal must be humiliated.

They contended that South Africa would be lost to England unless energetic intervention took place without delay, and that this menace to English rule was due to the Republican propaganda which the South African Republic had set in motion. That as long as the South African Republic refused to humiliate itself before British authority, but on the contrary kept its youthful head on high with national pride, other parts of South Africa would be inclined to follow its example, and there would thus be no certainty for British supremacy in this quarter of the globe. The South African Republic would have to be humiliated and to be crushed into the dust; the Africanders in other parts of South Africa would then abandon their alleged hope of a more extensive Republican South Africa.

The Necessity for Constitutional Means.

But how was this humiliation to be brought about, and how, above all, was it to be brought about by those "Constitutional means," which, since the failure of the conspiracy, had become a sine qua non?[209]

The new Governor of the Cape Colony and High Commissioner of South Africa,[210] who had enjoyed the distinction of a brilliant university career, who had learnt humility and moderation at the feet of Mr. W.T. Stead, and who had learnt by his experience with the fellaheen in Egypt how to govern the descendants of the Huguenots and the "Beggars of the Sea," would know very well how to evolve "Constitutional means" in order to humiliate the South African Republic, and to crush it into the dust.

[209] An essential condition; a thing that is absolutely necessary.
[210] Alfred Milner held both posts at this time.

The Suzerainty.

There was at any rate the burning question of suzerainty, which the South African Republic had unconsciously and innocently raised in the following way: -

After the Jameson Raid the Volksraad had passed certain laws with a view of removing some of the causes of that movement, as, for example, the law by which dangerous individuals could be expelled from the State, and the law by which paupers and people suffering from contagious diseases could be prevented from entering the Republic.[211] These laws were declared to be in conflict with Article XIV. of the London Convention. Violations of Article IV. were also said to have taken place in regard to certain extradition and other treaties, which had been concluded between the South African Republic and Foreign Powers.[212] On the 7th May, 1897, the Government of the South African Republic dispatched a very important reply to these accusations, in which, after fully stating the reasons why the Government differed from Her Majesty's Government, an appeal was made for arbitration as being the most suitable method of settling the dispute.

This appeal was couched in the following language:

The Appeal for Arbitration.

"While it respects the opinion of Her British Majesty's Government, it takes the liberty, with full confidence in the correctness of its own views, to propose to Her British Majesty's Government the principle of Arbitration, with which the honourable the First Volksraad agreed, in the hope that it will be taken in the conciliatory spirit in which it is made.

It considers that it has every reason for this proposal, the more so because the principle of Arbitration is already laid down in that Convention in the only case in which, according to its opinion at the time, a difference could be foreseen, to wit, with regard to Article I.; because it has already been proposed by Her British Majesty's Government, and accepted by this Government with regard to the difference in respect of Article 14 of the Convention arising in the matter of the so-called Coolie question, which was settled by Arbitration; because the Right Honourable the Secretary of State, Mr. Chamberlain, himself, in his letter of the 4th September, 1895, to His Excellency the High Commissioner at Cape Town, favours this principle in the same question, where he says: After 1886, as time went on, the manner in which the law was interpreted and was worked, or was proposed to be worked, gave rise to complaints on the part of the British Government, and as it seemed impossible to come to an agreement by means of correspondence, the Marquis of Ripon[213] took what is the approved course in such cases, of proposing to the South African Republic that the dispute should be referred to Arbitration.

This was agreed to ... because the principle of Arbitration in matters such as this appears to the Government to be the most impartial, just, and most satisfactory way out of the existing difficulty, and, lastly, because one of the parties to a Convention, according to all principles of reasonableness, cannot expect that his interpretation will be respected by the other party as the only valid and correct one.

And although this Government is firmly convinced that a just and impartial decision might be obtained even better in South Africa than anywhere else, it wishes, in view of the conflicting elements, interests, and aspirations which are now apparent in South Africa, and in order to avoid even the appearance that it would be able or desire to exercise influence in order to obtain a decision favourable to it, to propose that the President of the Swiss Bondstate, who may be reckoned upon as standing altogether outside the question, and to feel sympathy or antipathy neither for the one party nor for the other, be requested to point out a competent jurist, as has already often been done in respect of international disputes.

The Government would have no objection that the Arbitration be subject to a limitation of time, and gives the assurance now already that it will willingly subject itself to any decision if such should, contrary to its expectation, be given against it. The Government repeats the well-meant wish that this proposal may find favour

[211] [Dispatches of 12th August, 1896; 21st August, 1896; 17th February, 1897. C. 8423 and C. 8721.]

[212] [Dispatches of the 6th March, 1897. C. 8423.]

[213] George Frederick Samuel Robinson, 1st Marquess of Ripon, (24 October 1827–9 July 1909), was a British politician and Viceroy and Governor General of India who served in every Liberal cabinet between 1861 and 1908. George Robinson, 1st Marquess of Ripon - Wikipedia

with Her British Majesty's Government; and inasmuch as the allegations of breaches of the Convention find entrance now even in South Africa, and bring and keep the feelings more and more in a state of suspense, this Government will be pleased if it can learn the decision of Her British Majesty's Government as soon as possible."[214]

England Refuses to Arbitrate on Ground of Suzerainty.

To this the British Government replied that according to the Convention of 1884, taken in conjunction with the preamble of the Convention of 1881, the South African Republic was under the suzerainty of Her Majesty, and that it was incompatible with the subordinate position of the South African Republic to submit to Arbitration any matters in dispute as to the construction of the Convention between it and the suzerain Power.

In order to avoid any misunderstanding as to this very remarkable document, the exact wording of the British dispatch is given: - "Finally, the Government of the South African Republic propose that all points in dispute between Her Majesty's Government and themselves relating to the Convention should be referred to Arbitration, the Arbitrator to be nominated by the President of the Swiss Republic.

In making this proposal the Government of the South African Republic appear to have overlooked the distinction between the Conventions of 1881 and 1884 and an ordinary treaty between two independent Powers, questions arising upon which may properly be the subject of Arbitration.

By the Pretoria Convention of 1881 Her Majesty, as Sovereign of the Transvaal Territory, accorded to the inhabitants of that territory complete self-government, subject to the suzerainty of Her Majesty, her heirs, and successors, upon certain terms and conditions, and subject to certain reservations and limitations set forth in 33 articles; and by the London Convention of 1884, Her Majesty, while maintaining the preamble of the earlier instrument, directed and declared that certain other articles embodied therein should be substituted for the articles embodied in the Convention of 1881.

The articles of the Convention of 1881 were accepted by the Volksraad of the Transvaal State, and those of the Convention of 1884 by the Volksraad of the South African Republic. Under these Conventions, therefore, Her Majesty holds towards the South African Republic the relation of a suzerain who has accorded to the people of that Republic self-government upon certain conditions, and it would be incompatible with that position to submit to Arbitration the construction of the conditions on which she accorded self-government to the Republic."[215]

Reply of the Transvaal Government.

In its celebrated reply of the 16th April, 1898, the Government of the South African Republic proved with unanswerable force that the preamble of the Convention of 1881 had been abolished, that Lord Derby had himself in 1884 proposed a draft Convention, in which the preamble was erased (see Appendix B.), and that by the ultimate acceptance of that proposal, the suzerainty had ceased to exist.[216]

On this account, as well as for other reasons, it contended that as no suzerainty existed between the two countries, the objection to Arbitration as a means of settling disputes would disappear, and the Government reiterated their appeal to have such differences or disputes disposed of by Arbitration.

The Object of the Suzerainty Dispute.

Naturally this was exactly what Mr. Chamberlain did not want. He was opposed to Arbitration dispute, because it would have probably led to the humiliation of the British and not of the Boer Government. The suzerainty question was introduced in the meanwhile as a "Constitutional Proposal," which might be used for the purpose of humiliating the South African Republic.

In his answer to the arguments put forward by the South African Republic, Mr. Chamberlain could only persist in repeating his contention that suzerainty still existed, and did not even attempt to refute the statement that Lord

[214] [Dispatch, 7th May, 1897. No. 3, C. 8721.]
[215] [Dispatch, October, 1897. No. 7, C. 8721.]
[216] [Dispatch, 16th April, 1898. No. 4, C. 9507.]

Derby had himself erased the preamble of the Convention of 1881. It was clearly his opinion that Lord Derby had, through stupidity and thoughtlessness, abandoned the suzerainty in 1884, just as Lord Russell had abandoned the idea of obtaining the South African Republic in 1852, so that he would now, just as Shepstone in 1877, have to try and disconcert the Republic by a display of force and inflexible determination, so as not to be deprived of these eminently "Constitutional means."[217]

The Transvaal a Sovereign International State.

His arguments in this dispatch, that both the suzerainty of Her Majesty and the right of the South African Republic to self-government were dependent upon the preamble of the Pretoria Convention, and that if the preamble were null and void, not only would the suzerainty but also the right to self-government disappear, were clearly designed to intimidate the South African Republic; but in other respects the argument was perfectly correct. Accordingly the Government of the South African Republic replied that it did not base its claim to self-government on the preamble of the Convention of 1881, nor on the Convention of 1884 (for no mention is made of self-government in that document), but simply on the ground of its being a sovereign international state.[218]

In other words, it contended that the Convention of London implied that the South African Republic was a sovereign international state, and that it was therefore superfluous in that Convention to specify or define its rights. Into this answer, which is not only juridically and historically correct, but which rests on the basis of common sense, the astute High Commissioner was able to read a menace to Her Majesty's Government, although the Government of the Republic distinctly stated in that reply that it adhered to the Convention of London, an assurance which it had already made hundreds of times.

Justice of the Transvaal Contention.

This is the whole history of the suzerainty dispute between the two Governments. The South African Republic had asked for arbitration on certain questions, and England, with Mr. Chamberlain as spokesman, had refused, because a suzerain Power could not be expected to settle disputes with its vassal by means of arbitration. So that according to the new principles of International Law, based on the "screw" ethics of Birmingham, it was to be judge and jury in its own disputes with other people.

The position taken up by our Government in this remarkable controversy is substantiated by the actions of Lord Derby during the negotiations about the Conventions, as well as by the following telegram, which he sent to the High Commissioner for communication to the two Republics: -

High Commissioner, Cape Town.

To British Resident, Pretoria.

Please inform Transvaal Government that I have received the following from the Secretary of State: - 27th February. Convention signed to-day. New south-western boundary as proposed, following trade road. British Protectorate country outside Transvaal established with delegates' consent. They promise to appoint Border Commissioner inside Transvaal, co-operate with ours outside; Mackenzie - British Resident. Debt reduced to quarter million. Same complete internal independence in Transvaal as in Orange Free State. Conduct and control diplomatic intercourse Foreign Governments conceded. Queen's final approval treaties reserved. Delegates appear well satisfied and cordial feeling two Governments. You may make the above known.

This Convention is also substantiated by the express declarations of Lord Rosmead[219] and the Rev. D.P. Faure to the effect that it was clearly understood, at the time the London Convention was concluded, that the suzerainty was abolished. It is unnecessary to add anything about the evidence of the Members of the Transvaal Deputation. The suzerainty has thus not the slightest shadow of existence; and yet, as will be proved, Mr.

[217] [Footnote 38: Dispatch. C. 9507. Page 33.]

[218] [Dispatch, 17th March, 1899. C. 9507.]

[219] Hercules George Robert Robinson, 1st Baron Rosmead, GCMG, PC (19 December 1824–28 October 1897), was a British colonial administrator who became the 5th Governor of Hong Kong. Robinson arrived in South Africa shortly before the disaster of Majuba, and was one of the commissioners for negotiating a peace and determining the future status of Transvaal. Hercules Robinson, 1st Baron Rosmead - Wikipedia

Chamberlain is prepared to go to war with the South African Republic over this question, a war which will, according to his intentions, result in Annexation.

Uitlander Grievances and Capitalistic Agitation.

While the two Governments were occupied with this question the Capitalists were not idle. They were busy fanning the flame in another direction. It was not only a fact that Rhodesia was an unexpected failure, but it had proved far richer in native wars than in payable gold mines. The Capitalist groups possessing the greatest interests in the Witwatersrand gold mines were also the most deeply interested in Rhodesia, and it naturally occurred to them that their Transvaal mines ought also to bear the burden of their unprofitable investments in Rhodesia - an adjustment which would, however, necessitate the amalgamation of the two countries, especially when the interests of the shareholders were considered.

In order to attain this object a continual agitation was kept up at Johannesburg, so that English shareholders living far away should be prepared for the day when the Annexation would take place on Constitutional lines.

The argument which was calculated to impress these European shareholders was that the administration of the South African Republic had created a situation which was most prejudicial to the financial interests of the mining industry. Viewed from this standpoint the Uitlander grievances were an inexhaustibly rich and payable mine.

The Industrial Commission.

This agitation first of all emanated directly from the Capitalists, and had assumed such proportions in 1897 that the Government decided to appoint a Commission of officials and mining magnates in order to enquire searchingly into the alleged financial grievances. As far as the Government was concerned, the chief findings of the Commission were: -

(1). That the price of dynamite (85 shillings per case of 50 lbs.) was too high under the existing concession, and that a diminution in price was desirable either by cancellation of the concession, or by testing the legality of the concession in the High Court.

(2). That the tariffs of the Netherlands Railway Company for the carriage of coal and other articles were too high, and that it was necessary to expropriate the railway.

(3). That the import duties on necessaries of life were too high, and that the cost of living in Johannesburg for workmen was too high.

(4). That stringent measures ought to be adopted in order to prevent gold thefts, and that the law for the total prohibition of drink to native labourers ought to be more strictly enforced, and that there ought to be a more stringent application of the Pass Law (under which the traffic of the native labourers was regulated).

(5). With the object of carrying out the measures specified in Section 4, the Commission recommended that an Advisory Board should be nominated for the Witwatersrand gold fields for the purpose of advising the Government as to the enforcement of the said regulations.

Results of the Commission.

To what extent was effect given to these recommendations?

Dynamite.

1. As far as dynamite is concerned, it appeared that there was no chance of contesting the concession in the law courts with any success. Nor did the Volksraad or the Government feel justified in cancelling, without the consent of the owners, a contract which had been solemnly entered into, and upon which enormous sums of money had been expended. The Mining Industry was naturally eager for cancellation, even without adequate compensation; but the public were not at that time aware of a fact which was made public some months later, namely, that the De Beers Corporation intended to erect a dynamite manufactory, and that this agitation of the Capitalists was intended to obtain for themselves the control of this great source of income. People, however, knew that the Messrs. Chamberlain were interested in the English ammunition and dynamite house of

Kynoch,[220] but they hesitate to assume that the Colonial Secretary was actuated in his Transvaal policy by considerations of private financial interest.

The Government and Volksraad of the South African Republic adopted the wiser plan of lowering the price of dynamite to such an extent as to make it about equal to the local European price plus a protective tariff of 20s. per case.

It may here be remarked that Mr. Chamberlain, knowing how unpopular the Dynamite Concession[221] was in the South African Republic, intimated to the Government of the South African Republic, in a very threatening manner, that the Concession was in conflict with the London Convention.

The answer of the Government to this communication was so crushing that Mr. Chamberlain did not again return to the subject. In this he was, no doubt, also actuated by the fact that the most renowned English and European jurists had advised that the concession was in no sense a breach of the Convention. This, however, only became known later, and it is merely referred to now so as to show that no stone was left unturned in order to find a means of humiliating the South African Republic.

The Netherlands Railway Company.

2. With regard to the Netherlands South African Railway Company, it would appear that the Capitalists have altered their opinion, and now think that the administration of the Company is as good as can reasonably be expected, and that expropriation is now unnecessary. Perhaps, from their point of view, it would be better to buy up the shares of the Company, and thus become themselves masters, instead of the Government, of this source of income.

Respecting the Railway tariff, it is fair to assume that the cause of dissatisfaction has disappeared, for no complaints are now heard since the tariff was lowered in accordance with the recommendations of the Commission.

Reduction of Import Duties

This change in the tariff, together with the abolition of duties on nearly all necessaries of life have made a difference of about £700,000 in the income of the State during the last year. It will be admitted that this is an enormous item in comparison with the total income of the South African Republic. The above tends to show how anxious the Government of the South African Republic has been to remove all grievances as soon as it was proved that they actually existed.

Liquor, Pass, and Gold Thefts Laws.

3. As regards the administration of the Liquor Law, the Pass Law, and the Law dealing with Gold thefts, neither the Government nor the Volksraad felt at liberty to adopt the recommendation as to constituting an Advisory Board on the Witwatersrand. They decided to go deeper to the roots of the evil, and so altered the administration of the Laws that the evidences of dissatisfaction have disappeared. Indeed, no one ever hears of gold thefts now, and the representative bodies of the mining industry have repeatedly expressed their satisfaction with the administration of the Pass Law, and especially with that of the Liquor Law.

The Liquor Law.

In this very Liquor Law we have a test of a good administration. From the very nature of the drink question it is one of the most difficult laws that a Government can be called upon to administer, and the measure of success which has attended the efforts of the Government and its officials proves conclusively that the charges of incompetency so frequently brought against the Government of the South African Republic were devoid of

[220] Kynoch was a manufacturer of ammunition, later incorporated into ICI but remaining as a brand name for sporting cartridges. Kynoch - Wikipedia

[221] SAR President Paul Kruger became widely derided as corrupt and inefficient, especially the dynamite concession given to Edouard Lippert and a French consortium, a French consortium, which Kruger was forced to revoke in 1892 amid much scandal over misrepresentation and price gouging. Paul Kruger - Wikipedia

truth, and were only intended to slander and to injure the Republic. A combined meeting of the Chamber of Mines, the Chamber of Commerce, and the Association of Mine Managers - the three strongest and most representative bodies on the Witwatersrand Gold Fields - passed the following resolutions,[222] which speak for themselves: -

1. This combined Meeting, representing the Chamber of Mines, the Chamber of Commerce, and the Mine Managers' Association, desires to express once more its decided approval of the present Liquor Law, and is of opinion that prohibition is not only beneficial to the Natives in their own interest, but is absolutely necessary for the Mining Industry, with a view of maintaining the efficiency of labour.

2. This Meeting wishes to express its appreciation of the efforts made to suppress the Illicit Liquor Trade by the Detective Department of this Republic since it has been placed under the administration of the State Attorney, and is of opinion that the success which has crowned these efforts fully disproves the contention that the Liquor Law is impracticable.

The first resolution was carried by an overwhelming majority, and the second unanimously.

Compare this declaration of the representatives of the Mining and Commercial interests of the Witwatersrand with the allegation repeated by Mr. Chamberlain in his great "grievance" dispatch of the 10th May, 1899- that the Liquor Law had never been strictly enforced, but that this law was simply evaded, and that the Natives at the mines were supplied with drink in large quantities.[223]

When Mr. Chamberlain wrote these words they were absolutely untrue, and, like all his grievances, are of an imaginary character.

The results have clearly shown that the Government was quite correct in its conclusion that it was better to alter the administration of the laws complained of, than to adopt a principle (the advisory board), the consequences and eventual outcome of which no one was able to foresee.

The South African League.

The agitation in connection with the report of the Industrial Commission was followed by a great calm. If it had not been that the handling of the Swazie difficulty by the British Government gave colour to suspicion, one might have thought that there was no cloud upon the horizon. To a superficial observer, the two Governments seemed to be on the best and most friendly footing, and some of us actually began to think that the era of the fraternal co-operation of the two races in South Africa had actually dawned, and that the cursed Raid and its harvest of race hatred and division would be forgotten. Certain circumstances, however, indicated clearly that the enemy was occupied in a supreme effort to cause matters to culminate in a crisis.

The South African League,[224] a political organisation which sprang up out of, and owed its origin to, the race hatred which the Jameson Raid had called into being, and at the head of which Mr. Rhodes himself stands (a fact which places Capitalistic influence in a very clear light), began towards the latter part of last year to agitate against the Government in the most unheard-of way.

The individuals who stood at the head of this institution in Johannesburg were such that very little attention was paid to the League. It was, however, soon clearly shown that not only was the movement strongly assisted by the Capitalists, and strongly supported all along the mines, but that there was a close relationship in a mysterious way with Cape Town and London. The events of the last few months have brought this out very clearly. Meetings were arranged, memorials to Her Majesty about grievances were drawn up, and an active propaganda was preached in the Press; this all proved in a convincing way that a carefully planned campaign had been organised against the Republic.

As the Government of the South African Republic has set forth the trend of the agitation as well as the connection of the British Government with it in an official despatch, it is desirable to quote the language itself: -

[222] [17th August, 1899.]

[223] [Dispatch, 10th May, 1899. No. 83, C. 9345.]

[224] For a discussion of the Edgar Case and the South African League see portions of Jan Smuts' article: Jan Smuts in the South African Republic - Wikipedia

"But this Government wishes to go further. Even in regard to those Uitlanders who are British subjects it is a small minority which, under the pretext of imaginary grievances, promotes a secret propaganda of race hatred, and uses the Republic as a basis for fomenting a revolutionary movement against this Government. Ministers of Her Majesty have so trenchantly expressed the truth about this minority that this Government wishes to quote the very words of these Ministers, with the object of bringing the actual truth to the knowledge of Her Majesty's Government, as well as to that of the whole world, and not for the purpose of making groundless accusations."[225]

"The following words are those of the Ministers of the Cape Colony, who are well acquainted with local conditions, and fully qualified to arrive at a conclusion": -

"In the opinion of Ministers the persistent action, both beyond and within this Colony, of the political body styling itself the South African League in endeavouring to foment and excite, not to smooth and allay ill-will between the two principal European races inhabiting South Africa, is well illustrated by these resolutions, the exaggerated and aggravated terms of which disclose the spirit which informs and inspires them."

"His Excellency's Ministers are one in their earnest desire to do all in their power to aid and further a policy of peaceful progress throughout South Africa, and they cannot but regard it as an unwise propagandism, hostile to the true interests of the Empire, including this Colony as an integral part, that every possible occasion should be seized by the League and its promoters for an attempt to magnify into greater events minor incidents, when occurring in the South African Republic, with a prospect thereby of making racial antagonism more acute, or of rendering less smooth the relations between Her Majesty's Government or the Government of this Colony and that Republic."

"Race hatred is, however, not so intense in South Africa as to enable a body with this propaganda, aiming at revolutionary objects, to obtain much influence in this part of the world; and one continually asks oneself the question - 'How is it that a body, so insignificant both in regard to its principles and its membership, enjoys such a large measure of influence?' The answer is that this body depends upon the protection and the support of Her Majesty's Government in England, and that both its members and its organs in the Press openly boast of the influence they exert over the policy of Her Majesty's Government. This Government would ignore such assertions; but when it finds that the ideas and the shibboleths of the South African League are continually echoed in the speeches of members of Her Majesty's Government, when it finds that blue books are compiled chiefly from documents prepared by officials of the South African League, as well as from reports and leading articles containing 'malignant lies' taken from the press organs of that organisation, thereby receiving an official character, then this Government can well understand why so many of Her Majesty's right-minded subjects in this part of the world have obtained the impression that the policy advocated by the South African League is supported by Her Majesty's Government, and is thus calculated to contribute to the welfare and blessing of the British Empire."

"If this mistaken impression could be removed, and if it could be announced as a fact that the South African League, as far as its actions in the South African Republic are concerned, is only an organisation having as its object the fomentation of strife and disorder and the destruction of the independence of the Country, then it would very soon lose its influence, and the strained relations existing between the two Governments would quickly disappear.

The Africander population of this country would not then be under the apprehension that the interests of the British Empire imperatively demand that the Republic should be done away with, and its people be either enslaved or exterminated. Both sections of the white inhabitants of South Africa would then return to the fraternal co-operation and fusion which was beginning to manifest itself when the treacherous conspiracy at the end of 1895 awakened the passions on both sides."

As a result of the continual agitation of the South African League, three occurrences were selected and elevated by Mr. Chamberlain into culminating instances of the Uitlander grievances. To give the world a clear insight into the nature of the grievances in general, extracts are given from the official accounts both of the British and the Republican account of these occurrences. There were three - the "Lombard affair," with reference to the maltreatment of coloured British subjects at Johannesburg; the "Edgar case," in connection with the shooting of

[225] [Dispatch of the Transvaal Government, 26th September, 1899. Appendix C.]

an English subject by a police official; and the "Amphitheatre occurrence," in regard to a disorderly meeting of the South African League.

a. The Lombard Incident.

With regard to the "Lombard incident," Mr. Chamberlain says: -

"As an instance of such arbitrary action the recent maltreatment of coloured British subjects by Field Cornet Lombard may be cited. This official entered the houses of various coloured persons without a warrant at night, dragged them from their beds, and arrested them for being without a pass. The persons so arrested were treated with much cruelty, and it is even alleged that one woman was prematurely confined, and a child subsequently died from the consequences of the fright and exposure. Men were beaten and kicked by the orders of the Field Cornet, who appears to have exercised his authority with the most cowardly brutality. The Government of the Republic, being pressed to take action, suspended the Field Cornet, and an enquiry was held, at which he and the police denied most of the allegations of violence; but the other facts were not disputed, and no independent evidence was called for the defence. The Government have since reinstated Lombard.[226]

"Unfortunately this case is by no means unparalleled. Other British subjects, including several from St. Helena and Mauritius, have been arbitrarily arrested, and some of them have been fined, without having been heard in their own defence, under a law which does not even profess to have any application to persons from those Colonies."

"However long-suffering Her Majesty's Government may be in their anxious desire to remain on friendly terms with the South African Republic, it must be evident that a continuance of incidents of this kind, followed by no redress, may well become intolerable."

The answer of the Government of the South African Republic was as follows: -

"With reference to the Lombard case, this Government wishes to point out that no complaint was lodged with any official in this Republic for a full month after the ill-treatment of Cape coloured people[227] was alleged to have taken place, and that neither the Government nor the public was aware that anything had taken place. The whole case was so insignificant that some of the people who were alleged to have been ill-treated declared, under oath, at a later period before a court of investigation that they would never have made any complaint on their own initiative.[228] What happened, however?

"About a month after the occurrence the South African League came to hear of it; some of its officials sent round to collect evidence from the parties who were alleged to have been ill-treated, and some sworn declarations were obtained by the help of Her Majesty's Vice-Consul at Johannesburg (between whom and this League a continual and conspicuous co-operation has existed). Even then no charge was lodged against the implicated officials with the judicial authorities of the country, but the case was put in the hands of the Acting British Agent at Pretoria.

"When the allegations were brought under the notice of this Government, they at once appointed a commission of enquiry, consisting of three members, namely, Landdrost Van der Berg, of Johannesburg, Mr. Andries Stockenstrom, barrister-at-law, of the Middle Temple, head of the Criminal Section of the State Attorney's Department, and Mr. Van der Merwe, Mining Commissioner, of Johannesburg; gentlemen against whose ability and impartiality the Uitlander population of the Republic have never harboured the slightest suspicion, and with whose appointment the Acting British Agent also expressed his entire satisfaction. The instructions given to those officials were to thoroughly investigate the whole case, and to report the result to the Government; and they fulfilled these instructions by sitting for days at a time, carefully hearing and sifting the evidence of both sides. Every right-minded person readily acknowledges that far greater weight ought to be attached to the finding of this Commission than to the declarations of the complainants, who contradicted one another in nearly every particular, and who caused the whole enquiry to degenerate into a farce."

[226] [Dispatch, 10th May, 1899. Blue Book, C. 9345. Page 229.]

[227] Cape Coloureds are a South African ethnic group consisted primarily of persons of mixed race and Khoisan descent. Although Coloureds form a minority group within South Africa, they are the predominant population group in the Western Cape. Cape Coloureds - Wikipedia

[228] [Dispatch. Appendix C.]

"According to the report, nothing was proved as to the so-called ill-treatment; the special instances of alleged ill-treatment turned out to be purely imaginary; but it was clearly proved and found that the complainants had acted contrary to law, and the Commission only expressed disapproval of the fact that the arrests and the investigation had taken place at night, and without a proper warrant. It fills this Government with all the greater regret to observe that Her Majesty's Government bases its charges on ex parte, groundless, and, in many respects, false declarations of complainants who have been set in motion by political hatred, and that it silently ignores the report of the Commission."

b. The Edgar Case.

Mr. Chamberlain represented the Edgar case in the following way: -

"But perhaps the most striking recent instance of arbitrary action by officials, and of the support of such action by the Courts, is the well-known Edgar case. The effect of the verdict of the jury, warmly endorsed by the Judge, is that four policemen breaking into a man's house at night without a warrant, on the mere statement of one person, which subsequently turned out to be untrue, that the man had committed a crime, are justified in killing him there and then because, according to their own account, he hits one of them with a stick. If this is justification, then almost any form of resistance to the police is justification for the immediate killing of the person resisting, who may be perfectly innocent of any offence. This would be an alarming doctrine anywhere. It is peculiarly alarming when applied to a city like Johannesburg, where a strong force of police armed with revolvers have to deal with a large alien unarmed population, whose language in many cases they do not understand. The emphatic affirmation of such a doctrine by Judge and jury in the Edgar case cannot but increase the general feeling of insecurity amongst the Uitlander population, and the sense of injustice under which they labour. It may be pointed out that the allegation that Edgar assaulted the police was emphatically denied by his wife and others, and that the trial was conducted in a way that would be considered quite irregular in this country, the witnesses for the defence being called by the prosecution, and thereby escaping cross-examination."[229]

The answer of the Government of the South African Republic was: -

"The Edgar case is referred to by your Government as the most striking recent instance of arbitrary action by officials, and of the support of such action by the Courts," and this case is quoted as a conclusive test of the alleged judicial maladministration of this Republic; it will, therefore, be of interest to pause for a moment and consider it. What are the true facts?[230]

"A certain Foster, 'an Englishman,' was assaulted and felled to the ground, without any lawful cause, by a man named Edgar during the night of the 18th December, 1898; he lay on the ground as if dead, and ultimately died in the hospital. Edgar escaped to his room, and some police came on the scene, attracted by the screams of the bystanders. Amongst the police was one named Jones. When they saw the man who had been assaulted lying as if dead, they went to Edgar's apartment in order to arrest him as a criminal (he had, indeed, rendered himself liable for manslaughter, and apparently for murder). As he was caught in the very act, the police officers were, according to the Laws, not only of this Republic, but of all South Africa and of the United Kingdom of Great Britain and Ireland, justified in breaking open the door in order to arrest the culprit.

"While doing so, Edgar, with a dangerous weapon, struck Jones a severe blow. Under the stress of necessity the latter shot Edgar, from the effects of which he died. The question is not if Jones was justified in taking this extreme step, for the State Attorney of the Republic had already given effect to his opinion that this was a case for the jury by prosecuting him for manslaughter. The question is solely whether any jury in any country in the world would have found a man guilty of any crime under the circumstances set forth, and whether, if they did not find him guilty, the fact of their doing so would have been stamped and branded as a flagrant and remarkable instance of the maladministration of Justice.

"This Government is convinced that the English judicial administration affords numberless instances where the facts are as strong as in this case, and it cannot see why an occurrence which could happen in any part of the world would be especially thrown in their teeth in the form of an accusation.

229 [Dispatch, 10th May, 1899. C. 9345. Page 229.]

230 [Appendix C.]

"This Government does not wish to pass over in silence the censure which has been passed by Her Majesty's Government on the Public Prosecutor of Johannesburg, by whom the prosecution of this case was conducted; the fact that being of pure English blood, that he received his legal training in London, that he is generally respected by the Uitlander population on account of his ability, impartiality, and general character, will naturally not be of any weight with Her Majesty's Government against the facts of his action in calling witnesses for the prosecution who were intended for the defence, and thus rendering an imaginary cross-examination abortive.

"This Government only wishes to point out that the fact that the Edgar case is the strongest which Her Majesty's Government has been able to quote against the administration of Justice in this Republic affords the strongest and most eloquent proof possible that, taking it in general, the administration of Justice on the gold fields of this Republic not only compares favourably with that on other and similar gold fields, but even with that of old and settled countries.

"The untrue representations of this occurrence in the Press prove conclusively that the newspapers of the Witwatersrand, the atrocity-mongering tactics of which constitute a share of the organised campaign against the Republic and its Government, have been compelled to resort to mendacious criticisms on imaginary instances of maladministration, which were often simply invented. Where the Press is forced to adopt such methods, the true grievances must of necessity be unreal."

c. The Amphitheatre occurrence.

I now give Mr. Chamberlain's accusations about The Amphitheatre occurrence: -

"Some light upon the extent to which the police can be trusted to perform their delicate duties with fairness and discretion is thrown by the events referred to by the petitioners, which took place at a meeting called by British subjects for the purpose of discussing their grievances, and held on the 14th of January in the Amphitheatre of Johannesburg. The Government were previously apprised of the objects of the meeting, and their assent obtained, though this was not legally necessary for a meeting in an enclosed place. The organisers of the meeting state that they were informed by the State Secretary and the State Attorney that anyone who committed acts of violence or used seditious language would be held responsible, and in proof of the peaceful objects of the meeting, those who attended went entirely unarmed, by which it is understood that they did not even carry sticks. So little was any disturbance apprehended that ladies were invited to attend, and did attend. Yet, in the result, sworn affidavits of witnesses of different nationalities agree in the statement that the meeting was broken up almost immediately after its opening, and many of the persons attending it were violently assaulted by organised bands of hostile demonstrators, acting under the instigation and guidance of persons in Government employ, without any attempt at interference on the part of the police, and even in some cases with their assistance or loudly expressed sympathy.[231]

"The Government of the South African Republic has been asked to institute an inquiry into these disgraceful proceedings, but the request has been met with a flat refusal."

This accusation was answered in the following manner: -

"The Amphitheatre occurrence is used by Her Majesty's Government to show how incapable the police of the Witwatersrand are to fulfil their duties and to preserve order. The League meeting was held at the so-called Amphitheatre at Johannesburg, with the knowledge of the State Secretary and State Attorney, and the accusation is that in spite of that fact the uproar which arose at that meeting was not quelled by the police. The following are the true facts: -

Mr. Wybergh and another, both in the service of the South African League, informed the State Secretary and the State Attorney that they intended to call this meeting in the Amphitheatre, and asked permission to do so. They were informed that no permission from the authorities was necessary, and that as long as the meeting did not give rise to irregularities or disturbances of the peace, they would be acting entirely within their rights. Their attention was then drawn to the fact that owing to the action and the propaganda of the South African League, this body had become extremely unpopular with a large section of the inhabitants of Johannesburg, and that in all probability a disturbance of the peace would take place if a sufficient body of the police were not present to preserve order. To this these gentlemen answered that the police were in very bad odour since the Edgar case,

[231] [Dispatch, 10th May, 1899. Blue Book, C. 9345. Page 229.]

that the meeting would be a very quiet one, and that the presence of the police would contribute or give rise to disorder, and that they would on those grounds rather have no police at all.[232]

"The State Secretary[233] and State Attorney thereupon communicated with the head officials of the police at Johannesburg, with the result that the latter also thought that it would be better not to have any considerable number of police at the meeting. The Government accordingly, on the advice of these officials of the League as well as their own police officials, gave instructions that the police should remain away from this meeting; they did this in perfect good faith, and with the object of letting the League have its say without let or hindrance. The proposed meeting was, however, advertised far and wide.

As the feeling amongst a section of the Witwatersrand population was exceedingly bitter against the League, a considerable number of the opponents of that body also attended the meeting. The few police who were present were powerless to quell the disorder, and when the police came on the scene in force some few minutes after the commencement of the uproar, the meeting was already broken up. Taken by itself, this occurrence would not be of much importance, as it is an isolated instance as far as the gold fields of this Republic are concerned, and even in the best organised and best ordered communities irregularities like the above occasionally take place.

"The gravity of the matter, however, lies in the unjust accusation of Her Majesty's Government - that the meeting was broken up by officials of this Republic, and that the Government had curtly refused to institute an enquiry.

"This Government would not have refused to investigate the matter if any complaints had been lodged with it, or at any of the local Courts, and this has been clearly stated in its reply to Her Majesty's request for an investigation.

"This Government objects strongly to the systematic way in which the local authorities are ignored, and the continual complaints which are lodged with the Representatives of Her Majesty about matters which ought to be decided by the Courts of this Republic. Instead, however, of complaining to Her Majesty's Government after all other reasonable means of redress have been vainly invoked, they continually make themselves guilty of ignoring and treating with contempt the local Courts and authorities by continually making all sorts of ridiculous and ex parte complaints to Her Majesty's Government in the first instance; Her Majesty's Government is also thereby placed in the equivocal and undesirable position of intermeddling in the internal affairs of this Republic, which is in conflict with the London Convention.

Had the complaints been lodged with this Government, or with the proper officials or Courts, the facts could have been very easily arrived at, and it would have been proved that the few officials who were present at the meeting as a section of the public had done their best to prevent the irregularities, and that some of them had been hurt in their endeavours to preserve order. Instead of expressing their disapproval of such complaints, and referring the petitioners to the local Courts, Her Majesty's Government accepts those complaints, and gives them an official character by forwarding them for the information of this Government, and by publishing them in blue books for the information of the world.

"Her Majesty's Government will readily acknowledge that there is no State in the world with any sense of dignity, however weak and insignificant it may be, which can regard such matters with an indifferent eye; and when the relations of the two Governments are strained, then the mainspring must be looked for in this action of its subjects, which is not disapproved of by Her Majesty's Government, and not in imaginary or trumped-up grievances."

I have now examined the principal financial and administrative grievances of the English Uitlanders. I say English Uitlanders advisedly, because complaints are seldom or ever heard from other nationalities, either directly or by means of diplomatic representations.

Can it be contended with the slightest shadow of right and fairness that these grievances afford a reason for intervention? What crimes have been committed here against humanity or the law of nations? Do not the recorded grievances and abuses find a parallel in occurrences which are taking place every day in the most civilised countries? One can with perfect justice apply to the present circumstances the language which the

[232] [Appendix C.]
[233] Francis W. Reitz.

Russian Government used in stigmatising the illegal intervention of the British Government in the internal affairs of the Kingdom of Naples: -

"We would understand that, as a consequence of friendly forethought, one Government should give advice to another in a benevolent spirit; that such advice might even assume the character of exhortation; but we believe that to be the furthest limit allowable. Less than ever can it now be allowed in Europe to forget that sovereigns are equal among themselves, and that it is not the extent of territory, but the sacred character of the rights of each, which regulates the relations that exist between them. To endeavour to obtain from the King of Naples concessions as regards the internal government of his States by threats, or by a menacing demonstration, is a violent usurpation of his authorities, an attempt to govern in his stead; it is an open declaration of the right of the strong over the weak."[234]

In spite of all its hypocritical accusations, the British Government is perfectly well aware that, notwithstanding the unparalleled difficulties with which the Government and the Legislature have had to contend, the administration of the South African Republic is on a sound basis, and can, indeed, be favourably compared with that of other countries in a similar position.

It knows full well that the grievances which are used, by means of blue books, to stir up and excite the altruistic and humane feelings of the British public are for the most part imaginary, and that even if they were perfectly genuine, they nevertheless afford no ground for a justifiable interference in the internal affairs of the Republic. It is therefore necessary to have recourse to "Constitutional means" of another description.

Equal Political Rights.

The third and last "Constitutional" method which Mr. Chamberlain has had recourse to in order to forcibly intermeddle in the internal affairs of the South African Republic is the claim of equal rights for all the white inhabitants of the South African Republic. In this claim he has also followed the inspiration of Mr. Rhodes, for after the Jameson Raid Mr. Rhodes was prepared with a new programme for the "progressive policy" of South Africa, and made use of the formula "Equal rights for all white people south of the Zambesi."[235] Mr. Rhodes altered this cry afterwards, with an eye to the coloured vote in the Cape Colony, to "Equal rights for all civilised persons south of the Zambesi."

In due time the echo resounded from Downing Street "Equal political rights for all persons in the South African Republic." This formula may be either desirable or undesirable as a political aspiration in South Africa. But it is somewhat strange that Mr. Chamberlain should be one of the leaders of the party in England which has strenuously opposed the policy of manhood suffrage. In our case, however, Mr. Chamberlain does not confine himself to friendly advice, but he demands the franchise for all Uitlanders.

The South African Republic already possesses a franchise law, according to which every person is entitled to the full franchise after a seven years' residence in the Republic. But Mr. Chamberlain goes much further, and claims a far more extensive franchise. On what grounds does he base his claim?

The Royal Commission.

He appeals to the discussions which formed a prelude to the Convention of 1881. In the discussions, however, mention is only made of burgher rights or civil rights, with reference to which all possible equality has continuously existed since the Sand River Convention. To safeguard the equality of those civil as distinguished from political rights, Art. 12 of the Pretoria Convention provides "all persons (Her Majesty's loyal subjects) will have full liberty to reside in the country with the enjoyment, of all civil rights, and protection for their persons and property."

The period of the franchise was increased in 1882 from one year to five years, without, however, any protest from Her Majesty's Government, and in 1884 it was provided in the new Convention of that year in the most express and clear way possible that: -

(Art. XIV.). - All persons, other than natives, conforming themselves to the laws of the South African Republic (a) will have full liberty with their families, to enter, travel, or reside in any part of the South African Republic;

[234] [Life of Prince Consort, Vol. III., page 510.]

[235] The Zambezi River. Zambezi - Wikipedia

(b), they will be entitled to hire or possess houses, manufactories, warehouses, shops, and premises; (c), they may carry on their commerce either in person or by any agents whom they may think fit to employ; (d), they will not be subject, in respect of their persons or property, or in respect of their commerce or industry, to any taxes, whether general or local, other than those which are or may be imposed upon citizens of the said Republic.

In this way all white Uitlanders were guaranteed in their rights of free movement, ownership, and possession of property, trade, and commerce, and equal taxation with the burghers. There is no mention of political rights, nor has there ever been before this year - 1899. The Government of the South African Republic would be acting strictly in terms of the Convention if it informed Mr. Chamberlain that it alone has to determine upon the Franchise, as being a question of a purely internal nature; and further, that in claiming the right in terms of that Convention to force the Government to adopt a particular Franchise Law Mr. Chamberlain is the party who is violating the Convention.

The Bloemfontein Conference.

The Government of the South African Republic, however, took up a higher position; the State President [Kruger][236] went to Bloemfontein[237] for the purpose of discussing even internal affairs in a friendly spirit with the High Commissioner - inter alia - the question of the franchise, as he was actuated by the wish to consolidate and promote the peace of South Africa. Sir Alfred Milner said there: "If the question could be settled upon a broad and firm basis, the tension would disappear and everything come right in time." He has done his best latterly to prove that he did not say or mean anything of the kind, that the franchise question was only one of the burning internal matters in which Her Majesty's Government interested itself, and that a favourable understanding about the franchise would in no way pave the way to an agreement as to the other points of difference.[238]

Sir Alfred Milner's attitude.

The attitude of Sir Alfred Milner in this and other questions is, however, of such a nature that it is better to say nothing about his conduct, but to leave him to the judgment of public opinion and history. No agreement being possible between the parties, President Kruger left Bloemfontein and amended the Franchise Law in such a way that the Orange Free State, the Africanders of Cape Colony, and even Mr. Schreiner,[239] Premier of the Cape Colony, publicly signified their approval of the amendments which had been made.

[236] Stephanus Johannes Paulus Kruger (10 October 1825–14 July 1904) was a South African politician. He was one of the dominant political and military figures in 19th-century South Africa, and President of the South African Republic (or Transvaal) from 1883 to 1900. Nicknamed Oom Paul ("Uncle Paul"), he came to international prominence as the face of the Boer cause—that of the Transvaal and its neighbour the Orange Free State—against Britain during the Second Boer War of 1899–1902. He has been called a personification of Afrikanerdom, and remains a controversial figure; admirers venerate him as a tragic folk hero. Paul Kruger - Wikipedia

[237] The Bloemfontein Conference was a meeting that took place in Bloemfontein, capital of the Orange Free State from 31 May until 5 June 1899. The main issue dealt with the status of British migrant workers called "Uitlanders", who mined the gold fields in Transvaal.
The conference was initiated by Orange Free State president Martinus Theunis Steyn, in order to settle differences between Transvaal President Paul Kruger and British High Commissioner Alfred Milner. It was considered a last effort at reconciliation to prevent war between the two factions.
At the conference, Milner made three demands from Kruger:
Enactment by Transvaal of a law that would immediately give Uitlanders enfranchisement and the right to vote.
Use of the English language in the Volksraad (Transvaal Parliament).
All laws of the Volksraad would need to be approved by the British Parliament.
Kruger considered these demands an impossibility, however he was willing to reduce the period of Uitlander enfranchisement from the present fourteen years to seven years. Milner refused to compromise his original demands and, despite encouragement from British Colonial Secretary Joseph Chamberlain for him to continue the talks, Milner walked out of the conference on 5 June and no resolution concerning the fate of the Uitlanders was reached.
At this time, Milner composed a diatribe called the "Helot's Dispatch", which lambasted the Transvaal as a force that "menaces the peace and prosperity of the world". On 11 October 1899, the Second Boer War began. Bloemfontein Conference - Wikipedia

[238] [Blue Book, C. 9404.]

[239] William Philip Schreiner (30 August 1857–28 June 1919) was a barrister, politician, statesman and Prime Minister of the Cape Colony during the Second Boer War. William Schreiner - Wikipedia He is also the brother of Olive Schreiner.

President Kruger (to the British colonial): "There see what I am doing for you. Ain't you very grateful. Who is your true friend now?"[28] In the background is Joseph Chamberlin[240] looking stern and not satisfied.

The Joint Commission of Enquiry.

Mr. Chamberlain now discarded the appearance of friendliness, and began to adopt a menacing tone in his communications to the Government of the South African Republic. He proposed that the question as to whether the new Franchise Law was satisfactory or not should be discussed by a Joint Commission.

In the meanwhile, owing to informal conversations between the State Attorney [Reitz] and the British Government, there seemed to be a reasonable prospect of a speedy and satisfactory settlement.[241] The British Government, on being sounded by its agent, announced that if a five years' franchise, unhampered by complicated conditions, and with a quarter representation for the gold fields, were conceded, it would be prepared to consider the conditions, upon which the proposal depended, on their merits, and would not consider such a proposal as a refusal to accept the Joint Enquiry.

The conditions were that (a) no further interference should take place; (b), that the claim of suzerainty should drop; and (c) that further disputes should be settled by Arbitration. As soon, however, as the proposal was formally made the British Government refused to accept the condition with regard to the dropping of the suzerainty claim, notwithstanding the fact that the High Commissioner had declared in an official dispatch that the suzerainty controversy appeared to him to be etymological and not political.[242] Shortly afterwards the British Government made what was practically the same proposal, but without the condition as to the dropping of the suzerainty claim.

Bad Faith of the British Government.

As the Government of the South African Republic attached a vital importance to this condition, in view maintaining its international status, it refused to accept the proposal in this form; it, however, now reverted to the invitation for a joint enquiry, which it agreed to accept, but the British Government replied that it was too late, and that as a matter of fact it no longer adhered to the invitation.

Here we see in the clearest light -

(1). That, although the High Commissioner had stated that the suzerainty was only a question of etymological importance, that although the British Government had never been able to refute the arguments advanced by the South African Republic as to the abolition of the suzerainty in 1884, the British Government was nevertheless determined not to abandon its pretension, and is now prepared to make war in South Africa over this point.

[240] Joseph Chamberlain - Wikipedia

[241] [Blue Book, C. 9530.]

[242] [Blue Book, C. 9507. Page 6.]

(2). That the British Government invites the South African Republic to a joint enquiry, and, when this invitation, which had never been withdrawn, is accepted, the acceptance is refused with every mark of contempt.

Is there any instance in the history of civilised diplomacy of such trickery and such callous jugglery with the highest interests of South Africa?

Can anyone wonder that South Africa has lost all confidence in British statesmanship?

The British name has been sullied in this part of the world by many perfidious actions, but of a truth I cannot instance any more despicable and repellent incidents than those which have marked the course of events during the last few months.

And the consequence of this trickery will be written with the blood and the tears of thousands of innocent people.

Conclusion

I have now reviewed all the facts connected with the history of our oppression and persecution during the past hundred years. The allegations I have made are not invented, but are based upon the statements of the most reliable witnesses, nearly all of them of British nationality; they are facts that have been declared incontestable before the tribunal of history. [243]

As far as the more recent occurrences since 1898 are concerned, I may state that I have had personal knowledge of all the negotiations and questions at issue above referred to, and I can only declare that I have confined myself to facts; these will stand out in a much clearer light when the curtain is raised and the events of the last two years in this sorely afflicted part of the world are revealed.

In this awful turning point in the history of South Africa, on the eve of the conflict which threatens to exterminate our people, it behoves us to speak the truth in what may be, perchance, our last message to the world. Even if we are exterminated the truth will triumph through us over our conquerors, and will sterilise and paralyse all their efforts until they too disappear in the night of oblivion.

Up to the present our people have remained silent; we have been spat upon by the enemy, slandered, harried, and treated with every possible mark of disdain and contempt. But our people, with a dignity which reminds the world of a greater and more painful example of suffering, have borne in silence the taunts and derision of their opponents; indeed, they elected out of a sense of duty to remedy the faults and abuses which had crept into their public administration during moments of relaxed vigilance. But even this was ascribed to weakness and cowardice. Latterly our people have been represented by influential statesmen and on hundreds of platforms in England as incompetent, uncivilised, dishonourable, untrustworthy, corrupt, bloodthirsty, treacherous, etc., etc., so that not only the British public, but nearly the whole world, began to believe that we stood on the same level as the wild beasts.

In the face of these taunts and this provocation our people still remained silent. We were forced to learn from formal blue books issued by Her Majesty's Government and from dispatches of Her Majesty's High Commissioner in South Africa that our unscrupulous State Government, and our unjust, unprincipled, and disorderly administration, was a continual festering sore, which, like a pestilential vapour, defiled the moral and political atmosphere of South Africa.

We remained silent. We were accused in innumerable newspapers of all sorts of misdeeds against civilisation and humanity; crimes were imputed to us, the bare narration of which was sufficient to cause the hair to rise with horror. If the reading public believe a hundredth part of the enormities which have been laid at the door of our people and Government, they must be irresistibly forced to the conclusion that this Republic is a den of thieves and a sink of iniquity, a people, in fact, the very existence of which is a blot upon humanity, and a nuisance to mankind. Of the enormous sums which we are alleged to have spent out of the Secret Service Fund in order to purchase the good opinion of the world there has been no practical result or evidence, for the breath of slander went on steadily increasing with the violence of a hurricane. But our people remained silent, partly out of stupidity, partly out of a feeling of despairing helplessness, and partly because, being a pastoral people,

[243] PF: This is Jan Smuts writing in the first person.

they read no newspapers, and were thus unaware of the way in which the feeling of the whole world was being prejudiced against them by the efforts of malignant hate.

The practical effect has been that our case has been lost by default before the tribunal of public opinion. That is why I feel compelled to state the facts which have characterised the attitude of the British towards us during the Nineteenth century. Naboth's[244] title to his vineyard must be cancelled. The easiest way of securing that object, according to the tortuous methods of British diplomacy, was to prove that Naboth was a scoundrel and Ahab[245] an angel. The facts which have marked Ahab's career have been stated. I shall now proceed to draw my conclusions, which I submit must appeal irresistibly to every impartial and right-minded person.

During this century there have been three periods which have been characterised by different attitudes of the British Government towards us. The first began in 1806, and lasted until the middle of the century. During this period the chief feature of British policy was one of utter contempt, and the general trend of British feeling in regard to our unfortunate people can be summarised by the phrase, "The stupid and dirty Dutch." But the hypocritical ingenuity of British policy was perfectly competent to express this contempt in accents which harmonised with the loftiest sentiments then prevailing. The wave of sentimental philanthropy then passing over the civilised world was utilised by the British Government in order to represent the Boers to the world as oppressors of poor peace-loving natives, who were also men and brethren eminently capable of receiving religion and civilisation.

It may seem inexplicable that the Power which stood up boldly at the Treaty of Utrecht[246] as the shameless champion of negro slavery was the very one which was celebrated in South Africa for its morbid love of the natives; the explanation, however, is that it was not so much love for the native that underlay the apparent negrophilistic policy as hatred and contempt of the Boer.

As a result of this hatred of the Boer, disguised under the veneer of philanthropy in regard to the aborigines, the natives were employed as police against us; they were provided with arms and ammunition to be used against us; they were incited to fight us, and, wherever it was possible, they murdered and plundered us. In fact, our people were forced to bid farewell to the Cape Colony and all that was near and dear to them, and seek a shelter in the unknown wilderness of the North.

As an ultimate result of this hatred, our people had to pursue their pilgrimage of martyrdom throughout South Africa, until every portion of that unhappy country has been painted red with the blood, not so much of men capable of resistance as with that of our murdered and defenceless women and children.

The second period lasted until the year 1881. The fundamental principle then underlying British policy was no longer one of unqualified hatred. Results had already proved that hatred was powerless to subdue the Africander; it had, on the other hand, contributed largely to the consolidation of Africanderdom and to the fact that they spread over the whole of South Africa, thus forming the predominant nationality almost everywhere. In a moment of disinterestedness or absent-minded dejection England had concluded treaties with the Boers in 1852 and 1854, by which they were guaranteed in the undisturbed possession of certain wild and apparently worthless tracts of territory.

The fundamental sentiment which governed the policy of the second period was a feeling of regret at having made this mistake, coupled with the firm determination to set aside its results. These wild and useless tracts, which had been guaranteed to the Boers, appeared to be very valuable after the Boers had rescued them from barbarism, and opened them up for civilisation. It was felt that they ought to gleam amongst the jewels of Her Majesty's Crown, notwithstanding the obstacle in the treaties that had been concluded with the Boers. This was the concealed intention. As far as the means were concerned - they were, from the very exigency of inborn hypocrisy, partly revealed and partly concealed; the one differing from the other, as light from darkness. The secret means consisted in arming the Kaffir tribes against us in the most incredible manner, and in inciting them to attack us in violation of solemn treaties and promises.

[244] Naboth was a citizen of Jezreel. According to the Book of Kings in the Hebrew Bible, he was executed by Queen Jezebel so that her husband Ahab could possess his vineyard. Naboth - Wikipedia

[245] Ahab was the seventh king of Israel, the son and successor of King Omri and the husband of Jezebel of Sidon. Ahab - Wikipedia

[246] The Peace of Utrecht was a series of peace treaties signed by the belligerents in the War of the Spanish Succession, in the Dutch city of Utrecht between April 1713 and February 1715. The war involved three contenders for the vacant throne of Spain, and involved much of Europe for over a decade. Peace of Utrecht - Wikipedia

If this policy succeeded the real objects and means could be suppressed, and England could then come forward and pose openly as the champion of peace and order, and as the guardian angel of civilisation in this part of the world. The Republics could then be annexed under cover of these plausible pretexts. This policy failed as far as the Orange Free State was concerned, because the brave burghers of the neighbouring Republic succeeded, after great difficulty, in overcoming Moshesh, notwithstanding the fact that their arms and ammunition had been illegally stopped by the British Government. England was compelled in that case to confine itself to the protection of its "Basuto" tools. The British, however, succeeded in preventing the Boers from reaping the legitimate fruits of their victory, and in annexing the Diamond Fields - a flagrantly illegal act.

As far as the South African Republic is concerned, it was unfortunate that the burghers were not vigilant enough to foresee and prevent the crafty policy of the enemy. As the Transvaal Boers had subdued the most powerful Kaffir tribes, they never dreamt that the insignificant Kaffir wars in which they had been involved through English intrigue would have been seized as a pretext to annex their country to the British Crown. They had been remiss in not putting their full force into the field so as to bring these little wars to a speedy conclusion. And so the Magato and Socoecoeni[247] campaigns were conducted in a protracted and half-hearted way, much to the satisfaction of Sir Theophilus Shepstone, and those who were at his back.

The Annexation was brought about. It was announced that the extension of Her Majesty's sway and protection over the South African Republic could alone secure unity of purpose and trade, as well as open out a prospect of peace and prosperity. In these words of Shepstone's proclamation we see in all its repulsive nakedness the hypocrisy which openly masqueraded in the guise of the disinterested and pitiful Samaritan, while its true and secret object was to inflict a fatal wound upon the burgher Republic.

The third period of our history is characterised by the amalgamation of the old and well-known policy of fraud and violence with the new forces of Capitalism, which had developed so powerfully owing to the mineral riches of the South African Republic. Our existence as a people and as a State is now threatened by an unparalleled combination of forces.

Arrayed against us we find numerical strength, the public opinion of the United Kingdom thirsting and shouting for blood and revenge, the world-wide and cosmopolitan power of Capitalism, and all the forces which underlie the lust of robbery and the spirit of plunder. Our lot has of late become more and more perilous. The cordon of beasts of plunder and birds of prey has been narrowed and drawn closer and closer around this poor doomed people during the last ten years. As the wounded antelope awaits the coming of the lion, the jackal, and the vulture, so do our poor people all over South Africa contemplate the approach of the foe, encircled as they are by the forces of hatred and revenge, and by the stratagems and covetousness of their enemies.

Every sea in the world is being furrowed by the ships which are conveying British troops from every corner of the globe in order to smash this little handful of people. Even Xerxes, with his millions against little Greece, does not afford a stranger spectacle to the wonder and astonishment of mankind than this gentle and kind-hearted Mother of Nations, as, wrapped in all the panoply of her might, riches, and exalted traditions, she approaches the little child grovelling in the dust with a sharpened knife in her hand. This is no War - it is an attempt at Infanticide.

And as the brain of the onlooker reels, and as his thoughts fade away into uneasy slumbers, there arises before him in a dream the distant prospect of Bantu children playing amongst the gardens and ruins of the sunny south around thousands of graves in which the descendants of the European heroes of Faith and Freedom lie sleeping.

For the marauding hordes of the Bantu are once more roving where European dwellings used to stand. And when the question is asked - why all this has happened? Why the heroic children of an heroic race, to which civilisation owes its most priceless blessings, should lie murdered there in that distant quarter of the globe? An invisible spirit of mockery answers, "Civilisation is a failure; the Caucasian is played out!" and the dreamer awakens with the echo of the word "Gold! gold! gold!" in his ears.

[247] PF: Unable to identify these campaigns, tribes or rulers. In the index of the printed book Secoecoeni is referred to as a Zulu Chief. Magato may refer to the Malaboch War: The Malaboch War (1894) was between Chief Malaboch (Mmaleboho, Mmaleboxo) of the Bahananwa (Xananwa) people and the South African Republic Government led by Commandant-General Piet Joubert. Malboch refused to pay taxes to the Transvaal after it was given back to the Boers in 1881. This resulted in a military drive against him. The Malaboch war broke out when Chief Malaboch refused to leave his kingdom in Blouberg after being asked to leave by the government of South African Republic in April 1894. Piet Joubert led the Transvaal forces to an overwhelming victory leading to the surrender of the Bahananwa Malaboch War - Wikipedia

The orchids of Birmingham are yellow. The traditions of the greatest people on earth are tarnished and have become yellow.

The laurels which Britannia's legions hope to win in South Africa are sere and yellow.

But the sky which stretches its banner over South Africa remains blue. The justice to which Piet Retief appeals when our fathers said farewell to the Cape Colony, and to which Joachim Prinsloo called aloud in the Volksraad of Natal when it was annexed by England; the justice to which the burghers of the Transvaal entrusted their case at Paarde Kraal[248] in 1880, remains immutable, and is like a rock against which the yeasty billows of British diplomacy dissolve in foam.

It proceeds according to eternal laws, unmoved by human pride and ambition. As the Greek poet of old said, it permits the tyrant, in his boundless self-esteem, to climb higher and higher and to gain greater honour and might until he arrives at the appointed height, and then falls down into the infinite depths.

Africanders, I ask you but to do as Leonidas did with his 300 men when they advanced unflinchingly at Thermopylae against Xerxes and his myriads, and do not be disturbed by such men as Milner, Rhodes, and Chamberlain, or even by the British Empire itself, but cling fast to the God of our forefathers, and to the Righteousness which is sometimes slow in acting, but which never slumbers nor forgets. Our forefathers did not pale before the terrors of the Spanish Inquisition, but entered upon the great struggle for Freedom and Right against even the mighty Philip, unmindful of the consequences.

Nor could the rack and the persecuting bands of Louis XIV. tame or subdue the spirit of our fathers. Neither Alva nor Richelieu were able to compass the triumph of tyranny over the innate sentiment of Freedom and Independence in our forefathers. Nor will a Chamberlain be more fortunate in effecting the triumph of Capitalism, with its lust for power, over us.

If it is ordained that we, insignificant as we are, should be the first among all peoples to begin the struggle against the new-world tyranny of Capitalism, then we are ready to do so, even if that tyranny is reinforced by the power of Jingoism.

May the hope which glowed in our hearts during 1880, and which buoyed us up during that struggle, burn on steadily! May it prove a beacon of light in our path, invincibly moving onwards through blood and through tears, until it leads us to a real Union of South Africa.

As in 1880, we now submit our cause with perfect confidence to the whole world. Whether the result be Victory or Death, Liberty will assuredly rise in South Africa like the sun from out the mists of the morning, just as Freedom dawned over the United States of America a little more than a century ago. Then from the Zambesi to Simon's Bay it will be.

"Africa for the Africander."

[248] The Paardekraal Monument is situated in Krugersdorp, South Africa. The monument commemorates the original site of vow made by Transvaal Boers on 13 December 1880, prior to the armed rebellion known as First Boer War, when they vowed to regain their independence from the British Empire. Paardekraal Monument - Wikipedia

Century Appendices Appendix A

Lord Derby's Dispatch

Lord Derby's Dispatch on Convention of 1884
To Messrs. Kruger, Du Toit, And Smit.
Downing Street,
15 February, 1884.
Gentlemen,

I have the honour to acknowledge the receipt of your letter of the 13th inst., in which you intimate your readiness to accept the arrangement proposed by me at our recent interview, whereby the debt of the Transvaal State to Her Majesty's Government would be reduced by £127,000. I will not delay to recommend this proposal to the consideration of Her Majesty's Government.

I have considered the representations and suggestions made in the fourth and following paragraphs of your letter, and I do not think it would now be practicable to carry out the arrangements which you propose for the settlement of the questions referred to. Her Majesty's Government are willing, however, that the 20th Article of the Convention of Pretoria shall be retained in the new Convention, with such verbal alterations as are requisite, and I am glad to understand that this course will meet your views.

When I had the pleasure of receiving you here on the 8th inst. we discussed the other principal questions which, in addition to those of the boundary and the debt, you had submitted to me in previous correspondence, and I explained to you generally the nature and extent of the concessions which Her Majesty's Government would be able to make in regard to them. You were satisfied with these explanations, as far as they were put before you; and the progress which has been made appears to me to render it convenient that I should now transmit for your perusal a draft of the new Convention which Her Majesty's Government propose in substitution for the Convention of Pretoria.

In this draft the Articles of the Convention of Pretoria, which will be no longer in force, have been printed alongside of the proposed new Articles, and where an Article is retained and altered, the alterations have been shown in order to explain clearly the changes which will be made. You will find that in the draft, and the map which accompanies it, the conclusions which have been arrived at in the course of our communications have been closely adhered to and accurately expressed, and I trust that you will experience no difficulty in understanding and agreeing to each of its provisions. If, however, there should be any point as to which you are doubtful, it may be convenient that you should again meet me here and receive such further explanations as may be desirable.

It does not appear to me to be necessary that I should refer in detail to each Article of the draft. You will observe that in the preamble and throughout the Convention the wish of your Government that the designation "South African Republic" should be substituted for "Transvaal State" has been complied with. In the first Article the extension of the Western boundary is precisely defined as agreed to. By the omission of those Articles of the Convention of Pretoria which assigned to Her Majesty and to the British Resident certain specific powers and functions connected with the internal government and the foreign relations of the Transvaal State your Government will be left free to govern the country without interference, and to conduct its diplomatic intercourse and shape its foreign policy subject only to the requirement embodied in the fourth Article of the new draft—that any treaty with a foreign State shall not have effect without the approval of the Queen.

There are other provisions in the draft which have not been the subject of discussion with you; they are for the most part a renewal of those declarations made on behalf of the Transvaal State in the Convention of Pretoria, which it is desirable (as I trust you will agree in thinking) to maintain as an assurance to all parties that there will be no withdrawal of those securities for liberty and equal treatment which your State has always professed itself ready to afford. I would, however, refer more specifically to the 19th Article of the draft, in which it is proposed that in consideration of the discontinuance of all direct interference by this country in the government and control of the natives within the Transvaal, it should be formally declared that your Government will adopt and carry out the assurances which, with their assent and approval, were given to those natives by Her Majesty's Commissioners.

I trust that I may soon hear from you that there is no obstacle to my informing Her Majesty's Government that the Draft Convention can be adopted.

I have, etc., Derby.

Images of “Reviews” Edition

A CONVENTION CONCLUDED BETWEEN HER MAJESTY THE QUEEN, &C., &C., AND THE SOUTH AFRICAN REPUBLIC.

NOTE.—*The words and paragraphs bracketed or printed in italics are proposed to be inserted, those within a black line are proposed to be omitted.*

Her Majesty's Commissioners for the settlement of the Transvaal Territory, duly appointed as such by a Commission passed under the Royal Sign Manual and Signet, bearing date the 5th of April 1881, do hereby undertake and guarantee, on behalf of Her Majesty, that from and after the 8th day of August 1881, complete self-government, subject to the suzerainty of Her Majesty. Her Heir and Successors, will be accorded to the inhabitants of the Transvaal Territory, upon the following terms and conditions, and subject to the following reservations and limitations :—

Whereas the Government of the Transvaal State, through its Delegates, consisting of Stephanus Johannes Paulus Kruger, President of the said State, Stephanus Johannes Du Toit, Superintendent of Education ; Nicholas Jacobus Smit, a member of the Volksraad, have represented to the Queen that the Convention signed at Pretoria on the 3rd day of August, 1881, and ratified by the Volksraad of the said State on the 25th October, 1881, contains certain provisions which are inconvenient, and imposes burdens and obligations from which the said State is desirous to be relieved ; and that the south-western boundaries fixed by the said Convention should be amended, with a view to promote the peace and good order of the said state, and of the countries adjacent thereto ; and whereas Her Majesty the Queen, &c., &c., has been pleased to take the said representations into consideration : Now, therefore, Her Majesty has been pleased to direct, and it is hereby declared that the following articles of a new Convention * * * * * * * * * shall when ratified by the Volksraad of the South African Republic, be substituted for the Articles embodied in the Convention of 3rd August, 1881 ; which latter, pending such ratification, shall continue in full force and effect.

Signed at ~~Pretoria~~ *London* this ~~3rd day of August 1881.~~

~~HERCULES ROBINSON,~~
~~President and~~ High Commissioner
~~EVELYN WOOD, Major General,~~
~~Officer Administering the Government.~~
~~J. H. de VILLIERS.~~

We, the undersigned, Stephanus Johannes Paulus Kruger, ~~Martinus Wessel Pretorius,~~ and ~~Petrus Jacobus Joubert,~~ as ~~representatives~~ *delegates* of the ~~Transvaal Burghers,~~ *South African Republic*, do hereby agree to all the above conditions, reservations, and limitations, ~~under which self government has been restored to the inhabitants of the Transvaal Territory, subject to the suzerainty of Her Majesty, Her Heirs and Successors, and we agree to accept the Government of the said Territory, with all rights and obligations thereto appertaining, on the 8th day of August 1881,~~ and we ~~promise and~~ undertake that this Convention shall be ratified by a ~~newly elected~~ Volksraad of the ~~Transvaal State~~ *South African Republic* within ~~three~~ *six* months from this date.

Signed at ~~Pretoria,~~ *London*, this ~~3rd day of August 1881.~~

~~S. J. P. KRUGER.~~
~~M. W. PRETORIUS.~~
~~P. J. JOUBERT.~~

1881 Convention

Convention Concluded Between Her Majesty the Queen, &C., &C.,

And The South African Republic.

NOTE.—The words and paragraphs bracketed or printed in italics are proposed to be inserted, those within a black line are proposed to be omitted.

Her Majesty's Commissioners for the settlement of the Transvaal Territory, duly appointed as such by a Commission passed under the Royal Sign Manual and Signet, bearing date the 5th of April 1881, do hereby undertake and guarantee, on behalf of Her Majesty, that from and after the 8th day of August 1881, complete self-government, subject to the suzerainty of Her Majesty, Her Heir and Successors, will be accorded to the inhabitants of the Transvaal Territory, upon the following terms and conditions, and subject to the following reservations and limitations:—

Whereas the Government of the Transvaal State, through its Delegates, consisting of Stephanus Johannes Paulus Kruger, President of the said State. Stephanus Johannes Du Toit, [249] Superintendent of Education; Nicholas Jacobus Smit,[250] a member of the Volksraad, have represented to the Queen that the Convention signed at Pretoria on the 3rd day of August, 1881, and ratified by the Volksraad of the said State on the 25th October, 1881, contains certain provisions which are inconvenient, and imposes burdens and obligations from which the said State is desirous to be relieved; and that the south-western boundaries fixed by the said Convention should be amended, with a view to promote the peace and good order of the said state, and of the countries adjacent thereto; and whereas Her Majesty the Queen, &c., &c., has been pleased to take the said representations into consideration. Now, therefore, Her Majesty has been pleased to direct, and it is hereby declared that the following articles of a new Convention .... shall when ratified by the Volksraad of the South African Republic, be substituted for the Articles embodied in the Convention of 3rd August, 1881; which latter, pending such ratification, shall continue in full force and effect.

Signed at ~~Pretoria~~ London this ~~3rd day of August 1881~~,

~~Hercules Robinson~~,
~~President and~~ High Commissioner
~~Evelyn Wood,[251] Major General,~~
~~Officer Administering the Government~~
~~J.H. De Villiers~~.[252]

We, the undersigned, Stephanus Johannes Paulus Kruger, ~~Martinus Wessel Pretorius~~ and ~~Petrus Jacobus Joubert~~, as ~~representatives~~ delegates ~~of the Transvaal Burghers~~, South African Republic, do hereby agree to all the above conditions, reservations, and limitations, ~~under which self-government has been restored to the inhabitants of the Transvaal Territory, subject to the suzerainty of Her Majesty, Her Heirs and Successors, and we agree to accept the Government of the said Territory, with all rights and obligations thereto appertaining, on the 8th day of August 1881~~, and we ~~promise and~~ undertake that this Convention shall be ratified by a ~~newly elected~~ Volksraad of the ~~Transvaal State~~ South African Republic within three six months from this date.

Signed at ~~Pretoria~~, London, ~~this 3rd day of August 1881~~

~~S.J.P. Krueger~~
~~M.W. Pretorius~~
~~P.J. Joubert~~

[249] Stephanus Jacobus (S.J.) du Toit (9 October 1847, Daljosafat–28 May 1911, Daljosafat) was a Dutch Reformed minister, founding member and leader of the Fellowship of True Afrikaners, founder of the Afrikanerbond, superintendent of education in the Transvaal and editor of several newspapers and magazines, including Our Klyntji. Stephanus Jacobus du Toit - Wikipedia

[250] Nicolas Jacobus Smit (30 May 1837, Graaff-Reinet–4 April 1896) was a vice-president of the South African Republic and general during the First Boer War. Nicolas Jacobus Smit - Wikipedia

[251] Field Marshal Sir Henry Evelyn Wood, VC, GCB, GCMG (9 February 1838–2 December 1919) was a British Army officer. He served in several major conflicts including the Indian Mutiny where, as a lieutenant, he was awarded the Victoria Cross, for rescuing a local merchant from a band of robbers who had taken their captive into the jungle, where they intended to hang him. Wood further served as a commander in several other conflicts, notably the Third Anglo-Ashanti War, the Anglo-Zulu War, the First Boer War and the Mahdist War. His last appointment was as commander of 2nd Army Corps (later renamed Southern Command) from 1901 to 1904. Evelyn Wood (British Army officer) - Wikipedia

[252] J.H. de Villiers First Chief Justice of the Union of South Africa. From: Freemasonry in South Africa - Wikipedia

Appendix B Diamond Fields

The Annexation of the Diamond Fields

(Translation from Dutch).

In his speech at the opening of the Cape Parliament on the 18th April, 1872, Sir Henry Barkly said:—

The Sovereignty of Her Majesty was therefore proclaimed and brought into operation with the full consent of the diggers, and the Government has since been carefully and efficiently administered, notwithstanding considerable difficulties."

The Diamond News of the 1st May, 1872, says, in referring to this speech:—

Of the three short paragraphs which immediately concern us, the first is one of self-congratulation—the diggers and other inhabitants of Griqualand accept the British Government with heartfelt satisfaction. Sir Henry says nothing of the unaccountable and daily increasing dissatisfaction with that Government, and perhaps he knows nothing of it, as it would be an act of suicide for the Commissioners, which they would not be guilty of, to report about the prevailing feelings."

On the 30th May, 1872, the Diamond Fields said:—

There can be no doubt that the population of the Diamond Fields are strongly opposed to annexation to the Cape Colony.

If anything like a plebiscite could be taken, the votes against being put under the Cape Government would be in the proportion of nine to one ... even the Free State Government would get two votes to one if the Cape Town Government were the only other candidate."

In December, 1871, scarcely a month after the dispersion of the Free State authorities and the constitution of Sir Henry Barkly's junta, lynch law broke out. Lawlessness and general insecurity prevailed everywhere (see Diamond News, 17th January, 20th March, 17th July, 1872).

One reads in the Diggers' Gazette of the 26th April, 1872:—

No one would wish to ask for a continuation of the existing state of affairs. Only entirely mischievous people could wish for the continuation of such a failure as our Commissioners of British rule have brought about on these Fields. We have formerly expressed ourselves openly about this matter, and our local contemporaries have done the same."

The following remarks were made in the Diamond News of the 16th December, 1871:—

A description of Du Toit' span by night lately appeared in the Diamond News as it used to be under the admittedly unsatisfactory Free State police, and, by way of contrast, as it now is, after the withdrawal of that police. The comparison is not flattering to the strength of mind or administrative capability of our present rulers, and a comparison of Free State administration with Cape administration would in no way be more favourable to the latter.

The British Government, so highly prized, which would put everything to rights and would do so much for the diggers, has brought the camps back to their original position of having to protect themselves."

In the Diamond News of the 10th July, 1872 (eight months after the constitution of Sir Henry Barkly's rule), the following criticisms appear:—

Robberies are becoming so frequent that if we were only to relate the particulars of those that have been brought to our notice we would require more space than our limits will allow. Innumerable petty thefts are passed by without punishment. This is certainly a charming state of affairs! And the question naturally arises—how long will this continue? Thieves, black and white, experienced and dangerous, and yet no night police to stop their illegal actions! Shall we get no night police, or must the scoundrels, who are poisoning our camps continually, enjoy the immunity and freedom which they now appear to have?"

On the 26th July lynch law and revolt broke out afresh in an extensive way at New Rush, the principal diggings. The Diggers' Gazette made the following remarks about this:—

As long as Judge Lynch remains free to hold his court and to levy his punishments, for so long can the whole framework and machinery of lawful authority just as well cease to exist.

Authority cannot maintain its claim to be respected as long as persons suffering under the sense of having been injured take the law into their own hands, solely because of the proved incapability of those in authority to protect them where their interests mostly need protection.

Day after day, and night after night, the one or other part of the camp is entertained by the edifying spectacle of natives being thrashed, tents being burnt, and white people surrounded by ferocious crowds who can scarcely be kept back from carrying out their desire for vengeance by a small truncheon and a thick thong.

We do not wish to justify this state of affairs, but we cannot shut our eyes to the injustice which almost makes it a necessity.

No magistrate, however exceptional, counts against the absence of such laws, discipline, and police as our circumstances demand, and through want of which there is no other prospect than that terrorism which arises out of a blind struggle against anarchy."

The Diamond News, in its issue of 20th July, 1872, says:—

The copious news in our columns, and the reports of meetings, as well as the scenes which take place every night at mass meetings in this time of excitement, uproar and confusion, take up nearly all our principal columns. We heartily wish that the fire may be speedily got under, or else it is very much to be feared that the end will be dreadfully injurious to the safety and welfare of the innocent."

On the 19th July, 1872, a very large meeting of diggers was held at the Market Square, New Rush, when the following resolution, among others, was unanimously passed:—

As this meeting is of opinion that, with a view to the prevailing disturbances in this camp, the Commissioners ought at once, with the Diggers' Committee, to make such amendments in the existing unsatisfactory state of the law as will as far as possible prevent the thefts of diamonds by native labourers, and their purchase by unprincipled dealers, and will also make such alterations in the law so as to promote the general welfare."

In the Cape Parliament, commencing the 5th June, 1872, Mr. Merriman said:—

The Fields ... were annexed and a form of government was introduced there which could not be more ludicrous. A sort of irresponsible Commission (the Rovers junta) was established, in which the members could not agree, and were not responsible to anybody; he could imagine nothing more ridiculous or which worked worse. The Orange Free State had given the people a sort of representation, but the first act of our Government was to abolish all the Commissions, and the result was that the people were burdened with an irresponsible body.

The Orange Free State had appointed a responsible official ... who was efficient ... while we had established a court twenty miles away from the most populated part; whereby grinding expenses had been entailed on those who sought justice, just as if it was the only object of the British Government to pile up heavy law costs."

Mr. Knight said: "One of the chief reasons why he was against Annexation was that nine-tenths of the population on the fields would hold up their hands to get rid of the present Government because they felt that they were far better off before they were annexed."

Mr. Buchanan declared: "He himself, when he visited the Diamond Fields, had wandered from camp to camp, and from the one sorting table to the other, and had talked with the diggers in order to acquaint himself as to their feelings about various matters, and he had obtained the conviction that there was a great deal of feeling against the British Government."

In the subsequent debate in the Cape Parliament Mr. J.H. Brown said, in regard to Mr. Orpen's motion: "That the diggers look with the greatest contempt on the Government which was there now, and that this Government was quite as much hated as it deserved to be."—(Diggers' Gazette, 12th July, 1872).

In the Diamond News of the 8th October, 1872, one reads:—

Newspaper after newspaper comes out, and those who have a claim upon land look eagerly to see 'what is happening about the land?' and all the information the newspaper gives is that David Arnot, Esq.,[253] claims half the country, and that Francis Orpen, Esq., the Surveyor, has decided that £30 must be paid before the case of any claimant can be taken into consideration. It is Arnot and Orpen and land; and land and Orpen and Arnot, week after week. They appear to be made one for the other, and for nothing and nobody else.

Half a newspaper is filled with lists of claims of the said David, and it becomes daily clearer and clearer that the great head chief of Griqualand West cannot be Mr. Waterboer, but must be David Arnot—because all the claims and all the kopjes have been provided for, and all are for Mr. Arnot and nobody else.

The impression is everywhere that British protection is invoked not for British interests, nor for the interests of Britons working on the fields here, but for the sake of two gentlemen who hold the reins with far more power than ought to be given to anyone who is entrusted with the administration of this country.

Who has ever heard of a Government which binds itself to give the surveyorship of a new country to one man only? Mr. Francis Orpen is decidedly a first-class man in his profession ... but that does not justify any Government in agreeing that he, and he only, is to keep the survey of this territory entirely in his own hands. Everyone knows what that must lead to."

Appendix C Reply to Chamberlain Sept. 29, 1899

The Reply to Mr. Chamberlain's Dispatch on Grievances.

Department of Foreign Affairs, Pretoria.[254]

26th September, 1899.

Sir,

The Government of the South African Republic has the honour to acknowledge the receipt of a copy of a certain dispatch dated 10th May, 1899, addressed to His Excellency the High Commissioner by the Secretary of State for the Colonies, in consequence of a petition sent to Her Majesty the Queen of Great Britain and Ireland. 21,684 signatures appear on this petition, and are said to have been affixed thereto by an equivalent number of British subjects resident at Johannesburg, in this Republic.

This Government notes that Her Majesty's Government have thought fit, on the grounds of the information already in their possession, to make investigation into the subject matter of the aforesaid petition, and, as a result of such investigation, to express to this Government their views on the administration of the internal affairs of this Republic, which said views they have at the same time communicated to the memorialists as an answer to their petition.

This Government may be permitted to point out that the Convention of London of 1884, entered into between this Republic and the Government of Her Britannic Majesty, guarantees to the South African Republic full and free internal administration without any interference from anyone whatever. As Lord Derby notifies in his dispatch of the 15th February, 1884:—

Your Government will be left free to govern the country without interference, and to conduct its diplomatic intercourse, and shape its foreign policy, subject only to the requirements embodied in the fourth article of the new draft—that any treaty with a foreign State shall not have effect without the approval of the Queen."

In his despatch of the 4th February, 1896, the Colonial Secretary, Mr. Chamberlain, states:—

[253] Nicolaas Waterboer was whipped up by David Arnot, a lawyer from Colesberg, to lay claim to the Campbell grounds, among other things. The Free State disputed the claim, because with the Bloemfontein Convention of 1854 the territory was included in the OSCE and, moreover, in 1861 the republic bought all of Adam Kok's land from him. Arnot then referred to the whole dispute over the property rights over several diamond areas for arbitration. Keate, the Lieutenant Governor of Natal, was appointed arbitrator and in his infamous Keate judgment awarded the Campbell lands to Nicolaas Waterboer. Thereafter the Cape Colony incorporated the whole area under the name Griqualand West. Later, a special court under Judge Andries Stockenström determined that Waterboer had no right to the territory and that the British government had to pay significant damages to the Orange Free State. Campbell Grounds - Wikipedia

[254] Also reproduced in "Story of the Boers."

In the next place, it is necessary that I should state clearly and unequivocally what is the position which Her Majesty's Government claim to hold toward the Government of the South African Republic. Since the Convention of 1884, Her Majesty's Government recognised the South African Republic as a free and independent Government as regards all its internal affairs not touched by the Convention."

In a telegram, also from Mr. Chamberlain, dated 26th March, 1896, the same statement is substantially made, viz.:—"Her Majesty's Government do not claim any rights under the Conventions to prescribe particular internal reforms which should be made in South African Republic." in its entirety; at the same time, it has been consistent in protesting in the most forcible manner against any interference or intermeddling with the internal affairs of the Republic, and against the discussion or treatment of these affairs with or by any other than the Republic itself, and it can discover no reasons now which would either justify such interference or exempt it from the accusation of being a violation of the Convention of London.

This Government feels convinced that Her Majesty's Government would not favourably entertain a request from British subjects for intervention because the said British subjects are unwilling (as was agreed between this Republic and Her Majesty's Government in the Convention of London) to conform themselves to the laws of the land and to respect the legal institutions and customs of the South African Republic, and because they feel aggrieved that the laws are not altered in accordance with their demands.

The friendly relations so highly prized by this Government which have existed between this Republic and the United Kingdom, the other party to the Convention of London, have always been a safe guarantee to this Government against such a breach of the Convention on the part of Her Majesty's Government, and it greatly deplores the fact that Her Majesty's Government has now decided to act in conflict with the Convention of London by busying itself with the imaginary grievances of the Uitlanders, and making representations there anent[255] to this Government. Against such action this Government feels that it must earnestly and emphatically protest, and the Right Hon. Mr. Chamberlain could not take it amiss if this Government were to pay no further attention to the charges against its administration contained in the petition, or if they declined to discuss further the views of Her Majesty's Government about these charges.

This Government has, however, on more than one occasion, notified to Her Majesty's Government that it will attach great value to any suggestions which may be tendered in the interests of British subjects, and it will certainly lend a very willing ear to any friendly advice or hints which may be given by Her Majesty's Government as being the representative of a Power which, with this Republic and the Orange Free State, protects and fosters the paramount interests of South Africa.

His Honour the State President was animated by these sentiments when he accepted the courteous invitation of His Honour President Steyn to proceed to Bloemfontein in order to confer with Your Excellency about matters which are an equal source of interest to this Republic and Her Majesty's Government. These friendly sentiments now prompt it to take the liberty of drawing serious attention to the fact that Her Majesty's Government certainly appear to be supplied with insufficient and incorrect data about facts and occurrences from which erroneous ideas and conclusions are drawn, so that, although desirous of avoiding subjects the discussion of which would be contrary to the Convention, this Government nevertheless feels that it ought to convey to Her Majesty's Government the true position of affairs, and that it ought to point out how the latter is misled, the condition of affairs as depicted in the dispatch under reply being in all respects exaggerated, and in many instances entirely untrue.

In the first place, this Government wishes to point out that, so far from the petition which gave rise to the despatch under reply having been signed by 21,684 British subjects, it appears indeed that it was signed by very few people in the South African Republic—leaving aside all mention of British subjects.

This has been substantiated in many cases by sworn declarations, many of which were handed to His Excellency the High Commissioner during the Conference at Bloemfontein, and this Government feels that it may flatter itself that the British Government, after having examined these documents, will share with this Government the view that this memorial is in itself a matter of very slight importance, even although it may contain the signatures of a certain number of British subjects who hold the opinion that they are entitled to a change in the form of Government because, in violation of the Convention entered into between this Republic and Her

[255] (obsolete) Against, in front of, fronting; before; opposite; over against, on the other side. anent - Wiktionary

Majesty's Government, they will not conform themselves to the laws of the land, but claim alterations therein at their own caprice.

This Government is all the more convinced that this memorial is of no great moment, and that it certainly does not express the feelings of all the so-called Uitlanders, because another memorial has been received by it from about 23,000 inhabitants of this Republic, nearly all Uitlanders, and amongst whom are several British subjects. The High Commissioner was informed that the signatures to this memorial were obtained in a perfectly bona fide way, and this information was supported by sworn affidavits. The purport of this memorial bore evidence to the fact that the thousands of Uitlanders who signed it were satisfied with the administration and the Government of this Republic, and did not share the views of the memorialists to Her Britannic Majesty in respect of what the latter considered to be legitimate grievances.

This Government may further be permitted to point out that although the Uitlander population may have co-operated in effecting an increase in the revenues of the State, principally, as His Excellency has been informed, in custom dues, prospecting licences, railway receipts, etc., so that the revenue in 1898 amounted to £3,983,360, the fact must not be lost sight of, on the other hand, that gold to the value of £20,000,000 was exported from the State during the same year 1898, almost entirely by the Uitlanders.

At the same time, it must not be forgotten that although the, chief item in custom dues is collected on goods which are imported at Johannesburg, yet these goods are not entirely used or consumed by the Uitlanders, for a considerable quantity is sent over the whole Republic by the wholesale merchants to the retail dealers who do business with the burghers in the villages and the country, so that much of what is imported into Johannesburg is destined for consumption by the original burgher of the Republic.

With regard to the contention that the mining industry is more heavily taxed than in any other country, and that the cost of the necessaries of life is higher, this Government desires to remark that this contention is entirely contradicted by facts and statistics. The value of goods imported into the South African Republic during 1898 amounted to £9,996,575, and the custom duties levied thereon to £1,058,224, or 10.6 per cent. Under the Customs Union of the adjacent British Colonies the import duties amounted to 15 per cent, of the value of the goods, a comparison which yields a difference of nearly 50 per cent. in favour of the Republic. When the matter is examined in detail the case is even stronger. In the Colonies certain articles, such as bread stuffs, are subject to a special duty of 2s., say about 30 per cent, of the value, in corn, and 40 per cent. in meal. In this Republic the duty on both the foregoing articles is 7-1/2 per cent.; butter is especially taxed at 3d. per pound, or 30 per cent., under the Customs Union, while in the Republic it is subject only to the 7-1/2 ad valorem duty. Coffee and other necessaries of life, on being compared, would show a similar difference, and this Government therefore trusts that Her Majesty's Government will exonerate it when it points out the incorrectness and unreliability of the information supplied to the Secretary of State, on which he bases his conclusion that the cost of living is unusually high in consequence of the taxation levied by the State; that such is not the case will be at once shown by a comparison with the taxation of the neighbouring Colonies.

The character of the financial administration must have been erroneously represented to Her Majesty's Government if it was simply stated that defalcations to an amount of £18,590 had taken place. It would ex facie appear from such a statement that the above defalcations had taken place during the past year; as a matter of fact, the Inspection Department, which has only recently been called into existence, reported over financial matters covering the years 1884 to 1896.

It is unfair to characterise all deficiencies as defalcations, for from the nature of the case a deficiency does not always constitute a defalcation. The report specified the sub-divisions of monies which had yet to be accounted for. The first item in such deficiencies amounted originally to £12,000, and of this £6,000 was afterwards collected, and the balance was only brought forward; another item of £10,808 11s. was brought forward in its entirety, but £3,000 of this was eventually collected and accounted for, while continual efforts were made to secure the balance. Many items not brought forward were collected long before and accounted for, while during the inspection of last year it was found that a sum of £800 yet remained to be paid in out of the deficiencies, which balance has been accounted for.

The contention that advances to officials amounting to £2,398,506 16s. 8d. have remained unaccounted for is also absolutely incorrect; and the endeavour to pass this circumstance off as constituting defalcations on the part of officials bears ample witness to the strong desire to mislead which has actuated the informants of Her Majesty's Government.

Any person who is even superficially acquainted with financial administration will readily admit that this is due to a system of accounting which was followed until recently by Her Majesty's Government, and which obtains in some British Colonies, in Natal, for instance, at the present moment.

This system may deserve condemnation; it does not, however, necessarily follow that because the advances may not be speedily accounted for they have been embezzled, and it does not appear either from the report of the Inspector of Offices, or from the debates of the Volksraad, that such accusations were made. But in addition to this a sum of at least £1,968,306 is included in the aforesaid total of £2,398,506 16s. 8d. (but which is not comprised in the customary advances), such as Orphan Chamber £80,000, Indigent Burghers £150,000, Postal Orders £60,000, various loans to School Committees, Sanitary Boards, and for Waterworks, Hospitals, Committees, monies placed at interest in Europe, provisional loans to Railway Companies, purchases of food stuffs and mules in time of famine, and many others.

Items, too, of considerable importance appear in the advances, although they have really been accounted for up to within a pound or two, because for one reason or another it has not been possible to write off the exact total, the amounts still to be accounted for having dwindled to a very insignificant figure.

The contention that during 1896 a sum of £191,837 was paid out of the Secret Service Money is also absolutely unfounded, for in that amount a sum of £158,337 was included which was used for special Government Works, as was expressly stated in a foot-note on page 44 of the Estimates for 1897. The Secret Service Fund for that year (1896) did not amount to more than £33,500. This faulty information, supplied to Her Majesty's Government, is apparently taken from the said Estimates, it would seem with the fixed determination to ignore the explanatory foot-note on page 44.

It is incorrect to state that the system of granting concessions remains in full force. Where the Right Hon. the Secretary of State in his despatch refers to industrial concessions, this Government may remark that these are privileges granted in order to stimulate and protect local industry, and the contention that these concessions will develop into practical monopolies is not supported by any evidence; results will show that misleading information has been given here as well.

With regard to the question of education which has been dealt with in the dispatch of the Right Hon. the Colonial Secretary, this Government wishes to point out that the amount expended on education during the year 1898 was £226,219 4s. 8d. In the former year it was less. Of this amount £36,503 17s. 2d. was devoted to Education on the Gold Fields (for State as well as for subsidized schools). As the number of scholars under Act 15, 1896, as well as that of the teachers, have considerably increased, the amount during the current year will probably be £53,000. The conditions on which this money is given are certainly not such as to exclude the children of Uitlanders from its benefits. According to Volksraad Resolution of 1st June, 1892 (and amendments), schools where a foreign language was the medium of instruction were entitled to a subsidy of 20s. per pupil per quarter for the lower standard, and 25s. for the middle standard, provided that certain requirements as to knowledge of the official language of the country were complied with. These requirements are a standard lower than that for children of burghers in the country, who are taught in schools governed by Law No. 8 of 1892.

Few, if any, Uitlanders avail themselves of this offer; the few who have done so are now satisfied with it, and continue to enjoy the privileges of the resolution, although it was only renewed in 1898 for those schools which made a bona fide use of it. Law No. 15, 1896, made provision for the children of poor parents and strangers on the proclaimed gold fields entirely at State expense, and 13 schools have been established by this law—with 51 teachers and about 1,500 scholars—at Barberton, Pilgrims' Rest, Kaapsche Hoop, Johannesburg (5, viz., 1 in von Brandis Street, 1 at Braamfontein, 1 at Union Ground, 1 at Vredesdorp, and 1 in Market Street), Maraisburg, Krugersdorp, Randfontein, Klerksdorp, and Nigel. In addition to these, preparations are being made for State schools at the City and Suburban, Bertramstownship, Johannesburg, and at Roodepoort (Krugersdorp).

Out of the above-named 13 schools, English is the medium of instruction in four, and of the remaining nine English is the medium for the children of English-speaking parents, and Dutch for those of Dutch-speaking parents. In these nine schools a little more time is devoted to learning Dutch in each standard than was the case in the former standard, so that equality in both languages is reached at the 5th standard.

Altogether there are 27 Dutch Africander or Hollander teachers, and 24 teachers of English origin in these 13 schools. The Dutch Africander or Hollander teachers are obliged to possess a thorough knowledge of English, and have either to pass an examination or produce a certificate to that effect.

The object of the system of education in this Republic is to ensure in the first place the foundation of general knowledge. Law No. 8, 1892, provides this for the children of the original Boer population in their mother tongue, in which the necessary schoolbooks must be written, with this understanding, however, that in the 3rd standard three hours, and in the higher ones four hours, per week out of the 25 must be devoted to education in a foreign language.

With regard to the schools formed under the above-mentioned Resolution, teaching is carried on through the medium of a foreign language, but at least 5 hours per week must be devoted to the study of the official language of the country.

Of the 13 schools formed under Law 15 of 1896, the children of strangers are instructed in their own language, while the number of hours for instruction in and by means of Dutch is increased in each standard.

According to a Resolution of the First Volksraad, dated the 8th August, 1898, Article 731, a certain number of the School Board members required by Article I of Law 15 of 1896 have to be nominated and chosen by the Executive Council out of enfranchised persons (Article 2, Law 8, 1893) proposed by the fathers of the school children, on the understanding that the persons so chosen shall constitute less than half of the whole School Board, and further, that the persons so proposed shall always be double the number of the people actually nominated. The above facts clearly prove, according to the opinion of this Government, that Her Majesty's Government has also been misled in respect to the matter of education. It is clear that one-fourth of the whole educational vote has been devoted to the gold fields, so that the children of Uitlander residents can make use of it; that proper provision is made for education in the mother tongue whatever it may be, while at the same time compulsory education of the language of the country is also provided for. That both by the Resolution of the 1st June, 1892, as well as by the Law 15 of 1896, more has actually been done for the Uitlanders than for the original inhabitants, and that more time is given to the mother tongue of the children in the schools on the gold fields of this Republic than in any country in the world, and that here again information of a misleading character must have been given to His Excellency and the British Government.

Law No. 15, 1896, and the schools thereby established have been defended by Englishmen in various newspapers. (See the S.A. News, 10th May, 1899; The Star, 22nd March, 1899; Manchester Guardian, etc.).

With reference to the Municipality of Johannesburg, this Government desires to remark that in accordance with the promise made in 1896, the grant of Municipal Administration was made to the inhabitants of Johannesburg by which the control of that town and its suburbs was conferred upon them.

Her Majesty's Government seem to think that this Municipality does not answer its purpose, in the first place because half of the members must be naturalized burghers (not fully enfranchised burghers as the dispatch under reply erroneously contends), and in the second place because the financial powers of the town council are restricted.

With regard to the first objection, it is impossible that this should be a great grievance, because a residence of two years in the Republic is sufficient for naturalisation; as a matter of fact, more than the necessary half of the members are burghers; this shows conclusively that the requirement of burghership is in no sense an obstacle. The objection as to the restriction of the financial powers of the council is not conclusive, because there is no Municipality in the world the financial powers of which are not restricted by the law under which they are created, and the restrictions in the case of the town council of Johannesburg are the usual ones in such cases.

The Advisory Board recommended by the Industrial Commission would have proved inefficient because the laws with the administration of which that body would have had to concern itself can be carried out in a better and more efficient way by an official like the State Attorney, who has almost unlimited power and means of doing so. This is exactly what has happened. All complaints with regard to gold thefts have actually disappeared; one no longer hears of complaints as to the operation of the pass law; while latterly, as Her Majesty's Government must be well aware, the Chamber of Mines and other bodies of the Witwatersrand have repeatedly expressed their satisfaction with the stringent way in which the liquor law has been upheld. No local body, however well informed, would have been able to do what the State Attorney has done in this matter, and that is sufficient justification of the action of both Government and Volksraad in refusing to establish such an Advisory Board.

The Government now passes on to the discussion of the administration of justice, of which so much is made in the dispatch under reply.

With regard to these allegations, this Government perceives that much importance is attached in the dispatch to the so-called Lombard incident, the so-called Edgar case, and the so-called Amphitheatre occurrence.

A brief consideration of the facts referring to these three matters will show how unfounded are the accusations of Her Majesty's Government.

With reference to the Lombard incident, this Government wishes to point out that no complaint was lodged with any official in this Republic for a full month after the ill-treatment of Cape coloured people was alleged to have taken place, and that neither the Government nor the public was aware that anything had taken place. The whole case was so insignificant that some of the people who were alleged to have been ill-treated declared under oath at a later period before a court of investigation that they would never have made any complaint on their own initiative. What happened, however?

About a month after the occurrence the South African League came to hear of it; some of its officials sent round to collect evidence from the parties who were alleged to have been ill-treated, and some sworn declarations were obtained by the help of Her Majesty's Vice-Consul at Johannesburg (between whom and this League a continual and conspicuous co-operation has existed). Even then no charge was lodged against the implicated officials with the judicial authorities of the country, but the case was put in the hands of the Acting British Agent at Pretoria.

When the allegations were brought under the notice of this Government, they at once appointed a commission of enquiry consisting of three members, namely, Landdrost Van der Berg, of Johannesburg, Mr Andries Stockenstrom, barrister-at-law of the Middle Temple, head of the Criminal Section of the State Attorney's Department, and Mr. Van der Merwe, mining commissioner, of Johannesburg; gentlemen against whose ability and impartiality the Uitlander population of the Republic have never harboured the slightest suspicion, and with whose appointment the Acting British Agent also expressed his entire satisfaction. The instructions given to these officials were to thoroughly investigate the whole case, and to report the result to the Government; and they fulfilled these instructions by sitting for days at a time, and carefully hearing and sifting the evidence of both sides. Every right-minded person readily acknowledges that far greater weight ought to be attached to the finding of this Commission than to the declarations of the complainants, who contradicted one another in nearly every particular, and who caused the whole enquiry to degenerate into a farce.

According to the report, nothing was proved as to the so-called ill-treatment; the special instances of alleged ill-treatment turned out to be purely imaginary; it was clearly proved and found that the complainants had acted contrary to Law, and the Commission only expressed disapproval of the fact that the arrests and the investigation had taken place at night, and without a proper warrant. It fills this Government with all the greater regret to observe that Her Majesty's Government bases its charges on ex parte, groundless, and in many respects false declarations of complainants who have been set in motion by political hatred, and that it silently ignores the report of the Commission.

The Amphitheatre occurrence is used by Her Majesty's Government to show how incapable the police of the Witwatersrand are to fulfil their duties and to preserve order. The League meeting was held at the so-called Amphitheatre at Johannesburg, with the knowledge of the State Secretary and State Attorney, and the accusation is that in spite of that fact, the uproar which arose at that meeting was not quelled by the police.

The following are the true facts:—Mr. Wybergh and another, both in the service of the South African League, informed the State Secretary and the State Attorney that they intended to call this meeting in the Amphitheatre, and asked permission to do so; they were informed that no permission from the authorities was necessary, and that as long as the meeting did not give rise to irregularities or disturbances of the peace, they would be acting entirely within their rights. Their attention was then drawn to the fact that owing to the action and the propaganda of the South African League, this body had become extremely unpopular with a large section of the inhabitants of Johannesburg, and that in all probability a disturbance of the peace would take place if a sufficient body of the police were not present to preserve order.

To this these gentlemen answered that the police were in very bad odour since the Edgar case, that the meeting would be a very quiet one, and that the presence of the police would contribute, or give rise to, disorder, and that they would on those grounds rather have no police at all. The State Secretary and State Attorney thereupon communicated with the head officials of the police at Johannesburg, with the result that the latter also thought that it would be better not to have any considerable number of police at the meeting. The Government accordingly, on the advice of these officials of the League as well as their own police officials, gave instructions that the police should remain away from the meeting; they did this in perfect good faith, and with the object of letting the League have its say without let or hindrance.

The proposed meeting was however advertised far and wide. As the feeling amongst a section of the Witwatersrand population was exceedingly bitter against the League, a considerable number of the opponents of that body also attended the meeting. The few police who were present were powerless to quell the disorder, and when the police came on the scene in force some few minutes after the commencement of the uproar, the meeting was already broken up. Taken by itself, this occurrence would not be of much importance, as it is an isolated instance as far as the gold fields of this Republic are concerned, and even in the best organised and best ordered communities irregularities like the above occasionally take place.

The gravity of the matter, however, lies in the unjust accusation of Her Majesty's Government—that the meeting was broken up by officials of this Republic, and that the Government had curtly refused to institute an enquiry.

This Government would not have refused to investigate the matter if any complaints had been lodged with it, or at any of the local Courts, and this has been clearly stated in its reply to Her Majesty's request for an investigation.

The Government objects strongly to the systematic way in which the local authorities are ignored, and the continual complaints which are lodged with the Representatives of Her Majesty about matters which ought to be decided by the Courts of this Republic. Instead, however, of complaining to Her Majesty's Government after all other reasonable means of redress have been vainly invoked, they continually make themselves guilty of ignoring and treating with contempt the local Courts and authorities, by continually making all sorts of ridiculous and ex parte complaints to Her Majesty's Government in the first instance; Her Majesty's Government is also thereby placed in the equivocal and undesirable position of intermeddling in the internal affairs of this Republic, which is in conflict with the London Convention.

Had the complaints been lodged with this Government, or with the proper officials or Courts, the facts could have been very easily arrived at, and it would have been proved that the few officials who were present at the meeting as a section of the public had done their best to prevent the irregularities, and that some of them had been hurt in their endeavours to preserve order.

Instead of expressing their disapproval of such complaints, and referring the petitioners to the local Courts, Her Majesty's Government accepts those complaints, and gives them an official character by forwarding them for the information of this Government, and by publishing them in blue books for the information of the world.

Her Majesty's Government will readily acknowledge that there is no State in the world with any sense of dignity, however weak and insignificant it may be, which can regard such matters with an indifferent eye; and when the relations of the two Governments are strained, then the mainspring must be looked for in this action of its subjects, which is not disapproved of by Her Majesty's Government, and not in imaginary or trumped-up grievances.

The Edgar case is referred to by your Government as "the most striking recent instance of arbitrary action by officials, and of the support of such action by the Courts," and this case is quoted as a conclusive test of the alleged judicial maladministration of this Republic; it will therefore be of interest to pause for a moment and consider it. What are the true facts?

A certain Foster, "an Englishman," was assaulted and felled to the ground, without any lawful cause, by a man named Edgar during the night of the 18th December, 1898; he lay on the ground as if dead, and ultimately died in the hospital. Edgar escaped to his room, and some police came on the scene, attracted by the screams of the bystanders. Amongst the police was one named Jones. When they saw the man who had been assaulted lying as if dead, they went to Edgar's apartments in order to arrest him as a criminal (he had indeed rendered himself liable for manslaughter, and apparently for murder).

As he was caught in the very act, the police officers were, according to the Laws not only of this Republic, but of all South Africa and of the United Kingdom of Great Britain and Ireland, justified in breaking open the door in order to arrest the culprit. While doing so, Edgar, with a dangerous weapon, struck Jones a severe blow. Under the stress of necessity the latter shot Edgar, from the effects of which he died. The question is not if Jones was justified in taking this extreme step, for the State Attorney of the Republic had already given effect to his opinion that this was a case for the jury by prosecuting him for manslaughter. The question is solely whether any jury in any country in the world would have found a man guilty of any crime under the circumstances set forth, and whether, if they did not find him guilty, the fact of their doing so would have been stamped and branded as a flagrant and remarkable instance of the maladministration of justice.

This Government is convinced that the English Judicial administration affords numberless instances where the facts are as strong as in this case, and it cannot see why an occurrence which could happen in any part of the world should be especially thrown in their teeth in the form of an accusation.

This Government does not wish to pass over in silence the censure which has been passed by Her Majesty's Government on the Public Prosecutor of Johannesburg, by whom the prosecution of this case was conducted; the fact that he is of pure English blood, that he received his legal training in London, that he is generally respected by the Uitlander population on account of his ability, impartiality, and general character, will naturally not be of any weight with Her Majesty's Government against the facts of his action in calling witnesses for the prosecution who were intended for the defence, and thus rendering an imaginary cross-examination abortive.

This Government only wishes to point out that the fact that the Edgar case is the strongest which Her Majesty's Government has been able to quote against the administration of justice in this Republic affords the strongest and most eloquent proof possible that, taking it in general, the administration of justice on the gold fields of this Republic not only compares favourably with that on other and similar gold fields, but even with that of old and settled countries.

The untrue representations of this occurrence in the Press prove conclusively that the newspapers of the Witwatersrand, the atrocity-mongering tactics of which constitute a share of the organised campaign against the Republic and its Government, have been compelled to resort to mendacious criticisms on imaginary instances of maladministration which were often simply invented. Where the Press is forced to adopt such methods, the true grievances must of necessity be unreal.

Her Majesty's Government now proceeds to discuss certain laws of this Republic, with the object of showing that the Uitlander population is also oppressed by the legislature of this country, the Press Law, the Aliens Expulsion Law, and Law No. 1 of 1897 being especially instanced. But it can also be proved that the population of the gold fields have no solid grounds of complaint in regard to the laws in question.

Respecting the existing Press Laws, No. 26 of 1896, and No. 14 of 1898, it is necessary to remark that no printer, issuer, or editor of a newspaper can be prosecuted unless he has made himself guilty of criminal libel, so that the principle of the Grondwet of 1858[256] has in this respect been rigidly adhered to. Her Majesty's Government will at once see that these laws cannot in any way bear harshly upon the writing public, a fact which is clearly borne out by the way in which the newspapers of this country are edited. Nowhere else in the world has the liberty of the Press so degenerated into license. No newspaper in any country in the world would for one moment dare to speak of the Government, the Legislature, and authorities of the country as the Star, the Transvaal Leader, and similar newspapers do every day in this Republic.

The imaginary nature of these grievances is not dispelled by the fact that the power is vested in the State President of prohibiting either entirely or provisionally the circulation of any printed matter which is contrary to good morals or public order, because the very same Supreme Court, which in the opinion of Her Majesty's Government only exists at the mercy of this Government, has pronounced that it has no power to prohibit the circulation of any newspaper; the freedom of the regular Press thus remains as unrestricted as under the old Grondwet.

As a matter of fact, any person who has any practical experience of the Press of this Republic will regard the accusation as ridiculous, and as evincing an entire ignorance of the true facts. This power has not been exercised by the Judges on many occasions, but only once, and in that instance the High Court annulled the decision.

With regard to the Aliens Expulsion Law, this, like the Press Law, ought to be estimated according to its spirit and operation. Since this law has come into force the State President has only on one occasion made use of the power vested in him of expelling an undesirable individual, and his action was endorsed by the approval of the Press and the public of the country. As similar laws exist in nearly every civilised country in the world, it is difficult to see why such a law in this Republic should prove so objectionable in the eyes of Her Majesty's Government.

[256] Grondwet, noun. The constitution of any of the republics proclaimed by Boers during the nineteenth century. The constitution of the Transvaal was promulgated in 1858. Grondwet - definition of Grondwet in A Dictionary of South African English - DSAE

With regard to Law No. 1 of 1897, and the dismissal of Chief Justice Kotze[257] by virtue of its provisions, this Government can only state that it was with the bitterest regret that it felt itself compelled, in consequence of the arbitrary action of the said Chief Justice, to take comprehensive measures in order to prevent absolute constitutional and judicial disorder and chaos. It was an instance where a Chief Justice in conflict with a law existing for, at least, forty years, and in direct contradiction of his own decisions, suddenly adopted and applied a new principle, which affected the legality of the laws of the Republic, and produced real constitutional chaos. Would not any other Government under similar circumstances have done exactly what this Republic did, namely, pass a special law in this unusual case, in order to remove the exceptional difficulties?

This law was only applicable to this particular instance, and became inoperative immediately after its application; and this Government cannot understand how suspicion can therefore fall upon the impartial administration of Justice in this Republic.

If the Government had acquiesced in the position taken up by the late Chief Justice, then all titles dependent upon Volksraad resolutions would have been called in question, which would not only have dealt a heavy blow to existing rights, but also have plunged the administration of Justice in great uncertainty and doubt.

By this law the Judges, instead of being brought under the influence of the Executive Council, were really placed in the same constitutional position as any Judge in the Supreme Court of England, who is unable to question the validity of any law.

This Government has now traversed the various contentions of Her Majesty's Government, which have been submitted in order to prove that the policy of this Government, with regard to the Uitlander population and the administration of the laws, especially on the gold fields, are the causes of the strained relationship at present existing between the two Governments. This Government believes that this explanation and answer will clearly show that these causes are in no way sufficient to have resulted in the aforesaid tension.

It is of opinion that the source of evil must be sought for elsewhere, and it trusts that Her Majesty's Government will not take it in bad part if it now proceeds to explain what the real root of the evil is from its point of view; and in the first place it remarks as a very noticeable and prominent fact that although there are thousands of subjects of other Powers in Johannesburg, there are few complaints heard from them or from their Governments about the so-called grievances of the Uitlanders.

If these grievances existed in reality, and if they pressed equally on all so-called Uitlanders (and Her Majesty's Government does not contend that in this respect a difference is made between British subjects and subjects of other Powers), how does it happen that the complaints always come from British subjects, and that the subjects of other Powers, as a rule, express their sympathy with this Government and promise it their support?

But this Government wishes to go further. Even in regard to those Uitlanders who are British subjects, it is a small minority which, under the pretext of imaginary grievances, promotes a secret propaganda of race hatred, and uses the Republic as a base for fomenting a revolutionary movement against this Government. Ministers of Her Majesty have so trenchantly expressed the truth about this minority that this Government wishes to quote the very words of these Ministers with the object of bringing the actual truth to the knowledge of Her Majesty's Government, as well as to that of the whole world, and not for the purpose of making groundless accusations.

The following words are those of the Ministers of the Cape Colony, who are well acquainted with local conditions and fully qualified to arrive at a conclusion:—

In the opinion of Ministers the persistent action, both beyond and within this Colony, of the political body styling itself the South African League in endeavouring to foment and excite, not to smooth and allay, ill-will between the two principal European races inhabiting South Africa is well illustrated by these resolutions, the exaggerated and aggravated terms of which disclose the spirit which informs and inspires them.

His Excellency's Ministers are one in their earnest desire to do all in their power to aid and further a policy of peaceful progress throughout South Africa, and they cannot but regard it as an unwise propagandism, hostile to the true interests of the Empire, including this Colony as an integral part, that every possible occasion should be

[257] This is the judicial crisis. Kotze, together with the rest of the High Court, was unceremoniously dismissed by Paul Kruger following a dispute–as a result of his judgement in the case over mining rights. Kotze had stood in 1893 as a rival to Kruger in the presidential elections and was seen by Kruger as his long term political rival. Kruger was enraged at the judgement of the High Court in the case of Brown v. Leyds and he dismissed Chief Justice Kotzé in 1898 as President Kruger held his own opinion on the case outcome. Kruger's action was widely seen as unwarranted interference with the independence of the judiciary. John Gilbert Kotzé - Wikipedia

seized by the League and its promoters for an attempt to magnify into greater events minor incidents when occurring in the South African Republic, with a prospect thereby of making racial antagonism more acute, or of rendering less smooth the relations between Her Majesty's Government or the Government of this Colony and that Republic."

Race hatred is, however, not so intense in South Africa as to enable a body with this propaganda, aiming at revolutionary objects, to obtain much influence in this part of the world; and one continually asks oneself the question—"How is it that a body so insignificant, both in regard to its principles and its membership, enjoys such a large measure of influence?" The answer is that this body depends upon the protection and the support of Her Majesty's Government in England, and that both its members and its organs in the Press openly boast of the influence they exercise over the policy of Her Majesty's Government.

This Government would ignore such assertions, but when it finds that the ideas and the shibboleths of the South African League are continually echoed in the speeches of members of H.M. Government, when it finds that blue books are compiled chiefly from documents prepared by officials of the South African League, as well as from reports and leading articles containing "malignant lies" taken from the Press organs of that organisation, thereby receiving an official character, then this Government can well understand why so many of Her Majesty's right-minded subjects in this part of the world have obtained the impression that the policy advocated by the South African League is supported by Her Majesty's Government, and is thus calculated to contribute to the welfare and blessing of the British Empire.

If this mistaken impression could be removed, and if it could be announced as a fact that the South African League, as far as its actions in the South African Republic are concerned, is only an organisation having as its object the fomentation of strife and disorder and the destruction of the independence of the country, then it would very soon lose its influence, and the strained relations existing between the two Governments would quickly disappear. The Africander population of this country would not then be under the apprehension that the interests of the British Empire imperatively demand that the Republic should be done away with and its people be either enslaved or exterminated. Both sections of the white inhabitants of South Africa would then return to the fraternal co-operation and fusion which was beginning to manifest itself when the treacherous conspiracy at the end of 1895 awakened the passions on both sides.

Appendix D March 1899 Despatch

The Final Dispatch of Mr. State Secretary Reitz[258]

Enclosure.

Department For Foreign Affairs,
Government Office, Pretoria,

3rd March, 1899.

To The Hon. Cunynghame Greene, C.B., British Agent, Pretoria.

Sir,

Acknowledging the receipt of your letter of the 11th inst. re the meeting of the South African League held in the Amphitheatre at Johannesburg on the 14th January, 1899, I have the honour to communicate the following to you.

The complaint that the Government, or its duly authorised officials, have acted with partiality in this matter is entirely devoid of truth, and this Government regrets that such an unfounded and insulting accusation should have been made nearly a month after the occurrence in question.

Messrs. Dodd and Webb have been duly arrested and committed for trial on account of what took place on the 24th December, 1898, upon sworn affidavits which left nothing else for the proper officials to do but to prosecute.

With reference to the Amphitheatre occurrence, not a single British subject has lodged a sworn complaint against anybody with the proper officials, so that it can hardly be expected that this Government should now take any steps against the alleged disturbers of the peace.

Regarding the accusation that officials of this Government have contributed to the instigation of uproar on the said occasion, this Government can only state that no complaints have been made to it or the proper authorities, either from British subjects or from subjects of other Powers, so that this Government, to its regret, can do nothing in this matter. In case, however, of such complaints being lodged with the proper authorities, the Courts of the country are open to them.

I have the honour to be, Sir,

Your obedient servant,

F.W. Reitz,

State Secretary.

[258] PF: An accurate recital of the published title and text. Not sure that it titled correctly as per the content.

Appendix E Conventions (Texts)

Texts of the Conventions of 1852, 1881, and 1884

Sand River Convention of 1852

Conventions Between Her Majesty The Queen And The Transvaal Or South African Republic.

Sand River Convention, 1852. [259]

Minutes of a meeting held in the place of Mr. P.A. Venter,[260] Sand River, on Friday, the sixteenth day of January, 1852, between Major W. Hogge[261] and C.M. Owen, Esq., [262] Her Majesty's Assistant Commissioners, for the settling and adjusting of the affairs of the eastern and north-eastern boundaries of the Colony of the Cape of Good Hope on the one part, and the following deputation from the emigrant farmers residing north of the Vaal River:

A.W.J. Pretorius,[263] Commandant-General.
H.S. Lombard, Landdrost.[264]
W.F. Joubert, Commandant-General.
G.J. Kruger, Commandant.
J.N. Grobbelaar, Raadslid.
P.E. Scholtz.
P.G. Wolmarans,[265] Ouderling.
J.A. Van Aswegan, Veld-Cornet.
F.J. Botes, Veld-Cornet.
N.J.S. Basson, Veld-Cornet.
J.P. Furstenberg, Veld-Cornet.
J.P. Pretorius.
J.H. Grobbelaar.
J.M. Lehman.
P. Schutte.
J.C. Kloppers: on the other part.

1. The Assistant Commissioners guarantee in the fullest manner, on the part of the British Government, to the emigrant farmers beyond the Vaal River the right to maintain their own affairs, and to govern themselves according to their own laws without any interference on the part of the British Government, and that no encroachment shall be made by the said Government on the territory beyond to the north of the Vaal River, with the further assurance that the warmest wish of the British Government is to promote peace, free trade, and friendly intercourse with the emigrant farmers now inhabiting or who hereafter may inhabit that country, it being understood that this system of non-interference is binding upon both parties.

[259] Sand River Convention - Wikipedia The convention was signed on 17 January 1852, by Commandant-General Andries Pretorius and others, on behalf of the new country, and Major William Samuel Hogge and Charles Mostyn Owen, clerk to the Civil Commissioner of Winburg, duly authorised to, and on behalf of, the British government. The treaty was signed on the farm called Sand River belonging to P. A. Venter, near Ventersburg.

[260] Pieter Johannes Venter (Colesberg district, Cape Colony, c. 1820–Bloemfontein, Orange Free State, 3 January 1899) was, a founder of the Reformed Church in the Orange Free State and for many years elder of Reddersburg and Ladybrand. Pieter Venter - Wikipedia

[261] Major William Samuel Hogge.

[262] Charles Mostyn Owen.

[263] Andries Wilhelmus Jacobus Pretorius: Andries Pretorius - Wikipedia

[264] Hermanus Antonie Lombard List of participants in the Battle of Blood River - Wikipedia

[265] A.D.W. Wolmarans - Wikipedia W was the grandson of F.G. Wolmarans of George who accompanied the Great Trek to the Transvaal, one of the signatories to the Sand River Convention in January 1852 and an avid supporter of kmdt. A.W.J. Pretorius.

2. Should any misunderstanding hereafter arise as to the true meaning of the words "the Vaal River," this question in so far as regards the line from the source of that river over the Drakenberg shall be settled and adjusted by Commissioners chosen by both parties.

3. Her Majesty's Assistant Commissioners hereby disclaim all alliances whatever and with whomsoever of the coloured nations to the north of the Vaal River.

4. It is agreed that no slavery is or shall be permitted or practised in the country to the north of the Vaal River by the emigrant farmers.

5. Mutual facilities and liberties shall be afforded to traders and travellers on both sides of the Vaal River, it being understood that every waggon containing ammunition and firearms coming from the south side of the Vaal River shall produce a certificate signed by a British magistrate or other functionary duly authorised to grant such, and which shall state the quantities of such articles contained in said waggon to the nearest magistrate north of the Vaal River, who shall act in the case as the regulations of the emigrant farmers direct.

6. It is agreed that no objection shall be made by any British authority against the emigrant Boers purchasing their supplies of ammunition in any of the British Colonies and possessions of South Africa, it being mutually understood that all trade in ammunition with the native tribes is prohibited both by the British Government and the emigrant farmers on both sides of the Vaal River.

7. It is agreed that so far as possible all criminals and other guilty parties who may fly from justice either way across the Vaal River shall be mutually delivered up if such should be required, and that the British courts as well as those of the emigrant farmers shall be mutually open to each other for all legitimate processes, and that summonses for witnesses sent either way across the Vaal River shall be backed by the magistrates, on each side of the same respectively, to compel the attendance of such witnesses when required.

8. It is agreed that certificates of marriage issued by the proper authorities of the emigrant farmers shall be held valid and sufficient to entitle children of such marriages to receive portions accruing to them in any British Colony or possession in South Africa.

It is agreed that any and every person now in possession of land, and residing in British territory, shall have free right and power to sell his said property and remove unmolested across the Vaal River, and vice versa, it being distinctly understood that this arrangement does not comprehend criminals or debtors, without providing for the payment of their just and lawful debts.

This done and signed at Sand River aforesaid, this 17th day of January, 1852.

(Signed) A.W.J. Pretorius, Comdt.-General.
H.S. Lombard, Landdrost.
W.F. Joubert, Commandant-General.
G.J. Kruger, Commandant.
W.I. Hogge, Assistant Commissioner.
C. Mostyn Owen, Assistant Commissioner.
J.N. Grobbelaar, R.L.
P.E. Scholtz.
P.G. Wolmarans, Ouderling.
J.A. Van Aswegan, Veld Cornet.
F.J. Botes.
N.J.S. Basson, Veld Cornet.
J.P. Furstenberg, Veld Cornet.
J.P. Pretorius.
J.H. Grobbelaar.
J.M. Lehman.
P. Schutte.
J.C. Kloppers.

In Presence Of—
(Signed) John Burnet, Clerk to the Civil Commissioner of Winburg.
(Signed) J.H. Visagie, Secretary.

Convention of 1881

Convention for the Settlement of the Transvaal Territory[266]

Preamble. Her Majesty's Commissioners for the Settlement of the Transvaal territory, duly appointed as such by a Commission passed under the Royal Sign Manual and Signet, bearing date the 5th of April, 1881, do hereby undertake and guarantee on behalf of Her Majesty that, from and after the 8th day of August, 1881, complete self-government, subject to the suzerainty of Her Majesty, her heirs and successors, will be accorded to the inhabitants of the Transvaal territory, upon the following terms and conditions, and subject to the following reservations and limitations:—

Article I. The said territory, to be hereinafter called the Transvaal State, will embrace the land lying between the following boundaries, to wit: [Here follow three pages in print defining boundaries. See 1884 Convention Infra]

Article 2. Her Majesty reserves to herself, her heirs and successors—(a), the right from time to time to appoint a British Resident in and for the said State, with such duties and functions as are hereinafter defined; (b), the right to move troops through the said State in time of war, or in case of the apprehension of immediate war between the Suzerain Power and any Foreign State or Native Tribe in South Africa; and (c) the control of the external relations of the said State, including the conclusion of treaties and the conduct of diplomatic intercourse with Foreign Powers, such intercourse to be carried on through Her Majesty's diplomatic and consular officers abroad.

Article 3. Until altered by the Volksraad, or other competent authority, all laws, whether passed before or after the Annexation of the Transvaal territory to Her Majesty's dominions, shall, except in so far as they are inconsistent with or repugnant to the provisions of this Convention, be and remain in force in the said State in so far as they shall be applicable thereto, provided that no future enactment especially affecting the interest of natives shall have any force or effect in the said State, without the consent of Her Majesty, her heirs and successors, first had and obtained and signified to the Government of the said State through the British Resident, provided further that in no case will the repeal or amendment of any laws enacted since the Annexation have a retrospective effect, so as to invalidate any acts done or liabilities incurred by virtue of such laws.

Article 4. On the 8th day of August, 1881, the Government of the said State, together with all rights and obligations thereto appertaining, and all State property taken over at the time of Annexation, save and except munitions of war, will be handed over to Messrs. Stephanus Johannes Paulus Kruger, Martinus Wessel Pretorius,[267] and Petrus Jacobus Joubert,[268] or the survivor or survivors of them, who will forthwith cause a Volksraad to be elected and convened, and the Volksraad, thus elected and convened, will decide as to the further administration of the Government of the said State.

Article 5. All sentences passed upon persons who may be convicted of offences contrary to the rules of civilised warfare committed during the recent hostilities will be duly carried out, and no alteration or mitigation of such sentences will be made or allowed by the Government of the Transvaal State without Her Majesty's consent conveyed through the British Resident. In case there shall be any prisoners in any of the gaols of the Transvaal State whose respective sentences of imprisonment have been remitted in part by Her Majesty's Administrator or other officer administering the Government, such remission will be recognised and acted upon by the future Government of the said State.

Article 6. Her Majesty's Government will make due compensation for all losses or damage sustained by reason of such acts as are in the 8th Article hereinafter specified, which may have been committed by Her Majesty's

[266] For comparison see: Pretoria Convention - Wikisource, the free online library And Creswicke SA War Vol. 1.

[267] Marthinus Wessel Pretorius (17 September 1819–19 May 1901) was a South African political leader. An Afrikaner (or "Boer"), he helped establish the South African Republic, was the first president of the ZAR, and also compiled its constitution. Marthinus Wessel Pretorius - Wikipedia

[268] Petrus Jacobus Joubert (20 January 1831–28 March 1900), was Commandant-General of the South African Republic from 1880 to 1900. He also served as Vice-President to Paul Kruger from 1881 - 1883. He served in First Boer War, Second Boer War, and the Malaboch War. Piet Joubert - Wikipedia

forces during the recent hostilities, except for such losses or damage as may already have been compensated for; and the Government of the Transvaal State will make due compensation for all losses or damage sustained by reason of such acts as are in the 8th Article hereinafter specified, which may have been committed by the people who were in arms against Her Majesty during the recent hostilities, except for such losses or damages as may already have been compensated for.

Article 7. The decision of all claims for compensation, as in the last preceding article mentioned, will be referred to a Sub-Commission, consisting of the Honourable George Hudson[269], the Honourable Jacobus Petrus de Wet,[270] and the Honourable John Gilbert Kotze.[271] In case one or more of such Sub-Commissioners shall be unable or unwilling to act the remaining Sub-Commissioner or Sub-Commissioners will, after consultation with the Government of the Transvaal State, submit for the approval of Her Majesty's High Commissioner the names of one or more persons to be appointed by them to fill the place or places thus vacated. The decision of the said Sub-Commissioners, or of a majority of them, will be final. The said Sub-Commissioners will enter upon and perform their duties with all convenient speed. They will, before taking evidence or ordering evidence to be taken in respect of any claim, decide whether such claim can be entertained at all under the rules laid down in the next succeeding Article. In regard to claims which can be so entertained the Sub-Commissioners will, in the first instance, afford every facility for an amicable arrangement as to the amount payable in respect of any claim, and only in cases in which there is no reasonable ground for believing that an immediate amicable arrangement can be arrived at will they take evidence or order evidence to be taken. For the purpose of taking evidence and reporting thereon, the Sub-Commissioners may appoint Deputies, who will, without delay, submit records of the evidence and their reports to the Sub-Commissioners. The Sub-Commissioners will arrange their sittings and the sittings of their Deputies in such a manner as to afford the earliest convenience to the parties concerned and their witnesses. In no case will costs be allowed to either side, other than the actual and reasonable expenses of witnesses whose evidence is certified by the Sub-Commissioners to have been necessary. Interest will not run on the amount of any claim, except as is hereinafter provided for. The said Sub-Commissioners will forthwith, after deciding upon any claim, announce their decision to the Government against which the award is made and to the claimant. The amount of remuneration payable to the Sub-Commissioners and their Deputies will be determined by the High Commissioners. After all the claims have been decided upon, the British Government and the Government of the Transvaal State will pay proportionate shares of the said remuneration and of the expenses of the Sub-Commissioners and their Deputies, according to the amount awarded against them respectively.

Article 8. For the purpose of distinguishing claims to be accepted from those to be rejected, the Sub-Commissioners will be guided by the following rules, viz.:—Compensation will be allowed for losses or damage sustained by reason of the following acts committed during the recent hostilities, viz., (a), commandering, seizure, confiscation, or destruction of property, or damage done to property; (b), violence done or threats used by persons in arms. In regard to acts under (a), compensation will be allowed for direct losses only. In regard to acts falling under (b), compensation will be allowed for actual losses of property, or actual injury to the same proved to have been caused by its enforced abandonment. No claims for indirect losses, except such as are in this Article specially provided for, will be entertained. No claims which have been handed in to the Secretary of the Royal Commission after the 1st day of July, 1881, will be entertained, unless the Sub-Commissioners shall be satisfied that the delay was reasonable. When claims for loss of property are considered, the Sub-Commissioners will require distinct proof of the existence of the property, and that it neither has reverted nor will revert to the claimant.

Article 9. The Government of the Transvaal State will pay and satisfy the amount of every claim awarded against it within one month after the Sub-Commissioners shall have notified their decision to the said Government, and in default of such payment the said Government will pay interest at the rate of six per cent. per annum from the date of such default; but Her Majesty's Government may at any time before such payment pay

[269] Possibly: George Bickersteth Hudson JP DL (16 March 1845–29 February 1912) was a British Conservative politician and barrister who served as the Member of Parliament for Hitchin, Hertfordshire from 1892 to 1906. George Hudson (MP) - Wikipedia

[270] Sir Jacobus Petrus de Wet (25 August 1838–19 April 1900) was the 15th Chief Justice of Ceylon. He was appointed on 31 May 1882. Wet came from a well to do Dutch speaking Cape family. Jacobus de Wet - Wikipedia

[271] Sir John Gilbert Kotzé KC (5 November 1849–1 April 1940) was an eminent South African jurist. John Gilbert Kotzé - Wikipedia

the amount, with interest, if any, to the claimant in satisfaction of his claim, and may add the sum thus paid to any debt which may be due by the Transvaal State to Her Majesty's Government, as hereinafter provided for.

Article 10. The Transvaal State will be liable for the balance of the debts for which the South African Republic was liable at the date of Annexation, to wit, the sum of £48,000 in respect of the Cape Commercial Bank Loan, and £85,667 in respect to the Railway Loan, together with the amount due on 8th August, 1881, on account of the Orphan Chamber Debt, which now stands at £22,200, which debts will be a first charge upon the revenues of the State. The Transvaal State will, moreover, be liable for the lawful expenditure lawfully incurred for the necessary expenses of the Province since the Annexation, to wit, the sum of £265,000, which debt, together with such debts as may be incurred by virtue of the 9th Article, will be second charge upon the revenues of the State.

Article 11. The debts due as aforesaid by the Transvaal State to Her Majesty's Government will bear interest at the rate of three and a-half per cent., and any portion of such debt as may remain unpaid at the expiration of twelve months from the 8th August, 1881, shall be repayable by a payment for interest and sinking fund of six pounds and nine pence per cent, per annum, which will extinguish the debt in twenty-five years. The said payment of six pounds and nine pence per £100 shall be payable half yearly in British currency on the 8th February and 8th August in each year. Provided always that the Transvaal State shall pay in reduction of the said debt the sum of £100,000 within twelve months of the 8th August, 1881, and shall be at liberty at the close of any half year to pay off the whole or any portion of the outstanding debt.

Article 12. All persons holding property in the said State on the 8th day of August, 1881, will continue after the said date to enjoy the rights of property which they have enjoyed since the Annexation. No person who has remained loyal to Her Majesty during the recent hostilities shall suffer any molestation by reason of his loyalty, or be liable to any criminal prosecution or civil action for any part taken in connexion with such hostilities, and all such persons will have full liberty to reside in the country, with enjoyment of all civil rights, and protection for their persons and property.

Article 13. Natives will be allowed to acquire land, but the grant or transfer of such land will, in every case, be made to and registered in the name of the Native Location Commission, hereinafter mentioned, in trust for such natives.

Article 14. Natives will be allowed to move as freely within the country as may be consistent with the requirements of public order, and to leave it for the purpose of seeking employment elsewhere or for other lawful purposes, subject always to the pass laws of the said State, as amended by the Legislature of the Province, or as may hereafter be enacted under the provisions of the Third Article of this Convention.

Article 15. There will continue to be complete freedom of religion and protection from molestation for all denominations, provided the same be not inconsistent with morality and good order, and no disability shall attach to any person in regard to rights of property by reason of the religious opinions which he holds.

Article 16. The provisions of the Fourth Article of the Sand River Convention are hereby re-affirmed, and no slavery or apprenticeship partaking of slavery will be tolerated by the Government of the said State.

Article 17. The British Resident will receive from the Government of the Transvaal State such assistance and support as can by law be given to him for the due discharge of his functions; he will also receive every assistance for the proper care and preservation of the graves of such of Her Majesty's forces as have died in the Transvaal, and if need be, for the expropriation of land for the purpose.

Article 18. The following will be the duties and functions of the British Resident:—

Sub-section 1. He will perform duties and functions analogous to those discharged by a Charge d'Affaires and Consul-General.

Sub-section 2. In regard to natives within the Transvaal State he will (a) report to the High Commissioner, as representative of the Suzerain, as to the working and observance of the provisions of this Convention; (b), report to the Transvaal authorities any cases of ill-treatment of natives or attempts to incite natives to rebellion that may come to his knowledge; (c), use his influence with the natives in favour of law and order; and (d), generally perform such other duties as are by this Convention entrusted to him, and take such steps for the protection of the person and property of natives as are consistent with the laws of the land.

Sub-section 3. In regard to natives not residing in the Transvaal (a) he will report to the High Commissioner and the Transvaal Government any encroachments reported to him as having been made by Transvaal residents upon the land of such natives, and in case of disagreement between the Transvaal Government and the British

Resident as to whether an encroachment has been made, the decision of the Suzerain will be final; (b) the British Resident will be the medium of communication with native chiefs outside the Transvaal, and, subject to the approval of the High Commissioner, as representing the Suzerain, he will control the conclusion of treaties with them; and (c) he will arbitrate upon every dispute with Transvaal residents and natives outside the Transvaal (as to acts committed beyond the boundaries of the Transvaal) which may be referred to him by the parties interested.

Sub-section 4. In regard to communications with foreign powers, the Transvaal Government will correspond with Her Majesty's Government through the British Resident and the High Commissioner.

Article 19. The Government of the Transvaal State will strictly adhere to the boundaries defined in the First Article of this Convention, and will do its utmost to prevent any of its inhabitants from making any encroachment upon lands beyond the said State. The Royal Commission will forthwith appoint a person who will beacon off the boundary line between Ramatlabama and the point where such line first touches Griqualand West boundary, midway between the Vaal and Hart Rivers; the person so appointed will be instructed to make an arrangement between the owners of the farms Grootfontein and Valleifontein on the one hand, and the Barolong authorities on the other, by which a fair share of the water supply of the said farms shall be allowed to flow undisturbed to the said Barolongs.

Article 20. All grants or titles issued at any time by the Transvaal Government in respect of land outside the boundary of Transvaal State, as defined, Article 1, shall be considered invalid and of no effect, except in so far as any such grant or title relates to land that falls within the boundary of the Transvaal State, and all persons holding any such grant so considered invalid and of no effect will receive from the Government of the Transvaal State such compensation either in land or in money as the Volksraad shall determine. In all cases in which any native chiefs or other authorities outside the said boundaries have received any adequate consideration from the Government of the former South African Republic for land excluded from the Transvaal by the First Article of this Convention, or where permanent improvements have been made on the land, the British Resident will, subject to the approval of the High Commissioner, use his influence to recover from the native authorities fair compensation for the loss of the land thus excluded, and of the permanent improvement thereon.

Article 21. Forthwith, after the taking effect of this Convention, a Native Location Commission will be constituted, consisting of the President, or in his absence the Vice-President, of the State, or some one deputed by him, the Resident, or some one deputed by him, and a third person to be agreed upon by the President or the Vice-President, as the case may be, and the Resident, and such Commission will be a standing body for the performance of the duties hereinafter mentioned.

Article 22. The Native Location Commission will reserve to the native tribes of the State such locations as they may be fairly and equitably entitled to, due regard being had to the actual occupation of such tribes. The Native Location Commission will clearly define the boundaries of such locations, and for that purpose will, in every instance, first of all ascertain the wishes of the parties interested in such land. In case land already granted in individual titles shall be required for the purpose of any location, the owners will receive such compensation either in other land or in money as the Volksraad shall determine. After the boundaries of any location have been fixed, no fresh grant of land within such location will be made, nor will the boundaries be altered without the consent of the Location Commission. No fresh grants of land will be made in the districts of Waterberg, Zoutpansberg, and Lydenburg until the locations in the said districts respectively shall have been defined by the said Commission.

Article 23. If not released before the taking effect of this Convention, Sikukuni, and those of his followers who have been imprisoned with him, will be forthwith released, and the boundaries of his location will be defined by the Native Location Commission in the manner indicated in the last preceding Article.

Article 24. The independence of the Swazies within the boundary line of Swaziland, as indicated in the First Article of this Convention, will be fully recognised.

Article 25. No other or higher duties will be imposed on the importation into the Transvaal State of any article, the produce or manufacture of the dominions and possessions of Her Majesty, from whatever place arriving, than are or may be payable on the like article, the produce or manufacture of any other country, nor will any prohibition be maintained or imposed on the importation of any article, the produce or manufacture of the dominions and possessions of Her Majesty, which shall not equally extend to the importation of the like articles, being the produce or manufacture of any other country.

Article 26. All persons other than natives conforming themselves to the laws of the Transvaal State (a) will have full liberty with their families to enter, travel, or reside in any part of the Transvaal State; (b) they will be entitled to hire or possess houses, manufactures, warehouses, shops, and premises; (c) they may carry on their commerce either in person or by any agents whom they may think to employ; (d) they will not be subject in respect of their persons or property, or in respect of their commerce or industry, to any taxes, whether general or local, other than those which are or may be imposed upon Transvaal citizens.

Article 27. All inhabitants of the Transvaal shall have free access to the Courts of Justice for the protection and defence of their rights.

Article 28. All persons other than natives who established their domicile in the Transvaal between the 12th day of April, 1877, and the date when this Convention conies into effect, and who shall within twelve months after such last-mentioned date have their names registered by the British Resident, shall be exempt from all compulsory military service whatever. The Resident shall notify such registration to the Government of the Transvaal State.

Article 29. Provision shall hereafter be made by a separate instrument for the mutual extradition of criminals, and also for the surrender of deserters from Her Majesty's forces.

Article 30. All debts contracted since the Annexation will be payable in the same currency in which they may have been contracted; all uncancelled postage and other revenue stamps issued by the Government since the Annexation will remain valid, and will be accepted at their present value by the future Government of the State; all licenses duly issued since the Annexation will remain in force during the period for which they may have been issued.

Article 31. No grants of land which may have been made, and no transfer of mortgage which may have been passed since the Annexation, will be invalidated by reason merely of their having been made or passed since that date. All transfers to the British Secretary for Native Affairs in trust for natives will remain in force, the Native Location Commission taking the place of such Secretary for Native Affairs.

Article 32. This Convention will be ratified by a newly-elected Volksraad within the period of three months after its execution, and in default of such ratification this Convention shall be null and void.

Article 33. Forthwith, after the ratification of this Convention, as in the last preceding Article mentioned, all British troops in Transvaal territory will leave the same, and the mutual delivery of munitions of war will be carried out.

Articles end. Here will follow signatures of Royal Commissioners; then the following, to precede signatures of triumvirate.

We, the undersigned, Stephanus Johannes Paulus Kruger Martinus Wessel Pretorius, and Petrus Jacobus Joubert, as representatives of the Transvaal Burghers, do hereby agree to all the above conditions, reservations, and limitations under which self-government has been restored to the inhabitants of the Transvaal territory, subject to the suzerainty of Her Majesty, her heirs and successors, and we agree to accept the Government of the said territory, with all rights and obligations thereto appertaining, on the 8th day of August; and we promise and undertake that this Convention shall be ratified by a newly-elected Volksraad of the Transvaal State within three months from this date.

1884 London Convention.

A Convention Between Her Majesty The Queen Of The United Kingdom Of Great Britain And Ireland And The South African Republic.[272]

Whereas the Government of the Transvaal State, through its Delegates, consisting of Stephanus Johannes Paulus Kruger, President of the said State, Stephanus Jacobus Du Toit, Superintendent of Education, and Nicholas Jacobus Smit, a member of the Volksraad, have represented that the Convention signed at Pretoria on the 3rd day of August, 1881, and ratified by the Volksraad of the said State on the 25th October, 1881, contains certain provisions which are inconvenient, and imposes burdens and obligations from which the said State is desirous to be relieved, and that the south-western boundaries fixed by the said Convention should be amended, with a view to promote the peace and good order of the said State, and of the countries adjacent thereto; and whereas Her Majesty the Queen of the United Kingdom of Great Britain and Ireland has been pleased to take the said representations into consideration: Now, therefore, Her Majesty has been pleased to direct, and it is hereby declared, that the following articles of a new Convention, signed on behalf of Her Majesty by Her Majesty's High Commissioner in South Africa, the Right Honourable Sir Hercules George Robert Robinson, Knight Grand Cross of the Most Distinguished Order of Saint Michael and Saint George, Governor of the Colony of the Cape of Good Hope, and on behalf of the Transvaal State (which shall hereinafter be called the South African Republic) by the above-named Delegates, Stephanus Johannes Paulus Kruger, Stephanos Jacobus Du Toit, and Nicholas Jacobus Smit, shall, when ratified by the Volksraad of the South African Republic, be substituted for the articles embodied in the Convention of 3rd August, 1881; which latter, pending such ratification, shall continue in full force and effect.

Article 1. The Territory of the South African Republic will embrace the land lying between the following boundaries, to wit:—

Beginning from the point where the north-eastern boundary line of Griqualand meets the Vaal River, up the course of the Vaal River to the point of junction with it of the Klip River; thence up the course of the Klip River to the point of junction with it of the stream called Gansvlei; thence up the Gansvlei stream to its source in the Drakensberg; thence to a beacon in the boundary of Natal, situated immediately opposite and close to the source of the Gansvlei stream; thence in a north-easterly direction along the ridge of the Drakensberg, dividing the waters flowing into the Gansvlei stream from the waters flowing into the sources of the Buffalo, to a beacon on a point where this mountain ceases to be a continuous chain; thence to a beacon on a plain to the north-east of the last described beacon; thence to the nearest source of a small stream called "Division Stream"; thence down this division stream, which forms the southern boundary of the farm Sandfontein, the property of Messrs. Meek, to its junction with the Coldstream; thence down the Coldstream to its junction with the Buffalo or Umzinyati River; thence down the course of the Buffalo River to the junction with it of the Blood River; thence up the course of the Blood River to the junction with it of Lyn Spruit or Dudusi; thence up the Dudusi to its source; thence 80 yards to Bea. I., situated on a spur of the N'Qaba-Ka-hawana Mountains; thence 80 yards to the N'Sonto River; thence down the N'Sonto River to its junction with the White Umvulozi River; thence up the White Umvulozi River to a white rock where it rises; thence 800 yards to Kambula Hill (Bea. II.); thence to the source of the Pemvana River, where the road from Kambula Camp to Burgers' Lager crosses; thence down the Pemvana River to its junction with the Bivana River; thence down the Bivana River to its junction with the Pongolo River; thence down the Pongolo River to where it passes through the Libombo Range; thence along the summits of the Libombo Range to the northern point of the N'Yawos Hill in that range (Bea. XVI.); thence to the northern peak of the Inkwakweni Hills (Bea. XV.); thence to Sefunda, a rocky knoll detached from and to the north-east end of the White Koppies, and to the south of the Musana River (Bea. XIV.); thence to a point on the slope near the crest of Matanjeni, which is the name given to the south-eastern portion of the Mahamba Hills (Bea. XIII.); thence to the N'gwangwana, a double-pointed hill (one point is bare, the other wooded, the beacon being on the former) on the left bank of the Assegai River and upstream of the Dadusa Spruit (Bea. XII.); thence to the southern point of Bendita, a rocky knoll in a plain between the Little Hlozane and Assegaai Rivers (Bea. XI.); thence to the highest point of Suluka Hill, round the eastern slopes of which flows the Little Hlozane, also called Ludaka or Mudspruit (Bea. X.); thence to the beacon known as "Viljoen's," or N'Duko Hill; thence to a point north-east of Derby House, known as Magwazidili's Beacon; thence to the Igaba, a small knoll on the Ungwempisi River, also called "Joubert's Beacon," and known to the natives as "Piet's Beacon" (Bea. IX.); thence to the highest point of the N'Dhlovudwalili or Houtbosch, a hill on the northern bank of the Umqwempisi River (Bea. VIII.); thence to a beacon on the only flat-topped rock, about 10 feet

[272] For comparison see: London Convention - Wikisource, the free online library And Creswicke SA War Vol. 1.

high and about 30 yards in circumference at its base, situated on the south side of the Lamsamane range of hills, and overlooking the valley of the great Usuto River, this rock being 45 yards north of the road from Camden and Lake Banagher to the forests on the Usuto River (sometimes called Sandhlanas Beacon) (Bea. VII.); thence to the Gulungwana or Ibubulundi, four smooth bare hills, the highest in that neighbourhood, situated to the south of the Umtuli River (Bea. VI.); thence to a flat-topped rock, 8 feet high, on the crest of the Busuku, a low rocky range south-west of the Impulazi River (Bea. V.); thence to a low bare hill on the north-east of and overlooking the Impulazi River, to the south of it being a tributary of the Impulazi, with a considerable waterfall, and the road from the river passing 200 yards to the north-west of the beacon (Bea. IV.); thence to the highest point of the Mapumula range, the watershed of the Little Usuto River on the north, and the Umpulazi River on the south, the hill, the top of which is a bare rock, falling abruptly towards the Little Usuto (Bea. III.); thence to the western point of a double-pointed rocky hill, precipitous on all sides, called Makwana, its top being a bare rock (Bea. II.); thence to the top of a rugged hill of considerable height falling abruptly to the Komati River, this hill being the northern extremity of the Isilotwani range, and separated from the highest peak of the range Inkomokazi (a sharp cone) by a deep neck (Bea. I.). (On a ridge in the straight line between Beacons I. and II. is an intermediate beacon). From Beacon I. the boundary runs to a hill across the Komati River, and thence along the crest of the range of hills known as the Makongwa, which runs north-east and south-west, to Kamhlubano Peak; thence in a straight line to Mananga, a point in the Libombo Range, and thence to the nearest point in the Portuguese frontier on the Libombo Range; thence along the summits of the Libombo Range to the middle of the poort where the Komati River passes through it, called the lowest Komati Poort; thence in a north by easterly direction to Pokioens Kop, situated on the north side of the Olifant's River, where it passes through the ridges; thence about north north-west to the nearest point of Serra di Chicundo; and thence to the junction of the Pafori River with the Limpopo or Crocodile River; thence up the course of the Limpopo River to the point where the Marique River falls into it. Thence up the course of the Marique River to "Derde Poort," where it passes through a low range of hills, called Sikwane, a beacon (No. 10) being erected on the spur of said range near to and westward of the banks of the river; thence in a straight line through this beacon to a beacon (No. 9) erected on the top of the same range, about 1,700 yards distant from beacon No. 10; thence in a straight line to a beacon (No. 8) erected on the highest point of an isolated hill called Dikgagong, or "Wildebeest Kop," situated south-eastward of and about 3-1/3 miles distant from a high hill called Moripe; thence in a straight line to a beacon (No. 7) erected on the summit of an isolated hill or "koppie" forming the eastern extremity of the range of hills called Moshweu, situated to the northward of and about two miles distant from a large isolated hill called Chukudu-Chochwa; thence in a straight line to a beacon (No. 6) erected on the summit of a hill forming part of the same range, Moshweu; thence in a straight line to a beacon (No. 5) erected on the summit of a pointed hill in the same range; thence in a straight line to a beacon (No. 4) erected on the summit of the western extremity of the same range; thence in a straight line to a beacon (No. 3) erected on the summit of the northern extremity of a low, bushy hill, or "koppie," near to and eastward of the Notwane River; thence in a straight line to the junction of the stream called Metsi-Mash wane with the Notwane River (No. 2); thence up the course of the Notwane River to Sengoma, being the Poort where the river passes through the Dwarsberg Range; thence, as described in the Award given by Lieutenant-Governor Keate, dated October 17, 1871, by Pitlanganyane (narrow place), Deboaganka or Schaapkuil, Sibatoul (bare place), and Maclase to Ramatlabama, a pool on a spruit north of the Molopo River. From Ramatlabama the boundary shall run to the summit of an isolated hill, called Leganka; thence in a straight line, passing north-east of a Native Station, near "Buurman's Drift," on the Molopo River, to that point on the road from Mosiega to the old drift, where a road turns out through the Native Station to the new drift below; thence to "Buurman's Old Drift"; thence in a straight line to a marked and isolated clump of trees near to and north-west of the dwelling-house of C. Austin, a tenant on the farm "Vleifontein," No. 117; thence in a straight line to the north-western corner beacon of the farm "Mooimeisjesfontein," No. 30; thence along the western line of the said farm "Mooimeisjesfontein," and in prolongation thereof, as far as the road leading from "Ludik's Drift," on the Molopo River, past the homestead of "Mooimeisjesfontein" towards the Salt Pans near Harts River; thence along the said road, crossing the direct road from Polfontein to Sehuba, and until the direct road from Polfontein to Lotlakane or Pietfontein is reached; thence along the southern edge of the last-named road towards Lotlakane until the first garden grounds of that station is reached; thence in a south-westerly direction, skirting Lotlakane, so as to leave it and all its garden ground in native territory, until the road from Lotlakane to Kunana is reached; thence along the east side, and clear of that road towards Kunana, until the garden grounds of that station are reached; thence, skirting Kunana, so as to include it and all its garden ground, but no more, in the Transvaal, until the road from Kunana to Mamusa is reached; thence along the eastern side and clear of the road towards Mamusa, until a road turns out towards Taungs; thence along the eastern side and clear of the road towards Taungs, till the line of the district known as "Stellaland" is reached, about 11 miles from Taungs; thence along the line of the district Stellaland to the Harts River, about 24 miles below Mamusa; thence across Harts River to the junction of the roads from Monthe and Phokwane; thence along the western side and clear of the nearest road towards "Koppie Enkel," an isolated hill about 36 miles from Mamusa, and about 18 miles north of Christiana, and to the summit of the said hill; thence in a straight line to that point on the north-east boundary of Griqualand West as beaconed by Mr. Surveyor Ford, where two farms, registered as Nos. 72 and 75, do meet, about midway between the Vaal and Harts Rivers, measured along the said boundary of Griqualand West; thence to the first point where the north-east boundary of Griqualand West meets the Vaal River.

Article 2. The Government of the South African Republic will strictly adhere to the boundaries defined in the first Article of this Convention, and will do its utmost to prevent any of its inhabitants from making any encroachments upon lands beyond the said boundaries. The Government of the South African Republic will appoint Commissioners upon the eastern and western borders whose duty it will be strictly to guard against irregularities and all trespassing over the boundaries. Her Majesty's Government will, if necessary, appoint Commissioners in the native territories outside the eastern and western borders of the South African Republic to maintain order and prevent encroachments.

Her Majesty's Government and the Government of the South African Republic will each appoint a person to proceed together to beacon off the amended south-west boundary as described in Article 1 of this Convention; and the President of the Orange Free State shall be requested to appoint a referee to whom the said persons shall refer any questions on which they may disagree respecting the interpretation of the said Article, and the decision of such referee thereon shall be final. The arrangement already made, under the terms of Article 19 of the Convention of Pretoria of the 3rd August, 1881, between the owners of the farms Grootfontein and Valleifontein on the one hand, and the Barolong authorities on the other, by which a fair share of the water supply of the said farms shall be allowed to flow undisturbed to the said Barolongs, shall continue in force.

Article 3. If a British officer is appointed to reside at Pretoria or elsewhere within the South African Republic to discharge functions analogous to those of a Consular officer he will receive the protection and assistance of the Republic.

Article 4. The South African Republic will conclude no treaty or engagement with any State or nation other than the Orange Free State, nor with any native tribe to the eastward or westward of the Republic, until the same has been approved by Her Majesty the Queen.

Such approval shall be considered to have been granted if Her Majesty's Government shall not, within six months after receiving a copy of such treaty (which shall be delivered to them immediately upon its completion), have notified that the conclusion of such treaty is in conflict with the interests of Great Britain or of any of Her Majesty's possessions in South Africa.

Article 5. The South African Republic will be liable for any balance which may still remain due of the debts for which it was liable at the date of Annexation, to wit, the Cape Commercial Bank Loan, the Railway Loan, and the Orphan Chamber Debt, which debts will be a first charge upon the revenues of the Republic. The South African Republic will moreover be liable to Her Majesty's Government for £250,000, which will be a second charge upon the revenues of the Republic.

Article 6. The debt due as aforesaid by the South African Republic to Her Majesty's Government will bear interest at the rate of three and a-half per cent, from the date of the ratification of this Convention, and shall be repayable by a payment for interest and Sinking Fund of six pounds and nine pence per £100 per annum, which will extinguish the debt in twenty-five years. The said payment of six pounds and nine pence per £100 shall be payable half-yearly, in British currency, at the close of each half year from the date of such ratification: Provided always that the South African Republic shall be at liberty at the close of any half year to pay off the whole or any portion of the outstanding debt.

Interest at the rate of three and a-half per cent, on the debt as standing under the Convention of Pretoria shall, as heretofore, be paid to the date of the ratification of this Convention.

Article 7. All persons who held property in the Transvaal on the 8th day of August, 1881, and still hold the same, will continue to enjoy the rights of property which they have enjoyed since the 12th April, 1877. No person who has remained loyal to Her Majesty during the late hostilities shall suffer any molestation by reason of his loyalty; or be liable to any criminal prosecution or civil action for any part taken in connexion with such hostilities; and all such persons will have full liberty to reside in the country, with enjoyment of all civil rights, and protection for their persons and property.

Article 8. The South African Republic renews the declaration made in the Sand River Convention, and in the Convention of Pretoria, that no slavery or apprenticeship partaking of slavery will be tolerated by the Government of the said Republic.

Article 9. There will continue to be complete freedom of religion and protection from molestation for all denominations, provided the same be not inconsistent with morality and good order; and no disability shall attach to any person in regard to rights of property by reason of the religious opinions which he holds.

Article 10. The British Officer appointed to reside in the South African Republic will receive every assistance from the Government of the said Republic in making due provision for the proper care and preservation of the graves of such of Her Majesty's Forces as have died in the Transvaal; and if need be, for the appropriation of land for the purpose.

Article 11. All grants or titles issued at any time by the Transvaal Government in respect of land outside the boundary of the South African Republic, as defined in Article I, shall be considered invalid and of no effect, except in so far as any such grant or title relates to land that falls within the boundary of the South African Republic; and all persons holding any such grant so considered invalid and of no effect will receive from the Government of the South African Republic such compensation, either in land or in money, as the Volksraad shall determine. In all cases in which any Native Chiefs or other authorities outside the said boundaries have received any adequate consideration from the Government of the South African Republic for land excluded from the Transvaal by the first Article of this Convention, or where permanent improvements have been made on the land, the High Commissioner will recover from the native authorities fair compensation for the loss of the land thus excluded, or of the permanent improvements thereon.

Article 12. The independence of the Swazis, within the boundary line of Swaziland, as indicated in the first Article of this Convention, will be fully recognised.

Article 13. Except in pursuance of any treaty or engagement made as provided in Article 4 of this Convention, no other or higher duties shall be imposed on the importation into the South African Republic of any article coming from any part of Her Majesty's dominions than are or may be imposed on the like article coming from any other place or country; nor will any prohibition be maintained or imposed on the importation into the South African Republic of any article coming from any part of Her Majesty's dominions, which shall not equally extend to the like article coming from any other place or country. And in like manner the same treatment shall be given to any article coming to Great Britain from the South African Republic as to the like article coming from any other place or country.

These provisions do not preclude the consideration of special arrangements as to import duties and commercial relations between the South African Republic and any of Her Majesty's colonies or possessions.

Article 14. All persons, other than natives, conforming themselves to the laws of the South African Republic (a) will have full liberty, with their families, to enter, travel, or reside in any part of the South African Republic; (b), they will be entitled to hire or possess houses, manufactories, warehouses, shops, and premises; (c) they may carry on their commerce either in person or by any agents whom they may think fit to employ; (d), they will not be subject, in respect of their persons or property, or in respect of their commerce or industry, to any taxes, whether general or local, other than those which are or may be imposed upon citizens of the said Republic.

Article 15. All persons, other than natives, who established their domicile in the Transvaal between the 12th day of April, 1877, and the 8th August, 1881, and who within twelve months after such last-mentioned date have had their names registered by the British Resident, shall be exempt from all compulsory military service whatever.

Article 16. Provision shall hereafter be made by a separate instrument for the mutual extradition of criminals, and also for the surrender of deserters from Her Majesty's Forces.

Article 17. All debts contracted between the 12th April, 1877, and the 8th August, 1881, will be payable in the same currency in which they may have been contracted.

Article 18. No grants of land which may have been made, and no transfers or mortgages which may have been passed between the 12th April, 1877, and the 8th August, 1881, will be invalidated by reason merely of their having been made or passed between such dates.

All transfers to the British Secretary for Native Affairs in trust for natives will remain in force, an officer of the South African Republic taking the place of such Secretary for Native Affairs.

Article 19. The Government of the South African Republic will engage faithfully to fulfil the assurances given, in accordance with the laws of the South African Republic, to the natives at the Pretoria Pitso by the Royal Commission in the presence of the Triumvirate and with their entire assent (1), as to the freedom of the natives to buy or otherwise acquire land under certain conditions; (2), as to the appointment of a commission to mark out native locations; (3), as to the access of the natives to the courts of law; and (4) as to their being allowed to move freely within the country, or to leave it for any legal purpose, under a pass system.

Article 20. This Convention will be ratified by a Volksraad of the South African Republic within the period of six months after its execution, and in default of such ratification this Convention shall be null and void.

Signed in duplicate in London this 27th day of February, 1884.

(Signed) Hercules Robinson.

(Signed) S.J.P. Kruger.

(Signed) S.J. Du Toit.

(Signed) M.J. Smit.

End Text of Century of Wrong.

March 1900 Peace Offer and Reply

In March of 1900 the Presidents of both Republics wrote directly to Robert Cecil[273] (Marquess of Salisbury) who was serving as the Prime Minister of the United Kingdom; in an attempt to negotiate an end to the conflict on honorable terms.[274] [275]

Letter to Lord Salisbury

From the States-President of the South African Republic and the Orange Free State

Bloemfontein, 5th March, 1900.

To His Excellency Lord Salisbury, London.

The blood and tears of the thousands who have suffered through this war, and the prospect of all the moral and material ruin which now threatens South Africa, render it necessary for both parties carrying on the war to ask themselves calmly, and in the faith of the Trinity, for what they are fighting and if the aims of both justify all this horrible misery and devastation.

On this account, and with an eye to the assertion of several English Statesmen that the war was begun and carried on with the determined end to undermine Her Majesty's authority in South Africa, and to establish in the whole of South Africa a Government independent of Her Majesty's Government, we consider it our duty to declare that this War was only commenced as a measure of defence and for the purpose of obtaining a guarantee for the threatened independence of the South African Republic, and was only continued in order to ensure the indisputable independence of both Republics as Sovereign International States, and to obtain the assurance that the subjects of Her Majesty who have taken part with us in the war will not suffer the least hurt either in their lives or their possessions.

On these conditions alone we demand, as in the past, to see peace restored in South Africa, and an end made to the wrong that now exists there.

But if Her Majesty's Government has decided upon destroying the independence of the Republic, nothing remains to us and our people but to persist to the bitter end on the road now taken, notwithstanding the overpowering might of the British Empire, trusting that God, who has lit the inextinguishable fire of the love of liberty in our hearts, and in the hearts of our fathers, will not abandon us, but will fulfil His work in us, and in our descendants.

We hesitated to lay this declaration earlier before Your Excellency, because we were afraid that as long as the advantage was on our side, and our Army had in their occupation positions of defence far into the British Colonies, such a declaration would have hurt the feelings of the English nation; but now that the prestige of the British Empire may be considered to be restored, through the capture of one of our armies, and we are compelled by this to sacrifice other positions which our armies occupied, this difficulty is removed, and we can no longer hesitate to tell you, in the face of the whole civilized world, why we are fighting, and on what conditions we are prepared to make peace.

[273] Robert Arthur Talbot Gascoyne-Cecil, 3rd Marquess of Salisbury (3 February 1830–22 August 1903), known as Lord Salisbury, was a British statesman and Conservative politician who served as Prime Minister of the United Kingdom three times for a total of over thirteen years. He was also Foreign Secretary before and during most of his tenure. He avoided international alignments or alliances, maintaining the policy of "splendid isolation". Robert Gascoyne-Cecil, 3rd Marquess of Salisbury - Wikipedia

[274] Three Years' War By: Christiaan Rudolf De Wet. Charles Scribner's Sons, (1902) Trow Directory Printing And Bookbinding Company New York. Harvard Copy: https://archive.org/details/threeyearswar00wetgoog/mode/2up

[275] In Dr. Conan Doyle's work, Cause and Conduct, these two communications are reproduced as well. The differences in language are notable, since each purports to be a full transcription.

Reply

From Lord Salisbury

To their Excellencies the States-Presidents of the South African Republic and Orange Free State.

London, 11th, March, 1900.

I have the honour to acknowledge the receipt of your Honour's cable, dated 5th March, from Bloemfontein, of which the purport is principally whether Her Majesty's Government will acknowledge the indisputable independence of the South African Republic and Orange Free State and treat them as Sovereign International States, and will offer to conclude the war on these conditions.

In the beginning of October of this year, there was peace between the Queen and the two Republics, under the Convention which then held good. There was a discussion carried on during a few months between Her Majesty's Government and the South African Republic, of which the purport was the amendment of very serious grievances under which English inhabitants suffered in the South African Republic.

In the course of these negotiations, the South African Republic obtained the knowledge that Her Majesty's Government had made considerable preparations for war, and had taken steps to provide the necessary reinforcements for the English garrisons at Cape Colony and Natal. No inroad on the rights guaranteed by the Conventions had, until then, taken place on the English side.

Suddenly the South African Republic, after having two days previously issued an insulting ultimatum, declared War on Her Majesty; and the Orange Free State, with which there had been no disagreement, took a similar step.

Thereupon an inroad was made into Her Majesty's territory by the two Republics; three towns within the British frontier were besieged, a great part of the two Colonies was over-run, with great destruction of property and life, and the Republics claimed the right to treat the inhabitants of Her Majesty's territory as if this territory had been annexed by one of these States.

The Transvaal having these actions in view, had for years stored up, on an enormous scale, military provisions, which could only have been destined for use against England.

Your Excellencies made some remarks of a negative nature concerning the aim for which these preparations were made. I do not consider it necessary to discuss the question which you have thus raised, but the consequences of the preparations, made in great secrecy, have been that the British Empire has found itself forced to repel an inroad which has brought on a costly war, and caused the loss of thousands of valuable lives.

This great misfortune has been the punishment that Great Britain has had to undergo during the last few years for having suffered the two Republics to exist.

Keeping in sight the use which the two Republics have made of the position presented to them, and the misfortunes which their unprovoked attacks on Her Majesty's territory have brought, Her Majesty's Government can only reply to Your Honour's telegram by saying that they are not prepared to acknowledge the independence either of the South African Republic, or of the Orange Free State.

Robert Gascoyne-Cecil, 3rd Marquess of Salisbury.[29]

Quote from De Wet

It was decided to send a deputation to Europe. This deputation, consisting of Abraham Fissher,[276] Cornelius H. Wessels,[277] and Daniel Wolmarans,[278] sailed from Delagoa Bay.[279]

The reader may ask the object which this deputation had in view. Was it that our Governments relied on foreign intervention? Emphatically, no! They never thought of such a thing. Neither in his harangue to the burghers at Poplar Grove, nor in any of his subsequent speeches, did President Steyn give any hint of such an intention. The deputation was sent in order that the whole world might know the state of affairs in South Africa. It fulfilled its purpose, and was justified by its results. It helped us to win the sympathy of the nations.

Diplomatic Delegation of the Boer Republics to Europe and America, 1900, l.t.r. front: A.D.W. Wolmarans, A. Fischer, C. H. Wessels, [Cornelius Hermanus Wessels] and back: Dr. W.J. Leyds and Dr. H.P.N. Muller.[30] [280]

[276] Member of the Free State Volksraad and Executive Council.

[277] Member of the Free State Volksraad and Executive Council, and also President of the Volksraad.

[278] Member of the first Volksraad of the South African Republic.

[279] This harbour, then the only harbour in South Africa open to us, was subsequently forbidden us by the Portuguese Government, whose officials even went so far as to arrest eight hundred of our burghers (who, for want of horses, had taken refuge in Portuguese territory), and to send them to Portugal. The ports of German West Africa cannot be counted among those which were available for us. Not only were they too far from us to be of any service, but also, in order to reach them, it would have been necessary to go through English territory, for they were separated from us by Griqualand West, Bechuanaland, and isolated portions of Cape Colony. We had, therefore, during the latter portion of the war, to depend for supplies upon what little we were able to capture from the enemy.

[280] Special Diplomatic Delegation of the Boer Republics to Europe and America, 1900, l.t.r. front: A.D.W. Wolmarans, A. Fischer, C. H. Wessels, Cornelius Hermanus Wessels and back: Dr. W.J. Leyds and Dr. H.P.N. Muller.

Buller & Botha Peace Negotiations June 1900

Buller - Laing's Nek

From the General Officer Commanding in Natal to the Secretary for War.[281]

(Through the Field-Marshal Commanding the Forces in South Africa.)

Newcastle, Natal, 4th June, 1900.

Sir,

In my letter of the 24th ultimo, I reported that on reaching Laing's Nek on the 19th. [May] I found it too strongly occupied for me to force it with the troops then at my disposal.

2. I have since ascertained that the Wakkerstrom Commando, which had left the force opposing Lord Roberts' advance, reached Laing's Nek just in time to rally sufficient of the fugitives I was pursuing to stop our pursuit.

3. For the next few days the enemy were able to concentrate on and about Laing's Nek quicker than I could bring my force forward, and on the 28th I calculated that they had about 8,000 men distributed in very strong positions in Keteni Nek, Laing's Nek, Molls Nek, and the defiles of the Utrecht—Wakkerstrom road, with some 13 to 15 guns in well-selected positions, while some 6,000 Free Staters were in the north-east corner of the Free State, of whom at least 3,000 were holding Botha's Pass and the tracks adjoining it on my left.

4. On the 28th May I sent a force under General Hildyard across the Buffalo [River] at Wools Drift with instructions to march on Utrecht, and another under General Lyttelton at Ichanga Drift, with orders to turn south and clear the Dornberg, which was at the time held by the enemy in some force.

5. The enemy evacuated the Dornberg on General Lyttelton crossing the Buffalo River, and he then turned north and came up on the left flank of General Hildyard, who, on the 29th, had occupied the Belẹlas Berg, south and in front of the town of Utrecht.

Commandant Grobelaar, who was commanding the 1,500 men holding the Wakkerstrom—Utrecht road, withdrew from the town, giving a promise that no armed men should enter the town while we were there. On the following day, the Landrost surrendered the town, had several copies of attached Proclamation posted, and asked for more for distribution.

Buller Proclamation:

> The troops of Queen Victoria are now passing through the Transvaal. Her Majesty does not make war on individuals, but is on the contrary anxious to spare them as far as may be possible the horrors of war. The quarrel England has is with the Government, not with the people of the Transvaal.
>
> Provided they remain neutral no attempt will be made to interfere with persons living near the line of march, every possible protection will be given them, and any of their property that it may be necessary to take will be paid for.
>
> But on the other hand those who are thus allowed to remain near the line of march must respect and maintain their neutrality, and the residents of any locality will be held responsible, both in their persons and their property, if any damage is done to railway or telegraph, or any violence done to any member of the British Forces in the vicinity of their homes.

6. On the 30th May, I heard that Lord Roberts had occupied Elandsfontein Junction, and I at once sent a flag of truce to the Commandant at Laing's Nek, asking him, now his communications were cut, whether it was worth his while to continue the struggle. He replied that he had referred the question to his Commandant-General.

7. On the 2nd June, I met Assistant Commandant-General Chris. Botha between our outposts. I attach notes of the conversation that ensued. I may add that my Staff elicited from his Staff that at least half the burghers are

[281] South Africa Despatches: Presented to Parliament by Command of His Majesty, London: Printed for H. M. Stationery Office, by Harrison and Sons 1901. Vol I 286 pages. https://archive.org/details/southafricadespa00lond/page/n3/mode/2up
See Page 146- Start of Natal Field Army Despatches: (Buller & Botha page 228-231) Also: HathiTrust Page 298: Pages 84-87 of the online Volume I and II document: https://babel.hathitrust.org/cgi/pt?id=hvd.32044089026009&seq=298&view=1up&q1=Laing%27s+
And: Proclamations Issued In South Africa. Robert, Frederick Sleigh Roberts, 1st earl. Proclamations Issued in South Africa. London, 1900. 820 pages. Vol I & II 1900. https://babel.hathitrust.org/cgi/pt?id=hvd.32044089026009&seq=15
Start Vol II Page 355. https://babel.hathitrust.org/cgi/pt?id=hvd.32044089026009&seq=355&view=1up

anxious for peace, that they have telegraphic communication with Lydenburg through Standerton and Middelburg, and that their supplies also now come by wagons by the same route.

8. With regard to the terms I offered the troops on Laing's Nek, viz., that their homes should be unmolested, provided they now dispersed, taking their small-arms but leaving their artillery, I may mention that even if I attack and take the position, I cannot hope to get any result better than these terms involve. The position admits of such facilities for escape that I cannot hope to make any prisoners, or indeed capture many guns, and I reserved the right of further disarmament.

In these circumstances, should my terms be accepted (though this is I fear unlikely), I shall have obtained the occupation of Laing's Nek without loss of life and without prejudice to our position.

I have the honour to be,
Sir,
Your obedient Servant,
Redvers Buller, General

The Boer commando guarding Van Reenan's Pass.[31]

Drakensberg Railway Switchbacks.[32]

Tunnel Near Laing's Nek Wrecked by the Boers. North View.[33] Tunnel Near Laing's Nek Wrecked by the Boers. South View.[34] Laing's nek Tunnel reopened.[35]

Buller's Interview Notes

General Christian Botha.[36] Botha. General Sir Redvers Henry Buller.[37] Cape Cart, Requisitioned by Roberts for Peace Negotiations with Louis Botha, Driven by the Military Secretary, Captain Waterfield, to the Boer Lines.[38]

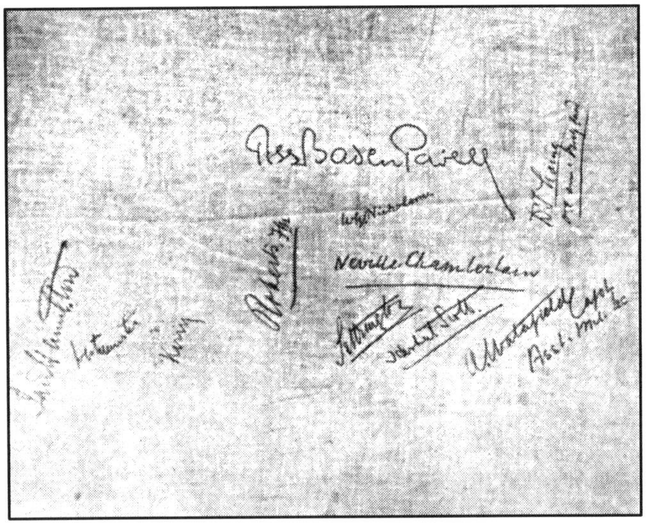

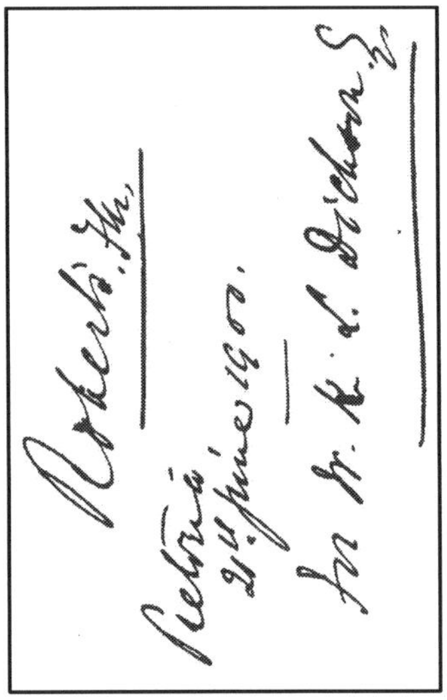

Flag of Truce:[39] What is most instructive is how the flag of truce was authenticated. It is inscribed with the following signatures for authenticity: Roberts (Vertical in Center), Baden Powell, Roberts' Secretary Neville Chamberlain,[282] Kerry, Nicholson, Scott, and others. Roberts' Autograph for comparison.[40]

Notes on interview between Sir Redvers Bailer and Assistant Commandant-General C. Botha, near Laing's Nek, 2nd June, 1900.[283,284]

Sir R. Buller told [Chris] Botha[285] that he had asked him to meet him with a view to avoid, if possible, the useless sacrifice of brave lives. Lord Roberts was in Johannesburg. There was a large army with many guns in Natal, and he hoped Botha would see that to go on fighting here was only throwing lives away to no purpose.

[282] Sir Neville Francis Fitzgerald Chamberlain (13 January 1856 – 28 May 1944) was an officer in the British Indian Army. He was later Inspector-General of the Royal Irish Constabulary, and resigned in the aftermath of the 1916 Easter Rising in Ireland. He is credited with having invented the game of snooker while serving in Jubbulpore (Jabalpur), India, in 1875. https://en.wikipedia.org/wiki/Neville_Chamberlain_(police_officer)

[283] Proclamations in SA, Interview Notes. https://babel.hathitrust.org/cgi/pt?id=hvd.32044089026009&seq=299&view=1up

[284] The Times' History of the War in South Africa 1899-1902 by Amery, L. S. (Leopold Stennett), Volume 5 pages 604- 606.

[285] Christiaan Botha (also Chris Botha and in English language literature mistakenly Christian Botha, 6 October 1864 – 29 October 1902) was a younger brother of Louis Botha (1862–1919) and Philip Botha (1851-1901) , but an older brother of Theunis Jacobus Botha (1867-1930), and likewise a Boer general in the Second Boer War. Chris Botha - Wikipedia

Commandant Botha asked Sir Redvers to give him his proposals in writing so that he could lay them before his Government. He cannot take upon himself not to fight any more; if he did so he would be a traitor to his country.

Sir R. Buller replied that Botha had received, four days ago, a letter laying the case before him.

Commandant Botha admitted that he did receive Sir Redvers' letter, but the information given in it was not so definite as this conversation was.

Sir R. Buller said that he had stopped all firing since he sent the letter, but in the meantime the Boers had gone on digging trenches. This state of things cannot continue.

Commandant Botha replied that he also had not fired. He then asked Sir Redvers to make a proposal.

Sir R. Buller said he expected the proposal from Botha. He had done the best he could, but he cannot wait long, and he understands that the Boer Government has moved to Lydenburg.

Commandant Botha said he had no proposition to make.

Sir R. Buller said he hates war—it is a miserable thing. A brave man knows when the time comes when to continue fighting means only useless loss of life, and slaughter.

Commandant Botha said it was not for him but for his Government to decide such a question.

Sir R. Buller said he had not asked Lord Roberts about it; but he had many friends in the force opposed to him, and he wished them well. He has so many men that Botha must see it is useless to go on fighting.

Commandant Botha said if he gave in now, Sir Redvers would have a big advantage and he would have great loss.

Sir R. Buller said that on the contrary if war goes on, the Boers' stock would he lost, their homes destroyed, and their property would suffer a great deal of damage, and he wants to avoid that.

Commandant Botha replied that all they have to fight for is their independence. Their stock, &c., is only a secondary consideration to them.

Sir R Buller said "But behind independence is life."

Commandant Botha said he would deserve to be hated by his country if he gave in.

Sir R. Buller said that the Boer Government has been telling the burghers that the English wish to destroy their farms. This is not true.

Commandant Botha said he knows it is not true, and that it is only a rumour and a fiction.

Sir R. Buller said that he was afraid that there was nothing more to be said, and if Botha must go on fighting it could not be helped.

Commandant Botha replied, "If it has to be, it must be." He would heartily welcome a peace if possible, but in present circumstances he would rather not be there to see it made.

The conference was then on the point of breaking up, when—

Commandant Edwards asked Sir Redvers for a definite proposition.

Sir R. Buller replied that the burghers should disperse home, leaving their artillery behind; they might take their small-arms with them. The question of the ultimate surrender of these arms would have to be settled afterwards. Sir Redvers does not want to take away their arms now, that would be a question for Lord Roberts and Mr. Kruger to settle. He, personally, had no power to make peace. He has met the deputation because he deplores the war. He has had many friends in the Transvaal, and he would like them to live happily and peacefully for the remainder of their lives.

Commandant Botha said he had the same wish, but it was impossible for him to accept or offer terms; he would be a traitor if he did.

Commandant Edwards asked whether Sir Redvers could not make definite proposals for peace.

Sir R. Buller asked whether the commandos here would authorise him to ask Lord Roberts to offer terms.

Commandant Botha agreed, on condition that they retained their independence.

Sir R. Buller replied that he was not in communication with the Government and he could not speak officially, but he had reason to believe that the present Government will not be allowed to continue, that there will be some English form of government, and that the burghers will come in time to participate in the government of the country.

Commandant Edwards said that if the burghers knew what they are to expect, it would facilitate matters, and suggested that Sir Redvers should communicate with Lord Roberts, and ask definitely what the terms of peace are to be.

Sir R. Buller said he would telegraph to Lord Roberts and enquire as to whether he was now in a position to formulate terms of peace.

Commandant Edwards said that his Government knew of this meeting, and they would inform it of Sir Redvers proposals.

Sir R. Buller said he could not wait long, but on being told that a reply could be received in three days, he agreed to an armistice up till Tuesday evening, 5th June.

Commandant Botha said that if he entered into this agreement the English forces must remain where they are.

Sir R. Buller said he could not agree to this as he cannot stop movements now in progress, but he will not fire, nor will he advance his troops in [the] front line beyond their present outposts.

Commandant Botha replied that all he wanted was an assurance that no forces will advance to attack his forces.

It was then agreed that Commandant-General Botha will communicate with his Government as to whether Sir Redvers' proposal should be accepted, and Sir Redvers said he would ask Lord Roberts whether he was yet in a position to formulate his terms of peace.

The meeting then ended.

Buller to Roberts

From General Buller, Newcastle, to Lord Roberts, Front. 2nd June, 1900.[41]

On the 30th May I sent to [the] Commandant on Laing's Nek, and told him that Lord Roberts had crossed the Vaal and that further fighting was useless. This eventually produced a meeting between our outposts today of Assistant Commandant-General Chris Botha and myself.

He asked me what terms of peace you would offer, and I undertook to make no advance for three days while he was communicating to his Government. Can you let me know your terms of peace for individual and separate commandos?

I told him that any terms were that his men should surrender all guns and return to their farms, and if they did that they could take their rifles with them, subject to the understanding that Lord Roberts will later probably order their disarmament.

I thought this would not be wrong, as they can at this moment, if they wish, run away and take both guns and rifles with them. I said that to talk about independence was nonsense, if hereafter they behave themselves they might become an independent colony, that was the only chance they had.

I think they are inclined to give in, and that I have in front of me about half the Transvaal forces now in the field. If you think it worth while, please let me know if may (sic) mention any terms of peace to them. I think that even if assisted from the Orange Free State it will cost me about 500 men killed and wounded to get out of Natal.

Roberts' Reply

From Lord Roberts, Johannesburg, to General Buller, Newcastle. 3rd June, 1900. [42]

Your telegram of yesterday. My terms with the Transvaal Government are unconditional surrender. With regard to troops, those who deliver up their arms and riding animals are allowed to go to their homes on signing pledge that they will not fight again during present war.

The exceptions to this rule are those who have commanded portions of the Republican forces or who have taken an active part in the policy which brought about the war, or who have been guilty of or been parties to wanton destruction of property, or guilty of acts contrary to the usages of civilised warfare.

Principal Officers should remain with you on parole, until you receive instructions regarding their disposal.

Buller's Report

From the General Officer Commanding in Natal to the Secretary of State for War. (Through the Field-Marshal Commanding the Forces in South Africa.) Laing's Nek, Natal, 19th June, 1900.[43] [286]

Sir, The armistice that I reported in my letter of the 4th June[287] ceased on the 5th, as Assistant Commandant-General Chris. Botha wrote on that day declining the terms I had offered. ....

[286] PF: On the 11th, General Buller was able to outflank the Boer position and they retreated. Buller's forces suffered minimal casualties during this operation.

Oath of Neutrality -Proclamation XLI.

Oath of Neutrality.[288]

I, the undersigned, in the District of ________________________

Do hereby solemnly make Oath and declare that I have handed in and given up all the Arms and Ammunition demanded of me by the British Authorities, namely, all Rifles and Rifle Ammunition of whatsoever description they may be.

And I solemnly swear that I have no Rifle or Rifle Ammunition remaining, and that I know of none such being concealed or withheld by anybody whatsoever.

And I further swear that I will not take up Arms against the British Government during the present War, nor will I at any time furnish any member of the Republican Forces with assistance of any kind, or with information as to the numbers, movements, or other details of the British Forces that may come to my knowledge.

I do further promise and swear to remain quietly at my home until the war is over.

I am aware that if have in any way falsely declared in the Premises, or if break my Oath or Promise as above set forth I, shall render myself liable to be summarily and severely punished by the British Authorities.

I make the above declaration solemnly believing it to be true,

So Help Me God.

____

Before me

____

See the Century of Wrong Volume for other proclamations by Roberts relating to the conduct of military operations.

Buller & Botha June Newspaper Coverage June 11

The Commanders' Interview. [Reuter's Special Service.] Mount Prospect, June 2.[289]

General Buller met Christian Botha at O'Neill's Farm, between Umquela and Majuba.

Botha, who met General Buller because his brother Louis could not be found, said that he was not in a position to discuss anything, but as Sir Redvers Buller said "Very well," and turned to go, he pressed him for a proposal.

Sir Redvers said he had no proposal to make, but wished to point out that the Boers were surrounded, and that it was useless to shed more blood.

"What do you want us to do?" asked Botha beseechingly.

"Go back to your farms, leave your big guns, and await Lord Roberts's decision," replied General Buller, at the same time impressing on the Boer officer that lie was not committing Lord Roberts to any definite step.

Botha said he would have to refer the question to the Burghers. General Buller agreed to his appeal for time, and the armistice was arranged.

Operations in Natal. Proposal to Surrender. From Our War. Newcastle, June 4.[290]

Christian Botha, commandant of the forces at Volksrust and brother of the Boer Commandant-General, met Sir Redvers Buller, at the British commander's request, at **Mount Prospect on Saturday**.

[287] This letter is not reproduced in the document. Only the letter of the 2nd.
[288] Proclamations in SA, Nov. 18th 1900: https://babel.hathitrust.org/cgi/pt?id=hvd.32044089026009&seq=377&view=1up
[289] Morning Post, Buller & Chris Botha 11 June https://www.britishnewspaperarchive.co.uk/viewer/bl/0000174/19000611/058/0007
[290] Morning Post, Buller & Chris Botha 11 June https://www.britishnewspaperarchive.co.uk/viewer/bl/0000174/19000611/058/0007

Botha was asked to surrender, and it was agreed that active hostilities should cease for three days, expiring at noon on Tuesday, pending the receipt of Botha's answer.

It is understood that the terms offered were easy.

Before General Hildyard left the vicinity of Utrecht a Proclamation was read to the Landdrost advising the Burghers to return to their farms and promising lenient treatment.

Terms Rejected. Ingogo, June 5.

The terms of surrender have not been accepted by Botha.

Hostilities were renewed on Wednesday, the Creusot on Pogwani Hill firing a few shots at Mount Prospect Camp.

The naval guns replied.

No casualties occurred on our side.

The enemy are still holding their former positions.

The Capture of Van Wyk's. Ingogo, June 7.[291]

The South African Horse were smartly engaged yesterday in taking Van Wyk's Hill, which commands Botha's Pass. They held a front of several miles against a strong force of the enemy until the afternoon, when they were reinforced by the 11th Brigade.

Our casualties were slight.

Through The Drakensberg. Headquarters, June 10.[292]

Yesterday we were engaged in getting our transport through the pass. General advance was begun to-day. We met with opposition eight miles out, but eventually forced the enemy to retire.

Numbers were seen trekking.

A squadron of South African Horse, in trying to cut the enemy off, was engaged all the afternoon at close quarters with a superior force of Boers, probably covering the main retreat.

We are now at the junction of Gans Vlei and the Klip River.

[291] Morning Post, Buller & Chris Botha 11 June https://www.britishnewspaperarchive.co.uk/viewer/bl/0000174/19000611/058/0007

[292] Morning Post, Buller & Chris Botha 11 June https://www.britishnewspaperarchive.co.uk/viewer/bl/0000174/19000611/058/0007

Middleburg Conference, Feb. 1901

Almost a year later, in early February of 1901, General Kitchener, with the consent of the Government decided to make peace overtures to General Botha well before the February 14th debate in the House of Commons. The actual conference took place from February 28th, until its unsuccessful conclusion on March 16th 1901.

On February 13,[293] a week after the failure of his night attack at Lake Chrissie,[294] [295] Louis Botha received a message through his wife, a verbal message, from Kitchener.

If General Botha desired Kitchener, it, so the message ran, a meeting could be held with the British Commander to arrange terms of peace; the one condition being that the question of the independence of the two republics was not to be discussed in any way.

The invitation arrived at an opportune moment; for Botha, though he had effectively countered the converging movement on Ermelo, had nevertheless seen French's columns sweeping unchecked across the high veld, and was fully aware of the searchings of heart which this great display of force had caused among his burghers.

The reply, despatched the same day, but not received by Kitchener until the 22nd, was an acceptance. In the same letter Botha suggested Middelburg as a meeting-place, and requested a safe conduct to and from that place. Kitchener agreed, and February 28 was fixed for the conference.

Middleburg stands on a tributary of Olifant's River and is 94 miles from Pretoria.[44]

Kitchener had no illusions as to the character of the struggle in which he was engaged. Even without the eloquent policy examples of history, events in South Africa since his accession to the command had shown the enormous capacity for resistance possessed by a pastoral race skilled in arms. He was conscious, too, that his mounted army was passing through a period of transition and for a time, at any rate, must inevitably decline in usefulness. The efforts of the Burgher Peace Committee[296] [297] having totally failed, there were two courses open:

[293] The Times' History of the War in South Africa 1899–1902 by Amery, L. S. (Leopold Stennett), Vol 5 Ch. VII pages 183–193.

[294] In an attempt to invade Natal in force and later his unsuccessful attempt to overwhelm a British Column. He eventually did break out back to his base area which the British operation had been designed to deprive him of access to.

[295] The Battle of Chrissiesmeer (Lake Chrissie) during Anglo-Boer War 2 started with an attack by General Louis Botha on the British forces under General Smith-Dorrien. Botha's main aim was to cripple the advance of Smith-Dorrien into the eastern Transvaal. According to oral tradition Smith-Dorrien's march had been kept under observation by San (Bushmen) who also acted as messengers. The Boers capitalised on the San's knowledge of the terrain and attacked at 02:50 in pitch darkness.
The burgers achieved initial success, but could not gain a foothold on the slopes and were not able to open direct fire on the main camp situated on a plateau. At 04:30, covered by thick morning mist, Botha ordered them to retreat. The Boer commando suffered about eighty casualties and the British seventy-five. About 300 horses of the British force were killed or stampeded. Despite heavy losses on the Boer side the British advance into the eastern Transvaal was delayed by the loss of their horses, which gave the Boer commandos time to re-group. https://sahistory.org.za/dated-event/san-involvement-battle-chrissiesmeer See Also: Lake Chrissie is a lake in Msukaligwa Local Municipality, Mpumalanga, South Africa. It is a shallow and large lake, with a maximum depth of about 6 metres (20 ft), 9 kilometres (5.6 mi) long, 3 kilometres (1.9 mi) wide. https://en.wikipedia.org/wiki/Lake_Chrissie

[296] Peace Committee Times History Vol 5. P. 91–93 In December of 1900 Kitchener placed himself in communication with influential men among the surrendered Boers, and it was partly on their advice that the proclamation of December 20 was framed. Nor did he stop here. At a meeting held early in December, under the presidency of Mr. Meyer de Kock, of Belfast, a Peace Committee was formed, with de Kock as secretary, for the purpose of urging upon the commandos the hopelessness of resistance and the need for a general surrender.

to maintain an attitude of unbending reserve, and accept with philosophy the prospect of an incalculably long and costly struggle; or, should a favourable opportunity arise, to persuade the enemy, on the promise of certain terms from which independence was rigidly excluded, to abandon a ruinous and futile resistance.

In the middle of February such an opportunity appeared to have arrived. De Wet and Steyn, the two most stubborn foes of British supremacy, were riding for their lives in Cape Colony. In the Transvaal French's great movement was throwing into panic the whole of a very important district. Kitchener, … . resolved to seize the opportunity; and, while de Wet and Steyn were incapable of interference, to effect a settlement with Botha. ………………On February 28 Kitchener and Botha met at Middelburg. By a stroke of dramatic irony this was the very day on which de Wet and Steyn, after a period of desperate peril, crossed the Orange and won their freedom. It might have been read as a bad omen for peace.

The Middleburg[298] Conference. Group photograph of the participants in the Middelburg peace conference. (February-March 1901)[45 46] Standing (left to right); Colonel G. F. R. Henderson, Dirk Overgauwe ("Dick") van Velden,[299] Major Watson, H. Fraser, Captain Maxwell, H. de Jager. Sitting (left to right); Christiaan de Wet, (Sic. Possibly Wynand Viljoen) General Louis Botha, General Kitchener, Colonel Ian S. M. Hamilton. Note the black armbands worn by all five British officers to commemorate Queen Victoria's death a month earlier. (January 22nd, 1901). See Annie Botha Cite on next page.

A meeting of surrendered Boers convened by this Committee was held in Pretoria on December 21, and was addressed sympathetically by Kitchener. He promised the Committee his advice and support, spoke of the military conditions which exacted the formation of concentration camps, of his determination to give the enemy every possible chance of submitting voluntarily and of the just and progressive government which at the end of the war it was proposed to establish. The speech was printed in Dutch and English, and steps were promptly taken to give it and the proclamation of December 20 wide circulation. To this end emissaries were appointed to visit the commandos and preach the gospel of peace.

Like the proclamation itself the peace propaganda produced the contrary effect to that hoped for. It exasperated the fighting burghers, who viewed its promoters, sincerely patriotic as they were, as cowards and traitors, and, when they obtained the opportunity, treated them as such. Though most of the emissaries escaped in the course of time to the British lines, many were tried by court-martial and sentenced to fines and imprisonment. Meyer de Kock himself, having ridden into Viljoen's lines at the end of January, was tried, sentenced to death for high treason, and executed. In one notorious case there is, at least, a grave suspicion that an irregular and violent course was taken.

On the whole, however, the treatment accorded to the peace emissaries was regular and not, under the circumstances, unduly harsh. In taking the risk of attempting to seduce the men on commando, they acted with their eyes open according to their own sense of patriotism. The fighting burghers, holding a different standard of patriotism, were within their rights in applying even extreme penalties.

[297] Meyer de Kock (5 October 1849 – 12 February 1901) After the British had captured the capital Pretoria and annexed the Transvaal, he surrendered on 10 December 1900. In January 1901, he went to the eastern Transvaal to persuade burghers still in the field to surrender. He was arrested, court-martialed, and later, on 12 February 1901, executed by firing squad. https://en.wikipedia.org/wiki/Meyer_de_Kock See also Viljoen Chapter 30.

[298] It was initially established as a halfway station between Lydenburg and Pretoria. The British built a large concentration camp in Middelburg during the Second Boer War. A Memorial Museum was built at the site next to the 1,381 graves of women and children who died in the concentration camp. Middelburg, Mpumalanga - Wikipedia

[299] Van Velden Dirk Overgauwe Kaptein Commando: Staf General Botha. Awarded the DTD.

Annie Botha, the wife of general Louis Botha.[47] [300] "Mrs. Botha is descended from Robert Emmet,[301] the famous "United Irishman" who was executed for high treason, September 20, 1803."

Newspaper Coverage.

There were several fragmented reports that a meeting was taking place published at the time.

Several of the reports were of this brief nature.

Highland News - Saturday 02 March 1901—The Fighting in South Africa—Reported Surrender of Botha.

Various reports were current on Thursday [February 28th] that General Louis Botha had formally surrendered to Lord Kitchener at Middleburg, but they remain totally unconfirmed. The War Secretary, replying to a question on the subject in the House of Commons, said no official report of the surrender had come to his Department.

The most accurate summary appeared in the Weekly Irish Times on Saturday 09 March 1901.[48]

SOUTH AFRICA.

PEACE PROSPECTS.

Meeting of Kitchener and Botha.

Armistice Granted for Seven Days.

(REUTER'S TELEGRAMS.)

LOURENCO MARQUEZ, FRIDAY.

News has reached here that Lord Kitchener has granted General Louis Botha a seven days' armistice to enable him to confer with the other Boer generals.

PRETORIA, TUESDAY.

Lord Kitchener met General Botha and other Boer leaders at Middleburg on 27th ult., when the question of the possibility of a termination of hostilities was discussed.

PRETORIA, WEDNESDAY.

The fact of the meeting between Lord Kitchener and General Botha is regarded as of great moment, and favourable expectations are formed concerning the probable outcome.

JOHANNESBURG, WEDNESDAY.

The news that General Botha has had a conference with Lord Kitchener at Middelburg, has been received here with great satisfaction, and a most hopeful feeling prevails in all quarters.

(CENTRAL NEWS TELEGRAM.)

LONDON, FRIDAY.

Ministers regard the meeting between Lord Kitchener and General Botha as of very good augury. Lord Kitchener is acting with a free hand, but is most fully aware of the views of His Majesty's Government, and that the Government most earnestly desires the end of the war on satisfactory terms to England.

Peace Prospects. Meeting Kitchener and Botha. Armistice Granted for Seven Days. (Reuter's telegrams.) Lourenco Marquez, Friday.

New has reached here that Lord Kitchener has granted General Louis Botha seren days' armistice to enable him to confer with the other Boer generals.

PRETORIA, Tuesday.

Lord Kitchener met General Botha and other Boer leaders Middleburg on 27th inst., when the question the possibility of termination of hostilities was discussed.

Pretoria, Wednesday.

The fact of the meeting between Lord Kitchener and General Botha is regarded as of great moment, and favourable expectations are formed concerning the probable outcome.

Johannesburg, Wednesday

The news that General Botha has had a conference with Lord Kitchener Middelburg, has been received here with great satisfaction, and a most hopeful feeling prevails in all quarters.

(Central News Telegram.) London, Friday. Ministers regard the meeting between Lord Kitchener and General Botha as of very good augury. Lord Kitchener is acting with free hand, but is most fully aware the views of His Majesty's Government, and that the Government most earnestly desires the end of the war on satisfactory terms to England.

[300] Annie Botha (née Emmett; 3 July 1864 – 20 May 1937) was a South African civic leader and political hostess. She was the wife of Louis Botha, who served as the first Prime Minister of South Africa. She established an orphanage in South Africa and, with Georgiana Solomon, co-founded and chaired the South African Women's Federation. Annie Botha - Wikipedia

[301] Robert Emmet (4 March 1778 – 20 September 1803) was an Irish Republican, orator and rebel leader. Emmet's Proclamation of the Provisional Government to the People of Ireland, his Speech from the Dock, and his "sacrificial" end on the gallows inspired later generations of Irish republicans. Robert Emmet - Wikipedia

In spite of the express condition laid down by Kitchener draft terms. and implicitly accepted in the letter of the Boer general, Botha began by asking that the Republics should retain some sort of independence. Kitchener having refused to discuss the point, a conference began upon the details of a possible settlement. At the end of the discussion, which was conducted in a very friendly and reasonable spirit, Botha took his departure, and the terms of a proposed settlement were thrown into the shape of a draft letter from the British to the Boer general. This letter was submitted to Milner, who met Kitchener at Bloemfontein, and was sent by him for approval to the Home Government.

The terms subsequently published in England for general readership.

THE BOER WAR.

THE RECENT PEACE NEGOTIATIONS.

THE TERMS REJECTED.

The official papers relating to the recent negotiations between Lord Kitchener and General Botha were issued this (Friday) morning. After detailing the events leading up to the interview, the following terms are specified by Lord Kitchener:—That, in the event of a general and complete cessation of hostilities and the surrender of all rifles, ammunition, cannon, and other munitions of war in the hands of burghers or in Government depots or elsewhere, His Majesty's Government is prepared to adopt the following measures:—His Majesty's Government will at once grant an amnesty in the Transvaal and Orange River Colonies for all bona-fide acts of war committed during the recent hostilities. British subjects belonging to Natal and Cape Colony, while they will not be compelled to return to those colonies, will, if they do so, be liable to be dealt with by the law of those colonies, specially passed to meet the circumstances arising out of the present war. As you are doubtless aware, the special law in the Cape Colony has greatly mitigated the ordinary penalties for high treason in the present cases.

All prisoners of war now in St. Helena, Ceylon, or elsewhere, will, on the completion of the surrender, be brought back to their country as quickly as arrangements can be made for their transport.

At the earliest practicable date military administration will cease and will be replaced by civil administration in the form of Crown colony government. There will, therefore, be in the first instance in each of the new colonies a Governor and an executive council, consisting of a certain number of official members to whom a nominated unofficial element will be added. But it is the desire of His Majesty's Government as soon as circumstances permit to introduce a representative element, and ultimately to concede to the new colonies the privilege of self-government. Moreover, on the cessation of hostilities a high court will be established in each of the new colonies to administer the law of the land, and this court will be independent of the executive.

Church property, public trusts, and orphans' funds will be respected.

Both the Dutch and English language will be used and taught in the public schools where parents of the children desire it, and allowed in courts of law.

As regards the debts of the late Republican Governments, His Majesty's Government cannot undertake any liability. It is, however, prepared as an act of grace to set aside a sum not exceeding £1,000,000 to repay the inhabitants of the Transvaal and Orange River Colonies for goods requisitioned from them by the late Republican Government or subsequent to annexation by commandants in the field being in a position to enforce such requisitions. But such claims will have to be established to the satisfaction of a judge or Judicial Commission, appointed by the Government, to investigate and assess them, and, if exceeding in the aggregate £1,000,000, they will be liable to reduction pro rata. I also beg to inform your honour that the new Government will take into immediate consideration the possibility of assisting by loan the occupants of farms, who will take the oath of allegiance to repair any injury sustained by destruction of buildings or loss of stock during the war, and that no special war tax will be imposed on farmers to defray the expense of the war.

As regards the extension of the franchise to Kaffirs in the Transvaal and Orange River Colony, it is not the intention of His Majesty's Government to give such franchise before representative government is granted to those colonies, and, if then given, it will be so limited as to secure the just predominance of the white races. The legal position of the coloured person will, however, be that which they hold in Cape Colony. In conclusion, I must inform your honour that if the terms now offered are not accepted, after a reasonable delay for consideration, they must be regarded as cancelled.

The terms were published in England on March 23rd.[49]

Previously the Government made changes to Kitchener's proposed language and this was sent to Botha on the 7th. (March) In its final form it ran as follows :-

THE BOER WAR.

THE RECENT PEACE NEGOTIATIONS.

THE TERMS REJECTED.

The terms were published in England on March 23rd.[50] Previously the Government made changes to Kitchener's proposed language and this was sent to Botha on the 7th. (March) In its final form it ran as follows:—

To his Honour Commandant-General Louis Botha. Pretoria, March 7, 1901.[302]

Your Honour,

With reference to our conversation at Middelburg on the 28th February, I have the honour to inform you that, in the event of a general and complete cessation of hostilities, and the surrender of all rifles, ammunition, cannon, and other munitions of war in the hands of the burghers, or in Government depots, or elsewhere, His Majesty's Government is prepared to adopt the following measures. His Majesty's Government will at once grant an amnesty in the Transvaal and Orange River Colony for all bona fide acts of war committed during the recent hostilities. British subjects belonging to Natal and Cape Colony, while they will not be compelled to return to those Colonies, will, if they do so, be liable to be dealt with by the laws of those Colonies specially passed to meet the circumstances arising out of the present war. As you are doubtless aware the special law in the Cape Colony has greatly mitigated the ordinary penalties for High Treason in the present case. All prisoners of war, now in St. Helena, Ceylon, or elsewhere, being burghers or Colonists, will, on the completion of the surrender, be brought back to their country as quickly as arrangements can be made for their transport.

At the earliest practicable date military administration will cease, and will be replaced by civil administration in the form of Crown Colony Government.

There will, therefore, be, in the first instance, in each of the new Colonies, a Governor and an Executive Council, composed of the principal officials, with a Legislative Council consisting of a certain number of official members to whom nominated unofficial element will be added.

But it is the desire of His Majesty's Government, as soon as circumstances permit, to introduce a representative element, and ultimately to concede to the new Colonies the privilege of self-government. Moreover, on the cessation of hostilities a High Court will be established in each of the new Colonies to administer the laws of the land, and this Court will be independent of the Executive.

Church property, public trusts, and orphan funds will be respected. Both the English and Dutch languages will be used and taught in public schools when the parents of the children desire it, and allowed in Courts of Law.

As regards the debts of the late Republican Governments, His Majesty's Government cannot undertake any liability. It is, however, prepared, as an act of grace, to set aside a sum not exceeding one million pounds sterling to repay inhabitants of the Transvaal and Orange River Colony for goods requisitioned from them by the late Republican Governments, or subsequent to annexation, by Commandants in the field being in a position to enforce such requisitions.

But such claims Will have to be established to the satisfaction of a Judge or Judicial Commission, appointed by the Government, to investigate and assess them, and, if exceeding in the aggregate one million pounds, they will be liable to reduction pro rata.

I also beg to inform your Honour that the new Government will take into immediate consideration the possibility of assisting by loan the occupants of farms, who will take the oath of allegiance, to repair any injuries sustained by destruction of buildings or loss of stock during the war, and that no special war tax will be imposed upon farms to defray the expense of the war.

[302] Part of appendix B from Three Years' War By: Christiaan Rudolf De Wet. Charles Scribner's Sons, (1902)

When burghers require the protection of fire-arms, such will be allowed to them by licence, and on due registration, provided they take the oath of allegiance. Licences will also be issued for sporting rifles, guns, &c., but military fire-arms will only be allowed for purposes of protection.

As regards the extension of the franchise to Kaffirs in the Transvaal and Orange River Colony, it is not the intention of His Majesty's Government to give such franchise before representative Government is granted to those Colonies, and if then given it will be so limited as to secure the just predominance of the white race. The legal position of coloured persons will, however, be similar to that which they hold in the Cape Colony.

In conclusion, I must inform your Honour that, if the terms now offered are not accepted after a reasonable delay for consideration they must be regarded as cancelled.

I have, &c.,

Kitchener, General,

Commander-in-Chief, British Forces, South Africa.

But in the meantime the prospects of peace had been declining. French, hampered by rain and scarcity, had for some time been at a complete standstill on the Swazi frontier, and the burghers behind him had had time to recover their spirits. Botha had consulted his Government and found it stubborn; he had corresponded with De la Rey and had met with no encouragement. Before the time came to reply, it was known that de Wet and Steyn had escaped capture, and their opinion of the negotiations scarcely needed asking.[303] Nor would they have held themselves bound by any decision of the Transvaal.

In a letter dated March 16 Botha, without Botha giving any reasons, declined to go any further with the negotiations.

Botha's Reply. These terms were refused by Botha and reported on March 23rd, in the following message:[51]

I have the honour to acknowledge the receipt of your Excelleney's letter stating what steps your Excellency's Government is prepared to take in the event of a general and total cessation of hostilities. I have advised my Government of your Excellency's said letter, and, after. mutual exchanges of views at Middleburg on the 28th February, it will certainly not surprise your Excellence to know that I do not feel disposed to recommend that the terms of the said letter shall have the earnest consideration of my Government. I may add also that my Government and my chief officers here entirely agree to my views.

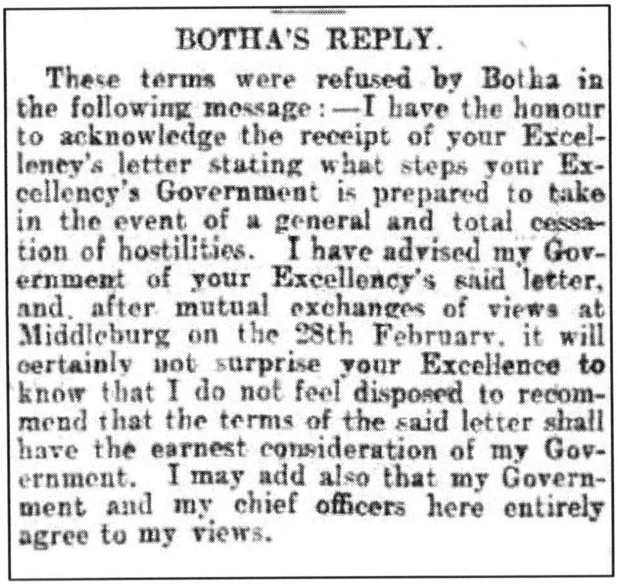

BOTHA'S REPLY.

These terms were refused by Botha in the following message:—I have the honour to acknowledge the receipt of your Excelleney's letter stating what steps your Excellency's Government is prepared to take in the event of a general and total cessation of hostilities. I have advised my Government of your Excellency's said letter, and, after mutual exchanges of views at Middleburg on the 28th February, it will certainly not surprise your Excellence to know that I do not feel disposed to recommend that the terms of the said letter shall have the earnest consideration of my Government. I may add also that my Government and my chief officers here entirely agree to my views.

[303] Original footnote: * Botha. wrote to de Wet and Steyn, asking them to come north and confer with him, but the letter arrived too late and the meeting did not take place till April. De Wet's secretary, however, went by train to Pretoria, only to find that negotiations had been broken off. He could have been of no use, for his master's temper, as shown by a circular to his burghers, was as unbending as ever. In this circular, which is dated April 1, he inveighs against various points in the proposed settlement, and asks finally, what is the use of examining it in detail, since nothing short of independence will induce the Boers to make peace.

Kitchener was always inclined to feel that with a little a little stronger support, especially on the question of amnesty, he might have obtained peace. However long the war lasted, it must, he held, eventually end in some such settlement as this. There was much truth in that; but the time had not yet come. His overtures were a bold but premature experiment. The Boer spirit-that new spirit born amidst the disasters of the previous year and matured in an offensive revival still quite recent, was far from being broken.

Although exhaustion and despondency existed in some quarters, when it was put to the Boers in black and white that their cause was lost irretrievably and that it only remained to settle subordinate issues, the national will revolted. The conditions which favoured this revolt are conditions which it can never be easy for a highly civilised industrial nation fully to understand.

The causes which bring such a nation to its knees were absent here. There were no vital industries to dislocate, no teeming population of peaceful workers to plunge into starvation. The people lived on the land, and though its fruits could be destroyed and the farms upon it gutted, the land could not be damaged. A year's crops were a relatively small matter, farm-buildings were of little value, and when a farm was once gutted it signified little whether it was rebuilt a year sooner or later.

Meanwhile, the male population, in other words the army, was inured by habit and inherited instinct to a life of peril and adventure under the stars. These men, moreover, were scattered over a vast expanse of territory under circumstances so varied as to render a common judgment unattainable. A few were suffering acutely; some were fighting with fair success; some were living in perfect safety and comfort. In short, there had never come to the Boers one of those moments of national agony which wring from a people a cry for peace.

As events fell out, Botha had effected a very useful reconnaissance in two directions. He had tested the sentiment of his burghers, made them familiar-and that was something-with the idea of negotiation; and he had found out on what lines an ultimate settlement was to be framed. ………………………………..

Commander-in-Chief by right of undoubted military merit, he nevertheless had not risen without effort. A keen ambitious purpose had helped him to gain the high position which he occupied. To crown its tenure by signing away independence as long as there remained the faintest hope of carrying his career to a triumphant military climax, was a hard step to take.

He knew very well that it was impossible to recover the lost territories with the forces at his disposal, but there always remained the chance of a general rising in Cape Colony. The chimera of foreign intervention still survived, as did the dim hope that pro-Boer sentiment in Great Britain would grow and triumph.

Meanwhile he could salve his conscience with the knowledge that the British policy of concentration camps freed him from responsibility for the women and children, whose misery was the most cogent argument for submission. There was little to lose; there was much to gain. For Botha had the shrewd perception that, whatever the ultimate issue, the Boers could fare no worse than they would fare under the proposed settlement.

His mental attitude is revealed clearly in a letter addressed to his burghers on March 15.

"Virtually, "he writes, "Lord Kitchener's letter contains nothing more, but rather less than what the British Government will be obliged to do should our cause go wrong." ……………..

"The cause is not yet lost," he writes, "and since nothing worse than this can befall us, it is well worth while to fight on." …………………..

Such were the abortive negotiations of 1901. Their failure caused much disappointment in England.

On public platforms and in Parliament the Government was bitterly attacked by a section of the Opposition for having thrown away the chances of peace by attempting to exact too much, and the differences of opinion, frankly set forth in the despatches, between Mr. Chamberlain, Lord Milner and Lord Kitchener, were used to further the argument. …………………

The nation at large instinctively grasped the truth, and resigned itself with unflinching determination to a further struggle of indefinite length and severity.

Philip Botha

General Botha's brother, Philip,[304] was killed in action and his two nephews wounded on March 6th.[52] while the negotiations at Middleburg were proceeding. It was reported: "From Lord Kitchener to Secretary of State for War. Pretoria, Wednesday, 4.30 p.m.—General P. Botha, brother of the Commandant-General, was killed on the Doornberg. His two sons were wounded."

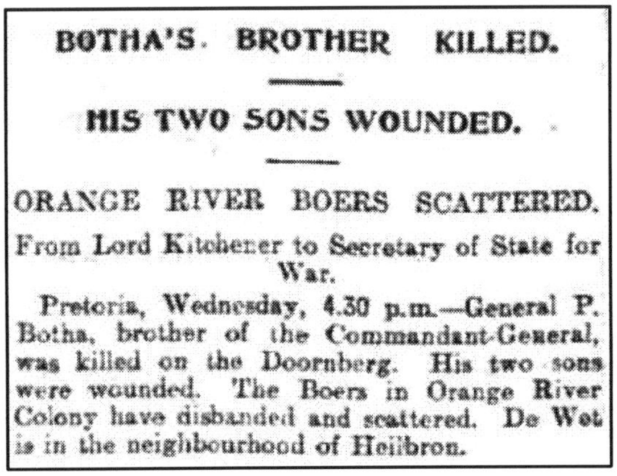

BOTHA'S BROTHER KILLED.

HIS TWO SONS WOUNDED.

ORANGE RIVER BOERS SCATTERED.

From Lord Kitchener to Secretary of State for War.

Pretoria, Wednesday, 4.30 p.m.—General P. Botha, brother of the Commandant-General, was killed on the Doornberg. His two sons were wounded. The Boers in Orange River Colony have disbanded and scattered. De Wet is in the neighbourhood of Heilbron.

Philip Rudolph Botha.[53]

Treaty of Vereeniging Terms

On May 31st this resolution was notified to Lord Kitchener, and at half-past ten of the same night the delegates arrived at Pretoria and set their names to the treaty of peace. ....

The following were in brief the terms of surrender:—

1. That the burghers lay down their arms and acknowledge themselves subjects of Edward VII.
2. That all prisoners taking the oath of allegiance be returned.
3. That their liberty and property be inviolate.
4. That an amnesty be granted—save in special cases.
5. That the Dutch language be allowed in schools and law-courts.
6. That rifles be allowed if registered.
7. That self-government be granted as soon as possible.
8. That no franchise be granted for natives until after self-government.
9. That no special land tax be levied.
10. That the people be helped to reoccupy the farms.
11. That 3,000,000 pounds be given to help the farmers.
12. That the rebels be disfranchised and their leaders tried, on condition that no death penalty be inflicted.

These terms were practically the same as those which had been refused by Botha in March 1901. [At the Middleburg Conference] Thirteen months of useless warfare had left the situation as it was."

Quote from The Great Boer War by Arthur Conan Doyle.[305] [306]

[304] Botha Philip Rudolf, was born in 1851. While in command of the Harrismith burghers, he made a breakthrough at Sprinkaan's Nek. He was killed in action while attacking the British position near Ventersburg on March 6th, 1901. See Also: Philip Botha - Wikipedia

[305] Doyle, Arthur Conan. The Great Boer War 17th Edition, 1902 with the two volumes as one document: The Great Boer War by Arthur Conan Doyle - Free Ebook (gutenberg.org) Chapter 39. Pages 232–234 of the Word document.

[306] General Article: Treaty of Vereeniging - Wikipedia

Final Peace Negotiations

Handbook of the Boer War

From A Handbook of the Boer War.[307]

Nearly two years had passed by since the negotiations for peace between Lord Roberts and L. Botha and between Sir Redvers Buller and C. Botha had fallen through shortly before the battle of Diamond Hill. In February, [and March of] 1901, another conference for peace was held at Middelburg in the Transvaal between Lord Kitchener and L. Botha, who after parleying for a fortnight, abruptly broke off the negotiations. ....

In January, 1902, an offer made by the Government of the Netherlands to mediate between the combatants was declined by the British Government. The incident of the offer was, however, communicated to the Transvaal Government, which was then lying north of Balmoral, and which asked for and received permission to discuss proposals for peace with the Free State Government at Kroonstad. Schalk Burger, the Acting President of the Transvaal, arrived at Kroonstad on March 22. Steyn, who was with Delarey, was sent for; De Wet was searched for, and for the first time found; and the allied Governments, the chief members of which were, on the one side, Schalk Burger and Delarey, and on the other De Wet and Steyn, met in conference on April 9 at Klerksdorp, which was, at Steyn's suggestion, chosen as a more convenient place of meeting than Kroonstad.

It was soon decided to open negotiations with Lord Kitchener, at whose invitation the Governments proceeded to Pretoria, where they met him and Lord Milner. The Boer proposals, which postulated the continued independent existence of the two shattered Republics, were rejected; it seemed that the war must be fought to a still bitterer end. Finally, it was agreed that the negotiations should be adjourned for a month, in order to allow the feelings of the burghers at large to be ascertained, and reported at a Convention to be held at Vereeniging on May 15. In the meantime the military operations were to be continued, subject to the permission to be given to the Boer leaders to go freely among and consult their people.[308]

When the Convention assembled it was found that while the Transvaal was generally in favour of submission, the Orange River Colony was still implacable. A compromise was effected between them, and the heads of a treaty, of which the chief clause ensured a qualified independence to the late Republics, under the guise of British Protectorates, were drawn up by J.C. Smuts, who had come from Ookiep to resume his former profession and to act as legal adviser to his colleagues. It was submitted to Lord Kitchener at Pretoria, who, as the delegates might have foreseen, refused to consider it and handed to their counsel Smuts a document, in which the Boer leaders were required, on their own behalf as well as on their followers' behalf, to acknowledge themselves as British subjects.

The negotiations at Pretoria were conducted by a deputation from the Vereeniging Convention: Delarey, Botha, Smuts, De Wet, and Hertzog. These did their best, and even obtained some verbal changes of phraseology which made Lord Kitchener's terms less unpalatable. The question of British nationality was waived for the moment to allow of the other stipulations of the document being discussed; and the general subject was referred to a minor convention consisting of Lord Milner and his legal adviser on one side, and of Smuts and Hertzog on the other.

A proposal for a final settlement was drawn up, which, with certain alterations insisted on by the Colonial Office, was presented by Lord Kitchener as his ultimatum, to be accepted within three days by the Vereeniging Convention. Botha and his colleagues returned to Vereeniging and laid it before the delegates. Steyn refused to entertain it and immediately resigned his titular office of President of the Orange Free State; De Wet, implacable almost to the last, protested against its terms. The hopelessness of the Boer cause in South Africa was, however, manifest. Even De Wet yielded, and voted with the majority in favour of accepting the British terms of peace.

On May 31, 1902, the Treaty of Vereeniging brought to an end the War of 960 days.

[307] A Handbook of the Boer War With General Map of South Africa and 18 Sketch Maps and Plans Gale And Polden Limited London 1910 A Handbook of the Boer War - Free Ebook (gutenberg.org)

[308] The delegates left Pretoria on April 18th. Times History p. 567.

Conan Doyle Discussion

Quote from The Great Boer War by Arthur Conan Doyle.

Chapter 39. The End.[309]

It only remains in one short chapter to narrate the progress of the peace negotiations, the ultimate settlement, and the final consequences of this long-drawn war. ……… it was announced upon March 22nd [1902] that the acting Government of the Transvaal, consisting of Messrs. Schalk Burger, Lucas Meyer, Reitz, Jacoby, Krogh, and Van Velden had come into Middelburg and requested to be forwarded by train to Pretoria for the purpose of discussing terms of peace with Lord Kitchener. ……

On March 23rd the Transvaal representatives were despatched to Kroonstad for the purpose of opening up the matter with Steyn and De Wet. Messengers were sent to communicate with these two leaders ….at the end of the month the message was conveyed, and resulted in the appearance of De Wet, De la Rey, and Steyn at the British outposts at Klerksdorp.

General Christiaan de Wet [Far Right] on his way to peace talks at Vereeniging, in April of 1902.[310] Christiaan de Wet, photographed at the end of the Second Boer War in Bloemfontein on June 6th 1902.[311]

On April 11th, after repeated conferences, both parties moved on to Pretoria,……After conferring with Lord Kitchener the Boer leaders upon April 18th left Pretoria again and rode out to the commandos to explain the situation to them. The result of this mission was that two delegates were chosen from each body in the field, who assembled at Vereeniging upon May 15th for the purpose of settling the question by vote. Never was a high matter of state decided in so democratic a fashion.

Up to that period the Boer leaders had made a succession of tentative suggestions, each of which had been put aside by the British Government. Their first had been that they should merely concede those points which had been at issue at the beginning of the war. This was set aside. The second was that they should be allowed to consult their friends in Europe. This also was refused. The next was that an armistice should be granted, but again Lord Kitchener was obdurate. A definite period was suggested within which the burghers should make their final choice between surrender and a war which must finally exterminate them as a people.

It was tacitly understood, if not definitely promised, that the conditions which the British Government would be prepared to grant would not differ much in essentials from those which had been refused by the Boers a twelvemonth before, after the Middelburg interview.

On May 15th the Boer conference opened at Vereeniging. Sixty-four delegates from the commandos met with the military and political chiefs of the late republics, the whole amounting to 150 persons.

A more singular gathering has not met in our time. There was Botha, the young lawyer, who had found himself by a strange turn of fate commanding a victorious army in a great war.

309 Doyle, Arthur Conan. The Great Boer War 17th Edition, 1902 with the two volumes is available as one document from Project Gutenberg: The Great Boer War by Arthur Conan Doyle - Free Ebook (gutenberg.org) Pages 232-234 of the Word document.

310 Description: Boer general Christiaan de Wet on his way to peace talks at Vereeniging. 13 April 1920, Source Scan of a publicly available post card from 1920. Author Unknown. File:De Wet by Ferreirastasie oppad na Vereeniging.jpg - Wikimedia Commons

311 Boer general Christiaan de Wet, photographed at the end of the Second Boer War in Bloemfontein on 6.6.1902, before embarking for Europe. Source: S. King File:Generaal Christiaan de Wet - Bloemfontein 6.6.1902.jpg - Wikimedia Commons

De Wet was there, with his grim mouth and sun-browned face; De la Rey, also, with the grizzled beard and the strong aquiline features. There, too, were the politicians, the grey-bearded, genial Reitz, a little graver than when he looked upon 'the whole matter as an immense joke,' and the unfortunate Steyn, stumbling and groping, a broken and ruined man. The burly Lucas Meyer, smart young Smuts fresh from the siege of Ookiep, Beyers from the north, Kemp the dashing cavalry leader, Muller the hero of many fights—all these with many others of their sun-blackened, gaunt, hard-featured comrades were grouped within the great tent of Vereeniging. ....The [Final] vote showed that the great majority of the delegates were in favour of surrender upon the terms offered by the British Government.

On May 31st this resolution was notified to Lord Kitchener, and at half-past ten of the same night the delegates arrived at Pretoria and set their names to the treaty of peace. ....

The following were in brief the terms of surrender:—

1. That the burghers lay down their arms and acknowledge themselves subjects of Edward VII.
2. That all prisoners taking the oath of allegiance be returned.
3. That their liberty and property be inviolate.
4. That an amnesty be granted—save in special cases.
5. That the Dutch language be allowed in schools and law-courts.
6. That rifles be allowed if registered.
7. That self-government be granted as soon as possible.
8. That no franchise be granted for natives until after self-government.
9. That no special land tax be levied.
10. That the people be helped to reoccupy the farms.
11. That 3,000,000 pounds be given to help the farmers.
12. That the rebels be disfranchised and their leaders tried, on condition that no death penalty be inflicted.

These terms were practically the same as those which had been refused by Botha in March 1901. [At the Middleburg Conference] Thirteen months of useless warfare had left the situation as it was.

Times History Discussion

Quote from The Times' History of the War. [312]

From the 12th of May onwards the tension of war relaxed.

From far and wide the delegates elected by the commandos travelled to the meeting-place. Though the rules governing the armistice did not, of course, apply to Cape Colony, General Smuts, interrupted in the middle of the siege of Ookiep, was transported by sea from Port Nolloth to Cape Town and thence sent to Vereeniging. Nine hundred miles from Ookiep, Beyers left his ragged bands in the Waterberg to travel to the same destination. Chris Botha came from the Swazi Border, Van Heerden from the Zwartruggens, Meuwhoudt and Brand from the banks of the Orange, Wessels from the rushing rivers and wild ravines of the Drakensberg. From north, south, east and west of the vast theatre of war they came to decide their nation's destiny.

On the 15th of May, 1902, a cold, misty morning, the sixty delegates and the members of the two Governments came together at Vereeniging. Two camps, one for each

In the appointment of the sub-committee the military element was eliminated, and the negotiations were left in the hands of Smuts and Hertzog, the legal advisers of the two Republics, and, on the British side, to Lord Milner and his legal adviser, Sir Richard Solomon.

Even so, agreement was only secured by the suggestion that the acceptance of the British terms should be accompanied by a formal statement which made clear that the acceptance was under protest and due to the hopelessness of continuing the struggle. The statement was drawn up by Hertzog and Smuts, and was moved as a substantive proposal at the afternoon session by Commandant H. P. Pretorius and seconded by General C. [Christian] Botha. [313]

[312] Times History Vol 5 Re: Peace Chapter p. 564–606 Attendees: Page 583.

[313] Christiaan Botha, 6 October 1864–29 October 1902) was a younger brother of Louis Botha and likewise a Boer general in the Second Boer War who fought the British to the end. Chris Botha - Wikipedia

Three Years' Appendices

This material is reproduced from the Appendices included in Christiaan Rudolf De Wet's work, Three Year's War.[314] The Ultimatum correspondence was included supra.

In particular, I have been looking for the material in General de Wet's Appendices regarding the Middleburg Conference in 1901, supra; and the deliberations during the final negotiations concluding the Peace Treaty of Vereeniging. I am grateful that he published a record of these important negotiations.

A.—Report of the Meeting of the General Representatives held at Vereeniging in the South African Republic on the 15th of May, 1902, and the Following Days

B.—The Conference at Pretoria between the Commission of the National Representatives and Lords Kitchener and Milner (May 19th-May 28th, 1902)

C.—Minutes of the Meeting of the Special National Representatives at Vereeniging, South African Republic, Thursday, the 29th of May, 1902, And the Following Days

Intro-Times History Discussion

From the 12th of May [1902] onwards the tension of war relaxed. From far and wide the delegates elected by the commandos travelled to the meeting-place.

Though the rules governing the armistice did not, of course, apply to Cape Colony, General Smuts, ...was transported by sea from Port Nolloth to Cape Town and thence sent to Vereeniging. Nine hundred miles from Ookiep, Beyers left his ragged bands in the Waterberg to travel to the same destination. Chris Botha came from the Swazi Border, Van Heerden from the Zwartruggens, Meuwhoudt and Brand from the banks of the Orange, Wessels from the rushing rivers and wild ravines of the Drakensberg. From north, south, east and west of the vast theatre of war they came to decide their nation's destiny.

On the 15th of May, 1902, a cold, misty morning, the sixty delegates and the members of the two Governments came together at Vereeniging. Two camps, one for each [Republic].

In the appointment of the sub-committee the military element was eliminated, and the negotiations were left in the hands of Smuts and Hertzog, the legal advisers of the two Republics, and, on the British side, to Lord Milner and his legal adviser, Sir Richard Solomon.[315]

Even so, agreement was only secured by the suggestion that the acceptance of the British terms should be accompanied by a formal statement which made clear that the acceptance was under protest and due to the hopelessness of continuing the struggle.

The statement was drawn up by Hertzog and Smuts, and was moved as a substantive proposal at the afternoon session by Commandant H. P. Pretorius and seconded by General C. [Christian] Botha.[316] [317]

[314] Three Years' War By: Christiaan Rudolf De Wet. Charles Scribner's Sons, (1902) Trow Directory Printing And Bookbinding Company New York. Harvard Copy: https://archive.org/details/threeyearswar00wetgoog/mode/2up

[315] The Times' History of the War in South Africa 1899-1902 by Amery, L. S. (Leopold Stennett), Volume 5 p. 592.

[316] Christiaan Botha, 6 October 1864–29 October 1902) was a younger brother of Louis Botha and likewise a Boer general in the Second Boer War who fought the British to the end. Chris Botha - Wikipedia

[317] The Times' History of the War in South Africa 1899-1902 by Amery, L. S. (Leopold Stennett), Volume 5 pages 604–606.

Meeting on 15th of May, 1902,

Appendix A

Report of the Meeting of the General Representatives Held at Vereeniging, in the South African Republic, on the 15th of May, 1902, and the Following Days

The first meeting of the representatives of the two Governments took place at 11.30 a.m. on May 15th.

There were present:—

For the South African Republic—His Honour the President, S.W. Burger, F.W. Reitz, Commandant-General L. Botha, Messrs. J.B. Krogh, L.J. Meijer, L.J. Jacobs, and His Honour the Staats-Procureur.

For the Orange Free State—States-President, M.J. Steyn; Judge, J.B.M. Hertzog; Secretary of State, W.J.C. Brebner; Commander-in-Chief, C.R. de Wet; and Mr. C.H. Olivier.

The first matter discussed was the formula for the oath which the delegates were to take, and it was decided that it should run as follows:—

"We, the undersigned, duly swear that we, as special national representatives, will remain true to our people, country, and Government, and that we will serve them to the best of our ability, and fulfil our duties faithfully and with all necessary secrecy, as is the duty of all faithful burghers and representatives of the nation. So help us God."

The question now arose as to whether the representatives had the right to decide, if circumstances rendered it necessary, upon any matter touching the independence of the country, irrespective of the powers given to the various delegates, for at some of the meetings the delegates had only received limited powers, whilst at others full authority had been given them to act according to their own judgment.

After considerable discussion it was decided to lay the matter before the delegates themselves.

The following representatives were called into the tent, and took the oath:—

For the South African Republic.

1. H.A. Alberts, Vechtgeneraal; for Heidelberg.
2. J.J. Alberts, Commandant; for Standerton and Wakkerstroom.
3. J.F. De Beer, Commandant; for Bloemhof.
4. C.F. Beijers, Assistant-Commandant-General; for Waterberg.
5. C. Birkenstock, burgher; for Vrijheid.
6. H.J. Bosman, magistrate; for Wakkerstroom.
7. Christiaan Botha, Assistant-Commandant-General; for Swaziland and the States Artillery.
8. B.H. Breijtenbach, Veldtcornet; for Utrecht.
9. C.J. Brits, Vechtgeneraal; for Standerton.
10. J.B. Cilluos, Vechtgeneraal; for Lichtenburg.
11. J. De Clercq, burgher; for Middelburg.
12. T.A. Dönges, Veldtcornet; for Dorp Middelburg in Regeeringswacht.
13. H.S. Grobler, Commandant; for Bethal.
14. J.L. Grobler, burgher; for Carolina.
15. J.N.H. Grobler, Vechtgeneraal; for Ermelo.
16. B.J. Van Heerden, Veldtcornet; for Rustenburg.
17. J.F. Jordaan, Commandant; for Vrijheid.
18. J. Kemp, Vechtgeneraal; for Krugersdorp.
19. P.J. Liebenberg, Vechtgeneraal; for Potchefstroom.
20. C.H. Muller, Vechtgeneraal; for Boksburg.
21. J.F. Naude, burgher; for Pretoria, late Commandant with General Kemp.
22. D.J.E. Opperman, Veldtcornet; for Pretoria.
23. B.J. Roos, Veldtcornet; for Piet Retief.
24. P.D. Roux, Veldtcornet; for Marico.
25. D.J. Schoeman, Commandant; for Lijdenburg.

26. T.C. Stoffberg, Landdrost; for Zoutpansberg.
27. S.P. Du Toit, Vechtgeneraal; for Wolmaransstad.
28. P.L. Uijs, Commandant; for Pretoria.
29. P.R. Viljoen, burgher; for Heidelberg.
30. W.J. Viljoen, Commandant; for Witwatersrand.

For the Orange Free State.

1. C.C.F. Badenhorst, Vice-Commandant-in-Chief; for Boshof, Hoopstad, West Bloemfontein, Winburg, and Kroonstad.
2. A.J. Bester, Commandant; for Bethlehem.
3. A.J. Bester, Commandant; for Bloemfontein.
4. L.P.H. Botha, Commandant; for Harrismith.
5. G.A. Brand, Vice-Commandant-in-Chief; for Bethulie, Rouxville, Caledon River, and Wepener in the eastern part of Bloemfontein.
6. H.J. Brouwer, Commandant; for Bethlehem.
7. D.H. Van Coller, Commandant; for Heilbron.
8. F.R. Cronje, Commandant; for Winburg.
9. D.F.H. Flemming, Commandant; for Hoopstad.
10. C.C. Froneman, Vice-Commandant-in-Chief; for Winburg and Ladybrand.
11. F.J.W.J. Hattingh, Vice-Commandant-in-Chief; for the eastern part of Kroonstad, in the district of Heilbron.
12. J.B.M. Hertzog, Commandant; for Philippolis.
13. J.N. Jacobs, Commandant; for Boshof.
14. F.P. Jacobsz, Commandant; for Harrismith.
15. A.J. De Kock, Commandant; for Vrede.
16. J.J. Koen, Commandant; for Ladybrand.
17. H.J. Kritzinger, Veldtcornet; for Kroonstad.
18. F.E. Mentz, Commandant; for Heilbron.
19. J.A.P. Van der Merwe, Commandant; for Heilbron.
20. C.A. Van Niekerk, Commandant; for Kroonstad.
21. H. Van Niekerk, Commandant.
22. J.J. Van Niekerk, Commandant; for Ficksburg.
23. I.K. Nieuwouwdt, Vice-Commandant-in-Chief; for Fauresmith, Philippolis, and Jacobsdal.
24. H.P.J. Pretorius, Commandant; for Jacobsdal.
25. A.M. Prinsloo, Vice-Commandant-in-Chief; for Bethlehem in Ficksburg.
26. L.J. Rautenbach, Commandant; for Bethlehem.
27. F.J. Rheeder, Commandant; for Rouxville.
28. A. Ross, Commandant; for Vrede.
29. P.W. De Vos, Commandant; for Kroonstad.
30. W.J. Wessels, Vice-Commandant-in-Chief; for Harrismith and Vrede.

The meeting now proceeded to choose a chairman, and the following were proposed:—J. De Clercq, C.F. Beijers, C.C. Froneman, W.J. Wessels, and G.A. Brand.

The choice of the meeting fell on General C.F. Beijers, who called upon the Rev. Mr. Kestell to offer prayer.

His Honour, S.W. Burger, now declared that the meeting was formally opened, and after the Chairman had spoken a few words, the representatives adjourned until three o'clock.

When they reassembled, the Chairman requested President Burger to explain the objects for which the meeting had been called.

Then the President spoke a few words of welcome to all; he expressed his sorrow for the absence of some who would certainly have been present had they not given their lives for their country. But still there were many left to represent the two Republics.

"The difficulties which confront us," continued the President, "are like a great mountain, at the foot of which we have just arrived. Everything now depends on us who are assembled together here. It is impossible to deny that the state of affairs is very serious, and that the future looms dark before us. Our position requires the most careful consideration, and as there are sure to be differences of opinion, it will be necessary for us to bear with one another, and yet, at the same time, to speak our minds freely."

The President proceeded to refer to the correspondence which had taken place between Holland and England. A copy of this correspondence had been sent, through Lord Kitchener, to the Governments of the two Republics. The opinion of the Transvaal Government (which was the first to receive the correspondence) was that advantage should be taken of this opportunity. It was proposed to ask Lord Kitchener to allow the Transvaal Government to meet that of the Orange Free State, so that they might discuss the desirability of making a peace proposal to England. The two Governments had accordingly met, and had corresponded with Lord Kitchener and Lord Milner. As a result of this, a letter, with the above correspondence annexed, had been sent to the various commandos.

"We felt," continued President Burger, "that we had no power to surrender our independence, and that we were only justified in making such terms of peace as would not endanger our national existence. Whether it is or is not our duty to surrender our independence is a question that must be left to the decision of our people. And it is to represent the people that you are here. It is from your lips, then, that our Governments must learn the opinions of the two nations. It is clear enough that the English Government has no idea of allowing us to remain independent—it expresses surprise that we even dare to speak of such a thing.

"You have now to report upon the condition of the country, and upon the circumstances in which your wives and children are placed. You have also to decide whether you are willing to make any further sacrifices. We have lost so much already that it would be hard, indeed, to lose our independence as well. But, although this matter is so near to our hearts, we must still listen to the voice of reason. The practical question, then, which we have to ask ourselves is, whether we are prepared to watch our people being gradually exterminated before our eyes, or whether we should not rather seek a remedy.

"The Government can do nothing without the support of the nation. You, therefore, must determine our best course. For instance, if you come to the conclusion that we have exhausted every expedient, will you still continue the struggle? Are we not to desist until every man of us is in captivity, in exile, or in his grave? Again let me urge you to speak freely, and yet with consideration for the feelings of others. For myself, I can truly say that my spirit is not yet broken; but I would hear from you what the feeling of the people is."

"At this point, however, a difficulty arises. Some of you, having only received limited powers from your constituencies, appear to think that you would not be justified in exceeding your mandates, while others have been authorized to act as circumstances may seem to require. But I do not think that this difficulty should be insurmountable. At least I beg of you not to allow it to cause any dissension among you. Let us all be of one mind. If we are united, then will the nation be united also; but if we are divided, in what a plight will the nation find itself?"

A letter was then read from the deputation in Europe, which had been written five months previously, and which had been brought through the English lines in safety. It contained little more than an assurance that our cause occupied a better position in Europe than it had ever done before.

The Chairman then asked Commandant L. Botha to address the meeting.

Complying with this request, the Commandant said that he wished to be assured, before anything further was done, that the fact that some of the representatives had been entrusted with limited powers, whereas others had been given a free hand, was not going to prove to be an insurmountable obstacle to united action on their part.

To this Judge Hertzog replied that it was a principle in law that a delegate is not to be regarded as a mere agent or mouthpiece of his constituents, but, on the contrary (when dealing with public affairs), as a plenipotentiary—with the right, whatever his brief might be, of acting to the best of his judgment.

States-Procureur Smuts concurred in this opinion, which appeared to satisfy both the Commandant-General and also all the other representatives, for no further allusion was made to the subject by anybody.

Commandant-General Botha now made his report.

In the districts of Vrijheid and Utrecht, he stated, the store of maize was so small that it could not last for more than a short time; but there was still a great number of slaughter-cattle. In the districts of Wakkerstroom there was hardly sufficient grain for one month's consumption. Two other districts had still a large enough number of slaughter-cattle—enough, in fact, to last for two or three months. In Ermelo, to the west and north-west of the blockhouses, and in Bethal, Standerton, and Middelburg, there was grain for one month. But the Heidelberg and Pretoria commandos had now, for the first time, no corn remaining for food. In the neighbourhood of Boksburg the only grain left was the old maize of the previous year, whilst there were no cattle at all in the district. When he had visited Boksburg he had found that the commandos had had no meat for three days. In the country between Vereeniging and Ermelo there were only thirty-six goats, and no cattle whatsoever. In the Wakkerstroom district, however, there were still a few slaughter-cattle. The horses were everywhere worn out and exhausted. They had been so constantly kept on the move, owing to the enemy's increasing attacks, they could now only cover the shortest distances.

The Kaffir question was becoming from day to day more serious. At Vrijheid, for instance, there was a Kaffir commando which had already made several attacks upon the burghers. This attitude of the Kaffir population was producing a very dispiriting effect upon the burghers.

The women were in a most pitiable state, now that the lines of blockhouses had been extended in all directions over the country. Sometimes the commandos had to break through the lines and leave the women behind alone; and when the burghers later on returned they would perhaps find that the women had been driven from their houses, and, in some instances, treated with atrocious cruelty.

Referring to the numbers in the field, he said that there were, in the whole of the Transvaal, ten thousand eight hundred and sixteen men, and that three thousand two hundred and ninety-six of them had no horses. The enemy during the summer had taken many of the burghers prisoner; and since June, 1901, the commandos had diminished to the extent of six thousand and eighty-four men. The burghers thus lost to them had either been killed, or taken prisoner, or had surrendered their arms.

The number of households was two thousand six hundred and forty.

The Commandant-General concluded by saying that the three greatest difficulties with which they were confronted were their horses, their food supply, and the miserable condition of their women and children.

Commander-in-Chief de Wet then spoke. He said he would leave it to the delegates who were officers to make reports. They had come from far and near, and knew exactly what the condition of things was. He, however, could state that the number of burghers in the Orange Free State was six thousand one hundred and twenty, of whom about four hundred were not available for service. The Basutos, he found, were more favourably inclined to the Boer cause than ever before.

"General De la Rey," continued General de Wet, "like myself, does not quite know what task he has to perform here, but he thinks with me that the duty of making reports belongs to the delegates. However, he feels bound to state that in his divisions there is a great scarcity of everything. But precisely the same state of affairs existed there a year ago. And when his burghers were at that time without food—well, he went and got it for them." (Cheers.)

General Beijers (Waterberg) then addressed the delegates, telling them that he would not detain them long. In Zoutpansberg, he stated, they had still a plentiful supply of food, for they were able to buy from the Kaffirs. At Waterberg the Kaffirs were neutral, but at Zoutpansberg they were getting out of hand. Yet, since no co-operation existed amongst them, they were not to be feared, and any uprising could easily be quelled.

Besides this trouble, they had many difficulties to face, which were produced by horse-sickness and fever.

As to the question of grain, there was food enough for the whole of the Transvaal and the Orange Free State. But now the English were beginning to buy up the maize at £1 a sack.

General Muller (Boksburg) reported that in his division the burghers had never suffered from hunger. He could still hold out for a few months more, as food could be obtained from the Kaffirs. There was, it could not be denied, a tendency to mutiny amongst the Kaffirs, but he did not think that this need cause any anxiety. He believed that he would be able to carry on operations until the end of the winter.

General Froneman (Ladybrand) said that the condition of his divisions, namely Winburg and Ladybrand, gave no cause for uneasiness. There were still eighty families in the districts, but they were able to provide for all their necessities. The Kaffirs were peaceable and well disposed, and were of great service to the burghers, for whom they bought clothing in Basutoland. It was possible for the burghers, he considered, to hold out for more than a year.

General Hattingh (Kroonstad) declared that in one part of the Kroonstad district there were still plenty of sheep and cattle, and that seed had been sown for next year's harvest. But another part of the district was entirely exhausted, and had to obtain its supplies from Bethlehem.

General Badenhorst (Boshof) stated that he could report on the Boshof district and the parts of the Winburg and Bloemfontein districts to the west of the railway. There were enough cattle to last his commandos for years, even if they had no other food at all. Recently he had captured fifteen hundred head of cattle, and he was in a position to give assistance to other districts. Grain, however, was not so plentiful as it had been the previous year, but nevertheless there was still a large enough supply to permit him to send help to others.

General Nieuwouwdt (Fauresmith) reported that his district was entirely devastated, and that for the last seven months there had been a dearth of all provisions; nevertheless, his burghers had contrived to live. There was, moreover, enough corn left to last them for another year. There were now only three women in the whole of his district.

General Prinsloo (Bethlehem) declared that he would be telling a falsehood if he were to say that there was no food in his district. He possessed slaughter-cattle and corn, and could help other districts. One of his commandants had recently found a store of maize (consisting of one hundred and thirty sacks) buried in the ground. The enemy had made many inroads into his district, and especially during the last few months. The blockhouses were a source of constant annoyance to him.

General Brand (Bethulie) reported upon the south-western part of the Orange Free State, where he commanded. There were some parts of his division, he said, which had been entirely laid waste. Everything had been carried off; there was not a sheep left; and the burghers had been without meat for days. But he was able to capture booty, and could still hold out for a year.

General Wessels (Harrismith) drew attention to the constant passage of large Kaffir families through the districts of Harrismith and Vrede. He could tell the delegates that the Kaffirs had been quite astonished that there were still cattle and sheep and supplies of grain in the districts. He had not yet come to the end of his provisions; but, even if everything were taken, he saw a chance of obtaining food from elsewhere.

Commandant C.A. Van Niekerk (Kroonstad) declared that if there was one part of the country which was entirely exhausted it was the part where he was in command, namely Hoopstad and a portion of Kroonstad. But yet, during the last twelve months, they had been able to obtain food, and even to sow for the ensuing year. There were no cattle in his district; but he had taken a thousand sheep and fifty-two cattle from the English.

Commandant Van der Merwe (Heilbron) spoke to the same effect.

General Smuts was the next to address the meeting. He began by saying that his expedition into Cape Colony had been the outcome of the advice which the deputation had given in July, 1901, namely to continue the war. That he had been in command of it had come about in the following way. News had been received in the Transvaal that affairs in Cape Colony were taking a favourable turn, and accordingly General De la Rey had received orders to go thither, and to take over the command there. But afterwards it was thought wiser to annul these orders, because De la Rey could not well be spared from the western parts of the Transvaal. Owing to this, he (General Smuts) took the task upon his own shoulders, and crossed the Orange River with two hundred men. He had had a difficult task to accomplish. He had marched through Cape Colony to Grahamstad, and from thence he had pushed on towards the coast, through Graaff Reinet. Thence he had proceeded to the neighbourhood where he was now carrying on operations.

He had visited every commando, and as he had seen that there were signs of disorder amongst them he had taken them all under his own command. In this way he had found himself at the head of some fifteen hundred men. During his expeditions Commandant Lotter had been captured with a hundred men; this had reduced his force to only fourteen hundred. But since then the number had nearly doubled, so that they now had two thousand six hundred men (divided into twenty commandos) under arms in Cape Colony. In addition to these men there was a division under General De Villiers operating in Griqualand West, and another under Commandant Van der Merwe in Bechuanaland. The total numbers of these two divisions amounted to about seven hundred men.

Passing on to the question whether help was to be expected from Cape Colony, General Smuts declared that there would be no general rising. The reports which represented such a rising as possible had exaggerated matters. There were great difficulties in the way of a general rising. First, there was the question of horses—and in Cape Colony the want of horses was as great, if not greater, than in the Republics. Secondly, it was exceedingly difficult for Colonials to rise, for they knew that not only would they have to be voetgangers,[318] but also that if they were captured they would be very severely punished by the English. The scarcity of grass was also greatly against any such attempt. The horses had to be fed, and, as the enemy had forbidden any sowing, it was almost impossible to find food for them. A counter proclamation had indeed been issued by the Republics, but it had been of no avail.

He was of opinion that the small commandos which had already been in Cape Colony had done the best they could. The question that now arose was whether the whole of their forces ought to be sent from the Republics into Cape Colony. He himself thought that there was an opening for them, but the difficulty was to find a method of getting them there. The existence of this difficulty, and the facts which he had brought before the delegates, had forced him to the conclusion that a general rising in Cape Colony was an impossibility.

As to the continuation of the war and matters of that nature, they must naturally be settled by the Republics, and not by Cape Colony.

The meeting was then adjourned until eight o'clock in the evening.

Upon its reassembling, Commandant Nijs (Pretoria, North) said that in that part of the district of Pretoria which lay to the north of the Delagoa Bay Railway there were still cattle enough to last for a considerable time, but that the store of grain would be exhausted within a fortnight. The number of horses also was insufficient. The district could muster one hundred and fifty-three mounted men and one hundred and twenty-eight voetgangers. In the division of Onderwijk, Middelburg, there were twenty-six mounted men and thirty-eight voetgangers.

Commandant Grobler (Bethal) stated that in his district they had not been left undisturbed during the summer. Only a short time previously he had lost sixty-three men in an engagement, where he had been besieged in a kraal, out of which he, with one hundred and fifty-three burghers, had managed to escape. Bethal had been laid waste from one end to the other, and he had no provisions for his commandos. He had on his hands three hundred women and children; these were in a serious position, owing to the lack of food; some of the women had also been assaulted by Kaffirs.

General Christiaan Botha (Swaziland) then reported on the condition of the Swaziland commando. They had no provisions in hand, and were simply living by favour of the Kaffirs. They had no women there. His commando of one hundred and thirteen men was still at Piet Retief. As there was no grain to be had, they were compelled to go from kraal to kraal and buy food from the Kaffirs, and this required money. Yet somehow or other they had managed to keep soul and body together. "I have fought for the Transvaal," he concluded, "for two and a half years, and now, since I hear that there is food in the Free State, I shall fight for the Free State for two and a half years more."

General Brits (Standerton) said that he had still provisions for two months, but no cattle. He had sixty-five families with him, and found it very difficult to provide them with the necessaries of life. Altogether, things were in a most critical state.

Mr. Birkenstock (Vrijheid) spoke as follows:

"I shall go deeper into some of the points which the Commandant-General has brought forward in his general report of the matter. At Vrijheid we have been harassed by large forces of the enemy for six or eight months, and the district is now completely devastated. The presence of women and children causes great difficulty, for of late the English have refused to receive the families which, compelled by absolute famine, wished to take refuge with them. There is also continual danger from the Kaffirs, whose attitude towards us is becoming positively hostile. Both horses and grain are scarce; but as far as the latter is concerned there will be sufficient, provided that the enemy does not return. One morning recently a Kaffir commando, shortly before daybreak, attacked a party of our men, who lost fifty-six killed out of a total of seventy. That peace must be made at all costs is the opinion of all the families in my district, and I feel it my duty to bring this opinion before you."

Commandant Alberts (Pretoria and Middelburg) said that his burghers had had no rest for a year, and that during that period no ploughing or sowing had been done in the district. Consequently a commando would not be able to find the means of subsistence there. On three occasions he had been forced to take refuge in a kraal, but fortunately had always been able to make his escape. They had no cattle which they could use for food, although

[318] Infantry.

he had received some, through Commandant Roos, from the Free State. Their horses were in the worst possible condition.

Landdrost Bosman (Wakkerstroom) then gave an account of the condition of affairs in his district. They were dependent for everything, except meat, upon the Kaffirs, giving them meat in exchange. This year there had been a very poor crop of mealies, and, such as it was, it had been much damaged by the enemy. Still the burghers might manage, with what mealies they had, to last out for another two months; but the women and children also needed to be provided for. The cattle were beginning to run short, and the few horses that they had were so weak that they would require a fortnight's rest before they could be used. It might become necessary for the commandos to leave the district, and if so, what was to become of the families?

Mr. De Clercq (Middelburg) regretted that he was unable to give as cheery a report as some of the gentlemen present had done. The part of Middelburg which he represented was in an almost hopeless condition. There were no slaughter-cattle, and only enough grain to last for a very short time. Out of five hundred horses only one hundred now remained, and these could do no work, being too weak even to get away when it became necessary to retreat from the enemy. The state of the burghers was very discouraging; if they should be compelled to leave the district the question would arise whether, considering the condition of their horses, it would be possible for them to reach their new destination. There were fifty families in Middelburg, and things were going very badly with them. The district would have to be abandoned, and what would then be the fate of the families, which even now could only be scantily provided for? The women had wished to go on foot to the English, but he had advised them to wait until the results of the present negotiations should become known.

Commandant David Schoeman (Lijdenburg) said that although but a short time ago there had been eight hundred head of cattle in his district, they had now all been carried off. Grain there was none. Should fighting be continued, he was at a loss to know how he could provide for the women.

Commandant Opperman (Pretoria, South) reported on that part of the Pretoria district which lies south of the line. What he said agreed substantially with the report of Commandant Alberts. (See page 343.)

Commandant Liebenberg (Potchefstroom) stated that during the last eight or nine months blockhouses had been erected in his district. All that was now left to him was a strip of country about twelve miles long; here he could still exist. A good deal of seed had been sown, but the crops had of late fallen into the hands of the English. The grain was altogether spoilt; some of it had been burnt, the rest trodden down by the horses. There were ninety-three households in his district. Between Lichtenburg and Potchefstroom there were some women from the Orange Free State who were reduced to the most dire straits. They had told him that if things did not improve they intended to go on foot to Klerksdorp, and he had replied that they must wait for the result of the negotiations. He had still four hundred mounted men, in addition to one hundred voetgangers. He could hold out for a short time longer, and then would have to look for some way out of his difficulties.

General Du Toit (Wolmaransstad) said that there were five hundred families in his district, but little enough for them to live on. Though his horses were weak, he would be able to save himself by strategy if he should get into a tight corner. His commandos were small—only four hundred and fifty mounted men. The cattle were in good condition, but grain was scarce.

Commandant De Beer (Bloemhof) had still under his command as many as four hundred and forty-four mounted men and one hundred and sixty-five voetgangers. Both grain and cattle were scarce, but then Bloemhof had never possessed many head of cattle. So far the families had not suffered from want. He would be able to hold out for another year.

General Kemp reported that he had under him Krugersdorp, Rustenburg, and parts of Pretoria and Johannesburg. In the district of Krugersdorp no more sowing was possible, and the majority of cattle had been carried away. Yet there was no want. Why should he lack for anything when he was in possession of a great "commissariat" extending as far as the Zoutpansberg, where General Beijers was in command? He took what he wanted from the Kaffirs—it was not their property; he was only taking back what really belonged to the burghers.

Commandant-in-Chief de Wet here asked why the eastern divisions of the Transvaal could not do like General Kemp, and take what they required from the Kaffirs?

General Kemp replied that the fact that in the eastern parts the Kaffirs were united with the English made the difference. The Kaffirs there, he said, gave all they looted to the English, who then sold them the cattle back again. If then cattle were taken in those parts, it would be cattle which was really the property of the Kaffirs.

Moreover, the Zulus were Kaffirs of a different sort to those with which he (the General) had to deal. General Botha also had said that among the Kaffirs in the Eastern Transvaal there were not to be found any cattle belonging to the burghers.

Mr. J.L. Grobler (Carolina) had not as yet had to complain of any lack of cattle or grain in his district. The English, however, by their system of blockhouses, had cut the burghers off from the greater part of the crop. If nothing happened, the newly-sown crops ought to produce a good harvest; but he did not like the temper of the Kaffirs. His men could still hold out for another six or seven months. The three hundred horses still remaining to them were in a weak condition; such as they were, there was not one apiece for the burghers.

Mr. J. Naude (Pretoria) said that he represented a part of Pretoria and General Kemp's flying column. In his district sowing and harvesting went on as usual. There were fortunately no women and children. Although the commandos had not a superabundance of cattle, yet no one lacked for any of the necessaries of life.

The meeting was then closed with prayer, and adjourned until the following morning.

Friday, May 16th, 1902.

The meeting opened with prayer a little after nine a.m. The correspondence which the two Governments had addressed to the burghers, in order that it might be communicated to their representatives at one of these meetings, was first read. It was then debated whether the meeting should request Lord Kitchener to put it into communication with the deputation in Europe. After speeches pro and con, it was decided not to do so.

Thereupon General Froneman proposed the following resolution:

"This meeting is of opinion that the Governments should be asked in the first place to thank His Majesty the King of England and Her Majesty the Queen of the Netherlands, through Lord Kitchener, for the efforts which (as appears from the correspondence between the said Governments) they have made to set on foot negotiations for peace; and, in the second place, to express to them the regret of this meeting that His Majesty's Government has not accepted the proposal of Her Majesty's Government that the representatives of the two Republics now in Europe (who still enjoy the full confidence of their fellow-countrymen) should be allowed to return home, and also that Lord Kitchener has declined a similar request addressed to him by the Governments of the two Republics."

This proposal was seconded by Commandant Flemming, and carried.

After another proposal, made by H.J. Bosman, and seconded by J.L. Grobler, had been rejected, the correspondence referred to above came under discussion.

The first speaker was Mr. P.R. Viljoen, who spoke as follows:

"We can apply to our own country those words of Scripture, 'The place whereon thou standest is holy ground.' The soil on which we are now standing, wet as it is with the blood and tears of our forefathers and also of the many who have fallen in this present struggle, may well be regarded as 'holy ground.'

"That we should ever have to surrender this country is a horrible thought. Yet it must be faced. It is certain at least that many districts must be abandoned, for the enemy is doing his utmost to collect us together at a few isolated places, where he will be able to concentrate his forces upon us.

"From the reports which we have received it appears that the state of affairs in the Orange Free State is still hopeful. Not so in the Transvaal. There our prospects are of the gloomiest.

"My opinion is that we must endeavour to bring this war to an end. If there was the least chance of our being able to maintain our independence, we would still fight on, and not even the bitterest sufferings would appear unendurable. But have we any such chance?—that is the question which we have got to answer.

"We know nothing, it will be said, of the present state of affairs in Europe, for the report from our deputation, which has just been read in your presence, is six months old. Nevertheless, if anything favourable to us had occurred since then, we must have heard of it by now.

"It is evident that we must endeavour to obtain peace on terms honourable to ourselves. But how are we to do so? By keeping our independence in view when making terms with the enemy, you will answer. Nevertheless, I think it would be advisable for us to commission our Governments to ask the English Government once more what concessions it is prepared to make to us on condition of our surrendering our independence. Until we know this we can come to no final decision.

"Though it is a bitter thing to have to say, yet I feel it my duty to tell you that I honestly believe it to be impossible for us to carry on the war any longer."

Mr. De Clercq then addressed the meeting in the following words:

"The question before us is, whether or not the war can be continued? To answer it, we must look forward into the future. We must ask ourselves what consequences will ensue from a continuance of hostilities, and what will be the result of their cessation.

"We have only fifteen thousand men against the enemy's quarter of a million. Our food and horses are scarce, and we have other difficulties besides these. It is impossible to go on with the struggle.

"Nevertheless, if I believed that to do so would give us a chance of retaining our independence, I also would be ready for further sacrifices. But as it is impossible to retain our independence, surely we shall only be storing up misery for the future if we continue fighting until every man of us is a prisoner or in his grave. I am of opinion that our most reasonable course is to save what is still left to us—our existence as a nation. It is not too late to save it now, but who can tell what the future holds in store for us? If we are to be still further reduced in number, we shall soon cease to exist as a nation. Can it be right to sacrifice a nation which has fought as the African nation has done?"

Commandant Rheeder (Rouxville) then spoke as follows:

"I know that the times are very dark, but still there are some rays of light. You have been asked whether you will continue fighting until you are exterminated. But there is another alternative. Will you not continue fighting until you are relieved? I maintain that our independence must be a sine qua non of any negotiations that we make—we cannot give it up. So long as we have life we must continue to fight, and we must only lay down our arms when relief arrives."

General Kemp now rose to his feet. "I am fully aware," he said, "of the very serious position in which we are placed. Yet, when the war began, the position was no less grave. We must continue our resistance. When we recall to our minds how much this war has cost us, and what rivers of blood have flowed, we feel that it is impossible to surrender. As far as I am concerned, unless relief comes, I will fight on till I die.

"But one should not look only at the dark side of the picture. It is true enough that in some districts food is scarce, but there are none in which it is absolutely unobtainable. The districts threatened by famine must be abandoned—that is the way to deal with the difficulty.

"It has been pointed out that a large number of our men have been killed or taken prisoners. This fact, however, only fills me with courage. A cause that has cost us so dearly must never be forsaken. To own ourselves beaten would be to dig a grave for the African nation, out of which it would never rise. Why should we lose our trust in God? Up to this moment He has aided us, and He will always be our Helper."

Vice-Commandant Breijtenbach (Utrecht) then spoke as follows:

"The burghers whom I represent have told me to inform them, when these deliberations have come to an end, whether a continuation of the war is possible, and if it be possible, how it is to be accomplished. If I cannot assure them that we are able to continue the struggle, the men of Utrecht will not fight any more. As you know, I can give them no such assurance.

"There are ten districts in the Transvaal which are unable to fight any longer. It surely is not proposed to leave these districts in the lurch! We must not only consult our sentiments, but also our reason. And what does the voice of reason say? This—that the continuation of the war is an impossibility. Should you decide now to continue the war, you would have to start a fresh campaign; and you know that that is beyond our powers.

"A previous speaker has referred to the help of the Lord, but who is able to fathom His counsels? Yet we can understand the answer God has given to our prayer—that prayer which we offered with the Mausers in our hands when the war began. And what was the answer we received ... I leave it to you to reply.

"Yes, we must use our reason. If we continue the struggle we give the death-blow to our existence as a nation. We have been told that there are ten districts that cannot go on fighting. Are we going to say, 'We will continue the struggle and leave these districts to their fate'? No! We must save what we can."

General Liebenberg then spoke. "I am able to give my support," he said, "to all that has fallen from the lips of Messrs. Viljoen and De Clercq. It cannot be doubted that the future is very dark. Yes, we can only trust in God, and use our reason to the best of our ability. I have been commissioned by those whom I represent to retain our independence if possible, and if it be not possible to make peace on the best terms that we can get."

Commandant Uijs was the next speaker. He explained that if the war were to be continued he would have to leave his district and abandon the women and children to the mercy of the Kaffirs. He could see a chance of saving the mounted men if only he could feel certain that they would all follow him, but the case of the women and children would be hopeless. A serious difficulty confronted the delegates, and it was with them, and no longer with the Government, that its solution rested. Never before had he been called upon to face so gigantic a task. It was not the time now to criticize one another, but to practise mutual forbearance. The Bible had been quoted by one of the speakers, but let them not forget the text in which the king is spoken of who calculated whether he was strong enough with ten thousand to encounter him who marched against him with twenty thousand. Then there was the question as to the disposal of the widows and orphans. What was to become of them if the burghers, by refusing to come to terms with the enemy, should no longer be able to act as their mutual protectors? Let them make no more widows and orphans, but let them open their eyes and recognize that the hand of God was against them.

The next business was the reading of two letters—one from General Malan and the other from General Kritzinger. Malan reported on his doings in the Cape Colony, while Kritzinger advised that the war should be discontinued.

General Du Toit then spoke, emphasizing the responsibility of the delegates and the importance of the occasion. He went on to say that he represented a part of the nation which had suffered very severely, but which nevertheless had commissioned him to stand up for independence, if by any means it could be retained; if he failed in this, he was to take whatever course seemed best to him. In his district the burghers were not reduced to such a pass as to oblige them to surrender, but the condition of other districts must also be taken into consideration, and if it appeared that the war could not be continued, the delegates must get the best terms they could. In their demands they must be united—this was the principal reason why dissension was so much to be avoided. For himself, he could only say that whether the meeting voted to continue the war or to bring it to a conclusion, he would fall in with the wishes of the majority. Any decision would be better than the failure of this conference, as that would leave everything undecided.

He was followed by Secretary of State Reitz, who said:

"You all know what the Governments have done. The question now is, Is there anything further that we can do? For my part, I think that there is. We might offer to surrender Witwatersrand and Swaziland; we might also relinquish our rights to a foreign policy; we might even accede to an English Protectorate. If France has been able to do without Alsace and Lorraine, surely we can do without the goldfields. What benefit have they ever done us? Did the money they brought ever do us any good? No! rather it did us harm. It was the gold which caused the war. It is then actually to our advantage to cede the goldfields, and moreover by so doing we shall be rid of a very troublesome part of our population."

Mr. Reitz then went on to discuss in detail the position in regard to Swaziland, the question of a British Protectorate, and the surrender of our right to treat with foreign powers.

General Muller (Boksburg) expressed sympathy with the views of the Secretary of State, while Vice-Commandant Roux (Marico) said that he was prepared to sacrifice many things, but that he intended to hold out for independence.

The next speech was made by Landdrost Stoffberg (Zoutpansberg), who said:

"I agree with General Du Toit in what he said about the necessity for unity amongst us. Disunion must not be so much as mentioned. I have a mandate from the burghers of Zoutpansberg not to sacrifice our independence. But if anything short of this will satisfy the English, I am quite prepared to make concessions. Some of the burghers think that it might be well to surrender the goldfields for a certain sum of money, while others point out that the gold was the cause of the war. I also think that we have suffered through the gold, and that we might give up the goldfields without doing ourselves any harm. For what has the gold done for us? It has enriched us, many will say. Yes! but it has also been a stumbling-block to many a man. And is it not better to be a poor but independent nation than to be rich and at the same time subject to another Power. Let the goldfields go. We shall still, with our markets, be rich enough."

Commandant Mentz (Heilbron) then rose.

"I appeal to the forbearance of the delegates," he said, "for making any speech at this meeting. I fear I am unable to give as rose-coloured a report as my brother Free-Staters have done: My district has been continually harassed by the enemy's troops, and great devastation has been wrought. But the greatest trouble I have is the presence of so many families, for there are still two hundred in the district. I have only eighty burghers under my command, and it is clear to me that I shall soon be obliged to leave the district. What will then become of these families? I received a commission not to sacrifice our independence. But since my burghers met more than half of them have been made prisoners. The remainder have instructed me to do my best to preserve our independence, but if I find that it cannot be maintained to act according to my own judgment. It appears to me that it may be possible to retain our independence by ceding some part of the country; if this be the case it ought most certainly to be done. I can remember the late President Brand saying in connexion with the diamond fields, 'Give them up; you will gain more by giving them up than by keeping them.' This remark may well apply to the present situation."

Commandant Flemming (Cape Town) reported that his district was well-nigh devastated. But they still possessed a fair number of cattle, which they had carried away with them. But even if they had no cattle, that would be no excuse for surrender, for in his district it was possible to live on the game. The view which he and his burghers had taken was that since they had already sacrificed nearly everything they possessed, they would not now sacrifice their independence. For should this also be lost, then there would be nothing left to them. That had been their opinion, but they had not then known how matters stood in the Transvaal. Now that he was aware of the state of affairs, he agreed with State Secretary Reitz that their best course was to cede a part of their territory.

Vice-President Burger now rose from his seat, and said:

"This meeting has to formulate a fresh proposal to the English Government, and to await its answer. If this proposal be rejected, well, you will be no worse off than you are at present. If there be a man who has earnestly considered what the sacrifice of everything means to us, then I am that man. It has been said, we must retain our independence, or else continue to fight; and we are still able to hold out for another six months, or even a year. Now, supposing that we can hold out another year, what should we gain by doing so? Why, we should only grow weaker, whilst the enemy grew stronger! I emphatically state that the war cannot be carried on any longer; and I ask if there is any man here who can maintain with a clear conscience that the struggle can be successfully continued.

"Some of you may tell me that complications may arise in Europe. But that is a groundless hope. Others may say that it is astonishing enough that we have been able to hold out till now, and that we still have the power of making our voices heard. Yes! that is very surprising; but shall we retain this power long? I heard some delegates say, 'We shall fight till we die!' That is a manly sentiment. But was it not, perhaps, prompted by a desire to make a fine speech, which would go down to posterity? Was not the aim in some cases that future generations might recall these speeches when they were told of the brave fight our men had made?

"Let every one consider this well: Is he prepared to sacrifice the nation on the shrine of his own ambition? Ambition, although it may cost us our lives, can never lead to martyrdom. A martyr is made of finer stuff!

"Have we not arrived at the stage of our history when we must pray, 'Thy will be done'? That prayer, considered rightly, is a prayer of faith. Do not let us imagine that we can compel God to do our will—that is not faith.

"I beg of you to consider what will become of the women and the children and the banished burghers if you still persist until your last shot has been fired. What right shall we have to intercede for these unfortunate ones when we have rejected the proposals of the English Government? We shall have no right whatsoever.

"Perhaps it is God's will that the English nation should oppress us, in order that our pride may be subdued, and that we may come through the fire of our troubles purified.

"My opinion is that we should make a peace proposal to England, yielding as much as we rightly can; and if England rejects our proposal, it will be time enough then to see what other course is open to us.

"There is one fact which we cannot allow ourselves to forget. There are ten districts in the Transvaal which must be abandoned. In the Free State, too, there are districts in a similar plight. It is the opinion of lawyers that so long as the inhabitants remain in a district their property cannot lawfully be confiscated; but if the district be abandoned, then confiscations can take place.

"It is criminal to say, 'Come what may, we will fight till everything is lost and all of us are dead!'"

The following resolution was then proposed by General Kemp, and seconded by Mr. J. Nand:

"This meeting decides, in order to expedite the work in hand, to depart from the original programme; and to constitute a Commission, to be composed of the Hon. Jacob Smits and the Hon. Judge Hertzog, and to give this Commission authority to draw up, conjointly with the two State Presidents, a draft proposal, to be laid before the delegates to-morrow morning."

This resolution was put to the meeting, and accepted by the delegates. The meeting then adjourned.

At half-past seven in the evening the delegates reassembled.

General Cilliers (Lichtenburg and Marico) was the first to make a report. "In my division," he said, "things are in a very favourable condition. Yet we are bound to take the other divisions into consideration. My burghers said to me, 'Stand firm for independence!' But when they gave me the order they did not know about the condition of the other districts. Will those other districts—such of them, I mean, as are in a worse predicament than ourselves—be able to co-operate with us in continuing the war? Some of them have already answered my question in the negative. Must we then not ask ourselves, What will be the best for the nation as a whole? Shall we say continue the war, or shall we approach the enemy and make a proposal?

"But are we really justified in prolonging the struggle, and making still further sacrifices? Some will answer, 'Yes, for we have a God in whom we have trusted from the beginning; shall we not continue to trust in Him who has worked such wonders for us already?' But I have heard a brother say, 'God's hand is against us.' It was bitter to hear these words from him, and for myself I will have none of them. My vote is given here and now for a continuance of the war.

"But we must hear what the rest of the delegates have to say, and if they can point out some other way by which we can retain even a portion of our national independence, we must be ready to follow it."

General Froneman next addressed the meeting.

"I fear," he began, "that too much is being made of the condition of my division: things are not so prosperous with us as some here appear to imagine. But for all that, my burghers are for nothing short of absolute independence. They cannot forget the blood which has already been spilt in our cause. They mean to hold out until they are relieved.

"I sympathize deeply with those districts that are less happily circumstanced than my own, but it pains me to discover that there are some here who doubt that God is for us. For what has supported us up till now save faith in God?—the faith of those who first prayed God to prevent the war, and then, when they saw that this was not His will, fought like men, putting all their trust in Him.

"Up till now the Lord hath been my helper; the enemy has cut us off from everything, and yet we see our two little Republics still full of hope, still holding out."

He concluded his speech by saying that he would like to hear the opinions of Generals Botha, De Wet, and De la Rey. They ought to be able to throw much light upon the matter.

Commandant General Botha then rose, and said:

"I am glad to have an opportunity of giving my views upon the present state of affairs. We know that differences of opinion are to be found everywhere and on every question; when, therefore, a man differs from those who think that this war can and ought to be continued, we must ascribe his opinion to discouragement, weakness, or cowardice. We must acknowledge the truth of the facts from which he draws his conclusions, and which have compelled him to utter it. His object is to make known the true state of the country—which indeed is his plain duty. Were he not to do so on the present occasion he would be accused, later on, of having kept secret what he ought to have revealed. Differences of opinion then need not, and must not, cause a disunion and discord. Whatever our private opinions may be, yet, as delegates of the burghers, we must speak and act as one man.

"The war has now lasted two years. But the question for us to answer is this: Are we going forwards or backwards? My own conviction—a conviction founded upon the views expressed by my commandos and the speeches which I have listened to at this meeting—is that we are not gaining, but losing ground. There is nothing, in my opinion, more evident than that, during the last six months, the tide has been setting steadily against us, and in favour of the enemy.

"A year ago there were no blockhouses. We could cross and recross the country as we wished, and harass the enemy at every turn. But now things wear a very different aspect. We can pass the blockhouses by night indeed, but never by day. They are likely to prove the ruin of our commandos.

"Then, as regards food. We are told that there is food here, and food there; but how are we to get at it? How are we to transport it from one district to another? Outside the frontiers of our Republics there are plenty of provisions, but it becomes daily more difficult to get them into our hands. The cattle, for instance, that used to be at Ladysmith have now been removed to Estcourt. Even the friendly Kaffirs, from whom we are now able to obtain provisions, may quite possibly soon turn against us. The time is coming when we shall be compelled to say, 'Hunger drives us to surrender.'

"The horses have been chased about so incessantly, and have suffered so much from want of forage, that their strength is almost exhausted. They are so weak that it is almost impossible to accomplish any long distance with them.

"As to the Cape Colony, I had always understood that the Colonists were going to rise en bloc, but General Smuts has just told us that there is no chance of such a thing happening. And he speaks from personal knowledge, having just returned from paying them a visit. Moreover, he has seen our horses, and says that it is impossible for them to go into the Colony, so it appears that our successes there are over. This is a severe check indeed; but it could not have been otherwise. We have not enough horses to enable us to give the Colonists effectual help, and they themselves have been cowed by the heavy penalties imposed upon all those who did rise. Many of those who are well disposed towards us dare not join us now.

"Again, there is no chance of European intervention: not one of the Powers will do anything for us. To see this it is only necessary to peruse that correspondence between the Netherlands and England, which was the cause of these negotiations. There we shall find that the Dutch Minister says that our deputation is only accredited to Holland, whereas it had been accredited by the two Republics to all the Governments in Europe. Moreover, the correspondence makes it very plain that England will not tolerate the intervention of any foreign Power whatsoever. But the truth is, that no foreign Power wants to help us. When the women were first made prisoners I thought that European intervention might perhaps be attempted, because to make prisoners of women is a thing quite outside the usual methods of warfare. But nothing was done even then. We were told that we had the sympathy of the nations of Europe—their sympathy, and nothing more!

"I have come to a subject that is very near our hearts—our women-folk. If this meeting decides upon war, it will have to make provision for our wives and children, who will then be exposed to every kind of danger. Throughout this war the presence of the women has caused me anxiety and much distress. At first I managed to get them into the townships, but later on this became impossible, because the English refused to receive them. I then conceived the idea of getting a few of our burghers to surrender, and sending the women in with them. But this plan was not practical, because most of the families were those of prisoners of war, and the men still on commando were not so closely related to these families as to be willing to sacrifice their freedom for them.

"We have heard much talk about fighting 'to the bitter end.' But what is 'the bitter end'? Is it to come when all of us are either banished or in our graves? Or does it mean the time when the nation has fought until it never can fight again? As to myself, personally, I can still continue the struggle. I have horses, my household is well provided for, and as far as my own inclination goes I am all for going on. But am I only to consider myself? Is it not my first duty to look at the interests of my nation? I have always been, and still am, of the opinion that, before letting the nation go to rack and ruin, it is our duty to parley. We must not let the chance for negotiations slip out of our hands. When our numbers have fallen to only four or five thousand men under arms we shall no longer have that chance, and this will undoubtedly happen if we hold out for another year, or even six months.

"There are some who say, 'We must trust in God and keep on fighting,' and I grant them that miracles are possible at all times. But it is beyond our power to say whether God will work a miracle for us. We do not know what His will may be. If we continue the war, and if it should afterwards appear that everything has been in vain, our responsibility will be only the heavier, the blinder our confidence now is. And over and over again we shall hear, 'He is dead,' 'and he, and he.' Will not this make our remorse all the more bitter? Our commandos are so weak, our country so exhausted, that the loss of one great battle, the surrender of a single strong force, would spell ruin for us.

"'But we have managed to hold out for so long.' Yes, but there is a natural reason, a military reason, why this has been the case. The fact that our commandos have been spread over so large a tract of country has compelled the British, up to the present time, to divide their forces. But things have changed now; we have had to abandon district after district, and must now operate on a far more limited territory. In other words, the British army can at last concentrate its forces upon us.

"I firmly believe that, under like circumstances, no other nation in the world would have fought as our nation has done. Shall such a nation perish? No! we must save it. If we delegates are convinced that we can no longer offer resistance to the enemy, it is our plain duty to tell the people so. We must not let them be exterminated for want of timely advice. More than twenty thousand women and children have died in the camps during this one year.

"There are men of our own kith and kin who are helping to bring us to ruin. If we continue the war, it may be that the Afrikanders against us will outnumber our own men.

"What is there left to hope for? Are we to retain our independence by ceding a part of our territories? Most assuredly yes, if such a compromise is feasible. As regards Swaziland, it is of so little importance to us that we can give it up without a thought. Then there are the goldfields—let them go. They are but a cancerous growth, sapping the very life of our country.

"We must face the fact that things are not at a standstill: we are slipping back every moment. We must all pull together, or everything is lost. If our sacrifices will buy our independence, well and good. But suppose that we are compelled to give it up—well, if it even comes to this, we must never do so unconditionally. An unconditional surrender would be well enough if the leaders only had to be considered. But we must think of the interests of the nation. We must say to our people, 'We have no thought of ourselves: our only desire is to place ourselves in the breach, if so we may save you.'"

General Botha then proceeded to discuss eventualities in the event of independence being lost. Representative government, he said, might perhaps still be retained, and the national language need not necessarily be supplanted. Thus the nation would still retain its old ideals and its old customs. General Roux had been pertinently asked whether it were better to strive for the recuperation of the people now or to wait until they were altogether overpowered and reduced to such straits that it would require some thirty years before they could once more call themselves a nation. He then went into the terms of the proposal by the British Government, and repeated that there must be no idea of unconditional surrender.

The General concluded in the following words:

"Although we do not wish to accept terms, we have no right to refuse them altogether. On the other hand we must not say to the English, 'Do with us as you like.' For then our descendants would eternally reproach us. We should have lost the privilege of looking after our own wives and children. They would be handed over to strangers. No! we must secure by some means or other that we ourselves shall be able to provide for them. The fate of our country is in the hands of the men in this tent. It has been bitter, indeed, for me to have to speak as I have done. But if I have not spoken the truth, convince me of my error, and I will be the first to own it. But do not condemn me, for I have had no other object than to tell you what I believe to be the truth."

General De la Rey spoke.

"I will not detain you long," he began, "but there are a few points to which I wish to draw attention. In regard to the districts under my command, every one will understand that my burghers, after their recent brilliant successes, are firmly resolved not to sacrifice their independence. If I allude to the battles which I have just fought it is with no thought of boasting, but only that you may picture to yourselves the effect which they must have had upon the enemy; and that no one may be angry with myself and my burghers for standing firm when our feet are on such solid ground.

"But since my arrival at Vereeniging I have heard about our districts where matters are in a far less favourable condition than in my own. So far as I myself am concerned, I cannot think of laying down my arms. Yet it appears to me that some parts of the country will be compelled by starvation to give up the struggle. It is well that those who represent these parts have spoken openly, and not left this meeting in ignorance of the state of affairs only to go and lay down their arms.

"I myself have never thought intervention possible. Even before the war broke out I said that nothing would come of it. I saw that South Africa was divided between Germany and England. And that if only the Republics could be extinguished, then England and Germany would be the only Powers left, and Germany would be safe. But if the Republics were victorious, then Germany would be in danger. Why then should Germany interfere in favour of the Republics, when she has everything to lose by such a course of action? No! intervention was entirely out of the question.

"There has been talk about fighting to the bitter end; but has not the bitter end already come? Each man must answer that question for himself.

"You must remember that everything has been sacrificed—cattle, goods, money, wife, and child. Our men are going about naked, and some of our women have nothing but clothes made of skins to wear. Is not this the bitter end?

"I believe that the time has now come to negotiate. England will never again give us the chance of doing so, should we allow this opportunity to slip by. But how shall we negotiate? I must leave it to this meeting to answer that question. If we do not obtain what we ask for, we shall at least stand or fall together. Yet let us act with reason.

"I cannot agree with one of the opinions expressed by Commandant-General Botha and States-Secretary Reitz. They have stated that they are against surrendering the goldfields to England; firstly, because England would never accept such a proposal, for by doing so she would declare to the whole world that she had only been fighting for the goldfields; and, secondly, because if we gave up the goldfields we should lose a source of revenue, without the aid of which we could not repair the damages which the war has wrought."

Commandant-in-Chief de Wet spoke as follows:

"I am of opinion that the circumstances in the Orange Free State are no less critical than those in the Transvaal. Nine districts were entirely ruined; but these, though at one time abandoned by the burghers, have now been reoccupied.

"If I now differ from those who are of opinion that it is useless to prolong the war, it must not be thought that I am lacking in respect for their judgment. By no means. I know that what has been said about the wretched plight of the people is only too true; but they must not take it amiss if I point out that the same condition of affairs was described in the correspondence from the Transvaal which fell into the hands of the English at Reitz. But, granting that the facts have been correctly stated, even then the Orange Free State will refuse to give in. Let me be candid with you, and say frankly that, in my opinion, this is virtually the Transvaal's war. This, however, makes no difference to me. For me the barrier of the Vaal River has never existed. I have always endeavoured to maintain the Nauwere-Vereeniging, [319]and I feel strongly the obligation which the union of the two States casts on each one of us. They are two nations, but their cause is one.

"What, then, is the prevailing feeling in the Orange Free State? Of the six thousand burghers who have been attending meetings, I myself have been in command of five thousand, and I can confidently say that never were five thousand men more unanimous in their opinion than were those I led when they cried, as with one voice, 'Persevere; we have everything to lose, but we have not yet lost it.' What, then, is the answer to be? I am firmly persuaded that we have only one course before us. If we are unable to obtain what we are asking for, then it only remains for us to alleviate as best we may the lot of those who cannot help themselves. I do not as yet clearly see how this is going to be done, but, at all costs, let us continue fighting. What was our total strength when we began this war? Sixty thousand men all told. Against this the English had a standing army of seven hundred and fifty thousand troops. Of these two hundred and fifty thousand, or one-third, are now in South Africa. We know from experience that they are unable to send more than one-third. And we? Have we not also one-third of our army left?

"I do not wish to imply that I am not prepared to concede something, but nothing will induce me to consent to any part of the country in our territory being given up. It will never do to have an English colony planted in our midst, for England then would have far too firm a hold upon our country.

"It is said, and with some truth, that the goldfields have been a curse to us, but surely there is no reason why they should continue to be so. I fail to see how, without retaining possession of these goldfields, the Republics are to be saved. Swaziland perhaps could be ceded, but never the goldfields. I feel that any intervention is out of the question; but is not the very fact that it has not taken place a sure proof that it was not the will of God? Does it not show that He is minded to form us, by this war, into a nation worthy of the name? Let us then bow to the will of the Almighty.

"My people will perhaps say, 'Our Generals see only the religious side of the question.' They will be right. Without faith we should have been foolish indeed to have embarked on this war and to continue it for so many months. Indeed, it must be a matter of faith, for the future is hidden from us. What has been is within our ken, but what is before is beyond the knowledge of the wisest man.

[319] Closer Union.

"Cape Colony is a great disappointment to me. I do not refer so much to what we have learnt about it from the reports as to the fact that no general uprising can be expected in that quarter. So much we have heard from General Smuts. But though there is to be no uprising, we have no reason to think that there has been any falling off in the number of our adherents in the Colony. The little contingent there has been of great help to us: they have kept fifty thousand troops occupied, with which otherwise we should have had to reckon.

"I feel deeply for our women and children; I am giving earnest consideration to their miserable plight. But their sufferings are among what we may call the necessary circumstances of the war. I have nothing to do with the circumstances. For me, this is a war of religion, and thus I can only consider the great principles involved. Circumstances are to me but as obstacles to be cleared out of the road.

"If we own ourselves defeated—if we surrender to the foe—we can expect little mercy from him. We shall at all events have dug the grave of our national independence, and, as things are, what difference is there between this and digging our own graves?"

Mr. Birkenstock said that the question about the goldfields must be carefully considered. This source of income must not be given up.

The meeting was then closed with prayer.

Saturday, May 17th, 1902.

The Chairman first called upon Chief Commandant de Wet to offer up prayer.

A private report from Mr. J. Schmorderer, who had brought the missive from the deputation in Europe, was then read.

The first delegate to speak was Landdrost Bosman (Wakkerstroom), who said:

"My opinion is that the best way of ascertaining the probable future course of events is to see what has already happened in the past. A year ago there were six hundred burghers in my district, and each man had a horse; now there are not more than half that number, and many of them have to go on foot. Last year we had from three to four thousand bags of maize ready to hand; this year there are not more than as many hundred, and how to get at them is more than I can tell. If such has been the history of the past year, in what sort of condition shall we be at the end of the present one?

"The great difficulty with regard to our families is not how to clothe them, but how to feed them. I know of a woman who has lived for weeks on nothing but fruit. I myself have had to satisfy my hunger with mealies for days together, although I have no wish to complain about it. Even the scanty food we can get has to be obtained from the Kaffirs by persuasion. Moreover, the Kaffirs side with the English, who in their counter-marches are clearing all the food out of the country.

"The men in my district told me that if I came back and reported that the war was to be continued, they would be obliged—for the sake of their wives and children—to go straight to the nearest English camp and lay down their arms. As to the women it is true that they are at present full of hope and courage, but if they knew how matters stood in the veldt, they would think very differently. Even now there are many of them who say that the war ought to be put a stop to, if only for their sakes.

"The Kaffirs are another great source of trouble; in this problem they are a factor which cannot be neglected.

"There is no hope of intervention, nor can we expect anything from the English nation. Facts that have come to my knowledge prove to me that England has become more and more determined to fight to the bitter end.

"I do not see what we can possibly gain by continuing the war. Our own people are helping the English, and every day the enemy are improving their position. What advantage can there then be in persisting in the struggle? We have now a chance of negotiating, and we should seize that chance. For we have the opportunity given us of obtaining some help for our ruined compatriots, who would be entirely unable to make a fresh start without assistance.

"As to the religious side of this matter, I am not ashamed to say that I believe I am serving God in the course which I am taking. We must not attempt to obtain the impossible against all reason. If we make any such attempt, the results will probably be exactly opposite to what we wish. I have the greatest doubt whether it really is in order to give glory to God that the nation wishes to retain its independence. On the contrary I believe that the motive is obstinacy, a vice to which human nature is always prone.

"It has been said that it would be shameful to disregard the blood already spilt; but surely one ought also to consider the blood that might yet be shed in a useless struggle."

The proposal of the Commission was now read, and after some discussion accepted. It ran as follows:

The meeting of national representatives from both Republics—after having considered the correspondence exchanged, and the negotiations conducted, between the Governments of the two Republics and His Excellency Lord Kitchener, on behalf of the British Government; and after having heard the reports of the deputies from the different parts of both Republics; and after having received the latest reports from the representatives of the two Republics in Europe; and having taken into consideration the fact that the British Government has refused to accept the proposal of our Governments made on the same basis; and notwithstanding the above-mentioned refusal of the British Government—still wishes to give expression to the ardent desire of the two Republics to retain their independence, for which already so much material and personal sacrifice has been made, and decides in the name of the people of both Republics to empower both Governments as follows:—To conclude a peace on the following basis, to wit: the retention of a limited independence offering an addition to what has already been offered by the two Governments in their negotiations, dated the 15th of April, 1902.

(a) To give up all foreign relations and embassies.

(b) To accept the Protectorate of Great Britain.

(c) To surrender parts of the territory of the South African Republic.

(d) To conclude a defensive alliance with Great Britain in regard to South Africa.

During the discussion it was clearly explained that the territory which it was suggested should be ceded was the already mentioned goldfields and Swaziland. The question was put whether the South African Republics would have to pay for the damage done during the war. "By all means let us pay," said Mr. De Clercq. "If I could only buy back the independence of the Orange Free State, I would gladly give all I possess."

Several other Transvaal delegates expressed themselves in the same sense, and said that they fully appreciated the sacrifices which the Orange Free State had made. General Froneman thanked them in the name of the Free State.

He felt that the two Republics no longer thought of themselves as having conflicting interests. In the fire of this war they had been firmly welded together.

Commandant Ross (Vrede) thought it wrong even to discuss the possibility of giving up independence. The delegates had received a definite mandate. They had been com missioned to see that the national independence had remained untouched, whatever else might have to be given up. This being the case, they might come to decisions on all other points, so long as they remembered that independence was not an open question.

Commandant J. Van Niekerk (Ficksburg) spoke to the same purpose. He could not even think of sacrificing independence.

After some other delegates had made a few short remarks, General Brand, seconded by Commandant A.J. De Kock, proposed the following resolution, which was accepted by the meeting:

"This meeting of the national representatives of the two Republics hereby charge the Governments to nominate a Commission for the purpose of entering upon negotiations with His Excellency Lord Kitchener, acting on behalf of His Britannic Majesty's Government. The Commission is to endeavour to make peace on satisfactory terms, and is then to lay the result of its negotiations before this meeting, for the sanction of the two Governments." The meeting was then closed with prayer.

The Conference at Pretoria (May 19th–May 28th, 1902)

Appendix B

The Conference at Pretoria Between the Commission of the National Representatives and Lords Kitchener and Milner (May 19th-May 28th, 1902)

Minutes of the Conference held at Pretoria on May 19th, 1902, between Lord Kitchener and Lord Milner, representatives of the British Government, and Commandant-General L. Botha, Commander-in-Chief C.R. de Wet, General J.H. De la Rey, Judge J.B.M. Hertzog, and General J.C. Smuts, delegates of the national representatives, who had met at Vereeniging on May 15th, 1902.

Mr. N.J. de Wet acted as interpreter; Mr. O. Walrond was secretary for the English Government; and the Rev. J.D. Kestell and D. Van Velden acted in a similar capacity for the Commission.

The Conference met at ten o'clock in the morning at the house of Lord Kitchener. After having greeted each other, the members took their seats at the table in the centre of the room.

Commandant-General L. Botha opened the proceedings in the following words:

"Allow me to state that, although the negotiations have taken a longer time than we expected, I am able to assure your Excellencies that we are acting in good faith, and that everything has been done with the sole aim of concluding the peace which we all desire.

"I must also draw attention to the fact that everything we transact here must be submitted to our national representatives, in order to obtain their sanction."

The suggestion was then made that the proposals which the Commission was prepared to make should be laid before the Conference, whereupon the following letter was read to the meeting:

Pretoria, 19th May, 1902.

To their Excellencies, Lord Kitchener and Lord Milner, Pretoria.

Your Excellencies,—

With a view to finally concluding the existing hostilities, and being fully empowered by the Government of the two Republics, we have the honour to propose the following points—in addition to the conditions already offered in the negotiations of April last—as a basis for negotiations:

(a) We are prepared to cede our independence as regards our foreign relations.

(b) We wish to retain self-government in our country, under British supervision.

(c) We are prepared to cede a part of our territory.

Should your Excellencies be prepared to negotiate on this basis, then the above-mentioned points can be elaborated.

We have the honour to be,

Your Excellencies' most obedient servants,

Louis Botha.

C.R. De Wet.

J.H. De La Rey.

J.B.M. Hertzog.

J.C. Smuts.

When this letter had been read, a discussion followed.

Lord Milner: "Considering the wide difference between this proposal and that made by His Majesty's Government, when we last met, I fear that I can hold out very little hope of any good results following negotiations on the basis you have suggested."

Lord Kitchener: "We can take those proposals into consideration, but I cannot see how it is possible to bring them into harmony with those of His Majesty's Government."

Commandant-General Botha: "If this is the position you take, we should like to receive from you a final answer to our proposals."

Lord Milner: "Do you wish us to refer your proposals to His Majesty's Government?"

Commandant-General Botha: "Yes, unless you have full powers to give us a final reply."

Lord Milner: "I am quite convinced that your proposal will be rejected; and I feel bound to say that to refer it, as it stands, to His Majesty's Government will only do you harm."

Commandant-General Botha: "If you have no power to decide upon this proposal here, we should like you to refer it to His Majesty's Government."

Lord Milner: "I have no objection to taking the responsibility of refusing your proposal on myself. The instructions received by myself and Lord Kitchener are quite clear on this point."

Commandant-General Botha: "I must then understand that when Lord Salisbury said that this war was not carried on with a view to annex territory, he did not mean it."

Lord Kitchener: "It is no longer a question of territory, for annexation is an accomplished fact."

Commandant-General Botha: "I am unable to see how our proposal is inconsistent with annexation."

Lord Milner: "I cannot now recall the exact words used by Lord Salisbury, but it is true that Lord Salisbury declared that his Government did not begin the war with the intention of obtaining territory. But in the course of the war circumstances developed in such a way that the decision to annex the Republics became a necessity, and the British Government have pronounced their firm intention not to withdraw from this decision."

Judge Hertzog: "I should like to be informed as to what the great difference is between the basis now proposed by us and that laid down by His Majesty's Government during the negotiations of last year—I do not mean the difference in details, but in principle."

Lord Kitchener: "Do you mean by your proposal that the Boers will become British citizens?"

General Smuts: "I cannot see that our proposal is necessarily in contradiction to that of last year. Our proposal only makes provision concerning the administration."

Lord Milner then quoted from the terms offered at Middelburg by the British Government the previous year:—

"At the earliest possible date military administration shall cease, and be replaced by civil administration in the form of a Crown Colony Government. At first there will be in each of the new Colonies a Governor, an Executive Council consisting of the highest officials, and a Legislative Council, which latter shall consist of a certain number of official members and also of a nominated non-official element. But it is the wish of His Majesty's Government to introduce a representative element as soon as circumstances permit, and, in course of time, to grant to the new colonies the right of self-government.

"It may be that I do not properly understand your proposal, but it seems to me to differ not only in detail, but also in spirit from the scheme I have just read to you."

Judge Hertzog: "I entirely agree with you that there is a difference in idea between the two proposals; but only such a difference in idea as might well be found between Colonies of the same State. In other words, one constitution is adapted for one colony, whilst another constitution is found fitting for another colony, but yet they all belong to the same Empire."

Lord Milner: "Exactly. There are different constitutions in different Colonies; but it seems to me that the policy laid down in your proposal differs from that laid down by His Majesty's Government."

Judge Hertzog: "I think that I am expressing the opinion of the whole Commission when I say that we wish for peace. I draw attention to this to show the way in which, according to my opinion, we should consider the matter. For if we on both sides are really desirous of coming to a settlement, we should not make too much of theoretical difficulties, so long as the practical aim has been obtained. For instance, the different Colonies which now are joined to form the United States once possessed constitutions differing much from one another. Now the constitution laid down in our proposal does not differ so much from that laid down in yours that a practical difference should arise therefrom; and such a practical difference would arise if you insisted upon carrying on negotiations on your own basis. I imagine that England has a certain object before her in South Africa, and I believe that that object can be as well obtained by our proposal as by that of Middelburg. I therefore ask, Is the difference so great that, in order for England to obtain her object, an entirely new status must be called into existence?"

Lord Milner: "We are comparing two different things. Here in the Middelburg scheme there are a number of definite proposals, which enter upon a great mass of particulars. I do not mean to imply that we have not the power to go into particulars. I perfectly understand that it lies within the power of Lord Kitchener and myself to carry on further deliberations with you about details, so as to throw light on any doubtful points, and, perhaps, to make such changes as would not fundamentally affect the scheme. As you say that your proposals are not in contradiction with those formulated at Middelburg, then there is no reason why you should not lay aside your proposals and discuss the Middelburg proposals, which are definite."

Judge Hertzog: "I quite admit that you, Lord Milner, are entitled to say that there is a fundamental difference between our proposals. But it is another question whether the difficulty that thus arises is of such a nature that we—those of us who on both sides are anxious to conclude peace—should not be able to find a solution to it satisfactory to both parties. I cannot answer that question; nor can I see why the same result would not be reached by negotiating on the basis proposed by us as by carrying on negotiations on the Middelburg proposal."

Lord Milner: "I understand, then, that you acknowledge that there is a fundamental difference between the two bases. Well, I do not think that we are empowered to negotiate on a basis differing from that laid down in the last report of His Majesty's Government, and also differing from the tenor of the Middelburg proposal. I may say that I believe that His Majesty's Government in their latest message went as far as it was possible for them to go with the object of meeting you. The whole spirit of the telegram was to that effect."

Commander-in-Chief de Wet: "I hope you will understand that I do not speak as a lawyer. (Lord Kitchener, laughing: "That's the case with me too!") I fully concur with what General Botha and Judge Hertzog have said in regard to our eagerness to establish peace. In order to be brief, I will only remark that I did not understand His Excellency, Lord Milner, to mean—any more than I myself meant—that we should go to the nation with the Middelburg proposal, with the idea of coming back with it unaltered."

Lord Milner: "No; if I gave that impression, I did not intend to do so. But I believe that when you went to your people with the last message from His Majesty's Government it was with the knowledge—which the message itself made clear—that His Majesty's Government was not prepared to take into consideration any terms which differed widely from the policy laid down in the Middelburg proposal."

Commander-in-Chief de Wet: "That was indeed what I understood; and accordingly we have now come with a proposal which does not differ very much from the Middelburg proposal."

General Smuts: "I thought that the vital principle your Government had in view was the destruction of our independence, and in our proposal the independence of the two Republics with regard to foreign relations is given up. I was therefore of opinion that the two parties might come to an arrangement on this basis. I did not think that for the restoration of peace the Middelburg terms were essential."

Lord Milner: "Not in the details, but in the general ideas. As the British Government has laid down a basis, and you have had weeks in which to consider the matter, it would never do for you now to put it on one side. Lord Kitchener has given your nation considerable time in which to take counsel; and now you come back, and, ignoring the Middelburg terms, you propose entirely different ones of your own, and say, let us negotiate on these. I do not believe that I and Lord Kitchener would be justified in doing this. But in case he is of another opinion, the British Government can be asked if they are prepared to set on one side all the former deliberations and begin again on a new basis."

Commander-in-Chief de Wet: "We cannot, of course, prevent Lord Kitchener from asking his Government any questions he pleases, but, at the same time, we request that you will cable our behests to the English Government."

Commandant-General Botha: "I cannot see that we are beginning again on a new basis, for, in consequence of the negotiations in April last, you were ordered by the British Government to encourage us to make fresh proposals. Our present proposal is the direct result of that order."

Lord Milner: "I did my best to get fresh proposals from you, but you would not make any. You forced the British Government into making proposals."

Commandant-General Botha: "I am of opinion that we must both work together in this matter of formulating proposals."

Lord Kitchener: "You were asked to make proposals, but you did not do so; and now, after the British Government has made a proposal, you yourselves come forward with one of your own."

General De la Rey: "I think that it was the encouragement given us by correspondence between the Netherlands and the British Government that caused us to make our proposals."

Lord Milner: "That correspondence was at the beginning of the negotiations."

Commander-in-Chief de Wet: "If we had been obliged to make a new proposal in April, we would not have been able to make one so fair, and so much to the advantage of the British Government, as our present one, for, not having consulted the nation, we would have been compelled to insist on entire independence."

Lord Milner: "I must remind you of what has taken place; not with the object of putting you in the wrong, but in order to make the position clear, for there are some points about it which are not very clear. You came and made a proposal. The British Government gave you a distinct answer—they refused to accept it. Their answer was perfectly outspoken, and perfectly intelligible. At the same time they said, 'We are anxious for peace; will you make other proposals?' You then said, 'No! we have no power to do so; we must first consult the nation.' We admitted that argument. Then you said, 'Let the British Government make proposals.' The British Government did so, and they are fully entitled to an answer. In what position do you think you are placing Lord Kitchener and myself? You come back with a totally fresh proposal, and do not say anything about ours. This is not fair treatment to the British Government, and we are not bound to take your proposal into consideration."

Judge Hertzog: "I have endeavoured to show that our reply really cannot be taken as ignoring the proposal of the British Government. The great question in the correspondence in April between us and the British Government was the question of independence; and now, after having consulted the nation, we come here and say that we are prepared to sacrifice in some degree our independence, and we indicate how far we will give it up. And, as General Smuts has said, that is the basis which we have laid down in our present proposal."

Lord Milner: "You say that you give up your independence as regards foreign relations."

Judge Hertzog: "Yes. But then you must understand that this is only a general principle, which we treat in detail later on."

General Smuts: "The independence is given up both in regard to our foreign relations and in regard to interior administration, which will be placed under the supervision of the British Government. So that the effect of these two articles is, that the independence is sacrificed, and that the two Republics will not in the future be able to be regarded as Sovereign States."

Lord Milner: "I understand perfectly well that they would not be Sovereign States any longer, but my intellect is not bright enough for me to be able to say what they really would be."

Lord Kitchener: "They would be a new kind of 'international animal.'"

General Smuts: "It has more than once happened in the course of history that difficulties have been solved by compromise. And this draft proposal goes as near as seems possible towards making us a Colony."

Lord Kitchener: "Do you accept the annexation?"

General Smuts: "Not formally; but I do not see in what way this proposal is in opposition to the annexation proclamation."

Lord Kitchener: "I am afraid I am not clever enough to comprehend this. There would be two Governments in one State. And how do you imagine that this arrangement could be carried on?"

General Smuts: "A more ample explanation will have to be given of the word 'supervision'; and I thought that this was just one of the points on which we could carry on further discussions and negotiations."

Lord Milner: "I am certainly not going to give up an explicit basis for a vague proposal."

Lord Kitchener: "I feel convinced that your proposal would never be able to be carried out in the practical governing of a country."

Commander-in-Chief de Wet: "I agree that our proposal has not been fully worked out, but neither have the Middelburg proposals. This was clearly indicated by Lord Kitchener and Lord Milner when these proposals were made, and they were only looked upon as a basis on which we could negotiate, so that the business might be begun. We naturally cannot compel the British Government to accept our proposal; but, at all events, it is a basis."

Lord Milner: "I am very anxious that these discussions should not end in smoke, and I shall not allow any formalities to stand in the way, but to abandon the definite proposals of Middelburg (March 7th) for a thing like this, and to begin a fresh discussion on the basis of something which is so very vague will surely land us in trouble. I believe we are quite entitled to keep you to the Middelburg proposal, which we might modify in regard to details."

Commandant-General Botha: "Perhaps it would be well if you would first give an answer to our proposals."

Commander-in-Chief de Wet: "I think that (unless your Excellencies have power to give a final answer to our terms) it would not be unfair if we were to ask you to lay our proposal before your Government."

Commandant-General Botha: "We are come here with the earnest intention of concluding peace; and I think that if our proposal is carried out Boer and Briton will be able to live side by side in this country. I presume that it is the wish of both parties to be fair and just, and to make a peace by which both can abide, and which will be permanent in South Africa."

Lord Milner: "That is certainly our aim."

Lord Kitchener: "Your proposal would involve important changes in our own—changes which, so far as I understand them, we should be unable to permit."

Commandant-General Botha: "I am of opinion that before a proposal is made from your side you should give a definite answer to ours."

Lord Kitchener and Lord Milner: "Well, then, change your proposal into ours."

Lord Milner: "I do not believe that the British Government is prepared to go any further to meet you than they have done in their last proposal. They think that they have already gone far in their efforts for peace—further, indeed, than the general opinion of the British public would warrant."

Lord Kitchener: "The difference between our proposals seems to be too great."

Commandant-General Botha: "We shall always remain under the supervision of the British Government."

Lord Kitchener: "Will you then consider yourselves British subjects? 'Supervision' is a new word, and 'suzerainty' has already caused us too much trouble."

Judge Hertzog: "The idea is not so very new. There are several kinds of different States, all belonging to the British Empire. For instance, there is Basutoland."

Lord Milner: "There are many different kinds, but this one is a new variety."

Judge Hertzog: "If your Excellencies could only understand us! We have no wish to lose a single minute. We have been to the nation, and we know what the nation wants and what their temper is. If, then, we are to make a proposal here, it must be:—Firstly, a proposal which shall meet the English Government in a fair way; and, secondly, a proposal which we are honestly convinced will be acceptable to our nation. And such a proposal we have laid before you. And now we are placed in a disadvantageous position, for we are here before your Excellencies, who have not full power finally to decide the matter."

Lord Kitchener: "We are in the same position as yourselves."

Judge Hertzog: "We offer you here what we know is in accordance with the mind of the nation; we cannot possibly do anything that is against it."

Lord Milner: "Are we to understand that the Middelburg proposals are not according to the mind of your people?"

General Smuts: "As yet no answer has been given to them. The only decision come to by the national meeting is that which we are now laying before you."

Lord Kitchener: "Are you prepared to set aside your present proposal and to hand in another one bearing a closer resemblance to that of Middelburg? We must try and find some middle course; and as we are here to endeavour to arrive at something definite, let us try to obtain a basis for discussion. Shall we make a new proposal?"

General Smuts: "As soon as there is a final answer to our proposal we shall be able to take a fresh one into consideration."

Lord Milner: "I believe that the fact that you have refused to enter upon the proposal made by the British Government justifies us in not considering your proposal. Let us rather say that your very refusal implies your answer to what we have proposed."

General Smuts: "I understand the position to be as follows—The British Government has declined our proposals, and at the same time holds fast to the old basis, but without prejudice to its power of making a new proposal."

Lord Milner: "The whole difference between you and myself is that I take the letter of 7th March to be the utmost concession that the British Government is able to grant; not that that letter binds us down to every clause of the proposal, but that it is an indication of how far our Government is prepared to go on the general question. Your answer, however, is no answer at all."

Lord Kitchener then read his telegram, dated 14th April. "A difficulty has arisen in getting on with the proceedings; the representatives state that constitutionally they have no power to discuss terms based on the surrender of independence, inasmuch as only the burghers can agree to such a basis. Therefore, if they were to propose terms, it would put them in a false position with regard to the people. If, however, His Majesty's Government could state the terms which, subsequently to a relinquishment of independence, they would be prepared to grant, the representatives, after asking for the necessary explanations, and without any expression of approval or disapproval, would submit such conditions to their people."] "Clearly you have not kept to what you undertook in this telegram."

Commander-in-Chief de Wet: "If it had only been a question of our feelings being hurt by having to give an answer on the basis proposed to us by the British then it would not have been necessary for the people to come together at Vereeniging. But in matter of fact we have come here with a proposal, which, rightly understood, is nearly equivocal to the Middelburg proposal, and which meets the wishes of the English Government as far as possible."

Commandant-General Botha: "I do not see why we should insist so much on our proposal. If it is not to the mind of your Excellencies, if it is an unacceptable proposal, then let us have a definite answer to it."

Lord Milner: "We wish to have an answer to the proposal made by us."

General Smuts: "I do not see that any proposal has been made by the British Government. A certain basis only has been laid down, and therefore no formal answer is required."

Lord Milner: "Our proposal is six times as definite as yours, and I believe that the British Government is justified in wanting to know if your people are inclined to come to terms on the general lines which have been placed before them."

Lord Kitchener: "Here is quite an original suggestion: How would it be if you were to go back to your people and ask them if they would not make a proposal?"

General Smuts: "You must understand that the Middelburg proposal, with all that took place in April, has been read to the people. Their answer was neither 'Yes' nor 'No.' They simply elected the delegates. The delegates as yet have not given any answer. They are still considering the matter, and, in order to gain time, they have commissioned us to see whether we could not come to some arrangement."

Lord Milner: "We are getting away from the subject. Tell us what alterations you want, and then place our proposal before your people."

Lord Kitchener: "Should you agree that your proposal is not in opposition to the annexation, we shall have accomplished something."

General Smuts: "Is it your opinion that our proposal must be set aside?"

Lord Kitchener: "Yes, surely. It is impossible for us to act on it."

Lord Milner: "It is impossible for us to take your proposal into consideration. We can send it to England, but this would certainly tend to hinder the negotiations. This is my personal opinion, which naturally you are not bound to accept. All that we can say is, that this is the only answer that we can give you."

Lord Kitchener: "It would be better to draw up a new document, in which everything of importance would be noted down, and all unimportant matters left out."

General Smuts: "But paragraph 3 of our proposal has not even been mentioned. We are prepared to cede a part of our territory."

Lord Milner: "This would be in contradiction to the annexation of the whole. If the whole becomes annexed by us, how then can a part be ceded by you?"

General Smuts: "The ceded part would then become a Crown Colony, the remaining part being governed as is here proposed."

Lord Milner: "You mean that one part would become a British Colony of the ordinary type, and another part a protected Republic?"

Lord Kitchener: "Two forms of government in the same country would lead to great friction. Our proposals are too divergent. From a military point of view, the two forms of government could not co-exist. Before a year was over we should be at war again."

The meeting was then adjourned till the afternoon.

During the interval the Commission discussed the situation, and sent General J.C. Smuts to deliberate on several points with Lord Kitchener and Lord Milner.

The meeting opened again at four o'clock.

Lord Milner: "In consequence of an informal conversation with General Smuts, Lord Kitchener and I have drawn up a document, which will show the form in which, as we think, the only agreement that can be arrived at must be worded. It is a draft document, and we believe the Governments will be able to sign it. Our idea is that after it has been taken into consideration here it might be laid before the burghers, and you could ask them, 'Are you willing that we should put our signatures to it?'"

This document ran as follows:—"The undersigned, leaders of the Boer forces in the Veldt, accepting, in their own name, and in that of the said burghers, the annexations as mentioned in the proclamations of Lord Roberts, dated respectively the 24th May, in the year of our Lord nineteen hundred, and number 15, dated 1st day of September, in the year of our Lord nineteen hundred, and accepting as a consequence thereof their status of British citizens, agree herewith immediately to lay down their weapons, and to hand over all guns, small arms, ammunition, and stores in their possession, or under their hold, and to cease all further resistance against the Government of His Majesty King Edward Seventh, or his successors. They do this trusting in the assurance of His Majesty's Government that neither their personal freedom nor their property shall be taken away from them, or from the burghers who surrender with them; and that the future action of His Majesty's Government in relation to the consequences of the war shall be in harmony with the declaration mentioned below. It is clearly understood that all burghers who at present are prisoners of war, in order to be able to enjoy the above-mentioned assurance, will have to notify their acceptance of the status of British citizens."

Commandant-General Botha: "Are we to understand that our proposal is now altogether rejected?"

Lord Milner and Lord Kitchener: "Yes."

Commandant-General Botha: "Then I understand that you are going to be guided only by the Middelburg proposals?"

Lord Kitchener: "No; we can alter them."

Lord Milner: "This draft document was originally written out in order to be annexed to the Middelburg proposals. But instead of the Middelburg proposals, this document is now drawn up, in order to place us in the position to formulate the proposals differently."

General Smuts: "If the idea is then that the Middelburg proposals should be amended, would it not be best to do so now, and then to annex them to this document?"

Lord Milner: "That which will take the place of the Middelburg proposals has to be added as a schedule to this document, and we have to work out this schedule together."

General Smuts: "I think it would be far better if you were to alter the proposal yourselves, and then lay it before us for consideration; we could then see what we could do to meet you."

Lord Kitchener: "I think that a sub-committee should be formed by you in order to draw up the schedule."

Lord Milner: "My idea is that the schedule should be drawn up, so that it and the document could be taken into consideration together."

General Smuts: "We should like to consider first whether we will help in drawing it up."

Lord Milner: "I am willing to draw it up in conjunction with you, or to let it be drawn up by you alone, but, from past experience, I must decline to draw it up by myself."

General Smuts: "If we were to sign this document, would not the outcome be that we leaders made ourselves responsible for the laying down of arms by our burghers."

Lord Milner: "Yes. And should your men not lay down their arms it would be a great misfortune."

Lord Kitchener: "I do not think so, for if some of the burghers refused to lay down their arms, the signatories could not help it. There are sure to be some who are dissatisfied."

General Smuts: "The document does not mention this."

Lord Kitchener: "It can be amended."

General De la Rey: "Well, then, there can be no peace, for one part of the burghers will hold back and continue the war."

Lord Milner: "If the national meeting agrees to give you power to sign this document, it will certainly mean that the burghers as a whole are agreeable; and those who after this do not submit will be—well, I do not know what I can call them—outlaws. But we will not consider such an eventuality possible."

General Botha: "We desire a peace that will be honourable to both parties. And, as I understand this document, we are leaving honour behind us, for we are now not only surrendering our independence, but we are allowing every burgher to be fettered hand and foot. Where is the 'honourable peace' for us? If we conclude peace, we have to do it as men who have to live and die here. We must not agree to a peace which leaves behind in the hearts of one party a wound that will never heal. I will do everything in my power to obtain peace. But it seems to me that this document asks too much of us, because, if I interpret it aright, it means that we must surrender our independence, that every one must give up his weapons, and that the leaders, in addition, must sign an undertaking to this effect."

Lord Milner: "All that we wish is that the people should live peacefully together as British citizens. If we do not obtain this, then I do not know what we do obtain."

Lord Kitchener: "I do not think that the Commandant-General realizes what the schedule contains. In it we state what we are ready to grant. Perhaps it would be best that the schedule should be arranged now, and then you will see that an honourable peace is proposed."

General Botha: "Well, then, explain the document."

Lords Kitchener and Milner: "You are to help us: we do not know what the burghers demand."

Commander-in-Chief de Wet: "By signing this document we shall place ourselves in the position which the Commandant-General has so clearly described."

General De la Rey: "We cannot form a judgment on anything that is not properly elaborated. I have no objection to the constitution of a sub-committee with the duty of helping in the work."

Commandant-General Botha: "I also have no objection, since I understand that it binds nobody to anything."

Lord Kitchener: "No, nobody will be bound."

General De la Rey: "We wish to have the matter concluded, so that we may know what is before us."

Commander-in-Chief de Wet: "I should like to have it clearly understood that I do not think there is the least chance of a Government of which Lords Kitchener and Milner are the heads being accepted. An arrangement of this nature would, it seems to me, be an insurmountable difficulty. When I feel so strongly in this matter, it would not be fair to their Excellencies for me to remain silent."

Lord Kitchener: "I think it would be better if General de Wet were to wait until he has seen the whole document before he gives his opinion."

It was then agreed that Judge Hertzog and General Smuts should act as a sub-committee, in order to draw up a complete draft with Lord Kitchener, who was to be assisted by Sir Richard Solomon.

The meeting then adjourned.

On Wednesday, 21st May, 1902, the Conference reassembled.

Lord Milner laid before the meeting the documents which he had drawn up with the help of the sub-committee. It was in the form of a contract, and the names of the members of both Governments were now filled in. The document was the same as that telegraphed, with the exception of Article 11, dealing with the notes and receipts and the sum of three million pounds.

It was read in Dutch and English, and ran as follows:—

"General Lord Kitchener of Khartoum, Commander-in-Chief, and His Excellency Lord Milner, High Commissioner, on behalf of the British Government;

"Messrs. S.D. Burger, F.W. Reitz, Louis Botha, J.H. De la Rey, L.J. Meijer, and J.C. Krogh, on behalf of the Government of the South African Republic and its burghers;

"Messrs. M.T. Steyn, W.J.C. Brebner, C.R. de Wet, J.B.M. Hertzog, and C.H. Olivier, on behalf of the Government of the Orange Free State and its burghers, being anxious to put an end to the existing hostilities, agree on the following points:—

"Firstly, the burgher forces now in the Veldt shall at once lay down their arms, and surrender all the guns, small arms and war stores in their actual possession, or of which they have cognizance; and shall refrain from any further opposition to the authority of His Majesty King Edward VII., whom they acknowledge as their lawful sovereign.

"The manner and details of this surrender shall be arranged by Lord Kitchener, Commandant-General Botha, Assistant-Commandant-General J.H. De la Rey, and Commander-in-Chief de Wet.

"Secondly, burghers in the Veldt beyond the frontiers of the Transvaal and of the Orange River Colony shall, on their surrender, be brought back to their homes.

"Thirdly, all prisoners of war, being at the time burghers out of South Africa, shall, on their declaring that they accept this status of subjects of His Majesty King Edward VII., be brought back to the farms on which they were living before the war.

"Fourthly, the burghers who thus surrender, or who thus return, shall lose neither their personal freedom nor their property.

"Fifthly, no judicial proceedings, civil or criminal, shall be taken against any of the burghers who thus return for any action of theirs in connexion with the carrying on of the war.

"Sixthly, the Dutch language shall be taught in the public schools of the Transvaal and of the Orange River Colony, where the parents of the children demand it; and shall be admitted in the courts of justice, wherever this is required for the better and more effective administration of justice.

"Seventhly, the possession of rifles shall, on taking out a license in accordance with the law, be permitted in the Transvaal and in the Orange River Colony, to persons who require them for their protection.

"Eighthly, military administration in the Transvaal and in the Orange River Colony shall, as soon as possible, be followed by civil government; and, as soon as circumstances permit it, a representative system tending towards autonomy shall be introduced.

"Ninthly, the question of granting the franchise to the natives shall not be decided until a representative constitution has been granted.

"Tenthly, no special tax shall be laid on landed property in the Transvaal and Orange River Colony to meet the expenses of the war.

"Eleventhly, a judicial Commission shall be appointed, to which the government bank notes, issued under Law No. 1 of the South African Republic, may be presented within six months. All such notes, if found to have been duly issued in conformity with the terms of the law, and if the presenting party shall have given consideration in value, shall be honoured, but without interest.

"All receipts issued in the Veldt by the officers of the late Republics, or by their orders, may also be presented to the said Commission within six months; and if they have been given bona fide in exchange for goods used by the burghers in the Veldt, they shall be paid in full to the persons to whom they were originally issued.

"The amount payable on account of the said Government's notes and receipts shall not exceed £3,000,000; and in case the whole amount of such notes and receipts accepted by the Commission should exceed that amount, a pro rata reduction shall be made.

"The prisoners of war shall be given facilities to present their notes and receipts within the above-mentioned six months.

"Twelfthly, as soon as circumstances shall permit, there shall be appointed in each district of the Transvaal and of the Orange River Colony a Commission, in which the inhabitants of that district shall be represented, under the chairmanship of a magistrate or other official, with a view to assist in the bringing back of the people to their farms, and in procuring for those who, on account of losses through the war, are unable to provide for themselves, food, shelter, and such quantities of seed, cattle, implements, etc., as are necessary for the resuming of their previous callings. Funds for this purpose, repayable by instalments extending over a number of years, shall be advanced—free of interest—by the Government."

Lord Milner: "If we come to an agreement, it will be the English document which will be wired to England, on which His Majesty's Government will decide, and which will be signed."

Commandant-General Botha: "Will not a Dutch translation be annexed?"

Lord Milner: "I have no objection to the addition of a Dutch translation. This, then, is the document which we are prepared to lay before the English Government."

Commandant-General Botha: "There are a few points on which I wish to speak. The first is in reference to the receipts given by our officers. It seems to me quite right that they should be mentioned in the paragraph about government notes. These receipts were issued, in accordance with instructions given by our Government, for the purchase of cattle, grain, and other necessaries for the support of our commandos; and the chief officers now present, as well as all other officers, have acted according to these instructions and issued receipts. Therefore I make this request. Some of these receipts were afterwards paid in part, and others in full, in government notes. But many were not paid at all. I do not believe that the amount is great, but it will strengthen our hands to be able to take up this affair honourably, for our honour is concerned in so far as we have signed the receipts. It will be a great point in our favour to be able to go before our delegates and tell them that they are guaranteed on this point, for most of them are officers."

Lord Kitchener: "I understand that General Botha refers not to commandeer or requisition notes, but only to actual receipts issued on the Treasury."

Lord Milner: "I do not see any difference between these receipts and commandeer notes. The willingness of persons to sell goods makes no difference in a legal document."

Lord Kitchener: "I mean that it makes a difference whether it is an order on the Treasury or a requisition note. I should limit this (guarantee) to receipts on the Treasury, issued in consequence of a law that permitted a certain sum to be issued."

Commander-in-Chief de Wet: "No decision was come to in the Free State as to how much was to be issued."

Lord Kitchener: "Am I to understand by this that it is an unlimited amount, or does it come within the amount decided on by the Volksraad?"

General Smuts: "While the Government existed the Volksraad empowered it to issue notes up to a certain amount. And this was done. Moreover the officers in the Veldt had the right to make purchases for the commandos and to give receipts for them."

Lord Milner: "I can see no difference between receipts and requisition notes, and they have been issued for an unlimited amount."

General Smuts: "These receipts were issued under a totally different law. They were not paid out of the credit voted by the Volksraad."

Commander-in-Chief de Wet: "I would have it clearly understood that I quite agree with what has been said by the Commandant-General, namely that the honour of every officer is engaged for these documents, and if your Excellencies agree it will give us a strong weapon with which to return to the delegates."

Lord Milner: "The proposal is de facto that the British Government shall repay all the monies which the Republics borrowed with the object of fighting against England."

Commander-in-Chief de Wet: "Yet we have fought honourably, and if we give up our independence it is no more than fair that you should meet us in this matter."

Commandant-General Botha: "Am I to understand your position to be that we must surrender everything, and that whilst you take away the freedom of our country (which amounts to many millions) you at the same time refuse all responsibility for our debts. We had been recognized by you as belligerent, and so are entirely in our rights in asking that when you seize the riches of the country you shall also take its debts upon your shoulders. So long as the British Government reaches the great goal at which it is aiming, a matter so easily arranged as this should not cause any difficulty: we are not bickering about trifles, but are bringing forward what to us is a real hardship, and you must take it for granted that when we say something here we really mean it. And now we tell you that this matter is an obstacle in our way. Personally, we have not signed many receipts: it was the officers of lower rank who signed the greater number, and it is these very officers who form the majority of the national meeting at Vereeniging. In some instances, I may add, special persons were appointed for the purpose of carrying out this work."

Lord Milner: "We do not take over the assets without taking also the liabilities. We take over all the debts owed by the country before the war, and we have even agreed to take over a debt—a legal debt—in the shape of notes, which notes we are fully aware it only became necessary to issue on account of the war, and thus we are already paying a part of the cost incurred in fighting us. I think this is a very great concession; and when I agreed that it should be put down I said that I believed (and I still am of the same opinion) that the English Government would take exception to it, although I hope that this will not be the case. But to go further than this, and to ask us to pay not only a debt contracted under a law for the furtherance of the war, but also every debt contracted by every officer in the armies of both Republics, for the purpose of fighting us, is to my mind a most extravagant proposal. In answer to what General Botha has said, I may observe that the Commission appears to think that we have no persons behind us whose feelings and prejudices (if you use that word) we are bound to take into consideration. If this matter causes a difficulty among your burghers, I can only say that I am sure that your proposal will cause the British Government the greatest trouble when dealing with the nation, with whose feelings they have to reckon."

Commander-in-Chief de Wet: "I should like to explain the position of the Orange Free State. In the Transvaal a law was passed empowering the Government to issue £1,000,000; but in the Orange Free State nothing was done, as the Government possessed the right to pay with receipts, and we thought that a receipt was as good and as legal as a note; and therefore, from my point of view, the two are of equal importance."

Commandant-General Botha: "I might point out that we should not insist so much on the technical meaning of words—and this is especially true for your side, because we have assembled here with the aim of stopping the hostilities which cause you such great expenses every month; and our meeting may be able to bring these expenses to an end. Therefore, if you accept our proposal and pay these receipts, you might save almost enough to cover the cost you incur. It would be much cheaper to make an end of the war by co-operation than to let matters drift on. Therefore I believe that it is the duty of both parties to be willing to make concessions when obstacles appear."

General de Wet: "I can assure His Excellency, Lord Milner, that the people always believed that should everything be lost they still would be able to obtain this money due on receipts. If this is not granted, I cannot imagine what the results will be. I am afraid of the consequences; and I trust that you will do your best to meet our wishes."

Commandant-General Botha: "It will not be a very large sum, but we cannot give you the exact amount."

Commander-in-Chief de Wet: "You can well understand that our expenses are only a drop in the ocean compared with yours. If I am right, the Orange Free State had three quarters of a million when the war began, and the issue of receipts only started when that sum was exhausted. Your Excellencies must acknowledge that we have the same obligation of creditor through these receipts as we should have in any other case."

Commandant-General Botha: "You have already many of our notes in your possession. In one case alone there were fifty thousand hidden away, and found by you. I have stated privately to Lord Milner that what we are now striving to obtain has already been granted to us de facto by Lord Kitchener. In Lord Kitchener's Middelburg proposal the paying of the Government notes was refused, but there was a proviso that the receipts should be paid to the amount of one million. Should this now be withdrawn, surely such a withdrawal would form a deviation from the Middelburg proposal. The paying of notes is legal, and is on quite another footing, and I cannot understand how it could have been refused in the Middelburg proposal. That it should be granted now is only reasonable. But as regards the payment of receipts, although it was allowed then up to a certain amount, it is now withdrawn. At this present stage of the proceedings I think that a point which had already been practically conceded in the previous negotiations should not be allowed to form a stumbling-block to a final agreement. I believe that the amount is only small; I was for one year in conjunction with De la Rey in command of the forces of the South African Republic. During that period of time an account was kept of all the receipts, and only a short time back the books were still in our possession. These receipts were issued in an orderly manner, and each of them was duly entered in a book, as far as I was able to judge. These receipts amounted to quite a small sum; and although Lord Milner would draw back if the sum was very big, the question how far he will go can be settled when the proposal is accepted. Yet I personally think that there are no grounds for fear, and the amount is really far smaller than you imagine."

Lord Milner: "I do not think it is so much a question of amount. This paying of notes and requisition notes appears to me very unreasonable. I believe that in this matter I am only voicing the opinion of the great majority of the British nation when I say that my countrymen would much prefer to pay a large sum at the conclusion of hostilities with the object of bettering the condition of the people who have been fighting against them than to pay a much smaller sum to meet the costs incurred by the Republics during the war. Whether such a view is right or wrong, it is a view you have to reckon with. We do not wish to pay the accounts of both parties; and my opinion of the clause quoted from the Middelburg proposal is that that clause was one of its faults. But should anything of the kind become necessary, then I think that the paying of the notes is less objectionable than the paying of the requisition notes. I placed this point about the payment of notes in the draft because I thought that if it came to a choice between paying one or the other you would prefer that the notes should be paid. However, if it should be thought better to return on this point to the Middelburg proposal, although I am greatly against the clause, I will waive my objection to it if Lord Kitchener is agreeable."

General Smuts: "I am afraid that we cannot agree to this, for we thought that the notes would be beyond all dispute."

Judge Hertzog: "I do not think that your Excellency is representing the matter fairly when you say that you will not pay the bills of both parties. There is one thing to be taken into consideration as regards the Orange Free State, and which must be considered before everything else, and that is, that we have made no loans nor have we given any government notes. The notes we used were notes of the South African Republic, which had been sent to the Orange Free State. Our law was formed on the idea that in case of war all the costs should be paid by commission notes. The Orange Free State acted on this principle, and receipts were issued. If we take into consideration at the same time that we have been and still are recognized by you as belligerent, then we can only say: On our side we surrender everything that we possess, and we only ask the other party to acknowledge the fact that if we had contracted a loan it would have been to the charge of the British Government, who, in taking everything from us, renders itself responsible for our public loans. Lord Milner should understand that it is of just as much importance to us for the receipts to be paid as it is to the South African Republic for the loan, which it contracted before the war, to be taken over by the British Government. But I can even go further and give Lord Milner the assurance that we have acted more economically when issuing these receipts than we should have done had we contracted the loan previous to the war. Now we have only what is absolutely necessary to meet our present needs. So that Lord Milner must own that we find ourselves in the same position towards those who are in possession of receipts, as we should have occupied towards any other creditor we might have had before the war began. I must give my support to what the Commandant-General has said; and I can only repeat what I have already informally told Lord Milner, namely, that this difficulty is almost insurmountable."

Lord Milner: "We can refer this to our Government. But your proposal is altogether antagonistic to the Middelburg proposal, which absolutely rejected the idea of taking over all the debts of the two States."

Lord Kitchener: "I should like to know the amount."

General De la Rey: "My issue of notes amounts to between twenty and fifty thousand pounds; but I cannot say what the issue in receipt has been."

Lord Milner: "There really is a feasible compromise, namely, to allow the notes and receipts to come in and to establish the suggested limit of £1,000,000."

Lord Kitchener: "Would that meet your difficulty?"

Commandant-General Botha: "No."

Lord Kitchener: "Well, would two or three million be sufficient? We must have a limit before we can do anything."

Commander-in-Chief de Wet: "It is impossible to stipulate the amount."

Lord Kitchener: "If you were in a position to give a limit, it would simplify matters."

Commander-in-Chief de Wet: "I agree with that entirely, and I can quite understand the position in which you are placed. Yet it is absolutely impossible to assign an amount. Will you give us your permission to adjourn for a moment in order to discuss the matter?"

The meeting was then adjourned. It reassembled at 2.30 p.m.

Commander-in-Chief de Wet: "We have agreed to fix on a sum of £3,000,000 for the government notes and receipts; their amount paid pro rata can be lowered should this sum prove insufficient. We have drawn up an article to lay before the meeting."

General Smuts then read a draft which was inserted at the end of Article 11 in the draft agreement.

In answer to a question by Lord Kitchener, Commander- in-Chief de Wet said: "The prisoners of war on the different islands who are in possession of such notes should be given an opportunity of sending them in for payment."

Lord Milner: "What is the next point you wish to raise? We now understand what your position is."

Commandant-General Botha: "Am I to understand that you mean that we are getting away from the point in discussion?"

Lord Milner: "This document contains your view of the matter, so we are now aware of your idea."

Commandant-General Botha: "We must know what to say to the delegates."

Lord Kitchener: "Is this the only point you wish to bring forward, or are there others in addition?"

Commandant-General Botha: "There is another concerning the protection of debtors, which is a vital question for us."

Lord Milner: "We must not have any beating about the bush. Everything must appear in the document."

General Smuts: "Most of the debts contracted before the war will have to be paid after the war; and if the debtors cannot pay we are afraid that it will result in the ruin of a great part of the inhabitants. We should like to see steps taken to prevent this. If Lord Milner intends to take such steps, we should like to be informed what they are."

Lord Milner: "I think it would be best if you were to make a proposal on this point."

General Smuts: "Our proposal is roughly that all interest which became payable during the war should be joined to the principal, and that this should be payable six months after the war."

Lord Kitchener: "Is it necessary to make a proposal about this?"

General Smuts: "If the Government is prepared to meet us in this difficulty it will be unnecessary to place a formal clause in the draft agreement."

Lord Milner: "As I look at the matter, the Government is making certain promises in this document, and I consider that all promises to which a reference may be made later should appear in it. Everything to which the Government is asked to bind itself should appear in this document, and nothing else. I do not object to clauses being added, but I wish to prevent any possible misunderstanding."

General Smuts: "Well, in that case we are quite willing to propose such a paragraph."

Commandant-General Botha: "We waive this question, so that early measures may be taken to arrive at an understanding. In case a great number of the inhabitants become subjects of His Majesty, it is to every one's interest, and principally to that of the Government, that these people should not be ruined. They will be thrown upon the mercy of a Government, whose duty it is to study their interests. If steps are not taken to prevent it, speculators who have been buying up the liabilities will, as soon as peace is concluded, enforce them, and directly the Courts of Justice are opened they will issue summonses. Against this we have to be on our guard."

Lord Milner: "I agree with the Commandant-General. I think that as these people become subjects of His Majesty, then some provision will have to be made for them. But I believe it to be neither necessary nor advisable to point out in every particular case the way in which His Majesty's Government has to provide for these people. I think that an idea exists—perhaps it is a very natural idea—because we have been fighting against the burghers that, therefore, after peace has been concluded we shall still retain a feeling of enmity against them. Just the opposite, however, is the truth. Our endeavour will naturally be, from the moment hostilities cease, to gain the confidence of the people and to do our best to promote their welfare. But if we have to bind ourselves beforehand in regard to the manner in which we shall deal with all sorts of involved legal questions, further misunderstandings are certain to occur. If you have not confidence in us—that we shall try to be a righteous Government, and to maintain the balance between the different classes of His Majesty's subjects—then you must put in writing every point that strikes you, and let them be laid before His Majesty's Government, to see what they think about them."

Commander-in-Chief de Wet: "I trust that you will not think that we are trying to tie the hands of His Majesty's Government. There are many other points which will give the Government opportunity to win the confidence of the people. But about things which concern the financial position of burghers who are entirely ruined we feel it our duty to obtain definite promises. They will be a weapon in our hands when we return to the delegates."

Commandant-General Botha: "I do not quite understand, Lord Milner. I did not interpret Mr. Chamberlain's telegram in the sense that we had to present new proposals in order to bind our hands further. I thought that proposals were to be made with a view to establishing peace."

Lord Kitchener: "I do not think that it is altogether necessary to include this proposal in the document. It concerns the very involved legal questions as to what the rights of creditor and debtor shall be, and as to what the law in the Transvaal may be on the matter. I think that every one can rest assured that the interests of the Boers will be protected by the Government in every way; and this, whether the point is put down now or left in the hands of the Government with the recommendation from this Commission to take the matter into serious consideration.

"I think that I know of a better way to deal with this involved question. Let this matter be brought under the consideration of the Government. I may be mistaken, but, as far as I can see, it will prove a very thorny question for the lawyers, and will take a long time before it can be clearly stated. It is, however, the wish of us all that you should return to the delegates equipped in such a way that you will be able to arrive at a decision. You may rest assured that the matter which you have brought before us has been included in the minutes of this meeting. I do not think that it is necessary for you to go further than this. The matter can now be carefully considered, not only here, but also in England; and you may be quite sure that your interests will receive, in every way, full consideration."

General De la Rey: "I think that the matter has been sufficiently discussed in the presence of your Excellencies, and that it need not be placed in the draft contract, for by so doing one might stumble on legal questions."

Commander-in-Chief de Wet: "This is my point of view: There are two parties, and one of them is about to cease to exist. It is, therefore, natural that this party cannot allow a vital question to pass unnoticed. It is for this reason that I cannot agree that this matter should be omitted from the draft contract. It will not be necessary that the military Government which now exists should continue after the war."

Lord Kitchener: "But the question will have to be settled by the Civil Government. It is a matter for lawyers, and must be laid before them, and will require much consideration."

Commandant-General Botha: "When hostilities are concluded it will be possible to summon a burgher for a debt contracted before the war. I put this request because our law states that no burgher can be summoned till sixty days have elapsed since the conclusion of peace."

Lord Kitchener: "You may entirely rely upon this, that whenever the war is over each burgher will have the absolute right to obtain consideration for his position in every way, and that his interests will be protected under the new as under the old regime."

Commandant-General Botha: "I understand that perfectly. But the possibility exists that syndicates may be formed to buy up all the debts, and the people may be ruined before a single burgher is in the position to earn anything or to have his position restored."

Lord Kitchener: "I quite agree with what the Commandant-General has said, and he is quite right to bring the question up. Yet I do not think that the draft contract is the best place in which to bring it forward. Once peace is a fact, then it will be the duty of every one to draw the attention of the Government to what is required to aid the nation; but to bring up difficulties at the present moment, and to attempt to right them, seems to be an endless task, and one for which this document was not destined."

Commander-in-Chief de Wet: "I am of opinion that this is a matter which should be settled by a proclamation; but I want to have as many weapons as possible in my hands when I return to the national delegates, and one of the first questions that will be asked me is this, 'What guarantee do we possess that we shall not be ruined by our creditors?' It would not be much trouble to you to give us now a draft of the proclamation which would be issued as soon as peace is concluded."

Lord Kitchener: "But this would be something quite apart from the matter under discussion."

Commander-in-Chief de Wet: "Yes."

Lord Milner: "What is the good then?"

Commander-in-Chief de Wet: "It is such a vital question for us that you cannot take it amiss if we insist upon it, for we have to give up everything."

Lord Kitchener: "Of course, no one is blaming you."

Lord Milner: "But without any thought of blame, I must point out that the effect of their proposal would be that another clause would have to be inserted in the draft contract, undertaking that such a proclamation would be issued."

Lord Kitchener: "I think that as long as the delegates receive an assurance that the Government will take this matter into consideration, in the interests of their subjects, whom they are bound to protect, that such an assurance ought to suffice. There should be no written undertaking, but only a promise that the matter shall receive attention. It is not advisable after the subject has been brought before the Government to press the matter further. The feelings of the burghers, moreover, in other ways than this, will be brought before Lord Milner."

Commander-in-Chief de Wet: "If we wished to do so, we could insist upon many other little points, but we only bring up vital questions."

Lord Kitchener: "This is one of the questions which, when once brought under the consideration of the Government cannot be put aside; and you may tell the burghers that their interests will be protected as fully as is possible. I think that, in so complicated a matter, this ought to be sufficient for them. All that is debated here is recorded in the minutes, and these minutes will be considered not only here, but also in England. Are you satisfied with this?"

Commandant-General Botha: "Yes, so far as I am concerned."

Commander-in-Chief de Wet: "I also am satisfied."

Lord Milner: "I hope it is quite understood that if the matter is allowed to remain where it is, my Government will be under no obligation to treat the matter in any particular way."

Lord Kitchener: "But there is a pledge that the matter will be properly considered."

Lord Milner: "Yes, naturally; if we put anything down in writing. I am convinced that it is necessary to make it quite clear that this document must contain everything about which there is anything in the form of a pledge."

Lord Kitchener: "There is, then, a pledge that the point upon which you have touched will be considered in your interests."

General Smuts: "There still remains the question of the payment of receipts."

Lord Kitchener: "That will be placed before the Government. The sum is an essential point; I believe the amount to be considerable. I should now like to know that it is understood that we are agreed about all these draft proposals, including your amendments, and that there are no further questions to be brought forward—it is necessary to know this, as they would have to be telegraphed to England."

Commander-in-Chief de Wet: "We have no further points to raise."

Lord Milner: "The telegram that I shall despatch is as follows:

'The Commission is prepared to lay before their burgher meeting the following document (in the event of it being sanctioned by His Majesty's Government), and to ask of the meeting a "Yes" or "No."'

"Is that satisfactory?"

Commander-in-Chief de Wet: "Yes, naturally. Only I cannot say that this document has my approval. Yet I shall be content to abide by the decision of the delegates."

Judge Hertzog: "I should not like to think that we are bound to use our influence with the delegates."

Lord Milner: "I think that is understood. I understand that the members of the Commission are not bound in respect of the opinions they may express before the burghers. They are only bound, if the British Government approves of the document, to lay it before the people. I propose to send the following telegram:

'The Commission is prepared to lay the following document before the burgher meeting at Vereeniging, for a "Yes" or "No" vote, in the event of His Majesty's Government approving of it.'

"I want also to state that we have completely deviated from the Middelburg proposal. I believe everyone is fully aware that the Middelburg proposal has been annulled altogether. Should an agreement be arranged in conformity with this document, and signed, then no attempt must be made to explain the document, or its terms, by anything in the Middelburg proposal."

The meeting was now adjourned.

Wednesday, May 28th, 1902.

The Commission met Lord Kitchener and Lord Milner at eleven o'clock with the purpose of hearing the British Government's answer to the draft proposal sent by their Lordships.

Lord Milner read the following memorandum:

"In answer to the telegram composed at our last meeting with the consent of the Commission and of which the members have received a copy, the following message has been received from His Majesty's Government:—

'His Majesty's Government sanctions the laying before the meeting for a "Yes" or "No" vote the document drawn up by the Commission and sent by Lord Kitchener on the 21st May to the Secretary of War, with the following amendments:

'The final proposal made by the British Government, on which the national representatives at Vereeniging have to answer "Yes" or "No."

'General Lord Kitchener of Khartoum, Commander-in-Chief, and His Excellency Lord Milner, High Commissioner, on behalf of the British Government;

'Messrs. S.W. Burger, F.W. Reitz, Louis Botha, J.H. De la Rey, L.J. Meijer, and J.C. Krogh on behalf of the Government of the South African Republic and its burghers;

'Messrs. M.T. Steyn, W.J.C. Brebner, C.R. de Wet, J.B.M. Hertzog, and C.H. Olivier on behalf of the Government of the Orange Free State and its burghers, being anxious to put an end to the existing hostilities, agree on the following points:

'Firstly, the burgher forces now in the Veldt shall at once lay down their arms, and surrender all the guns, small arms, and war stores in their actual possession, or of which they have cognizance, and shall abstain from any further opposition to the authority of His Majesty King Edward VII., whom they acknowledge as their lawful sovereign.

'The manner and details of this surrender shall be arranged by Lord Kitchener, Commandant-General Botha, Assistant-Commandant-General J.H. De la Rey, and Commander-in-Chief de Wet.

'Secondly, burghers in the Veldt beyond the frontiers of the Transvaal and of the Orange River Colony, and all prisoners of war who are out of South Africa, who are burghers, shall, on their declaration that they accept the status of subjects of His Majesty King Edward VII., be brought back to their homes, as soon as transport and means of subsistence can be assured.

'Thirdly, the burghers who thus surrender, or who thus return, shall lose neither their personal freedom nor their property.

'Fourthly, no judicial proceedings, civil or criminal, shall be taken against any of the burghers who thus return for any action in connexion with the carrying on of the war. The benefit of this clause shall, however, not extend to certain deeds antagonistic to the usages of warfare, which have been communicated by the Commander-in-Chief to the Boer Generals, and which shall be heard before a court martial immediately after the cessation of hostilities.

'Fifthly, the Dutch language shall be taught in the public schools of the Transvaal and of the Orange River Colony when the parents of children demand it; and shall be admitted in the Courts of Justice, whenever this is required for the better and more effective administration of justice.

'Sixthly, the possession of rifles shall, on taking out a licence in accordance with the law, be permitted in the Transvaal and the Orange River Colony to persons who require them for their protection.

'Seventhly, military administration in the Transvaal and in the Orange River Colony shall, as soon as it is possible, be followed by civil government; and, as soon as circumstances permit it, a representative system tending towards autonomy shall be introduced.

'Eighthly, the question of granting a franchise to the native shall not be decided until a representative constitution has been granted.

'Ninthly, no special tax shall be laid on landed property in the Transvaal and Orange River Colony, to meet the expenses of the war.

'Tenthly, as soon as circumstances permit there shall be appointed in each district in the Transvaal and the Orange River Colony a Commission, in which the inhabitants of that district shall be represented, under the chairmanship of a magistrate or other official, with the view to assist in the bringing back of the people to their farms, and in procuring for those who, on account of losses in the war are unable to provide for themselves, food, shelter, and such quantities of seed, cattle, implements, etc., as are necessary for the resuming of their previous callings.

'His Majesty's Government shall place at the disposal of these Commissions the sum of £3,000,000 for the above-mentioned purposes, and shall allow that all notes issued in conformity with Law No. 1, 1900, of the Government of the South African Republic, and all receipts given by the officers in the Veldt of the late Republics, or by their order, may be presented to a judicial Commission by the Government, and in case such notes and receipts are found by this Commission to have been duly issued for consideration in value, then they shall be accepted by the said Commission as proof of war losses, suffered by the persons to whom they had originally been given. In addition to the above-named free gift of £3,000,000, His Majesty's Government will be prepared to grant advances, in the shape of loans, for the same ends, free of interest for two years, and afterwards repayable over a period of years with three per cent. interest. No foreigner or rebel shall be entitled to benefit by this clause.'

Lord Milner: "In making this communication to the Commission we are instructed to add that if this opportunity of concluding an honourable peace is not taken advantage of within a time to be fixed by us, then this conference shall be regarded as closed, and His Majesty's Government shall not be bound in any way by the present terms. I have, in order that there may be no mistake about these terms, made a copy of the documents and of Lord Kitchener's telegram, also of the amendments and additions determined on by His Majesty's Government, and of the memorandum to which I have just drawn your attention."

A debate now followed on the time that should be allowed for the discussion of the proposals at Vereeniging, and it was agreed that Commandant-General Botha should propose a term that very day before the Commission left Pretoria.

It was subsequently settled that the delegates must arrive at a decision before Saturday evening, May 31st.

General Botha asked if there were any objection to the delegates erasing any paragraph of the proposal sent by the British Government.

Lord Milner: "There must be no alteration. Only 'Yes' or 'No' is to be answered."

Commandant-General Botha: "I think that the burghers have the right to erase any article they may wish, for they have the right to surrender unconditionally."

Lord Milner replied that the burghers certainly had the power to do so, but the document of the British Government could not be changed.

There now followed an informal discussion about the colonists who had been fighting on the side of the Republics.

Lord Milner communicated what the British Government's intentions were with regard to these colonists; and read the following document:—

"His Majesty's Government has to formally place on record that the colonists of Natal and the Cape Colony who have been engaged in fighting and who now surrender shall, on their return, be dealt with by the Colonial Governments in accordance with the laws of the Colonies, and that all British subjects who have joined the enemy shall be liable to be tried under the law of that part of the British Empire to which they belong.

"His Majesty's Government has received from the Government of Cape Colony a statement of their opinion as regards the terms to be offered to British subjects of the Cape Colony who are still in the Veldt or who have surrendered since April 12th, 1901. The terms are as follows:—In regard to the burghers, they all, on their surrender, after having laid down their arms, shall sign a document before a resident magistrate of the district in which their surrender has taken place, in which document they shall declare themselves guilty of high treason; and their punishment, in the event of their not having been guilty of murder, or of other deeds in contradiction to the customs of civilized warfare, shall be that for the rest of their lives they shall not be registered as voters, nor shall they be able to vote in Parliamentary, district, or municipal elections.

As regards justices and veldtcornets of the Cape Colony, and all other persons who had occupied official positions under the Government of Cape Colony, and all who held the rank of commandant in the rebel or burgher forces, they shall be brought on the charge of high treason before the ordinary Courts of the country, or before such special Courts as later on may legally be constituted. The punishment for their misdeeds shall be left to the discretion of the Court, with this reservation, that in no case shall capital punishment be inflicted.

"The Government of Natal is of opinion that the rebels should be judged by the laws of the Colony."

The meeting now adjourned.

The secretaries and Messrs. de Wet and J. Ferreira, with the help of lawyers, set themselves the task of making copies of the proposal of the British Government for the use of the national representatives at Vereeniging. This work kept them engaged until the evening.

At seven o'clock the Commission left Pretoria and returned to Vereeniging.

Appendix C Special Representatives Meetings

Meeting on Thursday, May 29th, 1902, and the Following Days

Minutes of the Meeting of the Special National Representatives at Vereeniging, South African Republic, Thursday, the 29th of May, 1902, and the Following Days

May 29th, 1902.

The Rev. J.D. Kestell having offered prayer, the Chairman requested Vice-President Burger to address the meeting.

Vice-President Burger said that the documents laid before the Governments by the Commission would now be read to the meeting. Thereupon Mr. D. Van Velden read the following letter:

Report of the Commission.

Pretoria, 28th May, 1902.

To the Governments of the Orange Free State and the South African Republic:

Honble. Gentlemen,—

In accordance with instructions received from you, we went to Pretoria in order to negotiate with the British authorities on the question of peace. We have the honour to make the following report:

The meetings lasted from Monday, May 19th, to Wednesday, May 28th, its prolongation having been principally caused by the length of time taken up by the cable correspondence with the British Government.

We first handed in a proposal (annexed under A)[320] in which we attempted to negotiate on the basis of a limited independence with surrender of part of our territory. Lords Kitchener and Milner refused emphatically to negotiate on this basis, and expressed the opinion that to cable this proposal to the British Government would be detrimental to the objects of these negotiations. They told us they had already informed the two Governments that the British Government would only negotiate on the basis of an amended form of the Middelburg proposal. In order finally to formulate this proposal, Lord Milner asked the assistance of some members of the Commission; and this was granted, on the understanding that the assistance of these members of the Commission should be given without prejudice to themselves.

As the result of the deliberations of this sub-committee, Lord Milner produced a draft proposal, in which we insisted that a fresh clause (No. 11) should be inserted; and this was done. This draft proposal (annexed under B)[321] was then cabled to the British Government, revised by them, and then communicated to us in its final shape (annexed under B).[322] We were informed by the British Government that no further revision of this proposal would be allowed, but that it must now be either accepted or rejected in its entirety by the delegates of the two Republics; and that this acceptance or rejection must take place within a stipulated time. We then told Lord Kitchener that he should know our final decision by the evening of the next Saturday at latest.

During our formal negotiations certain informal conversations took place in reference to the British subjects (in Cape Colony and Natal) who have been fighting on our side. As a result of these informal conversations a communication from the British Government was imparted to us (annexed under B).[323]

We have the honour to remain, etc.,

Louis Botha.

J.H. De La Rey.

C.R. De Wet.

J.B.M. Hertzog.

J.D. Smuts.

[320] See Appendix A

[321] See Appendix B.

[322] See Appendix B.

[323] See Appendix B.

Vice-President Burger said that the delegates must proceed to discuss this document, and that they would then be asked to decide—firstly, whether the struggle should be continued; secondly, whether the proposal of the British Government should be accepted; and, thirdly, whether they were prepared to surrender unconditionally.

It was decided that minutes of the meeting should be kept, and the delegates then proceeded to discuss the different articles of the British Government's proposal. The whole of the morning and a part of the afternoon sitting were devoted to questions dealing with the meaning of the several clauses, the members of the Commission answering to the best of their ability.

After these questions had been disposed of, Mr. De Clercq rose to speak. He said that he had already given his own opinion, but that now it was for the whole meeting to decide whether they would give up the war, and, if they resolved to do so, whether they would accept the proposal unconditionally. As to the proposal, it could not be denied that it did not give all that they themselves desired, but that could not have been expected. Should they now return to their commandos and be asked by their burghers what they had effected, they would have to reply, "Nothing." How would they be able to meet their burghers with such an answer as that? It would therefore be better to get terms from the British Government; and by doing so they would also gratify the British nation. As for himself, he was for accepting the proposal, unless it could be proved to him that unconditional surrender would be a still better course to take.

General Nieuwouwdt then proposed that the meeting should, without further delay, proceed to vote whether the war should be terminated, and whether the terms offered to them should be accepted.

General Froneman seconded this proposal.

Mr. Birkenstock (Vrijheid) felt that this was too important a matter to be treated with such haste. A decision about such a document as the one now lying before the meeting could not be come to in a moment. The delegates would hardly agree with the last speaker in his opinion that they should at once proceed to vote whether the war should or should not be continued. Time was required before coming to such a decision. Moreover it had to be proved whether it were possible to continue the war. There were some districts where it certainly could no longer be carried on. Was it possible for one part of the nation to continue fighting without the other? Then there was the question whether their resources and the troops which they still had were sufficient to justify them in prolonging the struggle. If they were insufficient the war must be discontinued and terms must be accepted. It would not be an easy thing to do; one could not, with a light heart, give up the independence of their country; but half a loaf was better than no bread,[324] and even such a sacrifice as this might be necessary if the nation was to be saved.

Commandant Jacobsz (Harrismith) was at one with the last speaker in holding that they must not be in too great a hurry to vote on the proposal.

Mr. P.R. Viljoen (Heidelberg) felt that the proposal of the British Government would so tightly bind them that they would never again be free. They were knee-haltered[325] now, but under certain circumstances they might even be hobbled.[326]

He considered that the meeting should ask the Governments to stop the war.

General Du Toit (Wolmaransstad) said that the times through which they were passing were very critical; every one ought to say exactly what he thought, and no one ought to be condemned for doing so. A delegate who should say that the war could not be continued must not be considered disloyal to his country because he did so. As regarded the three questions before the meeting, according to the opinion of his burghers the war ought to be continued. The views of his burghers when he left the commandos had been clearly expressed. "Let us retain our independence, or go on fighting," they had said. But why were they of this mind? Because they were unaware how matters stood in other districts. The eyes of the delegates, however, while directed towards God, were also able to observe the condition of the eastern parts of their country. If the burghers in those parts could not hold out, it would be impossible for the other commandos to do so. It could not be denied that some of the commandos were no longer able to continue fighting. That being the case, even if there were a majority in

[324] The Boer form of this proverb is: Half an egg is better than an empty shell.

[325] The head fastened to the knee.

[326] Having two legs fastened together.

favour of prolonging the struggle, that majority would have to yield to the wishes of the minority, and for this reason: if the war were to be continued in conformity with the wishes of the majority, and if the minority were to be compelled to surrender (and nobody would be surprised at this), then the majority would find themselves too weak to go on fighting. Thus there were clear reasons why the war must be ended. Moreover, its continuation would involve not only the national but also the moral death of the Republics. But it was still to be proved that a continuation of the war was even possible; for himself he feared that it was not so, and if fight he must he could only fight without hope and without heart. If he were now to go back to his burghers, and they were to ask him why he persisted in the war, and he was compelled to reply that he was doing so on the strength of opinions expressed in newspapers, and on the encouragement given to the cause of the Republics in their pages, he would be told that he was building on sand. Again, he feared that if the war were to be continued, detached parties would be formed which would try to obtain terms from the English for themselves. And should the commandos in time become so weak as to be forced to surrender unconditionally, what then would be the fate of the officers? Would they not lose everything, and be banished into the bargain? Let no one think, however, that he was trying merely to do what was best for himself. No. There was now a chance for negotiating; should the meeting let slip that chance, unconditional surrender would most certainly result, and that would be disastrous to all. He hoped that he would not be misunderstood; if the meeting decided to go on with the war, he, for one, would not lay down his arms. No, he would actively prosecute the war, and operate in conjunction with the other generals. But what would be the use of it: he sided with those who held that the struggle could no longer be carried on.

Commandant Rheeder (Rouxville) wished to reply to those who demanded reasons for the continuation of the war. One reason, he said, was to be found in the fact that England would not allow them to have any communication with the deputation in Europe; that meant that something advantageous to us was being held back. Another was the consideration of what their descendants in time to come would say. "How is it," they would ask, "that we are not now free men? There were a large number of burghers in the veldt to continue the war—what has become of our independence?" And what answer shall we be able to make?—we whose courage failed us before such tremendous odds, and who laid down our arms when victory was still possible? The speaker would only be satisfied if the meeting were unanimous for stopping the war, not otherwise. He thought of the families. How would the delegates face their families on their return, after the sacrifice of independence? He considered that the commandos should leave those districts where resistance was no longer possible and go to others. If to discontinue the war meant to surrender independence, then the war must not be discontinued.

Vice-President Burger said that he had not heard from the last speaker any reasons whatsoever for continuing the war.

Commandant Rheeder then remarked that if they wanted to surrender their country they should have done so earlier, when the burghers were not entirely destitute. But now nothing was left to them. As to the narrowness of the field of operations, there was still room enough to fight.

Commandant P.L. Uijs (Pretoria) referred to the frequent allusion which had been made to their European deputation. That deputation was now in Holland, and must know if anything was going on there to the advantage of the Republics. If there were any hopeful signs there, their comrades would certainly have informed them. They had not done so, and therefore the meeting should dismiss this subject from its thoughts.

The meeting then adjourned until 7.15 p.m.

Upon reassembling, Commandant Cronje (Winburg) said that he would not detain the meeting for long; he only wished to say a very few words. It had been rightly said that they were passing through a momentous period of their history. To his mind the present was the critical epoch in the existence of the African nation, whose destinies they had now to decide. Delegates were asking what hopes they could now entertain. But what grounds for hope were there when the war began? In his opinion there were none. It was only that men believed then that Right was Might, and put their trust in God. And God had helped them. When the enemy had entered their country everything was dark. There had been a day on which more than four thousand men had surrendered. Then, even as now, they had been without hope. Then, even as now, those who wanted to continue the war had been told that they were mad.

That had been some two years ago, and yet the war was still going on. Then, even as now, there had been no food, and yet they had managed to live. The delegates represented a free people; let them not take a step of which they would afterwards repent. As regarded intervention, he had often said that one could not rely on it.

But they could rely on God. When he returned to his burghers, and was questioned as to his reason for the course of action which he had advocated, he hoped to be able to answer, "Belief in God." There had always been times when there was no food, and yet they had always managed to live. A deputation had been officially sent to Europe, and was now there to represent their interests. Had the meeting lost its confidence in that deputation? Did it not realize that if the case of the Republic was hopeless in Europe the deputation would send word to that effect? It had been said that by continuing the war they would be exterminating the nation. He did not believe this. The way to exterminate the nation was to accept the British proposal. To go on with the war was their only policy, and it was a very good policy. The deputation had claimed that their advice should be taken before any negotiations were attempted. What right, then, had the delegates to give up the war on the basis of the proposal now before them? To do so was to give the death blow to their national existence; later on they would have cause to rue it. Moreover, the proposal did not safeguard the interests of their brethren in Cape Colony. Again, landed property belonging to burghers had already been sold, and in all probability these burghers would never see any of the proceeds. The sum (£3,000,000) which the proposal offered to compensate for all damages, was not sufficient to cover damage already done. For these and other reasons the proposal could not be accepted. No other course was open to them except to reject the proposal and to continue hostilities.

General Froneman (Ladybrand) agreed with the last speaker. He loved his country, and could not think of surrendering it. The reasons which had induced them to begin the war were still in force. He had been through the whole campaign, and saw stronger reasons now than ever before for the continuing of the war. His districts, like those of others, were exhausted, and yet his burghers remained in the veldt. He had been present at the surrender of the four thousand; he had seen General Cronje give up his sword. Those had been dark days, but the struggle still went on; they could still keep on their legs. It had been God's will that this war should take place. Prayers had been offered that it might be averted, but God had ruled it otherwise. Therefore they must carry the war through, and never think of surrender. They were Republicans. What would it be to have to give up that name for ever? He had consulted his burghers and their women-folk; he had asked them, "What conditions of peace will you accept?" They had answered, "No peace at all, if it means any loss of independence." And so, before he could vote for peace, he would have again to take the opinion of his burghers.

Veldtcornet B.H. Breijtenbach (Utrecht) urged that a definite yes or no must be given to the question, Is the war to continue? The general condition of the country had been laid before the meeting, and it had been clearly shown that its condition made the carrying on of the war impossible. One could not escape from that fact. Why then should they argue any longer? What reason had they for wishing to prolong this struggle? They surely would not do so blindfold. Unless good reasons could be alleged for continuing it, the war would have to be stopped. As those good reasons were not forthcoming, he would vote with those who were for peace. To continue the war would be a crime. Some of the last few speakers had stated that there had been no sufficient reasons for commencing the war. That might be true. They might have been over-confident then. Be that as it might, they certainly had lost so much ground since then that they must now give up the struggle. This was his irrevocable opinion. It had been clearly shown that fourteen commandos were unable to continue in the veldt. This made peace a necessity, for what was to be gained by continuing a struggle without a proper army. The war might last a few months longer, but it must end then—and end in disaster.

Commandant W.J. Viljoen (Witwatersrand) said that some speakers were for and others against the continuation of hostilities. The first were guided by faith alone; the second had brought forward definite grounds for their opinion. A year ago both parties had been inspired by faith, but what had been the result? He would be glad enough to be convinced, but those who wished to continue the war must show grounds for such a line of action.

General De la Rey would only say a few words. He had received definite instructions before he went to his burghers neither to encourage nor discourage them, whatever they might say at their meetings. He had strictly observed these instructions, and had never attempted to influence them. There were present among the delegates nine men (one being from Cape Colony) who represented his burghers, and who would testify as to their state of mind and temper; he need not therefore say anything. The delegates could bear witness how full of courage the men were. Nevertheless, the war could not be continued. Say or do what they would at that meeting, the war must cease. Some had talked about faith. But what was faith? True faith consisted in saying, "Lord, Thy will, not mine, be done." They must bow before the will of God. The delegates, he continued, must choose one of the three courses which were open to them. It would be a great calamity if they were to decide to surrender unconditionally. Had it been necessary to do so it should have been done while they still possessed something. Should they then continue the war? But the question as to what would become of the people under those circumstances must be faced—to continue fighting would be the ruin of the nation. The delegates might go away determined to fight, but the burghers would lay down their arms, and the state of affairs which would thus ensue would not redound to their honour. But the British Government offered guarantees; it would help the nation so that the nation might help itself. If any one were to say now, "Continue fighting," he and his generals might have the heart to do so if they kept their minds fixed on their recent exploits. For himself, however, he would refuse absolutely to accede to that request. And what real advantage had accrued from his successes in the veldt? What had followed on them? All his cattle had been taken away, some three hundred of his men had been killed, wounded, or taken prisoner. Some of the delegates set their hopes on the European deputation, but what did that deputation say a year ago? It said that all depended on their continuing to fight. They had continued to fight. What more, then, was there left for them to do? Some gentlemen present had definite mandates from their burghers, who very likely had no knowledge of the actual state of affairs when they gave those mandates. He himself had not known at that time in what a plight the country was. He challenged each and all of the delegates to show their burghers the proposal of the British Government, and then to see if those burghers were not in favour of unconditional surrender. But if the meeting insisted on the continuation of hostilities, the nation would be driven into hands-upping; thus the war would end in dishonour and disgrace.

Landdrost Bosman (Wakkerstroom) was glad that General De la Rey had spoken out so boldly; it was every one's duty to do so. He himself also was against the continuance of the war.

Although it had been said that the war had been begun in faith, it ought not to be forgotten that it had also been begun with hope of intervention, as was shown by the sending of the deputation to Europe—that deputation which, as they had often heard, had done so much good work. Another proof that there had then been hope of intervention was that the burghers had ordered the delegates to keep them in communication with the deputation. And that they had not relied exclusively on faith at the beginning of the war was shown by the fact that they had founded great hopes on what their brethren in Cape Colony might accomplish. These hopes had now been dissipated by General Smuts, who had just said that there was no chance of a general insurrection.

Again, could the war be continued when their commandos were so much weakened, and when food was so scarce? It was nonsense to say that food had been scarce a year ago; there had been a sufficiency then, and at the present time there was not. One could ride from Vereeniging to Piet Retief without seeing more than two or three herds of cattle. Moreover, the women and children were in a most pitiable condition. One delegate had spoken against any scheme which would be as it were a trampling on the blood which had already been spilt—he shared that delegate's sentiments; but he considered that to shed yet more blood in a cause which was to all appearance hopeless would be still more reprehensible. He should prefer not to enter into the religious aspect of the question. It was difficult to fathom the purposes of God; perhaps it might be the Divine will that they should lose their independence. All that they could do was to follow the course which seemed to be good and right. Were they, then, to surrender unconditionally? He would say no. It would be giving the enemy opportunities for doing things from which they might otherwise desist. Moreover, by voting for such a policy the leaders would incur the displeasure of the nation. In choosing what course they would pursue the delegates should let nothing else sway them save the good of the nation. They must not be carried away by their feelings; they must listen only to the voice of reason.

Commandant H.S. Grobler (Bethal) felt that, under the circumstances, the war could not be continued. It had already reduced them to such straits that they would soon have to fly to the utmost borders of their territories, leaving the enemy unopposed in the very heart of the country. At the beginning of the war they had not relied on faith alone; there had also been guns, war material and provisions. But now none of these things were left to them. It was terrible to him to think that they must sacrifice the independence of their country. He was a true son of his country, and could not consent to the surrender of her independence unless that were the only way of saving the women and children from starvation. But it was not only the women and children who were on the verge of starvation; the burghers still left in the laagers were in the same predicament. What, moreover, was to happen to the prisoners of war, if the struggle were to be continued? And to the families in the camps? The delegates must not forget those families. If the people generally were dying a national, the families were dying a moral, death. It was a sad thought that there were among their women in the camps, many who were thus losing their moral vitality. It was a thought which should make them determined to conclude the war.

Commandant Van Niekerk (Ficksburg) said that his commandos had commissioned him to hold out for independence. The proposal of the British Government could not be accepted. They must take no hasty step. If they persevered in the war, the enemy would grant them better terms. All they had to do was to act like brave men.

General J.G. Celliers (Lichtenburg) had already told the meeting what mandate he had received from his burghers. But he was there to do the best he could for the nation as a whole. The condition of the country was very critical. The fact that his own commandos were faring well was not a sufficient reason for continuing the war. He must take all circumstances into consideration. He had said that he was in favour of an arrangement by which peace should be made without the sacrifice of independence. Such an arrangement they had attempted to bring about. They had elected a Commission, which had done all in its power to give effect to their wishes in this matter. And the result was the proposal of the British Government now lying before them. That was what the Commission had obtained for them. Which of them could say that he could have obtained better terms for the people than those contained in that proposal? Or that, if the war were to be continued, the people would gain any advantage which that proposal did not give them? It had been said that the deputation in Europe had encouraged the burghers in their prolonged struggle. The last message they had received from the deputation had been: "Go on till every remedy has been tried." Could that be called encouragement? It had also been said that the nation must have faith. He admitted the necessity—but it must not be the sort of faith which chose what it would believe, and what it would disbelieve. They must be prepared to believe that it might be the will of God that they should yield to the enemy. As he had more insight into the state of affairs than his burghers, and therefore was better qualified to form a judgment, he did not feel himself bound by their mandate. Had the burghers known what he now knew, they would have given him a very different commission. He felt that it was a serious thing to continue sacrificing the lives of his fellow-countrymen. Moreover, however dear independence might be, it was useless to attempt impossibilities. Their one aim should be to safeguard the interests of the nation. His vote would be with those who were for accepting the proposal of the British Government.

Commander-in-Chief de Wet was the next to address the meeting. His speech was as follows:—

"As I feel it to be my duty to speak out all my mind before this meeting, I shall go back to the very beginning of the war. And recalling my feelings at that period, I can say that I had less hope then for intervention than I have now. I do not mean to say that I am sanguine about it even now; but I know to-day, what I did not know then, that great sympathy is felt for us by other nations. Even in England this sympathy is to be found, as is shown by the largely-attended 'Pro-Boer' meetings which have been held in that country. And that the feeling in our favour is widespread is evident from the reports which we received by word of mouth from the messenger to whom the deputation entrusted its recent letter, for we cannot believe that the deputation would have employed an unreliable person. And what did that messenger say? Among other things, he said that our cause was winning new adherents every day. It may be asked, however, why the deputation did not send a report of its own? I reply that it had its hand upon the pulse of the Governments, and that the information it was thus gaining was of such a character that it could not be entrusted to any messenger whatsoever. Perhaps the deputation was unable in any way to communicate what it knew to us—it would never do to noise abroad the secrets of European policy. The silence of the delegates ought not, then, to discourage us; on the contrary, we should regard it as a hopeful sign.

"If there is any one man who feels deeply for the critical condition of our country, I am that man. And critical our condition certainly is; so that I am not surprised that some of us are asking, 'What hope have we now in continuing the struggle?' But I would ask another question: 'What hope had we at the beginning of the war?' Our faith in God—we had nothing else to rely on! At the very outset of the war I knew that we, with our forty-five thousand troops, were engaged in a contest against a nation that had no less than seven hundred and fifty thousand men under arms, and who could easily send against us a third of that number. And to counterbalance the terrible odds against us, we had nothing, as I knew, but our faith. At that time there were some who expected that effectual help would come from Cape Colony. I was never deluded by this hope. I knew of course that there were men there who would fight with us against England; I knew how much those men sympathized with our cause; but I also knew that the circumstances of that country would make it impossible for the colonists to help us more than they have, as a matter of fact, done. No! God was our one Hope when the war began. And if, when the war is over, victory lies with us, it will not be the first time that faith in God has enabled the weaker nation to overthrow the stronger.

"Those of you who urge that the war should be discontinued, ask us, who are for carrying it on, what tangible reason we have for our hope. But what tangible reason for hope was there at the beginning of the war? Are our affairs darker now? Quite the contrary—miracles have been worked in our favour during the last twenty-two months. General Botha wrote to me some time ago, saying that the scarcity of ammunition was causing him much anxiety. And he had good cause for that anxiety—ammunition was exhausted. When a burgher came to me at that time with an empty bandolier, it absolutely terrified me. But now, to use an expression of General Joubert's, my pleasure is tempered with shame when I think of the plentiful store of ammunition which we possess. I am not angry with those of my compatriots who ask for reasons—I give my reasons—nor have I given a thousandth part of them.

"The enemy has already made us some concessions. There was a time when Lord Salisbury said that the English Government would be satisfied with nothing short of unconditional surrender. He does not say so to-day. England is negotiating with us—that is to say, she shows signs of yielding to our demands. If we continue the war, England will negotiate again; she will offer still more favourable terms; she will not even stick at independence.

"Do you want more of my reasons? Look back once more upon our past history, and you shall find them. Recall the time when the Transvaal was at war with England. At that time we did not know the English so well as we now know them; we had only thirteen cartridges for each man; and there were the so-called 'Loyalists'—a chicken-hearted crew—to hamper us. Faith was our only support then—and you all know how that war resulted.

"I am asked what I mean to do with the women and children. That is a very difficult question to answer. We must have faith. I think also that we might meet the emergency in this way—a part of the men should be told off to lay down their arms for the sake of the women, and then they could take the women with them to the English in the towns. This would be a hard expedient, but it may be the only one possible.

"America has been referred to by some of the speakers, who have compared our circumstances with those of the United States, when they made war upon England. The comparison is, in one respect at least, an apt one, for we also have large territories to which we can always retreat.

"As to Europe—we know little of the condition of things there. Our information about Europe comes only from newspapers, and 'Jingo' newspapers at that. If there is not a great deal going on in Europe which England wants to hide from us, why is she so careful not to let us see European journals? If there were anything in them unfavourable to our cause, England would flood our country with them in her own interests. We must also note that England will not permit our deputation to return to us.

"Taking all these facts into consideration, and remembering that the sympathy for us, which is to be found in England itself, may be regarded as being, for all practical purposes, a sort of indirect intervention, I maintain that this terrible struggle must be continued. We must fight on, no matter how long, until our independence is absolutely secure."

General Beijers (Waterberg) said that he had to give an answer to the question whether he ought to follow his reason or his conscience; he could only reply that conscience had the first claim upon him. If he were to perish whilst following the guidance of reason, he would feel that he had been unfaithful; whereas, were he to die whilst obeying the dictates of conscience, he would not fear death. Martyrs of old had died for their faith; but he feared that the martyr spirit was now only to be met with in books! Those martyrs had died, and with their death it had seemed that all was lost; but the truth, for which they had given up their lives, had lived!

But how is it now with us? We think our cause a righteous one, but are we willing to die for it? Some spoke of our existence as a nation—but whether that were to be preserved or lost, did not lie with us—it was in the hands of God—He would take care of it. Right must conquer in the end. They must take care to be on the side of right, should it even cost them their lives. He agreed with those who said that, even if the present deliberations were to come to nothing, they would have another chance, later on, of negotiating. This had been proved by what had already happened. General de Wet had shown them how Lord Salisbury had gone back upon his first demands; he (General Beijers) could tell them that on one occasion Lord Roberts had declined even to speak to General Botha—and yet the English were negotiating with them now. He was quite open to conviction, but at present he could not see that the war ought to be stopped. Nevertheless he was not blind to the critical state of their affairs. But their case was not yet hopeless; their anxiety about food, their lack of horses—these were not insurmountable difficulties. They might even find some means by which to save their womenfolk.

No. These difficulties were not insuperable; but there was one difficulty which was insuperable—the present spirit of the nation. When a spirit, be it what it might, inspired or ruled a man, then that man would submit to no other sway. The spirit that now ruled the burghers was a spirit that was driving them over to the enemy. Against that spirit it was impossible to contend. General De la Rey had said that, if the proposal now before the meeting were to be shown to the burghers, they would at once accept it—that was the sort of spirit that was in them, and one must take it into consideration, for he was convinced that it presented an insurmountable obstacle to the continuation of the war.

The meeting was then closed with prayer.

Meeting on Friday, May 30th, 1902.

After the preliminary prayer had been offered, Vice-President Burger said that before beginning the business of the day, it was his sad duty to inform the meeting that the President of the Orange Free State had been obliged to resign, on account of serious illness. President Steyn had been compelled, in order to obtain medical assistance, to put himself in the hands of the enemy. He had further to communicate that Commander-in-Chief de Wet had been appointed Vice-President of the Orange Free State. He wished to express his deep sympathy with the representatives in the severe loss which they had sustained. President Steyn, he said, had been a rock and pillar to their great cause.

Vice-President de Wet having thanked the Vice-President of the South African Republic for his kind and sympathetic words, Mr. J. Naude (the representative of Pretoria, and of General Kemp's flying columns) put some questions with regard to the colonists who had been fighting on the Boer side. These questions were answered by General Smuts. Mr. Naude then asked if the delegates were expected to come to any decision about independence.

General Botha replied that the Governments had informed Lords Kitchener and Milner that they were not in a condition to decide that question—that it was a matter for the nation to settle. The delegates had then gone to their burghers, and now had returned, and were present.

Mr. Naude said that it must therefore have been known at Klerksdorp that the delegates had to decide upon the question of independence. If that were so, he found himself in a difficulty. Either the delegates had been misled, or they were the victims of a mistake, for they had never been told that they had been elected as plenipotentiaries. Notwithstanding all that the lawyers might say, he considered himself as having a certain definite mission. He had obtained the votes of his burghers on the understanding that he would take up a certain position. He had asked them whether independence was to be given up, and they had answered in the negative. He could not therefore vote for the acceptance of the proposal now before the meeting, for that proposal demanded the surrender of independence. His burghers had also insisted on being allowed to keep their arms, and on the use of their language in schools and Courts of Justice, both of which conditions were refused by the British proposal. Since, therefore, he could not agree to the proposal, he was for continuing the war. Some asked what were the chances of success? He remembered the state of feeling among the burghers at Warmebad—that was a dark time indeed. The Commandant-General had paid those burghers a visit, and had told them that they had nothing to lose, but everything to win, by continuing the struggle. That had been enough for them. They had not had much prospect then; they could not see whither their road was leading. But they had found out afterwards. It had been a dark time too when Pretoria was taken, but most of the burghers had remained steadfast. And after the darkness the light had come back. Again a dark cloud was over them—it would pass away, and the light would reappear.

General De la Rey explained that he had not intended to mislead anybody at the gatherings of the burghers. Every document which the Government had handed over to him had been laid before those gatherings. Mr. Naude had asked whether the delegates at that meeting had to decide about independence. Most certainly they had. And to do so was a duty devolving upon Mr. Naude as much as on any other delegate present. They would have to decide, not for their own districts alone, but for the whole country.

Mr. Naude said that he had no wish to free himself from his responsibility, but he could not forget that he had come there with a definite mission.

Judge Hertzog wished again to explain the rights of the question from a legal point of view. One must ask: If the nation were here, what would it wish to be done? And one must act in conformity with what one thinks its answer would be. The Judge then proceeded to speak on the matter in general. What, he asked, were the arguments in favour of continuing the war? In the first place, England was growing weaker just as their own nation was. Any one could see that with their own eyes. It was true as regarded the financial side of the question. No doubt England could still collect millions of pounds, if she wished, but the time would come when she would have trouble with her tax-payers. Already the British Government found it difficult to pay the interest on the sum borrowed for war expenses, as was proved by the fact that a corn tax had been levied in England. That tax would not have been levied unless things had been in a serious condition. In the second place, he would ask how it was they had not been allowed to meet their deputation? It would only have taken the deputation fourteen days to perform the journey; by now it would have been among them. But permission had been refused them. And why? It was said that to grant a permission would have been a military irregularity. But the present meeting was also a military irregularity. There must be something more behind that refusal. But what were the arguments against going on with the war? He would enumerate them—the situation in which they found themselves was critical; the country as a whole was exhausted. Nearly all the horses had died or had been captured. The strongest argument of all, however, was that some of their own people had turned against them, and were fighting in the ranks of the enemy. Then the condition of the women caused great anxiety; a fear had been expressed that a moral decay might set in among the families in the camps. That consideration had great weight with him. No one with any heart could remain indifferent to it. If there was one thing which more than anything else made him respect Commandant-General Botha, it was that the Commandant-General had the heart to feel, and the courage to express, the importance of that consideration. The present war was one of the saddest that had ever been waged. He doubted if there had ever been a war in which a nation had suffered as they had. But all those sufferings, horrible though they were, did not influence his decision. Did he but see the chance of finally securing freedom for the nation, he would put all such considerations on one side, and go on fighting till death. No; it was not the horror of the situation which influenced him; there was something that weighed upon his heart yet more heavily—it was the holding of that meeting at Vereeniging. He reproached no one. Every one had acted with the best intentions. Nevertheless that meeting was a fatal error; it would give them their death blow. For what had it produced—a statement from the lips of the Commandant-General himself that the condition of the country was hopeless. If there were yet any burghers whose courage was not gone, would they not be utterly disheartened when they heard what their leaders had said at that meeting? That was the saddest thought of all. He could understand that those burghers who had already lost heart should be leaving the commandos, but now those who had never yet been disheartened would become so. But notwithstanding all this, it was difficult to feel certain which was the right course to pursue—to give up the war or to continue it. He could only suggest that those who were now in doubt on the matter should support the line of action which, before their doubt began, had appeared to them to be best.

Mr. L.J. Meijer (a member of the Government of the South African Republic) then gave some account of the devastation of that part of the country which lay to the north of the Eastern Railway, and on the further side of the Sabi River. (This report coincided with those already given by the delegates.) He went on to say that as they were all in the dark, and could not see the road they were travelling along, they must take reason and conscience for their guide. They had already lost much: let them not lose everything. And what could they hope to gain by continuing the struggle? To do so might be to throw away their last chance of peace. What would their progeny say of them if they were to persist in the struggle and thus lose everything they had possessed? They would say, "Our forefathers were brave, but they had no brains." Whereas, if they were to stop the war, their progeny would say, "Our forefathers did not fight for their own glory." He pointed out that however little the British proposal contained of what they desired, it nevertheless promised them representative government. In the past he had been against the war; he had wished that the five years' franchise should be granted. Although the people had opposed this measure he had always supported it. And why? Because he had feared that were that measure not conceded African blood would stain the ground. Must they still continue to shed blood? After the capture of Bloemfontein there had been a secret meeting of the council of war at Pretoria. His Government had then been willing to surrender, but the Free State had refused. The two Governments had therefore decided to go on with the war. A year later, in the month of June, there had been another meeting. A letter had been sent to the Free State. The two Governments had met at Waterval, and had once more decided to continue the struggle. Later on, again, the Government of the South African Republic wrote another letter to the Free State; but there had been no opportunity of meeting until the present occasion, which saw them assembled together at Vereeniging. Were they again going to decide to continue their resistance? It was a matter for serious consideration. There was but little seed-corn left. This must, if they had to go on fighting, be preserved from the enemy at all costs; were it to be destroyed, the African nation must cease to exist. But they could not continue the war. It was the Boers now who were teaching the English how to fight against us; Boers now were with the enemy's forces, showing them how to march by night, and pointing out to them all the foot passes.

Commandant Van Niekerk (Kroonstad) pointed out that the Colonists had already rendered them valuable aid, and could still do so. Were they now to abandon these Colonists, and—thinking only about saving themselves—leave them to fight on alone? It would be sad indeed if the burghers were compelled to lay down their arms.

Commandant-General L. Botha said that in regard to the holding of a national meeting, he had already chosen delegates with power to act. He spoke of the state of affairs at the beginning of the war—the two Republics had then at least sixty thousand men under arms. In reference to the Cape Colony, he said that it had never been expected that that country would allow its railways to be used for the transport of troops. The Commandant-General then proceeded as follows:—

"I used to entertain hopes that the European Powers would interfere on our behalf. All that they have done, however, has been to look on while England was introducing all sorts of new methods of warfare, methods, too, which are contrary to all international law.

"When the war began we had plenty of provisions, and a commando could remain for weeks in one spot without the local food supply running out. Our families, too, were then well provided for. But all this is now changed. One is only too thankful nowadays to know that our wives are under English protection. This question of our womenfolk is one of our greatest difficulties. What are we to do with them? One man answers that some of the burghers should surrender themselves to the English, and take the women with them. But most of the women now amongst us are the wives of men already prisoners. And how can we expect those not their own kith and kin to be willing to give up liberty for their sakes?

"As to the deputation, we must remember that it was accredited to all the Powers of Europe. And yet it has only been able to hand in its credentials to the Netherlands Government. Does not this prove that no other Government is willing to receive it? If you need further proof, I refer you to the letter in which the deputation—they were still allowed to write to us then—said: 'There is no chance for us in Europe.' The deputation wanted to be allowed to return home, but our Government advised them to remain in Europe, because their arrival in South Africa would be a death blow to the hopes of many. That is why the deputation is still in Europe. Later on they said that, although they knew that there was no chance of intervention, yet they felt that they ought to persist in their efforts, because of the sacrifices which we had already made. It is possible that a war may arise in Europe from which we shall gain something, but what right have we to expect such a contingency? Moreover, great nations take but little interest in the fate of small ones—indeed, it is to the advantage of the former that the small nations should be wiped out of existence.

"I cannot refrain from alluding to the faithlessness of some of our burghers, who are to be found in the ranks of the enemy. But this is not the only sign of the way in which affairs are trending—I look back on the past. I remember that we have been fighting a full year since we last heard of our deputation. What have we gained since June, 1901? Nothing. On the contrary, we have been going backwards so fast that, if this weakening process goes on much longer, we shall soon find ourselves unable any more to call ourselves a fighting nation. What have we not undergone in the course of this year which is just over! In the concentration camps alone, twenty thousand women and children have died. When I was in Pretoria I received reports from our information office, and otherwise, of our losses. I found that there were thirty-one thousand six hundred prisoners of war, of whom six hundred had died, and that three thousand eight hundred of our burghers had been killed in the war. Is not a loss such as this, in so short a time as two and a half years, a serious matter? Think, too, of the sufferings which those twenty thousand women who died in the camps must have endured!

"I am not deaf to the claims of the colonists who have been fighting for us. I have said that if we surrender our independence, we must provide for them. Should we serve their interests by continuing the war? No, indeed! The best thing for them would be that we should bring it to a close. But if we are absolutely determined to go on fighting, let us at least say to them, 'We advise you to desist.'

"What I am saying now is in substance what I said at Warmbad at a time when there were two thousand men of that district in the Veldt. How many are there now? Four hundred and eighty! On that occasion I also said that we must continue the war until we were driven by sheer starvation to make peace. Well, in some divisions starvation has already come. The delegates themselves have had to confess that our strength up till now has lain in the fact that we have been able to continue the struggle in every district. In this way we have divided the enemy's forces. But if we are compelled to abandon some of our districts, and to concentrate on certain points, then the English also will concentrate, and attack us with an irresistible force.

"It has been suggested that we ought to march into Cape Colony. I know, however, what that would mean—Commander-in-Chief de Wet marched into the colonies. He had a large force, and the season of the year was auspicious for his attempt, and yet he failed. How, then, shall we succeed in winter, and with horses so weak that they can only go op-een-stap.[327]

"What, then, are we to do? Some will reply, 'Go on with the war,' Yes, but for how long? For ten or twelve years? But would that be possible? If in two years we have been reduced from sixty thousand fighting men to half that number, where will our army be after another ten years of war? It is clear enough to me that if we go on any longer, we shall be compelled to surrender. Would it not be better to come to some agreement with the enemy, while we have the opportunity? We have all received the gift of reason; let us use it on the present occasion.

"As far as I and my own burghers are concerned, to continue the struggle is still possible. But we must not only think of ourselves. We must almost think of others. There are, for instance, the widows and orphans. If we accept the terms now offered to us, they will remain under our care. But if we go on with the war until we are forced to surrender, who will then take care of them? Or if we were all killed, what could we do for them? We should not even be able to send a deputation to Europe, to ask for money to help us to rebuild our farms, and to feed our burghers.

"There are three questions now before us—three alternatives between which we have to choose—the continuing of the war, unconditional surrender, and the acceptance of the British proposal. With regard to the first, I fail to see what satisfactory result can come to us from persisting in this unequal contest, which must result in the end in our extermination. As to the choice between the other two, in many ways unconditional surrender would be the better. But, for the sake of the nation, we may not choose it. Although to reject it may involve us in many hardships, yet we must think of nothing else but the interests of the nation. Our only course, then, is to accept the proposal of the English Government. Its terms may not be very advantageous to us, but nevertheless they rescue us from an almost impossible position."

After a short adjournment the delegates again assembled at about 2 p.m.

General C.H. Muller (Boksburg) said that his burghers had sent him to defend their menaced independence. One part of them had authorized him to act as his judgment should dictate; another part had ordered him to hold out for independence and to try to get into communication with the European deputation. He had long ago told his burghers that they must trust in God if they wished to continue the war, for they could not do so by relying only on their guns and rifles. He did not like to think of what they would say if he were to go back to them and tell them that he had not been in communication with the deputation, and that the proposal of the English Government had been accepted. He could not bring himself to surrender. Nevertheless, having in view what the Commandant-General and others had said, he felt that he must do so, for it was impossible for him to prosecute the war single-handed. But could not the delegates continue to stand by one another, and make a covenant with the Lord? The district which he represented was one of the poorest in the whole country, and the £3,000,000 offered by the enemy did not include any provision for those who, like his burghers, could do nothing to help themselves. He would again suggest that the delegates should make a vow unto the Lord. For himself, he could not vote for the acceptance of the British proposal.

General J.H. Smuts then spoke as follows:—

"Up till now I have taken no part in this discussion, but my opinions are not unknown to my Government; we have arrived at a dark period both in the history of our war, and in the course of our national development. To me it is all the darker because I am one of those who, as members of the Government of the South African Republic, provoked the war with England. A man, however, may not draw back from the consequences of his deeds. We must therefore keep back all private feeling, and decide solely with a view to the lasting interests of our nation. This is an important occasion for us—it is perhaps the last time that we shall meet as a free people with a free government. Let us then rise to the height of this occasion; let us arrive at a decision for which our posterity shall bless, and not curse us.

"The great danger for this meeting is that of deciding the questions before it on purely military grounds. Nearly all the delegates here are officers who in the past have never quailed before the overwhelming forces of the

[327] The step of a tired horse.

enemy, and who therefore are never likely to do so in the future. They do not know what fear is, and they are ready to shed the last drop of their blood in the defence of their country.

"Now if we look at the matter from their point of view, that is to say, if we look at it merely as a military question, I am bound to admit that we shall come to the conclusion that the war can be continued. We are still an unconquered power; we have still about eighteen thousand men in the field—veterans, with whom one can accomplish almost anything. From a purely military standpoint, our cause is not yet lost. But it is as a nation, and not as an army, that we are met here, and it is therefore for the nation principally that we must consult. No one sits here to represent this or that commando. One and all, we represent the African nation, and not only those members of it which are now in the field, but also those who rest beneath the soil, and those yet unborn, who shall succeed us.

"No! We do not only represent our burghers on commando, the troops over which we are placed in command; we represent also the thousands who have passed away, after making the last sacrifice for their country; the prisoners scattered all the world over; the women and children dying by the thousand in the prison camps of the enemy; we represent the blood and the tears of the whole African nation. From the prisons, the camps, the graves, the veldt, and from the womb of the future, that nation cries out to us to make a wise decision now, to take no step which might lead to the downfall or even to the extermination of their race, and thus make all their sacrifices of no avail. Our struggle, up to the present, has not been an aimless one. We have not been fighting in mere desperation. We began this strife, and we have continued it, because we wanted to maintain our independence and were prepared to sacrifice everything for it. But we must not sacrifice the African nation itself upon the altar of independence. So soon as we are convinced that our chance of maintaining our autonomous position as Republics is, humanly speaking, at an end, it becomes our clear duty to desist from our efforts. We must not run the risk of sacrificing our nation and its future to a mere idea which can no longer be realized.

"And ought we not to be convinced that independence is now irretrievably lost? We have been fighting without cessation for nearly three years. It is no exaggeration to say that during that period we have been employing all the strength and all the means which we possess, in the furtherance of our cause. We have sacrificed thousands of lives; we have lost all our earthly goods; our dear country is become one continuous desert; more than twenty thousand of our women and children have perished in the camps of the enemy. And has this brought us independence? Just the reverse; it is receding further and further from us every day. The longer we fight, the greater will be the distance between us and the aim for which we are fighting.

"The manner in which the enemy has been conducting, and still continues to conduct, this war, has reduced our country to such a state of exhaustion, that it will soon be a physical impossibility for us to fight any longer. Our only hope lies in the chance of help from outside. A year ago I, in the name of my Government, communicated the condition of our nation to His Honour States-President Kruger, in Europe. He wrote in reply that we must rely on the state of affairs in Cape Colony—and the sympathy of European nations—and that we must continue the war until all other means were exhausted."

The speaker here enlarged upon the political developments which had taken place in the United States and in the principal European countries during the preceding two years, and then continued:—

"So far as we are concerned, the sum total of the foreign situation is that we obtain a great deal of sympathy, for which we are naturally most grateful. More than this we do not obtain, nor shall obtain for many a long year. Europe will go on expressing sympathy with us until the last Boer hero has died on the field and the last Boer woman has gone down to her grave—until, in fact, the whole Boer nation has been sacrificed on the altar of history and of humanity.

"I have already, on a former occasion, told you what I think about the situation in Cape Colony. We have made great mistakes there; perhaps even now Cape Colony is not ripe for the sort of policy which we have been pursuing with regard to it. At all events, we cannot entertain any hopes of a general rising of the Colonists. We cannot, however, give too much honour to those three thousand heroes in the Colony who have sacrificed all in our behalf, even though they have not succeeded in securing our independence for us.

"Thus we have given President Kruger's advice a fair trial. For twelve months we have been testing the value of the methods which he urged upon us. And, as a result of it all, we have become convinced that those methods are of no avail—that if we wish to remain independent we must depend upon ourselves alone. But the facts which the various delegates have brought before our notice show that we cannot thus depend upon ourselves;

that, unless we obtain outside help, the struggle must come to an end. We have, then, no hope of success. Our country is already devastated and in ruins; let us stop before our people are ruined also.

"And now the enemy approaches with a proposal, which, however unacceptable it may be to us in other respects, includes the promise of amnesty for our Colonial brethren who have been fighting side by side with us. I fear that the day will come when we shall no longer be able to save these so-called rebels, and then it will be a just ground for reproach that we sacrificed their interests in a cause that was already hopeless. Moreover, if we refused the proposal which the British Government now makes to us, I am afraid that we shall considerably weaken our position in the eyes of the world, and thus lose much of the sympathy which to-day it evinces in our favour.

"Brethren, we have vowed to stand fast to the bitter end; but let us be men, and acknowledge that that end has now come, and that it is more bitter than ever we thought it could be. For death itself would be sweet compared with the step which we must now take. But let us bow before the will of God.

"The future is dark indeed, but we will not give up courage, and hope, and trust in God. No one shall ever convince me that this unparalleled sacrifice which the African nation has laid upon the altar of freedom will be in vain. It has been a war for freedom—not only for the freedom of the Boers, but for the freedom of all the nations of South Africa. Its results we leave in God's hands. Perhaps it is His will to lead our nation through defeat, through abasement, yes, and even through the valley of the shadow of death, to the glory of a nobler future, to the light of a brighter day."

Commandant A.J. Bester (Bloemfontein) said that at the meeting at which he had been elected his burghers had told him that they were resolved not to become the subjects of England. The arguments now urged against the continuation of the war were not new—they had been used in former times of depression. History gave many instances in which their nation had been delivered out of the most critical positions. One could not help believing that Right would conquer. How was it to be explained that two hundred and forty thousand troops had failed to exterminate two small Republics? Then there had been miraculous escapes; surely the thoughts of these ought to encourage them. They must all be of one mind. His own decision was to stand or to fall for his freedom.

Mr. Birkenstock (Vrijheid) asked whether the proposal could not be accepted under protest.

General J.C. Smuts answered that the meeting could empower the Governments to accept the proposal, and to add that they did so with such and such provisos.

Commandant A.J. Bester (Bloemfontein) thought that there had been enough said, and recommended that the discussion be closed.

Commandant F.E. Mentz (Heilbron) also thought that it was not necessary to argue any more. He believed that the war could not be continued. In Heilbron, Bloemfontein, and part of Bethlehem there were not five head of cattle left. The helpless condition of the women and children also demanded consideration. The state of the country was becoming so desperate that they were now obliged to break away from the kraals. He himself had been compelled to this not long ago, and had lost forty men in one day. He would have to leave his district, but could not bring it to his heart to leave the women behind. It was quite clear to him that the war must be stopped, for some parts of the Transvaal were absolutely unable to go on fighting. Moreover, were the war to continue, commando after commando would go over to the enemy.

General Kemp (Krugersdorp) took a more encouraging view of affairs. He would stand or fall with the independence. His mandate was to that effect. His conscience also would not justify him in taking any other course. He thought that the proposal of the English Government was vague, that there was not sufficient provision for the Boer losses in it, and that it treated the Dutch language as a foreign tongue. Circumstances had often been dark, and the darkness would pass away this time as it had done before. Remembering the commission which had been given to him by the burghers, he could not do otherwise than vote for a continuation of the war.

Vice-President Burger: "I have already given my opinion. I am sorry that the meeting seems to be divided. It is necessary for the welfare of our nation that we should be of one mind. Are we to continue the war? From what I have seen and heard, it is clear to me that we cannot do so. I repeat that there is no possibility of it, neither does any real hope exist that by doing so we should benefit the nation. It is idle to compare our condition in the struggle in 1877–1881 with that in which we now find ourselves; I speak from experience.

"It is true that the victory was then ours; that it was so is due to the help which we received from outside. The Orange Free State remained neutral, but assistance came from President Brand in South Africa and from Gladstone in England: thus it was not by our own sword that we were enabled to win.

"It will be asked why, if we have kept up the struggle for two years and a half, can we not still continue to do so?

"Because, in the meantime, we have become weaker and weaker, and if we persist the end must be fatal. What grounds have we for expecting that we may yet be victorious? Each man we lose renders us weaker; every hundred men we lose means a similar gain to the enemy. England's numerical strength does not diminish; on the contrary, there are even more troops in the country at this moment than when Lord Roberts had the command. England also has used our own men against us, and has not been ashamed of arming the Kaffirs; the enemy are learning from our own men in what way they should fight—he must be blind indeed who cannot see these facts.

"I do not think we can appropriately call this altogether a 'war of faith.' Undoubtedly we began this war strong in the faith of God, but there were also two or three other things to rely upon. We had considerable confidence in our own weapons; we under-estimated the enemy; the fighting spirit had seized upon our people; and the thought of victory had banished that of the possibility of defeat.

"The question still remains, What are we to do? I have no great opinion of the document which lies before us: to me it holds out no inducement to stop the war. If I feel compelled to treat for peace it is not on account of any advantages that this proposal offers me: it is the weight of my own responsibility which drives me to it.

"If I think that by holding out I should dig the nation's grave, nothing must induce me to continue the struggle.

"Therefore I consider it my duty, as leader of our nation, to do my utmost that not one man more shall be killed, that not one woman more shall die.

"The sacrifice must be made; is not this also a trial of our faith? What shall we gain by going on? Nothing! It is obvious that further surrenders will take place—here of a few, there of many—and our weakness will increase.

"We shall also be obliged to abandon large areas of the country. Will this make us stronger? Rather, will it not enable the enemy to concentrate still more? And the abandoned tracts—to whom will they belong? To the enemy!

"In all probability this is our last meeting. I do not believe that we shall be given another chance to negotiate: we shall be deemed too insignificant. If we reject this proposal, what prospects have we in the future? If we accept it, we can, like a child, increase in size and strength, but with its rejection goes our last opportunity.

"Fell a tree and it will sprout again; uproot it and there is an end of it. What has the nation done to deserve extinction?

"Those who wish to continue the war are influenced chiefly by hope; but on what is this hope founded? On our arms? No. On intervention? By no means. On what then? No one can say.

"I am sorry that the Transvaal and the Orange Free State are at variance on this point, and I regret that it is the Transvaal which has to declare itself unable to proceed further; but the enemy have concentrated all their forces in this State, and we can hold out no longer."

Mr. L. Jacobsz: "I have hitherto not spoken, because I am a non-combatant. I have also suffered much, although less than others. I have listened to what has been said, but my opinion is not changed by the views I have heard expressed.

"I repeat now what I said at Klerksdorp, namely that the struggle cannot continue. I have noted the condition of the country, which is such that the commandos can no longer be supported. I would point out the condition of the women and children, of whom many are dying, and all are exposed to great dangers. If there was a chance of succeeding in the end, then we might hold out, but there is no such chance; there is no possibility of intervention, and the silence of the deputation is ominous.

"I sympathize with the heroes present at this meeting; we must have a foundation for our faith, and we cannot altogether compare our people with the people of Israel. Israel had promises made to them; we have none. I would further point out that, in the interests of the nation, it will not do to surrender unconditionally: the terms before us may be deceptive, but they are the best obtainable.

"With regard to the difficulty of those delegates who consider that they are bound to act as they have been commissioned, I am of the same opinion as Judge Hertzog and General Smuts."

Commandant J.J. Alberts (Standerton) spoke more or less in the same strain. He was of opinion that the war should be finished by ceding territory, but, failing this, that it should be ended on any terms obtainable.

Vice-President de Wet expressed his opinion that, considering the short time at their disposal, they should proceed, if possible, to make some proposal.

General D.A. Brand said that he would have spoken if he had not thought that enough had been said; he considered it desirable to close the discussion, and was willing to make a proposal.

Veldtcornet D.J.E. Opperman (Pretoria South) considered that the difficulties of continuing the war, and of accepting the proposal, were equal. Some of his burghers would fight no longer. What troubled him most was the condition of the women; it went to his heart to see these families perish. He was of opinion that, for the sake of the women and children who were suffering so intensely, the proposal should be accepted under protest.

Veldtcornet J. Van Steedden, seconded by Veldtcornet B.J. Roos, moved that the discussion be now closed.

The meeting was adjourned after prayer.

Meeting on Saturday, May 31st, 1902.

The meeting was opened with prayer.

General Nieuwouwdt, seconded by General Brand, made the following proposal:—

"This meeting of special deputies from the two Republics, after considering the proposal of His Majesty's Government for the re-establishment of peace, and taking into consideration (a) the demands of the burghers in the veldt and the commissions which they had given to their representatives; (b) that they do not consider themselves justified in concluding peace on the basis laid down by His Majesty's Government before having been placed in communication with the delegates of the Republic now in Europe, decides that it cannot accept the proposal of His Majesty's Government, and orders the Governments of the two Republics to communicate this decision to His Majesty's Government through its representatives."

Mr. P.R. Viljoen, seconded by General H.A. Alberts, made a proposal, amended afterwards by General Smuts and Judge Hertzog, which appears later on under the proposal of H.P.J. Pretorius and C. Botha.

A third proposal by General E. Botha and General J.G. Celliers was laid upon the table, but subsequently withdrawn.

Mr. F.W. Reitz considered it to be his duty not only to the nation but also to himself as a citizen, to say that, in case the proposal of the British Government should be accepted, it would be necessary for the meeting to make provisions as to whose signatures should be attached to the necessary documents. He himself would not sign any document by which the independence would be given up.

Remarks were made by several members on the first proposal, and Mr. P.R. Viljoen asked that no division should arise.

Vice-President de Wet then said that, as the time was limited, and all could not speak, he would propose that a Commission should be nominated in order to draw up a third proposal in which various opinions of the members should be set down; and that, whilst the Commission was occupied in this way, the Orange Free State delegates on their part and those of the South African Republic on their part, should meet in order that an understanding might be come to between them. They must endeavour to come to a decision, for it would be of the greatest possible advantage to them.

Commandant-General Botha thought that this hint should be taken. They had suffered and fought together: let them not part in anger.

The above-mentioned Commission was then decided upon, and Judge Hertzog and General Smuts were elected.

Then the Orange Free State delegates went to the tent of Vice-President de Wet, whilst those of the South African Republic remained in the tent in which the meeting was held.

After a time of heated dispute—for every man was preparing himself for the bitter end—they came to an agreement, and Judge Hertzog read the following proposal:—

"We, the national representatives of both the South African Republic and the Orange Free State, at the meeting held at Vereeniging, from the 15th of May till the 31st of May, 1902, have with grief considered the proposal made by His Majesty's Government in connexion with the conclusion of the existing hostilities, and their communication that this proposal had to be accepted, or rejected, unaltered. We are sorry that His Majesty's Government has absolutely declined to negotiate with the Governments of the Republics on the basis of their independence, or to allow our Governments to enter into communication with our deputations. Our people, however, have always been under the impression that not only on the grounds of justice, but also taking into consideration the great material and personal sacrifices made for their independence, that it had a well-founded claim for that independence.

"We have seriously considered the future of our country, and have specially observed the following facts:—

"Firstly, that the military policy pursued by the British military authorities has led to the general devastation of the territory of both Republics by the burning down of farms and towns, by the destruction of all means of subsistence, and by the exhausting of all resources required for the maintenance of our families, the subsistence of our armies, and the continuation of the war.

"Secondly, that the placing of our families in the concentration camps has brought on an unheard-of condition of suffering and sickness, so that in a comparatively short time about twenty thousand of our beloved ones have died there, and that the horrid probability has arisen that, by continuing the war, our whole nation may die out in this way.

"Thirdly, that the Kaffir tribe, within and without the frontiers of the territory of the two Republics, are mostly armed and are taking part in the war against us, and through the committing of murders and all sorts of cruelties have caused an unbearable condition of affairs in many districts of both Republics. An instance of this happened not long ago in the district of Vrijheid, where fifty-six burghers on one occasion were murdered and mutilated in a fearful manner.

"Fourthly, that by the proclamations of the enemy the burghers still fighting are threatened with the loss of all their movable and landed property—and thus with utter ruin—which proclamations have already been enforced.

"Fifthly, that it has already, through the circumstances of the war, become quite impossible for us to keep the many thousand prisoners of war taken by our forces, and that we have thus been unable to inflict much damage on the British forces (whereas the burghers who are taken prisoners by the British armies are sent out of the country), and that, after war has raged for nearly three years, there only remains an insignificant part of the fighting forces with which we began.

"Sixthly, that this fighting remainder, which is only a small minority of our whole nation, has to fight against an overpowering force of the enemy, and besides is reduced to a condition of starvation, and is destitute of all necessaries, and that notwithstanding our utmost efforts, and the sacrifice of everything that is dear and precious to us, we cannot foresee an eventual victory.

"We are therefore of opinion that there is no justifiable ground for expecting that by continuing the war the nation will retain its independence, and that, under these circumstances, the nation is not justified in continuing the war, because this can only lead to social and material ruin, not for us alone, but also for our posterity. Compelled by the above-named circumstances and motives, we commission both Governments to accept the proposal of His Majesty's Government, and to sign it in the name of the people of both Republics.

"We, the representative delegates, express our confidence that the present circumstances will, by accepting the proposal of His Majesty's Government, be speedily ameliorated in such a way that our nation will be placed in a position to enjoy the privileges to which they think they have a just claim, on the ground not only of their past sacrifices, but also of those made in this war.

"We have with great satisfaction taken note of the decision of His Majesty's Government to grant a large measure of amnesty to the British subjects who have taken up arms on our behalf, and to whom we are united by bonds of love and honour; and express our wish that it may please His Majesty to still further extend this amnesty."

Mr. P.R. Viljoen then withdrew his proposal.

Commandant H.P.J. Pretorius, seconded by General C. Botha, presented the proposal, as read by the Commission.

General Nieuwouwdt also withdrew his proposal, but it was at once taken over by General C.C.J. Badenhorst, seconded by Commandant A.J. Bester, of Bloemfontein.

The meeting then adjourned till the afternoon.

In the afternoon at 2.05 it again met.

Proceeding to the voting, the proposal of H.P.J. Pretorius, seconded by General C. Botha, was accepted, by fifty-four votes against six. Then Vice-President Burger spoke a few words suitable to the occasion as follows:—"We are standing here at the grave of the two Republics. Much yet remains to be done, although we shall not be able to do it in the official capacities which we have formerly occupied. Let us not draw our hands back from the work which it is our duty to accomplish. Let us ask God to guide us, and to show us how we shall be enabled to keep our nation together. We must be ready to forgive and forget, whenever we meet our brethren. That part of our nation which has proved unfaithful we must not reject."

Later, Vice-President Burger spoke a few words of farewell to the Commandant-General, to the Members of the Executive Councils, and to the delegates.

In the afternoon, as it turned out for the last time, Commandant Jacobsz, seconded by General Muller, made the following proposal, which was unanimously accepted by the meeting:—

"This meeting of Delegates, having in view the necessity of collecting means to provide for the wants of the suffering women and children, widows and orphans, and other destitute persons, who have through this war come to a condition of want, and also having in view the desirability of nominating a Committee, whose duty it shall be to arrange the necessary steps in this matter, and to finally decide on the management and distribution of the donations received, decides:—

"To nominate the Hon. Messrs. M.J. Steyn, S.W. Burger, L. Botha, C.R. de Wet, J.H. De la Rey, A.P. Kriel, and J.D. Kestell, as the Committee, to carry out all arrangements for the above-mentioned purposes, that may seem desirable and expedient to them, and also to appoint new Members, Sub-Committees and working Committees; and the said Committee is empowered to draw up regulations, and to amend them from time to time as shall seem to them expedient.

"This meeting further decides to send abroad from the above-mentioned Committee, Messrs. C.R. de Wet, L. Botha, and J.H. De la Rey, in order that they may help in collecting the above-mentioned donations."

Then this—the last meeting of the two Republics—was closed with prayer.

Boer Declaration & Signing

The Boer Declaration prior to signing the peace treaty in May of 1902. [328]

"We, the national representatives of both the South African Republic and the Orange Free State, at the meeting held at Vereeniging, from the 15th of May till the 31st of May, 1902, have with grief considered the proposal made by His Majesty's Government in connexion with the conclusion of the existing hostilities, and their communication that this proposal had to be accepted, or rejected, unaltered. We are sorry that His Majesty's Government has absolutely declined to negotiate with the Government of the Republics on the basis of their independence, or to allow our Government to enter into communication with our deputation. Our people, however, have always been under the impression that not only on the grounds of justice, but also taking into consideration the great material and personal sacrifices made for their independence, that it had a well-founded claim for that independence.

"We have seriously considered the future of our country, and have specially observed the following facts :

"Firstly, that the military policy pursued by the British military authorities has led to the general devastation of the territory of both Republics by the burning down of farms and towns, by the destruction of all means of existence, and by the exhausting of all resources required for the maintenance of our families, the existence of our armies, and the continuation of the war."

"Secondly, that the placing of our families in the concentration camps has brought on an unheard-of condition of suffering and sickness, so that in a comparatively short time about twenty thousand of our beloved ones have died there, and that the horrid probability has arisen that, by continuing the war, our whole nation may die out in this way."

"Thirdly, that the Kaffir tribe, within and without the frontiers of the territory of the two Republics, are mostly armed and are taking part in the war against us, and through the committing of murders and all sorts of cruelties have caused an unbearable condition of affairs in many districts of both Republics. An instance of this happened not long ago in the district of Vryheid, [329] where fifty-six burghers on one occasion were murdered and mutilated in a fearful manner." [330]

"Fourthly, that by the proclamations of the enemy the burghers still fighting are threatened with the loss of all their movable and landed property—and thus with utter ruin—which proclamations have already been enforced."

"Fifthly, that it has already, through the circumstances of the war, become quite impossible for us to keep the many thousand prisoners of war taken by our forces, and that we have thus been unable to inflict much damage on the British forces (whereas the burghers who are taken prisoners by the British armies are sent out of the country), and that, after war has raged for nearly three years, there only remains an insignificant part of the fighting forces with which we began."

"Sixthly, that this fighting remainder, which is only a small minority of our whole nation, has to fight against an overpowering force of the enemy, and besides is reduced to a condition of starvation, and is destitute of all necessaries, and that notwithstanding our utmost efforts, and the sacrifice of everything that is dear and precious to us, we cannot foresee an eventual victory."

"We are therefore of opinion that there is no justifiable ground for expecting that by continuing the war the nation will retain its independence, and that, under these circumstances, the nation is not justified in continuing the war, because this can only lead to social and material ruin, not for us alone, but also for our posterity. Compelled by the above-named circumstances and motives, we commission both Governments to accept the proposal of His Majesty's Government, and to sign it in the name of the people of both Republics."

"We, the representative delegates, express our confidence that the present circumstances will, by accepting the proposal of His Majesty's Government, be speedily ameliorated in such a way that our nation will be placed in a

[328] The Times' History of the War in South Africa 1899-1902 by Amery, L. S. (Leopold Stennett), Volume 5 pages 604- 606.

[329] Vryheid - Wikipedia And:

[330] The Battle of Holkrans or Holkrantz (6 May 1902) took place at Holkrans, near Vryheid. To stop the raids operated by the Boers on their cattle and crops as a punishment for helping the British, the leader of the abaQulusi, Sikhobobho, responded by assembling his forces and attacked the commando camp at the foot of Holkrans hill. The Zulus attacked at night, and in a mutual bloodbath, the Boers lost 56 killed and 3 wounded, while the Zulus suffered 52 killed and 48 wounded. This battle was the last victory of the abaQulusi to date Battle of Holkrans - Wikipedia

position to enjoy the privileges to which they think they have a just claim, on the ground not only of their past sacrifices, but also of those made in this war."

"We have with great satisfaction taken note of the decision of His Majesty's Government to grant a large measure of amnesty to the British subjects who have taken up arms on our behalf, and to whom we are united by bonds of love and honour; and express our wish that it may please His Majesty to still further extend this amnesty."

The motion was carried by fifty-four votes to six. The irrevocable decision had been made. The time for speech making had gone, but Schalk Burger closed the meeting in a few sentences of simple eloquence.

"We are standing here at the grave of the two Republics. Much yet remains to be done, although we shall not be able to do it in the official capacities which we have formerly occupied."

"Let us not draw our hands back from the work which it is our duty to accomplish. Let us ask God to guide us, and to show us how we shall be enabled to keep our nation together. We must be ready to forgive and forget whenever we meet our brethren."

"That part of our nation which has proved unfaithful we must not reject."

The Commissioners travelled to Pretoria, and on the same night, at five minutes past eleven, only an hour before the expiry of the term of grace, the Treaty was signed.

"We are good friends now," said Kitchener, as he shook hands with the representatives of the late Republics.[331]

General L. Botha [With 'Aussie' hat, right side pinned up.] in conversation with General Lyttelton and Staff at Newcastle Station.[54]

The Holkrans Monument commemorates the death of 56 Boers on May 6th, 1902 in Vryheid. Louis Botha represented this district in the Legislature.[55]

[331] The Times' History of the War in South Africa 1899–1902 by Amery, L. S. (Leopold Stennett), Volume 5 page 606.

Treaty of Vereeniging Terms

Quote from The Great Boer War by Arthur Conan Doyle.[332] [333]

On May 31st this resolution was notified to Lord Kitchener, and at half-past ten of the same night the delegates arrived at Pretoria and set their names to the treaty of peace. ....

The following were in brief the terms of surrender:—

1. That the burghers lay down their arms and acknowledge themselves subjects of Edward VII.
2. That all prisoners taking the oath of allegiance be returned.
3. That their liberty and property be inviolate.
4. That an amnesty be granted—save in special cases.
5. That the Dutch language be allowed in schools and law-courts.
6. That rifles be allowed if registered.
7. That self-government be granted as soon as possible.
8. That no franchise be granted for natives until after self-government.
9. That no special land tax be levied.
10. That the people be helped to reoccupy the farms.
11. That 3,000,000 pounds be given to help the farmers.
12. That the rebels be disfranchised and their leaders tried, on condition that no death penalty be inflicted.

These terms were practically the same as those which had been refused by Botha in March 1901. [At the Middleburg Conference] Thirteen months of useless warfare had left the situation as it was."

[332] Doyle, Arthur Conan. The Great Boer War 17th Edition, 1902 with the two volumes as one document: The Great Boer War by Arthur Conan Doyle - Free Ebook (gutenberg.org) Chapter 39. Pages 232-234 of the Word document.
[333] General Article: Treaty of Vereeniging - Wikipedia

Peace Treaty of Vereeniging

The Following Notice is hereby published for general information. By order of His Excellency the High Commissioner and Administrator of the Transvaal. W.E. Davidson, Acting Secretary to the Transvaal Administration 3rd June 1902. [334] [335]

Army Headquarters, South Africa

General Lord Kitchener of Khartoum, Command in Chief

And

His Excellency Lord Milner, High Commissioner, on behalf of the British Government,

And

Messrs S.W. Burger, F.W. Reitz, Louis Botha, J.H. de la Rey, LJ. Meyer, and J.C. Krogh, acting as the Government Of South African Republic,

And

Messrs W.J.C. Brebner, C.R. de Wet, J.B.M. Hertzog, and C.H. Olivier, acting as the Government of the Orange Free State, on behalf of their respective Burghers

Desirous to terminate the present hostilities, agree on the following Articles.

1. The Burgher Forces in the Field will forthwith lay down their Arms, handing over all Guns, Rifles, and Munitions of War, in their possession or under their control, and desist from any further resistance to the Authority of His Majesty King Edward VII, whom they recognise as their lawful Sovereign.
The Manner and details of this surrender will be arranged between Lord Kitchener and Commandant General Botha, Assistant Commandant General de la Rey and Chief Commandant De Wet.
2. Burghers in the field outside the limits of the Transvaal and Orange River Colony, and all Prisoners of War at present outside South Africa, who are burghers, will, on duly declaring their acceptance of the position of subjects of His Majesty King Edward VII, be gradually brought back to their homes as soon as transport can be provided and their means of subsistence ensured.
3. The Burghers so surrendering or so returning will not be deprived of their personal liberty, or their property.
4. No proceedings Civil or Criminal will be taken against any of the BURGHERS so surrendering or so returning for any Acts in connection with the prosecution of the War. The benefit of this clause will not extend to certain Acts contrary to the usage of War which have been notified by the Commander in Chief to the Boer Generals, and which shall be tried by Court Martial immediately after the close of hostilities.
5. The Dutch language will be taught in Public Schools in the Transvaal and the Orange River Colony where the Parents of the Children desire it, and will be allowed in Courts of Law when necessary for the better and more effectual Administration of Justice.
6. The Possession of Rifles will be allowed in the Transvaal and Orange River Colony to persons requiring them for their protection on taking out a license according to Law.
7. Military Administration in the Transvaal and Orange River Colony will at the earliest possible date be succeeded by Civil Government, and, as soon as circumstances permit, Representative Institutions, leading up to self-Government, will be introduced.
8. The question of granting the Franchise to Natives will not be decided until after the introduction of Self-Government.
9. No Special Tax will be imposed on Landed Property in the Transvaal and Orange River Colony to defray the Expenses of the War.
10. As soon as conditions permit, a Commission, on which the local inhabitants will be represented, will be appointed in each District of the Transvaal and Orange River Colony, under the Presidency of a Magistrate or

[334] Text: Peace Treaty of Vereeniging - transcript | South African History Online (sahistory.org.za)
[335] General Article: Treaty of Vereeniging - Wikipedia

other official, for the purpose of assisting the restoration of the people to their homes and supplying those who, owing to war losses, are unable to provide for themselves, with food, shelter, and the necessary amount of seed, stock, implements etc. indispensable to the resumption of their normal occupations.

His Majesty's Government will place at the disposal of these Commissions a sum of three million pounds sterling for the above purposes, and will allow all notes, issued under Law No. 1 of 1900 of the Government of the South African Republic, and all receipts, given by the officers in the field of the late Republics or under their orders, to be presented to a Judicial Commission, which will be appointed by the Government, and if such notes and receipts are found by this Commission to have been duly issued in return for valuable consideration they will be received by the first-named Commissions as evidence of War losses suffered by the persons to whom they were originally given.

In addition to the above named free grant of three million pounds, His Majesty's Government will be prepared to make advances as loans for the same purpose, free of interest for two years, and afterwards repayable over a period of years with 3 per cent interest. No foreigner or rebel will be entitled to the benefit of this Clause.

Signed at Pretoria this thirty first day of May in the Year of Our Lord Thousand Nine Hundred and Two.

[Signed for British] Kitchener of Khartoum,[336] Milner,[337]

[Signed for Transvaal and Orange Free State]
S. W. Burger,[338]
F. W. Reitz,[339]
Louis Botha,[340]
J. H. De La Rey,[341]
L. J. Meyer,[342]
J. C. Krogh,
C. R. De Wet,[343]
J. B. M Hertzog,[344]
W. J. C. Brebner,[345]
C. H. Olivier[346]

[336] Herbert Kitchener: Herbert Kitchener, 1st Earl Kitchener - Wikipedia
[337] Alfred Milner: Alfred Milner, 1st Viscount Milner - Wikipedia
[338] Schalk Willem Burger: Schalk Willem Burger - Wikipedia
[339] Francis William Reitz: Francis William Reitz - Wikipedia
[340] Louis Botha: Louis Botha - Wikipedia
[341] Jacobus Herculaas de la Rey: Koos de la Rey - Wikipedia
[342] Lucas Johannes Meyer: Lucas Johannes Meyer - Wikipedia
[343] Christiaan Rudolf de Wet: Christiaan de Wet - Wikipedia
[344] James Barry Munnik Hertzog: J. B. M. Hertzog - Wikipedia
[345] W J C. Brebner was Secretary of State for the Orange Free State.
[346] General C. H. Olivier was appointed a member of the Executive Council of the Orange Free State in place of General A. P. Cronje.

Treaty Images 1

The treaty was executed in duplicate. One copy has the British representatives signing first and the other has the Boer representatives doing so.

Peace Treaty of Vereeniging original documents.[347 348]

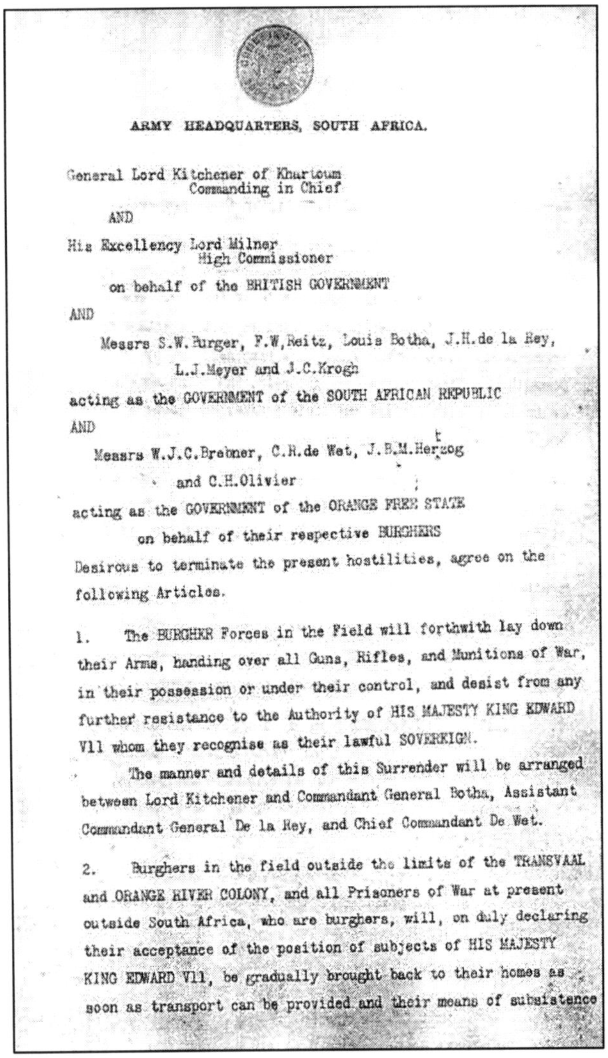

ARMY HEADQUARTERS, SOUTH AFRICA.

General Lord Kitchener of Khartoum
Commanding in Chief

AND

His Excellency Lord Milner
High Commissioner

on behalf of the BRITISH GOVERNMENT

AND

Messrs S.W.Burger, F.W,Reitz, Louis Botha, J.H.de la Rey,
L.J.Meyer and J.C.Krogh

acting as the GOVERNMENT of the SOUTH AFRICAN REPUBLIC

AND

Messrs W.J.C.Brebner, C.R.de Wet, J.B.M.Hertzog
and C.H.Olivier

acting as the GOVERNMENT of the ORANGE FREE STATE

on behalf of their respective BURGHERS

Desirous to terminate the present hostilities, agree on the following Articles.

1. The BURGHER Forces in the Field will forthwith lay down their Arms, handing over all Guns, Rifles, and Munitions of War, in their possession or under their control, and desist from any further resistance to the Authority of HIS MAJESTY KING EDWARD V11 whom they recognise as their lawful SOVEREIGN.

The manner and details of this Surrender will be arranged between Lord Kitchener and Commandant General Botha, Assistant Commandant General De la Rey, and Chief Commandant De Wet.

2. Burghers in the field outside the limits of the TRANSVAAL and ORANGE RIVER COLONY, and all Prisoners of War at present outside South Africa, who are burghers, will, on duly declaring their acceptance of the position of subjects of HIS MAJESTY KING EDWARD V11, be gradually brought back to their homes as soon as transport can be provided and their means of subsistence

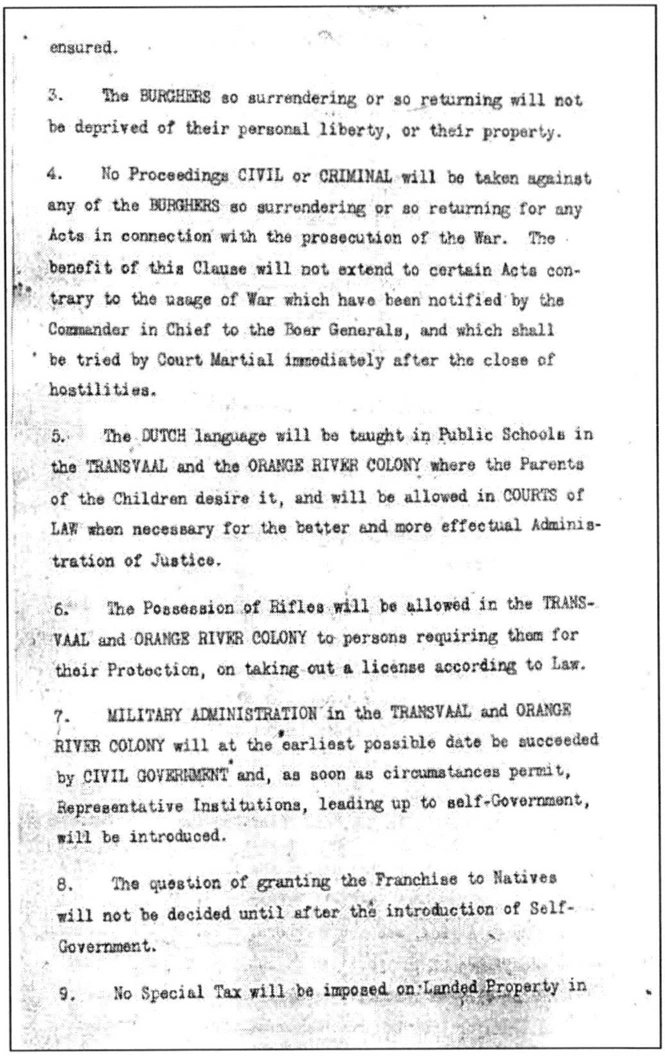

ensured.

3. The BURGHERS so surrendering or so returning will not be deprived of their personal liberty, or their property.

4. No Proceedings CIVIL or CRIMINAL will be taken against any of the BURGHERS so surrendering or so returning for any Acts in connection with the prosecution of the War. The benefit of this Clause will not extend to certain Acts contrary to the usage of War which have been notified by the Commander in Chief to the Boer Generals, and which shall be tried by Court Martial immediately after the close of hostilities.

5. The DUTCH language will be taught in Public Schools in the TRANSVAAL and the ORANGE RIVER COLONY where the Parents of the Children desire it, and will be allowed in COURTS of LAW when necessary for the better and more effectual Administration of Justice.

6. The Possession of Rifles will be allowed in the TRANSVAAL and ORANGE RIVER COLONY to persons requiring them for their Protection, on taking out a license according to Law.

7. MILITARY ADMINISTRATION in the TRANSVAAL and ORANGE RIVER COLONY will at the earliest possible date be succeeded by CIVIL GOVERNMENT and, as soon as circumstances permit, Representative Institutions, leading up to self-Government, will be introduced.

8. The question of granting the Franchise to Natives will not be decided until after the introduction of Self-Government.

9. No Special Tax will be imposed on Landed Property in

347 Peace Treaty of Vereeniging - original document | South African History Online (sahistory.org.za)

348 Treaty Page 1 File:Vereeniging1.jpg - Wikimedia Commons
Treaty Page 2 File:Vereeniging2.jpg - Wikimedia Commons
Treaty Page 3 File:Vereeniging3.jpg - Wikimedia Commons
Treaty Signatures 2 File:Vereeniging4.jpg - Wikimedia Commons

the TRANSVAAL and ORANGE RIVER COLONY to defray the Expenses of the War.

10. As soon as conditions permit, a Commission, on which the local inhabitants will be represented, will be appointed in each District of the TRANSVAAL and ORANGE RIVER COLONY, under the Presidency of a Magistrate or other Official, for the purpose of assisting the restoration of the people to their homes and supplying those who, owing to war losses, are unable to provide for themselves, with food, shelter, and the necessary amount of seed, stock, implements etc, indispensable to the resumption of their normal occupations.

His Majesty's Government will place at the disposal of these Commissions a sum of three million pounds sterling for the above purposes, and will allow all notes, issued under Law No.1 of 1900 of the Government of the SOUTH AFRICAN REPUBLIC, and all receipts, given by the officers in the field of the late Republics or under their orders, to be presented to a JUDICIAL COMMISSION, which will be appointed by the Government, and if such notes and receipts are found by this Commission to have been duly issued in return for valuable consideration they will be received by the first named Commissions as evidence of War losses suffered by the persons to whom they were originally given. In addition to the above named free grant of three million pounds, His Majesty's Government will be prepared to make advances as loans for the same purpose, free of interest for two years, and afterwards repayable over a period of years with 3 per cent interest. No foreigner or rebel will be entitled to the benefit of this Clause.

Signed at Pretoria this thirty first day of May in the Year of Our Lord One Thousand Nine Hundred and Two.

[Signed]
Kitchener of Khartoum,
Milner,
S. W. Burger,
F. W. Reitz,
Louis Botha,
J. H. De La Rey,
L. J. Meyer,
J. C. Krogh,
C. R. De Wet,
J. B. M Hertzog,
W. J. C. Brebner,
C. H. Olivier

Treaty Images 2

The treaty was executed in duplicate.[349]

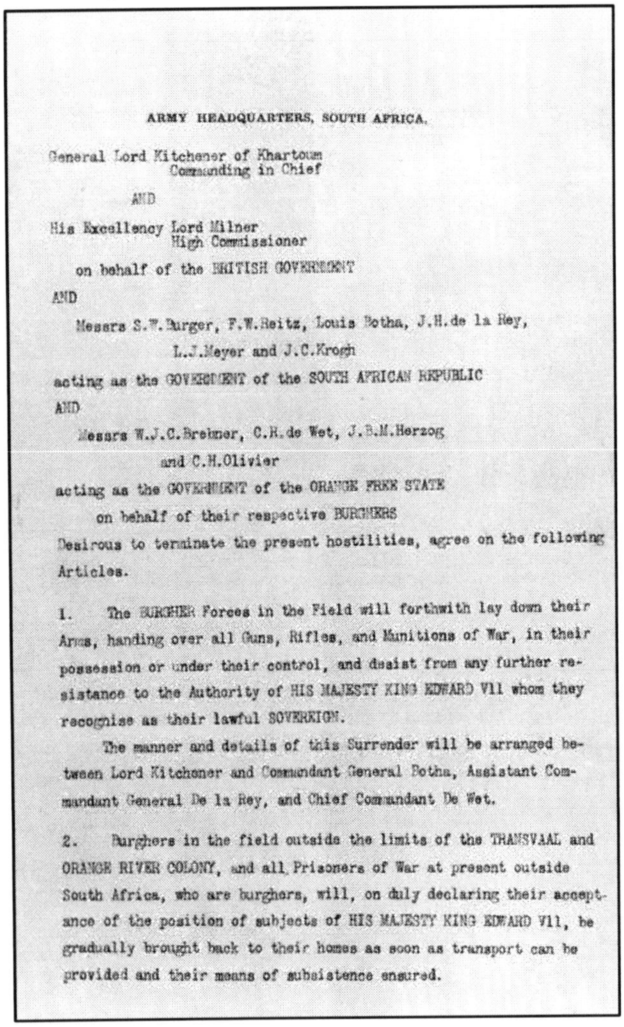

ARMY HEADQUARTERS, SOUTH AFRICA.

General Lord Kitchener of Khartoum
Commanding in Chief

AND

His Excellency Lord Milner
High Commissioner

on behalf of the BRITISH GOVERNMENT

AND

Messrs S.W.Burger, F.W.Reitz, Louis Botha, J.H.de la Rey,
L.J.Meyer and J.C.Krogh

acting as the GOVERNMENT of the SOUTH AFRICAN REPUBLIC

AND

Messrs W.J.C.Brebner, C.R.de Wet, J.B.M.Herzog
and C.H.Olivier

acting as the GOVERNMENT of the ORANGE FREE STATE
on behalf of their respective BURGHERS

Desirous to terminate the present hostilities, agree on the following Articles.

1. The BURGHER Forces in the Field will forthwith lay down their Arms, handing over all Guns, Rifles, and Munitions of War, in their possession or under their control, and desist from any further resistance to the Authority of HIS MAJESTY KING EDWARD V11 whom they recognise as their lawful SOVEREIGN.

The manner and details of this Surrender will be arranged between Lord Kitchener and Commandant General Botha, Assistant Commandant General De la Rey, and Chief Commandant De Wet.

2. Burghers in the field outside the limits of the TRANSVAAL and ORANGE RIVER COLONY, and all Prisoners of War at present outside South Africa, who are burghers, will, on duly declaring their acceptance of the position of subjects of HIS MAJESTY KING EDWARD V11, be gradually brought back to their homes as soon as transport can be provided and their means of subsistence ensured.

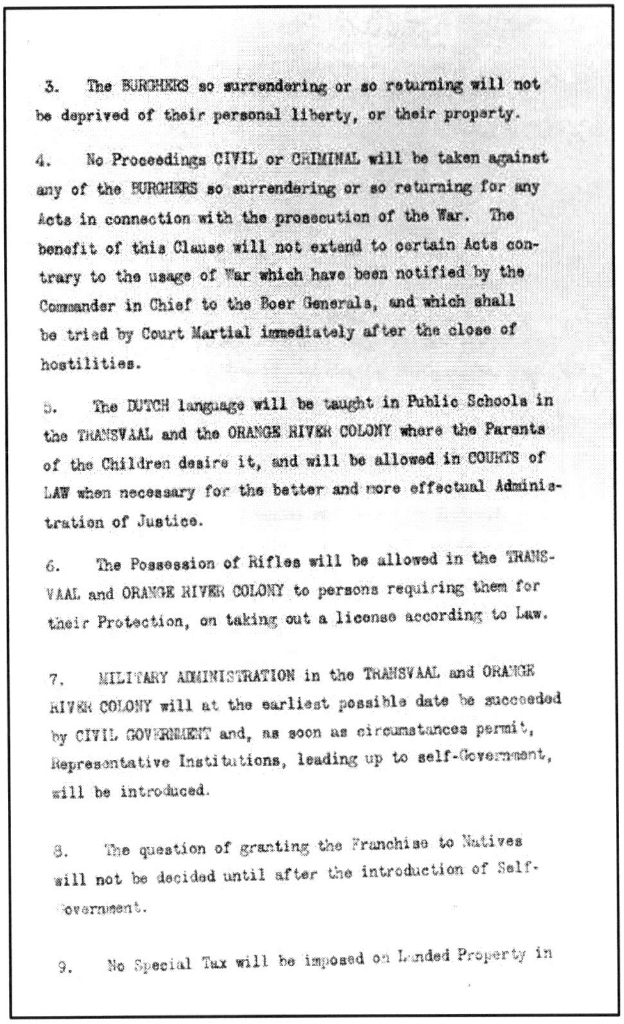

3. The BURGHERS so surrendering or so returning will not be deprived of their personal liberty, or their property.

4. No Proceedings CIVIL or CRIMINAL will be taken against any of the BURGHERS so surrendering or so returning for any Acts in connection with the prosecution of the War. The benefit of this Clause will not extend to certain Acts contrary to the usage of War which have been notified by the Commander in Chief to the Boer Generals, and which shall be tried by Court Martial immediately after the close of hostilities.

5. The DUTCH language will be taught in Public Schools in the TRANSVAAL and the ORANGE RIVER COLONY where the Parents of the Children desire it, and will be allowed in COURTS of LAW when necessary for the better and more effectual Administration of Justice.

6. The Possession of Rifles will be allowed in the TRANSVAAL and ORANGE RIVER COLONY to persons requiring them for their Protection, on taking out a license according to Law.

7. MILITARY ADMINISTRATION in the TRANSVAAL and ORANGE RIVER COLONY will at the earliest possible date be succeeded by CIVIL GOVERNMENT and, as soon as circumstances permit, Representative Institutions, leading up to self-Government, will be introduced.

8. The question of granting the Franchise to Natives will not be decided until after the introduction of Self-Government.

9. No Special Tax will be imposed on Landed Property in

[349] Treaty Page 1 File:The Second Boer War, 1899 - 1902 Q68896.jpg - Wikimedia Commons
Treaty Page 2 File:The Second Boer War, 1899 - 1902 Q68897.jpg - Wikimedia Commons
Treaty Page 3 File:The Second Boer War, 1899 - 1902 Q68898.jpg - Wikimedia Commons
Treaty Signatures 2 File:The Second Boer War, 1899 - 1902 Q68899.jpg - Wikimedia Commons

the TRANSVAAL and ORANGE RIVER COLONY to defray the Expenses of the War.

10. As soon as conditions permit, a Commission, on which the local inhabitants will be represented, will be appointed in each District of the TRANSVAAL and ORANGE RIVER COLONY, under the Presidency of a Magistrate or other Official, for the purpose of assisting the restoration of the people to their homes and supplying those who, owing to war losses, are unable to provide for themselves, with food, shelter, and the necessary amount of seed, stock, implements etc, indispensable to the resumption of their normal occupations.

His Majesty's Government will place at the disposal of these Commissions a sum of three million pounds sterling for the above purposes, and will allow all notes, issued under Law No.1 of 1900 of the Government of the SOUTH AFRICAN REPUBLIC, and all receipts, given by the officers in the field of the late Republics or under their orders, to be presented to a JUDICIAL COMMISSION, which will be appointed by the Government, and if such notes and receipts are found by this Commission to have been duly issued in return for valuable consideration they will be received by the first named Commissions as evidence of War losses suffered by the persons to whom they were originally given. In addition to the above named free grant of three million pounds, His Majesty's Government will be prepared to make advances as loans for the same purpose, free of interest for two years, and afterwards repayable over a period of years with 3 per cent interest. No foreigner or rebel will be entitled to the benefit of this Clause.

Signed at Pretoria this thirty first day of May in the Year of Our Lord One Thousand Nine Hundred and Two.

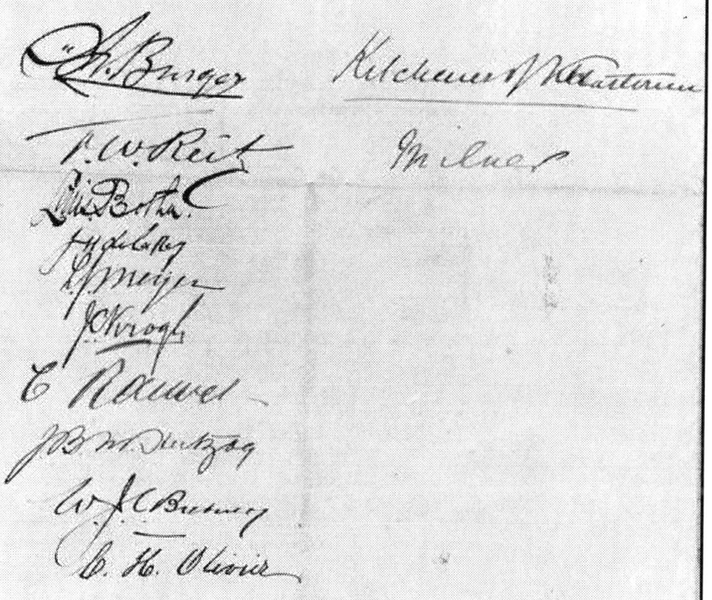

Kitchener's Final Despatch

Despatch by General H. Kitchener, dated 23rd June, 1902, relative to Military Operations in South Africa.[350]

From Lord Kitchener to the Secretary of State for War. Cape Town, 23rd June, 1902.

Sir, I have the honour to submit a final despatch which covers the period between the signature of the terms of peace at Pretoria and my departure from Cape Town. ………………………..

2. In my last despatch dated 1st June, I had the pleasure of reporting the conclusion of peace. Directly the terms were signed I appointed the following three Peace Commissioners to receive the surrenders in the territories of the new Colonies:

General Bruce Hamilton for the Eastern Transvaal.

General W. [Walter] Kitchener for the Western Transvaal.

General Elliot[351] for the Orange River Colony.

I also directed General French to make the necessary arrangements for the same purpose in the Cape Colony.

3. The reports of General French and the three Peace Commissioners are herewith submitted. ……………….... The Boer leaders concerned, played their part with loyalty and in a thoroughly straightforward manner, whilst the burghers and rebels on commando also accepted the situation in a manly spirit which augurs well for the future of South Africa. So strongly did I feel this that I sent the following telegram to Generals Louis Botha, De la Rey, and Christian de Wet:

> "Now that the surrender of the arms in the hands of the burghers in the Transvaal and Orange River Colony has been completed, I desire to place on record my high appreciation of the unflagging energy and unfailing tact with which you have facilitated the work of my Commissioners. I recognize how much it is due to your exertions that the burghers have displayed everywhere such a loyal spirit in accepting the change of Government that has taken place, and I can inform you that the manner in which the burghers have come in has greatly pleased His Majesty, the King, and deeply impressed the British people, who are heartily anxious to welcome them as fellow citizens. I feel confident that a new era of complete reconciliation between all races has now dawned in South Africa."[352]

The total numbers of the surrenders of armed burghers [were]

in the Transvaal were	11,166
in the Orange River Colony	6,455
in the Cape Colony	3,635
Total	21,256

4. I well understand that the accompanying list, ………… who have in my opinion rendered exceptionally good service during the campaign, is incomplete, …………… there must necessarily be a proportion of Officers omitted, who have rendered equal or even better service than those who have been mentioned. This, however, is the fortune of war, and will, I am sure, be well understood by the Army I have been so proud to command. What follows are 21 pages of lists of individuals and units and their service.]

350 Proclamations Issued In South Africa: Vol II p. 757 https://babel.hathitrust.org/cgi/pt?id=hvd.32044089026009&seq=757&view=1up

351 Lieutenant General Sir Edward Locke Elliot, KCB, KCIE, DSO (28 January 1850–12 December 1938) was a British Army General during the Second Boer War and in British India. Edward Locke Elliot - Wikipedia

352 At this time the Dutch and English were thought of and considered different 'races'. It was also British policy and thought that the conclusion of the conflict would materially improve the condition of all people in South Africa.

Appeal of the Generals

Soon [353]after the conclusion of the war Generals Botha, De Wet, and Delarey, in the hope of making favourable arrangements with the Government on behalf of their fellow countrymen, sailed for England. They were greeted by the British people with unusual cordiality, not because of any sympathy with the Republics they came to represent, but because it is a characteristic of the British people to honour brave men, even when they are defeated foes. General Botha was received by Mr. Chamberlain, and the Boer future was discussed. A few days later the public was startled to read in the daily journals the following manifesto entitled, "Appeal of the Boer Generals to the Civilised World."

"It is still fresh in the memory of the world how the Boers, after a terrible struggle lasting more than two and a half years, were at last obliged to accept through their representatives at Vereeniging the terms of peace submitted to them by the Government of King Edward VII. At the same time the representatives commissioned us to proceed to England in order, in the first place, to appeal to the new Government to allay the immense distress everywhere devastating the new colonies. If we did not succeed we were to appeal to the humanity of the civilised world for charitable contributions. As we have not succeeded up to the present in inducing the British Government to grant further assistance to our people in their indescribable distress, it only remains for us to address ourselves to the peoples of Europe and America."

"During the critical days through which we have passed it was sweet for us and ours to receive constant marks of sympathy from all countries. The financial and other assistance given to our women and children in the concentration camps, and to the prisoners of war in all parts of the earth contributed infinitely to mitigate the lot of those poor sufferers, and we take advantage of this opportunity to express in the name of the people of the late Republics our fervent thanks to all those who have charitably assisted us in the past. The small Boer nation can never forget the help it received in its dark hours of suffering."

"The people of the Republics were ready to sacrifice everything for their independence, and now the struggle is over and our people are completely ruined. Though we have not had the opportunity of drawing up an exact inventory of the destruction done, we have the conviction, based on personal experience, that at least thirty thousand houses on Boer farms and a number of villages were burnt or destroyed by the British during the war.

Our homes with their furniture were burned or destroyed, our orchards were ruined, all our agricultural implements broken, our mills were destroyed, every living animal was carried off or killed. Nothing, alas, remained to us. The country is laid waste. The war demanded many victims, and the land was bathed in tears. Our orphans and widows have been abandoned. Besides, it is needless to recall the fact how much will be needed in the future for the education of the children of the Burghers, who are in great distress."

"We address ourselves to the world, with the prayer to help us by charitable contributions for our widows and orphans, for the maimed and other needy ones, and for the satisfactory education of our children. We allude to the terrible results of the war in order to bring to the knowledge of the world our urgent needs, by no means to inflame people's minds. The sword is now sheathed, and all differences are silent in presence of such great misery. The ruin caused by the war is indescribable, so that the small amount which Great Britain is to give us, in accordance with the terms of surrender, even were it multiplied tenfold, would be wholly insufficient even to cover the war losses alone. The widows, orphans, maimed, needy, and children, on whose behalf alone we appeal, will receive little of this sum, and in most cases nothing."

"All contributions will be assigned to a fund to be called 'General Fund of Help for the Boers,' which will be devoted solely to supplying the wants of those for whom we are collecting, and to provide for their future. We solicit the hearty co-operation of the committees existing in the various countries of Europe and in America. We are now on the point of visiting these countries in succession with the object of establishing a satisfactory organisation."

Botha.

De Wet.

De La Rey.

[353] See Appendix of Volume 8 p. 189 of South Africa and the Transvaal War, Louis Creswicke, Edinburgh : T. C. & E. C. Jack, 1900. Vol 8 https://archive.org/details/southafricatrans08cres

British Repatriation Procedures.

This material appeared in John Blake's 'A West Pointer with the Boers.' [354] It has an authentic ring to it and seems appropriate to the circumstances at the end of the conflict.

Colonel Blake's introduction:

"The Peace Terms required that all burghers should lay down their guns and acknowledge King Edward VII. as their lawful sovereign, and no more. This applied to prisoners of war in the same way as to the burghers in the field. Here I insert a private document giving private instructions, and it shows plainly what an unscrupulous thing an English official or officer is."

[By] W. Lambton, Lieut. Colonel, Military Secretary, South Africa. Pretoria, Fourth of July, 1902.

Procedure to Be Adopted in Selecting Prisoners of War for Return to South Africa.

I. Classification of Prisoners in Order of Return.

The selection of prisoners of war for return to South Africa should be made in the following order:

1. Those who have volunteered for active service, [National Scouts] and are considered likely to become loyal subjects and useful settlers; and those who appear willing to accept the new order of things cheerfully.
2. Those who have shown no particular bias.
3. Irreconcilables, and men who have given trouble in the camps.

Lists of all prisoners of war have been prepared by the D. M. I., S. A., in conjunction with the local authorities of each district, divided into three categories, and it is desirable that this order should be maintained, as far as possible, and the lists made out by commandants of oversea camps, combined with the lists forwarded from South Africa, the corresponding classes being merged together.

It is to be understood that the lists supplied from South Africa are merely a general guide, and commandants of camps are invited to use their discretion in modifying the order, where their experience of the individual convinces them that an alteration is necessary.

No shipload of prisoners of war should include more than 100 men belonging to any one district.

II. Oath of Allegiance.

No prisoner of war should be embarked without taking the Oath of Allegiance, **or the approved equivalent declaration**. The oath or declaration must be signed in triplicate, and it is of the greatest importance that the prisoner should retain one copy of the form, for purposes of identification, and that one copy should be forwarded to the Colonial Secretary of the prisoner's Colony for record.

III. Nominal Rolls to Be Sent in Advance of Prisoners. To facilitate the work of repatriation in South Africa, a nominal roll of all prisoners should be posted to the Military Secretary to the High Commissioner, at least a fortnight before embarkation. This nominal roll should give the prisoner of war's number, and the farm, district and colony to which he belongs.

IV. Special Lists. Special lists will be forwarded from time to time, of men whose early release is approved by the High Commissioner, and these men should have precedence of all others; similarly, names may be sent of men whose early return is not considered advisable, and such men should in each case remain till the last.

[354] Blake, John Y. Fillmore, A West Pointer with the Boers: A Personal Narrative of Colonel J Y F Blake, Commander of the Irish Brigade (Angel Guardian Press, 1903). Also a Reprint, Kessenger Publishing Co LLC, Whitefish, MT, 2007). Catalog Search: https://archive.org/search?query=title%3A%28West%20Pointer%20with%20the%20Boers%29%20AND%20date%3A%5B1899-01-01%20TO%201905-01-01%5D U. Cal Scan: https://archive.org/details/westpointerwithb00blakrich
U. Michigan Scan: https://archive.org/details/awestpointerwit00blakgoog

V. Prisoners Allowed to Go at Own Expense.

Prisoners of war who take the Oath of Allegiance, and who belong to Class 1, may be permitted to proceed forthwith—

(a) To South Africa, (provided they have the means of supporting themselves on arrival.)

(b) Elsewhere.

In each case at their own expense.

The names of prisoners released under this clause, and the ships by which they sail, should be communicated to the Military Secretary to the High Commissioner, by telegraph, in the case of persons returning to South Africa, and by post in other cases.

VI. Preference to Be Given to Men with Families in South Africa and to Farm Owners.

It will be advisable in compiling the lists mentioned in par. I, to include only a small percentage of unmarried men without farms or means of livelihood, and to push forward as much as possible, men having families who need their support, and farms to which they can go immediately on arrival in South Africa, as it is this class who provide the work for the bijwoner [as printed] class, whose return for this reason, it is necessary to retard.

VII. Foreigners. Foreigners will not be allowed to return to South Africa.

VIII. Procedure on Arrival in South Africa.

On arrival of prisoners in South Africa, the S. O. Prisoners of War at the port of disembarkation will take over the prisoners of war, classify them according to districts, and arrange with the Repatriation Board in the two colonies for their distribution.

The Repatriation Board will then make all necessary arrangements at the district concentration camp for the accommodation of the burghers, and for returning them to their homes as soon as transport is available. In the ease of prisoners of war released in accordance with par. V. of these instructions, the S. O. Prisoners of War at port of disembarkation will arrange to meet them and take the particulars necessary for keeping all complete records.

[By] W. Lambton, Lieut. Colonel, Military Secretary, South Africa. Pretoria, Fourth of **July, 1902**.

Webster Davis Interviews with Kruger & Reitz

Before we embark on these two interviews I would like to introduce the American to whom they were granted.

Mr. Kruger and Mr. Reitz must have given similar recitations hundreds of times during their tenure. These probably are partially compendiums of several texts that were generally recited to given to journalists and others. They represent a full recapitulation of their justifications assembled in one place.

First we need to go back to the circumstances in the United States at the time and to the man, Mr. Webster Davis, who obtained and published them in his book, John Bull's Crimes.

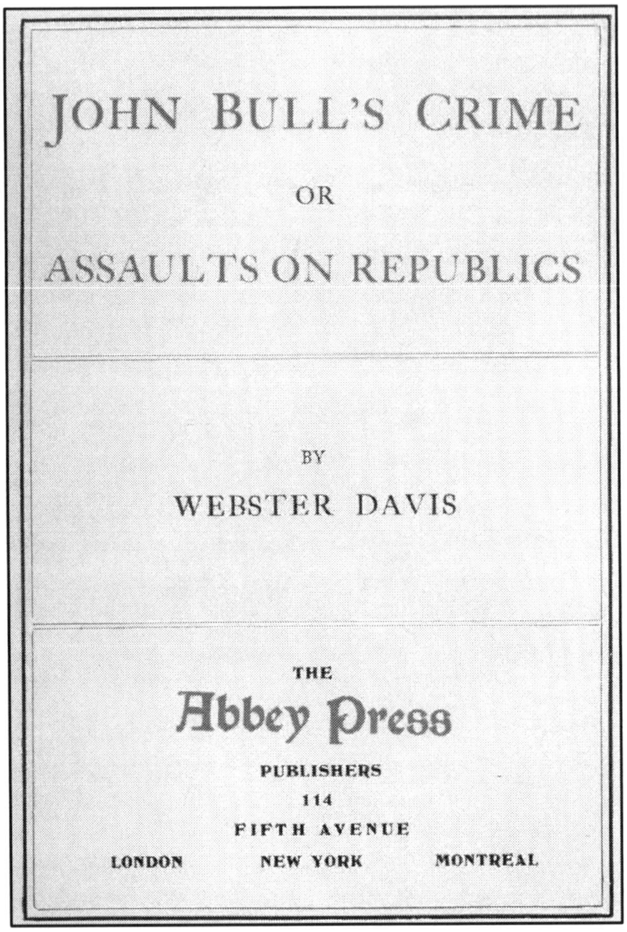
JOHN BULL'S CRIME

OR

ASSAULTS ON REPUBLICS

BY

WEBSTER DAVIS

THE

Abbey Press

PUBLISHERS

114

FIFTH AVENUE

LONDON NEW YORK MONTREAL

Upon his return from SA he published an account of his journey in 1901 under the title 'John Bull's Crimes.'[355]

[355] John Bull's crime; or, Assaults on republics. 1901 New York The Abbey Press HathiTrust Catalogue Record: Catalog Record: John Bull's crime | HathiTrust Digital Library U. Cal. https://babel.hathitrust.org/cgi/pt?id=uc2.ark:/13960/t0ht2s59k&seq=9 U. Michigan: https://babel.hathitrust.org/cgi/pt?id=mdp.39015070386605&seq=11
Internet Archive Records: https://archive.org/search?query=title%3A%28John%20Bull%27s%20Crime%29
Internet Archive Copy: https://archive.org/details/johnbullscrimeor0000unse/mode/2up
NYPL Copy: https://archive.org/details/johnbullscrimeo02davigoog/mode/2up

Webster Davis Intro

Webster Davis (June 1, 1861–February 22, 1923)[356] was a senior American politician who went to South Africa ostensibly on a well-deserved leave of absence to visit both the British and Boer governments at that time. Upon his return he resigned his post so that he could speak freely about the cause of the Boer Republics.

In 1898 the US President was William McKinley, a Republican, who had just led the Government in successfully prosecuting the Spanish-American War between April and December of that year.[357] The United States also annexed the Republic of Hawaii in August of 1898.

US support for Cuban independence had been prevalent across the body politic; even William Jennings Bryan, the Democratic Party candidate in the 1896 presidential election supported Cuban independence in order to bring an end to Spanish colonial rule. A rule which had devolved into a brutal counter insurgency program that was devolving into a military and humanitarian disaster, and saw one of the first uses of concentration camps[358] to imprison civilians in an effort to deprive the Cuban revolutionaries of rural support. The British would adopt this same tactic in their conflict with the Boer republics as well.

After concluding the Treaty of Paris to end the Spanish-American War, the issue of the United States becoming an imperial power with colonies of its own was hotly debated. Historically, George Washington, the first president of the United States, began a policy of US non-interventionism which lasted into well into the 1800's. The United States promulgated the Monroe Doctrine in 1823, in order to stop further European colonialism in Latin America. Abraham Lincoln, while a congressman in 1847, opposed the Mexican-American War, which he imputed to President James K. Polk's desire for "military glory - that attractive rainbow, that rises in showers of blood".[359]

With respect to the British Empire, the United States itself being a former British colony which had fought two wars to obtain and maintain its independence was at this time hoisted on its own petard with respect to British colonial expansion since the United States was engaging in the exact same expansionist and imperialist behaviour.

While the American administration may not have been in any place to object; in the country at large in the 1890s there many United States citizens whose grandfathers had fought against the British in the War of 1812 and one only needed to scratch the surface to expose a deep undercurrent of distrust and resentment towards the British Empire amongst the American public.

The 1896 Presidential Election had been fought over whether the United States would adopt a gold or silver standard for its currency. William Jennings Bryan had lost that election and the gold standard won out.

[356] Davis was born in Ebensburg, Pennsylvania. In 1868 his family moved to Chillicothe, Missouri and then to Gallatin, Missouri where his father began a shoemaking operation. In 1881 Davis moved to Chicago, Illinois where he was a lamplighter. In 1884 he attended the University of Kansas and became a lawyer initially practicing in Garden City, Kansas and becoming active in the Republican Party. After graduating from the University of Michigan Law School he moved to Kansas City, Missouri where he unsuccessfully ran for Congress in 1892. After Davis' successful run for mayor he was appointed by President William McKinley as Assistant Secretary of the Interior.
He was forced to resign after an 1898 visit to South Africa when he sympathized with the Boers. Unable to get a plank supporting them in the Republican Party platform, he switched to being a Democrat. He wrote a book about the Boer War entitled John Bull's Crime: Or, Assaults on Republics which was published in 1901.
He died in Kansas City on February 22, 1923, and is buried in Elmwood Cemetery. See: Webster Davis - Wikipedia

[357] The Spanish–American War (April 21–December 10, 1898) was fought between Spain and the United States in 1898. It began with the sinking of the USS Maine in Havana Harbor in Cuba, it resulted in the U.S. acquiring sovereignty over Puerto Rico, Guam, and the Philippines, and a protectorate of Cuba. It represented U.S. intervention in the Cuban War of Independence and Philippine Revolution, with the latter later leading to the Philippine–American War. See: Spanish–American War - Wikipedia

[358] The reconcentration policy was a plan implemented by Spanish military officer Valeriano Weyler during the Cuban War of Independence to relocate Cuba's rural population into concentration camps. Reconcentration policy - Wikipedia

[359] Heidler, David Stephen; Heidler, Jeanne T. (2006). The Mexican War. ISBN 978-0-313-32792-6. pp. 181–183.

"The two Williams—the striking facial resemblance of the U.S. presidential candidates."[56] (L. William McKinley, R. William Jennings Bryan, August 4th, 1900)

The 1900 election would be contested over whether to retain the Spanish possessions islands or give them independence. With McKinley again carrying the election over Bryan's and the Democrats the Pro-Imperialists Republicans won their way over what would prove to be vocal and long lasting opposition. In September of 1901 William McKinley was assassinated six months into his second term. He was succeeded by Theodore Roosevelt who proved to be far more expansionist and imperialist than his predecessor.

With the Republican victory in 1900, Congress began to pass legislation that marked the United States' deliberate turn toward imperialism. This was cast into form with Congress' increased funding of the Navy and the creation of America's first substantial pre-dreadnaught fleet, the Great White Fleet.[360]

When the Great White Fleet circled the globe on a Goodwill Tour in 1909 it had to go around Cape Horn to reach the Pacific since the Panama Canal would not be completed until 1914. This fleet of six pre-dreadnaught battleships were already functionally obsolete as battleships by the time they were commissioned since HMS Dreadnaught was already in commission in 1906. As a naval power the United States was emerging from under the umbrella of the Pax Britannica but was in no position militarily to object to or obstruct the British efforts in South Africa. This fleet was however on par with the Japanese navy which had recently defeated the Russian navy in the battle of Tsushima during the Russo-Japanese war. A conflict for which Teddy Roosevelt won the Nobel Peace Prize in 1906 for brokering the Treaty of Portsmouth in September of 1905.

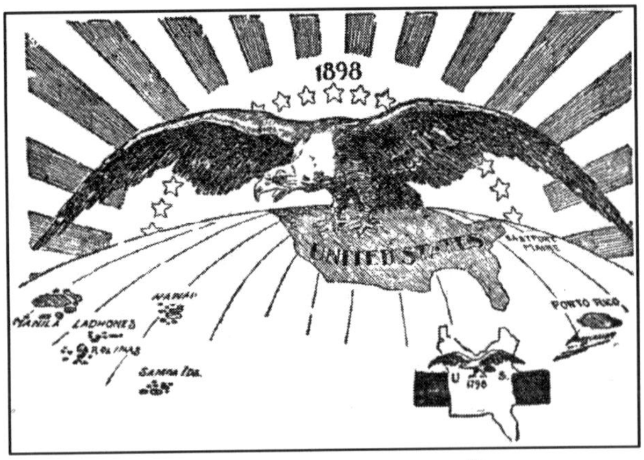

Ten Thousand Miles from Tip to Tip.[57]

[360] Great White Fleet - Wikipedia

Over the course of the Boer War the United States would engage in a vigorous trade with South Africa, supplying horses, railroad locomotives, steel rail, saddles and all manner of supplies that were needed by the British during the course of the conflict. Even Winston Churchill commented on the superiority of American railroad locomotives that were employed during by the British during the Mahdist War in the Sudan in 1898. Over and over, industrialization drives expansionism.

By 1900, the American Anti-Imperialist League,[361] which included individuals like Benjamin Harrison, Andrew Carnegie, Carl Schurz and Mark Twain, emerged as the primary domestic organization opposed to the continued American control of the Philippines and colonialism in general.

Taking just a moment to survey the other major powers which could have intervened in this conflict, France had substantial colonial assets in Africa in the form of Algeria and much of central Africa;[362] but during the course of the Fashoda Incident[363] in 1898, a European war scare resulted from this dust up, and France had been forced by the British to back down in its attempt to expand its sphere of influence from the French Congo to the Arabian sea. In the present conflict, the French had no strategic interest in southern Africa other than as a means to access their Asian colonies and were not likely to renew any confrontation with the British after so recently having climbed down from their recent confrontation which had threatened to evolve into a European war over an issue in Africa.

The Dutch (Netherlands[364]) were a neutral state and also beholden to the British for naval protection for their Asian colonies. While sympathetic to their African brethren they were in no position to impose their will.

The German Empire had expanded into New Guinea, Namibia (German West Africa) and German East Africa to some degree with the acquiescence of the British. This was all part of the Scramble for Africa[365] represented by the General Act concluding the Berlin Conference of 1884,[366] in which the participants resolved to end slavery by African and Islamic powers but in general negotiated a way to carve out spheres of influence for subsequent colonial expansion within those boundaries.

Germany did stand to gain the most from meddling in southern Africa. In the first instance their industry was able to sell its superior military hardware to the gold and diamond rich republics while also observing the effectiveness of those weapons in combat.

With respect to naval assets at their disposal with which to oppose the British, in 1899 the High Seas Fleet[367] was no more than a twinkle in Admiral von Tirpitz's eye. Like the Great White Fleet, it would not become a viable force until 1905 only to be made obsolete by again, HMS Dreadnaught, requiring the German fleet to start again from scratch to meet the British on near equal terms.

As far as America was concerned, this was a European affair that happened to be taking place in Africa. Despite our sympathy there was no way to oppose the British efforts particularly while America was engaged in dismembering the Spanish Empire. No matter how one framed the issue it would have been a case of the pot calling the kettle black.

If there ever was a time for the British to engage in a 'Forward Policy' such as they had recently pursued in the North-West Frontier between Indian and Afghanistan;[368] an episode in the Great Game[369] to prevent Russia from obtaining direct military access to Britain's Indian frontier, this was it.

It was Salisbury, Chamberlain and Alfred Milner who saw this opening to consummate the consolidation of Southern Africa under British suzerainty. This scheme had been taking shape in one form or another ever since

361 American Anti-Imperialist League - Wikipedia
362 French colonial empire - Wikipedia
363 Fashoda Incident - Wikipedia
364 History of the Netherlands (1900–present) - Wikipedia
365 Scramble for Africa - Wikipedia
366 Berlin Conference - Wikipedia
367 High Seas Fleet - Wikipedia
368 Military history of the North-West Frontier - Wikipedia
369 Great Game - Wikipedia

George Grey's[370] efforts in the 1850s and Carnarvon's[371] in the 1870s, following his success with the Canadian Federation in 1866–7.

Of course the tremendous wealth being generated by the diamond and gold mines was attractive as a short term goal but it was the strategic location that mattered more. With the German Empire ensconced in German South West Africa,[372] ultimately resulting in the Herero and Nama genocide,[373] the prospect that the German interests would combine with those of the Transvaal and Orange Free state to invade and overwhelm the British Cape Colony and Natal was too great a threat to ignore.

This proved to be a remarkably prescient piece of statesmanship. Despite the tragedy of the Second Boer War, the dimly perceived prospect of the First World War; beginning for the British with a land war in Europe and possibly one in South Africa as well would have taxed the British Empire to even greater extremes than it was in the eventual conflict.

Instead of dealing with the Martiz Rebellion[374] lasting four months and being extirpated using local forces loyal to Britain, a full out land war in South Africa, with heavily armed, militarily capable, and gold rich states would have erupted and could have resulted in the territorial loss Natal and the Cape Colony entirely.

From an Empire wide perspective this would not have been territorially fatal but from the standpoint of the British Empire as a whole, despite the existence of the Suez Canal, the denial of the Cape of Good Hope as a transit point or uncontested seaway would have been a serious blow to the British war effort overall.

If the German/Afrikaans coalition had been able to maintain commerce raiding cruisers or even WWI endurance submarines along the south African coast, or in a worst case, to berth a portion of the High Seas Fleet at the Cape it would have constricted Britain's access to India and its other far eastern colonies, including Australia; all of which were essential to maintaining its armies in Europe. The same holds true for France in its efforts by employing resources from its African and eastern colonies.

While the British were able to defend the Suez canal against an overland attack by the Ottoman Army in 1915,[375] it is by no means certain that Britain and France, deprived of resources available via the Cape route could not have been defeated at Suez as well.

The map following shows just how much territory in Africa was or could have been controlled by powers hostile to Britain. These geographical facts were also observed by others looking for opportunities during the high tide of colonialism and in the midst of the scramble for Africa.

See the map of Southern Africa at the beginning of this volume. Also of not is the East Africa Campaign which the British fought against primarily the Italian Army from June of 1940 to November of 1941 resulting in the dissolution of Italian East Africa.[376]

Had a Fascist, racist, Italian or Teutonic coalition of South African governments maintained their holdings the consequences for Britain and Free France in the Second World War would have been even more dire. Commerce raiding in the Southern Ocean was a serious issue even with control of South African waters, if a portion of the German Fleet had been roaming around as well as the submarines that already were, nothing good for Britain's war effort would have resulted. This is particularly so in light of the fact that both the Western and

[370] George Grey - Wikipedia

[371] Henry Herbert, 4th Earl of Carnarvon - Wikipedia

[372] German South West Africa - Wikipedia

[373] The Herero and Nama genocide or Namibian genocide, was a campaign of ethnic extermination and collective punishment which was waged against the Herero (Ovaherero) and the Nama in German South West Africa (now Namibia) by the German Empire. It was the first genocide to begin in the 20th century, occurring between 1904 and 1908. Herero and Nama genocide - Wikipedia

[374] The Maritz rebellion, was an armed pro-German insurrection in South Africa in 1914, at the start of World War I. It was led by Boers who supported the re-establishment of the South African Republic in the Transvaal. Many members of the South African government were themselves Boers who had fought with the Maritz rebels against the British in the Second Boer War, which had ended twelve years earlier. Maritz rebellion - Wikipedia

[375] Raid on the Suez Canal - Wikipedia

[376] East African campaign (World War II) - Wikipedia

Eastern African coast and the Mediterranean Sea were hotly contested areas.[377] Even with maximum effort Britain was only just able to maintain Malta and lost Greece and Crete.[378]

It was in fact a categorical imperative that the British secure Eastern and Southern Africa. The British knew this and acted upon it. Despite the oppressiveness of colonialism South Africa, in the long run it was better served under British suzerainty than any other available alternative.[379]

Even with all this effort at confederation and assimilation the medicine did not take. Starting in 1948 when Jan Smuts party was narrowly defeated and the National Party took control this continued up through the closely contested 1960 referendum[380] that ultimately ended the Union of South Africa[381] to become the Republic of South Africa ostensibly to pursue nationalism against imperialism but in reality to pursue apartheid.[382] The Afrikander's had their way for the next 34 years enduring political isolation and domestic unrest throughout that time until finally the government relented and Following the election of 27 April 1994, Nelson Mandela was sworn in as President of South Africa.[383] [384]

[377] For the West Coast of Africa See: Battle of Gabon - Wikipedia and related articles. For East Africa, the first British strategic victory occurred when they were able to defeat the Italian forces both ground and naval, in the East African Campaign, East African campaign (World War II) - Wikipedia which took a year of concerted effort extending from June of 1940 until May of 1941 to secure the Red Sea and the destruction of ground forces in Italian East Africa. Italian East Africa - Wikipedia

[378] The worst case and somewhat catastrophizing would be the Japanese and German fleets combining early in the war to menace India and cut off Australia. In April of 1942, that drove the British naval forces out of the Indian Ocean and back to East Africa.

In February of 1942 the Japanese navy had the run of the Indian Ocean having driven the Dutch and British back to defending coastal India and ultimately back to East Africa. See: Indian Ocean raid - Wikipedia

A portion of the German navy was based on the French coast, including submarines conducting the Battle of the Atlantic but also the flotilla that later made up the Channel Dash Channel Dash - Wikipedia consisting of 2 battleships, Gneisenau and Scharnhorst, 1 heavy cruiser and 6 destroyers along with other assets. Had this force headed south to meet up with the Japanese while refueling along the way at Vichy French ports and possessions, the consequences could have been dire. Imagine the battle of Coral Sea reinforced with a portion of the German Fleet. Port Moresby falls to the Japanese.

In March and April of 1942, there was nothing to stop the German and Japanese forces from meeting at Madagascar, a Vichy French outpost, to use as a base in order to block both the Arabian Sea approaches to the Suez Canal and the Cape route from the East. The Battle of Madagascar did not start until May of 1942. See: Battle of Madagascar - Wikipedia Prior to that time the British were fully engaged in defeating the Italian land and naval forces. There were very few naval assets in East Africa that could have prevented this combination and by staying out of range of land based aircraft the Japanese could have choked off all shipping though both routes. Augmented by German submarines this could have established a killing zone in the Indian Ocean and the South Atlantic. Instead of Midway, a worthless target, you would have had Japanese aircraft carriers in the Arabian sea preventing the replenishment route through and Iraq/Iran route fed by Suez and the southerly route via the Cape that fed into the Artic convoy system to Archangel, both blocking the flow of war materiel to Russia. Those materials allowed Russia to blunt the German offensives in 1942. As a result, Stalingrad might have had a different result. Britain was not in any position to invade Norway in 1942. Germany consolidating its fleet in the Baltic was superfluous. It was a waste of the fleet to recall it back to Germany. This scheme also has the advantage of making the conflict in North Africa irrelevant. There is no need to waste the Italian Army and the Afrika corps in questing towards Cairo. Nor any need to take Crete. Those resources could have be redirected towards other theatres of the war with significant consequences. Even the Italian navy could have been freed up for other action if the Mediterranean was not the primary scene of action in 1941-43. And where exactly would have the Americans have tried to break into the Atlantic Wall in 1943 if there was no reason for Operation Torch, Dieppe, and with what likelihood of success? Actually much of this did occur. See: German Subs based in Malay. Monsun Gruppe - Wikipedia and scuttling German ships in neutral Goa Operation Creek - Wikipedia. Defending Oceania was a waste of resources for the Japanese when all of Eurasia was available for the taking by meeting Germany in the middle. Why didn't the Japanese attack Russia to get oil instead of the US?

[379] The Afrikaans Republics' conception of self-determination was more closely aligned with that of Leopold of Belgium and his administration of the Congo Free State and Belgian Congo that Queen Victoria's 1858 Proclamation at the conclusion of the Indian Rebellion of 1857. See: Congo Free State - Wikipedia Belgian Congo - Wikipedia Indian Rebellion of 1857 - Wikipedia Proclamation by the Queen in Council, to the princes, chiefs, and people of India - Wikisource, the free online library

[380] 1960 South African republic referendum - Wikipedia

[381] Union of South Africa - Wikipedia

[382] Apartheid - Wikipedia

[383] History of South Africa (1994–present) - Wikipedia

[384] One last aside. The advent of the Cold War and its concomitant possibility of thermonuclear mutually assured destruction resulted in a diminished importance of South Africa and the Cape of Good Hope as a strategic waterway. Even apart from de-colonialism as a social movement whatever future war would break out would not be decided by fleets and in combat or long term commerce across its waters. It is too far away from China for its fleet to remain active in the area, the same holds true for Russia which also no longer maintains a substantial surface fleet. The Strait of Malacca has taken over the Cape's former place as the choke point for international commerce.

Webster Davis Prelude

In late 1899 Webster Davis is a Republican politician in good standing with the McKinley administration; having begun his political career as mayor of Kansas City, Missouri. He was an experienced politician and on that merit and as a reward for his activities during the 1896 election he was appointed as Assistant Secretary of the Interior.

With the outbreak of hostilities in South Africa and America's need for all the commerce and connections it could make, along with the money it might generate for the US, it made sense to send a representative of the Administration to South Africa, even informally, to make those connections and observations. By inclination and position, Webster Davis was in a position to fill both roles.[385]

With the permission of President McKinley, Davis accepted the invitation of his friend Colonel J G. Stowe the United States Consul General to visit South Africa and he departed in December of 1899[386] at a time near the nadir of the British military effort. Upon his arrival in Cape Town he was treated cordially as a ranking member of the United States and the McKinley administration.

> I found Sir Alfred Milner, the British Governor of Cape Colony, a most able, affable, genial gentleman. He impressed me as being a man of great ability, and an exceedingly clever diplomat. His frankness was especially notable. I had the pleasure of being his guest at a public dinner and was shown every courtesy by him. He also honored me with an invitation to meet Lord Roberts and Lord Kitchener, who arrived in Cape Town the day before I left it. The American residents of the city also tendered me a public banquet at the City Club, at which Sir Alfred Milner and the Lord Mayor of Cape Town were guests, and publicly extended me a cordial welcome to the city.
>
> While there I also had an opportunity of seeing much of the British army. I met many of the distinguished commanders and many of the now famous troops. Among them was a regiment of Uitlanders encamped near Stellenbosch under command of Colonel Seymour. Colonel Seymour invited Consul Stowe and myself to visit the camp, which we did and took dinner with them. We found them a jolly lot of fellows, mostly British and a few Americans among them, most of them from Johannesburg. They were men who had been employed in the mines at Johannesburg, most of them as superintendents and high officers in the employ of British companies who owned the large mines there. These Americans were friendly to the British cause, for, in fact, they were in the employ of the British, some of them receiving large salaries. Colonel Seymour was reported to be receiving a salary of $50,000 a year to superintend the mines of a large British company. These Americans, of course, because of their being in the employ of Britishers, were ardent sympathizers of the British cause. They were drilling every day and preparing to go to the front.[387]

Davis then made his way to Natal and on to Lorenco Marques where he was extended a formal invitation to visit the Transvaal and Orange Free state. President Kruger even sent his personal train car.

The reason for this extensive survey is to reproduce the interviews which Webster had with President Kruger and Secretary Reitz. Both men probably gave dozens if not hundreds of similar interviews and the themes are by now familiar. However, since these interviews are extensive and authoritatively sourced they are included. But before we get to those discussions we need to follow Mr. Davis' journey back to the United States and the consequences of his decision to espouse the Boer side of the conflict to the American public.

[385] Quote: After a hard campaign tour of six weeks in Ohio and other states during the months of September and October, 1899, I immediately thought of a trip to Cape Town, South Africa, as my old friend and neighbor Colonel J G. Stowe United States Consul General [had asked him to come].
Having been Assistant Secretary of the Interior for three years and had never taken a vacation, while the law entitled me to thirty days' leave of absence and thirty days' sick leave each year, therefore it seemed to me that I was entitled to a good, long vacation. The President [McKinley] said I had certainly earned it and should take it.

[386] He departs New York on December 6th, 1899(.p. 1) He arrives back in New York on April 1st, 1900. (page 150)

[387] p. 11.

His expressed opposition to the foreign policy of President McKinley required that he resign his post so that he could speak as a private citizen against the policy of the current administration and he switched his party affiliation to the Democratic party.

The following article published on the day of his resignation contains all of the various angles that journalism could provide on the circumstances of his departure from Government Service.

THE ST. LOUIS REPUBLIC.

NINETY SECOND YEAR. ST. LOUIS, MO., TUESDAY, APRIL 3, 1900. PRICE {In St. Louis, One Cent. Outside St. Louis, Two Cents. On Trains, Three Cents.

RESIGNATION OF DAVIS IN PRESIDENT'S HANDS.

Assistant Secretary of Interior Quits Office to Espouse the Boer Cause.

Declines to Support the Administration's Pro-British Policy—Says That a Nobler, Braver or More God-Fearing People Than the Boers Never Lived.

McKINLEY: "BOYS, THE MINUTE HE SAYS SOMETHING THAT DOESN'T SUIT US, WE'LL TURN LOOSE ON HIM."

BROADWOOD LOST ALL HIS BAGGAGE.

British Disaster at Bloemfontein Waterworks a Serious Setback.

Seven Guns and the Transport Train Captured and 350 Casualties Sustained—Fighting Resumed.

St. Louis Republic, Tuesday April 3rd, 1900.[388] Note John Bull, lower right, looking smug.

St. Louis Republic Article

Resignation of Davis in President's Hands.

Assistant Secretary of Interior Quits Office to Espouse the Boer Cause.

Declines to Support the Administrations Pro-British Policy—Say's that a Nobler, Braver or More God-Fearing People Than the Boers Never Lived.

Webster Davis of Kansas City today sent in his resignation as Assistant Secretary of the Interior.[389] ....

The cause for this action is stated by Mr. Davis in a candid and manly way. He cannot, after his personal study of the war in South Africa, and of all the causes leading tip to it, remain longer with an administration he believes is in sympathy with the monarchy against the Republic, and which has omitted to do many things it might have done to prevent the slaughter of thousands of patriotic men. Since his return from South Africa there has been a sharp struggle between, the loyalty to party and the dictates of his conscience and honor. .... Upon his retirement Mr. Davis, by writing and lectures and speeches throughout the country, will make known to the world both sides of the South African war.

It promises to be a recital which will stir the blood of liberty-loving Americans to deep and bitter distrust of the of this Government, too willing to remain a silent onlooker in the death struggle of two weak Republics against

[388] St. Louis Republic, Tuesday April 3rd, 1900. 0060.pdf

[389] The Republican Bureau 14th St. and Pennsylvania Ave, Washington, April 2nd 1900.

the resistless armies of invading Britons. Forced by his conscience to perform this work fearlessly, the Assistant Secretary found but one course open to him to separate himself immediately from the administration, with whose policies he can no longer be in sympathy

Saw the President

Mr. Davis has talked with the President [McKinley] twice since his return. The interviews were brief, but an intimation was made to Mr. Davis, unequivocally, that if he insisted on making public his expressions of sympathy for the Boers he must at once tender his resignation from office. There was then a sharp struggle between duty and party loyalty. The decision was taken. The Missourian could not smother the cries of his conscience. He preferred to retire from office, retaining his self-respect and leaving the future to take care of itself. He has received many requests for lectures, speeches and letters upon South Africa. ....In leaving the administration Mr. Davis realizes fully that by that action he separates himself from the Republican party. To the consequences of that he is indifferent.

He believes the administration, before the outbreak of hostilities in the Transvaal should have made a manful effort to prevent the slaughter and horrors which would follow. He holds that it could have made vigorous efforts for peace, and in so doing would have found justification in reason, liberty and Christianity, if not in strict diplomatic procedure. And, inasmuch as Mr. Davis cannot reconcile the course of his party with what he considers the plain dictates of humanity, it is of little concern to him whether he remains longer in such company or not.

His Opening Gun

Mr. Davis will begin his discussion of the South African question next Sunday evening at the Grand Opera house in this city. He has been invited to address a mass meeting then, assembled under the auspices of Reverend Doctor Stafford and other leading churchmen at the capital. ....

Mr. Davis was not in his office today and has not been since his return from Africa, excepting for a few moments Saturday. when he signed a few routine papers and dictated replies to private correspondents.

His decision to retire seems to have been reached quite suddenly, as he stated Saturday the probably he would continue in his present office.

It became rumored about the city, however, that Mr. Davis was to speak at a mass meeting of Boer sympathizers. The intimation was given him then so plainly that this would be an action highly offensive to his administration, that the Missourian decided to resign.

Republicans Disgruntled.

At the Capitol today there was considerable discussion of Mr. Davis's intended resignation. His action generally was commended. Some of the Republican leaders pretended to be skeptical about the sincerity of his motives. Representative Dick, who is secretary of the Republican National Committee, has known Mr. Davis intimately. At his request the Missourian has gone to help in critical campaigns. When told that Mr. Davis purposed to resign, Colonel Dick said sarcastically: "Resigns to speak for the Boer cause, does he? Well, well, well!" There was little in Dick's language but there was a whole sermon of mockery in the manner of its utterance.

Littlehead of Maine, the brilliant Republican who succeeds Dingley and has no great love for the administration said: "Well, isn't it rather late for him to take this course? The Britons have got the Boers nearly wiped of the earth by this time."

Others asserted that there was nothing in Davis's retirement but a shrewd move to market valuable literary material which he has collected under exceptional advantages as an American official.

Naturally there is general resentment..................

Say It Was Demanded

The Republicans seek to break the force of the resignation by asserting that it was practically was demanded for other reasons. It is set forth by them that Davis went to South Africa on an indefinite leave of absence with the understanding that his official duties were at an end in December. They refer to the friction existing between Secretary Hitchcock[390] and Mr. Davis because of pension matters and say that as soon as the Ohio election was

[390]Ethan Allen Hitchcock (September 19, 1835–April 9, 1909) served under Presidents William McKinley and Theodore Roosevelt as U.S. Secretary of the Interior. Ethan A. Hitchcock (Interior) - Wikipedia

decided it was concluded that he should be made acquainted with the fact that his presence was no longer wanted in the Interior Department.

Undoubtedly there have been awkward relations between Mr. Davis and Commissioner Evans of the Pension Bureau. The latter complained that Mr. Davis overruled many of his decisions adverse to pension claimants for the sole purpose of seeking popularity with the veterans: that many of the reversals were not in accordance with law nor made with good legal grounds assigned for the change. This friction increased during the encampment of the Grand Army at Philadelphia when Commissioner Evans believed he discovered quiet efforts on the part of Mr. Davis to increase the clamor by the veterans for the removal of Evans for the purpose of posing as the special friend of the soldier and thereby gaining some political strength in Missouri.

It is said that Mr. Davis was somewhat disgruntled at not being promoted to the Secretary-ship upon the retirement of Mr. Bliss[391] and especially after the place was given to another Missourian. While the relations of Secretary Hitchcock and Mr. Davis ostensibly were friendly, it is a fact that after the St.. Louisan became Secretary, the importance of Colonel Kerens and Mr. Davis in Missouri patronage matters shrank very perceptibly: and this did not make the Kansas-Cityan's position more enjoyable during the latter months of his service.

Say He'll Be Well Paid

His detractors state that his work for creating Boer sympathy will be entirely for hire: that some time ago he entered into negotiations with literary and lecture bureaus for marketing his South African views at very profitable rates: and that the tears he evokes for the struggling patriots in the Transvaal will be charged for at good round rates. In line with the, they cite the fact that Mr. Davis's secretary foreseeing that his chief soon would be crowed out of the Interior Department resigned in advance and went to South Africa as a war correspondent.

In letters to his former chief, Mr. Easton made it clear that there was an excellent field for and exceptional material could be procured by a man high in official life visiting Pretoria and making use of all the opportunities which his official position gave him. Therefore it is asserted by his critics that Mr. Davis did not resign before he left, but retained his office until his return, thereby facilitating the gathering of news and remaining on the Government payroll at one and the same time—a most happy combination.

The character of the criticisms indicates the soreness of the Republicans at the Missourian's retirement and the cause assigned by him therefor.

Davis is Popular

Republican Special. Washington, April 2nd

Since his advent in Washington, Davis, Assistant Secretary Davis has been a much more prominent official that the grad of the position of itself would entitle him to. He is a man in the prime of life, of many and pleasing personality, popular to a marked degree; and without being at all [illegible word] has impressed people generally with a good opinion of his character and ability. He has been in every sense a popular man.

……. Party calamities have accumulated with great rapidity upon the administration during the past three months. The retirement of Mr. Davis to take up the work he has outlined is not the least of them.

Why Davis Resigned

Webster Davis, when asked why he had accepted the invitation of certain prominent citizens of Washington to deliver and address on the war in South Africa, and why, in accepting the same, he had tendered his resignation as Assistant Secretary of the Interior, gave the Republic the following signed statement:

It is simply a matter of conscience and sympathy for the Boers on my part. Shortly after the close of the last campaign in Ohio I found myself worn out with continuous speaking for several weeks during that campaign, and my physician told me it was absolutely necessary for me to take a long sea voyage. My old friend and neighbor Colonel J. G. Stowe, now United Stated Consul General at Cape Town, Africa had been importuning me for two years to visit South Africa. I concluded the proper time for me to make such a visit had arrived. Not

[391] Cornelius Newton Bliss (January 26, 1833–October 9, 1911) was an American merchant, politician and art collector, who served as Secretary of the Interior in the administration of President William McKinley and as Treasurer of the Republican National Convention in four successive campaigns. Cornelius Newton Bliss - Wikipedia

having had any vacation for three years of my official term, I asked leave of absence, which was kindly granted by the President and Secretary of the Interior.

First I went to Cape Town and was treated very nicely there by my friend and also his Excellency, Sir Alfred Milner, Governor of Cape Colony and other officials, and this, too, when it was well understood that I was on a visit simply for health and recreation, and not on any Government mission whatsoever.

After this I went to Lorenzo Marquez for the purpose of trying to get into the South African Republic, as I had great anxiety to see and hear the Boer side of the controversy for I had a suspicion that their side was not getting properly before the public, as it was well known that all cable lines were under the control of the British and the censor made it absolutely impossible for the Boers to get anything favorable to them either over the wires or through the mails. At Lorenzo Marquez after a most cordial reception tendered me voluntarily by the Governor and Governor General of the Portuguese Province of Mozambique, I received a telegram from Secretary Reitz of the South African Republic inviting me to become the guest of the Government and that President Kruger would send his private car to take me to Pretoria.

President Kruger's private car.[58] Hon. Webster Davis traveling in President Kruger's Private Car.[392 59]

I accepted this hospitality, just as I had accepted the hospitality of the British officials at Cape Town and the Portuguese officials at Delagoa Bay.

At Pretoria I was given a most hearty reception. Secretary Reitz and the other Government officials met me at the station and conducted me to the hotel. I spent considerable time in the Orange Free State and the South African Republic, saw much of the Boer people aid the cities, on the farms, in public and private life; saw them in laager on the way to the front and on the battlefields and I soon concluded that no people in the world had ever been so badly abused and so badly misrepresented for a kinder hearted, a more generous or nobler people cannot be found anywhere.

Not wishing to embarrass the administration in any way, I have resigned my office in order that I may feel free to give expression to my views. My heart bleeds for those poor unfortunate Boers who without money and without resources are making the most gallant fight for liberty and justice yet recorded in the histories of nations and I feel that if I were standing absolutely alone in America for their cause, yet I would do so with courage and firmness.

[Signed] Webster Davis.

[392] Anxious to visit the battlefields and see the Boer in camp and on the firing line, President Kruger's private car was placed at my disposal. It was well stocked with provisions, and the President's private porter was in charge, with instructions to take good care of me until I returned. Page 133.

Effect In Missouri.

Davis's Resignation May Cause a Republican Split. [393]

What effect Mr. Davis's resignation will have In Missouri politics is a matter of speculation. Mr. Davis has hosts of political friends. He has already been practically slated as one of the "big four" delegates-at-large to the Philadelphia convention.

If the administration forces should attempt to keep him from going as a delegate they will have a hard time of It. If the friends of the administration in Missouri care to take up its fight, there will be a general split in the ranks in the State. Already the signs of disaffection over the attitude of the President towards the Boers are becoming evident. With Webster Davis to take the lead, the revolt may grow to such proportions that a part of the delegation to Philadelphia will be in open opposition to McKinley.

PF: In the event Mr. Davis was not able to secure a plank in the Republican platform supporting the Boer cause.

Other Coverage

A Home Opinion of Webster Davis.

From the Kansas City Star.

The generous devotion which Davis professes to a forlorn cause is hardly consistent with that love of self which leads a man to practice the ingratitude toward his friends and benefactors which has been proven against Davis. As a matter of fact, Davis is the victim of that vaunting ambition which overleaps itself. He was not content to occupy the post of assistant secretary in the Interior Department. To borrow an expression from Mr. Ingalls, he became "swelled up to the point of inconceivable tumidity," and wanted to be the whole thing. Secretary Hitchcock very properly objected and Davis had to go. The estimate in which persons are held in the community where they live and where they are best known is the one which is verified before the world in the end. Davis has really lasted longer at Washington than was expected in Kansas City when he went there.

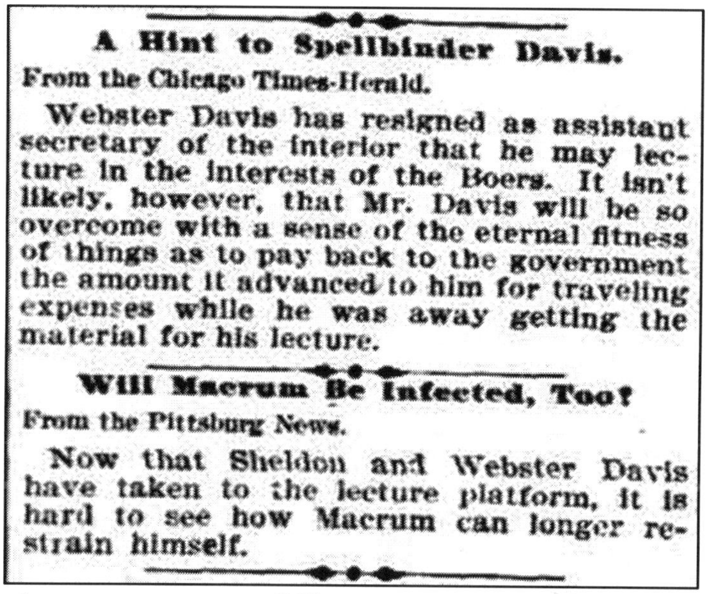

A Hint to Spellbinder Davis.

From the Chicago Times-Herald.

Webster Davis has resigned as assistant secretary of the interior that he may lecture in the interests of the Boers. It isn't likely, however, that Mr. Davis will be so overcome with a sense of the eternal fitness of things as to pay back to the government the amount it advanced to him for traveling expenses while he was away getting the material for his lecture.

Will Macrum Be Infected, Too?

From the Pittsburg News.

Now that Sheldon and Webster Davis have taken to the lecture platform, it is hard to see how Macrum can longer restrain himself.

Both from Washington Evening Star, Friday April 6th, 1900 page 6. Col 3.[60 394]

[393] St. Louis Republic, Tuesday April 3rd, 1900. 0060.pdf

[394] During the time intervening between Mr. Macrum's dismissal [As Counsel in Pretoria.] and Mr.[Adlebert] Hay's arrival, Mr. W. J. Hollis, United States Consul at Lorenzo Marquez, was stationed in the consulate at Pretoria.

The Eccentric Mr. Webster Davis.

We look upon Mr. Webster Davis' resignation as Assistant Secretary of the Interior, that he may stump the United States in behalf of the Boers as a case in which he either mad a bargain with President Kruger while at Pretoria that he would do the thing for so much a stump speech or as one of those grand-stand plays to the galleries that weak-minded people think will add very much to their consequences and importance. If it be the first, then Mr. Webster Davis has operated a very clever bit of business that may make him quite comfortable for the rest of his life. If it be the latter, then Mr. Webster Davis is one of those impressionable individuals of whom we find a very charming specimen in the veracious chronicles of Don Quixote.

Mr. Webster Davis may make his speech from every stump in the united states, and it will have about as much influence upon Great Britain as one drop of rain has upon the tallest peak in the Himalayas.

The speeches of Mr. Webster Davis from American stumps notwithstanding, Great Britain will go right along in the vigorous prosecution of the war until the Boers have made absolute submission or until the dogged obstinacy and good marksmanship of the Boers have made such havoc in the ranks of her soldiers that Great Britain concluded the game is not worth the candle and abandons the struggle.

But either event, whichever it may be, will be arrived at without the smallest regard to Mr. Webster Davis' stump speeches, though he should make two when he only contemplates making one now; and if Mr. Webster Davis has not sense enough to know this, then we seriously question the wisdom of his friends in allowing him to go from stump to stump without a guardian in charge of him.

Mr. Webster Davis will very probably have the male and female old women who attend his stump speeches dissolving in tears at the pictures he will paint, and the small boys will yell when he tells them of the real gallantry and marksmanship of the Boers. But there is about as much probability that he will get the American people to demand of this government that it shall abandon neutrality and fight out the Boers' quarrel for them as there is that Webster Davis will be made President of the United States and immediately thereafter Czar of Russia.

Upon the whole then, what can be at the bottom of this most eccentric action of Mr. Webster Davis?

We are absolutely at a loss to account for it unless it be a fact that it was all arranged between him and President Kruger at Pretoria for a consideration.

THE ECCENTRIC MR. WEBSTER DAVIS.

We look upon Mr. Webster Davis' resignation as Assistant Secretary of the Interior, that he may stump the United States in behalf of the Boers, as a case in which he either made a bargain with President Kruger while at Pretoria that he would do the thing for so much a stump speech, or as one of those grand-stand plays to the galleries that weak-minded people think will add very much to their consequence and importance. If it be the first, then Mr. Webster Davis has operated a very clever bit of business, that may make him quite comfortable for the rest of his life. If it be the latter, then Mr. Webster Davis is one of those impressionable individuals of whom we find a very charming specimen in the veracious chonicles of Don Quixote.

Mr. Webster Davis may make his speech from every stump in the United States, and it will have about as much influence upon Great Britain as one drop of rain has upon the tallest peak in the Himalayas.

The speches of Mr. Webster Davis from American stumps, notwithstanding, Great Britain will go right along in the vigorous prosecution of the war until the Boers have made absolute submission or until the dogged obstinacy and good markmanship of the Boers have made such havoc in the ranks of her soldiers that Great Britain concludes the game is not worth the candle and abandons the struggle. But either event, whichever it may be, will be arrived at without the smallest regard to Mr. Webster Davis' stump speeches, though he should make two when he only contemplates making one now; and if Mr. Webster Davis has not sense enough to know this, then we seriously question the wisdom of his friends in allowing him to go from stump to stump without a guardian in charge of him.

Upon the other hand, if Mr. Webster Davis thinks he is going to stir up such a ruction in this country as will cause it to intervene and fight out the battle of the Boers with the British the case becomes still clearer as one for a guardian, and in that event ordinary prudence would suggest two guardians at least.

Mr. Webster Davis will very probably have the male and female old women who attend his stump speeches dissolving in tears at the pictures he will paint, and the small boys will yell when he tells of the real gallantry and marksmanship of the Boers. But there is about as much probability that he will get the American people to ·mand of this government that it shall abandon neutrality and fight out the Boers' quarrel for them as there is that Webster Davis will be made President of the United States and immediately thereafter Czar of Russia.

Upon the whole, then, what can be at the bottom of this most eccentric action of Mr. Webster Davis?

We are absolutely at a loss to account for it unless it be a fact that it was all arranged between him and President Kruger at Pretoria for a consideration.

The Richmond, (Virginia) Times.[395] Veracious.[396] [397]

[395] The times. [volume] (Richmond, Va.) 1890-1903, April 05, 1900, Page 4, Image 4 « Chronicling America « Library of Congress

[396] Veracious, superlative, most veracious.

[397] It's not clear from his writing when Webster had his Road to Damascus moment but somewhere along the way he decided to throw himself from the top of the ladder much like Randolph Churchill did.

The Evening Tribune.

ESTABLISHED 1888 PAWTUCKET R. I TUESDAY, APRIL 10 1900. PRICE ONE CENT

WEBSTER DAVIS' GREAT SPEECH.

The Boer-British War as Seen by an American.--British Cupidity and Boer Bravery.

An Eloquent Statement of the State of Affairs in South Africa.-- Appeal to America.

HON. WEBSTER DAVIS.

GENERAL BOTTLED.

Roberts Tied Up by Enemy.--Cut Off from Cape Town.

Will Postpone His Visit to Pretoria.--Boers Massing Around Bloemfontein.

April 8th Speech Coverage.[398]

Washington DC coverage of the April 8th speech.

At the Grand Opera House. He did not criticize McKinley. [399]

……after my resignation was accepted, a committee of citizens of Washington, D. C., waited upon me and extended an invitation to address a mass meeting in the Grand Opera House on the evening of April 8th, subject, 'The Boers of South Africa.'

Within a few days after the delivery of this address, invitations were received from every State in the Union to address mass meetings in behalf of the Boers. I accepted more than two hundred of these invitations, and was everywhere greeted by large audiences who were very enthusiastic in their sympathy for the struggling Boers of the two South African republics.

Speeches

Davis reproduced some of his speeches in the latter part of his book.

1. Address delivered at a Boer mass meeting at the Academy of Music in New York City on the night of May 6th, 1900.[400]

2. Speech delivered at the Democratic National Convention at Kansas City, Mo., July 5th, 1900.[401] Anti-Imperialist in tone with respect to Spanish War.

3. Extract of speech delivered before the Fusion Convention at Fort Scott, Kansas. July 25, 1900.[402]

4. Extract of a speech delivered on September 15th, 1900, in the Coliseum, St. Louis, Mo., the occasion being a great mass meeting in honor of William J. Bryan, candidate for President of the United States, who also delivered an address. [403] "The colonial system of Europe must not be established in this country. And we are compelled now to put ourselves on record at the coming election as either favoring or approving the English colonial system."

5. Address before the Jacksonian club at their annual celebration August 25th, 1900, at Omaha, Nebraska. An address was also delivered by William Jennings Bryan on that occasion.[404]

[398] The evening tribune. (Pawtucket, R.I.) 189?-190?, April 10, 1900, Image 1 « Chronicling America « Library of Congress

[399] The times. [volume] (Washington [D.C.]) 1897-1901, April 09, 1900, Image 1 « Chronicling America « Library of Congress

[400] Coverage: The sun. [volume] (New York [N.Y.]) 1833-1916, May 07, 1900, Image 1 « Chronicling America « Library of Congress Davis was the principal speaker and the coverage made several remarks about his style of delivering his remarks. Book P.196

[401] P. 207.

[402] P. 210.

[403] P. 213.

[404] P. 215.

Webster Davis With the Irish Brigade.

Just before leaving the Boer army for Pretoria, I visited the camp of the famous Irish Brigade. This was a body of three hundred Americans, mostly Irishmen, from almost every state in the Union, who had been working in the mines at Johannesburg, but when the war began, believing in the justness of the Boer cause, they enlisted in the Boer army and selected as their commander Colonel J. Y. F. Blake, a native Missourian, and a graduate of West Point.[405]

He was unfairly accused of carrying arms in this reproduced photograph.

Americans in the Boer Army Besieging Ladysmith.[61]

Webster Davis Portrait.[62] And[63].

"This photograph shows Mr. Webster Davis, Rifle In hand, amidst the American mercenaries serving with the Boer army. Mr. Davis was formerly Assistant Secretary of the Interior Department of the United States Government. He proceeded to South Africa during the course of the war. and after following some of the Boer commandos into the field. he returned to America. where be took a prominent part in a Pro-Boer agitation making public speeches in favour of the Independence of the Boer Republics."

Irish Brigade of Boer Army—Mr. Davis is next to the flag with the black cowboy hat on and is standing next to Blake.[64]

[405] P. 143

The Irish Brigade—Mr. Davis Under Peak of Right Hand Tent.[65]

Officers of the Brave Irish Brigade, Near Ladysmith [Blake Center in White Jacket].[66]

Mr. Davis and Escort Ascending Spion Kop After Battle.[67] Mr. Davis [Center]Viewing Buller's Army from Spion Kop.[68]

Kruger Interview

[Interview with President Kruger.][406]

.... in the company of Mr. Groebler,[407] Secretary of Foreign Affairs, I called upon President Paul Kruger.

As the President refrains from the use of the English language, Secretary Groebler acted as interpreter. After a pleasant greeting, the President said to me: One hundred or so years ago the people of the United States Republic were compelled to fight the same British nation to secure their liberty that we are now fighting, hence your people ought to sympathize with this little sister republic which has dared to fight a mighty power to maintain its own independence.

The main question in dispute between this government and that of England was in regard to the franchise. I have always been willing to have this question and others settled by arbitration, but England has always 'declined arbitration. At the very start we wanted the President of the United States of America to intervene as arbitrator. Nothing- would please us better, and we would be perfectly satisfied to abide by his decision. The franchise law adopted by the legislature at the commencement of the present year would, according to the existing lists of field cornets, give the vote to fifty thousand new electors; and, as there are only thirty thousand of the older inhabitants on the voters' lists, this would immediately have given a superiority in numbers to the new population. Instead of accepting this, the British nation has declined and forced us into war by bringing thousands of troops into South Africa and up to our borders with the avowed object of forcing us to do whatever it considers right.

During this century there are three stages which characterize the relations of the British government with our people. The first stage began in 1806 and lasted to the second half of the century. During this period British policy toward our people is marked by a simple contempt.

'The stupid and dirty Dutch' was the simple idea then prevalent in the British mind respecting our little people. According to the hypocritical nature of British policy, however this contempt was expressed in terms of the loftiest ideas then prevailing in the civilized world.

A sentimental philanthropy then ruled in the civilized world and was used by the British government to represent the Boers to mankind as the oppressors of the poor, peaceful natives, so amenable to religion and civilization, and in every respect men and brothers.

If it should appear inexplicable why the power that under the treaty of Utrecht[408] stood forth as the unblushing champion of negro slavery distinguished itself in South Africa by a nauseous love for the native, then the explanation is that in this latter case it was not so much love for the native as hatred and contempt for the Boer which characterized its South African policy.

[406] Chapter III, Page 25–31.

[407] Esaias Reinier Grobler cited supra.

[408] The Peace of Utrecht was a series of peace treaties signed by the belligerents in the War of the Spanish Succession, in the Dutch city of Utrecht between April 1713 and February 1715.

> In a major coup for the British delegation, the British government emerged from the treaty with the Asiento de Negros, which referred to the monopoly contract granted by the Spanish government to other European nations to supply slaves to Spain's colonies in the Americas.
>
> The Asiento de Negros had come about due to the fact that the Spanish Empire rarely engaged in the transatlantic slave trade itself, preferring to outsource this to foreign merchants. Bourbon France had previously held the Asiento de Negros, allowing French slave traders to supply 5,000 slaves to the Spanish Empire each year; France had gained control over this contract after Philip V had become King of Spain.
>
> After the British government gained access to the Asiento de Negros, the economic prominence held by Dutch Sephardic Jewish slave-owners began to fade, while the South Sea Company was established in hopes of gaining exclusive access to the contract.
>
> The British government sought to reduce its debt by increasing the volume of trade it had with Spain, which required gaining access to the Asiento de Negros; as historian G.M. Trevelyan noted: "The finances of the country were based in May 1711 on the assumption that the Asiento, or monopoly of the slave trade with Spanish America, would be wrested from France as an integral part of the terms of peace". Following the passage of the treaty, the British government gained a thirty-year access to the Asiento de Negros. Peace of Utrecht - Wikipedia

As a result of that hatred toward the Boer, concealed under that simulated love for the native, the natives were used as police against us, were furnished with weapons of war and ammunition, and incited to fight us and, where possible, rob and murder us. As a result of that hatred our people were obliged to bid farewell to Cape Colony with all that they loved and cherished, and to seek a refuge in the unknown wildernesses of the North, and as a result of that hatred our people had to continue their crusade of martyrdom over South Africa until every part of South Africa's soil was to be reddened with the blood, not so much of able-bodied men, as of murdered women and children.

The second stage lasted till 1881. During this period the basis of British policy toward us was not so much simple hatred of the Afrikander (history had already shown that that hatred was powerless to keep the Afrikander down); on the contrary it had contributed greatly toward dispersing the Afrikanders as the ruling race over the whole of South Africa.

In a moment of apathy and thoughtless disinterestedness England had entered into treaties (1852, 1854) with the Boers by which they were placed in possession of certain wild and seemingly useless parts of the country. The basis of the policy of the second stage was a feeling of remorse over this mistake and a firm resolve to forestall the consequences thereof.

The wild and useless parts assigned to the Boers proved to be very valuable after these Boers had opened them up to civilization; they ought therefore again to sparkle as pearls in Her Majesty's crown in spite of the treaties entered into with the Boers.

This was the disguised object. As to the means employed, innate hypocrisy caused these means to be partly disguised and partly open, and the one kind of means to differ essentially from the other. The disguised means was to arm the Kaffir races against us in an unprecedented manner, in spite of solemn treaties and promises, and to incite them to attack us. If this policy was successfully carried out, then England could conceal her true object and means, and openly come forward for the preservation of peace and order and for the maintenance of civilization in this part of the world, and could annex the republics on such false pretenses.

As regards the Orange Free State, this policy was a failure, as the above burghers of the neighboring republic, after great trouble, succeeded in defeating Moshesh, notwithstanding the unlawful stoppage of their arms and ammunition by the British government.

England was in that case compelled to rest satisfied with the protection of her Basuto interests and the prevention of all the advantages which the Boers might have derived from their victory, and with the openly illegal annexation of the diamond fields.

As regards the South African Republic, her burghers were unfortunately not careful enough to guard against this insidious policy of the enemy. The Transvaal Boers had defeated the mightiest Kaffir tribes, and therefore never for a moment dreamed that the small Kaffir wars, into which they were drawn by the English inciting the Kaffirs, and which were not immediately put down by every possible means, would be used as a pretext to annex their country to the British Empire.

Thus the Magato war and the Secucuni war[409] dragged on to the endless satisfaction of Sir Theophilus Shepstone and his principals. And thus the annexation came about with the extension of Her Majesty's jurisdiction and protection over the South African Republic, by which means alone unity of purpose and action could be secured, and a beautiful prospect of peace and prosperity for the future could be opened up. In these words of Shepstone's annexation proclamation we see in all its hideous nakedness the Hypocrisy which gave a secret fatal stab to the Boer Republic and then publicly came forward as the disinterested good Samaritan!

The third stage in our history is characterized by the combination of the old well-known policy of fraud, with the new forces of capitalism, called into being by the mineral wealth of the South African Republic. Our existence as a people no less than as a state is at present threatened by this unparalleled combination of powers and forces. But we shall continue the struggle against the overwhelming British odds so long as a single Boer still lives to wield a Gun. [End Interview text.]

[409] Kgosi Sekonyela (c. 1804–20 July 1856) was a chief of the Batlokwa people; settling in Jwalaboholo in modern day northern Lesotho. He regularly engaged in cattle raids on neighbouring tribes, often to the detriment of his own people. In late 1853, Sekonyela's Tlôkwa Chiefdom was defeated by the army of Basotho king Moshoeshoe I. Most of his tribesmen were subsequently dispersed or absorbed by the victors. Sekonyela moved to Herschel where he died three years later. Kgosi Sekonyela - Wikipedia

There can be no doubt but that President Kruger is the proper man for the present crisis. The week before I met him he was at the front in Natal praising the burghers for the great things they had done and exhorting them to still greater efforts in the future. After his visit to the burghers of the Transvaal in Natal he then visited the burghers of the Free State strongholds, and inspired them with confidence wherever he went. His speeches gave the keynote to the presidential mood and presidential mind and left no room for mistaking the set purpose and the steadfast spirit that possessed the head of the state.

On the 13th of October, 1899, the president put his hand to the plow and there is not to be any turning back. He started out to defend his country's independence. The vigor, determination and confidence of President Kruger was very impressive.

Despite his seventy-six years of age, despite all the stress of stormy seasons of the past, with all his manifold responsibilities, he appeared at that time buoyant and confident, and his strong patriotism and courage seemed to fire the imagination even of his enemies, and inspired all the burghers to their best efforts. The effect of his visits to the laagers and to the Boers fighting in the trenches was that there was renewed federal activities, reinvigorated camps and a movement which presaged fresh purposes.

At Bloemfontein, the capital of the Orange Free State, President Kruger received a magnificent ovation, though his visit occurred but a short time after the surrender of poor Cronje. He is a man of few words, but they are ever weighty.

In his speech at Bloemfontein on this occasion he expressed in half a dozen words his great determination when he said: "This far and no farther."

First Reitz Interview

This is the first of two interviews that Webster Davis has with Secretary Reitz.[410] They are both quite extensive amounting to almost 20,000 words in total.

> [The] Boer case as set forth by Mr. F. W. Reitz, Secretary of State of the South African Republic.
>
> Of all the statesmen of the two Boer republics none is so well qualified to state the Boer side of the case in the South African controversy as Mr. F. W. Reitz, Secretary of State of the South African Republic, and a former president of the Orange Free State. In an interview with him, he said to me.

The struggle which has now lasted almost a century, which began with the forcing of a foreign ruler upon the Dutch population of the Cape of Good Hope, is rapidly nearing its end; we have reached the last act in the great drama fraught with such tremendous issues for the whole of South Africa; we have arrived at that point at which it must be decided whether all the sacrifices which our fathers and ourselves have laid upon the altar of liberty have been in vain, whether all the blood of our people by which, as it were, every part of South Africa is consecrated has been shed in vain; or whether, by God's grace. the copestone[411] shall now be placed upon the building that our forefathers began with so much suffering and sorrow. The hour has come when it shall be decided whether, by vindicating her liberty, South Africa shall enter upon a new and grander period of her history, or whether our people shall cease to exist, shall be extirpated in the struggle for that liberty which it has always valued above all earthly treasures, and South Africa shall in future be governed by soulless gold kings acting in the name and under the protection of an unjust and hated government 7,000 miles away.

The allegations of humanity, civilization and equal rights, upon which the British government bases its actions, is nothing but a cloak for that hypocritical spirit of annexation and piracy which has always characterized her actions in all her relations with our people.

After thirty years of English government it was conclusively proved that it brought no salvation, but rather oppression, for the Boer. His elementary rights were violated and without the least security; his situation was intolerable in the British colony, which had then as its northern boundary the Groot River. It was therefore decided to sacrifice home, property and the possessions that yet remained after the Kaffir devastations and to quit the British jurisdiction.

410 (pages 43–61) ~8,000 words.

411 Coping is the capping or covering of a wall. Coping (architecture) - Wikipedia

Lieut. Governor Stockenstrom was first consulted. but he said that there was no law to forbid his leaving the Colony and settling elsewhere, and if such a law existed it would be a tyrannical law which could not be put into force.

The Cape Attorney-General Oliphant, consulted by Lord Charles Somerset,[412] gave the same advice, saying that the emigrants were apparently resolved to go to another land and not to consider themselves any longer as British subjects (as was taking place daily in the emigration from England to North America), that the government was powerless and could do nothing to stop the evil.

Now, outside the British jurisdiction lay the countries north of the Orange River and east of the Drakensbergen, and as far as known at that time these countries were inhabited by barbarians. But rather than remain any longer under British rule our fathers resolved to risk the dangers of the wilderness and there purchase from the Kaffirs a stretch of land and establish an independent society.

After untold hardships and much suffering at the hands of the Zulus, the Republic of Natal[413] was founded by our fathers.

But the history of this republic was destined to be a short one. The British Colonial office was on the trail of our people. At first the British government resolved to effect a military occupation of Natal, because, as Governor Napier[414] wrote to Lord Russell, the Secretary of State, on June 22nd, 1840, it was evidently the fixed determination of Her Majesty's government not to extend her possessions in Africa.' The military occupation was simply intended to oppress and harass the Boers, as Governor Napier declares with brutal frankness in his despatch to Lord Glenelg of January 16th, 1838. In other words. the intention was to prevent the Boers from obtaining ammunition and from establishing an independent republic. By this means he considered that the emigration would cease.

Again, on April loth, 1842, Lord Stanley instructs Governor Napier to cut off the Boers from all communication and to inform them that the British government \would assist the barbarians against them and treat them as rebels. The military occupation was resisted by us and the English troops were on two occasions beaten off. More of them however, were drowned in their flight than perished from our bullets. Later on Commissioner Cloete was despatched to annex the young republic, as a reward to the Boers for their services. in reclaiming it for civilization. Not without powerful protest from our side did this annexation take place. On February 1st, 1842, the Volksraad of Maritzburg under the chairmanship of Joachim Prinsloo, wrote to Governor Napier as. follows:

We know that there is a God who is ruler of heaven and earth and who has the power and the will to protect the weak against their oppressors. To Him we entrust the righteousness of our cause. If it is His will that we, our wives and children shall be totally extirpated, we shall humbly submit to such a fate. We will not challenge the might of England, yet we cannot allow that might shall triumph over right, without having made every effort in our power to resist such might.'

When our noble leader Andries Pretorius, who had ridden on horseback to Grahamstown, hundreds of miles distant, in order to acquaint Governor Pottinger with the true state of affairs, and was sent back unheard, reached the Drakensbergen, he found almost the entire population trekking away over the Drakensbergen-away from British authority. His own wife lay dying in her wagon; his daughter was leading the oxen and had been painfully gored by them. And this was but one instance out of innumerable others.

Sir Henry Smith, who had succeeded Pottinger as Governor, described the condition of these trekking Boers as 'a state of misery which he had not seen equaled except in Massena's invasion of Portugal. The scene was truly heartrending.'

Thus had we fared at the hands of the British government in connection with the founding of Natal.

[412] Lord Charles Henry Somerset PC (12 December 1767–18 February 1831), was a British soldier, politician and colonial administrator. He was governor of the Cape Colony, South Africa, from 1814 to 1826. Lord Charles Somerset - Wikipedia

[413] The Natalia Republic was a short-lived Boer republic founded in 1839 after a Voortrekker victory against the Zulus at the Battle of Blood River. The area was previously named Natália by Portuguese sailors, due to its discovery on Christmas ("Natal" is the Portuguese word for Christmas). The republic came to an end in 1843 when British forces annexed it to form the Colony of Natal. After the British annexation of the Natalia Republic, most local Voortrekkers trekked northwest into Transorangia, later known as the Orange Free State, and the South African Republic. See: Natalia Republic - Wikipedia

[414] Sir George Thomas Napier KCB (30 June 1784–16 September 1855) was a British Army officer who saw service in the Peninsular War and later commanded the army of the Cape Colony. George Thomas Napier - Wikipedia

We trekked away over the Drakensbergen to the Orange Free State, where some of us remained, while the others trekked northwards across the Vaal River.

After this compulsory emigration from Cape Colony, how long were the Boers permitted by the British government to rest in peace, without being further molested? I asked of Secretary Reitz.

Only a short time, he answered, for the British government soon appointed an official to preside over the Orange Free State known as a British Resident.

Pretorius, however, gave him forty-eight hours to quit the republic. Thereupon Sir Harry Smith collected an army, consisting chiefly of colored troops against us and fought a battle with us at Boomplaats on August 29th, 1848.

After the battle, which was a very tough one, a Boer, called Thomas Dreijer, was caught by Smith's colored troops, and to the shame of the English name was butchered by the English Governor for no other crime than that, having been a British subject many years before, he now dared to fight against the Queen's flag.

Another murder and atrocity put to the account of England.

In the meantime Sir Harry Smith had also annexed the country under the name of the Orange River Sovereignty, on the pretext that four-fifths of the inhabitants favored British rule and were only intimidated by the threats of Pretorius.

Not long after this, however, the British Resident involved himself in difficulties with Moshesh, the great and astute paramount chief of the Basutos. The Resident invoked the assistance of the Boers, but, of the thousand called out only seventy-five responded. The English troops got the worst of it. As the Resident wrote to his government, the existence of the Orange River Sovereignty now depended on Andries Pretorins, the man on whose head Sir Harry Smith had put a price of two thousand pounds.

Earl Grey censured Sir Harry Smith and the Resident Warden, and recalled the latter, saying in his despatch of December 15th, 1851, to the Governor, that the British government had annexed the land under the representation that the general body of inhabitants were in favor of such a measure, that, if the inhabitants were unwilling to support the authority of the British government, which was established solely for their benefit, then there was no reason for the maintenance of such authority.

When the British government retired from the sovereignty it was, however, to be clearly understood that no wars, however bloody, which might arise between the various native tribes and the white communities in a state of independence beyond the colonial boundaries would be considered as constituting a ground for interference.

In other words, as Froude puts it, 'In 1852 we discovered that wars with natives and Dutch were expensive and useless, that sending troops out and killing thousands of natives was an odd way of protecting them.

We resolved to keep within our territories, not meddle beyond the Orange River, and leave natives and Dutch to settle their differences.' And again, 'Grown sick of enterprises which led neither to honor nor peace, we resolved to make the Orange River, in 1852, the boundary of British responsibilities. We made formal treaties with the two Dutch States, binding ourselves not to interfere between them and the natives and leaving them either to become a barrier, or, as we considered most likely, to sink in an unequal struggle with warlike tribes by whom they were infinitely outnumbered.'

The administration of the Free State cost the British taxpayer too much. Besides, there was an idea that if the Boer were given rope enough he would hang himself.

A new Governor, Sir George Cathcart, was sent out with two special commissioners to carry out the new policy, and a treaty was entered into between England and the Free State by which complete independence was guaranteed to the Free State, and the British undertook not to interfere with native races north of the Great Orange River.

As Cathcart says in his letters, 'The sovereignty bubble is at an end,' and 'The foolish sovereignty farce is over.'

It must not be forgotten that as long as the Free State was English territory it included the tract of country now known as Kimberley and the diamond fields, that English mortgages under the Orange Free State Sovereignty had been issued for the ground in question as belonging to the Sovereignty, and that the tract of country formed part of the jurisdiction of a Sovereignty magistrate, and that therefore this, at the retrocession of the Free State, formed part of that territory.

The convention between England and the Free State, vas not fifteen years old before it was broken by the English. Though they had solemnly undertaken not to interfere in native affairs north of the Groot River, yet, when the Basutos had murdered and robbed the Free Staters, ravished their women and committed innumerable acts of violence, and the Free Staters had succeeded, after three years of warfare, in severely chastising them, the English interfered in favor of the Basutos in 1869.

In the Aliwal convention, however, they again promised not to interfere.

The ink of this treaty was scarcely dry before diamonds were discovered in that part of the Free State between the Groot and Vaal Rivers, to which reference has already been made. Instead of frankly confessing that it (the British government) was the strongest, and therefore demanded the ground in which the richest diamond mine in the world was situated, the hypocritical allegation was resorted to, that the true cause for the seizure of this ground from the Free State was that it belonged to a native, notwithstanding the fact that this assertion was proved and adjudged to be false, even in the English law courts.

There was an idea, says Froude, that the richest diamond mine in the world should not be lost to the British Empire. The ground was taken from the Boer, and since then the Boer in South Africa can rely on English promises less than ever before.

This business, Froude, who died before the Jameson invasion, calls 'perhaps the most discreditable page in British colonial history.'

Afterward, When Brand went to England, the government pleaded guilty and paid a paltry ninety thousand pounds as compensation for seizing the richest diamond fields in the world, where almost daily diamonds in greater value than this sum are dug up. But in spite of the Free State convention, in spite of the repeated promises in the Aliwal convention, the Free State had yet to suffer a third scandalous breach of the convention from England. Tens of thousands of guns were imported through the colony to Kimberley, and there sold to the Kaffirs, who surrounded and threatened the two Dutch republics.

General Sir Arthur Conynghame, the English commander in South Africa, says that under his rule four hundred thousand guns were in this way sold to the Kaffirs. Protests from the Transvaal and Free State were of no avail, and when the Free State made use of its rights and stopped wagons loaded with guns on the way to the Free State, it was moreover forced to give compensation to the British government.

The Free State, says the English historian Froude, 'paid the compensation under protest with an old fashioned appeal to the God of righteousness, whom, strange to say, they considered a reality.'

The history of the following decades was to give even greater point to this sarcasm.

At this point the Secretary controlled his emotions with great difficulty, for he had once been honored with the highest office in the gift of the Boers of the Orange Free State, and his love for them and their republic was exceedingly strong.

Three of his stalwart sons, one but sixteen years of age, were then fighting on the Modder River as members of a Free State commando. In response to my request to give me some facts as to the early settlement of the Transvaal or South African Republic, he said:

The Boers first found the Transvaal overrun with the warriors of Moselikatze[415] (the Matabele king, father of Lobengula).

When he heard of the approaching, emigrant Boers he sent an impi[416] to extirpate them. They murdered a few whites who had wandered away from the rest, but were defeated at Vechtkop by a small laager under Sarel Celliers, where the Boer women also distinguished themselves by deeds of heroism.

Shortly afterwards the emigrant Boers crossed the Vaal river and, after two battles, succeeded in driving Moselikatze and his barbarians across the Limpopo River into Matabeleland.

After the annexation of Natal Andries Pretorius had also come to the Transvaal and lived there peacefully as Commandant General, notwithstanding the price placed on his head by Sir Harry Smith. The British Resident in the Free State, which then still belonged to England, had however to confess to the English Governor that the

[415] Mzilikazi, Moselekatse, Khumalo (c. 1790–9 September 1868) was a Southern African king who founded the Ndebele Kingdom now called Matebeleland which is now part of Zimbabwe. In his autobiography, David Livingstone referred to Mzilikazi as the second most impressive leader he encountered on the African continent. Mzilikazi - Wikipedia

[416] Impi is a Nguni word meaning war or combat and by association any body of men gathered for war also a term denoting an army.

fate of the Free State was in the hands of this same Pretorius, to whose influence it was due that Moshesh had not extirpated the British soldiers. It had been determined in England, as Froude says, to leave the Afrikanders and Kaffirs in peace beyond the borders in the hope that the Kaffirs would exterminate the Afrikanders.

The colonial office was therefore glad, says the English Member of Parliament, :Molesworth, when the Governor, in 1851, received a letter from Andries Pretorius, Commandant General of the Transvaal Boers, in which he offered in the name of his people to enter into negotiations with the British government with the object. of forming a treaty of peace and friendship.

The price on his head was at once cancelled, and when Harry Smith had been recalled in dishonor, Governor Cathcart was sent out by Earl Grey to recognize the independence of the Boers.

The Aberdeen ministry, which immediately followed, declared through its spokesman in the English House of Commons: 'They regretted that they had ever crossed the Great Orange River.

Lord Grey had done this for the sake of Sir Harry Smith, though the latter knew better and had also a different opinion, as the Boers were opposed to British rule.'

This policy was confirmed by the almost unanimous voice of the British House of Commons.

Thereupon the proposal of Pretorius was accepted and the two assistant high commissioners, Hogge and Owen, sent out with Governor Cathcart, held a conference with the delegates of the Boers at Sand River in the Free State, which resulted in the signing of the Sand River convention by both parties. In this convention, as later in the Free State convention, the Transvaal Boers were secured in fullest measure against interference or intervention on the part of England, either with them or w:th the natives north of the Great River, while both sides bound themselves not to provide these natives with arms or ammunition. The British commissioners reported that the acknowledgment of the independence of the Transvaal Boers had several advantages, as it would secure their friendship, prevent their alliance with Moshesh, and guarantee that no slavery should exist and that criminals should be extradited.

On May 13th, 1852, Sir George Cathcart, the Governor, in a proclamation expressed his satisfaction that one of the first acts of his administration was the approval of this Sand River convention. In June, 1852, the British colonial secretary also approved of the convention.

But England's' word could not be relied on even in a convention solemnly approved and signed by her. When the diamonds were discovered in the Free State, scarcely seventeen years after the signing of this convention, England claimed part of the Transvaal territory adjacent to that taken from the Free State.

It was decided to have recourse to arbitration. The arbitrators differed and the umpire, Governor Keate of Natal, gave his award against the Transvaal.

It then appeared that the British arbitrator had purchased 12,000 morgen from the Kaffir chief Waterboer for a mere song and that Governor Keate had already received Waterboer as a British subject, in direct opposition to the convention.

Even Dr. Moffat, who was no friend of the Boers, protested against this in a letter to the London Times, because the territory in question had always belonged to the Transvaal.

But this was only one of the breaches of the convention. When the four hundred thousand guns were sold to Kaffirs at Kimberley, according to the account of Conynghame and Moodie, the Transvaal government protested strongly in 1872 to the Cape High Commissioner, but they had to content themselves with an impudent answer from Sir Henry Barkly.

And to crown all the deeds of infamy committed by England, Shepstone, on April 12, 1877, annexed the Transvaal.

Lord Carnarvon, to complete his South African confederation policy, sent Sir Bartle Frere as Governor to Cape Town. He also sent Shepstone to the Transvaal to annex the country, provided the consent of the Volksraad or of the majority of the inhabitants was obtained. The Volksraad protested against the annexation. The President protested. Out of a possible population of eight thousand burghers, six thousand and eight hundred protested, but all in vain.

Bishop Colenso declared that 'the sly, underhand way in which the Transvaal has been annexed appears to me to be unworthy of the English name.'

The Free State expressed her heartfelt regret at the annexation.

Even Gladstone expressed his sorrow and acknowledged that in the Transvaal England was placed in the position of the free subjects of a kingdom coercing the free subjects of a republic to accept a citizenship to which they were averse.

But everything was of no avail.

Sir Garnet Wolseley declared: 'As long as the sun shines the Transvaal will remain British territory,' and again' that the Vaal River would sooner return to its source over the Drakensbergen than England would give up the Transvaal.'

Shepstone's principal reasons for the annexation were that the Transvaal could not conquer Secucuni and that the Zulu nation threatened to overwhelm the Transvaal. As regards Secucuni he had a little earlier prayed for peace and had been made to pay a fine of two thousand head of cattle by the republic.

As regards the Zulu nation the menacing danger had never been felt by the Republic. Four hundred burghers had broken the Zulu power in 1838 and crowned Panda, the father of Ceteywayo, in 1840.

Sir Bartle Frere, in a letter to Sir Robert Herbert on January 12th, 1879, admits that it had appeared strange to him that the Zulus had so long left Natal unmolested, until he found that the Zulus had been time after time completely crushed by the Boers in the time of Dingaan.

Shortly before the annexation a small patrol of Transvaal burghers had pursued the paramount chief Umbeline into the heart of Zululand. But Colenso shows what a treacherous stalking-horse the Zulu trouble was.

There was a dispute lasting several years between the Transvaal and the Zulus concerning a strip of land on the border which had been in possession of the Boers and had been inhabited by them since 1869. Before the annexation, when Shepstone was still in Natal, the matter had been referred to him and he had given his verdict in favor of the Zulus and against the Boers.

There could thus be no reason for a Zulu attack upon the Transvaal. But Shepstone was scarcely ruler in the Transvaal before he proclaimed it British territory, and he then found that the evidence in favor of the contention of the Boers was so strong that the Zulus had no claim to the land in question.

The Governor of Natal, Bulwer, appointed a border commission who decided in favor of the Zulus, but Shepstone was furious against this award and Sir Bartle Frere and the High Commissioner followed him blindly.

In consequence of this, England sent an ultimatum to the Zulus, and the Zulu war followed, which has done incalculable harm to the English name in South Africa among the natives.

We thus see that Shepstone's two principal motives were without foundation.

It was, of course, difficult for the Secretary of State to abide by his instructions, 'to annex, if the majority of the people. were in favor of such a measure,' in face of the fact that six thousand eight hundred out of the eight thousand burghers had protested against it; but without any semblance of reason both Shepstone and Carnarvon declared that the signatures to the protesting petition had been obtained by intimidation.

The case was, however, exactly the reverse. When the meeting was held at Pretoria to sign the petition, Shepstone had the cannons directed at the assembled multitude. And not content with this, he published a proclamation warning and threatening those who should sign the petition.

When it was pointed out what a gross violation of the Sand River convention the annexation was. Sir Bartle Frere said in 1870 that if we wished to go back to the Sand River convention we might as well go back to the creation!

It must also not be forgotten that the ground, which according to the Keate verdict in 1870 fell outside the republic was now incorporated with the Transvaal as belonging to the Transvaal.

There were also other things which had been wrong under the republican rule of the Transvaal. but which were perfectly right under the British rule. In the Secucuni war against the republic the British High Commissioner had protested against the use by the republic of Swazies and volunteers against Secucuni's people. Under British rule the war was continued first with troops, but when they were beaten by the Kaffirs an army of Swazies and volunteers was levied. How great the number of Swazies thus employed must have been can be judged from the fact that five hundred Swazies were killed. The atrocities committed by the Swazie allies of the English at this time were horrible.

Colenso, who had the opportunity for judging, in dealing with the consequences of the annexation of the republic, says: 'The Zulu trouble, as well as the war with Secucuni, is the direct result of that unfortunate annexation of the Transvaal, which would have met us half way if we had not taken possession of the land as a lot of freebooters, partly by trickery and partly by bullying.'

And in another place: 'And thus we annexed the Transvaal, and that deed brought in its train as its Nemesis the Zulu trouble.'

That it was always the intention of the British government to make use of the Zulus to crush the Transvaal at the proper moment is evident from a letter written by Sir Bartle Frere, the then High Commissioner, to General Ponsonby, in which he says: 'It is a fact that when the Boer republic was a rival and a half hostile power, it was a weakness in Natal to pat the Zulus as we pat a tame wolf which only devours our neighbor's sheep.

It is true, we always said, 'Don't,' but now that both flocks belong to us we feel a bit perplexed when we must check them.'

And again in a letter to Sir Robert Herbert: The English were well inclined to help the Zulus against the Boers. It was a shock to us to find out how close to the wind the predecessors of the present Natal government had sailed in supporting the Zulus against the Boers. John Dunn declares that he furnished Zulus with guns with the knowledge of the government. [Thus here was also a breach of the Sand River convention.]

It is undoubted that in Natal sympathy was strongly in favor of the Zulus against the Boers, and what is still worse, it is so to-day.

Under these circumstances the annexation took place. The English did not scruple to make use of Kaffir allies against the Boers as they had done at Boomplaats. And in every way we tried to bring home to the British nation the gross injustice that was done here, but even the High Commissioner, while he heard the words uttered from our bleeding hearts, wished that he had brought artillery with him to disperse us, and misrepresented and slandered us without ceasing.

We had hopefully said that our people believed that if the Queen of England and the English nation knew that a people was being oppressed in the Transvaal they would never permit it.

But now we were forced to say that we could no longer talk to England, as there was no one there who heard us. With confidence in the Almighty God of Right and Justice we girt our loins for a seemingly hopeless struggle, firmly convinced that whether we won or whether we perished, the sun of liberty would rise out of the morning clouds in South Africa. By the omnipotence of God we were victorious, and our liberty again seemed secure for a time.

At Bronkhorst Spruit, at Langsnek, at Ingogo and at Amajuba God gave us the victory, though in all these battles the British troops were more numerous and better equipped than ourselves. After these victories had added new strength to our arguments, the British government decided, under the leadership of the never-to-be-forgotten Gladstone, to nullify the annexation and reinstate us in the possession of our violated rights.

A simple minded person would think that the only proper way to effect this retrocession would have been for the British government in future to stick to the terms of the Sand River convention. If the annexation was in itself wrong, and not only because it had been followed by the Boer victories, then it ought to have been abolished with all its consequences and a restitution integrum of that republic should have taken place; in other words, the Boers should have been placed in the same position they had occupied before the annexation.

But what happened? With a magnanimity which the English press· and orators never weary of holding before our eyes, they gave back our land, but the violation of the Sand River convention was not nullified. Instead of sovereign liberty, we were allowed internal government with the reservation to Her Majesty of the suzerain power over the republic.

This took place in the Pretoria convention, the preamble of which gave self-government to the 'Transvaal State' with the distinct reservation of the suzerainty, and the articles of which tried to establish a modus vivendi between that self-government and the suzerainty.

Under this twofold administration the republic was for three years governed by two heterogeneous principles, that of representative self-government and that represented by the British Resident. This system of course could not work in practice. The settlement of 1881 also does not seem to have been intended. as a final one. Above all, the suzerainty was a monstrosity that could not be reconciled with practical reality. With the approval of the British government, therefore, a republican deputation repaired to London in order to get the status of the republic altered and to obtain a new convention instead of that of Pretoria.

They proposed to return to the position under the Sand River convention, and that would have been the only honest and statesmanlike settlement. The ministry, however, which (according to one of the witnesses on the British side, the Rev. D. P. Faure) stood in unwholesome awe of the British Parliament, refused to accede to this and made a counter proposal, which was eventually accepted by the deputation, and the terms of which are therefore to-day of the greatest importance.

That draft law comprised the Pretoria convention with certain alterations which were intended to make it acceptable to the deputation. The preamble in which self-government. with the reservation of the suzerainty, was given to the republic was altogether struck out by Lord Derby, the then Secretary of State for the Colonies, and in this way, as a matter of course, the suzerainty also fell away when the draft proposal was eventually accepted.

To make it still more tangible that the status of the Transvaal was placed on another basis, the name 'Transvaal State' was altered into 'South African Republic' the name it had borne under the Sand River convention. All the articles in the Pretoria convention which gave the British government any authority to meddle in the internal affairs of this republic were struck out.

As to foreign affairs a great, one may say a radical, alteration was made. The Pretoria convention stipulated, in Article II, that 'Her Majesty reserved to herself the control of the foreign relations with the said state, including the making of treaties and the regulation of diplomatic and consular agents in foreign parts.'

For this was substituted Article IV. of the London convention, which ran as follows:

The South African Republic will conclude no treaty or engagement with any state or nation other than the Orange Free State, nor with any native tribe to the eastward or westward of the republic, until the same has been approved by Her Majesty the Queen.

Such approval shall be considered to have been granted if Her Majesty's government shall not within six months after receiving the copy of such treaty (which shall be delivered to them immediately on its completion) have notified that the conclusion of such treaty is in conflict with the interests of Great Britain or of any of Her Majesty's possessions in South Africa.

Thus the right of the British government to control all our foreign relations and to carry on all our diplomatic intercourse by means of our treaties and conventions after they were completed, and then only in the interests of Great Britain or Her' Majesty's possessions in South Africa.

It was this Article IV. which gave the semblance, but only the semblance, of truth to Lord Derby's declaration in the House of Lords that, though he had dropped the 'suzerainty', its substance remained. It would have been more correct to say that by the disappearance of the suzerainty the South African Republic could no longer be called a half-sovereign state; that it had emerged as a free. independent, sovereign, international state, the only limit to its sovereignty being the one mentioned in Article IV.

Sovereignty need not necessarily be absolute. Belgium is certainly a sovereign international state, though it is bound to a position of permanent neutrality. In this category of states, whose sovereignty is definitely limited in this or that respect, but is nevertheless indispensable, the South African Republic also falls.

After this narration of the true facts concerning the laying of the foundation stones of the Boer republics by one who is most competent and reliable, it would seem that no fair-minded person could for a moment refrain from sympathizing with the Boers, who love liberty and independence, and who feel that the two little republics are their country, that they have a personal proprietorship in their history, and who are jealous of their rights and want their children and their children's children to be the inheritors of a glorious heritage. bequeathed to them by ancestors whose blood and tears cemented together the stones of these republics.

Second Reitz Interview

Webster Davis has a second interview with Francis Reitz in which he recites many of the same facts as are related in A Century of Wrong but the exposition is in a more conversational style that is easier to follow and also contains some emotional content that is lacking in the more formal style of the published book. As mentioned above it is ~12,000 words amounting to 25 pages.[417] [418]

> Desiring to know the facts from the Boer standpoint as to the exact conditions prevailing in the gold fields that gave rise to the bitter controversy concerning them, I took occasion to ask Secretary Reitz to give me a correct statement on this very important matter.

He said that the whole question had already been discussed quite fully in a pamphlet recently published entitled 'A Century of Wrong', and with which he had something to do, but that he would gladly set forth the real facts again, which he proceeded to do as follows:

The natural inequality of mankind finds expression in the different kinds of influence which one man can possess and exert over another; this influence may be religious, moral, political or purely material. This last (material) sort of influence usually takes the form of money, the monetary nexus as an English writer has expressed it. An unusual collection of this kind of influence leads to so-called capitalism, just as an unusual collection of political influence leads to tyranny and an unusual collection of religious influence to hierarchical despotism. This capitalism threatens to become as dangerous to mankind in our time as the political tyranny of the old Eastern World and the religious tyranny of the middle ages were in their respective times.

In, a country full of rich mines, as in South Africa, capitalism has as a matter of course a great natural function to fulfil. Unfortunately it has from the very commencement tried to exceed its natural limits, to obtain political influence and in this way to make all other forms of power and influence subservient to its designs.

The spirit of South African capitalism has its incarnation in Mr. C. J. Rhodes. who succeeded in bringing about the amalgamation of the thousand and one conflicting interests of the diamond fields into one large corporation, of which he was himself the head. Though he had perhaps no unusual natural genius for politics, yet he was irresistibly drawn in that direction, and by means of his financial influence, in addition to a double share of the elasticity of conscience common to his class, he succeeded in obtaining for himself the post of Prime Minister of the Cape Colony and the support of the Afrikander party in all its power and solidarity. The Afrikanders of the Cape Colony believed in him, because they were fully convinced of the great necessity of the co-operation and fusion of the white races in South Africa, and he, a loyal Englishman, possessing the fullest confidence of the colonial Afrikanders, seemed to them the very person to realize their ideal.

A thoughtful spectator of this brotherhood of Afrikanderdom and capitalism could have foretold that a breach would occur sooner or later. For Afrikander policy is based on a deeply rooted and truly national sentiment, on a pure political conviction, which could never become subservient to financial interests.

On the other side was the so-called jingoism - a form of party politics without any solid or real faith, which busies itself in using big words and playing with high-sounding ideas and principles, a policy which always appeals to motives of self-interest, of illegal annexation of what belongs to others, a policy which springs from that spirit of brag so deeply rooted in human nature-a policy, in fact, in direct conflict with the true spirit of religion, with the aesthetic sentiment of mankind and with the sentiments of humility and moderation which form the natural basis of all morality.

Here then was an opportunity for establishing a lasting alliance, between capitalism with its tremendous material influence, but without any exalted ideas or principles, on the one side and jingoism, poor, empty, soulless, but with a rich store of high-flown ideas and principles and selfish inclinations, on the other side. The one was just suited to supplement the other, and thereby enter into a natural alliance, which is now becoming a menace throughout the world to the greatest and most lasting interests of mankind. That capitalistic jingoism is the tree from which poor South Africa is at present plucking such bitter fruit.

Mr. Rhodes, with that treacherous duplicity which is the abiding characteristic of British policy in South Africa, worked openly in the fullest sympathy with the Colonial Afrikanders, while in secret he was plotting with jingoism against the Afrikanders and the South African republics.

[417] Pages 65–107 ~12,000 words.

[418] PF: Once again the use of quotation marks was so idiomatic and the conversation so easy to follow that I have deleted most of them.

In the Cape Colony he had the Afrikanders in his power. He would now try to obtain the same influence-not so much for himself personally as for capitalism with which his own interests were identified-in the South African Republic with its rich gold mines. If he succeeded in doing this, he would have gained his personal object, and capital would be crowned absolute despot of South Africa.

With his eye fixed on this purpose, he and other capitalists began to set on foot a political agitation against the republic in Johannesburg in 1892. In a place like Johannesburg, where much liquor is consumed, where minds are always in a state of excitement, on account of the high altitude[419] and the rush of business, and where there is just that measure of real grievances calculated to give the semblance of truth to imaginary grievances, it was easy enough to bring about a political fermentation in a very short time by the lavish use of money.

Such was the beginning of the National Union movement, which began in Johannesburg in 1892, and whose followers almost exclusively consisted of creatures and instruments of the capitalists and a small number of honest blockheads and enthusiasts who, of course, do not think deep enough to penetrate the purpose and tendency of such movements and are generally found on the wrong side.

The capitalists certainly kept themselves altogether in the background so that the movement might appear to be a popular one. The capitalists of Johannesburg, however, were too theatrical, and their thirst for notoriety was too great to be suppressed forever. And thus it came about that in the course of a few years they took their natural place at the head of the opera-bouffe[420] agitation.

They commenced by undermining the Boer policy through the lowest and dirtiest means, so that they might in this way obtain control of all the legislative and administrative power in reference to the mines. They had persuaded themselves and the world that the Boers were a corrupt lot and they therefore at once resorted to bribery to effect their object.

Thus Lionel Phillips[421] wrote to Beit in London, on June 10, 1894:

I don't, of course, want to meddle in politics, and as to the franchise, do not think many people care a fig about it.

And again, on the 16th of June, 1894:

I may here say that, as you, of course, know, I have no desire for political rights, and believe as a whole the community is riot ambitious in this respect.

The bewaarplaatsen [Repositories] question will, I think, be settled in our favor, but at a cost of twenty-five thousand pounds. . . .

It is proposed to spend a good deal of money in order to secure a better Raad, [Volksraad] but it must be remembered that the spending of money on elections has by recent legislation been made a criminal offence, and the matter will have to be carefully handled.

And again, on July 15th, 1894:

Our trump card is a fund of ten to fifteen thousand pounds to improve the Raad. Unfortunately the companies have no secret service fund. I must devise a way. We don't want to shell out ourselves.

Here we get a peep behind the curtains and see how already in 1894 the capitalists tried to degrade and to destroy our public life by means which did not even stop at the criminal laws of the land, to say nothing of elementary morality.

And have they been successful? Are the people and the Volksraad as corruptible as they thought and as they still wish to persuade the world? Their failure is the best and most convincing answer to this.

If bribery on a great scale was not able to secure the triumph of capitalism over society, then there yet remained the other trump card of political jingoism.

The High Commissioner was sounded by Mr. Phillips. And what was the answer of Sir Henry Loch,[422] Her Majesty's representative in South Africa? In the same book of secret correspondence we find the following letter, dated July 1st, 1894, to Wernher, another member of the gigantic firm of Wernher,[423] Beit[424] & Co. :

419 1,753 m (5,751 ft).

420 Opéras bouffes are known for elements of comedy, satire, parody and farce.

421 Sir Lionel Phillips, 1st Baronet (6 August 1855–2 July 1936) was a British-born South African financier, mining magnate and politician. Lionel Phillips - Wikipedia

Sir Henry Loch (with whom I had two long private interviews alone) asked me some very pointed questions- such as: What arms we had in Johannesburg, whether the population could hold the place for six days until help could arrive, etc., etc.-and stated plainly that if there had been three thousand rifles and ammunition here, he would certainly have come over, and so on in the same strain. Sir Henry Loch has corroborated these assertions by openly boasting of his plans to make an attack on the South African Republic two years later in the House of Lords.

And all this happened while he was the guest of our government and was engaged in friendly negotiations concerning the interests of British subjects. To such a low level British policy in South Africa had then already sunk! Within two years, however, a yet deeper abyss was to reveal itself.

The secret conspiracy of capitalists and jingoes to overthrow the Republic now began to grow rapidly, for just at this critical period Mr. Chamberlain became Secretary of State for the Colonies.

In the secret correspondence of the conspirators continual reference is made to the colonial office in Downing street in a way, which, taken in connection with later disclosures and later suppression of the truth, has left the public over the whole world under the impression that the colonial office was cognizant of, if not accessory to, the mean attack on the South African Republic.

It is not necessary to go into the details of the Jameson invasion. The world has not yet forgotten how the administrator of a British territory, in execution of the purpose of a conspiracy at whose head stood the Prime Minister of the Cape Colony, entered the South African Republic with an armed body of troops in order to assist the capitalistic revolution of Johannesburg in overthrowing the Boer government; how that invasion and that revolution were frustrated by the vigilance of the Boers; how Jameson and his band of robbers were handed over to the English government for trial, though the Boers had the power and the right to shoot them down as robbers; how the whole lot of Johannesburg capitalists pleaded guilty to high treason and sedition; how, instead of confiscating all their possessions according to the law, and in this way giving the final blow to capitalism in South Africa, the government of the South African Republic pardoned them (a magnanimity which they repaid three years afterward by setting on foot a still more dangerous agitation against the republic); how at the instance of the Afrikander party in the Cape Colony an inquiry was held into the causes of the raid; how that inquiry degenerated into a base attack on the government of the deeply injured South African Republic, and how finally when the truth was at the point of being revealed and the conspiracy traced to its source in the British cabinet, the commission suddenly decided not to publish the compromising documents.

Here we see to what a depth the grand old traditions of the British constitution had sunk, under the influence of the ever increasing and all-devouring money spirit and in the hands of a sharp-tongued wholesale merchant, who, like Cleon[425] of old, posed as a statesman!

Treachery and violence had not succeeded in attaining their object, and therefore, as Mr. Rhodes openly boasted before the above mentioned commission of inquiry, 'constitutional means' would be employed to make capitalistic jingoism master of the situation in South Africa.

[422] Henry Loch, 1st Baron Loch - Wikipedia

[423] Sir Julius Charles Wernher, 1st Baronet (9 April 1850–21 May 1912) was a German-born Randlord, diamond magnate, and art collector who became part of the English establishment. With the discovery in 1886 of gold on the Witwatersrand, the firm appointed Hermann Eckstein as their representative in Johannesburg, while Cecil Rhodes and Beit effectively amalgamated the Kimberley diamond mines by 1888 and enabled Wernher, Beit & Co. to acquire a controlling interest in De Beers Consolidated Mines. Wernher by now was managing over 70 South African companies from his London office, and developing a passion for collecting art. Julius Wernher - Wikipedia

[424] Alfred Beit (15 February 1853–16 July 1906) was an Anglo-German gold and diamond magnate in South Africa, and a major donor and profiteer of infrastructure development on the African continent. He also donated much money to university education and research in several countries, and was the "silent partner" who structured the capital flight from post-Boer War South Africa to Rhodesia. Beit's assets were structured around the so-called Corner House Group, which through its holdings in various companies controlled 37 per cent of the gold produced at the Witwatersrand's goldfields in Johannesburg in 1913. Alfred Beit - Wikipedia

[425] Cleon (died 422 BC) was an Athenian general during the Peloponnesian War. He was an early representative of the commercial class in Athenian politics; which during the early Peloponnesian war was coming into prominence - although he was an aristocrat himself. He strongly advocated for an offensive war strategy and is remembered for being ruthless in carrying out his policies. He was often depicted in a negative way, predominantly by Thucydides and the comedic playwright Aristophanes, who both represent him as an unscrupulous, warmongering demagogue. Cleon - Wikipedia

It was, therefore, only to be expected that such a treacherous attack on the republics would thoroughly rouse the colonial Afrikanders and bring new forces into the political arena. To show the character of the feeling roused by the Jameson raid, I wish here to quote a few sentences from an article which appeared a few months after the invasion in Ons Land, [Our Land] the organ of the colonial Afrikander party, an article which undoubtedly expressed the feeling of the Afrikanders:

Has Providence not overruled the painful circumstances of South Africa since the beginning of this year to a higher purpose? who can doubt this?

The stab which was intended to paralyze Afrikanderdom in the republics once for all has sent an electric shock to the national heart. Afrikanderdom has waked up with an earnestness and a consciousness which we had not been seen since the glorious War of Independence, in 1881. From the Limpopo to Cape Town the second Majuba has sent a new inspiration into our people and awakened a new movement. Through the whole of South Africa a new feeling has gone throbbing through our people. The faint and enervating imperialism, which was already beginning to make our national blood thin and meagre, is gradually disappearing in the fresh air which is now blowing about our people. Many who had become tired of the slow progress of the national idea and had surrendered themselves to imperialism have become converted and have asked themselves what imperialism has accomplished in South Africa. Bitterness and race hatred, indeed. Since the days of Sir Harry Smith and Theophilus Shepstone and Sir Bartle Frere until the days of Leander Jameson and Cecil Rhodes imperialism in South Africa has been accompanied by a policy of blood and deceit. whatever the good fruits of imperialism may be elsewhere, in our country its constant tendency in all these years has been to force our national life and national character into foreign grooves, and to consummate that force with blood and tears. . . . Truly, Afrikanderdom over the whole. of South Africa finds itself at present at the most critical moment of its existence. N ow or never: now or never must the foundation of an all embracing nationalism be laid. - The iron is glowing and the hour for striking has come.

The partition wall has disappeared. Let us now stand firmly together. The danger is not yet past; on the contrary, Afrikanderdom has never been more in need of a policy of colonial and republican union. And now that the-psychological moment has come, now that our people over the whole of South Africa have awakened, now that a new flame has been lit in our hearts, let us lay the cornerstone of a truly United South Africa on the foundation of a pure and all-embracing national sentiment. Language like this frightened the jingoes, not because it was disloyal, which it obviously was not, but because it was an indication that the Afrikanders had been awakened, and that this defeat of the jingoes has opened the way for still greater defeats in the future. A policy of annexation of the republics, for instance, would in future have to reckon also with the colonial Afrikanders. For some time the jingoes hoped that under an altered redistribution scheme they would secure the majority in the Cape Parliament. The general election of 1898, however, gave the Afrikander party a small majority, which was later on increased under a redistribution scheme which the jingo opposition had been strong enough to force on the government.

Instead of frankly recognizing that this Afrikander victory was a natural consequence of the Jameson raid, the jingoes, not only in South Africa, but also in England, began to scream that the authority and prestige of England was menaced in South Africa; that, unless a striking display of British power was soon made, South Africa would speedily be lost to England, and that this menace to British authority originated with the republican propaganda which they alleged the South African Republic had begun to spread in South Africa. As long as the South African Republic would not bow before British authority, but with national pride carried its youthful head high, the other parts of South Africa would be tempted to follow this pernicious example, and there was thus no security for British supremacy on this sub-continent. The South African Republic must be humbled and bent in the dust; thereby the Afrikanders in other parts of South Africa would, as a matter of course, relinquish their alleged hope of a greater republican South Africa.

But how could this humiliation be brought about? And how could it be brought about through those 'constitutional means' which the failure of the Jameson conspiracy had made necessary?

The new Governor of Cape Colony and High Commissioner for South Africa knew well enough how to devise 'constitutional means' for humiliating the South African Republic.

For was there not the burning question over the suzerainty, to which the South African Republic itself had given rise, and in the following manner?

After the Jameson raid, and with a view to removing some of its causes, the Legislature of the South African Republic had passed certain laws-as, for instance, a law for the expulsion of dangerous persons, a law whereby persons without means, or suffering from diseases, could be prevented from entering the country-which the British government considered to be a breach of Article XIV. of the London convention.

Article IV. of the London convention was similarly alleged to have been broken by the conclusion of several extradition and other treaties with foreign powers. On May 7, 1897, the government of the South African Republic replied to these charges in a very important despatch which, after fully setting forth the reasons which induced that government to differ from Her Majesty's government, concluded with an appeal to arbitration as the fittest means of deciding the dispute. The words of the government of the South African Republic were as follows:

While the government of the South African Republic respect the views of Her Majesty's government, they nevertheless feel confident of the correctness of their own contentions, and therefore wish to propose to Her Majesty's government the principle of arbitration, with which the first Volksraad of the South African Republic also agrees, in the hope that the proposal will be accepted in the same spirit of conciliation in which it has been made. They feel all the more confidence in making this proposal because the arbitral principle has already been laid down in the London convention, in the only case in which, according to their opinion, a difference could at the time of its completion have been anticipated, namely, with reference to Article 1.; because, further, arbitration was proposed by Her Majesty's government and accepted by this government with regard to the dispute under Article XIV. of the convention over the so-called Coolie question which was settled by arbitration; because the Right Honorable Secretary of State for the Colonies favors the same principle in his despatch of September 4th, 1895, to the High Commissioner in Cape Town, in which he says:

After 1886 as time went on the manner in which this law was interpreted and worked gave rise to complaints on the part of the British government, and as it seemed impossible to come to an agreement by means of correspondence, the Marquis of Ripon took what is the approved course in such a case-of proposing to the South African Republic that the dispute should be referred to arbitration. This was agreed to."

And, finally, because the arbitral principle in cases like these appears to the government to be the most impartial, just and satisfactory way out of an existing dispute, and because one of the parties to a convention cannot, on any principle of fairness, expect that his interpretation shall be accepted by the other party as the only valid and correct one.

And although this government is fully convinced that a just and impartial decision is perhaps more likely to be obtained in South Africa than elsewhere, yet considering the contradictory elements, interests and aspirations which are to-day asserting themselves in South Africa, and \with a view to avoiding even the appearance of wishing to influence a decision favorable to itself, they wish to suggest that the President of the Swiss Republic, who can be considered as standing entirely outside the question and not to be animated by sympathy or antipathy for either party, be invited to appoint a competent jurist as arbitrator, as has often been done in the case of international disputes. This government would have no objection to the arbitrator being subjected to a time limit and wish to give the assurance in advance that they will with the greatest pleasure submit to any decision which might unexpectedly be given against them.

The government repeats the well-meant wish that this proposal may be acceptable to Her Majesty's government, and, as the allegations of breaches of the convention appear to be believed in South Africa and bring and keep the public mind in a state of tension, this government would be pleased if Her Majesty's government could come to a speedy decision on this matter.

To this Her Majesty's government answered that under the convention of 1884, taken in connection with the preamble of the convention of 1881 (which it considered to be still existing), the South African Republic was under Her Majesty's suzerainty, and that it was inconsistent with that subordinate position of the South African Republic to submit to arbitration questions arising between the South African Republic and the suzerain power on the interpretation of the convention of 1884.

To prevent all misunderstandings as to this amazing answer I repeat the words of the British despatch:

Nineteenth-Finally, the government of the South African Republic propose that all points in dispute between her Majesty's government and themselves relating to the convention should be referred to arbitration, the arbitrator to be nominated by the President of the Swiss Republic.

Twentieth-In making this proposal the government of the South African Republic appear to have overlooked the distinction between the conventions of 1881 and 1884 and an ordinary treaty between two independent powers, questions arising upon which may properly be the subject of arbitration.

Twenty-first-By the Pretoria convention of 188??! Her Majesty, as sovereign of the Transvaal territory. accorded to the inhabitants of that territory complete self-government subject to the suzerainty of Her Majesty, her heirs and successors, upon certain terms and conditions, subject to certain reservations and limitations set forth in thirty-three articles, and by the London convention of] 884. Her Majesty, while maintaining the preamble of the earlier instrument, directed and declared that certain other articles embodied therein should be substituted for the articles embodied in the convention of 1881. The Articles of the convention of 1881 were accepted by the Volksraad of the Transvaal State, and those of the convention of 1884 by the Volksraad of the South African Republic. Under these conditions, therefore, Her Majesty holds toward the South African Republic the relation of a suzerain who has accorded to the people of that republic self-government upon certain conditions, and it would be incompatible with that position to submit to arbitration the construction of the conditions on which she accorded self-government to the republic.

In its famous reply of April 16th, 1898, the Government of the South African Republic proved irrefutably that the preamble of the convention of 1881 had disappeared, that Lord Derby had himself substituted a draft convention in which the preamble of 1881 was struck out, and that by the final acceptance of that proposal the suzerainty had for good ceased to exist. Now that there was therefore no suzerain relation, for this as well as for other reasons, between the two countries, and the objection to arbitrate over mutual differences had disappeared, the South African Republic repeated its request to the British government for arbitration on mutual differences.

But that was, of course, just what Mr. Chamberlain did not want. He objected to arbitration because it would probably lead to the defeat of the British and not of the republican government; for, as we have already shown, the suzerainty question had been expressly brought forward by him for the purpose of being used as a 'constitutional means' to humble the South African Republic. In his answer to the arguments of the South African Republic, Mr. Chamberlain could thus only persist in his assertion of suzerainty, though he made no attempt to refute the argument concerning Lord Derby's striking out of the preamble of the Pretoria convention. It was clearly his opinion that Lord Derby had sacrificed this suzerainty by his stupidity and thoughtlessness in 1884, even as Lord Grey had let the South African Republic go in 1852, and therefore it was now necessary for him, by a great show of power and immovable determination, like Shepstone in 1877, to attempt to bluff the republic in order not to be deprived of this eminent, constitutional means.

His assertion in this despatch that both the suzerainty of Her Majesty and the right of the South African Republic to self-government depended on the preamble of the Pretoria convention, and that, if the preamble had disappeared, our right to self-government had likewise disappeared, was clearly also intended to bully the government of the South African Republic; but in other respects, it was quite correct. Therefore the government of the South African Republic replied that they no longer claimed the right to self-government under that preamble nor by the convention of 1884 (since that said nothing about self-government), but simply by their right as a sovereign international state.

In other words, according to their contention it was a necessary implication of the convention of 1884 that the South African Republic was a sovereign state and should derive its right from that source, that it was therefore considered unnecessary to say anything concerning its rights in the convention of 1884. In that answer, which is not only judicially and historically correct, but is moreover based on simple common sense, our High Commissioner was clever enough to find a defiance' to Her Majesty's government, though even in that answer the government of the South African Republic submitted to the London convention. as they had done hundreds of times before this.

This is the whole history of the suzerainty dispute between the two governments. The South African Republic had asked for arbitration in certain disputes. and England, with Chamberlain acting as spokesman, refused because a sovereign power cannot be expected to settle disputes with her vassal by arbitration, and because, according to the new principles screwed into international law at Birmingham, she must be judge in her own dispute with others. The position occupied by the South African Republic in this remarkable correspondence is supported by the actions of Lord Derby at the time of the negotiations concerning the conventions, and also later in a cablegram in which he summarized the contents of this convention to the High Commissioner for the information of the two republics, which were as follows:

High Commissioner, Cape Town, to British Resident, Pretoria:

'Twenty-eighth Please inform Transvaal government that I have received the following from the Secretary of State: Begins, February 27th. Convention signed to-day. New South Western Boundary as proposed, following Trade road. British Protectorate country outside Transvaal established with delegates' consent. They promise to appoint Border Commissioner inside Transvaal co-operate with ours outside, Mackenzie British Resident. Debt reduced to quarter million. Same complete internal independence in Transvaal as in Orange Free State. Conduct and control diplomatic intercourse foreign government conceded. Queen's final approval treaties reserved. Delegates appear well satisfied and cordial feeling between two governments. You may make the above known'

This contention is further also confirmed by the positive declarations of Lord Rosmead and the Rev. D. P. Faure, that it was distinctly understood when the London convention was made that suzerainty had disappeared, to say nothing of the evidence of the Transvaal deputation.

While the two governments were engaged with this question, the capitalists of course were also busy keeping their fire burning. Rhodesia was not only an unexpected failure, but was in short richer in Kaffir wars than in paying mines. The capitalistic groups which had the greatest interest in the Witwatersrand were also most interested in Rhodesia, and it very naturally seemed advisable to them that their Transvaal mines should be responsible for the obligations of their undertakings in Rhodesia-a settlement which could, however, only be carried out by a political fusion of the two countries.

To accomplish this object a constant agitation had to be kept up in Johannesburg, so that the English shareholders living at a distance might be prepared for the day on which the annexation of the Transvaal by, constitutional means' was to take place.

The argument that was calculated to find easy credence among these European shareholders was that on account of the maladministration of the South African Republic a state of affairs existed on the gold fields which was very· detrimental to the financial interests of the mining industry; in other words, considered from this point of view, the so-called' Uitlander grievances' were an inexhaustibly rich and paying mine.

This agitation emanated, at first, directly from the capitalists and became in the course of 1897 so serious that the government resolved to appoint a commission of officials and mining magnates in order to institute a searching investigation into the alleged financial grievances. As regards the government, the principal findings of the commission were as follows:

First, that the price of dynamite (85 shillings per case of 50 pounds) under the existing concession was too high and that a reduction was desirable, either by means of cancelling the concession or by testing the validity thereof in a court of law.

Second, that the tariffs of the Netherlands South African Railway Company for the conveyance of coal and other articles were too high, and that it was also desirable to expropriate the company.

Third, that the customs dues on necessaries of life were too high and that in consequence the workingman's expense of living at Johannesburg was too high.

Fourth, that strict measures ought to be adopted to prevent the theft of gold, and that the law on total prohibition of sale of liquor to native laborers had to be applied much more stringently, and that it was also necessary to apply the pas& law' (whereby native labor is controlled) more carefully.

Fifth, with a view to carrying out the recommendations in four the commission suggested that an advisory board be appointed for the Witwatersrand, to advise the government with regard to the application of the laws in question.

In how far have these recommendations been carried out?

First, as regards dynamite it appeared that the existing concession could not with any measure of success be challenged in a court of law, and neither government nor Volksraad was willing to cancel, without consent of the contracting party, a contract solemnly entered into and under which enormous sums of money had been spent. The mining industry, as a matter of course, worked heart and soul for the cancellation, even without adequate compensation, but the public did not yet know, what has leaked out within the last few months, that the De Beers Corporation had itself formed the intention of erecting dynamite factories in South Africa, and that the agitation of the capitalists on this point was simply intended to obtain for themselves the control of this important source of income.

Of Mr. Chamberlain's interest in the well known ammunition and explosive firm of Kynoch, the public are very well aware, although one hesitates to assume that the South African policy of the Secretary of State for Colonics is influenced by considerations of a private financial nature.

Both government and Legislature of the South African Republic have adopted the wiser course of lessening the price of dynamite to such an extent that it is at present about equal to European market price increased by a protective tariff of twenty shillings per case.

Here it may be noted that Mr. Chamberlain, knowing how unpopular the dynamite concession is in the South African Republic, has not hesitated to inform the government of the republic in a menacing tone that the concession is in conflict with the London convention.

The answer of this government was so crushing that this circumstance, in addition to the fact, which only became known later, that some of the most important English and European jurists had given it as their opinion that the concession was in no way in conflict with the convention, has prevented Mr. Chamberlain from returning to the subject. I mention this matter to show how every trifle is resorted to in order to discover a ground for humiliating the South African Republic.

Second, as regards the Netherlands South African Railway Company, the capitalists seem to have changed their opinion since the time of the industrial concession, and now think that the administration of the company is as reasonable as can be expected, and that expropriation has thus become unnecessary. Perhaps, too, they think that, from their point of view, it would be better that they themselves should buy the shares, and that thus the mining industry instead of the government should become masters of that source of income.

As regards the railway tariffs these have been so far lowered in accordance with the recommendation of the Industrial Commission that no complaints are any longer made, and therefore we come to the conclusion that all cause for complaints has disappeared.

The lowering of these rates in addition to the removal of customs duties from almost all necessaries of life has brought about a change of about seven hundred thousand pounds in the state revenues of the last year, an enormous sum compared with the total of the state revenues in the South African Republic.

This is a proof of how eager the government of the South African Republic is to remove grievances as soon as they are clearly convinced that they really exist.

Third, as regards the administration of the liquor law, pass law and gold theft law, neither the government nor the Legislature has felt at liberty to recommend the formation of an advisory board on the Witwatersrand. They have penetrated deeper to the root of the evil, and have made such changes in the administration of the laws that no signs of dissatisfaction are any longer apparent. On the contrary, we no longer hear of gold thefts, and the representatives of the mining industry have repeatedly expressed their satisfaction with the administration of the pass law, and more especially the liquor law,

In this liquor law we have a proof of a good administration. The nature of the liquor law is such that it is one of the most difficult laws that a government can ever be called upon to carry out, and the measure of success attained by this government and its officials' has proved irrefutably that the accusations of incompetent administration so often brought against the government of the South African Republic are devoid of all truth, and are only intended to calumniate and abjure it. Thus, for instance, a combined meeting of the Chamber of Mines, the Chamber of Commerce and the Mine Managers' Association, the three most powerful and most representative bodies on the Witwatersrand gold fields, passed the following two resolutions on August 17th last, which were:

First, This combined meeting, representing the Chamber of Mines, Chamber of Commerce and the Mine Managers' Association, again records its decided approval of the liquor law as it now stands, and is of opinion that prohibition is not only salutary for the natives in their own interests, but absolutely essential to the mining industry for the conservation of its labor.

Second, This meeting hereby places on record its appreciation of the efforts to put down the illicit liquor traffic, which has been made by the detective department of this state since that department was placed under the control of the State Attorney, and is of the opinion that the success which has thus far attended those efforts amply disproves the contention that the liquor law is unworkable.

The first motion was carried by an overwhelming majority, and the second unanimously.

Compare this declaration of the representatives of the mining and commercial interests of the Witwatersrand with the assertion repeated by Mr. Chamberlain in his great grievances despatch of May 15th last: 'Stringent application of the liquor law has not yet taken place and the law is simply evaded and liquor sold to the natives on the mines in unlimited quantities.'

When Mr. Chamberlain wrote these words they were absolutely untrue, but almost all of his grievances are of this imaginary stamp.

The result has thus fully shown that the government was correct in its opinion that it was better to change the administration of laws about which complaints were made than to introduce a principle of which no one was able to predict the consequences and final results.

The agitation in connection with the report of the Industrial Commission was followed by a great calm. If it were not that the Swazieland trouble gave cause for Suspicion, we might readily have thought that there was no cloud on the horizon. The two governments were seemingly on very good and friendly terms, and some of us had already begun to think that the period of brotherly co-operation between the two white races in South Africa had finally dawned. and that the cursed Raid and all its consequences of race hatred and discord were at an end. Certain circumstances, however, indicated that the calm was not peace, but that on the contrary the enemy was engaged in making a final attempt to bring affairs to a crisis.

The South African League, a political organization, which originated in the race hatred to which the Jameson raid had given birth, and at whose head, to place the capitalistic connection in its truest light, Mr. Rhodes himself stands, began to agitate against the government in an unheard of manner toward the end of last year. The Executive Committee for Johannesburg was such that at first no notice was taken of his movement. The chairman was a prizefighter, the secretary a former socialistic demagogue from London. etc., etc. It soon became evident, however, that the movement was not alone aided by the capitalists and strongly supported by the mines but was also in a mysterious way connected with London and Cape Town, a connection which the events of the last months have made still clearer. Meetings were called, petitions full of grievances drawn up

md sent to Her Majesty, and propaganda made in the press, which all went to prove that a well organized campaign was set on foot against the republic. As the government of the South African Republic has, in an official despatch, set forth the tendency of the agitation and the connection of the British government therewith, I wish to repeat their weighty words:

But this government wishes to go further. Even as regards those Uitlanders who are British subjects, they are a small minority who, under the pretext of imaginary grievances, have continued secret propaganda of race hatred and used this republic as a basis to set on foot a revolutionary movement against this government. Concerning this minority, ministers of Her Majesty have so forcibly set forth the true state of the case that this government, whose only object is to set things in their true light before Her Majesty's government and the world, and not to make groundless accusations, here wishes to repeat the words of these ministers-ministers of the Cape Colony, well acquaintance with local circumstances and capable of judging:

In the opinion of ministers, the persistent action, both beyond and within this colony, of the political body styling itself the South African League, in endeavoring to foment and excite, not to soothe and allay, ill will between the two principal European races inhabiting South Africa, is well illustrated by these resolutions, the exaggerated and aggravated terms of which disclose the spirit which informs and inspires them.

His Excellency's ministers are one in their earnest desire to do all in their power to aid and further a policy of peaceful progress throughout South Africa, and they cannot but regard it as an unwise propaganda, hostile to the true interests of the empire, including this colony as an integral part, that every possible occasion should be seized by the League and its promoters for an attempt to magnify into great events minor incidents, when occurring in the South African Republic, with a prospect thereby of making racial antagonism mare acute, or of rendering less smooth the relations between Her Majesty's government or the government of this colony and that republic.

The cause of race hatred is not So strong in South Africa, however, that a body with this propaganda, striving toward a revolutionary goal, would be able to exert great influence in this sub-continent; and it is constantly being asked why a body so insignificant in itself and its principles and as regards its members can yet enjoy such a measure of success. The answer is that this body relies on the protection and support of Her Majesty's government in England and that both its members and its press organs openly boast of the influence which it exerts over the policy of Her Majesty's government. This government would pay no attention to such assertions, but when they see that the ideas of this body are constantly echoed in the addresses of members of Her Majesty's government, when they see that bluebooks are compiled comprising to a great extent memoranda composed by members of the South African League, and the false articles and reports of the press organs of this body, which thereby acquire an official character, then this government can easily understand why so many of Her Majesty's right-minded subjects in this sub-continent come under the wrong impression that the policy followed by the

South African League is approved by Her Majesty's government and is thus destined for the welfare and prosperity of the British Empire in general.

'If this wrong impression can be removed and the fact become known that the South African League as far as the South African Republic is concerned, is an organization whose object is to cause bad blood and revolt and to undermine the independence of the country, then this body will soon lose its influence and the strained relations at present existing between the two governments will soon disappear. Then, too, the Afrikander republics and the Afrikander population of this subcontinent will no longer fear that the interests of the British Empire necessarily mean the downfall of those republics and the extermination or enslavement of that population; then, too, both parts of the white race in South Africa will return to that brotherly co-operation and fusion which had at least begun - before the treacherous conspiracy at the end of 1895 again roused the passions on both sides.'

As a result of the continual agitation of the South African League three events took place in Johannesburg which Mr. Chamberlain considered the climax of the Uitlander grievances. The three events were: The so-called' Lombard case' in connection with the alleged ill-treatment of colored British subjects in Johannesburg, the so-called 'Edgar case' in connection with the shooting, of a British subject' by a policeman, and the so-called 'Amphitheatre Case' in connection with a riotous meeting of the South African League.

As Regards the Lombard Case, Mr. Chamberlin Says:

As an instance of such arbitrary action, the recent maltreatment of colored British subjects by Field Cornet Lombard may be cited. This official entered the houses of various colored persons, without a warrant, at night, dragged them from their beds, and arrested them for being without a pass. The persons so arrested were treated with much cruelty, and it is even alleged that one woman was prematurely confined, and a child subsequently died from the consequences of the exposure.

Men were beaten and kicked by the orders of the Field Cornet, who appears to have exercised his authority with the most cowardly brutality. The government of the republic, being pressed to take action, suspended the Field Cornet) and an inquiry was held, at which he and the police denied most of the allegations of violence, but the other facts were not disputed, and no independent evidence was called for the defense.

The government have since reinstated Lombard. Unfortunately this case is by no means unparalleled. Other British subjects, including several from St. Helena and Mauritius, have been arbitrarily arrested, and some of them have been fined, without having been heard in their own defense, under a law which does not even profess to have any application to persons from those colonies. However long-suffering Her Majesty's government may be in their anxious desire to remain on friendly terms with the South African Republic, it must be evident that a continuance of incidents of this kind followed by no redress may well become intolerable.

The answer of the Government of the South African Republic to the accusations on this point was as follows:

As regards the Lombard case, this government wishes to point out that for a full month after the alleged ill-treatment of Cape colored persons had taken place no complaint was made to anyone in authority in this republic. and that neither the government nor the public was acquainted with what had taken place. The whole affair was so insignificant that some of the persons alleged to have been ill-treated afterwards declared on oath before the Court of Inquiry that they would never of their own accord have laid any complaints. But what happened? About a month after the events the so-called South African League chanced to hear of them; they sent some of their officials out to collect the evidence of the persons alleged to have been ill-treated, and with the assistance of Her Majesty's Vice Consul at Johannesburg, who always co-operated with the League in a striking manner, some sworn declarations were taken down.

Even then no complaints against the officials concerned were made to the lawful powers of the country, but the case was handed over to the acting British agent at Pretoria. When the attention of this government was called to the allegations, they immediately appointed a commission of inquiry, consisting of three gentlemen-Landdrost Van den Berg, of Johannesburg; :Mr. Andries Stockenstrom, barrister-at-law of the Middle Temple, head of the criminal department of the State's Attorney's office, and Mr. Van der Merwe, mine commissioner at Johannesburg-gentlemen against whose ability and impartiality no trace of suspicion had ever existed among the Uitlander population oi this republic, and with whose appointment the acting British agent also expressed himself perfectly satisfied. These officials were charged to examine the whole case thoroughly and to report the results of their investigations to the government, and they fulfilled their mandate by listening to and carefully considering the evidence of both sides for several days. Every right-minded person will readily acknowledge that infinitely more weight should attach to the findings of this commission than to the declarations of the complaining parties, who contradicted themselves on almost all particulars and well nigh turned that whole inquiry into a comedy.

Of the so-called facts of ill-treatment nothing was left over in this report; the special cases of alleged ill-treatment were evidently imaginary. It was clearly proved and felt that the complainants had acted contrary to the law, and the commission only disapproved of the arrests and investigations having taken place at night and without a warrant. This government regrets very deeply to see that Her Majesty's government bases its accusations on the ex parte, groundless, and in many respects false, declarations of complainants urged on by political hatred, and takes no notice of the report of the commission.

The Edgar Case Is Thus Represented by Mr. Chamberlain:

But perhaps' the most striking recent instance of arbitrary action by officials, and of the support of such action by the courts, is the wen known Edgar case. The effect of the verdict of the jury, warmly endorsed by the judge, is that four policemen breaking into a man's house at night without a warrant, on the mere statement of one person, which subsequently turned out to be untrue, that the man had committed a crime, are justified in killing him there and then because, according to their own account, he hits one of them with a stick.

If this is a. justification, then almost any form of resistance to the police is justification for the immediate killing of the person resisting, who may be perfectly innocent of any offense. This would be an alarming doctrine anywhere. It is peculiarly alarming when applied to a city like Johannesburg, where a strong force of police armed with revolvers have to deal with a large alien unarmed population, whose language in many cases they do not understand. The emphatic affirmation of such a doctrine by judge and jury in the Edgar case cannot but increase the general feeling of insecurity amongst the Uitlander population and the sense of injustice under which they labor. It may be pointed out that the allegation that Edgar assaulted the police was emphatically denied by his wife and others and that the trial was conducted in a way that would be considered quite irregular in this country, the witnesses for the defense being called by the prosecution and thereby escaping cross-examination. The reply of the government of the South African Republic was:

The Edgar case is then mentioned by your government as the most striking recent instance of arbitrary action by officials and of the support of such action by the courts.

That incident is used as a conclusive test of the alleged legal maladministration of this republic and it is thus important that we should pause a moment to consider it. What are the true facts? A certain Foster, an Englishman, was, without any lawful cause, attacked and knocked down by a certain Edgar, on the night of December 18th. 1898, so that he was picked up for dead and finally died in the hospital.

Edgar then escaped into his room, and in answer to the cries of bystanders, some policemen came hurrying upon the scene. Policeman Jones. among others. saw the person attacked lying like a dead man, and then went to Edgar's room to arrest him as a criminal, for he had indeed committed manslaughter and apparently murder. As he had been caught red-handed, the policemen were justified according to the laws, not alone of this republic, but of the whole of South Africa and of the United Kingdom of Great Britain and Ireland. to enter the house by force in order to arrest the criminal.

On their breaking into the room, Edgar gave Jones a tremendous blow with a formidable weapon, and in self-defense the latter fired at Edgar, in consequence of which he was killed. The question is not whether Jones was justified in taking this extreme step; the State Attorney of this republic by prosecuting him for manslaughter has already shown that in his opinion this case was one for the jury to decide. The question is only whether any jury in any country in the world would find a person guilty of any crime under circumstances such as these, and whether, if they did not find him guilty, it would be stigmatized as a flagrant and striking case of maladministration of justice.

This government feels convinced that the English administration of justice is also full of cases of which the facts are as strong as the facts of this case, and cannot understand why an incident which might occur in any country in the world should specially be used as an accusation against them.

This government does not wish to consider the blame cast by Her Majesty's government on the state prosecutor at Johannesburg, by whom the prosecution of this case was conducted. The fact that he is of pure English descent, that he received his legal education in London, that he is universally respected by the Uitlander population on account of his ability, his impartiality and his character, will of course not counterbalance, m the opinion of Her Majesty's government, his monstrous behavior in the calling up of witnesses for the prosecution who had been destined for the defense, and the consequent frustration of an imaginary cross-examination. This government only wishes to point out that the fact that the Edgar incident is the strongest that Her Majesty's government has been able to bring against the administration of justice in this republic is the strongest and most striking proof possible that, taken as a whole, the administration of justice on the gold fields of this republic compares most favorably with that of other similar gold fields even of old and long established countries.

The untrue representations made in the press concerning this incident prove sufficiently that the newspapers of the Witwatersrand, whose propaganda forms part of the organized campaign against this republic and its government, are obliged to exercise their false criticism on imaginary cases of maladministration which are often altogether unfounded. when the press must resort to such means, the real grievances must be insignificant.

Concerning the So-Called Amphitheatre Case, Mr. Chamberlain Says:

Some light upon the extent to which the police can be trusted to perform their delicate duties with fairness and discretion is thrown by the events referred to by the petitioners, which took place at a meeting called by British subjects for the purpose of discussing their grievances, and held on January 4th in the Amphitheatre of Johannesburg. The government were previously apprised of the objects of the meeting and their assent obtained, though this was not legally necessary for a meeting in an enclosed place. The organizers of the meeting state that they were informed by the State Secretary and the State Attorney that anyone who committed acts of violence or used seditious language would be held responsible, and in proof of the peaceful objects of the meeting, those who attended went entirely unarmed, by which it is understood that they did not even carry sticks.

So little was any disturbance apprehended that ladies were invited to attend and did attend. Yet in the result, sworn affidavits from many witnesses of different nationalities agree in the statement that the meeting was broken up almost immediately after its opening, and many of the persons attending it were violently assaulted by organized bands of hostile demonstrators actin!{ under the instigation and guidance of persons in government employ, without any attempt at interference on the part of the police, and even in some cases with their assistance or loudly expressed sympathy. The government of the South African Republic has been asked to institute an inquiry into these disgraceful proceedings, but the request has been met with a flat refusal.

To this accusation the following reply was made:

The Amphitheatre case is used by Her Majesty's government to prove how incapable the police on the Witwatersrand are to fulfil their duties and maintain order. - The League meeting was held in the so-called Amphitheatre in Johannesburg with the knowledge of the State Secretary and State Attorney and the accusation now is that in spite of that fact the tumult that took place at the meeting was not put down by the police.

The true facts of the case are these: Mr. Weyburgh and another, both in the pay of the South African League, informed the State Secretary and State Attorney that they intended calling this meeting in the Amphitheatre, and they, asked permission to do this. They were told that it was not necessary to receive the permission of the authorities, and that as long as the meeting did not cause disorder and disturbance of the peace they would be acting completely within their rights. Their attention was then directed to the fact that, on account of the behavior and propaganda of the South African League, this body was very unpopular among a considerable section of the population of Johannesburg, and that in all probability a disturbance would take place unless there was a sufficient number of the police present to maintain order. To this the gentlemen replied that since the Edgar incident the police were in bad repute, that the meeting would be very orderly and that the presence of police would contribute or give rise to disorder and that on these grounds they would rather not have any police. The State Secretary and State Attorney thereupon communicated with the chief of police in Johannesburg, with the result that he also was of the opinion that it would be better not to have an unusual number of police at the meeting. The government, acting on the advice of the officials of the League as well as their own police officials, gave instructions that the police should keep away from the meeting; they did this in good faith and with the object of letting the League have its say unhindered.

The proposed meeting was, however, advertised far and wide, and as the feeling among a certain section of the Witwatersrand population was very bitter against the League, a considerable number of its opponents was also present.

The few policemen present were powerless to stop the disorderly proceedings, and when the police came upon the scene a few minutes after the commencement of the uproar the meeting had broken up.

Taken by itself this incident would not be of much consequence, for it is an isolated case as regards the gold fields of this republic, and even in the best organized and controlled society, disorders like this sometimes take place. What makes the case serious, however, is the unjust accusation of Her Majesty's government that the meeting was broken up by officials of this republic and that this government flatly refused to inquire into the matter.

This government would not have refused to institute an inquiry if any complaints had been laid with them or with the local courts, and they said so in reply to Her Majesty's request for an inquiry. This government objects to the systematic habit of ignoring the local authorities and constantly complaining to Her Majesty's representatives about matters which ought to be decided by the courts of this republic. Instead, however, of complaining to Her Majesty's government only when all other reasonable means of redress have been tried in vain, Her Majesty's subjects are in the habit of ignoring and disregarding the local courts and authorities and of bringing forward all trivial and ex parte complaints in the first instance before Her Majesty's representatives, and thus also Her Majesty's government is constantly placed in the ambiguous and unenviable position of interfering in the internal affairs of this republic in conflict with the London convention. If a complaint had been laid with this government or the competent officials or courts, then the facts of the case could very easily have been investigated, and then, too, it would have been proved that a few officials who were present at the meeting as part of the public had done their best to stop the disorderly proceedings and that some of them were even wounded in their attempts to maintain peace.

Instead of showing their disapproval of such complaints and directing the complainants to the local courts, Her Majesty's government receives the complaints and then imparts an official character to them by sending them on to this government for notice and publishing them in due course in bluebooks for the information of the world. Her Majesty's government will readily admit that no state in the world, no matter how weak and small, that possesses any sense of honor can look on such things calmly, and if the relations between the two governments have become strained. then the true cause is to be found in the actions of Her Majesty's subjects which are not censured by Her Majesty's government, and not in imaginary and trivial grievances.

Is there the least semblance of right and justice in asserting that those grievances form a cause for intervention? What crimes have been perpetrated against humanity or the law of nations? Are the grievances and abuses brought up not equaled by events which take place almost daily in the most highly civilized countries in the world? We can with reason apply to the case in question the words with which the Russian government stamped the unlawful intervention of the British government in the internal affairs of Naples:

We could understand that as a consequence of friendly forethought one government should give advice to another in a benevolent spirit, that such advice might even assume the character of exhortation; but we believe that to be the farthest limit allowable. Less than ever can it now be allowed in Europe to forget that it is not the extent of territory, but the sacred character of rights of each state, which regulates the relations that exist between them. To endeavor to obtain from the government of the South African Republic concessions as concern the internal government of the republic by threats, or by a menacing demonstration, is a violent usurpation of its authority, an attempt to govern in its stead; it is an open declaration of the right of the strong· over the weak.

Notwithstanding all her hypocritical accusations the British government is very well acquainted with the fact that the administration of the South African Republic is on a sound basis, in spite of the almost unequalled difficulties with which the government and legislature have had to contend, and will stand comparison with that of other countries under similar circumstances; that the grievances by which, in the shape of bluebooks. the humane feeling of the British public is worked upon are to a great extent imaginary, and even if they were perfectly true, they yet offer no ground for interference in the internal affairs of the republic. It has thus become necessary to find some other constitutional means.'

The third and last 'constitutional means' which Mr. Chamberlain used as a pretext for interfering forcibly in the internal affairs of the South African Republic was the claim for equal political rights for all inhabitants of the South African Republic. In demanding- this he also followed the inspiration of Mr. Rhodes. For after the Jameson raid Mr. Rhodes had laid down, as a new programme for the progressive policy of South Africa the formula: Equal rights for all white men south of the Zambesi.

But with a view to the colored vote of the Cape Colony, Mr. Rhodes afterwards changed that cry to: Equal rights for all civilized men south of the Zambesi. And in due time the echo came from Downing Street: Equal political rights for all persons in the South African Republic.

As a political aspiration that may be as desirable or undesirable in South Africa as in England, where Mr. Chamberlain is now one of the leaders of the party which has always been opposed to all 'manhood suffrage.'

Mr. Chamberlain does not, however, confine himself to giving friendly advice, but demands the franchise for all Uitlanders. The South African Republic has already a franchise law by which every person who has already been. or shall yet be, seven years in this republic is entitled to the full franchise. On what grounds does he base his claim?

He appealed to the discussions which preceded the convention of 1881. In the discussions however mention is only made of civil rights, with regard to which all possible equality has always existed since the Sand River convention. For the maintenance of the equality of these civil . rights as distinguished from political rights, Article XII. of the Pretoria convention stipulates:

All such persons (loyal to Her Majesty) will have full liberty to reside in the country with enjoyment of all civil rights and protection for their persons and property.

In 1882 the franchise was altered from one year's to five years' residence, without any protest from Her Majesty's government. And in 1884 in the new convention of that year it was stipulated in the most emphatic and unequivocal manner:

Article XIV.-That all persons, other than natives, conforming themselves to the laws of the South African Republic will have full liberty with their families to enter, travel or reside in any part of the South African Republic; they will be entitled to hire or possess houses, manufactories, warehouses, shops and premises; they may carry on their commerce either in person or by any agents whom they may think fit to employ; they will not be subject, in respect of their person or property, or in respect of their commerce or industry, to any taxes, whether general or local, other than those which are or may be imposed upon citizens of the said republic.

Here, therefore, certain rights were guaranteed specifically to all white inhabitants-the rights of moving about as they wished, of possessing movable and fixed property, of trading and of equal taxation with the burghers. There is no question here of political rights and there was no question of those rights before this year 1899. The government of the South African Republic would thus be acting altogether within the limits of the convention if they informed Mr. Chamberlain that questions with regard to the franchise fell solely within their competence, it being a purely internal matter, and more over that by claiming the rights under this convention to force a franchise law upon the government, Mr. Chamberlain is the party guilty of breaking the convention.

The government of the South African Republic have, however taken up a much more exalted position. The President himself went to Bloemfontein to discuss even internal matters in a friendly spirit with the High Commissioner and among other things also the franchise, as his only desire was to maintain and promote the peace of South Africa and the welfare of its inhabitants.

Sir Alfred Milner had there said that' if that question could be settled on a satisfactory and permanent basis the tension would be lessened and everything would come right in time. Lately he has done his best to prove that he never said or meant such a thing, that the franchise law was only one of the burning internal questions in which Her Majesty's government was so deeply interested and that the favorable solution of the franchise difficulty by no means carried with it the agreement of the parties concerning the other points of difference. The attitude of Sir Alfred Milner on this and other points is of such a nature, however, that I would rather say nothing more about his conduct, but leave him to the judgment of public opinion and history.

As no agreement was possible between the parties President Kruger left Bloemfontein and improved the franchise law to such an extent that the Orange Free State, the Afrikanders of the Cape Colony and even Mr. Schreiner, premier of the Cape Colony, openly expressed their satisfaction with the improvements made.

Mr. Chamberlain, however, now began to write to the government of the South African Republic in a menacing tone and no longer in the friendly tone he had formerly used, and he finally proposed that a joint commission should inquire into the question and see whether the new law was satisfactory.

In the meantime informal conversations between the State Attorney of the South African Republic and the British agent had given rise to the prospect of a speedy and a satisfactory solution of the matter. Thereupon the British government was sounded by the British agent and said that, if the franchise was brought to five years without any complicated conditions, and if the gold fields could elect one-fourth of the members of the Volksraad, it was prepared to consider on their merits the conditions attached, namely, that the claim to the suzerainty should be dropped, that no future intervention would take place and that differences would be settled by arbitration.

When this proposal was formally made, however, the British government refused to accept the condition with regard to the dropping of the suzerainty claim. though the High Commissioner had already in a formal despatch declared that the suzerainty question appeared to him to be an etymological and not a political question. Soon afterwards the British government came forward with the same proposal, but with the omission of the condition concerning the dropping of the suzerainty claim. As the government of the South African Republic considered this condition of the greatest importance for the maintenance of its international status, it refused to accept the proposal in this form. It, however, accepted the invitation to the joint inquiry, but the British government replied that it was too late and that it now withdrew its invitation.

Here we thus see in its clearest light:

First. that. though the High Commissioner had said that the suzerainty was only of etymological importance, and though the British government has never been able to refute the arguments of the South African Republic concerning the dropping of the suzerainty in 1884, the British government is nevertheless unwilling to sacrifice its present claim thereto and is ready on that ground to begin a war in South Africa.

Second, that the British government invites the South African Republic to a joint inquiry, and when that invitation has been accepted without it having been withdrawn, that acceptance is declined with every mark of contempt.

Is there any example in the history of civilized diplomacy of such base deceit and hypocritical trifling with the most important interests of South Africa?

And is it to be wondered at that South Africa has lost faith in British statesmanship?

Truly, of all the disgraceful acts which have sullied the British name in this sub-continent I know none baser and more contemptible than this.

And the consequences of this deceit will be written with the blood and the tears of thousands of innocent persons.

I have now gone over the facts marking our oppression and persecution during this century. The statements made by me are not imaginary, but are taken from the mouth of the most credible historical witnesses, almost all of British nationality; they are facts which have been declared to be indisputable before the bar of history.

As regards the more recent events since 1898, I have been personally acquainted with all the negotiations and differences hereinbefore set forth, and can only affirm that I have confined myself to the facts, which will hereafter appear even more clearly when the curtain is raised, and the occurrences of the last two years in this deeply agitated subcontinent are revealed.

Hitherto our people have remained silent; the enemy has spat upon, slandered, beaten and treated us with every possible power of contempt and hatred. But with a dignity which reminds the world of a yet more tragic and exalted passion, our people have borne in silence the insults and contempt of the enemy, and under the sense of duty which inspired them have thought it better to remove the errors and abuses which had crept into our administration in moments of less thoughtfulness and care. Even this was accounted to us as weakness and fear. On hundreds of platforms in Great Britain, and by the most influential statesmen, our people have been called incompetent, uncivilized, dishonorable, faithless, corrupt, bloodthirsty, treacherous, etc., etc., until not only the British public, but almost the whole world, has begun to believe that we stand on a level with the wild beast.

Amid all this insult and contumely we have remained silent. From formal bluebooks of Her Majesty's government, from despatches of Her Majesty's High Commissioner in South Africa, we have had to learn that our unprincipled system of government and our unjust, chaotic and immoral administration have been a constantly festering sore by which, as by a contaminating pestilence, the moral and political atmosphere of South Africa has been poisoned.

In numberless newspapers we have been accused of every crime against civilization and humanity, and offenses are imputed to us the mere mention of which causes one's hair to stand on end. If the reading public believed only a hundredth part of all the atrocities of which our people and government are accused, then it must necessarily have been forced to the conclusion that this republic was a den of robbers and murderers, a people whose mere existence was a blot on humanity and a nuisance to mankind. To such a depth. according to these accounts, had the descendants of the moral aristocracy of Europe sunk!

Of the enormous sums which we are said to spend out of the secret service funds to secure for ourselves the support of the public opinion of the world, there was hardly any practical effect or trace; but the contumely raged on like an all devouring hurricane. But our people remained silent, partly from stolidity, partly from a feeling of hopeless [and] helplessness; partly because we as a simple agricultural people read no newspapers and were, therefore, not acquainted with the way in which the feeling of the whole world was being worked up against us with malicious fury. The practical effect was that our case went by default before the bar of public opinion.

Naboth's title deed to his vineyard had to be destroyed, and according to the hypocritical British diplomacy the shortest way to that end was to prove that he was a criminal and Ahab an angel.

End Second Interview

Bloemfontein Conference

Towards the end I would like to revisit the beginning of the end and look at the Bloemfontein Conference.[426]

Alfred Milner[427] was appointed as both Governor of the Cape Colony, and High Commissioner for Southern Africa in May of 1897.[428] His previous appointments, as under-secretary of finance in Egypt, and as chairman of the Board of Inland revenue, gave him an excellent background in finance but not necessarily in diplomacy. He was, by all accounts, competent, well liked, mannerly and intellectually gifted. He was not trained as a diplomat but he had spent several years in journalism, rising to the rank of assistant editor of the Pall Mall Gazette.

After more than a year of service in South Africa, Milner returned to England in November of 1898 for a working vacation and to have a private conversation with his superior, the Colonial Secretary, Joseph Chamberlain. Milner wanted to advocate for a more 'Forward Policy'[429] in South Africa similar to the one recently pursued by the government in the Kyber area of Afghanistan[430] as experienced and reported in the Malakand Field Force book penned by Winston Churchill. It should also be noted that the Battle of Omdurman

[426] Bloemfontein Conference - Wikipedia A very well written and scholarly article with an excellent timeline. And Mr. Cecil Headlam (19 September 1872–12 August 1934) was an English author and cricketer active in 1895–1908 Cecil Headlam - Wikipedia who compiled: The Milner papers / edited by Cecil Headlam. Publisher Cassell, London, 1931. The Milner papers / edited by Cecil Headlam - Catalogue | National Library of Australia https://catalogue.nla.gov.au/catalog/887984

[427] Alfred Milner, 1st Viscount Milner, (23 March 1854–13 May 1925) was a British statesman and colonial administrator. Subsequently, from December 1916 to November 1918, he was one of the most important members of Prime Minister David Lloyd George's War cabinet. Alfred Milner, 1st Viscount Milner - Wikipedia

[428] List of governors of British South African colonies - Wikipedia And: High Commissioner for Southern Africa - Wikipedia

[429] A forward policy is a set of foreign policy doctrines applicable to territorial ambitions and disputes in which emphasis is placed on securing control of targeted territories by invasion and annexation or by the political creation of compliant buffer states. Forward policy - Wikipedia

[430] Anglo-Afghan War - Wikipedia And: Mohmand campaign of 1897–1898 - Wikipedia

had taken place on September, 2nd 1898, effectively ending the Mahidist War in the Sudan, and with it, the last vestiges of the slave trade. This was a moral victory as well as a military one.[431]

Also of note is that the Fashoda Incident[432] resolved itself in Britain's favour, on November 3rd, 1898, only three weeks prior to Millner's meeting with Chamberlain. Britain forced France to climb down from what turned out to be a European 'war scare' while also evicting them from the Upper Nile Valley which the British had recently secured by their victory at the battle of Omdurman and their subsequent occupation of Khartoum.

This policy of intimidating other European powers to relinquish their claims in Africa was a repetition of the 1890 ultimatum to Portugal which dealt with their claims to the central portion of Southern Africa.

The British South Africa Co. and the 1890 Ultimatum

The 1890 British Ultimatum[433] was an ultimatum by the British government delivered on 11 January 1890 to the Kingdom of Portugal. Portugal had attempted to claim a large area of land between its colonies of Mozambique and Angola including most of present-day Zimbabwe and Zambia and a large part of Malawi, which had been included in Portugal's "Rose-coloured Map". The ultimatum led to the withdrawal of Portuguese forces from areas which had been claimed by Portugal on the basis of Portuguese exploration in the area, but which Britain claimed on the basis of uti possidetis. (possession by occupation)

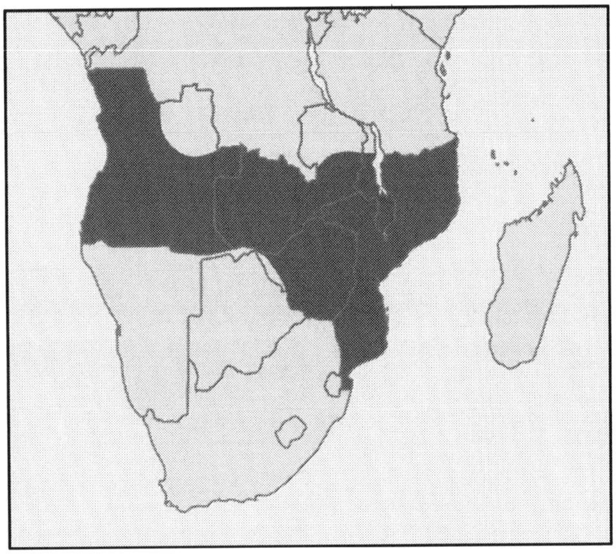

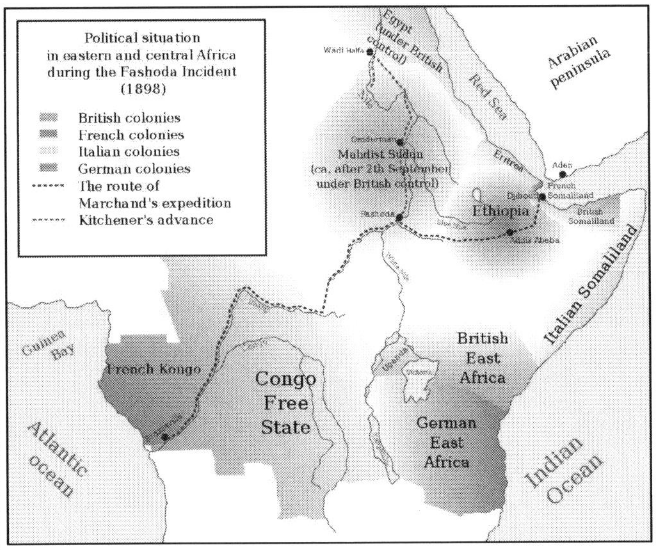

The Rose Colored Map of Portuguese claims in 1890.[69] Fashoda Incident Map taking place 10 years later. Fashoda is below the confluence of the Southerly White Nile with the North Branch of the Nile.[70]

It has sometimes been claimed that the British government's objections to the Portuguese claims arose because their claims clashed with its aspirations to create a Cape to Cairo Railway, linking its colonies from the south of Africa to those in the north. This seems unlikely, as in 1890 Germany already controlled German East Africa, now Tanzania, and Sudan was independent under Muhammad Ahmad.

[431] It is important to note that it was the British navy who established and maintained the blockade off the coast of Africa to prevent slave trafficking for 62 years from 1808 to 1870. The United States banned the importation of slaves beginning in 1807 but the U.S. Navy did not materially participate in the blockade until 1819 and the British formed the overwhelming majority of the ships employed previously and thereafter. It was slave transportation to America that provided the motivation for vessels to attempt running the blockade. The blockade represents a three generation effort by a country, at great expense, to eliminate a social evil. https://en.wikipedia.org/wiki/Blockade_of_Africa See Also: The Suppression of the Atlantic Slave Trade : British Policies, Practices and Representations of Naval Coercion ISBN: 071908511X ISBN13: 9780719085116 Robert Burroughs and Richard Huzzey And Royal Navy Versus the Slave Traders: Enforcing Abolition at Sea 1808-1898 ISBN-10: 1844156338 ISBN-13: 978-1844156337 by Bernard Edwards Also See: Drachinifel Channel: Anti-Slavery Patrols - The West Africa Squadron - YouTube

[432] The Fashoda Incident, also known as the Fashoda Crisis (French: Crise de Fachoda), was the climax of imperialist territorial disputes between Britain and France in East Africa, occurring between 10 July to 3 November 1898. A French expedition to Fashoda on the White Nile sought to gain control of the Upper Nile river basin and thereby exclude Britain from Sudan. The French party and a British-Egyptian force (outnumbering the French by 10 to 1) met on friendly terms. However, in Europe, it became a war scare. Both empires stood on the verge of war with heated rhetoric on both sides. Under heavy pressure, the French withdrew, ensuring Anglo-Egyptian control over the area. Fashoda Incident - Wikipedia

[433] 1890 British Ultimatum - Wikipedia

Rather, the British government was pressed into taking action by Cecil Rhodes, whose British South Africa Company[434] was founded in 1888 south of the Zambezi and the African Lakes Company and British missionaries to the and British missionaries to the north.

The British South Africa Company (BSAC) was chartered in 1889 following the amalgamation of Cecil Rhodes' Central Search Association and the London-based Exploring Company Ltd, which had originally competed to capitalize on the expected mineral wealth of Mashonaland but united because of common economic interests and to secure British government backing. The company received a Royal Charter modelled on that of the British East India Company. Its first directors included The 2nd Duke of Abercorn, Rhodes himself, and the South African financier Alfred Beit.

Rhodes hoped BSAC would promote colonisation and economic exploitation across much of south-central Africa, as part of the "Scramble for Africa". However, his main focus was south of the Zambezi, in Mashonaland and the coastal areas to its east, from which he believed the Portuguese could be removed by payment or force, and in the Transvaal, which he hoped would return to British control.

NO FIGHT.

FRENCH POODLE: "Well, if I can't have the bone I'll be satisfied if you'll give me one of the scraps."

French Poodle: "Well If I can't have the bone I'll be satisfied if you'll give me one of the scraps."

No Fight Cartoon by JM Staniforth: A French poodle begs for scraps from a British bulldog, who is guarding the bone named Fashoda in a bowl named Khartoum (26 October 1898).[71]

[434] British South Africa Company - Wikipedia

The Empire was consistent in its aims and policy. This Fashoda incident occurred just subsequent to Queen Victoria's Diamond Jubilee,[435] celebrating both the Queen and the Empire in a manner that reinforced the Empire's self conception as being entitled to its hegemony and a mandate to continue to do so on her behalf.

On November 22nd, 1898, Milner is able to meet with Joseph Chamberlain in order to put forward his case for 'working up to a crisis' in the Transvaal. It was clear from the recent Transvaal elections, which Paul Kruger had won overwhelmingly that the Transvaal Government would continue to arm itself with the best weapons that Germany and France could provide them and that the Transvaal Government had the resources to pay for them and more. Also that its race-oligarchy form of government would persist for the indefinite future, to the detriment of both the status of British emigrants, and other citizens of the Empire, particularly emigrants from India including Mohandas Gandhi who was then practicing law in both the Transvaal and Natal and vigorously advocating for their equal treatment out from under the same oppressive regime.

A timeline of Gandhi's activities shows that he would be doing his best to put forward the case for other subjects of Queen Victoria, who were entitled under the 1858 Proclamation to fair treatment throughout the Empire.[436]

11/3/1898 Cabled Colonial Secretary protesting against visitors' and embarkation fees imposed under Immigration Act.

12/31/1898 Drew up petition to Secretary of State for Colonies regarding Dealers' Licenses Act, 1897.

4/25/1899 Transvaal Government ordered Asiatics to remove to Locations before July 1.

5/17/1899 Gandhi addressed memorial to Chamberlain regarding Govt. steps to enforce Law 3 of 1885.

5/18/1899 Wrote to Colonial Secretary, Pietermaritzburg, pleading that Bill to amend Indian immigration law be modified in interests of indentured labour.

7/6/1899 Communicated to Colonial Secretary information about cases of hardship resulting from operation of Dealers' Licenses Act.

7/15/1899 Called on State Secretary and appealed for magnanimity towards Indians.

7/20/1899 Leads deputation to British Agent in Pretoria objecting to location laws.

7/31/1899 Petitions Natal Government for right of appeal to Supreme Court against arbitrary refusal of licenses to Indians by municipalities.

9/9/1899 Cabled Colonial Secretary for facilities to Indians to leave Transvaal, in view of imminent British-Boer hostilities.

While Gandhi would not have a seat at the table while Milner conversed with Chamberlain, he was doing his best to put the case forward for other subjects of the Queen to be treated equally to the fullest extent that the British Empire's writ would run.

[435] The Diamond Jubilee of Queen Victoria was officially celebrated on 22 June 1897 to mark the occasion of the 60th anniversary of Queen Victoria's accession. Diamond Jubilee of Queen Victoria - Wikipedia

[436] Chronology source(s) The Collected Work of Gandhi and https://www.sahistory.org.za/article/mohandas-karamchand-gandhi-mahatma-gandhi-timeline-1890-1899

Milner Interview with Chamberlain

Chamberlain listened to Milner's proposals and was reserved, cautious, even wary. The political and legal fallout from the Jameson Raid[437] only two years prior still had not settled. During that crisis, Chamberlain had only barely been able to cover up his complicity in the debacle with the thinnest veneer of plausible deniability. The was no possibility of any other adventure in freebooting.[438]

Even at this present summit of British hegemony in late 1898 he cautioned Milner that the most enduring way to achieve a union of South African states was without a war. Britain's overall policy going back thirty years was to duplicate the success of the Canadian Confederation of 1867.[439] Any armed conflict would make this goal harder, rather than easier. As far as he was concerned there would or could be no overt Government support for a forward policy, at the present time.

The only way that Chamberlain would countenance any change in his position would be if the Transvaal could be put in such a light that they were the aggressors. Milner took the hint.

One plausible reason for Britain to take up the cause of the Uitlander's in the Transvaal was that by allowing the Transvaal to deny political rights to emigrants and its subjects Britain would lose credibility with its colonists in Australia, India, Canada and Asia if it failed to protect them in South Africa.[440]

As we have seen, Milner did manage to 'work up a crisis' over the course of the next year, at first, in South Africa itself, and subsequently spilling over into British public opinion. In South Africa he did this with the help of local media like the Johannesburg Star,[441] and the Cape Times;[442] both of which were owned either by Cecil Rhodes or his affiliates these newspapers were able to portray the Uitlander situation as more onerous than it actually was.

The protection of capital, capitalists and their interests was also a factor. Virtually everybody with any money in Britain was investing in the gold and diamond mines of South Africa. It was the Internet Bubble or Tech Boom of its age. But it had gold and diamonds as it's work product. It had legs under it.

One of the earliest observers to note how this protectionism operated was J. A. Hobson.[443] He was an economist and journalist, who was in South Africa working for the Manchester Guardian in the months preceding the war's outbreak. As an eyewitness to events in South Africa, he argued that not only did the Uitlanders care little about the grievances that so aroused British national fury, but also that the most egregious offenses against them were largely apocryphal.[444] Hobson's central tenet was that British capitalism encouraged a misallocation of wealth that led investors to seek higher investment returns in developing foreign markets. Governments, seeking to protect their investors' commitments abroad, followed imperialist policies. Imperialism, argued Hobson, did not benefit the state as a whole but served the interests of financial strongmen.[445]

[437] The Jameson Raid ,(29 December 1895–2 January 1896) was a botched raid against the Transvaal carried out by British colonial administrator Leander Starr Jameson, under the employment of Cecil Rhodes. The raid was intended to trigger an uprising by the primarily British expatriate workers (known as Uitlanders) in the Transvaal but it failed. Jameson Raid - Wikipedia

[438] A filibuster, also known as a freebooter, is someone who engages in an unauthorized military expedition into a foreign country or territory to foster or support a political revolution or secession. Filibuster (military) - Wikipedia

[439] Canadian Confederation was the process by which three British North American provinces—the Province of Canada, Nova Scotia, and New Brunswick—were united into one federation, called the Dominion of Canada, Canadian Confederation - Wikipedia

[440] Arthur Keppel-Jones, South Africa: A Short History, 3rd revised edition. London: Hutchinson and Co., 1961. (pages 116–133).

[441] *The Star* newspaper appeared for the first time in Johannesburg as ***The Eastern Star***. It was founded in Grahamstown under that title on 6 January 1871 The Star (South Africa) - Wikipedia

[442] The Cape Times had its origins in the great economic and social boom years that followed the Cape's attainment of "Responsible Government" (local democracy) in 1872. It was the first daily paper in southern Africa, and soon became one of the principal newspapers of the Cape. Modelled on The Times, its primary target was the poor working class, as it attempted to expose early government corruption. Cape Times - Wikipedia

[443] John Atkinson Hobson (6 July 1858–1 April 1940) was an English economist and social scientist. Hobson is best known for his writing on imperialism, which influenced Vladimir Lenin, and his theory of under-consumption. J. A. Hobson - Wikipedia

[444] This and several subsequent quotes and citations are used by permission of Garrett B. Moritz, the author of "From the Jameson Raid to Bloemfontein: Debating the Origins of the Boer War."
https://web.archive.org/web/20061029192730/http:/www.gtexts.com/college/papers/s1.html Retrieved 1/22/25.

[445] Wolfgang J. Mommsen, Theories of Imperialism. Trans. P.S. Falla. Chicago: University of Chicago Press, 1982. (pages 11–15)

This quote which concludes his article nicely sums up his thesis.[446]

> Times change, men do not greatly change. The memorable saying of Sir Thomas More is still applicable in our day: "Everywhere do I perceive a certain conspiracy of rich men seeking their private advantage under the name and pretext of the Commonweal."

Hobson was struck by the ease with which a small group of raffish financiers could manipulate public opinion. The way in which a handful of Rand millionaires inspired jingoistic patriotism through a small but strategic press monopoly was further evidence for his thesis that the Boer War—and by association imperialism in general was instigated by a few powerful capitalists.[447]

As Paul Kruger had predicted upon the discovery of the Witwatersrand gold field in the Transvaal.

> "Instead of rejoicing you would do better to weep, for this gold will cause our country to be soaked in blood."[448]

Returning to the conference proceedings themselves. It was organized by Orange Free State president Martinus Theunis Steyn, to take place in Bloemfontein, and by late May of 1899 was considered a last effort at reconciliation to prevent war.

General view of Bloemfontein.[72]

By this time, the British had already begun to militarily reinforce both Natal and the Cape Colony. The British had no other significant conflicts that were taking up resources or the attention of the Empire as a whole. The Boxer Rebellion would not seriously disturb the Empire until a little bit later in 1899, if at all.

It was during this lull that Milner was able to get his foot in the door for and pitch his forward policy; and a less than optimal time for the Republics to resort to military conflict with the British.

On May 9th, 1899 the British Cabinet met to decide whether to commit themselves to intervention. As a result, Chamberlain telegraphed Milner; "The despatch, is approved, we have adopted your suggestion."[449] Per Milner's despatch he had advocated a 'franchise first' negotiating position.[450]

Milner had asked for this and the Cabinet had allowed him to do proceed with it. It was not that Chamberlain had told him to do so. However he was authorized by the Cabinet, including Chamberlain to place three demands on the agenda for the conference.

1: Enfranchisement [voting rights for Uitlanders], 2: language [English as well as Dutch], and 3: suzerainty [Some 'control' of foreign policy.]

The formula to be proposed was to place upon the table a demand that for a five year retrospective franchise (five years of residency to be eligible to vote), the placement of at least 7 members of the Rand [District] into

446 J. A. Hobson, The War in South Africa, Its Causes and Effects, 2nd ed. London: James Nisbet and Co., 1900.

447 J.A. Hobson, The Psychology of Jingoism. London: G. Richards, 1901. (pages 25–27)

448 Byron Farwell, The Great Anglo-Boer War. New York: Harper & Row, 1976. (page 21).

449 Pakenham, pages 59 and 60.

450 Pakenham page 58.

the Volksraad, and if Kruger refused, to try granting municipal government enfranchisement to English residents and control of the police.

It is generally agreed by historians that Milner's brief ran to the extent that if agreement couldn't be reached on the franchise, there was no need or obligation to discuss other issues.[451]

Milner had placed himself in this limited negotiating position to both his and Britain's detriment. On Milner's part he was not likely to climb down from it. It was a flawed strategy from the start. He had proposed it, the Cabinet had approved it, who was really to blame when he followed through with it?

Subsequent to the Cabinet's approval of intervention, Chamberlain was concerned that the British newspapers and the public in general were not paying attention to the situation in South Africa.[452] Chamberlain himself requested that Milner produce a despatch for publication in Chamberlain's upcoming Blue Book.[453]

Milner, putting his acquired journalism skills from the Pall Mall Gazette to good use wrote his famous Helot's Despatch which is reproduced infra. It was dated May 4th, and certainly was reviewed by the Chamberlain and the Colonial Office, but the Blue Book itself would not be published prior to the start of the Bloemfontein conference, which is one reason that Milner thought the conference was premature. Much of the despatch is related to putting 'franchise first' before the British public and having been asked to do some advocacy on behalf of policy it set the policy, for Milner, if not in concrete at least in hard mud, which further limited Milner's ability to be objective. He was rolling the dice on his career; as he said to Selborne the under secretary, while asking for more material/military support in order to threaten Kruger and the Transvaal. "...I myself am risking a lot, - indeed everything.?"[454]

Both parties were risking all on this conflict; Jan Smuts wrote a secret memorandum for the Transvaal Executive on September 4th, 1899 that said in part:

> 'South Africa stands on the eve of a frightful blood-bath out of which our volk shall come.....either as...... hewers of wood and drawers of water for a hated race, or as victors, founders of a United South Africa, one of the great empires [rifken] of the world......an Afrikaner republic in South Africa stretching from Table Bay to the Zambezi' [river][455] [456]

So, when Jan Hofmeyr[457] proposed the conference between Milner and Paul Kruger, that Milner not overly enthusiastic to participate because he did not think he had enough leverage yet. The 'crisis' had not adequately been 'worked up.'

On May 17th, Milner writes to under-secretary Selborne: 'Kruger is not capable of negotiating, so the upcoming meeting will likely fail.' In Chamberlain's view the British had suzerainty over Transvaal since 1881.[458]

Another means of keeping the issue of Uitlander representation in front of the public and the nation was by the use of petitions addressed to Queen Victoria, asking for her assistance in addressing their grievances. This was a recognized means of pleading cases for redress and was used extensively by ethnic and religious groups most notably by Gandhi in support of South African residents of Indian extraction.[459]

[451] J. Lee Thompson (2007). Forgotten patriot. Fairleigh Dickinson Univ Press. ISBN 978-0-8386-4121-7. pgs. 132–133.

[452] Pakenham page 59.

[453] The British Blue Book has the oldest history, going back at least as far as 1633. It was used in England as a means of publishing diplomatic correspondence and reports. Color book - Wikipedia And: United Kingdom National Accounts–The Blue Book - Wikipedia

[454] Pakenham p. 58 citing Selborne 17 May 99, MP I 384-5e.

[455] Pakenham, Introduction to Chapter 9 'The Ultimatum' p. 100.

[456] As mentioned above in the Webster Davis section, despite the trouble, treasure and blood caused, spent and shed during the conflict it helped ensure Britain and its allies' ability to secure lines of commerce and communication with India, Australia and the rest of the Far East during both the first and second world wars.

[457] Jan Hendrik Hofmeyr (Onze Jan) - Wikipedia

[458] Headlam, pgs. 384-385, 389-390 letters to Selborne & Chamberlain.

[459] Repeated Uitlander Petitions to the Queen, See the efforts of James Percy FitzPatrick James Percy FitzPatrick - Wikipedia [Pakenham, pages 54-55 56-57] and appendix F of his work. Anglo Boer War - Fitzpatrick: Appendix F The Great Franchise Debate And his book: Anglo Boer War - Fitzpatrick: The Transvaal from within Report of the great Franchise Debate, published in the Johannesburg Star, August 17, 1895: Extension Of The Franchise.—**Monster Uitlander Petitions**.—What The Burghers Wish.
For the text of the petition see Times History Vol. I pages 225–232.

Unlike so many administrators and military commanders in South Africa,[460] Milner was not exceeding his authority by adopting his uncompromising negotiating position which would precipitate Britain going to war. It was his show. Yet, like previous efforts of political amalgamation and consolidation in South Africa it would become a very deadly and expensive undertaking.

The conference took place in the railway station in Bloemfontein from May 31st, to June 5th, 1899.

The railway station at Bloemfontein.[73] Cartoon: Chamberlain, on the viewer right side: "I feel I am getting the best of it; in only needs time, and I shall throw him easily."[461] Kruger is shown putting his foot on the neck of a defeated Uitlander.

31 May 99 (2:30 to 4:30 pm): "Rather discursive, and we did not get very far."[462] (on the franchise question, Kruger said it would be worse than annexation and the "freedom of the Republic would not exist any longer").[463] The tone was friendly.

In the evening there was a huge reception at President Steyn's. Kruger was present for a little..." "The President rambles fearfully."

1 June 99: Morning: Kruger asked about threatening movements of soldiers near his border, which Milner denied. Milner countered by asking about the transfer of Transvaal (Afrikaner) troops near Natal, and recent purchases of heavy weapons. Kruger replied that the weapons were defensive, for protection against enemies or wild animals. Also, he stressed that the Boers were never an attacking force, and that "as long as your Excellency lives you will see that we shall never be the attacking party on another man's land".

Milner then brought the discussion back to the franchise. Afternoon: Kruger asked for time to consider Milner's proposals. He then talked about the Dynamite Monopoly (the Boers had a monopoly on dynamite). When asked to put his suggestions for reform in writing, Kruger said that would encroach upon his country's independence.

Milner then asked Kruger to prepare a counterproposal on the franchise question, which he agreed to do. Kruger then asked about various other issues (the annexation of Zambaansland and Swaziland,[464] Jameson Raid reparations, and arbitration), to which Milner said he would receive a reply.

[460] One example: Henry Bartle Frere - Wikipedia As High Commissioner for Southern Africa (1877–1880), he implemented a set of policies which attempted to impose a British confederation on the region and which led to the overthrow of the Cape Colony's first elected government in 1878 and to a string of regional wars, culminating in the invasion of Zululand (1879) and the First Boer War (1880–1881). The British Prime Minister, Gladstone, recalled Frere to London to face charges of misconduct; Whitehall officially censured Frere for acting recklessly.

[461] 'Breathing Time' – JM Staniforth political cartoon in which Joseph Chamberlain (right) complains of being unable to move Paul Kruger (State president of Transvaal) from the 'uitlander' (foreigners). Alfred Milner, then High Commissioner of Southern Africa, lays exhausted and prone to the left. 29 June 1899. File:Breathing Time - JM Staniforth.png - Wikimedia Commons

[462] For material in this chronology see: Headlam, Cecil, "The Milner Papers, Vol. I", pg. 405-406 And Bloemfontein Conference - Wikipedia

[463] Thompson, J. Lee, "Forgotten Patriot," pgs. 135–139.

[464] Eswatini - Wikipedia

2 June: Morning: Kruger asked Milner to agree to a plan for international arbitration before he settled the franchise question, because he needed something to take back to his countrymen first. Milner replied that foreign interference would not be allowed, but some other form of impartial tribunal might be found.

Milner then answered questions raised by Kruger at the end of the previous day regarding arbitration but nothing new was found. After a recess, Milner brought the topic back to the franchise, and asked for a serious discussion. He said he came "at a time of crisis in order to see if one big straightforward effort might not be made to avert a great disaster," and if they could not agree to discuss the matter on its merits, "everything else was a waste of time."

One of Milner's aides reported to his mother, "Paul Kruger wept this morning."[465] Afternoon: Kruger surprised Milner with a "complete Reform Bill worked out in clauses and subclasses" for a 7 year franchise to the Uitlanders (his previous stand was 14 years). However, it was non-retrospective[466] and loaded with qualifiers. Kruger also added two conditions: Britain's acceptance of international arbitration for future disputes, and the Transvaal's annexation of Swaziland. Milner asked for time to consider it all.

3 June: "Meeting this morning, at which time I read a memo, explaining why I could not accept President's counter proposal. We adjourned after short discussion. We were to have met again in the afternoon, but soon after lunch I received a message asking that the meeting might be put off until 9:30 am on Monday, to which I agreed..."

The plan lacked an allowance for Volksraad seats, the franchise was prospective only, and most Uitlanders would have to forfeit their British citizenship five years before they received new citizenship.

Also, Milner did not want to give in on arbitration. In his response, which took him most of the night to draft, Milner said the plan, while "a great advance", was so inadequate it would be a waste of time to consider its details.

In reply, Kruger said he meant to ask the Volksraad to create 4 or 5 new electoral divisions, but he couldn't let his people to be swamped with strangers.

4 June 99: Sunday (day off). Milner telegraphed Joseph Chamberlain and said the "Conference seems likely to fail".

Milner later confessed to Chamberlain "If we went on and no, we might get a little more and a little more, each concession being made to appear very big, and finally feel unable, after so many concessions, to break off, and yet find we had a perfectly hollow scheme."[467]

The cabled warning that Milner might have to break off negotiations did not reach Chamberlain until late on Sunday the 4th. Chamberlain immediately replied: "I hope you will not break off hastily. Boers do not understand quick decisions.......... I am by no means convinced that eh President has made his last offer, and you should be very patient and admit a good deal of haggling before you finally abandon the game."[468]

By the time the cable arrived, it was too late. The conference was over. Had he received the message earlier, Milner said the talks would have continued.[469]

5 June 99: "Close of Conference, of course result-less. We met at 11:30 when I put in [a] stiff memorandum, knocking about President's scheme. We adjourned for lunch. At 3 we met again. He adhered to his scheme and we parted at 4:30. .... Wild rush to send off telegrams..."

Kruger would not go further without concessions, and said he was "not ready to hand over his country to strangers." He stood with eyes watering and repeated: "It is our country you want."[470]

Milner closed his remarks by stating, chillingly, "This conference is absolutely at an end, and there is no obligation on either side arising from it."[471]

[465] Thompson, pg. 137.

[466] Non-retroactivity is the legal principle that laws do not apply retroactively. It means that laws or decisions cannot be applied to events that took place before the law was introduced.

[467] M-C 4 June 1899 CO 417/262.

[468] Pakenham p. 68 and C-M 5 June 1899, CO 417/262 (AF South 572-83-4).

[469] Thompson, pg. 138.

[470] Pakenham p. 68.

Milner's assessment was that the conference had been premature and that Kruger had not been scared enough. Milner's policy was to continue to turn the 'war screw' and force a climb down by Kruger. This was a fantasy if Kruger was negotiating from his capital, Pretoria. The only way any progress would be made if Kruger 'went to the mountain' like Anwar Sadat and Menachem Begin did when they accomplished the Camp David Accords in 1978.[472]

We will see in the following chronology that Kruger did continue to compromise of the voting rights issue when he was motivated by the seriousness of the British pursuit of their goals.

What we can also see from the above conference summary is that Milner had a point. Kruger bringing up, annexing Swaziland, Jameson Reparations, Arbitration, these were tertiary issues. Kruger was not negotiating in good faith by not focusing on the main topic that had brought them together, the Uitlander franchise situation and Taxation without representation. The non-retroactive 7 year residency and requiring surrender of British citizenship five years prior would mean that those seeking citizenship would be essentially stateless persons for those five years. A ludicrous proposition.

What could Kruger have done if he was serious about resolving the issues after the 'end' end of the conference. First, he could have gone over Milner's head to Chamberlain. He could have refused to end the conference, stayed in Bloemfontein and gone public with his offers to try and keep up pressure on the British.[473]

In hindsight a productive strategy might have been to take the gun out of Milner's hand by agreeing to his demands sufficiently to resolve the crisis and then dawdle, equivocate and finagle the outcomes over the next several years. Lull the British to sleep and come back at another time when the British were occupied elsewhere and revise or constrict the franchise. Maintaining a veneer of independence now and then ignoring, delaying or equivocating on the results in the succeeding years was one workable strategy.

Kruger also bears responsibility. Yes, he had won his recent election by a landslide but he only represented one party in the election and his nation.[474] Kruger's more conservative coalition had been raised, informed and battle tested on the thesis that they were the new Israelites, whose promised land was theirs for the taking, and that this gave them divine rights to subjugate any of the peoples they could conquer or 'annex'.

By the time the sabre rattling was done, the British had committed so many resources to South Africa that they were bound to use them. The Boers new that a defensive attack was their only hope to defeat the local British forces before more reinforcements arrived.

[471] Pakenham p. 68 and C 9404/44 PF: It seems both parties had reached the end of their ability to mediate their differences. Kruger walks away with nothing to show for the effort and Milner's hand is strengthened. There is a school of thought that Milner broke off negotiations precisely because he thought Kruger would give sufficient ground for a deal to be made. Milner was after big game, a confederation. He was in pursuit of a career 'victory' at the cost of so much suffering on both sides.

[472] The Camp David Accords were a pair of political agreements signed by Egyptian president Anwar Sadat and Israeli prime minister Menachem Begin on 17 September 1978, following twelve days of secret negotiations at Camp David, supported by US President Jimmy Carter. Camp David Accords - Wikipedia

[473] Gandhi would have stayed and gone on a hunger strike. Not a likely course of action for Kruger and Smuts.

[474] The Progressive party among the Boers, led by General Joubert, strongly espoused the cause of the Uitlanders. This party, among whose most prominent members were Mr. Ewald Esselen, who had been secretary to the 1883 delegates and a Judge of the High Court, and Mr. Eugene Marais, editor of the Progressive newspaper 'Land en Volk,' objected almost as strongly as the Uitlanders themselves to the manner in which they saw the public offices invaded by shoals of needy and unscrupulous Hollanders and the spirit of their local institutions perverted by foreign influence. Dr. Leyds especially, whom the Progressives credited with being the moving spirit in all the principal swindles and whom the President insisted on appointing to the important post of State Secretary in the spring of 1889, was the special object of their aversion. Times History Page 132.

Chronology

Returning to the Chronology leading up to the outbreak of hostilities.[475] This is a second look at the sequence of events that supplements the Brown and Guyot Summary that was set out supra. It is not as granular as that summary but it gives an another perspective with very authoritative citations. Dates with asterisks are not definite.

6 June 1899: From Chamberlain: "The new situation which the failure of the Conference has created will be carefully considered by the Government as soon as they receive your full despatches. Further instructions will then be given to you." Milner replied, "I think ultimatum now would be premature..."[476]

9 June: Francis Reitz approaches the British and proposes a treaty of arbitration, whose president would be neither Transvaal or British.[477]

15 June: Judicial Crisis in South African Republic.[478] Annexation of Zululand to Natal.

16 June: Milner calls for large increase in Natal.[479]

18 July: Kruger offers seven-year enfranchisement, completely retroactive. This franchise law is passed in the Transvaal on 20 July, but doesn't take effect until five years' time, in 1904.[480]

28 July: In Parliamentary debate in London, it was decided that a conciliatory message be sent to President Kruger.[481]

28 July: The British propose that a joint inquiry be held, by the Boer and British, to examine President Kruger's proposals.[482]

*1 Aug: Milner invites the Transvaal to appoint delegates to discuss the offer.[483]

3 Aug.: Chamberlain wires Milner that HMG has decided to reinforce Natal with 2,000 troops.[484]

12 Aug.: A 7 year franchise law is offered by Transvaal Attorney General Jan Smuts to Conyngham Greene, head of the British diplomatic mission in the Transvaal. The franchise was further reduced to 5 years, suzerainty would be tacitly dropped, and international arbitration would commence as soon as the franchise becomes law. The deal was forwarded to Milner on 14 August.[485]

15 Aug.: A 5-year franchise is offered. Milner telegraphed Chamberlain to be careful of the new talks, as negotiations must be direct.

16 Aug.: Chamberlain replied that the government was bound to look into it, for if the offer was genuine, it could be the way out.[486]

*17 Aug.: Milner invites the Transvaal to appoint delegates to discuss the new offer.[487]

*21 Aug.: An end to suzerainty and end to internal affairs is demanded by Kruger.[488]

*24 Aug.: Smuts's proposals were flatly refused by President Kruger.[489]

26 Aug.: Chamberlain's speech at a Garden party shows his turn of mind.[490] Chamberlain, learning that Smut's proposals were refused by Kruger, criticizes Kruger by saying, "he dribbles out reforms like water from a

475 Not all citations have been checked. Dates prefaced with an asterisk are difficult to verify.

476 Headlam, pg. 41.

477 "The Times, History of the War", pg. 303.

478 PF: Not able to identify this event with particularity. See other court cases and judicial v. legislative conflicts infra.

479 Headlam, pg. 512.

480 Headlam, pg. 468 and Worsfold, William Basil, "Lord Milner's Work in South Africa", footnote 107.

481 "The Times", pg. 308.

482 "The Times", pgs. 308–309.

483 (WTS, pg. 76.)

484 Headlam, pg. 512.

485 Headlam, pgs. 487–488 Levi, N, Jan Smuts, being a character sketch..., London: Longmans, 1917 Levi, pgs. 43–45.

486 (WTS, pg 76; TC, pg 90.)

487 (WTS, pg. 77.)

488 (TC, pg. 91.)

489 "The Times." pg. 331.

490 TC, pg. 92 (Highbury speech).

squeezed sponge", while "the sands are running down in the glass", and a "knot must be loosened...or we shall have to find other ways of untying it".[491]

28 Aug.: Chamberlain asks for a new peace conference in Cape Town based on Smut's proposals, to avoid the suzerainty matter, and arbitration that excludes foreigners.[492]

*2 Sep.: Transvaal assumes negotiations regarding 7-year offer is still on and asks for proposals regarding time and place, assuming 'that it is not intended to interfere in internal affairs'.[493]

*8 Sep.: British Cabinet decides to send 10,000 troops to Natal including the 2000 sent in Aug.[494] The Cabinet is persuaded that in the face of such force, Kruger will back down and not fight. The reinforcements will include 5,500 from India.

*8 Sep.: Chamberlain informs Boers that Britain cannot now go back to his own proposals of 17 Aug that 'were a substitute and demands withdrawal of conditions.'[495]

8 Sep, Chamberlain makes a final appeal to the Boers, asking for a deal based on Smuts's terms.[496]

16 Sep.: Transvaal, via Reitz asks Britain to abide by its own proposal and 'cannot understand...'[497]

16 Sep. Transvaal said it could no longer "comply with the far-reaching and insolent demands of the British Government".[498]

*16 Sep.: Generals White and Cols Hamilton and Rawlinson sail from UK for Durban via Cape Town to take command of the larger force in Natal.

*17 Sep.: Troops in India embark for Natal.

*17 Sep.: Transvaal Executive rejects British demands.[499]

*28 Sep.: Transvaal forces mobilized.

*7 Oct.: Orange Free State forces mobilized.

*7 Oct.: General George White lands at Durban and takes command of forces in Natal. Reinforcements disembark over next 2 days.

9 Oct.: Ultimatum delivered by Reitz to Conningham-Greene the British representative in Pretoria. Britain decides to send the Army Corps of 50,000 men under Sir. General Buller.

11 Oct.: Boer Ultimatum time-limit expired. Great Britain commenced to be at war with Transvaal and Orange Free State.

12 Oct.: Text of Great Britain's reply to Boer Ultimatum issued. It stated that the conditions demanded were such as her Majesty's Government deemed it impossible to discuss.

12 Oct.: The Battle of Kraaipan, begun on the night of the 11th, ends with surrender of the British manning the train.

> After the Potchefstroom and Lichtenburg commandos under General Koos de la Rey (one of General Piet Cronjé's field generals) attacked and captured the British garrison and railway siding at Kraaipan between Vryburg and Mafeking, some 60 kilometres (37 mi) south west of Mafeking. The armoured train, "Mosquito", carrying two 7-pounder cannons, rifles, ammunition and supplies was derailed and after a five-hour fight the British surrendered the next morning. The cannons, rifles, ammunition, supplies and prisoners were taken.[500]

[491] "The Times", pgs. 333–334.
[492] "The Times", pgs. 334–335.
[493] WTS p. 77.
[494] Pg. 96.
[495] WTS pg.78.
[496] Headlam, pgs. 533–534.
[497] WTS pg.78.
[498] Headlam, pg. 537.
[499] TC pg.77.
[500] Battle of Kraaipan - Wikipedia And: Crow Pan - Wikipedia

Helot's Despatch May 4th, 1899

Milner wrote this almost a month before the Bloemfontein Conference. It shows his state of mind and that he had fully bought in to the Uitlander cause and by implication the Queen's 1858 Proclamation to the limit of how far Britain could enforce its hegemony. As mentioned above it was not published in the Blue Book until after the conclusion of the conference.

Telegram from Sir A. Milner to Mr. Chamberlain.[501] [502]

4th May, [1899]. Having regard to critical character of South African situation and likelihood of early reply by Her Majesty's Government to Petition, I am telegraphing remarks which under ordinary circumstances I should have made by despatch. Events of importance have followed so fast on each other since my return to South Africa, and my time has been so fully occupied in dealing with each incident severally, that I have had no opportunity for reviewing the whole position.

The present crisis undoubtedly arises out of the Edgar incident.[503] But that incident merely precipitated a struggle which was certain to come. It is possible to make too much of the killing of Edgar. It was a shocking and, in my judgment, a criminal blunder, such as would have excited a popular outcry anywhere. It was made much worse by the light way in which it was first dealt with by the Public Prosecutor, and by the attitude of the Judge at the trial.

By itself, however, it would not have justified, nor, in fact, provoked the present storm. But it happened to touch a particularly sore place. There is no grievance which rankles more in the breasts of the mass of the Uitlander population than the conduct of the police, who, while they have proved singularly incompetent to deal with gross scandals like the illicit liquor trade, are harsh and arbitrary in their treatment of individuals whom they happen to dislike, as must have become evident to you from the recurrent ill-treatment of coloured people.

There are absolutely no grounds for supposing that the excitement which death of Edgar caused was factitious. It has been laid to the door of the South African League, but the officials of the League were forced into action by Edgar's fellow workmen. And, the consideration of grievances once started by the police grievance, it was inevitable that the smoldering but profound discontent of the population who constantly find their affairs mismanaged, their protests disregarded, and their attitude misunderstood, by a Government on which they have absolutely no means of exercising any influence, should once more break into flame.

We have, therefore, simply to deal with a popular movement of a similar kind to that of 1894 and 1895 before it was perverted and ruined by a conspiracy of which the great body of the Uitlanders were totally innocent. None of the grievances then complained of, and which then excited universal sympathy, have been remedied, and others have been added. The case is much stronger than it was. It is impossible to overlook the tremendous change for the worse which has been effected by the lowering of the status of the High Court of Judicature and by the establishment of the principle embodied in the new draft Grondwet[504] that any resolution of the Volksraad is equivalent to a law.

The instability of the laws has always been one of the most serious grievances. The new Constitution provides for the permanent instability of everything, the Judges being bound by their oath to accept every Volksraad Resolution as equally binding with a law passed in the regular form and with the provisions of the Constitution itself. The law prescribing this oath is one of which the present Chief Justice said that no self-respecting man could sit on the Bench while it was on the Statute Book.

Formerly the foreign population, however bitterly they might resent the action of the Legislature and of the Administration, had yet some confidence in the High Court of Judicature. It cannot be expected that they should feel the same confidence to-day. Seeing no hope in any other quarter, a number of Uitlanders who happen to be British subjects have addressed a Petition to Her Majesty the Queen.

[501] Compiler: Cecil Headlam (died in 1934)"The Milner Papers", Vol. I, Cassell & Co.: London, 1931 Pages 349–353. Milner's "Helot dispatch" to Secretary Joseph Chamberlain in 1899.

[502] Original footnote: This telegram was published ,as sent in C. 9345 No. 78 with the exception of a few verbal alterations made in a subsequent telegram and the paragraph here inserted in brackets.

[503] Edgar was a suspect in a murder and was shot and killed by the Transvaal police when he resisted arrest.

[504] Compound of grond ("ground, base") + wet ("law"). [government, law, constitution]

I have already expressed my opinion of its substantial genuineness and the absolute bona fides of its promoters. But the Petition is only one proof among many of the profound discontent of the un-enfranchised population, who are a great majority of the white inhabitants of the State.

The public meeting of 14th January was indeed broken up by workmen, many of them poor burghers, in the employment of the Government and instigated by Government officials, and it is impossible at present to hold another meeting of a great size. Open air meetings are prohibited by law, and by one means or another all large public buildings have been rendered unavailable. But smaller meetings are being held almost nightly along the Rand and are unanimous in their demand for enfranchisement. The movement is steadily growing in force and extent.

With regard to the attempts to represent that movement as artificial, the work of scheming capitalists or professional agitators, I regard it as a willful perversion of the truth. The defenceless people who are clamouring for a redress of grievances are doing so at great personal risk. It is notorious that many capitalists regard political agitation with disfavour because of its effect on markets. It is equally notorious that the lowest class of Uitlanders, and especially the illicit liquor dealers, have no sympathy whatever with the cause of reform. Moreover, there are in all classes a considerable number who only want to make money and clear out, and who, while possibly sympathizing with reform, feel no great interest in a matter which may only concern them temporarily.

But in very large and constantly increasing proportion of tile Uitlanders are not birds of passage; they contemplate a long residence in the country or to make it their permanent home. These people are the mainstay of the reform movement as they are of the prosperity of the country. They would make excellent citizens if they had the chance.

A busy industrial community is not naturally prone to political unrest. Hut they bear the chief burden of taxation; they constantly feel in their business and daily lives the effects of chaotic legislation and of incompetent and unsympathetic administration; they have many grievances, but they believe all this could be gradually removed if they had only a fair share of political power.

This is the meaning of their vehement demand for enfranchisement. Moreover, they are mostly British subjects, accustomed to a free system and equal rights; they feel deeply the personal indignity involved in position of permanent subjection to the ruling caste which owes its wealth and power to their exertion. The political turmoil in the Transvaal Republic will never end till the permanent Uitlander population is admitted to a share in the Government, and while that turmoil lasts there will be no tranquility or adequate progress in Her Majesty's South African dominions.

The relations between the British Colonies and the two Republics are intimate to a degree which one must live in South Africa in order fully to realize. Socially, economically, ethnologically, they are all one country, the two principal white races are everywhere inextricably mixed up; it is absurd for either to dream of subjugating the other. The only condition on which they can live in harmony and the country progress is equality all round.

South Africa can prosper under two, three, or six Governments, though the fewer the better, but not under two absolutely conflicting social and political systems, perfect equality for Dutch and British in the British Colonies side by side with permanent subjection of British to Dutch in one of the Republics. It is idle to talk of peace and unity under such a state of affairs.

It is this which makes the internal condition of Transvaal Republic a matter of vital interest to Her Majesty's Government No merely local question affects so deeply the welfare and peace her own South African possessions. And the right of Great Britain to intervene to secure fair treatment of the Uitlanders is fully equal to her supreme interest in securing it.

The majority of them are her subjects, whom she is bound to protect. But the enormous number of British subjects, the endless series of their grievances, and the nature of those grievances, which are not less serious because they are not individually sensational, makes protection by the ordinary diplomatic means impossible.

We are, as you know forever remonstrating about this, that, and the other injury to British subjects. Only in rare cases and only when we are very emphatic do we obtain any redress. The sore between us and the Transvaal Republic is thus inevitably kept up while the result in the way of protection to our subjects is lamentably small.

For these reasons it has been, as you know, my constant endeavour to reduce the number of our complaints. I may sometimes have abstained when I ought to have protested from my great dislike of ineffectual nagging. But

I feel that the attempt to remedy thee hundred and one wrongs springing from a hopeless system by taking up isolated cases is perfectly vain. It may easily lead to war, but will never lead to real improvement.

The true remedy is to strike at the root or all these Injuries, the political impotence of the injured. What diplomatic protests will never accomplish, a fair measure of Uitlander representation will gradually but surely bring about.

It seems a paradox but It is true that the only effective way of protecting our subjects is to help them to cease to be our subjects. The admission of Uitlanders to a fair share of political power would no doubt give stability to the Republic. But it would at the same time remove most of. our causes of difference with it, and modify and In the long run entirely remove the intense suspicion and bitter hostility to Great. Britain which at present dominates its internal and external policy.

The case for intervention is overwhelming. The only attempted answer is that things will right themselves if let alone. But, in fact, the policy of leaving things alone has been tried for years, and it has led to their going from bad to worse. It is not true that this is owing to the Raid. They were going from bad to worse before the Raid. We were on the verge of war before the Raid, and the Transvaal was on the verge of revolution. The effect of the raid has been to give the policy of leaving things alone a new lease of life and with the old consequences.

> [There is no doubt one thing which thrives mightily under that policy, I mean the military strength of the Transvaal. It has increased greatly since the Raid, and is still increasing. This is so far the one substantial result of trusting to time and patience. It may seem absurd that a State of 20,000 citizens which owes whatever measure of independence It possesses to the generosity of the British Government, and which is supported by the industry of a much larger alien population, mostly British subjects, should be a danger to a Power like Great Britain, and it is perfectly true that the Transvaal is not likely to invade British territories. Specious encroachments may be attempted from time to time; one of these is at present before you. But a deliberate invasion is most improbable. There are subtler and safer means of aggression.]

The spectacle of thousands of British subjects kept permanently in the position of helots, constantly chafing under undoubted grievances, and calling vainly to Her Majesty's Government for redress, does steadily undermine the influence and reputation of Great Britain and the respect for the British Government within its own dominions. A certain section of the press, and not in the Transvaal only, preaches openly and constantly the doctrine of a Republic embracing all South Africa, and supports it by menacing references to the armaments of the Transvaal, its alliance with the Orange Free State, and the active sympathy which in case of war it would receive from a section of Her Majesty's subjects.

I regret to say that this doctrine, supported as it is by a ceaseless stream of malignant lies about the intentions of the British Government, is producing a great effect upon a large number of our Dutch fellow colonists. Language is frequently used which seems to imply that the Dutch have some superior right even in this is [Cape] colony to their fellow-citizens of British birth. Thousands of men peaceably disposed, and, if left alone, perfectly satisfied with their position as British subjects, are being drawn into disaffection, and there is a corresponding exasperation on the side of the British.

I can see nothing which will put a stop to this mischievous propaganda but some striking proof of the intention, if it is the intention, of Her Majesty's Government not to be ousted from its position in South Africa. And the best proof alike of its power and its justice would be to obtain for the Uitlanders in the Transvaal a fair share in the Government of the country which owes everything to their exertions.

It could be made perfectly clear that our action was not directed against the existence of the Republic. We should only be demanding the re-establishment of rights which now exist in the Orange Free State, and which existed in the Transvaal itself at the time of and long after the withdrawal of British sovereignty. It would be no selfish demand, as other Uitlanders besides those of British birth would benefit by it. It is asking for nothing from others which we do not give ourselves. And it would certainly go to the root of the political unrest in South Africa, and, though temporarily it might aggravate, it would ultimately extinguish the race feud which is the great bane of the country.[505]

[505] Images of the despatch. Pages 340–350. [505] Pages 351–352.[505] Page 353.[505]

Judicial Conflicts and Crises

This material has primarily been condensed and paraphrased from the Times History of the War Vol. 1 edited by Leo Amery.[506] He is the older student that Churchill once pushed into the pool at public school. He also became a reporter during the Boer War and was in Estcourt with Churchill in November of 1899. He bunked with John Black Atkins and Churchill[507] and one evening they heard the sound of railcars being loaded with the cannons preparatory to retreating. They were having a discussion with Col. Long, in their tent about this topic (perhaps over drinks?) and by their persuasive reasoning they both convinced Colonel Long, to not retreat from Estcourt. After the discussion the operation to load cannons onto railcars stopped and they were brought back into defensive positions.

Winston's remark to his companions including was: "I did that", 'uhh, err', we did that!" [508] Soon after, when Haldane was given command of the next day's armoured train reconnaissance Winston agreed to go along.

On November 15th, 1899 It was dark and raining that morning. Winston tried to rouse Leo without success since usually the train did not leave till after 8:00 AM. Winston knew that Haldane was serious about getting an early start, so Winston went and Leo did not. Leo did not get captured, and missed out on the adventures that

[506] Leopold Charles Maurice Stennett Amery (22 November 1873–16 September 1955), was a British Conservative Party politician and journalist. During his career, he was known for his interest in military preparedness, British India and the British Empire and for his opposition to appeasement. He was Secretary of State for the Colonies (1924–29), opposed the National Government of the 1930's and served as Secretary of State for India during the Second World War (1940–45). Leo Amery - Wikipedia

[507] My Early Life Chapter XIX. We landed at Durban and travelled a night's journey to Pietermaritzburg. The hospital was already full of wounded. Here I found Reggie Barnes shot through the thigh. He had been hit at close range in our brilliant little victory at Elandslaagte Station in which my friend Ian Hamilton, now a General, had commanded. He told me all about the fighting and how skillful the Boers were with horse and rifle. He also showed me his leg. No bone was broken, but it was absolutely coal black from hip to toe. The surgeon reassured me afterwards that it was only bruising, and not mortification as I feared. That night I travelled on to Estcourt, a tiny tin township of a few hundred inhabitants, beyond which the trains no longer ran.

It had been my intention to get into Ladysmith, where I knew Ian Hamilton would look after me and give me a good show. I was too late, the door was shut. The Boers had occupied Colenso Station on the Tugela River and held the iron railway bridge. General French and his staff, which included both Haig and Herbert Lawrence, had just slipped through under artillery fire in the last train out of Ladysmith on his way to the Cape Colony, where the main cavalry forces were to be assembled. There was nothing to do but to wait at Estcourt with such handfuls of troops as were being hurriedly collected to protect the southern part of Natal from the impending Boer invasion. A single battalion of Dublin Fusiliers, two or three guns and a few squadrons of Natal Carabineers, two companies of Durban Light Infantry and an armoured train, were the only forces which remained for the defence of the Colony. All the rest of the Natal Army was blockaded in Ladysmith. Reinforcements were hurrying to the spot from all parts of the British Empire; but during the week I was at Estcourt our weakness was such that we expected to be ourselves surrounded almost every day, and could do little but fortify our post and wear a confident air.

At Estcourt I found old friends. Leo Amery, the monitor I had unluckily pushed into the bathing pool at Harrow ten years before, afterwards long my colleague in Parliament and Government, was now one of the war correspondents of the Times. We were able for the first time to meet on terms of equality and fraternity, and together with my friend of the Manchester Guardian [John Black Atkins] we took up our abode in an empty bell tent that stood in the shunting triangle of the railway station. That evening, walking in the single street of the town, whom should I meet but Captain Haldane, who had been so helpful in procuring me my appointment to Sir William Lockhart's staff during the Tirah Expedition. Haldane had been wounded at Elandslaagte, and had hoped to rejoin his battalion of Gordon Highlanders in Ladysmith, and being like me held up by the enemy, had been given the temporary command of a company of the Dublin Fusiliers. The days passed slowly and anxiously. The position of our small force was most precarious. At any moment ten or twelve thousand mounted Boers might sweep forward to attack us or cut off our retreat. Yet it was necessary to hold Estcourt as long and in as firm a posture as possible. Cavalry reconnaissances were pushed out every morning for ten or fifteen miles towards the enemy to give us timely notice of their expected advance; and in an unlucky moment it occurred to the General in command on the spot to send his armoured train along the sixteen miles of intact railway line to supplement the efforts of the cavalry.

Nothing looks more formidable and impressive than an armoured train; but nothing is in fact more vulnerable and helpless. It was only necessary to blow up a bridge or culvert to leave the monster stranded, far from home and help, at the mercy of the enemy. This situation did not seem to have occurred to our commander. He decided to put a company of the Dublin Fusiliers and a company of the Durban Light Infantry into an armoured train of six trucks, and add a small six-pounder naval gun with some sailors landed from H.M.S. Terrible, together with a break-down gang, and to send this considerable portion of his force out to reconnoiter towards Colenso. Captain Haldane was the officer he selected for the duty of commanding this operation. Haldane told me on the night of November 14 of the task which had been set him for the next day and on which he was to start at dawn. He did not conceal his misgivings on the imprudence of the enterprise, but he was of course, like everyone else at the beginning of a war, very keen upon adventure and a brush with the enemy. 'Would I come with him?' He would like it if I did! Out of comradeship, and because I thought it was my duty to gather as much information as I could for the Morning Post, also because I was eager for trouble, I accepted the invitation without demur.

[508] Quote from Hero of the Empire by Candice Millard, Page 113. Anchor Books Edition.

followed. Winston and Leo would have a long and productive career, mostly on the same side of the aisle in Parliament.[509] [510]

I see no real reason to completely re-write the factual Times History account. Leo and his fellow chroniclers were closer to the events than I am. I have tried to make a few improvements. The flow of the Times History is not chronological, despite its attempts to be so. The topics, characters, events and interconnections require a fair amount of jumping back and forth.

The series of judicial crises outlined below are punctuation points where a fledgling Transvaal Republic is trying its best to govern in the far outpost of the world while every swindler, con artist, and fortune seeker from the rest of the planet is flocking to their border.

The Boer protagonists in this course of events are navigating turbulent waters. Much like Lincoln's remark about guiding the Union through the maelstrom of the Civil War, they were, "steering from point to point." The buffeting the Transvaal was experiencing, in the face of so many immigrants coming to their borders

Ultimately, again quoting Lincoln, a house divided against itself cannot stand. Particularly when matters of race and origin are involved.

The Judicial Review of Constitutional provisions was originated and later accepted into American jurisprudence by Justice John Marshall deciding the case of Marbury v. Madison. This doctrine is truly an American invention. At the time, in 1804, and even subsequently the judiciary in the UK did not have the inherent ability to overrule Parliament's enactments.

In South Africa in 1899, it is the Wild West out there, and the carping by Chamberlain about the Convention of 1881 must have grown old after almost two decades of self-government.

We now turn to some of the main conflicts and grievances lodged against their nascent judicial system and government.

1886 Nellmapius Cases

In 1886 Kruger's friend and special favourite, the ex-valet and concessionaire Nellmapius, was tried for embezzlement of moneys belonging to the powder factory and condemned to eighteen months imprisonment.[511]

Kruger, acting as the Executive, promptly ordered his release. In effect he issued an immediate commutation of the sentence. This was unwise; far more statesmanlike to have waited a few months and granted parole from jail; but such was not the case.

[509] One seldom is blessed with the child they envision. Nevertheless, that child is yours and nature takes its course; to love, raise and guide. Leo had a the misfortune to have a son, John Amery, whose passion for anti-communism saw him collaborate with the Nazi's during the Second World War. John was executed for treason in the United Kingdom for his actions as an anti-communist in support of the Axis powers.

[510] John Amery (14 March 1912–19 December 1945) was a British fascist and Nazi collaborator during World War II. He was the originator of the British Free Corps, a volunteer Waffen-SS unit composed of former British and Dominion prisoners of war.
Amery conducted recruitment efforts, and made propaganda broadcasts for Germany. He later gave direct support to Italian dictator Benito Mussolini. He was prosecuted by the British authorities and pleaded guilty to eight counts of high treason, for which he was sentenced to death, seven months after the war in Europe ended.
Amery was prosecuted for treason in London. In a preliminary hearing, he argued that he had never attacked Britain and was an anti-Communist, not a Nazi. At the same time, his brother Julian attempted to show that John had become a Spanish citizen, and therefore would legally be incapable of committing treason against the United Kingdom.
His counsel, Gerald Osborne Slade KC, tried to show that the accused was mentally ill. Amery's sanity was questioned by his own father, Leo, but all efforts to have the court consider his mental state were unsuccessful. Further attempts at a defence were suddenly abandoned on the first day of his scheduled trial, 28 November 1945, when to general astonishment, Amery pleaded guilty to eight charges of treason, and was sentenced to death. The hearing lasted just eight minutes. John Amery - Wikipedia
Amery was hanged in Wandsworth Prison on 19 December 1945 by executioner Albert Pierrepoint and buried in the prison cemetery. Amery actually quipped as he was led to the scaffold, "I've always wanted to meet you, Mr. Pierrepoint, though not of course under these circumstances!"
An epitaph by his father appears in The Empire at Bay. The Leo Amery Diaries. 1929–1945:
At end of wayward days he found a cause–
'Twas not his Country's–Only time can tell
If that defiance of our ancient laws
Was treason or foreknowledge. He sleeps well.

[511] Times History Pages 129–130.

Judge Brand, whose sentence was thus set aside, promptly sent in his resignation, and a crisis between the President and the judiciary was with difficulty patched up.

1887 Doms Case

In 1887 a confrontation between the Executive\Legislative branches and the judiciary developed. A Mr. Doms brought an action against the Government for the transfer of certain properties.[512]

The Government refused to appear and defend themselves. The summons issued by the court hearing the case was put before the Volksraad. The legislature disposed of the question by resolution on the same day; issuing its statement that:

> "The Volksraad has considered the claim of Doms, denies it, and declares as a final decision that he is not entitled to the farms for which the action is instituted."

The failure of the Executive to even appear and defend itself before a judicial tribunal seeking to enforce laws passed by the Legislature that governed all civic and civil behavior in the nation was in effect placing itself above and not bound by that law. That this was done by resolution rather than legislation was equally dismissive of the judicial branch. It had the feel of something more along the lines of a Revolutionary Tribunal than a functioning Nation State.

Still, Sovereign Immunity[513] is a real and necessary adjunct of any government. It is only by permission that a Government can be hailed into a Court, without its consent, in order to answer in most circumstances.

1894

In 1894[514] a Committee appointed to revise the Constitution introduced modifications so important into the relations existing between the Judiciary and the Executive that Chief Justice Kotze,[515] speaking at Eustenburg in October of that year, solemnly warned the burghers that—

> "According to the altered provisions as recommended by the Volksraad Committee the Courts of Justice from the lowest to the highest in the land would have been so affected in the independent exercise of their functions that it would simply have been an impossibility to have dispensed justice between man and man without favour or prejudice. The altered provisions in question assign powers and functions to the Executive and the Legislature which at present belong exclusively to the Courts of Justice ...... The very independence of the Republic which is so inseparably connected with the independence of the Courts of Law would have come to an end."

1895 The Brown Case

It was in 1895[516] that the pretensions of the Government to control the Courts was again placed on record and brought to a definite test.

In 1895 goldfield at a place called Witfontein[517] had been proclaimed open by the Government for the pegging of public claims. As is usual in such cases the public waited anxiously for the day and hour of opening, and a rush then took place to secure claims.

[512] Times History Page 130.

[513] Sovereign immunity, or crown immunity, is a legal doctrine whereby a sovereign or state cannot commit a legal wrong and is immune from civil suit or criminal prosecution, strictly speaking in modern texts in its own courts. Sovereign immunity is the original forebear of state immunity based on the classical concept of sovereignty in the sense that a sovereign could not be subjected without his or her approval to the jurisdiction of another. Sovereign immunity - Wikipedia

[514] Times History Pages 145–146.

[515] Sir John Gilbert Kotzé KC (5 November 1849–1 April 1940) Kotzé undertook legal training in Britain as a student at the Inner Temple in London. In 1877 he was appointed judge of the High Court of the Transvaal, becoming Chief Justice in 1881. Kotze had stood in 1893 as a rival to Kruger in the presidential elections and was seen by Kruger as his long term political rival He, together with the rest of the High Court, was unceremoniously dismissed by Paul Kruger following a dispute over the Testing Rights issue. . Kruger, on this particular occasion, was enraged at the judgement of the High Court in the case of Brown v. Leyds and he dismissed Chief Justice Kotzé in 1898. John Gilbert Kotzé - Wikipedia

[516] Times History Page 146.

The Government, fearing a riot, cancelled the proclamation after the hour on which the ground had become open for pegging, and decided to dispose of the claims by lottery. The persons who had pegged claims protested that the action of the Government in changing their mind after the ground had been publicly proclaimed was illegal.

An American named Brown determined to test the case, and sued the Government in the High Court. The Executive, to dispose of this and other legal difficulties in connection with the matter, submitted a measure to the Volksraad that claims against the Government in regard to their action at Witfontein should not lie; that persons who thought they had claims for damages had none, and that the Government was absolved from all liability. The Volksraad obediently passed the measure.

Once again Sovereign Immunity is a necessary adjunct to any Government. This course of action was unwise but not unconstitutional.

The Court crisis, 1897.

Dismissal of Chief Justice Kotze, 1898.[518]

In February, 1897, the crisis between the Executive and the High Court became acute, in the Brown case regarding the Witfontein goldfield lottery.

Chief Justice Kotze had given judgment in favour of one of the plaintiffs, an American called Brown, ignoring as unconstitutional a special resolution of the Volksraad passed in order [to] retrospectively to absolve the Government from all liability.

The Volksraad, at the instance of the President, promptly replied with a Law, the well-known Law I. of 1897, which imposed upon all future judges and landdrosts an oath relinquishing the so-called "testing right," or right of testing the constitutionality of a law, and empowering the President to exact, on pain of instant dismissal, a similar pledge from the existing members of the judiciary.

The judges promptly protested in a body, but by the mediation of Sir Henry de Villiers,[519] a compromise was arranged, by which the President promised to pass a measure guaranteeing the independence of the High Court, and the crisis was for the moment averted.

A year later, however, as Kruger showed no signs of any intention to fulfil his promise, Mr. Kotze renewed his protest and was at once dismissed under Law I. of 1897, his place as Chief Justice being filled by Mr. Reinhold Gregorowski,[520] who, a year before, had been loudest in denunciation of the President's action.*[521]

Immigration

In the summer of 1896[522] an Expulsion of Aliens Act was passed in spite of the protest of Mr. Chamberlain that the law was inconsistent with the letter and spirit of the London Convention. Attempts were made to cut down the agreement made under the previous Government between Sir Henry Loch and President Kruger in respect of

[517] Witfontein is a town in Sekhukhune District Municipality in the Limpopo province of South Africa. Witfontein - Wikipedia

[518] Times History Page 216.

[519] John Henry de Villiers, 1st Baron de Villiers, (15 June 1842–2 September 1914) was a Cape lawyer and judge. He was Attorney-General in the Molteno Government, Chief Justice for the Cape Colony (1872–1914, and later the first Chief Justice for the Union of South Africa. As the country's most senior judge for 40 of its formative years, De Villiers is often considered the most influential judge in South African history. John de Villiers, 1st Baron de Villiers - Wikipedia

[520] 1881, Reinhold Gregorowski is appointed a judge in the Orange Free State at the age of 25. See: 1881 in South Africa - Wikipedia See: Hon. Mr. Justice Reinhold Gregorowski (1914). Judicial Commission of Inquiry into the circumstances leading up to and attending upon the deaths of General the ''J. H. de la Rey and Dr. G. Grace. Cape Times Limited. pp. 1–4, 7–11. https://archive.org/details/judicialcommissi00sout

[521] *[Original footnote.] In the abstract no doubt there is a great deal to be said for the complete freedom of the Legislature from such control by the judiciary as is created by the right of testing the constitutionality of a law, and no Englishman would wish to introduce the American system into this country. But the British system is only possible with a parliament where legislation receives the fullest discussion in a series of readings, and where the criticisms of every interest represented are freely heard. In the Transvaal a score of ignorant or interested farmers, swayed by one imperious will, claimed the right by mere resolution to alter the whole conditions of a complex industry in a morning's sitting, or to interfere in a case actually proceeding before the Courts. No judge with any proper respect for his profession could acquiesce in such a claim.

[522] Times History Page. 184.

commandeering, and to limit its application to white persons in place of the original assurance which covered all British subjects, white or coloured.* C. 8423, p. 62.

In November, 1896,[523] an Aliens Immigration Act, laying placing severe restrictions on the entrance of foreigners to the Transvaal, was passed by the Volksraad, Mr. Chamberlain at once objected that this law infringed Article XIV. of the London Convention, inasmuch as by it new and burdensome conditions, in most cases probably impossible to fulfil, were imposed on persons who, under the Convention, were at full liberty to enter and reside in the South African Republic on condition of conforming to its laws, and expressed his confidence that no attempt would be made to enforce the law.

The Transvaal Government refused to comply, basing its refusal on the grounds that the law was a mere police measure.

The Volksraad, under pressure of Mr. Chamberlain's ultimatum, had repealed the Aliens Immigration Law, and shortly after passed a resolution (never carried into effect) for amending the Aliens Expulsion Act by giving an appeal to a court of law.

He stated that the Convention of London was not, in the view of Her Majesty's Government, a treaty between two states on an equal footing, but"

"a declaration by the Queen of the conditions upon which she accorded complete self-government to the South African Republic, subject to her suzerainty, these conditions having been accepted by the delegates of the South African Republic and subsequently ratified by the Volksraad."

[523] Times History Pages 185 and 200.

Legislation Opposed in Monster Petition

A portion of the Uitlander's petition to Queen Victoria.[524]

8. Instead, however, of the admitted grievances being redressed, the spirit of the legislation adopted by the Volksraad during the past few years has been of a most unfriendly character, and has made the position of the Uitlanders more irksome than before.

9. In proof of the above statement. Your Majesty's petitioners would humbly refer to such measures as the following:—

The Immigration of Aliens Act (Law 30 of 1896)

The Press Law (Law 2G of 1896);

The Aliens Expulsion Law of 1896.

Of these, the first was withdrawn at the instance of Your Majesty's Government, as being an infringement of the London Convention of 1884.

By the second the President is invested with the powers of suppressing wholly, or for a stated time, any publication which in his individual opinion is opposed to good manners or subversive of order. This despotic power he has not hesitated to exercise towards newspapers which support British interests, while newspapers which support the Government have been allowed to publish inflammatory and libelous articles, and to advocate atrocious crimes without interference.

The Aliens Expulsion Act draws a distinction between the Burghers of the State and Uitlanders which your Majesty's petitioners humbly submit, is in conflict with the Convention of 1884. Thus, whilst Burghers of the State are protected from expulsion, British subjects can be put over the border at the will of the President, without the right of appealing to the High Court, which is, nevertheless, open to the offending Burgher. This law was repealed, only to be re-enacted in all its essential provisions during the last session of the Volksraad.[525]

…………..

The petition continues through another 6 pages with 32 two items numbered.

By: W. Wybeegh,

&c., P.O. Box 317,

Johannesburg, South African Republic,
And Others.

[524] For the text of the petition see Times History Vol. I pages 225–232. This from page 226.

[525] In the reply to the mining representatives: "On the question of coloured immigration they explain that they cannot intervene, as the matter is governed by the Convention; but they suggest that the Government should secure their wishes in the matter as part of a general settlement with the Imperial Government." Times History p. 237.

Piet Joubert's Petition to Victoria

P. J. Joubert, Vice-President of the South-African Republic and Commander in-Chief of the Burgher's Army.[526]

An Earnest Representation and Historical Reminder

Pretoria, June 15, 1899.[527] [528]

To Her Most Gracious Majesty the Queen of Great Britain and Ireland, Empress of India, etc., etc.

Your Majesty: It is with feelings of deepest pain and distress that the undersigned ventures to address Your Most Gracious Majesty at this critical period, and in view of the dark future, which, as a cloud, is hovering over South Africa, the land of his birth and home. This unhappy situation has been brought about by the unjust action of one of Your Majesty's Ministers, who, perhaps in good faith, though upon incorrect information, has allowed himself to be led by unscrupulous fortune-seekers, reckless speculators and insatiable capitalists.

This matter will be reverted to again during the course of this letter by Your Majesty's lowly petitioner, who desires, first, in all humility, to make known to Your Majesty who he is. He is a descendant of and great-great-grandson of Pierre Joubert, one of the Huguenots, who, because of their religious belief, were obliged to leave their homes and friends, and to seek refuge from persecution in flight to South Africa, where they could serve their God in freedom. He settled at Fransch Hoek, near Cape Town, which was then under the administration of the "Hollandsche Compagnie," and became soon, through the blessing of God, one of the richest and most influential farmers and landowners there. He resided there until compelled by circumstances to remove to the district of Graaff-Reinet, where he now lies buried—in the land of my birth, that passed for good under the rule of Great Britain, in 1806.

Alas! What has our nation not experienced and suffered under that rule? It has, perhaps, never been brought to Your Majesty's notice why these people could not live peacefully in their land of adoption and birth. And yet, who is there now to tell you thereof? And how would he begin? It would, indeed, be tedious to relate everything minutely, Your Majesty!

The discontent, so often, and to his detriment, ascribed to the Boer was exaggerated and misrepresented, as, for instance, in the matter of the freeing of the slaves, when he was described as being inhumanly against their liberation. No! Your Majesty, it was not the Christian Boers' repugnance to the emancipation, but his opposition to the means employed in effecting same under the blessed British rule. Is Your Majesty perhaps aware how the Boers became possessed of those slaves? They, the Boers, had no ships to convey the slaves from Mozambique

[526] A century of injustice; synopsis of a message to the people of South-Africa, sent by the government of the South-African republic. Baltimore Md. November1899. https://babel.hathitrust.org/cgi/pt?id=wu.89100085885&seq=5

[527] This was published in 'A Century of Injustice' in November of 1899. Not in 'Story of the Boers'.

[528] PF: Regretfully this ~9k word petition has been edited down to 2k words to make room for Dr. Conan Doyle's work.

and elsewhere, as none other than English vessels were allowed to bring slaves to the Cape market; therefore, it was from English slave-ships that the Boers first bought their slaves, and in this manner enjoyed a short season of prosperity; for, assisted by their dearly bought slaves, they could have their lands ploughed and sown with grain, which, under the blessings of Britannia's laws, could be sold for not more than 18d . per bag.

It was thereafter shipped abroad by English merchants and sold at immense profits. And then, Your Majesty, the Boer was suddenly told: "Your slaves are free, and you will receive compensation to such and such an amount for them, which you will have to go and get in England. Your Majesty, how could the Boer be expected with his ox-wagon or horses to go and fetch same? To have undertaken, at that time, a voyage so dangerous and lengthy (a hundred days or so being the time required to accomplish same) would have cost more than the small amount of the indemnity he was to receive for his dearly bought slaves. What could the Boer do? The only means left him was to engage the English dealer, from whom he had purchased the slaves at exorbitant prices, to go and fetch the money for him, or to sell his chance for what he could get.

How many unscrupulous agents and merchants took advantage of the opportunity thus offered, not to reconcile the Boer to the law and authority of the British Government, but to carry out their own designs, in order to satisfy their cupidity, thus nurturing the hostility of the Boer against the Government, hoping thereby, eventually, to acquire possession of his lands.

The population increasing, spread out further and further, gradually enlarging the Colony; and it is, perhaps, known to Your Majesty, how the poor Boers on the frontiers fared, how they were robbed of their cattle, and how, owing to the insufficient protection afforded them, they were often left to their fate, or more frequently persecuted and oppressed, so that it is not to be wondered at (although I do not seek to justify their conduct) that, disgusted and dissatisfied with the treatment meted out to them, they at last rebelled against the Government; thus originating what took place in 1815 and ended so disastrously. ....

Alas! Your Majesty, what had the Boer not to suffer, then, under the otherwise glorious British rule? Inquire of the border settlers of 1820 to 1834, when their eventful departure from the Colony took place. Is it, perhaps, known to Your Majesty how they were driven back from the boundaries by the natives who pursued them far into the country, harassing and molesting them? Yes, even murdering some, robbing them of their cattle, and burning and laying waste their homes.

What protection did they enjoy against the savages who had murdered their wives and children, who had lashed young girls to the trunks of trees, ravished them, cut off their breasts, and, after performing nameless other cruelties, killed them? They, the Boers, were called out for Commando Service at their own expense, under command and control of the British, to fight the Kaffirs. And with what result? The Boer was impoverished thereby, without the Kaffir being brought to a sense of his duty; for while on commando, his cattle were stolen from his farm and driven away into Kaffirland, whither he was prevented from going in order to recover them. No! they had no choice but to wait until the troops retook the cattle, which were afterwards publicly sold as loot in the presence of the owners thereof, the Boers being informed that they would receive compensation for same. But, Your Majesty, they received no recompense; not in money or goods, neither in rest nor peace, but, instead, abuse and indignities were heaped on them. They were told that they should be satisfied at not being punished as the instigators of the disturbance.

Your Majesty, this was the state of affairs in 1834. The dissatisfaction evinced at such treatment became more and more pronounced. The Boers were told by His Excellency, the Governor, that all who were not content or would not submit to British rule were at liberty to migrate beyond the borders of the Colony, out of British territory. With feelings of deep anguish at the thought of having to leave their motherland and the country of their birth, and with a weary sigh, the question escaped them, "Whither? To the dismal hinterland of savage South Africa?" Yes! yes! Your Majesty, rather the dangers of the wilderness, amidst wild animals and savage men, than to remain longer under the yoke of so iniquitous a Government. And then, "Come, friends; come, brothers! Pack your wagons, collect your flocks and herds, and let us go away over the border. God knows whither, and He will guide us." ....

How could they arm themselves against such dangers? They were not permitted to carry arms or ammunition along with them, but were even followed by British officials beyond the Orange River, to try and find out if there were not perhaps still one faithful slave with his master, and if the Boers were not perhaps carrying a quantity of arms and ammunition along with them.

Thanks to the kindness of those officials, the Boers were advised of the object of their coming, and were consequently enabled to conceal their guns and ammunition. Does Your Majesty not perceive in the aforementioned some analogy to certain facts in biblical history? For even as Pharaoh drove the Israelites through the Red Sea, were the Boers driven through the Great River. Is it, then, to be wondered at that, sad at heart and with intense bitterness, they preferred the perils of the desert?

Your Majesty, who can write the history of their lives? Who can describe the suffering they endured? They ventured forth, trusting in God, rid of all human despotism, surrounded by wild beasts, in search of a free land for their children and children's children. They wandered in small groups further and further, yet ever onward, until they arrived at the Vaal River. Here they pitched their tents and regarded the country as their Eldorado. Here were the means of subsistence—fish in the water, game on the veldt, and a prospect of being able to sow crops and to live in peace. They could clothe themselves with skins and subsist on flesh until God, in His bounty, provided other means; at least so reasoned the poor Boers. Come now, let us erect our tent (our tabernacle) to celebrate the Sabbath, for in our God we believe and trust; He has given unto us this glorious land and we shall live and praise Him here. It needs not that we go beyond the Jordan, we have no Babylon or Jericho to overthrow. No walls to be demolished for us, for our Canaan is an uninhabited land; therefore, ye Boers, be up, work and live.

Thus they thought, and thus they spoke; but how short-lived was their delight, when at break of day, one morning, the dread cry of "Murder! Murder!" awakened them. What could it be? Whence this uproar and confusion? Moselikatse, head of a cruel, unknown Kaffir tribe, had come with a large regiment of warriors from the far north, through a wild and unpopulated country, a distance of over a hundred miles, and attacked a small detachment of Boers near the river, no warning having reached them of the intended onslaught. "Up, now! Courage, men! Fight for your lives, for your wives and your children." The odds at first were three to one, then seven, and eventually increased to twenty to one; but God gave them courage and strength, and they not only repulsed the horde of savages, but succeeded in rescuing several children and severely wounded women who were captured. ....

Other parties of the Boers had gone eastward. With these they now decided to combine. But did the undaunted Moselikatse allow these few Boers to escape him? To the contrary, he immediately sent a second expedition, much stronger than the previous one, commanding it not to return so long as there remained a Boer living; that he did not thereafter wish to hear of a living Boer.

Thus it came to pass that this small party of fleeing Boers (thirty-eight only being capable of bearing arms), with their wives and children, together with cattle and thirty-four wagons, were followed by that great commando of savages, until they reached that ever memorable spot in the Orange Free State known as "Vechtkop," where the Boers, recognizing the futility of continuing their flight, drew up a laager or camp with their wagons, surrounding same with branches of trees, and calmly awaited their pitiless foe, who did not long delay in attacking them with all the fiendish courage of savages.

Prepared to die, in the face of overwhelming odds, they, nevertheless, determined to fight manfully to the last, trusting in God. The impending danger was awaited in earnest supplications before the Throne of the Triune God. As the enemy pressed on, each Boer made use of his rifle, causing the smoke to ascend in such volumes to heaven that even the flying enemy imagined the Boers had been vanquished, that their laager was in flames, and that they had been utterly annihilated. We were afterward told that when the intelligence reached Grahamstown, Cape Colony, Your Majesty's subjects were so elated thereat that they celebrated the receipt of the news by bonfires and other illuminations, thinking the last of the Boers had fallen, and that the extravagant expectations of the discontented rebels had now all ended in smoke.

But no! Your Majesty, our God in heaven had another destiny for the Boer. For, notwithstanding 1,333 assegais were hurled into the small laager, only two men were killed and six wounded, and their little camp, unlike the cities of Sodom and Gomorrah, was not laid waste. There was still to be found five just men before God, whose prayers had warded off disaster, and thwarted the wishes of Your Majesty's Grahamstown subjects. Not only did our God cause the smoke and mist to disappear, but he touched the heart of a noble native, Marroco, who, when he heard of the wretched plight that had overtaken the Boers, sent them, without delay, succor in the shape of milk, Kaffir corn and pack-oxen, thereby enabling them to rejoin their friends, who had passed over the Drakensberg into Natal.

Before further recording the history of this party, I would like to relate to Your Majesty about two other ill-fated parties of trekkers—that of Jansen van Rensburg, which proceeded northward, beyond Zoutpansberg, never to be heard of again, for all record of them is as absolutely lost to the world as that of the ten tribes of Israel. It was stated that, owing to the want of ammunition, which was denied them by the Government of the British Cape Colony, on their departure into the wilds, they were massacred, every one of them. However, what actually became of them we do not know.

The other party, under Louis Trichardt, also ventured as far as Zoutpansberg, thence proceeding southeastward until Delagoa Bay was reached, where he, the leader, and others succumbed to the there prevailing fever, and from which place the few survivors, together with their children, were conveyed by vessel to Natal, where they were enabled to rejoin their friends. The misery and suffering experienced and endured by these pioneers is likewise indescribable, and distresses one even to think of.

But now let us return to the history of those who passed over the Drakensberg and attached themselves to Piet Retief, Gert Maritz, and Uys, and let us see, Your Majesty, how they fared. Did they go to attack a peaceful people? Did they go as freebooters into a strange or friendly country? Did they go purposing to wrest territory from a lot of defenceless savages, or did they go to revenge themselves on the brother of Moselikatse for the iniquitous attack on them at the instigation of the latter?

Did they seek to avenge the blood of Van Rensburg and others, who were murdered by the same race of savages as that to which Dingaan belonged? No! Your Majesty, nothing of the kind. First they held communion with the Almighty God, and then approached the savage ruler of the land, King Dingaan, who had already promised them a tract of country, and requested him to grant them a written agreement to that effect. It is doubtless known to Your Majesty how this cruel and barbarous chief, after having given them the land, and after duly signing the agreement thereto, mercilessly and treacherously murdered Piet Retief and his seventy men, immediately afterward sending out his commandos to massacre those awaiting the return of Piet Retief and the unsuspecting women and children. Thus without warning were 600 helpless old men, women and children butchered in cold blood.

What a panic, what dismay, this caused among the Boers scattered about the country! Those remaining were robbed of all their cattle; and what could they do? Should they await other such onslaughts and perish eventually at the hands of a savage people, or die of hunger in the wilderness? Alas, how dismal their outlook seemed!

Whither could they go? Whence could they expect help? From Great Britain? Yes, and help came too! A vessel arrived at Port Natal, and Captain Jarvis stepped on shore. "Thank God, assistance was at hand; now no more starvation; no more fear of the sword of Dingaan. Succor has come at last!" Such were the thoughts of many a simple-minded Boer. But, alas! how soon was their joy to be turned into grief and indignation, for how terribly surprised were they to learn that, instead of having come to their aid, he was sent to forbid them to fight with the natives and to disarm them.

What was to be done? Should they offer Captain Jarvis resistance? Yes! Rather would they fight to the death than hand over their firearms. But what, then, if the Kaffirs should come to his aid? The Boers found their prospects more cheerless now than ever. They acted, therefore, with great cunning, yet with submissiveness. Rather than show antagonism they hid their guns and ammunition and submitted to the inspection and search of Captain Jarvis, anxiously praying to God to give them refuge. Captain Jarvis, having ascertained that there was no booty to be got from the poor Boers, and as Natal offered but few attractions then, was glad to take his departure.

Poor, deserted Boer, what was now your outlook? In a savage land, in the vicinity of a powerful and barbarous tribe, ruled over by the tyrant Dingaan. What was there to do but to avenge the murders committed and restore peace with the sword? Therefore, it behooved Pieter Uys, Hdk. Potgieter and every one to punish Dingaan and his tribe and to reestablish peace, otherwise the Boers would not have been able to live in the country. Therefore, "Two hundred men of you up and get at the mighty Dingaan!" This, however, was not owing to a lust for fighting, Your Majesty, but because the Boer adjudged it absolutely necessary, and no one in the world could have done otherwise.

A return to the Colony was not to be thought of. The only conclusion they could arrive at was to endeavor to compel Dingaan, at the edge of the sword, to promote peace. How unfortunate, though, was the outcome of this desperate effort of only two hundred men to advance against the might of Dingaan, in the midst of his people and in his own dangerous land, without the support of cannon or other instruments of war, but simply mounted on their horses, armed with flintlock guns. And yet they had no choice but to do it. The issue was only as could have been expected. Dingaan's regiments were too powerful for the little handful of Boers, who were forced to take refuge in flight, not, however, until after hundreds of the foe had bitten the dust. Their small stock of ammunition had run out; their brave commander, Piet Uys, his never-to-be-forgotten little son, and eight others lost their lives in this conflict. But in vain! Dingaan was conqueror and his courage revived immediately. He then sent a larger and more powerful commando than before, with instructions to completely destroy the Boers.

This time, however, the Boers were on their guard. They had constructed a laager on the banks of the Bosmans River, where the flourishing village of Escourt now lies, close to the village Weenen (to wail), so called in memory of the many wailing women and children massacred there.

It was here that Dingaan was to learn that, although but a mere handful of whites, the Boers, with righteousness as their cause, were not to be overthrown by his iniquitous hosts. No! they did not rely in the strength of their horses or the heroism of their men, but in the omnipotence of their God, who gave them the victory. For, although the Boers were surrounded by overwhelming odds and repeatedly stormed by thousands and thousands of the enemy, they lost but one killed.

The Zulus, however, after three days' fighting, were forced to retire, leaving so many of their dead on the field that for years after the veldt was white with their bones, testifying to the frightful carnage that took place there. God had protected the Boers and delivered the dearly bought land of Natal into their hands. They had, however, been robbed of all their cattle and knew not what to do.

Their God and His word still remained to them, and so they were comforted—for he who has faith in God has not built upon the sand—and in the sight of heaven their cause was just. Therefore he sent them help from above. Andries Pretorius had in company with other Boers recently arrived from the Cape, and he, having called together all the Boers to be found in Natal, and even as many of those to be found in the territory known as the Orange Free State, formed a commando about four hundred strong, with which he hazarded to invade Dingaan's country, and notwithstanding the fact that his men were armed only with flintlock guns, they succeeded, on December 16, 1838, in not only defeating him (Dingaan) in this battle, but in overthrowing his kingdom and destroying his chief kraal, driving him so far inland that he was nevermore able to return. In token of their gratitude for the victory gained, the Boers made a vow to ever afterward keep the date thereof as a day of thanksgiving, and so the 16th of December is always commemorated at Paardekraal.

One would have thought, Your Majesty, that the Boer after this would have been left alone to live peaceably, praising his God in the country he had bought so dear. But no! the yoke of oppression had not yet been broken. Their cup of bitterness was not yet emptied. Scarcely had the Boers laid out the village, Pietermaritzburg, dug a water-furrow, erected a church, started a small school for their children, and built a court-house and prison, when lo! threatening clouds began to gather and the alarm to sound again. What can it be—the Kaffirs? No! a thousand, thousand times worse. The English have come; an officer with a company of soldiers, equipped with cannon and shell, is here! "It is Captain Jarvis, that good—that brave old soldier. We will soon be able to adjust matters with him; he will presently be gone again." No! my poor fellow-Boers, you are deluded. The officer is Captain Smith; he has come to annex the country as a possession of that mighty empire, Great Britain—to make an end to our boasted independence and to destroy our peace.

Your Majesty, it is with a shudder I recall this deplorable incident. It cannot be wondered at that the Boers, who had endured and suffered so much to obtain this land and to form an independent people, should have declined to voluntarily submit to such an injustice, and have resisted any attempts to achieve the same. When they discovered that argument and fair words were of no avail, and that Major Smith was steadfast in his purpose to take possession of the country and crush the Boers, and, as a step in that direction, had already declared the bay annexed, they were driven to the verge of despair and so resorted to arms.

Having hastily collected together to the number of about two hundred, for they were but few and much scattered, they advanced toward the Congella. Major Smith, vainly imagining that this mere handful of Boers would be disconcerted and put to flight at the first firing of his cannon, advanced along the shore under cover of darkness, until he had almost reached the sleeping laager, when he opened fire on the picket guard, comprising about twenty-eight men, with the fatal result that one Boer was killed, Jan Greyling.

The remainder of the Boers repelled the attack, and obliged the Major to retreat, leaving his cannon behind. I may here mention that more of the troops got drowned in the sea than succumbed to the bullets of the Boers. Now they had to face the fact that, although thankful to God for his many mercies, and in deep sorrow at the loss of one of the bravest of their young men and for the many soldiers drowned, they had opposed the might of Britain. It was awful to contemplate; so young a nation as they, which had suffered so many hardships at the hands of the savages during the great trek, and that had just been visited by an epidemic of measles, which, owing to the lack of medical assistance and proper nourishment, had carried off many of them.

Should they fight or surrender? was the question asked. Certainly, fight for their just rights. But, see, two ships were coming; it is madness for this little handful of Boers to offer further resistance. They were not trained nor armed with cannon; and thus could not prevent the landing of a force stronger than they were themselves. They dared not longer to fight the English, for the Kaffirs had already commenced to harass them from the rear. A Boer had been killed on his farm, and another, named Van Rooyen, murdered, his wife and daughter being subjected to the most inhuman treatment, ravished and driven away naked. Others were assaulted and barely escaped with their lives. In this way the Kaffirs proved of great service to Major Smith and his soldiers, who were besieged by the Boers and had already been driven to the extremity of eating crows and horseflesh, and who would undoubtedly have been obliged to capitulate had it not been for the harassing attacks of the Kaffirs in the rear of the Boers, which necessitated them hastening out to their farms, in order to save their families from certain death.

And thus it came to pass that the Boers lost their sacred right to the territory of Natal, which had been purchased with the blood of their slain. What was to be done next? There was no other remedy for it but to trek again, and to trek inland, whither the English would not follow them, for if they remained they would once more have had to submit to the British yoke. They would, nevertheless, first give the latter a trial. "We will submit," they said; "perhaps England will deal with us more kindly here than she did in the Cape Colony, our motherland. Come, let us wait and see!" What happened after this, Your Majesty? The first thing Your Majesty's servants did was to banish certain of the Boers, who had to flee for their lives.

This was not all, however, for when the Kaffirs stole their cattle and brought them to Major Smith, the Boers were told they could not get same back, as he had run short of provisions and would require them as food. Thus were the prospects of the Boer growing darker and darker.

Colonel Cloete had arrived. What had he to tell them? Firstly, that they were to consider themselves the conquered subjects of Her Majesty. And, as such, what would they enjoy? Each one who had occupied a piece of ground could make application for same, which, after certain investigations, would be granted him. The country had been won and acquired by the Boers; consequently the Boer Volksraad had granted to each Boer capable of bearing arms two farms and one erf[529] at Pietermaritzburg. These farms were inspected, registered, and declared as marketable property some time before the appearance of the English.

When, however, several of the Boers, dissatisfied with the principle of British rule, began to leave the country, and tried to barter their farms and erven for wagons, trek-cattle, clothing, and other requisites for their fresh trek inland, they, as well as the few Boers who intended to remain under British rule in Natal and had bought or given something in exchange for the erven and farms, were profoundly astonished, not to say disappointed, when they approached Colonel Cloete for transfer of the property they had secured, to hear that as the erven and farms had not been bona-fide occupied, they had, therefore, reverted to the Government, and were now declared as crown lands. "The wagon and oxen or money and goods you gave for same can only be regarded as a dead loss to yourself," was the reply they got.

This was how the British Government in Natal introduced itself to the defeated Boers. Many and bitter were the tears shed by the thus oppressed and impoverished Boers.

Is Your Majesty, perhaps, acquainted with the fact that the Boers sent a delegate to lay their grievances before Your Majesty, who, after many weeks' traveling on horseback, reached Governor Pottinger and entreated him to listen to their complaints?

But, Your Majesty, this emissary was not given an audience. Thus it was obvious to all that the doors had been closed at them to be heard, and that they would have to patiently tolerate all that befell them, without the slightest prospect of ever obtaining justice or relief. Is it a matter of wonder, Your Majesty, that under these circumstances every Boer took advantage of the first opportunity that was offered to leave the Colony of Natal

[529] A small inherited house-and-garden lot in a village or settlement.

and trek beyond the Drakensberg to a haven of rest, where there was no British authority and where they could live and die in peace?

It was upon these trek-Boers that various deceptions were practised in Your Majesty's name. They were called together by the late General Pretorius to meet the Governor, Sir Harry Smith, who, it was stated, wished personally to see the Boers and to learn what the majority desired. It was announced that if the majority would remain under Her Majesty's rule he, the Governor, would give them land and would treat the minority with every degree of kindness and patience, always endeavoring to persuade them to be reconciled to British authority; but, on the other hand, should it appear that the majority were for freedom and antagonistic toward the authority of the British, they could go to perdition; Her Majesty's Government would not trouble itself further about them.

On this pretext as many of the Boers as could were prevailed upon to proceed to Winburg, a newly laid-out village, for the purpose of meeting Sir Harry Smith. But how ineffably deceived were they, for instead of finding Sir Harry Smith and obtaining a peaceful settlement of all their grievances, an ultimatum was presented to them reading as follows: "Your headman or leader is a rebel. I have put a price of a thousand pounds on his head, and woe unto any of you who connive at his escape. I will treat such as rebels."

Who can describe the feelings of disappointment and resentment that arose in the breasts of the Boers at these words, and to which can only be attributed what subsequently took place at Boomplaats on the 29th August, 1849? It is true that the forces of Sir Harry, reinforced by Basutos and Griquas, suffered a heavy reverse. The Boers, however, being armed only with flintlock guns, could not for long withstand a larger and better armed force, supported by cannon, and were eventually obliged to retreat, leaving six of their number dead on the field and several others prisoners in the hands of the English, none of whom we have ever seen again or heard of.

Thus ended this act in the drama of South Africa, creating new miseries for the Boers, who could not immediately trek or escape in flight beyond the Vaal River, where the Portuguese had conceded them a tract of country, decimated of its native population by the raiding of Moselikatse, previous to his attack upon the Boers in 1836, and for which he had been severely punished already by Piet Uys and Hendrik Potgieter. The country had, so to say, been cleared by the Boers, and they now availed themselves of the permission given them by the Portuguese to settle down north of the Vaal River, where they immediately founded a village which they named Potchefstroom. Having built a church and jail, they proceeded with the election of a Parliament and the enactment of laws, etc.

It had by this time begun to dawn upon Her Majesty's Government that it was more politic to leave the Boer severely alone than to be everlastingly pursuing him from place to place like a small bird, hopping from branch to branch and tree to tree. With the object of assuring the Boers that they would not be interfered with north of the Vaal River, and could administer their own affairs, Her Majesty's Special Commissioner, Mr. C. M. Owen, was sent, with the result that a convention was entered into on the 16th January, 1852, signed by Your Majesty's Commissioners, Major W. S. Hogg and Mr. C. M. Owen, the first three articles of which read somewhat as follows:

Art. 1. Her Majesty's Commissioners, on behalf of the British Government, do absolutely guarantee to the emigrant Boers north of the Vaal River the right of administering their own affairs and of governing in accordance with their own laws, without interference whatsoever on the part of the British Government, and that no extension shall be made by the said Government north of the Vaal, with the additional assurance that it is the fervent desire of the British Government to maintain peace and free trade, and to promote a friendly understanding with the emigrant Boers occupying or still to occupy the said territory, and it is further understood that these terms are to be mutually adhered to.

Art. 2. Should there arise any misunderstanding regarding the meaning of the word Vaalrivier, more particularly with respect to the tributaries of the Vaal, the question shall be decided by a mutually appointed commission.

Art. 3. That Her Majesty's commissioners disavow all compacts of whatever nature with the colored nations north of the Vaal.

See also the protocol, which defines the boundary along the Vaal River and the Orange Free State right unto the sea. The British evidently concluded that the Orange Free State was not worthy of being retained by so wealthy and good a Government as that of England. Therefore, Her Majesty's Government sent Sir Russel Clark, on the 4th of February, 1854, to abolish the suzerainty and give the Boers absolute independence and free government.

This just action on the part of the British Government, Your Majesty, was lauded and magnified by the Boer, whose confidence in the equity of the British had revived. No one dare say aught detrimental to the English. No! an Englishman was as good as any other man. This feeling toward the English can be testified to by the many soldiers who deserted hither, by every trader, and by the first gold-diggers in the country.

Have not English persons served as members of our Executive Council and as Landdrosts? Have not Englishmen sat as members of our Volksraad? Yes! even several who did not understand Dutch. Did not perfect harmony, co-operation, confidence, and friendship prevail then between the Englishman and the Boer all over South Africa? Would not, in this way, all the people of South Africa, irrespective of nationality, soon have been blended into one common people or nation?

Whence came this antagonism, this disruption, then? Your Majesty, it is to be ascribed to the diamonds, to the Basutoland question—ask but Theophilus Shepstone—to what took place on the 12th of April, 1878. Yes! Lord Carnarvon knows, as also does Sir Michael Hicks-Beach. Did the Boers not have to submit to the diamond fields south of the Vaal being taken from them? Was not the glory of having vanquished the Basutos, after a long and bloody struggle, and after having endured so much, snatched from the Orange Free State?

Was not the trust assured them by the Convention abused when they were dispossessed of a stretch of country where the diamond mines were situated, and for which they were subsequently obliged to accept a sum of ninety thousand pounds sterling—a ridiculously inadequate sum, considering that in one week the value of the diamonds procured exceeded this amount?

Was not the Transvaal annexed after all the native tribes had been subdued by the Boers? Did not the Boers for three whole years implore Lord Carnarvon, and also later Sir Michael Hicks-Beach, as it were, on their knees, for a restitution of their rights, sending two deputations to England for that purpose, yet without obtaining the least hope of ever having their legitimate rights restored to them? It was, therefore, in desperation that the Boers resolved, on the 13th of December, 1880, at Paardekraal, to recall the Government to resume their official duties, which had been interrupted owing to the annexation, and to govern the people in accordance with the laws of the land.

Your Majesty is probably aware that when the country was annexed, on the 12th of April, 1877, against which act President Thomas Burgers, however, resolutely protested, a proclamation was printed at Pretoria in the name of the British, without let or hindrance from the side of the Boer. No! the Boers, notwithstanding their indignation at this great wrong, submitted to the law and preserved order, intending to petition Your Majesty against this manifestly unjust breach of the Convention, committed in the name of Your Majesty. They, therefore, without murmur, permitted the publication of the document. When, however, they wanted to have a proclamation printed, declaring to the world their rights, Major Clark ordered his men to open fire on them—and this without previous warning or the proclaiming of war—wounding two and killing one of their horses. Thus, on December 16, 1880, war was declared by England against the Boers, regardless of the Convention of 1852, wherein their independence, etc., etc., was guaranteed to them.

This was how the war, which lasted almost three months, originated.

The wretched Boers had no experienced soldiers, nor did they possess cannon, ammunition, modern weapons or a full treasury; indeed, they were almost destitute of food and clothing. They were armed only with antique flintlock guns, and had at the most a hundred rounds of ammunition. Their officers had but recently been chosen; the majority of them had never been under fire before, and, in fact, knew not what war meant. Such were the men who were now obliged to take up arms and to give battle. Against whom? Against Your Majesty? Against Great Britain? No!

Your Majesty, happily not; but against those persons who, through misrepresentation, had beguiled the British Empire into the committal of a shameful deed, thereby seeking to cast a lasting reproach on Your Majesty's honored name, and that of the noble British race, at the same time straining to crush a people to whom Your Majesty had, by the terms of the Sand River Convention, etc., guaranteed their independence.

In this way the unfortunate struggle between the Boers and English came about. The Boers, perceiving that they could not move their pitiless oppressors by their protests and petitions, resolved to repurchase liberty with their blood. Although many more brave English soldiers fell than Boers, the loss of the Boer, however, was greater and more acutely felt, considering the status of the British soldier and how considerably it differs from that of the Boer. The Boer was fighting for his property, his home, and for his country. He is invariably the father of a family, and if he gets killed then he leaves behind him a widow and children, or, perhaps, the only son of a widow or of aged and decrepit parents, whose support he was, is killed.

A soldier knows none of these tender anxieties. He is instructed in the science of war, and thinks of nothing else; his greatest ambition is to carry out the orders of his commander and to gain a medal for bravery in the fight. They do not concern themselves with the question as to whether they are fighting in a good or bad, a just or unjust cause. No! it matters little to them. Those in high positions (who sit in safety) should know, for they have calculated how much glory and honor they can gain or purchase with the life and blood of the soldier, but they do not consider the amount of suffering and pain they inflict, and what their responsibility will be when they come before the judgment seat of the Great Judge of Heaven and Earth, before whom every one will one day have to stand, face to face with those who stood under their authority and were used to the destruction and downfall of others.

In this war, however, such was not the outcome, for, although the struggle was fierce and arduous and the Boers lost heavily, their God gave them the ultimate victory. There arose a man—Mr. Gladstone—at the head of affairs in Great Britain, an upright, God-fearing man, who could discern the directing finger of the Almighty, and was not too high-minded to acknowledge the same and boldly declare that righteousness exalteth a nation—his nation, Your Majesty's nation—while injustice and wrong-doing sully the fame of a nation. Actuated thereto by a generous and noble impulse, he caused the unjust war to cease, and restored the honor of Great Britain by transforming an act of violence into a magnanimous deed.

Peace was thereupon concluded at Lang's Nek, and the Boers might have again exulted at being in amity with Great Britain, although burdened now with a heavy debt—a liability which they respectfully protest they never incurred—an empty treasury, broken firearms, ammunition all spent, and a Convention that cannot be conformed with, which can be declared as infringed every day, with no impartial tribunal to determine one way or the other. The Boers were, however, free again, and they hoped it would now go better with them. They vainly imagined so, and frequently declared so. But, alas! Poor Transvaal! You have hardly survived one disaster when two others stand staring you in the face.

Unfortunately a rich gold mine has been discovered in your country. It is surely not meant for the poor down-trodden Boer. Poor and abandoned men soon began to flock to this New Eldorado, and were presently followed by a legion of unscrupulous speculators. Afterward certain ambitious capitalists arrived on the scene, who knew how to use their influence, and were indifferent as to what role they played or of what became of the country as long as they could increase their wealth tenfold. And to what end did they eventually apply their gold derived from the Transvaal mines? Let history tell Your Majesty, and it will prove that it was not devoted to the good of the country or the welfare of their fellow-men; but, to the contrary, to the detriment of the country whose hospitality they were enjoying.

Their object was to overthrow the Government and to rob the people of their liberty, by force if necessary. As they had money in abundance, the proceeds of the gold they had won from the mines, they bought thousands of rifles and Maxim cannons—smuggled these, concealed in oil-casks, into the country for the purpose of using them against the people of the Transvaal to oust them out of their country, whither the capitalist had come and possessed himself of the gold fields. With this aim in view they had made a compact with one Cecil Rhodes to undertake a raid into the Transvaal, Dr. Jameson acting as the tool.

Behold! Your Majesty, the conduct of these men—the same men who are to-day clamoring about grievances. Yes! grievances which have made them rich, richer than ever any of the Voortrekkers was or any of their children will be.

They, then, who tried to overthrow the South African Republic, who stirred up strife in Johannesburg, on account of which many anxious and timid people fled from the city to escape probable hardships, are responsible for that dreadful railway accident in Natal, through which so many mothers and children lost their lives. They shall also have to answer before the judgment seat of God for the blood that was spilt during this contemptible Jameson raid. Here, again, Your Majesty, six Boers fell defending their rights and the independence of their country.

Thus have the Boers, from time to time, been aggravated and harassed. But even in these troubles they were not deserted by their God, who gave them refuge and enabled them to prove to the world that they are a meek and enlightened people; for, although they had it in their power to refuse to grant quarter or pardon to Jameson or his gang of freebooters, they did not shoot them down as, perhaps, another military force would have done, or even follow the example set them at Schlachtersnek.

The thought alone that they were British subjects sufficed the Boers not to treat them according to their deserts, but to hand them over to the law officers of Your Majesty to be dealt with as Your Majesty deemed fit. And what are the thanks we get for our magnanimity in liberating Jameson, Rhodes' henchman? Instead of thanks we are cursed with the revival of the Johannesburg agitation of 1895 and 1896.

These are the men who, encouraged and assisted by Mr. Chamberlain, are trying once again to bring misery upon the Transvaal, and as a means to this end, and in order to mislead the generous British public, have caused a false document, stated to have been voluntarily signed by 21,000 oppressed aliens, to be addressed to Your Majesty.

If Your Majesty would have that petition sent to Johannesburg to be publicly and impartially scrutinized, it would soon be made manifest how many thousands of the names appended thereto are of persons who had neither read nor seen it, and of numerous others who have long been dead. Armed with such a document they are now endeavoring to bring another calamity upon the Transvaal, and, perhaps, upon the whole of South Africa. Were such a scrutiny to take place, it could be positively proved that many whose names appear as signatories, rather than being against the continuance of the independence of the Transvaal, have grievances against the framers of that notorious petition, and would like to bring them up for withholding their wages or ill-treatment.

Such, we are sure, will faithfully stand by the Boers and fight for their adopted country; unlike the authors of that petition, whose guilty consciences are prompting them to leave the country or send their wives and money away to Natal or the Cape Colony. All this for fear of the consequences of their own wickedness. They have insured the works at their gold mines against damage, which they recklessly wish to cause to others. The wire-pullers of this vile scheme are Messrs. Rhodes, Chamberlain, and Jameson.

Your Majesty, what are we expected to do? We are told to-day they demand the franchise. Would it not be better for the people and for the independence of the country to give a vote to every raw Englishman, just arrived in the country, or even an army deserter, than to such unscrupulous capitalists and dishonest speculators, whose only object is to rob the South African Republic of its independence, in order to be enabled to do the same here with the gold mines as they did with the diamond mines at Kimberley under British rule?

Your Majesty, it was with a deep sense of pain at the critical state of affairs in South Africa that I commenced to write this letter, but my pain and indignation have been intensified by what I have lately read in the newspapers of Mr. Chamberlain and his statements anent the Transvaal, which he fondly hopes will be accepted as gospel truth by every one. He has never yet been in the Transvaal. I have been to London and yet I do not pretend to know all about it. Would it not be presumption on my part to think so? And does he alone know everything about the Transvaal? No! Your Majesty.

Now I see clearly that he has been misled, that he has believed in fiction; for how otherwise could he have uttered such language? Witness his bitter speech at Birmingham when he referred to the shooting of Edgar. Your Majesty, this man had struck another a mortal blow, and when the police tried to arrest him, he struck and almost killed one of them, who thereupon shot him dead.

It was indeed a regrettable incident; but has it not often occurred at Hyde Park and Trafalgar Square, that the English police have found it necessary to fire on an unarmed mob, thereby killing and wounding private citizens? And did ever any foreign minister dream of declaring war against England or make unreasonable demands on account of such action? Mr. Chamberlain is alarmed, forsooth, because a woman is murdered in the streets of Johannesburg—a circumstance which we all deplore, yet cannot discover the murderer.

We have offered a reward of 500 pounds to any one giving information that will lead to the conviction of the person who committed this crime, but up to the present we have failed in tracking the culprit. Now, Your Majesty, how many women were murdered in London by the so-called Jack the Ripper, who, notwithstanding Mr. Chamberlain, has never been caught? And yet who would ever dream of going to war with England because of this Jack the Ripper? Mr. Chamberlain, however, would set the whole of South Africa ablaze just because we have not captured a murderer, or because a jury has not convicted an Englishman in our police service of certain murder.

Will Your Majesty permit a small, weak State, that has time after time relinquished its rights, and has ever tried to live in peace and harmony with Your Majesty's people and Government, to be oppressed and overthrown by the world-renowned power and might of Great Britain, simply owing to the misrepresentations of the persons I have already mentioned?

Such is the inquiry of one who considers it an honor and privilege to extol Your Majesty, the Queen of Great Britain and Ireland and the Empress of India, and to acknowledge the generosity of the British nation and of several British statesmen.

No! Your Majesty, ever in supplication to the Almighty, who ruleth over Kings and Princes, and inclineth all to His great will, I, Your Majesty's humble petitioner, will never believe that Your Majesty will suffer the sacred rights of a weak, peace-loving people to be violated in your name, and South Africa to be cast into grief and mourning. To the contrary, I pray Your Majesty that peace, rest, prosperity, union, and co-operation will reign in Your Majesty's name throughout South Africa, and endure as long as there remains a Boer or an Englishman on earth.

Such is the wish and prayer of

Your Majesty's most humble petitioner.

P. J. Joubert.

The Story of the Boers March 1900

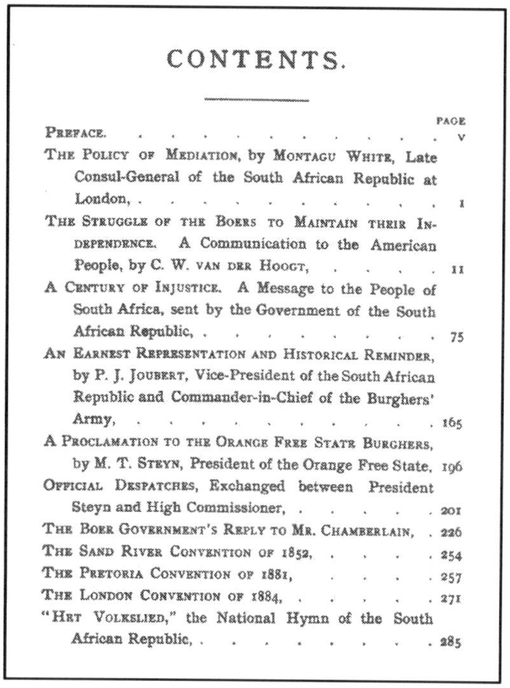

CONTENTS.

Cover and Contents.[530]

The
Story of the Boers
NARRATED BY
THEIR OWN LEADERS
Prepared under the Authority of
the South African Republics
By
C. W. VAN DER HOOGT
ILLUSTRATED
Preceded by
The Policy of Mediation
By MONTAGU WHITE
Late Consul-General to the South African Republics

NEW YORK AND LONDON
HARPER & BROTHERS, *Publishers*
1900

Harper Front.[531]

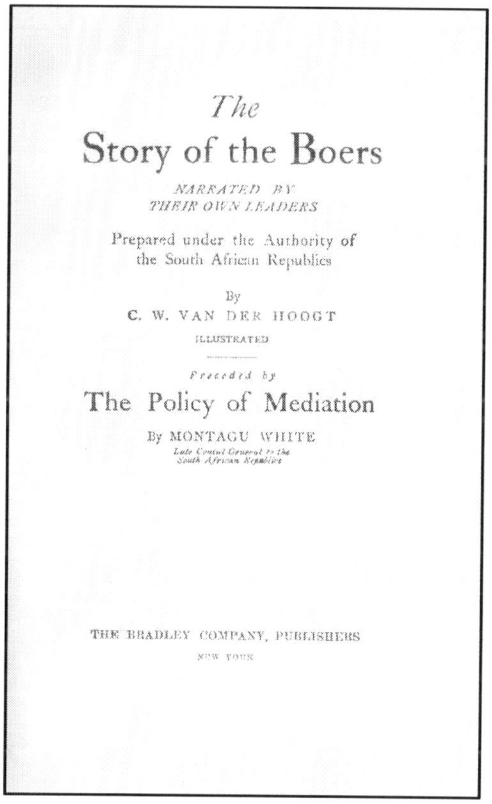

The
Story of the Boers
NARRATED BY
THEIR OWN LEADERS
Prepared under the Authority of
the South African Republics
By
C. W. VAN DER HOOGT
ILLUSTRATED
Preceded by
The Policy of Mediation
By MONTAGU WHITE
Late Consul-General to the South African Republics

THE BRADLEY COMPANY, PUBLISHERS
NEW YORK

Bradley Company Front.[532]

[530] Story of the Boers Harper & Brothers, New York and London, 1900 https://archive.org/details/storyboersnarra00whitgoog/mode/2up
[531] Story of the Boers. Harper & Brothers, NYPL Copy 1900: https://archive.org/details/storyboersnarra00whitgoog/mode/2up
[532] Story of Boers Bradley Co., U. Cal Copy, Bradley Co.: https://archive.org/details/storyofboersnarr00vand/page/n9/mode/2up

Quote

Nor Have I Ever Questioned That, In The Beginning Of The Trouble, The Boers Met With Much Of Which To Complain At The Hands Of The British Governments. Their Maltreatment Was Not Intentional, Indeed, But Rather A Result Of The Systematic Neglect,—To Use A Mild Word— Of Colonies And Their Inhabitants.

H. Rider Haggard,

In The Dedication of

The Swallow: A Tale Of The Great Trek

"NOR HAVE I EVER QUESTIONED THAT, IN THE BE- "GINNING OF THE TROUBLE, THE BOERS MET WITH "MUCH OF WHICH TO COMPLAIN AT THE HANDS OF "THE BRITISH GOVERNMENTS. THEIR MALTREAT- "MENT WAS NOT INTENTIONAL, INDEED, BUT RATHER "A RESULT OF THE SYSTEMATIC *NEGLECT*,—TO USE "A *MILD* WORD—OF COLONIES AND THEIR INHABI- "TANTS."

H. RIDER HAGGARD,

IN THE DEDICATION OF

"THE SWALLOW: A TALE OF THE GREAT TREK."

Sir Henry Rider Haggard.[533] [534]

March 1900 Preface #2

It is with some hesitation that I venture to undertake the rewriting and enlargement of the former issue of this work, which appeared in pamphlet form under the title of "A Century of Injustice," but complying with the wishes of our struggling brethren, my dear friends and kinsmen in far South Africa, I have endeavored to explain the real "grievances" of the Boer Governments against the wrongdoings of their oppressors. I had only one object in view—namely, to enlighten the American people, especially those in high authority. It is gratifying to state that the book has been favorably received, for many readers have assured me that, after the reading of the plain facts, they have become convinced that the cause of the Boers is right.

The unexpectedly large demand from all over the country and from all classes of people, as well as the urgent requests of many sympathizers and societies, has induced me to publish the work in a new and revised edition under the title of "The Story of the Boers." The new work has been prepared with great care and is much more complete. It contains, among other important official documents, the treaties of Sand River, of Pretoria, and of the London convention.

The friendly attitude of the press toward our sister republics, especially in my own city, has greatly encouraged me in undertaking this work.

I am indebted to my friend, Mr. H. H. de Vos, of New York, the ex-Vice-Consul of the Netherlands, for his valuable assistance. I express my renewed thanks to my friends in the East and West for their continued devotion to the good cause; and finally, I sincerely hope—it being my earnest desire to serve the Boers' cause—that the book in its new form may find its way into many homes, not for my own sake, but for that of the Boers.

Cornelius W. Van Der Hoogt.

Baltimore, Md., March, 1900

[533] Sir Henry Rider Haggard (22 June 1856–14 May 1925) was an English writer of adventure fiction romances set in exotic locations, predominantly Africa, and a pioneer of the lost world literary genre. He was also involved in land reform throughout the British Empire. His stories, situated at the lighter end of Victorian literature and including the eighteen Allan Quatermain stories beginning with King Solomon's Mines, continue to be popular and influential. H. Rider Haggard - Wikipedia See: List of works by H. Rider Haggard - Wikipedia

[534] The novel was adapted into a 1922 South African film. Swallow (novel) - Wikipedia

[Translation.] Department Of Foreign Affairs, Government Office, Pretoria, August 19, 1899.

To: The Honorable W. Conyngham Greene, C. B., British Agent, Pretoria.

Sir: With reference to your request for a joint inquiry, contained in your dispatches of 2 and 3 August, the Government of the South African Republic have the honor to suggest the alternative proposal for the consideration of Her Majesty's Government, which this Government trusts may lead to final settlement.

1. The Government are willing to recommend to the Volksraad and the People a five years' retrospective franchise, as proposed by His Excellency the High Commissioner at Bloemfontein on 1 June, 1899.

2. The Government are further willing to recommend to the Volksraad that eight new seats in the First Volksraad and, if necessary, also in the Second Volksraad, be given to the population of the Witwatersrand, thus with the two sitting members of the Goldfields, giving to the population thereof ten representatives in a Raad of thirty-six, and in future the representation of the Goldfields of this Republic shall not fall below the proportion of one-quarter of the total.

3. The new burghers shall, equally with the old burghers, be entitled to vote at the election for State President and Commandant General.

4. This Government will always be prepared to take into consideration such friendly suggestions regarding the details of the Franchise Law as Her Majesty's Government, through the British Agent, may wish to convey to it.

5. In putting forward the above proposals the Government of the South African Republic assumes:

a. That Her British Majesty's Government will agree that the present intervention shall not form a precedent for future similar action, and that in the future no interference in the internal affairs of the Republic will take place.

b. That Her Majesty's Government will not further insist on the assertion of the Suzerainty, the controversy on this subject being allowed tacitly to drop.

c. That arbitration (from which foreign element, other than Orange Free State, is to be excluded) will be conceded as soon as the franchise scheme has become law.

6. Immediately on Her British Majesty's Government accepting this proposal for a settlement, the Government will ask the Volksraad to adjourn for the purpose of consulting the people about it, and the whole scheme might become law, say, within a few weeks.

7. In the meantime the form and scope of the proposed tribunal are also to be discussed and provisionally agreed upon, while the franchise scheme is being referred to the people, so that no time may be lost in putting an end to the present state of affairs.

The Government trusts that Her Majesty's Government will clearly understand that in the opinion of this Government the existing franchise law of this Republic is both fair and liberal to the new population, and that the consideration that induces them to go further, as they do in the above proposals, is their strong desire to get the controversies between the two governments settled, and further to put an end to the present strained relations between the two governments, and the incalculable harm and loss it has already occasioned in South Africa, and to prevent a racial war, from the effects of which South Africa may not recover for many generations, perhaps never at all, and therefore this Government, having regard for all these circumstances, would highly appreciate it, if Her Majesty's Government, seeing the necessity of preventing the present crisis from developing still further and the urgency of an early termination of the present state of affairs, would expedite the acceptance or refusal of the settlement here offered.

I have the honor to be, Sir,
Your obedient servant,
F. W. Reitz, State Secretary.

[Translation.] Department of Foreign Affairs, Government Office. Pretoria, August 21, 1899.

To: The Honorable W. Conyngham Greene, C. B., British Agent, Pretoria.

Sir: In continuation of my dispatch of the 19th instant and with reference to the communication to you of the State Attorney this morning, I wish to forward you the following in explanation thereof, with the request that the same may be telegraphed to His Excellency the High Commissioner as forming part of the proposals of this government embodied in the above-named despatch:

1. The proposals of this Government regarding the question of franchise and representation contained in that despatch must be regarded as expressly conditional, on Her Majesty's Government consenting to the points set forth in par. 5 of the despatch—viz.:

a. In future not to interfere in the internal affairs of the South African Republic.

b. Not to insist further on its assertion of the existence of the Suzerainty.

c. To agree to arbitration.

2. With reference to par. 6 of the despatch, this Government trusts that it is clear to Her Majesty's Government that this Government has not consulted the Volksraad as to this question, and will only do so when an affirmative reply to its proposals has been received from Her Majesty's Government.

I have the honor to be, Sir,

Your obedient servant,

F. W. Reitz, State Secretary.

These letters were only written after the Boer Government had been confidentially assured by the British agent, Mr. Conyngham Greene, that the proposals formulated therein would be acceptable to this government.

And how were these proposals received? The following answer was sent by the British agent:

Her Majesty's Agency, Pretoria, August 30, 1899.

To: The Honorable the State Secretary.

Sir: With reference to your notes to me of the 19th and 21st instant I have to state to you that Her Majesty's Government have considered the proposals which the Government of the South African Republic have put forward therein as an alternative to those contained in the telegram from the Secretary of State to the High Commissioner of the 31st of July last, the substance of which I had the honor to communicate to you in my note of the 2nd of August.

Her Majesty's Government assume that the adoption in principle of the franchise proposals made by the High Commissioner at Bloemfontein will not be hampered by any conditions which would impair their effect, and that by the proposed increase of seats for the Gold Fields and by other provisions the Government of the South African Republic intend to grant immediate and substantial representation of the Uitlanders.

That being so, Her Majesty's Government are unable to appreciate the objections entertained by the Government of the South African Republic to a joint Commission of Inquiry into the complicated details and technical questions on which the practical effect of the proposals depends. Her Majesty's Government will, however, be ready to agree that the British Agent, assisted by such other persons as the High Commissioner may appoint, shall make the investigation necessary to satisfy them that the result desired will be achieved, and, failing this, to enable them to make those suggestions which the Government of the South African Republic state that they will be prepared to take into consideration.

Her Majesty's Government assume that every facility will be given to the British Agent by the Government of the South African Republic, and they would point out that the inquiry will be easier and shorter if the Government of the South African Republic will omit in the proposed new Law the complicated conditions as to previous registration, qualification and behavior which accompanied their previous proposals and which would have entirely nullified their beneficial effect. Her Majesty's Government hope that the Government of the South African Republic will wait to receive their suggestions founded on the report of the British Agent's investigation before submitting these new proposals to the Volksraad and the burghers.

With regard to the conditions of the Government of the South African Republic:

First, as regards intervention, Her Majesty's Government hope that the fulfilment of the promises made and the just treatment of the Uitlanders in future will render unnecessary any further intervention on their behalf, but Her Majesty's Government cannot of course debar themselves from their rights under the conventions, nor divest themselves of the ordinary obligations of any civilized power to protect its subjects in a foreign country from injustice.

Secondly, with regard to Suzerainty, Her Majesty's Government would refer the Government of the South African Republic to the second paragraph of the despatch of the Secretary of State to the High Commissioner of the 13th of July last, a copy of which I had the honor to forward to you in my note of the 18th instant.

Thirdly, Her Majesty's Government agree to a discussion of the form and scope of a tribunal of arbitration from which foreigners and foreign influence are excluded.

Such a discussion, which will be of the highest importance to the future relations of the two countries, should be carried on between the President of the South African Republic and the High Commissioner, and for this it appears to be necessary that a further Conference, which Her Majesty's Government suggest should be held at Cape Town, should be at once arranged.

Her Majesty's Government also desire to remind the Government of the South African Republic that there are other matters of difference between the two governments which will not be settled by the grant of political representation of the Uitlanders and which are not proper subjects for reference to arbitration. It is necessary that these should be settled concurrently with the questions now under discussion, and they will form with the question of arbitration proper subjects for consideration at the proposed conference.

I have the honor to be, Sir,

Your obedient servant,

Conyngham Greene.

The paragraph in the despatch of Mr. Chamberlain to Sir Alfred Milner, of July 13, 1899, above referred to, reads as follows:

"Her Majesty's Government concur generally in the views in your despatch and have no intention of continuing to discuss this question with the Government of the Republic, whose contention that the South African Republic is a sovereign international State is not in their opinion warranted either by law or history, and is wholly inadmissible. They therefore confine themselves to a very brief review of historical facts and of the opinions and intentions of their predecessors, on whose advice Her Majesty was pleased to grant—first the Pretoria Convention and later the London Convention—as shown in their official statements at the time."

Was this an acceptance or a rejection of the Boer proposals? Mr. Chamberlain has claimed recently that it was an acceptance. But the South African Republic took it for a refusal, and Mr. Chamberlain had the sad courage not to correct this wrong interpretation of his reply.

It will be noted that the Boer Government had made its proposal for a five years' retrospective franchise, subject to three conditions, viz., Her Majesty's Government:

(a) In future not to interfere in the internal affairs of the South African Republic.

(b) Not to insist further on its assertion of the existence of the suzerainty.

(c) To agree to arbitration.

Now we see that the answer to the first two conditions was no answer at all, and that the half affirmative answer to the third condition was deprived of all practical value by the additional statement that there were other matters of difference between the two Governments "which are not proper subjects for reference to arbitration."

If this answer of Mr. Conyngham Greene was not a rejection of the Boer proposals—and Mr. Chamberlain has claimed it was not—we can only assume that it was clothed in such obscure form that the Government of the Republic should take it as a refusal. As a matter of fact, it was so taken, and, under date of September 2, 1899, the South African Republic withdrew its offer of a five years' franchise, but declared its willingness to continue negotiations on the basis of its prior proposals. The subsequent answer of the British agent, under date of September 12, 1899, says that:

"Her Majesty's Government cannot now consent to go back to the proposals for which those in the note of the Government of the Republic of the 19th of August are intended as a substitute."

And he ends with the following ultimatum:

"If, however, as they most anxiously hope will not be the case, the reply of the Government of the South African Republic is negative or inconclusive, I am to state to you that Her Majesty's Government must reserve to themselves the right to reconsider the situation de novo and to formulate their own proposals for a final settlement."

And what was the positive and conclusive reply which Her Majesty's Government "most anxiously" hoped to receive? Nothing more or less than that the South African Republic would grant the five years' retrospective franchise with the increased number of Rand representatives in the Volksraad, and waive the three conditions enumerated in the letter of August 19th. And while asking the South African Republic to waive the conditions under which the offer was made, Mr. Chamberlain deemed it advisable to make some conditions himself, both of them humiliating to the Boers, and which he knew could not possibly be accepted.

These British conditions were that an inquiry should be made, either joint or unilateral, "that the new scheme of representation will not be encumbered by conditions which will nullify the intention to give substantial and immediate representation to the Uitlander"; and, furthermore, "Her Majesty's Government assume that, as stated to the British agent" (which was never done either officially or confidentially), "the new members of the Volksraad will be permitted to use their own language." And this demand was made by the same Government that, about seventy-five years before, had denied to the Boers the use of their own language, in violation of the guarantees given at the time of the transfer of the Cape Colony to the British in 1806.

The most important condition insisted upon by the South African Republic, in connection with its offer of a five years' franchise, was that the British Government should not insist further on its assertion of SUZERAINTY. The Boers were compelled to make this a "conditio sine qua non," in view of Mr. Chamberlain's assertion of the existence of British suzerainty.

In regard to the alleged suzerainty, it would be sufficient to call our readers' attention to the London Convention of 1884, the full text of which, and also of the Pretoria and Sand River conventions, are given in this book, to show that Mr. Chamberlain's claim was totally unjustifiable, and that the South African Republic was then and is still a sovereign and independent state.

This is the status of the Republic, notwithstanding Article 4 of that Convention provided that the South African Republic would conclude no treaty with any state or nation, other than Orange Free State, without Her Majesty's approval. At most, this was no more than a treaty stipulation between two sovereign powers. The present war has ended this treaty,

Mr. Chamberlain was evidently satisfied that he could not base his assertion of the existence of suzerainty on that article of the London convention, and he therefore made the discovery that only the articles of the Pretoria Convention of 1881, but not its preamble, were superseded by the 1884 Convention.

This novel claim was for the first time set up in Mr. Chamberlain's despatch of October 16, 1897, to the High Commissioner, in answer to the proposal of the South African Republic that all points in dispute between the two Governments relating to the convention should be referred to arbitration, the arbitrator to be nominated by the President of the Swiss Republic.

In reply to this proposal, Mr. Chamberlain said:

"Finally, the Government of the South African Republic propose that all points in dispute between Her Majesty's Government and themselves relating to the Convention should be referred to arbitration, the arbitrator to be nominated by the President of the Swiss Republic.

"In making this proposal the Government of the South African Republic appears to have overlooked the distinction between the Conventions of 1881 and 1884 and an ordinary treaty between two independent powers, questions arising upon which may properly be the subject of arbitration.

"By the Pretoria Convention of 1881 Her Majesty as Sovereign of the Transvaal Territory accorded to the inhabitants of that territory complete self-government subject to the suzerainty of Her Majesty, her heirs and successors, upon certain terms and conditions and subject to certain reservations and limitations set forth in 33 Articles, and by the London Convention of 1884 Her Majesty, while maintaining the preamble of the earlier instrument, directed and declared that certain other articles embodied therein should be substituted for the articles embodied in the Convention of 1881. The articles of the Convention of 1881 were accepted by the Volksraad of the Transvaal State and those of the Convention of 1884 by the Volksraad of the South African Republic.

"Under these conventions, therefore, Her Majesty holds towards the South African Republic the relation of a suzerain who has accorded to the people of that Republic self-government upon certain conditions, and it would be incompatible with that position to submit to arbitration the construction of the conditions on which she accorded self-government to the Republic."

Mr. Chamberlain has since insistently adhered to his contention, and in his subsequent despatches he has always referred to the conventions between Her Majesty's Government and the South African Republic, evidently meaning the London Convention of 1884 and the Pretoria Convention of 1881.

Now it is a fact beyond question that the principle of suzerainty as laid down in the 1881 Convention was from the very start the main cause of the objection on the Boer side. This objection was clearly expressed by the Transvaal deputation in its letter of November 14, 1883, to Lord Derby, at that time Secretary of State for the Colonies, and it was for this very reason that it was then asked that the Sand River Convention of 1852 be restored in force. In his reply of November 20, 1883, Lord Derby stated "that it is not possible to entertain the suggestion that the Sand River Convention has now any vitality, as that, if it could be revised, it would meet the requirements of the present case." "That Convention," Lord Derby further writes, "like the Convention of Pretoria, was not a treaty between two contracting Powers, but was a declaration by the Queen, and accepted by certain persons at that time her subjects, of the conditions under which, and the extent to which, Her Majesty could permit them to manage their own affairs without interference."

Could the difference between the Convention of 1881 and the new Convention under discussion be more distinctly expressed? And still, notwithstanding this clear statement, Mr. Chamberlain now holds that the preamble of the 1881 Convention, which gives it the character of the one-sided "declaration by the Queen," is still in existence.

Again, in his letter of February 15, 1884, transmitting the draft of the new Convention, Lord Derby says:

"By the omission of those Articles of the Convention of Pretoria which assigned to Her Majesty and to the British resident certain specific powers and functions connected with the internal government and the foreign relations of the Transvaal State, your Government will be left free to govern the country without interference, and to conduct its diplomatic intercourse and shape its foreign policy subject only to the requirement embodied in the fourth article of the new draft, that any treaty with a foreign state shall not have effect without the approval of the Queen."

We print below the first page of the draft of the new Convention, as transmitted with Lord Derby's letter, and call special attention to the head note.

A Convention Concluded Between Her Majesty the Queen, &C., &C., and the South African Republic.

NOTE.—The words and paragraphs bracketed or printed in italics [green text] are proposed to be inserted, those within a black link [black text] are proposed to be omitted.

A CONVENTION CONCLUDED BETWEEN HER MAJESTY THE QUEEN, &C., &C., AND THE SOUTH AFRICAN REPUBLIC.

NOTE.—*The words and paragraphs bracketed or printed in italics are proposed to be inserted, those within a black link are proposed to be omitted.*

Her Majesty's Commissioners for the settlement of the Transvaal Territory, duly appointed as such by a Commission passed under the Royal Sign Manual and Signet, bearing date the 5th of April, 1881, do hereby undertake and guarantee, on behalf of Her Majesty, that from and after the 8th day of August, 1881, complete self-government, subject to the suzerainty of Her Majesty, Her Heir and Successors, will be accorded to the inhabitants of the Transvaal Territory, upon the following terms and conditions, and subject to the following reservations and limitations:

Whereas, the Government of the Transvaal State, through its Delegates, consisting of Stephanus Johannes Paulus Kruger, President of the said State; Stephanus Johannès Du Toit, Superintendent of Education; Nicholas Jacobus Smit, a member of the Volksraad, have represented to the Queen that the Convention signed at Pretoria on the 3rd day of August, 1881, and ratified by the Volksraad of the said State on the 25th October, 1881, contains certain provisions which are inconvenient, and imposes burdens and obligations from which the said State is desirous to be relieved; and that the south-western boundaries fixed by the said Convention should be amended, with a view to promote the peace and good order of the said State, and of the countries adjacent thereto; and whereas Her Majesty the Queen, &c., &c., has been pleased to take the said representations into consideration: Now, therefore, Her Majesty has been pleased to direct, and it is hereby declared, that the following articles of a new Convention, signed on behalf of Her Majesty by Her Majesty's High Commissioner in South Africa, the Right Honorable Sir Hercules George Robert Robinson, Knight Grand Cross of the Most Distinguished Order of Saint Michael and Saint George, Governor of the Colony of the Cape of Good Hope, and on behalf of the Transvaal State (which shall herein-after be called the South African Republic) by the above-named Delegates, Stephanus Johannes Paulus Kruger, Stephanus Johannes Du Toit, Nicholas Jacobus Smit, shall, when ratified by the Volksraad of the South African Republic, be substituted for the articles embodied in the Convention of 3rd August, 1881; which latter, pending such ratification, shall continue in full force and effect.

Pages 37& 38 of Story of the Boers.

Her Majesty's Commissioners for the settlement of the Transvaal Territory, duly appointed as such by a Commission passed under the Royal Sign Manual and Signet, bearing date the 5th of April, 1881, do hereby undertake and guarantee, on behalf of Her Majesty, that from and after the 8th day of August, 1881, complete self-government, subject to the suzerainty of Her Majesty, Her Heir and Successors, will be accorded to the inhabitants of the Transvaal Territory, upon the following terms and conditions, and subject to the following reservations and limitations:

Whereas, the Government of the Transvaal State, through its Delegates, consisting of Stephanus Johannes Paulus Kruger, President of the said State; Stephanus Johannes Du Toit, Superintendent of Education; Nicholas Jacobus Smit, a member of the Volksraad, have represented to the Queen that the Convention signed at Pretoria on the 3rd day of August, 1881, and ratified by the Volksraad of the said State on the 25th October, 1881, contains certain provisions which are inconvenient, and imposes burdens and obligations from which the said State is desirous to be relieved; and that the south-western boundaries fixed by the said Convention should be amended, with a view to promote the peace and good order of the said State, and of the countries adjacent thereto, and whereas Her Majesty the Queen, &c.;, &c.;, has been pleased to take the said representations into consideration: Now, therefore, Her Majesty has been pleased to direct, and it is hereby declared, that the following articles of a new Convention, signed on behalf of Her Majesty by Her Majesty's High Commissioner in South Africa, the Right Honorable Sir Hercules George Robert Robinson, Knight Grand Cross of the Most Distinguished Order of Saint Michael and Saint George, Governor of the Colony of the Cape of Good Hope, and on behalf of the Transvaal State (which shall herein-after be called the South African Republic) by the above-named Delegates, Stephanus Johannes Paulus Kruger, Stephanus Johannes Du Toit, Nicholas Jacobus Smit, shall, when ratified by the Volksraad of the South African Republic, be substituted for the articles embodied in the Convention of 3rd August, 1881; which latter, pending such ratification, shall continue in full force and effect.

We see that immediately below the head note followed the preamble to the 1881 Convention, and that this preamble was within a black line, and consequently to be omitted. And still Mr. Chamberlain claims that this preamble is now in force, and on this contention he has gone to war with the South African Republic!

It is also to be noted that by the 1884 Convention the name of Transvaal State was changed into the South African Republic, in accordance with the wishes of the deputation. The only reason for this change was that the deputation desired to emphasize the difference between the status of their country under the 1881 and the 1884 Conventions.

In submitting the 1884 treaty to the Volksraad for ratification, the deputation said in its report of July 28, 1884:

"It (the treaty) is entirely bilateral, and your deputation was not placed in the humiliating situation of receiving from a Suzerain Government a one-sided document containing rules and provisions, but was recognized as a free contracting party.

"It (the treaty) therefore ends the British Suzerainty and restores, with the official recognition of her name, complete self-government to the South African Republic, with one single limitation regarding the conclusion of treaties with foreign Powers (Art. 4)."

The British Government never entered any protest against this interpretation of the 1884 Convention, as it would have been in duty bound to do, if in its opinion this Boer interpretation had been wrong.

As well might the United States claim suzerainty over the South American republics, because under the Monroe doctrine the former deny the right of European Powers to make conventions with them for territorial acquisitions on our continent.

From the foregoing it is plain that the South African Republic is a sovereign and independent state, and Great Britain has more than once admitted this status of the Republic prior to Mr. Chamberlain's discovery of 1897, and notably so in the convention concluded with the South African Republic in 1894, whereby Swaziland was placed under the protectorate of the Republic.

Who ever heard of a vassal state being made the protector of foreign territory? It was in accordance with the treaty of 1884, and shortly after its ratification, that Jonkheer Beelaerts van Blokland was recognized by Great Britain as minister plenipotentiary of the South African Republic, and held that position until his death in 1894. Moreover, the South African Republic appointed consuls throughout Europe, and the consul-general in London and consul in Durban were each granted exequatur by the British Government, and the latter has likewise asked exequatur for the British consuls in the Republic.

Another proof of its recognized sovereignty is that the Republic is admitted into the Postal Union, and is also a member of the Convention of Geneva. Furthermore, our own Government as well also as other Powers has been officially notified that there exists a state of war between Great Britain and the two South African Republics. Now, in view of the generally admitted doctrine that there cannot be a state of war between a suzerain and its vassal, Great

Britain in the face of this notice necessarily withdraws its claims of vassalage of the South African Republic, and it will require all of Mr. Chamberlain's eloquence to explain away the inconsistency between this notice of public war and his claim of suzerainty. Furthermore, our own Government and other Powers have also appointed consuls to and received exequaturs from the Government of the South African Republic.

Still stronger evidence of independent sovereignty is the fact that the United States consul at Pretoria is now acting in a protectorate capacity for British subjects; and, be it remembered, that this is at the special request of and as a matter of international courtesy to the British Government on the part of the United States, and by order of our courteous Secretary of State to that consul. Furthermore, it is well known that by international law, even with all these dealings between our Government and that of Great Britain, the American consul at Pretoria could not act in such capacity without the consent of the Government of the South African Republic, which could at any time withdraw his exequatur.

Taking all these facts into consideration, it is plain that there cannot be any question of suzerainty, and that the South African Republic was and is a sovereign independent state.

The American monthly Review of Reviews, one of the foremost magazines in this country, published in its "Leading Articles of the Month" (November number) under the title, "Mr. Chamberlain's Diplomacy," the following:

Diplomaticus' writes, in the Fortnightly Review for October, [1899] on 'Mr. Chamberlain's Mistakes.' This writer especially censures Mr. Chamberlain for putting forward a claim to the suzerainty of 1881:

Never,' says 'Diplomaticus,' 'was a good cause compromised in a more unhappy and gratuitous fashion. To have raised this question at any time would have been unwise and superfluous, but to do it at a time when the first object of statesmanship was avowedly to solve the franchise question was a fatal and unpardonable blunder. The claim was not only of very doubtful value, but it is absolutely futile and unprofitable. There was absolutely no necessity for raising it. Even if the whole of Mr. Chamberlain's case were granted, the suzerainty for which he contends is an empty thing. It would not give us a single right or advantage we do not already possess or which was not amply secured to us. The word alone, as used in the 1881 preamble, has no effective meaning.

A Grave Error.

But the worst of Mr. Chamberlain's blunder in putting forward this doubtful and unnecessary contention is that he thereby prejudiced the chances of an amicable settlement of the franchise question, inasmuch as he embittered the Boers and gave them a grievance with which to appeal not only to Dutch sympathy, but to the sympathy of not a few leaders of public opinion in Europe.

The extraordinary thing is that it was not raised in the heat of any controversy, but in the full tide of Sir Milner's conciliatory mission and before the High Commissioner had come to the conclusion that diplomacy was useless to liberate the Uitlanders and the moment for intervention had arrived. Mr. Chamberlain did not dream of it at the time of the raid, for when, in the negotiations which followed that deplorable act of folly, President Kruger referred to newspaper theories on the subject and declared roundly that the suzerainty "no longer exists" he abstained from controverting him and correctly took his stand by Article IV. It was in October, 1897, that, in answer to Proposals for a scheme of arbitration to settle all disputes between Pretoria and Downing Street, Mr. Chamberlain, for the first time for thirteen years, asserted the existence of the suzerainty in virtue of the 1881 preamble. The Transvaal repudiated the claim, and Sir Alfred Milner himself, following in the traditions of Sir Hercules Robinson and Lord Derby, was "unable to see anything material in this controversy." Nevertheless the Colonial Secretary persisted in it, with the result that, on May 9th of the present year, he received a note from Mr. Reitz, the ill-temper of which is apparent in every line, and especially in the extravagance and defiance of the claim that the South African Republic is a "sovereign international State."

It is not difficult to understand this ill-temper. The Boers honestly believed that in 1884 their diplomacy had obtained the revocation of the 1881 preamble. Now, on the morrow of the raid and on the eve of a fresh Uitlander campaign, when they had hoped to bargain for a further extension of their independence, they found themselves confronted by what they regarded as an attempt to reduce them to the status of the 1881 Convention. It was under this aggrieved impression that they went into the Bloemfontein conference. Can we wonder that the meeting failed?

How Mr. Chamberlain came to play this trump card into Mr. Kruger's hands passes my comprehension. The effect of the blunder is, however, clear, for if we have war it will not be on the question of a seven or five years' franchise, but, so far as Dutch public feeling is concerned, mainly on the question of the suzerainty.'"

Besides the clamor for franchise, the Uitlanders had a great many other "grievances," some of them of so puerile a character that it can be hardly understood how they could have been seriously brought forward. "Those poor, oppressed Uitlanders," who claimed that they came to the Republic on the "invitation" of the Government, thereby implying that they would not have come in the absence of such invitation! As if it ever needed an invitation to the class of people who principally compose the population of mining camps, to come to any gold-producing country. We know better; we know what hardships adventurous mining people will endure in their hunt for the yellow metal; and we know that not only is no invitation required, but they will flock to such a country, notwithstanding any and all cautions, warnings, and dangers.

The "cruel Boers" did not thank them for coming. They did not give at once these adventurers the franchise! They did not offer these Uitlanders the so-much-coveted citizenship of their Republic—in other words, did not extend to these strangers the privilege to rule the country of the Boers in accordance with the wishes of Cecil

Rhodes and others of his ilk! Just imagine how anxious men like Alfred Beit, Robinson, John Hays Hammond, and the like must have been to become burghers and to be commandeered into the Boer army, to serve the South African Republic without pay, in case of war!

The fact is that only an insignificant, small percentage of these Uitlanders came to the Republic with any purpose of staying there. The English Uitlanders wanted the franchise, not for the sake of the country, which they would not adopt as their own, but only for their own nefarious purpose. Yet the Boer Government was willing, for the sake of peace, to run the risk and to give them the franchise. But, as above shown, that offer, made as it was upon the suggestion of the British Government itself, was rejected by this Government and the rejection was accompanied by demands for further concessions!

As an illustration of the "liberality" shown by British colonial authorities, we might recall that at the very same moment these oppressed Uitlanders were complaining, 3,000 Dutch residents of British Guiana, born on its soil and about equal in number to the British subjects in that colony, were and still are not entitled to hold an office under either the executive, legislative, or judicial branches of the Colonial Government.

Then we have the cry of "taxation without representation." What is the rate of taxation of American mines in that part of Alaska claimed by England as British territory, and what representation have they?

That the Uitlander, who bought mineral property and became rich, has to pay taxes, is no more than reasonable, and that the English pay a large share no one denies; but that does not indicate that they have any right to dictate to the lawmakers to make laws to suit them. The Boer Government had always been courteous and ready to listen to the reasonable demands of this floating population, and it is admitted that the laws and taxation are as liberal as those of any other country. Does not the British Government itself, and its Colonial Government also, deny to denizens, of however long residence, the election franchise, and compel them to pay taxes at whatever rates the Parliament and Colonial legislatures are pleased to exact?

Moreover, the taxes levied on the Uitlanders are exactly the same as those levied on the burghers, and if the former have paid more it only shows that they soon became possessed of more assessable property. The taxes levied on the gold mines by the Republic were only 2.5 per cent. on the production; in the British Klondike it is 10 per cent.; and in Rhodesia, under the benevolent rule of that great philanthropist, Cecil Rhodes, it is even 50 per cent. It may be remarked here that no large quantities of gold are found in Rhodesia, and that this is one of the very evident reasons why Mr. Rhodes and his company are so anxious to take in the South African Republic under their own special suzerainty.

Another crying injustice to the Uitlander was the dynamite monopoly. Certainly we are no friends of monopolies, but we desire to submit that President Kruger had very good reasons for preferring that dynamite be made in his own country. Furthermore, the price as it was reduced was hardly higher than the cost of the imported article with the cost of transportation and duty added thereto, and it certainly was not higher than the prices charged at Kimberley and in Rhodesia.

Another "grievance" of the Uitlander was the language of the South African Republic. The British demanded that the English language should be made the official language on equal footing with the Dutch. Because in the Johannesburg district there lived more English-speaking people than in other parts of the Republic, they wished to make their own language the official one. Does not such a demand seem ridiculous? As a rule, the officials of the Government understand both English and Dutch, and the Uitlanders never found any difficulty in carrying on their business in their own language.

What an absurd claim of grievance this is, and is it not the universal custom that instruction in schools, supported by the Government, should be given in the language of the country? Does, for instance, the English Government support any schools in Great Britain where instruction is given in Dutch or other foreign language? But even in this respect the Boer Government has shown its extreme liberality by paying subsidies for English schools in the gold fields.

The Uitlanders further complained that their right of free speech and of holding meetings was not respected. This is wholly untrue. The authorities very wisely prohibited the holding of meetings when rebellion against the Government was openly preached, and for the same reason they did not allow the class of people who resorted to such meetings to carry weapons.

There are still a great many other grievances, most of them too puerile to deserve mention, but we wish with a single word to refer to one of the complaints, brought forward by a man of standing, Mr. Fitzpatrick, Secretary of the Uitlander Committee. Mr. Fitzpatrick felt that his rights as a free-born British subject were grievously infringed by a decree issued by the Boer Government, forbidding the employment of barmaids in Johannesburg. We must admit that this barbarous decree fully shows that the Boers have not the slightest appreciation of the blessings of British civilization of that kind.

One of the "sorely oppressed" Uitlanders is now travelling through this country denouncing the Boers, and even using churches for the purpose of bringing his false statements before the public. This is his mode of acknowledging the magnanimity shown him by President Kruger. I refer to Mr. John Hays Hammond, who has recently demonstrated in figures how much more profit the mine owners could make if the Republic were to be swallowed up by the British Empire. One of his arguments is that the Boer Government does not furnish sufficient native laborers for the gold mines and that the wages are too high. Under British rule this would soon be changed for the benefit of the Uitlander capitalist. There would be more laborers and the wages of the natives would be reduced. This is indeed an argument that should strongly appeal to the American public! It is no more ridiculous than the other British arguments, all based on greed.

We may ask here in what manner Mr. Hammond proposes to supply the increased number of natives. By compulsory laws? And this under the highly civilized British Government, which is always so anxious to protect the natives against the Boers, who, according to English slanderers, are nothing but "concealed slave-holders"!

Mr. Hammond is a perambulating monument of Boer clemency. He was arrested after the Jameson Raid and sentenced to death as one of the instigators of this infamous conspiracy, which was condemned by the whole civilized world. President Kruger magnanimously changed his sentence to a fine. But the fact remains that this man, a citizen of the United States, assisted the subjects of a European monarchy in their attempt to trample down the flag of a republic. My fellow-citizens, can you put any value upon the statements of such a man?

All these "grievances" and a great many others equally frivolous were taken up by Mr. Chamberlain and made the subject of official remonstrations lodged with the Boer Government. And yet all the time Mr. Chamberlain disclaimed any intention to interfere with the internal affairs of the Republic! Of course, his only purpose was to exasperate the Boers, to drive them into a war in which he fondly hoped to blot out the two Republics from the map of Africa. The Boers became soon firmly convinced that the final struggle was coming, and that no amount of concessions would avail. They knew that triumvirate Rhodes, Milner, and Chamberlain were bound to annex the Transvaal, and President Kruger and his people prepared to defend their land, their homes, and firesides.

Under the auspices of the South African League, a petition signed by "21,000" alleged English subjects was sent to the Queen, asking Her Majesty's interference. This was, of course, a new pretext for Mr. Chamberlain to become more persistent in his interference and to change his requests for concessions into demands.

Let me here pause a moment to show how the 21,000 signatures to this "petition" were obtained.

The following sworn affidavit from an American citizen, selected from the many similar documents published in the South African Republic Green Book, and submitted to the High Commissioner at the Bloemfontein Conference, will serve as an illustration:

Appearing before me, Justice of the Peace in Johannesburg, South African Republic, this day, the 24th of April, 1899, Thomas Bernard Regan swears and declares:

"I live at 33 Critic Building, Johannesburg, and I am an American citizen. Some time ago, before it became known that there was to be sent a petition to Her Majesty the Queen of England, claiming that it contained 21,000 signatures, a certain Alexander A. Banier approached me with a few sheets of blank paper, with some numbers of pages on the top, asking me to sign a petition. I asked him to show me the petition, and he answered that he had not the petition with him, but that the contents were to ask the British intervention in the affairs of the Transvaal. I refused to sign. He remained in my presence and approached a Mr. Schimmelbusch, asking him the same question. I overheard the conversation, and among other things, Schimmelbusch said: 'How do I know that I am not signing my death Warrant?' I was curious and gave all my attention to the incident. I saw that Banier went to a table, sat down and commenced to write. Afterwards he rose from the table and showed me the same sheets of paper. I discovered that they were now filled with from ten to fifteen names. When he showed this to me, he said: 'How's that?' I looked at him and his papers with astonishment. I swear positive that it had been utterly impossible to get these signatures and I am convinced that these names were forgeries."

Signed: T. B. Regan.
Sworn before me,
Signed: Smuts De Villiers,
Justice of the Peace.

A counter petition, genuinely signed by 23,000 Uitlanders, who declared their loyalty to the South African Republic Government, was simply ignored by Mr. Chamberlain and contemptuously brushed aside.

I think that it is now clear to every reader of this book that Mr. Chamberlain and his followers had made up their mind, long before the Boers took up the arms to defend their rights, that the South African Republic, and incidentally the Orange Free State, had to be conquered, and that no concessions on the part of the Boers would have prevented the consummation of that dastardly scheme. In the mean time, and previous to the negotiations already mentioned, war preparations were going on and a cry for war was heard in the English Parliament. To gain time until the British Government had a sufficient army landed so as to dictate to the Boers its own terms, was the purpose of the British negotiations.

The Government at Pretoria waited for Mr. Chamberlain's "new proposals" until October 9th, after which they demanded a withdrawal of the British troops from the borders of both Republics and that the despatch of troops to South Africa, pending the negotiations, should stop. Again the Government of the South African Republic pleaded for arbitration, and it was ready to name the Government of the United States or the Republic of Switzerland as the arbitrator; but the plea was ignored. Is not this fact of itself sufficient to convince every impartial person of the justice of the cause of the Boers, that they were anxious to arbitrate and let others decide upon the question, who is in the wrong? Would not that have been the honest way out of the difficulties?

My fellow-citizens, judge for yourselves, what could the two Republics do under these circumstances? There was nothing else to be done than to call the burghers to arms for the defence of their liberty, their independence, and their homes from ruthless foreign invasion. The war was forced upon them by a powerful and relentless foe, whose creed is that "might makes right," and who is bent upon the conquest of weaker nations wherever opportunity may safely offer. The Boers have made all the concessions they could make, far more than any people on earth could be expected to make in like case.

Would not it have been an unpardonable mistake on the part of President Kruger to tarry any longer after such gross denials of common justice by the British Government? Perhaps he waited too long, but up to the last moment he tried honestly to prevent the terrible war that has already cast the shadow of death into so many homes in both countries. It is due to Mr. Conyngham Greene, the British agent at Pretoria, to state that he also worked for peace up to the last moment, and it is a fact that Messrs. Chamberlain and Milner have not forgiven Mr. Greene for his honorable efforts. He is now in disgrace, so far as his government is concerned.

It is plain to everybody who is reasonably well informed that Messrs. Chamberlain and Milner have in effect openly admitted that the war in South Africa is not started for the purpose of obtaining redress for the grievances of the Uitlanders. Mr. Chamberlain has spoken of the "dangerous ideals of the two Dutch Republics," and Mr. Milner has distinctly stated that he was determined to "break the dominion of Afrikanderdom."

And what were these dangerous ideals of the two Republics? Simply the determination of the Boers to maintain their independence and liberty and to uphold their Dutch character. Is this a sin against civilization? Have not the Boers always been the pioneers of civilization in South Africa? It was they who first opened that region of country to commerce. Their natural desire to gather the fruits of their own toil, paid for in blood and tears, is now called "a dangerous ideal." Has not England had time and again every possible chance to reconcile the Dutch element in this region to British dominion? And what do we see? For almost a century the Cape Colony has been under English rule, and yet the Dutch language is still spoken by a majority of the population. The Afrikanders have a majority in the Cape Parliament, with an Afrikander Prime Minister. The Dutch element still has a dominating influence in South Africa. Superior power has taken the land from them, but it can never convert the Boer to British thought or rule.

Instead of treating the Dutch kindly, the English governments followed the policy of slandering, defaming and humiliating them, driving them again and again from their old settlements into the wilderness. And still the English think that the Dutch should accept them as masters. By a kind treatment they might have reconciled the Dutch, for as James Anthony Froude, the well known English historian, remarked: "The Boer responds more readily than most men to kindness and justice. If you try to drive him, there is no mule in either hemisphere more stubborn."

And yet the English boast that they can subdue the Dutch descendants of the heroes of the Eighty Years' War. For an answer to this I wish again to quote what Olive Schreiner says in her Essay:

I suppose it would be quite possible for the soldiers to shoot all male South Africans who appeared in arms against them. It might not be easy, a great many might fall, but a great Empire could always import more to take their places; we could not import more, because it would be our husbands and sons and fathers who were falling, and when they were done we could not produce more. Then the war would be over. There would not be a house in Africa—where African-born men and women lived—without its mourners, from Sea Point to the Limpopo; but South Africa would be pacified—as Cromwell pacified Ireland three centuries ago, and she has been being pacified ever since!

As Virginia was pacified in 1677;[535] its handful of men and women in defence of their freedom were soon silenced by hired soldiers. 'I care that for the power of England,' said 'a notorious and wicked rebel' called Sarah Drummond, as she took a small stick, and broke it, and lay it on the ground. A few months after her husband and all the men with him were made prisoners, and the war was over. 'I am glad to see you,' said Berkeley, the English governor, 'I have long wished to meet you; you will be hanged in half an hour!' and he (her husband?) was hanged and twenty-one others with him, and Virginia was pacified.[536]

But a few generations later in that State of Virginia was born George Washington, and on the 19th of April, 1775, was fought the battle of Lexington—Where once the embattled farmers stood, and fired a shot, heard round the world,—and the greatest crime and the greatest folly of England's career was completed. England acknowledges it now.

A hundred or a hundred and fifty thousand imported soldiers might walk over South Africa; it would not be an easy walk; but it could be done. Then from east and west and north and south would come men of pure English blood to stand beside the boys they had played with at school, and the friends they had loved; and a great despairing cry would rise from the heart of Africa. But we are still few. When the war was over the imported soldiers might leave the land—not all; some must be left to keep the remaining people down. There would be quiet in the land. South Africa would rise up silently, and count her dead and bury them. She would know the places where she found them. South Africa would be peaceful. There would be silence, the silence of a long exhaustion—but not peace!

Have the dead no voices? In a thousand farmhouses black robed women would hold memory of the count, and outside under African stones would lie the African men to whom South African women gave birth under our blue sky. There would be silence, but no peace.

You say that all the fighting men in arms might have been shot. Yes, but what of the women? If there were left but five thousand pregnant South African-born women, and all the rest of their people destroyed, those women would breed up again a race like to the first. Oh, lion-heart of the North, do you not recognize your own lineage in these whelps of the South? We cannot live if we are not free!

The grandchildren and great-grandchildren of the men who lay under the stones (who will not be English then, nor Dutch, but only Africans), will say, as they pass those heaps: 'There lie our fathers or great-grandfathers who died in the first great War of Independence,' and the descendants of the men who lay there will be the aristocracy of Africa. Men will count back to them and say: 'My father or my great-grandfather lay in one of those graves.' We shall know no more of Dutch or English then; we shall know only one great African people."

And now the war has come with all its terrors. Thousands of brave men have fallen already on both sides, either killed or maimed for life. Thousands of children have become fatherless, thousands of wives and mothers will vainly wait for the return of their husbands and sons. And for what purpose did the soldiers of England give their lives? For right, for justice, for civilization? No, a thousand times no! They died because Mr. Chamberlain and his party of stock jobbers and speculators, supported by the jingoes, want the Republics of South Africa and the gold mines therein. And all this happening at the end of the nineteenth century!

[535] Bacon's Rebellion was an armed rebellion by Virginia settlers that took place from 1676 to 1677. It was led by Nathaniel Bacon against Colonial Governor William Berkeley, after Berkeley refused Bacon's request to drive Native American Indians out of Virginia. Bacon's Rebellion - Wikipedia See Also: Treaty of 1677 - Wikipedia The treaty designated those that signed as "tributary tribes", which signified that they were guaranteed control over their traditional homelands, hunting and fishing rights, the right to keep and bear arms, and other rights so long as they maintained their loyalty towards the English Crown.

[536] Note Charles II's observation as to William Berkeley's conduct. "He has hung more men in that naked land than I have for the murder of my father." Berkeley was recalled.

Is there anything that can more strikingly describe the horrors of this war than the following touching story told in the letter of an English soldier:

We were out looking after the wounded at night when the fight was over, when I came across an old, white-bearded Boer. He was lying behind a bit of rock, supporting himself on his elbows....

I kept my eye on the old chap. But when I got near I saw that he was too far gone to raise his rifle. He was gasping hard for breath, and I saw he was not long for this world. He motioned to me that he wanted to speak, and I bent over him. He asked me to go and find his son—a boy of thirteen—who had been fighting by his side when he fell.

Well, I did as he asked me, and under a heap of wounded I found the lad, stone dead, and I carried him back to his father. Well, you know I'm not a chicken-hearted sort of a fellow. I have seen a bit of fighting in my time, and that sort of thing knocks all the soft out of a chap.

But I had to turn away when the old Boer saw his dead lad. He hugged the body to him and moaned over it, and carried on in a way that fetched a big lump in my throat. Until that very moment I never thought how horrible war is. I never wanted to see another shot fired. And when I looked round again the old Boer was dead, clasping the cold hand of his dead boy.

And how do the Boers carry on this War? Do they behave like half barbarians, as they were and still are called by the British? Do not they treat their wounded enemies and prisoners with the greatest kindness, even with true Christian forgiveness? And how do the highly civilized British behave? I need only refer to the slaughter of the sixty Boers at Elandslaagte in cold blood by the Royal Lancers, this is no Boer report; the atrocities were minutely described in the approving London Times in letters from soldiers and officers.

"Fine pig sticking;" "The bag was sixty," so writes one of Her Majesty's officers. [Regarding the charge at Elandslaagate] These men and officers of the Royal Lancers still serve Queen Victoria. They were not considered to have disgraced the uniform. But in every land outside of the British Empire they have placed themselves beyond the pale of humanity and have brought everlasting contempt and disgrace on the British army.

Allow me to refer to the behavior of an officer of our own country at the moment of victory—to the immortal words of Captain (now Rear Admiral) Philip of the United States Navy at the battle of Santiago:

"Don't cheer, boys, the poor fellows are dying!" The British officer boasting that he and his soldiers killed defenceless enemies, enjoying the sport as if it were a mere "pig sticking," and the other officer stopping the very natural cheering of his men at the moment of victory in the presence of a dying enemy, and all his men reverentially obeying his command!

Another instance of the brutal violation of civilized warfare as carried on by the mother of civilization was the tragic death of General Kock. By uncontradicted evidence it is shown that the general did not die of his wound, but only in consequence of the exposure and neglect. He was stripped by British soldiers while lying helpless on the field.

The following is a copy of the protest sent by the government of the South African Republic to the foreign consuls at Pretoria:

"I have the honor to call your Government's attention both to the report announcing the engagement last night (October 18) between a commando and the English near Mafeking, the English having 1,000 Kaffir auxiliaries (one of whom was wounded and is a prisoner), and the results of this information and other reports coming in from the east frontier where the Kaffirs have been called to arms by the British authorities."

This shows that the British Government commits the unpardonable crime of arming the blacks against the whites in a struggle unjustly forced on the South African Republic. This act may have the gravest consequences for all white Africa.

I am commanded to inform your Government that a further document received is General Joubert's protest to Secretary Reitz, at Pretoria, under six heads, as follows:

First.—That the British at Elandslaagte fired on an ambulance.

Second.—That a British lancer attempted to assassinate a doctor wearing the Geneva cross, missing the surgeon, but killing his horse.

Third.—The tying of thirteen prisoners, some of them wounded, behind a Maxim gun and dragging them along.

Fourth.—That at Dundee the fugitives retired under cover of a white flag while the main body was fighting the Orange Free State troops.

Fifth.—That an armored train, protected by a white flag, repaired a bridge.

Sixth.—That the British are recruiting mounted Basutos.

General Joubert appends a document seized among an officer's effects at Dundee. The paper is a communication from a Basutoland magistrate, informing the general commanding the Glencoe camp that there will be no difficulty in procuring Basutos at 5 shillings per day, and asking: 'Must they bring their horses?'

General Joubert added: 'I am preserving the original of this document.'

The terrible consequences of the use of Kaffirs by the English are illustrated by the following report:

Rustenburg, 16th of December, 1899.

At the Landdrost's office of the Rustenburg district has been deposited the evidence, confirmed by oath, of women and girls whom the English had caught by Kaffirs. They declare that while being held by the Kaffirs they were outraged by the English.

Do raise your voices in the name of humanity and civilization against such atrocities. The poor beings are at the hospital at this moment.

Baron Von Dalwig -Formerly Captain of the Royal Prussian Horse, now Captain and Commander of a Battery in the Boer Army.

How the Red Cross flag is respected by the English is fitly illustrated in a report of Dr. Ransbottom, head of the Boer Red Cross.

On November 28 Dr. Ransbottom was ordered by General Cronje to proceed with his ambulance to the battlefield. After finishing their work the doctors were informed by the British commander that they and all the nurses were considered as prisoners of war. Their protests were ignored, and the doctors were sent to Cape Town, and arrived there on December 4th, having made the trip in cattle trucks.

They were then informed that it was all a mistake and on the same day were returned to the Modder River. Upon their arrival there they asked for their wagons and material, and Captain Ross informed them that he had been instructed not to give them up, and the doctors and nurses had to walk with their baggage on their back to the Boer camp.

Of course this was merely a "mistake" of some overzealous British officer, but the question arises, Where are the Boer ambulance wagons?

I recall the slandering cablegrams, containing the accusations in the strongest language, that the Boers disregarded the white flag and were shooting upon the ambulances of the Red Cross Society. But General Buller was compelled to cable to his home government that this was "satisfactorily explained by the enemy." I wish to recall the official statement of Major Donegan, chief medical officer at Glencoe, who wired to the state secretary at Pretoria an expression of thanks on behalf of all the British officers and men in the hospitals at Glencoe, for the extreme kindness shown them by the Boer officers and men.

I wish to recall General Joubert's kind act toward Lady Symons. From an excellent sketch given by the New York Herald of November 12, describing "Slim Piet," his pet name among Afrikanders, which means literally crafty or clever Peter (or to put it in plain English: "He was one too many for me, or he outwitted me!"), as a kind gentleman, splendid general, the idol of his fighting men, I take the following:

Have not you English always followed on our heels—not on us here only, but all over the world, always conquering, always getting more land? We were independent when you came here. We are independent now, and you shall never take our independence from us. The whole people will fight. You may shed blood over all South Africa, but it will only be over our dead bodies that you will seize our independence. Every Dutchman in South Africa will fight against you. Even the women will fight. You may take away our lives, but our independence—never.'

That is what Pietrus Jacobus Joubert said to an English correspondent in Pretoria two years ago. It was printed in a London newspaper November 30, 1897. Joubert is showing the world to-day something of the fine old Dutch spirit he talked of in 1897. He is doing some of that fighting he predicted then.

It was very much like Joubert to talk like that to the English correspondent, and very much like him, too, to cable condolences to Lady Symons over the dead body of her fallen husband. He is frankness and honesty personified. He is a man and a soldier of the type Englishmen and Americans like. Nothing could be more courteous than his treatment of his English prisoners from Ladysmith. Nothing could be more kinder than his care for the wounded enemy.

Nothing is written about Joubert that is not comment on his fairness.

General Joubert told the truth when more than two years ago he predicted that even the women would fight for liberty, for I have found in the official lists of the wounded and killed which I received from South Africa lately, many names of young women, who fought side by side with their husbands and relatives.

And still the British press continue to call the Boers cowards, but the Boers can well afford to remain silent. Magersfontein, Colenso, Stormberg and Spion Kop speak louder than words can do. How can England expect sympathy from the descendants of the Dutch, who settled that country and who are one large family, related by kinship? Step by step England has, by its mighty power and money, taken the conquered land from the Dutch, who are a peaceful and God-fearing people. Are these Boers to blame if they prefer to die rather than give up their last acre of land?

They have been driven from the one place to the other, and they have found no rest. It is always England and English elements that disturb the peace.

A high official wrote to me from Pretoria in September:

"We desire peace and a quiet developing of our beloved country, and you may rest assured that if war breaks out it will be forced upon us by the impossibility of submitting to unreasonable demands. If it comes, we shall defend our fatherland to the last drop of our blood."

These patriotic people simply desire to keep their country, which they have developed and civilized.

I heard recently an Englishman say: "We are foolish to spill so much blood to get that little piece of land. Have we not territory enough?" I fully agree with him. How many lives of both countries have already been sacrificed? How much distress is already brought over so many families who mourn the loss of their beloved ones? But War, War! is still the cry in England, and still growing fiercer. Oorlog! Oorlog! was the signal heard over the veldts of South Africa. War among people made by the same Creator of mankind! Who is to blame for this terrible slaughter of men? I again call the attention of the reader to those dishonest men who created the so-called "grievances of the Uitlanders."

The Boers honestly tried to meet even the pretended grievances, but as Olive Schreiner sadly remarked: "There have been told so many lies about them."

And who are the people who have told these lies? They are the same British Uitlanders, now safely located at Cape Town and Durban, who, under the leadership of Rhodes, and aided by his subsidized press, have slandered the Boers for years.

But there are other Uitlanders: Americans, Germans, Hollanders, Belgians, Irish, Scandinavians, French, Swiss, Italians, even English, have of their own free will taken up arms against Great Britain and pledged fidelity to the Republic.

The Washington Post of January 15, 1900, contains an article written by my friend, Mr. Fred F. Schrader, from which I quote the following:

I know of no single instance that punctures the fabric of the luminous lie about the grievance of the Outlanders as simply and completely as the following letter, received by the secretary of state for the Transvaal republic, Mr. F. W. Reitz:

To: Hon. F. W. Reitz, State Secretary P. O. Box 5, Johannesburg, 14 Oct., '99.

Honored Sir—I have to request you will forward to the high commissioner at the earliest opportunity the enclosed medal for services rendered by me to Her Majesty the Queen. My other decorations will be forwarded to the military authorities in England.

So much for the agitation for the franchise.

I am, honorable sir, your obedient servant,

Edw. L. Stratton-Collins.

Mr. Collins was until four years ago a captain in the British army. He resigned and went to the gold fields. He lived peaceably and prospered until the agitation of the past three years almost ruined his business. When war was declared, he took the oath of allegiance to the Republic, has sent all his medals of honor and heroism back to the English Government, and is now on the border fighting as a true burgher against what he knows to be, by personal observation, the scheme of Rhodes to overthrow a peaceable government. There are other similar instances.

President Kruger has been accused of oppressing the Jewish population. The truth is that the Jews in the Transvaal are among his warmest friends and admirers. They have formed companies, which are now doing police duty to guard the towns.

It is an acknowledged fact that President Kruger is one of the greatest statesmen the world has ever produced. His diplomacy, knowledge of international affairs and his natural sagacity have astonished the nations of the world, although he never had any training in that direction. He remains, however, the humble Oom Paul, taking the natural-born talents as an undeserved gift from the hands of his Lord and Master, not to be tied up in a napkin, but to be accounted for as a faithful steward.

He has at his side, as State Secretary, the Hon. F. W. Reitz, ex-President of the Orange Free State, one of the ablest jurists in South Africa, a man who possesses the confidence of his people, and is admired and respected by every one with whom he comes in contact. Olive Schreiner describes him as a man who manifested in his career a beautiful character. Dr. Reitz is the successor of Dr. W. J. Leyds, who served the country in the same capacity for a number of years. Dr. Leyds has succeeded Jonkheer Beelaerts van Blokland as Minister Plenipotentiary of the Republic in Europe. He has been accredited to and fully recognized by the following powers: Russia, Germany, France, the Netherlands, Belgium and Portugal. He is a scholar and a distinguished lawyer, and is known as a specialist on international law. His working ability is well known, and he serves his adopted country in his present position with great devotion.

While the second gentleman of the land, the popular Commander-in-Chief of the Boer forces, General Joubert, is directing the military operations with his able generals, Schalk, Burger, Botha, De Wet and others in the field (alas! our brave Cronje, the "lion of South Africa," is now deprived of serving his beloved country), the President is surrounded at home with excellent men like Reitz, Wolmarans and other members of Council, directing the internal affairs of the Republic, and he is well represented in Europe by his former Secretary of State.

If we realize this situation of affairs, does it not stir up a feeling of admiration for these brave and patriotic men who are so well able to rule their own country if they were let alone? Is it not a shame that they are now compelled to fight for their liberties—a war declared for conquest by a lustful monarchy? But they will submit until the last extremity, for they are a brave people—free Republicans as we are here in America. They are our brethren, brethren in more than one sense. Their symbol is ours, their principles are ours, they love as we do freedom and independence.

They have the same flag—only they added the green to it, the color of hope—that same dear old red, white and blue, adopted as our flag after the Declaration of Independence. They are fighting the same nation that our people fought—not to gain independence, but to maintain their independence. My fellow-citizens, do you know that these South African burghers are the descendants of the same Dutch people who first settled Manhattan Island?

New York, formerly New Amsterdam; Breukelen, afterwards called Brooklyn, and Harlem, were each founded by these sturdy Dutch who came here with their Bible under their arm to build up a new country. There is no country whose history is more closely connected with the history of the United States of America than little Holland. It was the Dutch, who, for love of the principles of America, fought in the ranks of George Washington, the father of his country.

It was the Dutch who first took sides with the Americans in their struggle for liberty and independence, and the first who saluted the flag which was the same as theirs. It was the Dutch who sent their battleships to this coast and landed provisions to feed the soldiers, facing the fleet of England. It was the Dutch in Manhattan and Staten Island with whom the great founder of this country spent his happiest hours. He loved them and was by them beloved.

It was the "Unie van Utrecht" after which the Constitution of America was formulated, and the "Afzwering van Philip" on which the Declaration of Independence was founded—two of the most important Dutch national documents were thus taken as a model to aid the lawmakers of America to form the great Republic of the United States.

The Holland American has a right to be proud of his pedigree. There are thousands and thousands of Americans who can trace their ancestry to the land of the great "William the Silent," that little country small in compass, but great in history. We find them to-day, as in the past, among the most prominent men in this country, many in high authority. The nation is at present in mourning over the death of one of her noblest citizens, our esteemed Vice-President, who was on his mother's side of Dutch blood. We have lost in him one of the most popular Vice-Presidents this country ever had; President Kruger lost in him a warm sympathizer and friend.

My fellow-Americans, do you hear the voice of this people, who are fighting for the same principle this country fought for in 1776? Would it not be a crime against civilization to see our sister republics wiped out from the face of the earth and swallowed up by any European power, under the pretence of "protecting the rights of its subjects?" Can there be found one true American, born or adopted, who remembers George Washington and his patriot army—the great preserver of this country—and who does not sympathize with our brethren in South Africa? For almost a century they have been oppressed, gradually the richest land has been taken from them. Is it any wonder that their determination is now, "We shall not give up our land, unless they walk over our dead bodies?" Can it be a surprise that the true South Afrikander in Cape Colony and Natal takes the side of his friends and relatives when it is that of justice and of God-given right?

The Boers do not ask for mercy," says Dr. Engelenburg, editor of the Pretoria Volkstem, in his article "A Transvaal View of the South African Question," "they ask for justice.

Those who keep up the unfair agitation against the South African Republic are the last men, however, to listen to the voice of righteousness, or to be guided by any noble impulse; political corruption is the seed they sow, and by their unexampled opportunities they feel confident of reaping their criminal harvest. Up to the present they have gathered only tears; a still more bitter time of reaping has yet to come. In the past, the Boers have been able to fight against immensely superior odds. They feel that the final victory will be theirs; for they know they have right on their side.

Notwithstanding the many reverses to the British arms, Mr. Chamberlain and the majority of the British Parliament still profess to believe in the ultimate success of England; but the English never expected to lose their American colonies, but they did nevertheless.

It is my honest opinion that Great Britain will never conquer the Boers, and I believe with President Kruger, who believes that Providence is with them, because their cause is one of justice and righteousness.

If any one should ask me what special interest has America in the welfare of South Africa, or in what relation do we stand to them from a commercial standpoint, I would refer to the increasing demand of American machineries and other articles of commerce which were exported there in the last few years. England takes, at present, the lead in the trade, but America is next. In 1897, America had exported to the Transvaal alone merchandise to the amount of $13,500,000; and, as the South Afrikanders are in hearty sympathy with America and American institutions, you may rest assured—if they are not utterly crushed in their present struggle against English oppression—that the commercial transactions in the near future will be increased tenfold, for they are anxious to obtain close relations with the great sister Republic. The latter is certainly a consummation not hoped for by England or her merchants.

There is no doubt that the sympathy of the Americans in general is with the Boers. "An immense deal is being made of the American sympathy in this country," says the London correspondent of the Baltimore American, in his cablegram of November 18, 1899:

It is strange that so powerful an empire as Great Britain, with 400,000,000 of people and three-fifths of the wealth of the globe, should be specially anxious for the sympathy of anybody when trying to whip two little states, which have not all told more than 200,000 inhabitants. Great Britain is 8,000 times as great as the Transvaal and the Orange Free State combined, and she is probably a million times their superior in actual wealth. It is a sign of weakness, therefore, to be making so much of the alleged friendship of the United States, of which there is no evidence except the movement for the fitting out of a hospital ship, which is distinctly British. The women engaged in it are all married to Englishmen, and can in no sense be regarded as Americans. The London Times, through its correspondent, makes the assertion that the United States Government has granted British agents certain privileges at American ports in contravention of the neutrality laws, with the proviso that they are not to be regarded as a precedent, and the Times writes an editorial panegyric a column and a half long. The despatch is probably imaginary as to its facts. It is impossible to believe that the government of the United States could have done anything of the sort."

There is much talk about the close relationship which it is alleged exists between the two great countries, the United States and England, pointing in proof thereof to the ties of the "Anglo-Saxon" race, as though other nations should be excluded. Allow me to make the remark that the Dutch and Germans are a branch of that very same race. Or, to speak more correctly, the Angles and Saxons were low German tribes, as were the ancient Dutch.

We hear always of the English people as the great promoters of Anglo-Saxon civilization and progress, but I want better proof than mere boasting. Let me refer to the history of this great country and ask: Did not the Dutch bring civilization with them when they settled New York, and did the German and other nationalities leave civilization at home when they came to our shores? We absolutely deny the story that the English civilized South Africa. It was the Boers who have changed its wildernesses into a beautiful country. It was the Boers who educated the natives there. The Kaffirs, Malays and other tribes speak the language of the Boers, and even the Hottentots have adopted the Cape Dutch as their native tongue.

Really the Boers can govern the land of their fathers; they do not need British interference or civilization. They have been driven from their land every time as it was developed into prosperity, and perhaps they might have left it again and trek further into the interior if it were not that they are completely surrounded by British territory. So they can go no further. Therefore they have this time determined to conquer or to die.

The English historian Froude, admitting the wrong done by his country, referring to the annexation of the Transvaal by Shepstone in the name of the Queen of Great Britain and Ireland, said:

"We have annexed a country as large as France which belonged to Dutchmen. Dutchmen do not like to have their independence taken from them any more than we do, and nobody exactly knows why we did it. I believe that in our hearts we are sorry now that we annexed it at all, and we would be glad to get rid of it again if we only knew how to get rid of it without seeming ridiculous to the rest of the world."

The time might come that England's pride will receive a more severe blow than it received at Majuba Hill, for the Boer cause is one of justice and righteousness. No true Americans can help sympathizing with the God-fearing sturdy Boers.

The claim that England stood by us in the late war with Spain is not any reason why we should sympathize with a policy of injustice toward our brethren in South Africa, or that we should sympathize with a war uncalled for, condemned by the civilized people all over the world, and subjected to bitter criticism by many prominent men in Great Britain itself.

We should stand by the Boers and inspire them, even at this distance, with our hearty wishes for their success in their noble struggle. We send our greetings to Oom Paul, the beloved patriot of his country. We send our salute to the gallant Commander-in-Chief, General Joubert, and his army of brave men who defend their country and their homes so nobly and heroically. We should forward our sincere sympathy to the wounded and sufferers, our heartfelt condolence to the widows and orphans of those who gave their lives for a just cause, and every liberty loving American should pray that peace, an everlasting peace, may soon reign over South African soil.

The brave burghers might meet with reverses, if they are outnumbered ten to one, as recent events have shown; but their liberty, their republican principles, they will never surrender to British power.

The Boers do not ask for mercy; they ask for justice.

Cornelius W. Van Der Hoogt.

20 OFS Despatches

Official Despatches Exchanged Between President Stein and the High Commissioner

The following despatches have been exchanged between His Honor President Stein and His Excellency Sir Alfred Milner:[537]

1. High Commissioner, Cape Town, [to] State President, Bloemfontein:

19th Sept. I have the honor to inform Your Honor that it has been deemed advisable by the Imperial military authorities to send a detachment of the troops, ordinarily stationed at Cape Town, to assist in securing the line of communication between the Colony and the British territories lying to the north of it. As this force, or a portion of it, may be stationed near the borders of the Orange Free State, I think it desirable to acquaint Your Honor with this movement, and the reasons for it, in order to prevent any misconception on the part of the Burghers of the Orange Free State, of the object which the military authorities have in view.

The movement in question is in no way directed against the Orange Free State, nor is it due to any anxiety as to the intentions of the latter, as I rest fully satisfied with the declarations on this point contained in Your Honor's telegram of August 16 last. I take this opportunity of making a general statement of the attitude of H. M. Govt. at the present juncture which in view of the many current misapprehensions on the subject, H. M. Govt. have authorized me to convey to Your Honor. H. M. Govt. are still hopeful of a friendly settlement of the differences which have arisen between them and the South African Republic: but should this hope unfortunately be disappointed, H. M. Govt. look to the Government of the Orange Free State to preserve strict neutrality and to prevent any military intervention by any of its citizens, and are prepared to give formal assurances that in that case the integrity of the Orange Free State Territory will be strictly respected under all circumstances.

As far as H. M. Govt. are aware, there is absolutely no cause to justify any disturbance of friendly relations between Great Britain and the Orange Free State. Her Majesty's Government are animated by the most friendly sentiments toward the Orange Free State, and it is entirely untrue that they desire to impair the independence of that Republic.

2. State President, Bloemfontein, [to] His Excellency High Commissioner, Cape Town:

19th Sept.—Your Excellency's telegram of this day. I share with Your Excellency the hopefulness of a friendly settlement of the differences which have arisen between H. M. Government and the S. A. R. being still arrived at. I cannot even now see that those differences justify the use of force as the only solution thereof. Both on this account and seeing the existing state of tension here and elsewhere in South Africa, I note with apprehension and regret the intention of H. M. Government to send a detachment of the troops ordinarily stationed at Cape Town northward with a view to having same or a portion thereof stationed near the border of this State.

While this Government will continue to do all in its power to allay excitement, I cannot help impressing upon Your Excellency the fact that, if the proposed course be pursued, following as it will on other military preparations, near our borders, it will not improbably be considered by our Burghers as a menace to this State, and will in any case and naturally create a very strong feeling of distrust and unrest among them. If unwished for developments should arise therefrom, the responsibility will not rest with this Government. I will submit Your Excellency's telegram to the Volksraad early in its session, which opens on Thursday next, and meanwhile beg to assure Your Excellency that this Government would view with deep regret any disturbance of those friendly relations which hitherto existed between Great Britain and this State.

3. High Commissioner, Cape Town, [to] State President, Bloemfontein:

20th Sept. I have the honor to acknowledge receipt of Your Honor's telegram of yesterday. I propose to publish the telegram which I addressed to Your Honor. Does Your Honor desire that I should at the same time publish your reply?

[537] These 20 despatches appear in both Century of Injustice and Story of the Boers.

4. State President, Bloemfontein, [to] His Excellency High Commissioner, Cape Town:

20th Sept. I have the honor to acknowledge the receipt of Your Excellency's telegram of this day. I contemplate, as stated yesterday, submitting Your Excellency's telegram to the Volksraad if possible to-morrow, and at the same time to inform it of my reply thereto. I have no objection to my reply to Your Excellency being published.

5. State President, Bloemfontein, [to] His Excellency High Commissioner, Cape Town:

25th Sept. I have this day received information that considerable body of troops are being moved northward along and nearer our border, from Ladysmith by rail. With a view to allaying undue excitement, I trust and would be pleased to learn from Your Excellency that the report is devoid of truth.

6. From High Commissioner, Cape Town, [to] State President, Bloemfontein:

25th Sept. Your Honor's telegram of to-day. Governor of Natal informs me that some troops are being moved from Ladysmith to Glencoe, and will be replaced at Ladysmith by troops from Maritzburg. There is no advance toward the borders of the Orange Free State, nor is there any justification for alarm. I am not aware of any change in the situation since my telegram to Your Honor of the 19th. I adhere to the hope therein expressed as regards differences between Her Majesty's Government and the South African Republic and repeat the assurance given to the Orange Free State.

7. State President, Bloemfontein, [to] His Excellency High Commissioner, Cape Town:

27th Sept. have the honor to communicate, for information of Your Excellency and H. M.'s Government, the following resolution, this day unanimously adopted by the Volksraad. Translated begins:

The Volksraad having heard the second paragraph of His Honor's opening speech and the official documents and correspondence relating thereto which have been handed in;

Having regard to the strained state of affairs in South Africa, which has arisen in consequence of the differences between the Governments of the South African Republic and H. B. Majesty's, which constitute a threatening danger for bringing about hostilities, the calamitous effects of which would be incalculable for all white inhabitants of South Africa;

Being bound to the South African Republic by the closest bonds of blood and alliance, and standing in a most friendly relationship toward Her British Majesty's Government;

Fearing that should a war break out a hatred would be generated between the European races in South Africa, which still, in the far future, will impede and restrain the peaceful development of all the States and Colonies of South Africa;

Being sensible that the serious obligation rests upon the Volksraad to do all that is possible to prevent the shedding of blood;

Considering that in the course of negotiations with the British Government, which have extended over several months, every endeavor has been made by the Government of the South African Republic to arrive at a peaceful solution of the differences which have been brought forward by the Uitlanders in the S. A. Republic, and which have been adopted as its own cause by the Government of H. B. Majesty, which endeavors unfortunately have only had the result that British troops have been concentrated upon the borders of the South African Republic, and are still continually being reinforced

"Resolves to instruct the Government still further to do everything in their power to preserve and establish peace and to contribute by peaceful methods toward the solution of the existing differences, provided that can be brought about without injury to the Honor and Independence of this State or of the South African Republic, and wishes unmistakably to declare its opinion that there exists no cause for war, and that if a war is now begun or occasioned by H. B. Majesty's Government against the South African Republic this will morally be a war against the whole white population of South Africa, and would in its results be calamitous and criminal. Further, that the Orange Free State will honestly and faithfully observe its obligations toward the South African Republic arising out of the political alliance between the two Republics, whatever may happen."

8. From State President, Bloemfontein, [to] His Excellency the High Commissioner, Cape Town:

27th Sept. view of the ever-increasing gravity of the situation and the strained relations unfortunately existing between the Government of Great Britain and of the S. A. Republic, I deem it my duty to avail myself of this opportunity to address H. M.'s Government through Your Excellency.

The Free State Government, as H. M.'s Government are aware, is bound both to the people of the S. A. Republic and of the neighboring British Colonies by ties of blood and friendship. It is in addition bound on the one hand to the S. A. Republic by a solemn treaty, in which this State has undertaken to assist the Sister Republic in the event of its Independence being threatened or attacked, while on the other side there exists between it and the British Government and the Governments of the neighboring British Colonies long established and highly appreciated amicable relations.

It has ever been and still is the aim and object of Free State Policy heartily to support and continually to foster any measures tending to maintain not only, but to increase the spirit of harmony and co-operation among the Colonies and States of South Africa and their respective Governments, and it would most deeply regret the occurrence of any untoward event that would cause a break in the cordial relations hitherto so happily subsisting between this State and all its neighbors.

It is this strong feeling of good will and amity toward both the Government of Great Britain and of the S. A. Republic, between whom relations have now for some time been unfortunately, but, as I trust, only temporarily strained, that led me to bring about the Conference between Your Excellency and President Kruger in May last. I acted in the hope that thereby the basis for a good understanding and harmonious co-operation in the future might have been arrived at.

That Conference terminated without effecting the desired results, and ever since then this Government has been unceasing in its efforts and has done all in its power to obtain a peaceful and satisfactory solution of the differences between H. M.'s Government and the S. A. Republic, by influencing the Government of the S. A. Republic to make most important reforms in the matter of Franchise and representation for British subjects who are desirous of becoming burghers of that Republic.

In pressing those Franchise and representation reforms and concessions, this Government kept in view the spirit that animated Your Excellency at the Conference and in which they assumed that the British Government also was willing to act, viz., "to adopt an attitude of friendly suggestion and not of dictation in the internal affairs of the Republic." When it is borne in mind what the position was both in regard to the question of Franchise and of representation in the S. A. Republic at the time of the Conference, and what radical reforms have been effected by the Government and Legislature of that country in the comparatively short time that has elapsed since that date, I think it may be fairly claimed that our efforts, aided by the representations of other friends of peace and harmony in South Africa, have been crowned with a large measure of success.

While the Government of the S. A. Republic, encouraged thereto by the advice of the Free State and other friends, were busy inducing the Legislature and people of that Republic to accept reform in the direction suggested and desired by H. M.'s Government, and intended to meet the alleged wants of the Uitlander population, and even before the proposal was made by the British Government, that the Franchise Law and scheme of increased representation for the Witwatersrand Goldfields should be submitted to a Joint Commission for examination and report, this Government could not be blind to the fact that the tone of the dispatches had altered, and that the British Government had, in fact, departed from the basis on which negotiations were opened: that of not interfering in the internal affairs of the Republic.

The request for the Joint Commission of Inquiry emphasized that fact beyond any shadow of doubt. Notwithstanding this the Government of the O. F. State, in the hope that an impartial investigation might inaugurate a renewal of the employment of friendly methods tending toward a satisfactory solution of the questions in difference, and adopting the friendly suggestion received from several quarters, once more advised the Government of the S. A. Republic to make yet another concession, and to give yet another proof of its willingness to meet the British Government, by consenting to accept the invitation of the British Government to take part in such a Joint Commission; this advice was adopted, and at last it seemed that the efforts of the friends of peace and harmony in South Africa stood a fair chance of being crowned with success.

Great, therefore, was the disappointment of the Government and people of this State when it transpired that, from causes with which I am still unacquainted, our best efforts, culminating in the acceptance by the S.A. Republic of the proposals of the British Government for a Joint Commission of Inquiry on the seven years

Franchise Law and adopted increased representation scheme, proved unavailing, and that the unfortunate tension seemed, as it seems now, to be only increasing.

This Government are still prepared, and tender their services to further the interests of peace, and to continue in their endeavors to procure a satisfactory solution of existing difficulties on fair and reasonable lines: they feel themselves, however, hampered now as in the past:

a. By a want of knowledge as to the definite object and extent of the desires or demands of the British Government, compliance with which that Government consider themselves entitled to insist upon, and as to the grounds on which such insistence is based.

b. By the fact that, notwithstanding the repeated assurances of the British Government that it did not wish to interfere in the internal affairs of the S. A. Republic nor to disturb its independence, it has pursued a policy which seems to justify a contrary conclusion.

To give but one instance, which could not be otherwise than calculated to be a most disturbing element in the conduct of negotiations, I may mention the enormous and ever-increasing military preparations on the part of the British Government, indicating a policy of force and coercion during the whole course of negotiations which were stated to be of a friendly and conciliatory nature, those preparations, in the absence of any apparent cause justifying the same, being not unnaturally looked upon as a direct menace to the S. A. Republic. After all that has been done by the S. A. Republic to meet the wishes of H. M.'s Government for a Joint Commission to inquire into the scope and effect of those measures, and whether immediate and substantial representation would thereby be assured to the Uitlanders willing to avail themselves of the provisions thereof, this Government cannot conceive it possible that the points of difference that may exist on this subject justify those extensive and ever-increasing military preparations being carried out on the borders, not only of the S. A. Republic, but also of the 0. F. State, and it is, therefore, reluctantly compelled to conclude that they must be intended to secure other objects at present unknown to the Government of this State, and the knowledge whereof, if they prove to be fair and reasonable, might induce this Government to make necessary representations to secure their attainment and enable them to continue their efforts to secure a speedy, peaceful, and satisfactory solution of the difficulties and differences existing between H. M.'s Government and the Government of the S. A. Republic.

I beg to add that I am firmly convinced (and feel sure that any reasonable assurance could be obtained), that the Government of the S. A. Republic have been sincerely desirous to maintain in its integrity the Convention of 1884, both as regards its letter and its spirit, and that they do not contemplate or assert a claim to any absolute political status without the qualification arising out of Art. 4 of that Convention, and accordingly it does not appear to me that there is any misunderstanding hereon that could not promptly and without difficulty be settled.

I feel assured that there is no difference between their contention on that point and the communication made on behalf of H. M.'s Government by H. M.'s High Commissioner to the Governments, both of the S. A. Republic and of this State, on the 27th February, 1884, as to the import of that Convention. That communication was as follows:

"Same complete internal independence in Transvaal as in the Orange Free State. Conduct and control intercourse, Foreign Governments conceded. Queen's final approval Treaties reserved."

In the expectation that H. M.'s Government will share my views that no effort should be spared to effect a peaceable settlement, if possible, of the points in difference between them and S. A. Republic, and that consequently all causes of irritation likely to delay or prevent such settlement should be removed or at least not be aggravated.

I trust that H. M.'s Government may see their way clear pending the arrival of the further despatch intimated as about to be sent to the Government of the S. A. Republic, and pending further negotiations, to stop any further movements or increase of troops on or near the borders of the S. A. Republic and of this State, and further to give an assurance to that effect to allay the great excitement and irritation naturally aroused and increased thereby, and if H. M.'s Government should be pleased to accede to this request, this Government would be glad to be favored with the views of H. M.'s Government on the points raised herein, and more particularly as to the precise nature and scope of the concessions or measures, the adoption whereof H. M.'s Government consider themselves entitled to claim or which they suggest as being necessary or sufficient to insure a satisfactory and permanent solution of existing differences between them and the S. A. Republic, while at the same time providing a means for settling any others that may arise in the future. (Sig.) M. T. Steyn, State President.

9. High Commissioner, Cape Town, [to] His Honor State President, Bloemfontein:

28th Sept. I beg to acknowledge your Honor's two telegrams received last night, the contents of which I have communicated to H. M.'s Government.

10. State President, Bloemfontein, [to] His Excellency High Commissioner, Cape Town:

2nd Oct. have the honor to inform Your Excellency that I have deemed it advisable in order to allay the intense excitement and unrest among our Burghers arising from the totally undefended state of our Borders in the presence and continued increase and movement of troops on two sides of this State, to call up our Burghers to satisfy them that due precautions have been taken in regard to guarding our Borders and to insure their not acting independently of proper control. I am still strongly and sincerely desirous of seeing and, if possible, aiding in a friendly settlement of the differences between H. M. Government and the S. A. Republic being arrived at. I am still looking forward soon to be favored with the views of H. M. Government on the points touched upon in my telegraphic despatch to Your Excellency of the 27th ult., receipt whereof was acknowledged by Your Excellency on the following day.

11. High Commissioner, Cape Town, [to] His Honor State President, Bloemfontein:

2nd October. I have the honor to acknowledge Your Honor's telegram of to-day, the terms of which I am communicating to H. M. Government. With reference to the movements of troops to which you refer, I can only repeat the assurances given in my telegrams of the 19th and 25th September. I regret that Your Honor should have felt obliged to order up a large body of Burghers and to place them immediately on our Borders, whereas no Imperial troops have been so placed on the Borders of the Orange Free State, except the small detachment engaged in the defence of Kimberley, but as Your Honor has seen fit to take this course, I am glad to have Your Honor's assurance that your forces will be held in proper control.

As Your Honor is aware, the Government of the S. A. Republic has mobilized and placed upon the Borders of Natal a very considerable army and made dispositions which, unwilling as I am to believe such action possible, seem to indicate an immediate invasion of the Queen's dominions.

In view of the repeated declaration of Your Honor I feel confident that any invasion of H. M. territories by the S. A. Republic would not have the countenance and support of Your Honor's Government, all the more so as Your Honor continues to express the hope of a peaceful settlement, of which I likewise do not despair. I hope to be able very shortly to communicate to you the reply of H. M. Government to your telegram of the 27th of September.

12. State President, Bloemfontein, [to] His Excellency High Commissioner, Cape Town:

2nd October. I have the honor to acknowledge receipt of Your Excellency's telegram of this afternoon. I cannot help, regretfully, expressing my conviction that the action of the Transvaal in putting Burghers on their Borders is only the natural result, all along feared by me, of the constant increase of British troops and their movement in the direction of Transvaal Border. At the same time I have no reason to anticipate any immediate aggressive action on part of Transvaal, unless further forward movement of British troops should indicate intention of attack on Transvaal. I beg to urge upon Your Excellency the necessity of trying both to expedite the reply to my telegraphic despatch and to prevent further movement of troops.

13. High Commissioner, Cape Town, [to] State President, Bloemfontein:

3rd Oct. I have the honor to acknowledge Your Honor's telegram of yesterday evening. Your

Honor must be perfectly aware that all the movements of British troops which have taken place in this country since the beginning of present troubles, and which have been necessitated by the natural alarm of the inhabitants in exposed districts, are not comparable in magnitude with the recent massing of armed forces of the S. A. Republic on the borders of Natal. I do not suggest that Your Honor is in any way responsible for that action, which appears to me inconsistent with the tone of Your Honor's telegram of the 27th September, in which you expressed your conviction that a peaceful settlement of difficulties was still possible and ought to be arrived at.

14. State President, Bloemfontein, [to] High Commissioner, Cape Town:

3rd Oct. I have the honor to acknowledge Your Excellency's telegram of this morning. I am as sincerely and strongly desirous as ever to see a speedy, peaceful, and satisfactory solution being arrived at, and to do all that lies in my power to try even yet to attain that result. I deem it my duty, however, to state emphatically that I do not consider that the movements of British troops which have taken place in this country since the beginning of the present troubles have been necessitated by the natural alarm of the inhabitants in exposed districts, nor, in fact, have I ever thought that there were any fair grounds justifying such movements.

On the contrary, I have never for a moment had or expressed any other view than that the ever-increasing military preparations, which both in England and in South Africa have all along accompanied protestations for a desire to arrive at peaceful and friendly settlement, retarded and hampered the efforts of myself and all those who were sincerely working to maintain peace and effect fair settlement.

To the bitter and hostile tone of the utterances made both by responsible men and by almost the whole English press in South Africa and in England, bristling with misrepresentation and constant menace to the Transvaal, accompanied by ever-increasing military preparations on an extensive scale, not only in South Africa and in England, but throughout the British Empire, which are openly stated as being directed against and intended to coerce the Transvaal, I mainly attribute the failure hitherto of arriving at an amicable and satisfactory solution of existing difficulties.

I wish to place on record my earnest conviction, that on those in authority, who introduced the military element, and who thereby inaugurated and have since continued a policy of menace and forcible intervention, will rest the responsibility, should all efforts fail to secure peace and an honorable settlement of differences. After the proofs already given by the Transvaal since the Conference, to meet the views and wishes of the British Government, I consider the constant and systematic attempts to throw the blame for the present critical situation of affairs on the S. A. Republic unjust to and undeserved by the latter.

While I am not responsible for, but, on the contrary, for a long time successfully used my best endeavors to prevent the massing of burghers by the Government of the S. A. Republic on their borders, I cannot but recognize the fact that in view of the action of the British authorities already alluded to, the Transvaal Government cannot be blamed for acting as they have done. I am the more confirmed in this view by the fact that while I am still without any reply to my telegraphic despatch of the 27th ult., and in which I expressed my conviction as quoted by Your Excellency, the reasonable request therein made that the increase and further movement of British troops should be stayed, and which, if acceded to, would probably have prevented the calling out of the burghers both in the S. A. Republic and in this State, has not only been ignored, but activity in military preparations and the despatch of troops have been going on more persistently than ever.

I am not in a position to judge whether the movement of British troops on the Border of the S. A. Republic is comparable or not in magnitude with the recent massing of armed forces of the S. A. Republic on their Borders, but Your Excellency should not lose sight of the fact that on all sides in the English press and otherwise the assertion constantly finds expression that the British troops already in this Country, with their superior armament and discipline, are more than a match for the undisciplined Burgher force of the Republic, are intended forthwith to enforce British demands on the Transvaal, and that moreover troops are being despatched almost daily from England, and military preparations are in active and constant progress which are utterly incompatible with the requirements of defence, and which would seem to more than sufficiently justify a conviction, in the minds of the Burghers of the S. A. Republic, that England has abandoned any idea of attempting any longer to arrive at a solution of differences, except by force.

I trust that Your Excellency will receive this communication in the spirit in which it is honestly intended, namely, to put the facts of the case and the situation, as I see them, at this most critical time, clearly before you so as to prevent any misunderstanding, not only, but in the hopes that by a clear comprehension of the views I hold as to the causes which have brought about the present crisis, Your Excellency may the better be enabled to form a judgment not based on ex-parte information only.

I feel deeply impressed with the danger of delay, and with the urgent need of immediate action being taken if any further attempts are to be made to secure a peaceful solution. Once again I tender my best services toward the attainment of that object, but I fear that these will probably be useless and unavailing if not accompanied or preceded by the assurance requested in mine of 27th ult.

15. From High Commissioner, Cape Town, [to] His Honor the State President, Bloemfontein:

4th Oct. No. 2. I have the honor to acknowledge Your Honor's long telegram of yesterday afternoon, the substance of which I have communicated by wire to H. M.'s Government. There is, I think, a conclusive reply to Your Honor's accusations against the policy of H. M.'s Government; but no good purpose could be served by recrimination. The present position is that burgher forces are assembled in very large numbers in immediate proximity to the frontiers of Natal, while the British troops occupy certain defensive positions well within those borders. The question is whether the burgher forces will invade British territory, thus closing the door to any possibility of a pacific solution.

I cannot believe that the S. A. Republic will take such aggressive action, or that Your Honor would countenance such a course, which there is nothing to justify. Prolonged negotiations have hitherto failed to bring about a satisfactory understanding, and no doubt such understanding is more difficult than ever to-day after expulsion of British subjects with great loss and suffering. But till the threatened act of aggression is committed I shall not despair of peace, and I feel sure that any reasonable proposal, from whatever quarter proceeding, would be favorably considered by H. M.'s Government, if it offered an immediate termination of the present tension and prospect of permanent tranquility.

16. From State President, Bloemfontein, [to] His Excellency the High Commissioner, Cape Town

5th Oct. I have the honor to acknowledge the receipt of Your Excellency's telegram No. 2, of yesterday evening. I note with pleasure that Your Excellency does not despair of peace, and that you feel sure that any reasonable proposal, from whatever quarter proceeding, would be favorably considered by H. M. Government, if it offered an immediate termination of the present tension and a prospect of permanent tranquility.

I see no reason why such proposals should not be forthcoming, and I myself am prepared actively to assist to bring about the indicated and desirable result. I must, however, point out that it seems to me it would be most difficult to attempt to make friendly proposals or continue to negotiate while the armed forces on both sides remain in menacing positions now occupied by them, but above all do I consider it would not be practicable to induce the Government of the S. A. Republic to make or entertain proposals or suggestions, unless not only the troops menacing their State are withdrawn further from their border, but an assurance be given by H. M. Government that all further despatch and increase of troops will at once, and during negotiations, be stopped, and that those now on the water should either not be landed or, at least, should remain as far removed as can be from the scene of possible hostilities.

I trust Your Excellency will agree with me that these suggestions are only reasonable, as it would be manifestly unfair should further negotiations prove abortive result which I would earnestly endeavor to prevent and which I trust need not be anticipated that the forces of the S. A. Republic should be in a worse position or at a greater disadvantage than they are at present.

I must urge upon Your Excellency the urgent necessity of intimating to me without delay whether Your Excellency sees your way clear to give effect to these my views and wishes, and if so, I would be prepared to take steps at once and try and obtain any needful assurance to safeguard against any act of invasion of or hostility against any portion of H. M. Colonies or territories pending negotiations. If these preliminary but absolutely essential matters can be regulated between this and to-morrow, I would be further prepared to aid, if possible, in formulating and heartily to assist in dealing with and supporting any reasonable proposals which shall possess the element of finality and give the assurance of immediate and lasting peace.

A reply to the request made in the very last part of my telegraphic despatch to Your Excellency of 27th ultimo would enable me to judge in how far it would be possible for me to support the requests or requirements of H. M. Government in reopening negotiations with the Transvaal.

In regard to another point, touched upon by your Excellency in your telegram under reply, I have no information before me from which I can infer that H. M. subjects have been expelled with great loss and suffering from the S. A. Republic. The report, no doubt, has its origin, like many others, in the exaggerated statements of persons leaving that country in a panic.

17. From High Commissioner, Cape Town, [to] State President, Bloemfontein:

6th Oct. With reference to Your Honor's telegram of yesterday, I must demur to Your Honor's statement that British troops are in menacing positions. I regret that Your Honor should suggest as a condition precedent to further negotiations an assurance from H. M.'s Government hampering their freedom of action with regard to the disposition of British troops for defensive purposes in British territory. Such an assurance it is impossible for me to ask H. M.'s Government to give. If on the other hand Your Honor can obtain an assurance that, pending negotiations, no act of hostility will be committed against any of H. M.'s possessions, I am prepared to advise H. M.'s Government to give an assurance to the like effect.

18. From State President, Bloemfontein, [to] High Commissioner, Cape Town:

6th Oct. I have the honor to acknowledge the receipt of Your Excellency's telegram of to-day. I am earnestly desirous of meeting any reasonable suggestion that may tend to a continuance of friendly negotiations and to avert an issue for which, as I have frequently stated, I see no justification whatever. I trust that Your Excellency will, on reconsideration, see that the Government of the S. A. Republic, in only taking proper precautions for the future, might fairly decline, and I do not feel I could be expected to ask them to continue negotiations in the face of the fact that from all sides of H. M.'s Dominions troops are being poured into South Africa with the avowed object of coercing the S. A. Republic into accepting whatever terms H. M.'s Government might decide to impose.

I have no doubt in so far as H. M.'s troops are intended for the defence of H. M.'s possessions the same purpose, viz., fully safeguarding those possessions from invasion and subjects from molestation, could be effected. I would be willing to assist in its being effected without one side finding itself put at a great disadvantage during and because of further negotiations. The assurance asked for by Your Excellency could, I have no doubt, be obtained and satisfactorily arranged; but the point that I think it fair to urge is that it would be taken by the S. A. Republic as virtually amounting to an act of hostility on the part of Her Majesty's Government to be continuously and extensively increasing its forces during negotiation when all need for defensive measures can, as I firmly believe, be fully obviated without such increase.

19. From High Commissioner, Cape Town, [to] State President, Bloemfontein:

7th Oct. With reference to Your Honor's telegram of Sept. 27th, I am instructed by H. M.'s Government to inform Your Honor that H. M.'s Government have repeatedly explained their views on the questions at issue between them and the Government of the S. A. Republic, and especially in the note addressed to that Government, on September 12th. Her Majesty's Government do not think their position open to misunderstanding, but if Your Honor desires the elucidation of any specific point in their proposals, H. M.'s Government are prepared to give it.

As regards their military preparations, these have been necessitated by the action of the Government of the S. A. Republic, in converting that country into an armed camp. In view of the rejection of their last proposals by the Government of the S. A. Republic, H. M.'s Government are reconsidering the situation, having regard to the grave fact that both Republics have now placed themselves on a war footing. While intending shortly to put forward new proposals of their own, H. M.'s Government would even now be prepared to consider any definite suggestion from Your Honor for the termination of the present crisis, provided it was not inconsistent with the attempt of the objects avowed and pursued by them.

The above was received before Your Honor's telegram of yesterday afternoon, to which I will reply immediately.

20. From High Commissioner, Cape Town, [to] State President, Bloemfontein:

7th October. I have the honor to acknowledge Your Honor's telegram of yesterday afternoon. With every desire to relieve the strain of the present situation, I cannot go beyond the suggestions made by me in my telegram of yesterday morning. I have no right to attempt to influence Your Honor as to what advice it would be reasonable for you to give to the Government of the South African Republic, having regard to the impending increase of Her Majesty's forces in South Africa. My object, in all the communications which have passed between us since Your Honor's telegram of 2nd October, has been to leave nothing undone which could prevent action on the part of the South African Republic calculated to make a pacific solution finally impossible. But I cannot, even with that object ask Her Majesty's Government to pledge themselves either with regard to the disposition of troops within British territory in South Africa or to their despatch thither from other parts of the Empire.

The war in South Africa, its Cause & Conduct.[538]

The War in South Africa
Its Cause & Conduct
By
A. Conan Doyle
Author of
The Great Boer War

New York
McClure, Phillips & Co.
Mcmii

Contents

PF Introduction:

This Volume is primarily designed to compile as much material regarding the Century of Wrong text(s) as possible in order to fully represent the Boer's legal case and their efforts to maintain their independence.

Dr. Conan Doyle's work is to some degree an interloper in that context. Yet, his contribution belongs in this volume since the most probative parts of his work detail the events leading to the conflict, the negotiations and

[538] Doyle, Arthur Conan, 1859-1930 The war in South Africa, its cause & conduct; 1902 McClure, Phillips & Co. U. Cal. Copy: https://archive.org/details/warinsouthafrica00doylrich

the subsequent communications discussing peace negotiations; all supported by extensive quotations from the original documents.

This work of ~60k words has been edited down to ~28k words. The reason being that by this point in the series many of the topics have already been extensively covered. Dr. Conan Doyle, while not a 'fair witness' in the Heinleinien[539] sense is an articulate and observant, thoughtful and fact conscious author. That is the primary benefit of his work, to provide an additional layer of dates, events and participants along with quotes from the relevant documents under discussion. By excising out the journalism and opinion matter, we are left with a rational and insightful look at the British perspective as well as a wealth of original documentation and witness testimony that supplements and adds context to the Boer cause as well as the British.

Medical Training Sketch

Often overlooked is that Dr. Arthur Conan Doyle was an accomplished and highly educated physician, classically trained and to emphasize this aspect of his education I am including an excerpt from his Wikipedia biography that describes his medical training.[540]

From 1876 to 1881, Doyle studied medicine at the University of Edinburgh Medical School; during this period he spent time working in Aston and Ruyton-XI-Towns. Also during this period, he studied practical botany at the Royal Botanic Garden in Edinburgh. While studying, Doyle began writing short stories. His earliest extant fiction, "The Haunted Grange of Goresthorpe", was unsuccessfully submitted to Blackwood's Magazine. His first published piece, "The Mystery of Sasassa Valley", a story set in South Africa, was printed in Chambers's Edinburgh Journal on 6 September 1879. On 20 September 1879, he published his first academic article, "Gelsemium as a Poison" in the British Medical Journal….

Doyle was the doctor on the Greenland whaler Hope of Peterhead in 1880. After graduating with Bachelor of Medicine and Master of Surgery (M.B. C.M.) degrees from the University of Edinburgh in 1881, he was ship's surgeon on the SS Mayumba during a voyage to the West African coast. He completed his Doctor of Medicine (M.D.) degree (an advanced degree beyond the basic medical qualification in the UK) with a dissertation on tabes dorsalis in 1885.

In 1882, Doyle partnered with his former classmate George Turnavine Budd in a medical practice in Plymouth, but their relationship proved difficult, and Doyle soon left to set up an independent practice. Arriving in Portsmouth in June 1882, with less than £10 to his name, he set up a medical practice at 1 Bush Villas in Elm Grove, Southsea. The practice was not successful. While waiting for patients, Doyle returned to writing fiction.

Doyle was a staunch supporter of compulsory vaccination and wrote several articles advocating the practice and denouncing the views of anti-vaccinators.

In early 1891, Doyle embarked on the study of ophthalmology in Vienna. He had previously studied at the Portsmouth Eye Hospital in order to qualify to perform eye tests and prescribe glasses. …………

Doyle served as a volunteer physician in the Langman Field Hospital at Bloemfontein between March and June 1900, during the Second Boer War in South Africa (1899–1902). ………

Doyle was a supporter of the campaign for the reform of the Congo Free State that was led by the journalist E. D. Morel and diplomat Roger Casement. In 1909 he wrote The Crime of the Congo, a long pamphlet in which he denounced the horrors of that colony. …………..

Original Preface

For some reason, which may be either arrogance or apathy, the British are very slow to state their case to the world. At present the reasons for our actions and the methods which we have used are set forth in many Blue-books, tracts, and leaflets, but have never, so far as I know, been collected into one small volume. In view of the persistent slanders to which our politicians and our soldiers have been equally exposed, it becomes a duty which we owe to our national honour to lay the facts before the world. ………………….

There was never a war in history in which the right was absolutely on one side, or in which no incidents of the campaign were open to criticism. I do not pretend that it was so here. But I do not think that any unprejudiced

[539] See Robert Heinlein's novel, 'Stranger in a Strange Land.'

[540] Sir Arthur Ignatius Conan Doyle (22 May 1859–7 July 1930) was a British writer and physician. Arthur Conan Doyle - Wikipedia

man can read the facts without acknowledging that the British Government has done its best to avoid war, and the British Army to wage it with humanity.

I may add that I have not burdened my pages with continual references. My quotations are reliable and can always, if necessary, be substantiated.

A. Conan Doyle

Undershaw,[541] Hindhead:[542]

January, 1902.

Undershaw circa 1900. Several of Arthur Conan Doyle's children playing on the driveway.[74]

Arthur Conan Doyle in 1893.[75]

Arthur Conan Doyle in 1914.[76]

541 Undershaw was the residence of the author Arthur Conan Doyle, The house was built for Doyle at his order to accommodate his wife's health requirements, and is where he lived with his family from 1897 to 1907. Undershaw is where Doyle wrote many of his works, including The Hound of the Baskervilles. Undershaw - Wikipedia

542 Hindhead is a village in the Waverley district of the county of Surrey. Hindhead - Wikipedia

I. The Boer People

.... It was about the time when Oliver Cromwell was at his zenith—in 1652, to be pedantically accurate—that the Dutch made their first lodgment at the Cape of Good Hope. The Portuguese had been there before them, but, repelled by the evil weather, and lured forward by rumours of gold, they had passed the true seat of empire, and had voyaged farther, to settle along the eastern coast. ....

They built themselves houses, and they supplied the Dutch East India Company with food and water, gradually budding off little townlets, Wynberg, Stellenbosch, and pushing their settlements up the long slopes which lead to that great central plateau which extends for 1,500 miles from the edge of the Karoo to the Valley of the Zambesi.

.... Cattle raising became an industry, but in a country where six acres can hardly support a sheep, large farms are necessary for even small herds. Six thousand acres was the usual size, and five pounds a year the rent payable to Government.

The diseases which follow the white man had in Africa, as in America and Australia, been fatal to the natives, and an epidemic of smallpox cleared the country for the newcomers. Father and farther north they pushed, founding little towns here and there, such as Graaf-Reinet and Swellendam, where a Dutch Reformed Church and a store for the sale of the bare necessaries of life formed a nucleus for a few scattered dwellings.

Already the settlers were showing that independence of control and that detachment from Europe which has been their most prominent characteristic. Even the sway of the Dutch Company had caused them to revolt. The local rising, however, was hardly noticed in the universal cataclysm which followed the French Revolution. After twenty years, during which the world was shaken by the Titanic struggle in the final counting up of the game and paying of the stakes, the Cape Colony was added in 1814 to the British Empire.

In all the vast collection of British States there is probably not one the title-deeds to which are more incontestable than to this. Britain had it by two rights, the right of conquest and the right of purchase. In 1806 troops landed, defeated the local forces, and took possession of Cape Town.

In 1814 Britain paid the large sum of six million pounds to the Stadtholder for the transference of this and some South American land. It was a bargain which was probably made rapidly and carelessly in that general redistribution which was going on. As a house of call upon the way to India the place was seen to be of value, but the country itself was looked upon as unprofitable and desert.

What would Castlereagh or Liverpool have thought could they have seen the items which they were buying for six million pounds? The inventory would have been a mixed one of good and of evil; nine fierce Kaffir wars, the greatest diamond mines in the world, the wealthiest gold mines, two costly and humiliating campaigns with men whom we respected even when we fought with them, and now at last, we hope, a South Africa of peace and prosperity, with equal rights and equal duties for all men. ....

Had Great Britain bought those vast regions which extended beyond the settlements? Or were the discontented Dutch at liberty to pass onwards and found fresh nations to bar the path of the Anglo-Celtic colonists? In that question lay the germ of all the trouble to come.

An American would realise the point at issue if he could conceive that after the founding of the United States the Dutch inhabitants of the State of New York had trekked to the westward and established fresh communities under a new flag.[543] Then, when the American population overtook these western States, they would be face to face with the problem which this country has had to solve. If they found these new States fiercely anti-American and extremely unprogressive, they would experience that aggravation of their difficulties with which British states- men have had to deal. ....

Five thousand British emigrants were landed in 1820, settling on the eastern borders of the colony, and from that time onwards there was a slow but steady influx of English-speaking colonists. The Government had the historical faults and the historical virtues of British rule. It was mild, clean, honest, tactless, and inconsistent. ....

[543] The Mormons did. He mentions this later as well.

The Imperial Government has always taken an honourable and philanthropic view of the rights of the native and the claim which he has to the protection of the law. We hold, and rightly, that British justice, if not blind, should at least be colour-blind. ....

The British Government in South Africa has always played the unpopular part of the friend and protector of the native servants. It was upon this very point that the first friction appeared between the old settlers and the new administration, A rising with bloodshed followed the arrest of a Dutch farmer who had maltreated his slave. It was suppressed, and five of the participants were hanged. This punishment was unduly severe and exceedingly injudicious.[544]

A brave race can forget the victims of the field of battle, but never those of the scaffold. The making of political martyrs is the last insanity of statesmanship. However, the thing was done, and it is typical of the enduring resentment, which was left behind that when, after the Jameson Raid, it seemed that the leaders of that ill-fated venture might be hanged, the beam was actually brought from a farmhouse at Cookhouse Drift to Pretoria, that the Englishmen might die as the Dutchmen had died in 1816. Slagter's Nek marked the dividing of the ways between the British Government and the Africanders.

And the separation soon became more marked. With vicarious generosity, the English Government gave very lenient terms to the Kaffir tribes who in 1834 had raided the border farmers. And then, finally, in this same year there came the emancipation of the slaves throughout the British Empire, which fanned all smouldering discontents into an active flame.

It must be confessed that on this occasion the British philanthropist was willing to pay for what he thought was right. It was a noble national action, and one the morality of which was in advance of its time, that the British Parliament should vote the enormous sum of twenty million pounds to pay compensation to the slaveholders, and so to remove an evil with which the mother country had no immediate connection.

It was as well that the thing should have been done when it was, for had we waited till the colonies affected had governments of their own it could never have been done by constitutional methods. With many a grumble the good British householder drew his purse from his fob and paid for what he thought to be right. If any special grace attends the virtuous action which brings nothing but tribulation in this world, then we may hope for it over this emancipation. We spent our money, we ruined our West Indian colonies, and we started a disaffection in South Africa, the end of which we have not seen.

But the details of the measure were less honourable than the principle. It was carried out suddenly, so that the country had no time to adjust itself to the new conditions. Three million pounds were ear-marked for South Africa, which gives a price per slave of from 60*l.* to 70*l.*, a sum considerably below the current local rates. Finally, the compensation was made payable in London, so that the farmers sold their claims at reduced prices to middlemen.

Indignation meetings were held in every little townlet and cattle-camp on the Karoo. The old Dutch spirit was up—the spirit of the men who cut the dykes. Rebellion was useless. But a vast untenanted land stretched to the north of them. ....

One by one they were loaded up, the huge teams were inspanned, the women were seated inside, the men with their long-barreled guns walked alongside, and the great exodus was begun. Their herds and flocks accompanied the migration, and the children helped to round them in and drive them. One tattered little boy of ten cracked his sjambok whip behind the bullocks. He was a small item in that singular crowd, but he was of interest to us, for his name was Paul Stephanus Kruger.

It was a strange exodus, only comparable in modern times to the sallying forth of the Mormons from Nauvoo upon their search for the promised land of Utah. The country was known and sparsely settled as far north as the Orange River, but beyond there was a great region which had never been penetrated save by some daring hunter or adventurous pioneer. ....

It chanced—if there be indeed such an element as chance in the graver affairs of man—that a Zulu conqueror had swept over this land and left it untenanted, ...

544 Note Bacon's Rebellion in Western Virginia and Charles II's observation as to William Berkeley's conduct. "He has hung more men in that naked land than I have for the murder of my father."

They travelled in small detached parties, but their total numbers were considerable, from six to ten thousand according to their historian, or nearly a quarter of the whole population of the colony. Some of the early bands perished miserably. A large number made a trysting-place at a high peak to the east of Bloemfontein, in what was lately the Orange Free State. One party of the emigrants was cut off by the formidable Matabeli, a branch of the great Zulu nation.

The final victory of the 'voortrekkers' cleared all the country between the Orange River and the Limpopo, the sites of what have been known as the Transvaal and the Orange Free State. In the meantime another body of the emigrants had descended into Natal, and had defeated Dingaan, the great Chief of the Zulus.

.... the Boers saw at the end of their travels the very thing which they desired least—that which they had come so far to avoid—the flag of Great Britain.

The Boers had occupied Natal from within, but England had previously done the same by sea, and a small colony of Englishmen had settled at Port Natal, now known as Durban. The Home Government however, had acted in a vacillating way, and it was only the conquest of Natal by the Boers which caused them to claim it as a British colony. At the same time they asserted the unwelcome doctrine that a British subject could not at will throw off his allegiance, and that, go where they might, the wandering farmers were still only the pioneers of British colonies.

To emphasise the fact three companies of soldiers were sent in 1842 to what is now Durban—the usual Corporals guard with which Great Britain starts a new empire. This handful of men was waylaid by the Boers and cut up, as their successors have been so often since. The survivors, however, fortified themselves, and held a defensive position— as also their successors have done so many times since—until reinforcements arrived and the farmers dispersed. Natal from this time onward became a British colony, and the majority of the Boers trekked north and east with bitter hearts to tell their wrongs to their brethren of the Orange Free State and of the Transvaal. ....

[Here] there is a case for our adversary. Our annexation of Natal had been by no means definite, and it was they and not we who first broke that bloodthirsty Zulu power which threw its shadow across the country.

It was hard after such trials and such exploits to turn their back upon the fertile land which they had conquered, and to return to the bare pastures of the upland veldt. They carried out of Natal a heavy sense of injury, which has helped to poison our relations with them ever since. ....

This population was scattered over a space as large as Germany, and larger than Pennsylvania, New York, and New England. Their form of government was individualistic and democratic to the last degree compatible with any sort of cohesion.

Their wars with the Kaffirs and their fear and dislike of the British Government appear to have been the only ties which held them together. They divided and subdivided within their own borders, ... The Transvaal was full of lusty little high-mettled communities, who quarreled among themselves as fiercely as they had done with the authorities at the Cape.

Lydenburg, Zoutpansberg, and Potchefstroom were on the point of turning their rifles against each other. In the south, between the Orange River and the Vaal, there was no form of government at all, but a welter of Dutch farmers, Basutos, Hottentots, and half-breeds living in a chronic state of turbulence, recognising neither the British authority to the south of them nor the Transvaal republics to the north.

The chaos became at last unendurable, and in 1848 a garrison was placed in Bloemfontein and the district incorporated in the British Empire. The emigrants made a futile resistance at Boomplats[545] and after a single defeat allowed themselves to be drawn into the settled order of civilised rule.

At this period the Transvaal, where most of the Boers had settled, desired a formal acknowledgment of their independence, which the British authorities determined once and for all to give them. .... A convention was concluded between the two parties, known as the Sand River Convention, which is one of the fixed points in South African history.

[545] The Battle of Boomplaats on 29 August 1848 between the British and the Voortrekkers. The British were led by Sir Harry Smith, while the Boers were led by Andries Pretorius. The British were victorious after one Boer opened fire too early and betrayed their position. Battle of Boomplaats - Wikipedia

By it the British Government guaranteed to the Boer farmers the right to manage their own affairs, and to govern themselves by their own laws without any interference upon the part of the British. It stipulated that there should be no slavery, and with that single reservation washed its hands finally, as it imagined, of the whole question. So the Transvaal Republic came formally into existence.

In the very year after the Sand River Convention, a second republic, the Orange Free State, was created by the deliberate withdrawal of Great Britain from the territory which she had for eight years occupied. ....

Against the will of a large part of the inhabitants, whether a majority or not it is impossible to say, we withdrew our troops as amicably as the Romans withdrew from Britain, and the new republic was left with absolute and unfettered independence.

On a petition being presented against the withdrawal, the Home Government actually voted 48,000*l*. to compensate those who had suffered from the change. Whatever historical grievance the Transvaal may have against Great Britain, we can at least, save perhaps in one matter, claim to have a very clear conscience concerning our dealings with the Orange Free State. Thus in 1852 and in 1854 were born those sturdy States which have been able for a time to hold at bay the united forces of the Empire.

In the meantime Cape Colony, in spite of these secessions, had prospered exceedingly, and her population—British, German, and Dutch—had grown by 1870 to over two hundred thousand souls, the Dutch still slightly predominating.........

In 1872 complete self-government was given to it, the Governor, as the representative of the Queen, retaining a nominal unexercised veto upon legislation. According to this system the Dutch majority of the colony could, and did, put their own representatives into power and run the government upon Dutch lines. Already Dutch law had been restored, and Dutch put on the same footing as English as the official language of the country. ....

For twenty-five years after the Sand River Convention, the burghers of the Transvaal Republic had pursued a strenuous and violent existence, fighting incessantly with the natives and sometimes with each other, with an occasional fling at the little Dutch republic to the south. Disorganisation ensued. The burghers would not pay taxes and the treasury was empty.

One fierce Kaffir tribe threatened them from the north, and the Zulus on the east. It is an exaggeration to pretend that British intervention saved the Boers, for no one can read their military history without seeing that they were a match for Zulus and Sekukuni combined. But certainly a formidable invasion was pending, and the scattered farmhouses were as open to the Kaffirs as our farmers homesteads were in the American colonies when the Indians were on the warpath.

Sir Theophilus Shepstone, the British Commissioner, after an inquiry of three months, solved all questions by the formal annexation of the country. ....

This, then, in 1877, was a complete reversal of the Sand River Convention and the opening of a new chapter in the history of South Africa.

There did not appear to be any strong feeling at the time against the annexation. The people were depressed with their troubles and weary of contention. [Mr.] Burgers, the President, put in a formal protest, and took up his abode in Cape Colony, where he had a pension from the British Government. A memorial against the measure received the signatures of a majority of the Boer inhabitants, but there was a fair minority who took the other view. Kruger himself accepted a paid office under Government. ....

Through no bad faith, but simply through preoccupation and delay, the promises made were not instantly fulfilled. .... But the British Government had some other local matters to set right, the rooting out of Sekukuni and the breaking of the Zulus, before they would fulfil their pledges.

The delay was keenly resented. And we were unfortunate in our choice of Governor. The burghers are a homely folk, and they like an occasional cup of coffee with the anxious man who tries to rule them. The 300*l*. a year of coffee-money allowed by the Transvaal to its President is by no means a mere form. A wise administrator would fall into the social and democratic habits of the people. Sir Theophilus Shepstone did so. Sir Owen Lanyon[546] did not.

There was no Volksraad and no coffee, and the popular discontent grew rapidly. In three years the British had broken up the two savage hordes which had been threatening the land. The finances, too, had been restored. The reasons which had made so many burghers favour the annexation were weakened by the very power which had every interest in preserving them. ....

There were no Rand mines in those days, nor was there anything in the country to tempt the most covetous. An empty treasury and two expensive native wars were the reversion which we took over.

It was honestly considered that the country was in too distracted a state to govern itself, and had, by its weakness, become a scandal and a danger to its neighbours and to itself. ....

In December 1880, the Boers rose. Every farmhouse sent out its riflemen, and the trysting-place was the outside of the nearest British fort. All through the country small detachments were surrounded and besieged by the farmers. Standerton, Pretoria, Potchefstroom, Lydenburg, Wakkerstroom, Rustenburg, and Marabastad were all invested and all held out until the end of the war.

In the open country the troops were less fortunate. At Bronkhorst Spruit[547] a small British force was taken by surprise and shot down without harm to their antagonists. The surgeon who treated them has left it on record that the average number of wounds was five per man.

At Laings Nek[548] an inferior force of British endeavoured to rush a hill which was held by Boer riflemen. Half of the men were killed and wounded. Ingogo[549] may be called a drawn battle, though the British loss was more heavy than that of the enemy. Finally came the defeat of Majuba Hill,[550] where 400 infantry upon a mountain were defeated and driven off by a swarm of sharpshooters who advanced under the cover of boulders.

Of all these actions there was not one which was more than a skirmish, and had they been followed by a final British victory they would now be hardly remembered. It is the fact that they were skirmishes which succeeded in their object—which has given them an exaggerated importance.

The defeat at Majuba Hill was followed by the complete surrender of the Gladstonian Government, an act which was either the most pusillanimous or the most magnanimous in recent history. ....

An overwhelming British force was in the field and the general declared that he held the enemy in the hollow of his hand. British military calculations have been falsified before now by these farmers, and it may be that the task of [Evelyn] Wood[551] and [Frederick] Roberts would have been harder than they imagined; but on paper, at least, it looked as if the enemy could be crushed without difficulty. So the public thought, and yet they consented to the upraised sword being stayed.

With them, as apart from the politicians, the motive was undoubtedly a moral and Christian one. They considered that the annexation of the Transvaal had evidently been an injustice, that the farmers had a right to the freedom for which they fought, and that it was an unworthy thing for a great nation to continue an unjust war for the sake of a military revenge. ....

An armistice was concluded on March 5, 1881, which led up to a peace on the 23rd of the same month. The Government, after yielding to force what it had repeatedly refused to friendly representations, made a clumsy compromise in their settlement. ....

It was obvious that if the annexation were unjust, then the Transvaal should have reverted to the condition in which it was before the annexation, as defined by the Sand River Convention. But the Government for some

[546] Colonel Sir William Owen Lanyon KCMG CB (21 July 1842–6 April 1887) was an Irish colonial administrator and British Army officer. Owen Lanyon - Wikipedia

[547] The battle of Bronkhorstspruit was the first major engagement of the First Boer War. It took place by the Bronkhorstspruit river, near the town of Bronkhorstspruit, Transvaal, on 20 December 1880. Battle of Bronkhorstspruit - Wikipedia

[548] The Battle of Laing's Nek was a major battle fought at Laing's Nek during the First Boer War on 28 January 1881. Battle of Laing's Nek - Wikipedia

[549] Ingogo - Wikipedia

[550] Battle of Majuba Hill - Wikipedia

[551] Evelyn Wood (British Army officer) - Wikipedia

reason would not go so far as this. They niggled and quibbled and bargained until the State was left as a curious hybrid thing such as the world has never seen. ....

It was autonomous, and yet subject to some vague suzerainty, the limits of which no one has ever been able to define. ....

It was evident from the first that so illogical and contentious an agreement could not possibly prove to be a final settlement, and indeed the ink of the signatures was hardly dry before an agitation was on foot for its revision. The Boers considered, and with justice, that if they were to be left as undisputed victors in the war then they should have the full fruits of victory. ....

During eighteen years [1881-1899] our people saw, or thought that they saw, that one concession led always to a fresh demand, and that the Dutch republics aimed not merely at equality, but at dominance in South Africa.

.... The Government of the Transvaal after the war was left in the hands of a triumvirate, but after one year Kruger became President, an office which he continued to hold for eighteen years. ....

Continued rule for half a generation must turn a man into an autocrat. The old President has said himself; in his homely but shrewd way, that when one gets a good ox to lead the team it is a pity to change him. ....

Considering that it was larger than France and that the population could not have been more than fifty thousand, one would have thought that they might have found room without any inconvenient crowding. But the burghers passed beyond their borders in every direction.

The President cried aloud that he had been shut up in a kraal, and he proceeded to find ways out of it. A great trek was projected for the north, but fortunately it miscarried. To the east they raided Zululand, and succeeded, in defiance of the British settlement of that country, in tearing away one-third of it and adding it to the Transvaal.

To the west, with no regard to the three-year-old treaty, they invaded Bechuanaland and set up the two new republics of Goshen[552] and Stellaland.[553] So outrageous were these proceedings that Great Britain was forced to fit out in 1884 a new expedition under Sir Charles Warren[554] for the purpose of turning these freebooters out of the country.

It may be asked, Why should these men be called freebooters if the founders of Rhodesia were pioneers? The answer is that the Transvaal was limited by treaty to certain boundaries which these men transgressed, while no pledges were broken when the British power expanded to the north. ....

Once more the purse was drawn from the pocket of the unhappy taxpayer, and a million or so was paid out to defray the expenses of the police force necessary to keep these treaty-breakers in order. ....

In 1884 a deputation from the Transvaal visited England, and at their solicitation the clumsy Treaty of Pretoria was altered into the still more clumsy Convention of London. The changes in the provisions were all in favour of the Boers, and a second successful war could hardly have given them more than **Lord Derby** handed them in time of peace. Their style was altered from the Transvaal to the South African Republic, a change which was ominously suggestive of expansion in the future. The control of Great Britain over their foreign policy was also relaxed, though a power of veto was retained.

But the most important thing of all, and the fruitful cause of future trouble, lay in an omission. A suzerainty is a vague term, but in politics, as in theology, the more nebulous a thing is the more does it excite the imagination and the passions of men. This suzerainty was declared in the preamble of the first treaty, and no mention of it was made in the second. Was it thereby abrogated or was it not? The British contention is that only the articles were changed, and that the preamble continued to hold good for both treaties. They point out that not only the suzerainty, but also the independence, of the Transvaal is proclaimed in that preamble, and that if one lapses the other must do so also.

On the other hand, the Boers point to the fact that there is actually a preamble to the second convention, which would seem, therefore, to take the place of the first. As a matter of fact the discussion is a barren one, since both

552 https://en.wikipedia.org/wiki/State_of_Goshen

553 Stellaland - Wikipedia

554 Charles Warren - Wikipedia

parties agree that Great Britain retained certain rights over the making of treaties by the Republic, which rights place her in a different position to an entirely independent state. ....

II. The Cause of the Quarrel

Gold had been known to exist in the Transvaal before, but it was only in 1886 that it was realised that the deposits which lie some thirty miles south of the capital are of a very extraordinary and valuable nature. The proportion of gold in the quartz is not particularly high, nor are the veins of a remarkable thickness, but the peculiarity of the Rand mines lies in the fact that throughout this blanket formation the metal is so uniformly distributed that the enterprise can claim a certainty which is not usually associated with the industry.

It is quarrying rather than mining. Add to this that the reefs which were originally worked as out-crops have now been traced to enormous depths and present the same features as those at the surface. ....

A great number of adventurers flocked into the country, some desirable and some very much the reverse. There were circumstances, however, which kept away the rowdy and desperado element who usually make for this newly-opened goldfield. It was not a class of mining which encouraged the individual adventurer. It was a field for elaborate machinery, which could only be provided by capital.

Managers, engineers, miners, technical experts, and the tradesmen and middlemen who live upon them, these were the Uitlanders, drawn from all races under the sun, but with the Anglo-Celtic vastly predominant. The best engineers were American, the best miners were Cornish, the best managers were English, the money to run the mines was largely subscribed in England.

As time went on, however, the German and French interests became more extensive, until their joint holdings are now probably as heavy as those of the British. Soon the population of the mining centres became about as numerous as that of the whole Boer community and consisted mainly of men in the prime of life—men, too, of exceptional intelligence and energy.

The situation was an extraordinary one. I have already attempted to bring the problem home to an American by suggesting that the Dutch of New York had trekked west and founded an anti-American and highly unprogressive State. To carry out the analogy we will now suppose that that State was California, that the gold of that State attracted a large inrush of American citizens, that these citizens were heavily taxed and badly used, and that they deafened Washington with their outcry about their injuries. ....

That these Uitlanders had very real and pressing grievances no one could possibly deny. To recount them all would be a formidable task, ... There was not a wrong which had driven the Boer from Cape Colony which he did not now practise himself upon others—and a wrong may be excusable in 1835 which is monstrous in 1895. ....

The country Boers were little affected, some of them not at all, but the Pretoria Government became a most corrupt oligarchy, venal and incompetent to the last degree. Officials and imported Hollanders handled the stream of gold which came in from the mines, while the unfortunate Uitlander who paid nine-tenths of the taxation was fleeced at every turn ....

On the contrary, he was patient to the verge of meekness, as capital is likely to be when it is surrounded by rifles. But his situation was intolerable, and after successive attempts at peaceful agitation, and numerous humble petitions to the Volksraad, he began at last to realise that he would never obtain redress unless he could find some way of winning it for himself.

Without attempting to enumerate all the wrongs.....the more serious of them may be summed up in this way:

1. That they were heavily taxed and provided about seven-eighths of the revenue of the country. The revenue of the South African Republic—which had been 154,000*l*. in 1886, when the goldfields were opened—had grown in 1899 to 4,000,000*l*., and the country through the industry of the newcomers had changed from one of the poorest to the richest in the whole world (per head of population).

2. That in spite of this prosperity which they had brought, they were left without a vote and could by no means influence the disposal of the great sums which they were providing. Such a case of taxation without representation has never been known.

3. That they had no voice in the choice or payment of officials. ...... The total official salaries had risen in 1899 to a sum sufficient to pay 40*l*. per head to the entire male Boer population.

4. That they had no control over education. Mr. John Robinson, the Director-General of the Johannesburg Educational Council, has reckoned the sum spent on the Uitlander schools as 650*l*. out of 63,000*l*. allotted for education, making 1*s*. 10*d*. per head per annum on Uitlander children, and 8*l*. 6*s*. per head on Boer children—the Uitlander, as always, paying seven-eighths of the original sum.

5. No power of municipal government. Watercarts instead of pipes, filthy buckets instead of drains, a corrupt and violent police, a high death-rate in what should be a health resort—all this in a city which they had built themselves.

6. Despotic government in the matter of the press and of the right of public meeting.

7. Disability from service upon a jury.

8. Continual harassing of the mining interest by vexatious legislation. Under this head come many grievances, some special to the mines and some affecting all Uitlanders. The dynamite monopoly, by which the miners had to pay 600,000*l*. extra per annum in order to get a worse quality of dynamite; the liquor laws, by which the Kaffirs were allowed to be habitually drunk; the incompetence and extortions of the State-owned railway; the granting of concessions for numerous articles of ordinary consumption to individuals, by which high prices were maintained; the surrounding of Johannesburg by tolls from which the town had no profit—these were among the economical grievances, some large, some petty, which ramified through every transaction of life. These are the wrongs which Mr. W. T. Stead has described as 'the twopenny-halfpenny grievances of a handful of Englishmen'.

The manner in which the blood was sucked from the Uitlanders, and the rapid spread of wealth among the Boer officials, may be gathered from the list of the salaries of the State servants from the opening of the mines to the outbreak of the war: [in £]

1886 ---- 51,831
1887 ---- 99,083
1888 --- 164,466
1889 --- 249,641
1890 --- 324,520
1891 --- 332,888
1892 --- 323,608
1893 -- 361,275
1894 --- 419,775
1895 --- 570,047
1896 --- 813,029
1897 --- 996,959
1898 - 1,080,382
1899 - 1,216,394

which shows, as Mr. FitzPatrick has pointed out, that the salary list had become twenty-four times what it was when the Uitlanders arrived, and five times as much as the total revenue was then. ....

Out of twenty-five members of the first Volksraad twenty-one were, in the case of the Selati Railway Company, publicly and circumstantially accused of bribery, with full details of the bribes received, their date, and who paid them. The black-list includes the present vice-president, Schalk Burger; the vice-president of that date; Eloff, the son-in-law of Kruger; and the secretary of the Volksraad.

Apparently every man of the executive and the legislature had his price. [Anecdotes of Boer Legislative silliness omitted]........................... Except for this:

Pillar-boxes [a free standing post box] in Pretoria were opposed on the grounds that they were extravagant and effeminate. Deputy Taljaard said that he could not see why people wanted to be always writing letters; he wrote none himself. In the days of his youth he had written a letter and had not been afraid to travel fifty miles and more on horseback and by wagon to post it—and now people complained if they had to go one mile.

Were the Boers to lose by the ballot-box the victory which they had won by their rifles? Was it fair to expect it? These newcomers came for gold. They got their gold. Their companies paid a hundred per cent. Was not that enough to satisfy them? If they did not like the country, why did they not leave it? No one compelled them to stay there. But if they stayed, let them be thankful that they were tolerated at all, and not presume to interfere with the laws of those by whose courtesy they were allowed to enter the country.

That is a fair statement of the Boer position, and at first sight an impartial man might say that there was a good deal to say for it; but a closer examination would show that, though it might be tenable in theory, it is unjust and impossible in practice.

.... A handful of people by the right of conquest take possession of an enormous country over which they are dotted at such intervals that it is their boast that one farmhouse cannot see the smoke of another, and yet, though their numbers are so disproportionate to the area which they cover, they refuse to admit any other people upon equal terms, but claim to be a privileged class who shall dominate the newcomers completely. They are outnumbered in their own land by immigrants who are far more highly educated and progressive, and yet they hold them down in a way which exists nowhere else upon earth. ....

Again, the argument of the Boers would be more valid had they received no benefit from these immigrants. .... They grew rich at the Uitlanders expense. They could not have it both ways. It would be consistent to discourage him and not profit by him, or to make him comfortable and build the State upon his money; but to ill-treat him and at the same time to grow strong by his taxation must surely be an injustice.

And again, the whole argument is based upon the narrow racial supposition that every naturalised citizen not of Boer extraction must necessarily be unpatriotic. This is not borne out by the examples of history. The newcomer soon becomes as proud of his country and as jealous of her liberty as the old. Had President Kruger given the franchise generously to the Uitlander, his pyramid would have been firm upon its base and not balanced upon its apex.

It is true that the corrupt oligarchy would have vanished, and the spirit of a broader, more tolerant freedom influenced the counsels of the State. But the Republic would have become stronger and more permanent, with a population who, if they differed in details, were united in essentials. ....

In more ways than one President Kruger has been a good friend to the Empire.

At the time of the Convention of Pretoria (1881) the rights of burghership might be obtained by one years residence. In 1882 it was raised to five years, the reasonable limit which obtains both in Great Britain and in the United States. Had it remained so, it is safe to say that there would never have been either an Uitlander question or a war. Grievances would have been righted from the inside without external interference.

In 1890 the inrush of outsiders alarmed the Boers, and the franchise was raised so as to be only attainable by those who had lived fourteen years in the country. The Uitlanders, .. perceived that their wrongs were so numerous that it was hopeless to have them set right seriatim, and that only by obtaining the leverage of the franchise could they hope to move the heavy burden which weighed them down.

In 1893 a petition of 13,000 Uitlanders, couched in most respectful terms, was submitted to the Raad, but met with contemptuous neglect. Undeterred, however, by this failure, the National Reform Union, an association which was not one of capitalists, came back to the attack in 1894. They drew up a petition which was signed by 35,000 adult male Uitlanders, as great a number probably as the total Boer male population of the country. A small liberal body in the Raad supported this memorial and endeavoured in vain to obtain some justice for the newcomers.

Mr. Jeppe was the mouthpiece of this select band [of Boer supporters]. 'They [Uitlanders] own half the soil, they pay at least three-quarters of the taxes, said he. They are men who in capital, energy, and education are at least our equals. What will become of us or our children on that day when we may find ourselves in a minority of one in twenty without a single friend among the other nineteen, among those who will then tell us that they wished to be brothers, but that we by our own act have made them strangers to the Republic?' ....

The memorial was rejected by sixteen votes to eight, and the franchise law was, on the initiative of the President, actually made more stringent than ever, being framed in such a way that during the fourteen years of probation the applicant should give up his previous nationality, so that for that period he would really belong to no country at all. ....

It had been arranged that the town was to rise upon a certain night, that Pretoria should be attacked, the fort seized, and the rifles and ammunition used to arm the Uitlanders. It was a feasible device, though it must seem to us, who have had such an experience of the military virtues of the burghers, a very desperate one. But it is conceivable that the rebels might have held Johannesburg until the universal sympathy which their cause excited throughout South Africa would have caused Great Britain to intervene.

Unfortunately they had complicated matters by asking for outside help. Mr. Cecil Rhodes was Premier of the Cape, a man of immense energy, and one who had rendered great services to the empire. ....it is certain that he allowed his lieutenant, Dr. Jameson, to assemble the mounted police of the Chartered Company, of which Rhodes was founder and director, for the purpose of co-operating with the rebels at Johannesburg.

Moreover, when the revolt at Johannesburg was postponed, on account of a disagreement as to which flag they were to rise under, it appears that Jameson (with or without the orders of Rhodes) forced the hand of the conspirators by invading the country with a force absurdly inadequate to the work which he had taken in hand. Five hundred policemen and two field-guns made up the forlorn hope who started from near Mafeking and crossed the Transvaal border upon December 29, 1895.

On January 2 they were surrounded by the Boers amid the broken country near Dornkop, and after losing many of their number killed and wounded, without food and with spent horses, they were compelled to lay down their arms. Six burghers lost their lives in the skirmish. ....

The Uitlanders have been severely criticised for not having sent out a force to help Jameson in his difficulties, but it is impossible to see how they could have acted in any other manner. They had done all they could to prevent Jameson coming to their relief, and now it was rather unreasonable to suppose that they should relieve their reliever. Indeed, they had an entirely exaggerated idea of the strength of the force which he was bringing and received the news of his capture with incredulity. ....

The President had the raiders in his keeping at Pretoria, and let it be understood that their fate depended upon the behaviour of the Uitlanders.

They were led to believe that Jameson would be shot unless they laid down their arms, though, as a matter of fact, Jameson and his people had surrendered upon a promise of quarter. So skillfully did Kruger use his hostages that he succeeded, with the help of the British Commissioner, in getting the thousands of excited Johannesburgers to lay down their arms without bloodshed. ....

Completely out-manoeuvred by the astute old President, the leaders of the reform movement used all their influence in the direction of peace.....

To the raiders themselves the President behaved with generosity. Perhaps he could not find it in his heart to be harsh to the men who had managed to put him in the right and won for him the sympathy of the world. His own illiberal and oppressive treatment of the newcomers was forgotten in the face of this illegal inroad of filibusters. ....

From then onwards the government might grow worse and worse, but it was always possible to point to the raid as justifying everything. Were the Uitlanders to have the franchise? How could they expect it after the raid! Would Britain object to the enormous importation of arms and obvious preparations for war? They were only precautions against a second raid. For years the raid stood in the way, not only of all progress, but of all remonstrance. ....

The raiders were sent home, where the rank and file were very properly released, and the chief officers were condemned to terms of imprisonment which certainly did not err upon the side of severity. In the meantime, both President Kruger and his burghers had shown a greater severity to the political prisoners from Johannesburg than to the armed followers of Jameson. ....

The prisoners were arrested in January, but the trial did not take place until the end of April. All were found guilty of high treason. Mr. Lionel Phillips, Colonel [Frank] Rhodes (brother of Mr. Cecil Rhodes), George Farrar, and Mr. Hammond, the American engineer, were condemned to death, a sentence which was afterwards commuted to the payment of an enormous fine. The other prisoners were condemned to two years imprisonment, with a fine of 2,000*l*. each. The imprisonment was of the most arduous and trying sort, and was embittered by the harshness of the gaoler, Du Plessis.

One of the unfortunate men cut his throat, and several fell seriously ill, the diet and the sanitary conditions being equally unhealthy. At last, at the end of May, all the prisoners but six were released. Four of the six soon followed, two stalwarts, Sampson and Davies, refusing to sign any petition and remaining in prison until they were set free in 1897. Altogether the Transvaal Government received in fines from the reform prisoners the enormous sum of 212,000*l*. A certain comic relief was immediately afterwards given to so grave an episode by the presentation of a bill to Great Britain for 1,677,938*l*. 3*s*. 3*d*.—the greater part of which was under the heading of moral and intellectual damage. ……………………..

The grievances of the Uitlanders became heavier than ever. The one power in the land to which they had been able to appeal for some sort of redress amid their troubles was the law courts. Now it was decreed that the courts should be dependent on the Volksraad. The Chief Justice protested against such a degradation of his high office, and he was dismissed in consequence without a pension. …………

A commission appointed by the State was sent to examine into the condition of the mining industry and the grievances from which the newcomers suffered. The chairman was Mr. Schalk Burger, one of the most liberal of the Boers, and the proceedings were thorough and impartial. The result was a report which amply vindicated the reformers, and suggested remedies which would have gone a long way towards satisfying the Uitlanders. With such enlightened legislation their motives for seeking the franchise would have been less pressing. But the President and his Raad would have none of the recommendations of the commission.

The rugged old autocrat declared that Schalk Burger was a traitor to his country for having signed such a document, and a new reactionary committee was chosen to report upon the report. ……………………

The small spark which caused a final explosion came from the shooting of a British subject named Edgar by a Boer policeman, Jones, in Johannesburg. The action of the policeman was upheld by the authorities, and the British felt that their lives were no longer safe in the presence of an armed, overbearing police.

At another time the incident might have been of no great importance, but at that moment it seemed to be taken as the crowning example of the injustice under which the miners suffered. A meeting of protest called by the British residents was broken up by gangs of workmen under Boer officials. Driven to desperation the Uitlanders determined upon a petition to Queen Victoria, and in doing so they brought their grievances out of the limits of a local controversy into the broader field of international politics. Great Britain must either protect them or acknowledge that their protection was beyond her power.

A direct petition to the Queen praying for protection was signed in April 1899 by 21,000 Uitlanders. [555] The condition of Your Majesty's subjects in this State has indeed become well-nigh intolerable. ………….

Maladministration and peculation of public moneys go hand-in-hand, without any vigorous measures being adopted to put a stop to the scandal. The education of Uitlander children is made subject to impossible conditions. The police afford no adequate protection to the lives and property of the inhabitants of Johannesburg; they are rather a source of danger to the peace and safety of the Uitlander population.

A further grievance has become prominent since the beginning of the year. The power vested in the Government by means of the Public Meetings Act has been a menace to Your Majesty's subjects since the enactment of the Act in 1894. This power has now been applied in order to deliver a blow that strikes at the inherent and inalienable birthright of every British subject—namely, his right to petition his Sovereign. ………………..

Wherefore Your Majesty's humble petitioners humbly beseech Your Most Gracious Majesty to extend Your Majesty's protection to Your Majesty's loyal subjects resident in this State, and to cause an inquiry to be made into grievances and complaints enumerated and set forth in this humble petition, and to direct Your Majesty's representative in South Africa ………..

III. The Negotiations

The British Government and the British people do not desire any direct authority in South Africa. Their one supreme interest is that the various States there should live in concord and prosperity, and that there should be no need for the presence of a British redcoat within the whole great peninsula. ……………

It was in April, 1899, that the British Uitlanders sent their petition praying for protection to their native country. Since the April previous a correspondence had been going on between Dr. Leyds, Secretary of State for the South African Republic, and Mr. Chamberlain, Colonial Secretary, upon the existence or nonexistence of the suzerainty.

On the one hand, it was contended that the substitution of a second convention had entirely annulled the first; on the other, that the preamble of the first applied also to the second. If the Transvaal contention were correct it is

[555] See portions set forth in Monster Petition section.

clear that Great Britain had been tricked and jockeyed into such a position, since she had received no *quid pro quo* in the second convention, and even the most careless of Colonial Secretaries could hardly have been expected to give away a very substantial something for nothing.

But the contention throws us back upon the academic question of what a suzerainty is. The Transvaal admitted a power of veto over their foreign policy, and this admission in itself, unless they openly tore up the convention, must deprive them of the position of a sovereign State.

But now to this debate, which had so little of urgency in it that seven months intervened between statement and reply, there came the bitterly vital question of the wrongs and appeal of the Uitlanders. Sir Alfred Milner, the British Commissioner in South Africa, ... and a conference was arranged between President Kruger and him at Bloemfontein, the capital of the Orange Free State. They met on May 31, 1899.

There were three different classes of subject which had to be discussed at the conference. One included all those alleged breaches of the Convention of London which had caused so much friction between the two Governments and which had thrice in eighteen years brought the States to the verge of war. Among these subjects would be the Boer annexations of native territory, such interference with trade as the stopping of [crossing] the Drifts, the question of suzerainty, and the possibility of arbitration.

The second class of questions would deal with the grievances of the Uitlanders, which presented a problem which had in no way been provided for in the conventions.

The third class contained the question of the ill-treatment of British Indians, and other causes of quarrel. Milner was faced with the alternative either to argue over each of these questions in turn—an endless and unprofitable business—or to put forward someone test-question which would strike at the root of the matter and prove whether a real attempt would be made by the Boer Government to relieve the tension.

The question which he selected was that of the franchise for the Uitlanders, for it was evident that if they obtained not a fair share—such a request was never made—but any appreciable share in the government of the country, they would in time be able to relieve their own grievances and so spare the British Government the heavy task of acting as their champions.

But the conference was quickly wrecked upon this question. Milner contended for a five-years retroactive franchise, with provisions to secure adequate representation for the mining districts. Kruger offered a seven-years franchise, coupled with numerous conditions which whittled down its value very much; promised five members out of thirty-one to represent half the male adult population; and added a provision that all differences should be subject to arbitration by foreign powers—a condition which is incompatible with any claim to suzerainty.

This offer dropped the term for the franchise from fourteen years to seven, but it retained a number of conditions which might make it illusory, while demanding in exchange a most important concession from the British Government. ....nothing [was] settled except the extreme difficulty of a settlement.

On June 12 Sir Alfred Milner received a deputation at Cape Town and reviewed the situation. 'The principle of equality of races was,' he said, 'essential for South Africa. The one State where inequality existed kept all the others in a fever. Our policy was one not of aggression, but of singular patience, which could not, however, lapse into indifference.'

Two days later Kruger addressed the Raad. 'The other side had not conceded one tittle, and I could not give more. God has always stood by us. I do not want war, but I will not give more away. Although our independence has once been taken away, God had restored it.' He spoke with sincerity, no doubt, but it is hard to hear God invoked with such confidence for the system which encouraged the liquor traffic to the natives, and bred the most corrupt set of officials that the modern world has seen.

A despatch from Sir Alfred Milner, giving his views upon the situation, made the British public recognise, as nothing else had done, how serious the position was, and how essential it was that an earnest national effort should be made to set it right. In it he said: [See Helot's despatch supra.]

Throughout the end of June and the early part of July much was hoped from the mediation of the heads of the Afrikander Bond, the political union of the Dutch Cape colonists. On the one hand, they were the kinsmen of the Boers; on the other, they were British subjects and were enjoying the blessings of those liberal institutions which we were anxious to see extended to the Transvaal. 'Only treat our folk as we treat yours!' Our whole contention was compressed into that prayer.

But nothing came of the mission, though a scheme endorsed by Mr. Hofmeyr and Mr. Herholdt, of the Bond with Mr. [Abraham] Fischer of the Free State, was introduced into the Raad and applauded by Mr. Schreiner, the Africander Premier of Cape Colony. In its original form the provisions were obscure and complicated, the franchise varying from nine years to seven under different conditions.

In debate, however, the terms were amended until the time was reduced to seven years, and the proposed representation of the Goldfields placed at five. The concession was not a great one, nor could the representation, five out of thirty-one, be considered a generous provision for half the adult male population; but the reduction of the years of residence was eagerly hailed in England as a sign that a compromise might be effected.

A sigh of relief went up from the country. 'If,' said the Colonial Secretary, [Chamberlain] 'this report is confirmed, this important change in the proposals of President Kruger, coupled with previous amendments, leads Government to hope that the new law may prove to be the basis of a settlement on the lines laid down by Sir Alfred Milner in the Bloemfontein Conference.'

He added that there were some vexatious conditions attached, but concluded, 'Her Majesty's Government feel assured that the President, having accepted the principle for which they have contended, will be prepared to reconsider any detail of his scheme which can be shown to be a possible hindrance to the full accomplishment of the object in view, and that he will not allow them to be nullified or reduced in value by any subsequent alterations of the law or acts of administration.'

At the same time, the 'Times' declared the crisis to be at an end: 'If the Dutch statesmen of the Cape have induced their brethren in the Transvaal to carry such a bill they will have deserved the lasting gratitude, not only of their own countrymen and of the English colonists in South Africa, but of the British Empire and of the civilised world.'.............

But this fair prospect was soon destined to be overcast. Questions of detail arose which, when closely examined, proved to be matters of very essential importance. The Uitlanders and British South Africans, who had experienced in the past how illusory the promises of the President might be, insisted upon guarantees. .... But there were conditions which excited distrust when drawn up by so wily a diplomatist. One was that the alien who aspired to burghership had to produce a certificate of continuous registration for a certain time. But the law of registration had fallen into disuse in the Transvaal, and consequently this provision might render the whole bill valueless.

Since it was carefully retained, it was certainly meant for use. The door had been opened, but a stone was placed to block it. ....

It took the course, therefore, of suggesting that each Government should appoint delegates to form a joint commission which should inquire into the working of the proposed bill before it was put into a final form. The proposal was submitted to the Raad upon August 7, with the addition that when this was done Sir Alfred Milner was prepared to discuss anything else, including arbitration without the interference of foreign powers. ....there could be no rest in South Africa so long as one race tried to dominate the other.

It is futile to suggest analogies, and to imagine what France would do if Germany were to interfere in a question of French franchise. Supposing that France contained nearly as many Germans as Frenchmen, and that they were ill-treated, Germany would interfere quickly enough and continue to do so until some fair *modus vivendi* was established. ....

A long delay followed upon the proposal of the Secretary of the Colonies. No reply was forthcoming from Pretoria. But on all sides there came evidence that those preparations for war which had been quietly going on even before the Jameson Raid were now being hurriedly perfected. ....Huge packing-cases, marked 'Agricultural Instruments' and 'Mining Machinery,' arrived from Germany and France to find their places in the forts of Johannesburg or Pretoria. ....

For three years the Transvaal had been arming to the teeth. So many modem magazine-rifles had been imported that there were enough to furnish five to every male burgher in the country. The importation of ammunition was on the same gigantic scale. For what were these formidable preparations? Evidently for a war with Great Britain, and not for a defensive war. .... For three weeks and more, during which Mr. Kruger was silent, these preparations went on more energetically and more openly.

But beyond them, and of infinitely more importance, there was one fact which dominated the situation and retarded the crisis. A burgher cannot go to war without his horse, his horse cannot move without grass, grass will not come until after rain, and it was still some weeks before the rain would be due.

Negotiations, then, must not be unduly hurried while the veldt was a bare, russet-coloured, dust-swept plain. Mr. Chamberlain and the British public waited week after week for an answer. But there was a limit to their patience, and it was reached on August 26, when the Colonial Secretary showed, with a plainness of speech which is as unusual as it is welcome in diplomacy, that the question could not be hung up forever. 'The sands are running down in the glass,' said he. 'If they run out we shall not hold ourselves limited by that which we have already offered, but, having taken the matter in hand, we will not let it go until we have secured conditions which once for all shall establish which is the paramount power in South Africa, and shall secure for our fellow-subjects there those equal rights and equal privileges which were promised them by President Kruger when the independence of the Transvaal was granted by the Queen, and which is the least that in justice ought to be accorded them.'

Lord Salisbury, a short time before, had been equally emphatic: 'No one in this country wishes to disturb the conventions so long as it is recognised that while they guarantee the independence of the Transvaal on the one side, they guarantee equal political and civil rights for settlers of all nationalities upon the other. But these conventions are not like the laws of the Medes and the Persians. They are mortal, they can be destroyed . . . and once destroyed they can never be reconstructed in the same shape.' ....

Pressure was in the meanwhile being put upon the old President and upon his advisers, if he can be said ever to have had any advisers, in order to induce him to accept the British offer of a joint committee of inquiry. Sir Henry de Villiers, representing the highest Africander opinion of the Cape, wrote strongly pleading the cause of peace, and urging Mr. Fischer of the Free State to endeavour to give a more friendly tone to the negotiations. 'Try and induce President Kruger to meet Mr. Chamberlain in a friendly way and remove all the causes of unrest which have disturbed this unhappy country for so many years.' Similar advice came from Europe. The Dutch minister telegraphed as follows:

'August 4, 1899.—Communicate confidentially to the President that, having heard from the Transvaal Minister the English proposal of the International Commission, I recommend the President, in the interest of the country, not peremptorily to refuse that proposition.'

'August 15, 1899.—Please communicate confidentially to the President that the German Government entirely shares my opinion, expressed in my despatch of August 4, not to refuse the English proposal. The German Government is, like myself, convinced that every approach to one of the Great Powers in this very critical moment will be without any results whatever, and very dangerous for the Republic.'....................

For a long time he was silent, and when he at last spoke it was to open a new phase of the negotiations. .... The game must be kept going for a couple of months. 'You are such past-masters in the art of gaining time!' said Mr. Labouchere to Mr. Montague White. The President proceeded to prove it.

His new suggestions were put forward on August 12. In them the Joint Commission was put aside, and the proposal was made that the Boer Government should accede to the franchise proposals of Sir Alfred Milner on condition that the British Government withdrew or dropped her claim to a suzerainty, agreed to arbitration by a British and South African tribunal, and promised never again to interfere in the internal affairs of the Republic.

To this Great Britain answered that she would agree to such arbitration; that she hoped never again to have occasion to interfere for the protection of her own subjects, but that with the grant of the franchise all occasion for such interference would pass away; and, finally, that she would never consent to abandon her position as suzerain power.

Mr. Chamberlains despatch ended by reminding the Government of the Transvaal that there were other matters of dispute open between the two Governments apart from the franchise, and that it would be as well to have them settled at the same time. By these he meant such questions as the position of the native races and the treatment of Anglo-Indians.

For a moment there seemed now to be a fair prospect of peace. There was no very great gap between the two parties, and had the negotiations been really bond fide it seems incredible that it could not be bridged. But the Transvaal was secure now of the alliance of the Orange Free State; it believed that the [Cape] Colony was ripe for rebellion; and it knew that with 60,000 cavalry and 100 guns it was infinitely the strongest military power in Africa. ....

On September 2 the answer of the Transvaal Government was returned. It was short and uncompromising. They withdrew their offer of the franchise. They reasserted the non-existence of the suzerainty. The negotiations were at a deadlock. It was difficult to see how they could be reopened. ....

On September 8 there was held a Cabinet Council—one of the most important in recent years. The military situation was pressing. The handful of troops in Africa could not be left at the mercy of the large and formidable force which the Boers could at any time hurl against them. On the other hand, it was very necessary not to appear to threaten or to appeal to force. For this reason reinforcements were sent upon such a scale as to make it evident that they were sent for defensive, and not for offensive, purposes. Five thousand men were sent from India to Natal, and the Cape garrisons were strengthened from England.

At the same time that they took these defensive measures, a message was sent to Pretoria, ...it begins by repudiating emphatically the claim of the Transvaal to be a sovereign international State in the same sense in which the Orange Free State is one. Any proposal made conditional upon such an acknowledgment could not be entertained. The status of the Transvaal was settled by certain conventions agreed to by both Governments, and nothing had occurred to cause us to acquiesce in a radical change in it.

The British Government, however, was prepared to accept the five years franchise as stated in the note of August 19, assuming at the same time that in the Raad each member might use his own language.

'Acceptance of these terms by the South African Republic would at once remove tension between the two Governments and would in all probability render unnecessary any future intervention to secure redress for grievances which the Uitlanders themselves would be able to bring to the notice of the Executive Council and the Volksraad.

'Her Majesty's Government are increasingly impressed with the danger of further delay in relieving the strain which has already caused so much injury to the interests of South Africa, and they earnestly press for an immediate and definite reply to the present proposal. If it is acceded to they will be ready to make immediate arrangements ... to settle all details of the proposed tribunal of arbitration. ... If, however, as they most anxiously hope will not be the case, the reply of the South African Republic should be negative or inconclusive, I am to state that Her Majesty's Government must reserve to themselves the right to reconsider the situation *de novo*, and to formulate their own proposals for a final settlement.' ....

Mr. Morley, Mr. Leonard Courtney, the 'Daily Chronicle'—all the most strenuous opponents of the Government policy—were satisfied that it was a message of peace. But nothing at that time, save a complete and abject surrender upon the part of the British, could have satisfied the Boers, who had the most exaggerated ideas of their own military prowess and no very high opinion of our own. ....

On September 18 the official reply of the Boer Government to the message sent from the Cabinet Council was published in London. ....

It refused to recommend or propose to the Raad the five-years franchise and the other provisions which had been defined as the minimum which the Home Government could accept as a fair measure of justice towards the Uitlanders. The suggestion that the debates of the Raad should be bilingual, as they are in the Cape Colony and in Canada, was absolutely waved aside.

The British Government had stated in their last despatch that if the reply should be negative or inconclusive they reserved to themselves the right to 'reconsider the situation *de novo*, and to formulate their own proposals for a final settlement.' The reply had been both negative and inconclusive, and on September 22 a council met to determine what the next message should be.

It was short and firm but so planned as not to shut the door upon peace. Its purport was that the British Government expressed deep regret at the rejection of the moderate proposals which had been submitted in their last despatch, and that now, in accordance with their promise, they would shortly put forward their own plans for a settlement. The message was not an ultimatum, but it foreshadowed an ultimatum in the future.

In the meantime, upon September 21, the Raad of the Orange Free State had met, and it became more and more evident that this republic, with whom we had no possible quarrel, but, on the contrary, for whom we had a great deal of friendship and admiration, intended to throw in its weight against Great Britain.

Sometime before, an offensive and defensive alliance had been concluded between the two States, which must,.......appear to have been a singularly rash and unprofitable bargain for the smaller one.

She had nothing to fear from Great Britain, since she had been voluntarily turned into an independent republic by her and had lived in peace with her for forty years. Her laws were as liberal as our own. But by this suicidal treaty she agreed to share the fortunes of a State deliberately courting war, ...[This] one might imagine, have alienated the sympathy of her progressive [OFS] neighbour.

The trend of events was seen clearly in the days of President Brand, who was a sane and experienced politician. 'President Brand', says Paul Botha (himself a voortrekker and a Boer of the Boers), 'saw clearly what our policy ought to have been. ....

And in order to maintain its character he always strove for the friendship of England. President Brand realised that closer union with the turbulent and misguided Transvaal, led by Kruger's challenging policy, would inevitably result in a disastrous war with England.

I [Paul Botha] felt this as strongly and never ceased fighting against closer union. I remember once stating these arguments in the Volksraad, and wound up my speech by saying, "May Heaven grant that I am wrong in what I fear, because, if I am right, then woe, woe to the Orange Free State."

It is evident that if the Free State rushed headlong to utter destruction it was not for want of wise voices which tried to guide her to some safer path. But there seems to have been a complete hallucination as to the comparative strength of the two opponents, and as to the probable future of South Africa. ....

When I come to think of the abuse the pulpit made of its influence,' says Paul Botha, 'I feel as if I cannot find words strong enough to express my indignation. Gods word was prostituted. A religious peoples religion was used to urge them to their destruction. A minister of God told me himself, with a wink, that he had to preach anti-English because otherwise he would lose favour with those in power.' Such were the influences which induced the Free State to make an insane treaty, compelling it to wantonly take up arms against a State which had never injured it and which bore it nothing but good will.

The tone of President Steyn at the meeting of the Raad, and the support which he received from the majority of his burghers, showed unmistakably that the two republics would act as one. ....

Among the obvious military precautions which could no longer be neglected by the British Government, was the sending of some small force to protect the long and exposed line of railway which lies just outside the Transvaal border from Kimberley to Rhodesia. ....

On August 15, at a time when the negotiations had already assumed a very serious phase, after the failure of the Bloemfontein Conference and the despatch of Sir Alfred Milner, the British forces in South Africa were absolutely and absurdly inadequate for the purpose of the defence of our own frontier. Surely such a fact must open the eyes of those who, in spite of all the evidence, persist that the war was forced on by the British.

A statesman who forces on a war usually prepares for a war, and this is exactly what Mr. Kruger did and the British authorities did not. The overbearing suzerain power had at that date, scattered over a huge frontier, two cavalry regiments, three field batteries, and six and a half infantry battalions—say six thousand men. The innocent pastoral States could put in the field more than fifty thousand mounted riflemen, whose mobility doubled their numbers, and a most excellent artillery, including the heaviest guns which have ever been seen upon a battlefield.

At this time it is most certain that the Boers could have made their way easily either to Durban or to Cape Town. The British force, condemned to act upon the defensive, could have been masked and afterwards destroyed, while the main body of the invaders would have encountered nothing but an irregular local resistance, which would have been neutralised by the apathy or hostility of the Dutch colonists. It is extraordinary that our authorities seem never to have contemplated the possibility of the Boers taking the initiative, or to have understood that in that case our belated reinforcements would certainly have had to land under the fire of the republican guns.

They ran a great military risk by their inaction, but at least they made it clear to all who are not willfully blind how far from the thoughts or wishes of the British Government it has always been that the matter should be decided by force. In answer to the remonstrances of the Colonial Prime Minister the garrison of Natal was gradually increased, partly by troops from Europe, and partly by the despatch of 5,000 British troops from India. Their arrival late in September raised the number of troops in South Africa to 22,000, a force which was inadequate to a contest in the open field with the numerous, mobile, and gallant enemy to whom they were to be opposed, but which proved to be strong enough to stave off that overwhelming disaster which, with our fuller knowledge, we can now see to have been impending.

In the weeks which followed the despatch of the Cabinet message of September 8, the military situation had ceased to be desperate but was still precarious. Twenty-two thousand regular troops were on the spot who might hope to be reinforced by some ten thousand Colonials, but these forces had to cover a great frontier, ...

For purposes of comparison we may give some idea of the forces which Mr. Kruger and Mr. Steyn could put in the field. The general press estimated the forces of the two republics varied from 25,000 to 35,000 men. Mr. J. B. Robinson, a personal friend of President Kruger's and a man who had spent much of his life among the Boers, considered the latter estimate to be too high. ....

According to this the fighting strength of the Transvaal alone was 32,000 men, and of the Orange Free State 22,000. With mercenaries and rebels from the colonies they would amount to 60,000, while a considerable rising of the Cape Dutch would bring them up to 100,000. Our actual male prisoners now amount to 42,000, and we can account for 10,000 casualties, so that, allowing another 10,000 for the burghers at large, the Boer force, excluding a great number of Cape rebels, would reach 62,000.

Of the quality of this large force there is no need to speak. The men were brave, hardy, and fired with a strange religious enthusiasm. They were all of the seventeenth century, except their rifles. Mounted upon their hardy little ponies, they possessed a mobility which practically doubled their numbers and made it an impossibility ever to outflank them. As marksmen they are supreme. Add to this that they had the advantage of acting upon internal lines with shorter and safer communications, and one gathers how formidable a task lay before the soldiers of the Empire. ....

There was a lull in the political exchanges after the receipt of the Transvaal despatch of September 16, which rejected the British proposals of September 8. In Africa all hope or fear of peace had ended. The Raads had been dissolved and the old Presidents last words had been that war was certain, with a stern invocation of the Lord as the final arbiter. Britain was ready less obtrusively, but no less heartily, to refer the quarrel to the same dread judge.

On October 2 President Steyn informed Sir Alfred Milner that he had deemed it necessary to call out the Free State burghers—that is, to mobilise his forces. Sir A. Milner wrote regretting these preparations and declaring that he did not yet despair of peace, for he was sure that any reasonable proposal would be favourably considered by Her Majesty's Government. Steyn's reply was that there was no use in negotiating unless the stream of British reinforcements ceased coming into South Africa.

As our forces were still in a great minority, it was impossible to stop the reinforcements, so the correspondence led to nothing.

On October 7 the army reserves for the First Army Corps were sailed out in Great Britain, and other signs shown that it had been determined to send a considerable force to South Africa. Parliament was also summoned, that the formal national assent might be gained for those grave measures which were evidently pending.

It has been stated that it was the action of the British in calling out the reserves which caused the ultimatum from the Boers and so precipitated the war. Such a contention is absurd, for it puts the cart before the horse. The Transvaal commandos had mobilised upon September 27, and those of the Free State on October 2.

The railways had been taken over, the exodus from Johannesburg had begun, and an actual act of war had been committed by the stopping of a train and the confiscation of the gold which was in it. The British action was subsequent to all this and could not have been the cause of it.

But no Government could see such portents and delay any longer to make those military preparations which were called for by the critical situation..........

It was on October 9 that the somewhat leisurely proceedings of the British Colonial Office were brought to a head by the arrival of an unexpected and audacious ultimatum from the Boer Government. ....

The document was very firm and explicit, but the terms in which it was drawn were so impossible that it was evidently framed with the deliberate purpose of forcing an immediate war. It demanded that the troops upon the borders of the Republic should be instantly withdrawn, that all reinforcements which had arrived within the last year should leave South Africa, and that those who were now upon the sea should be sent back without being landed. Failing a satisfactory answer within forty-eight hours, The Transvaal Government will with great regret be compelled to regard the action of Her Majesty's Government as a formal declaration of war, for the consequences of which it will not hold itself responsible.'

The audacious message was received throughout the empire with a mixture of derision and anger. The answer was despatched next day through Sir Alfred Milner.

'October 10.—Her Majesty's Government have received with great regret the peremptory demands of the Government of the South African Republic, conveyed in your telegram of the 9th October. You will inform the

Government of the South African Republic in reply that the conditions demanded by the Government of the South African Republic are such as Her Majesty's Government deem it impossible to discuss.'

IV. Some Points Examined

PF: This chapter has been omitted as being simply journalism addressing calumny leveled at the British leaders and policies. These arguments have already been repeatedly discussed and Arthur takes a decidedly pro-British slant to all of them.

V. The Negotiations for Peace

.... every yard of British territory which was occupied was instantly annexed either by the Transvaal or by the Orange Free State. This is admitted and beyond dispute. What becomes then of the theory of a defensive war, and what can they urge against the justice which awarded the same fate to the land of the Boers when it in turn was occupied by us? The Boers did not use their temporary victory in any moderate spirit. At the end of January 1900, Dr. Leyds, while on a visit to Berlin, said:

I believe that England will have to give us back a good part of the territory formerly snatched away from us. . . The Boers will probably demand the cession of the strip of coast between Durban and Delagoa Bay, with the harbours of Lucia and Kosi. The Orange Free State and the Transvaal are to be united and to form one State, together with parts of Natal and the northern districts of Cape Colony.—('Daily News' Berlin correspondent, February 1, March 16, 1900.)

They were to go to the sea, and nothing but going to the sea would satisfy them. The war would end when their flag flew over Cape Town. But there came a turn of the tide. The resistance of the garrisons, the tenacity of the relieving forces, and the genius of Lord Roberts altered the whole situation. The Boers were driven back to the first of their capitals. Then for the first time there came from them those proposals for peace, which were never heard when the game was going in their favour. Here is President Kruger's telegram:

Kruger's March 1900 Proposal

[PF: This material is a repeat of the section titled 'March 1900 Offer and Reply' supra. It is reproduced here since there are slight differences in language used.

The Presidents of The Orange Free State and of The South African Republic

To The Marquis of Salisbury.

Bloemfontein: March 5, 1900.

The blood and the tears of the thousands who have suffered by this war, and the prospect of all the moral and economic ruin with which South Africa is now threatened, make it necessary for both belligerents to ask themselves dispassionately, and as in the sight of the Triune God, for what they are fighting, and whether the aim of each justifies all this appalling misery and devastation.

With this object, and in view of the assertions of various British statesmen to the effect that this war was begun and is being carried on with the set purpose of undermining Her Majesty's authority in South Africa, and of setting up an Administration over all South Africa independent of Her Majesty's Government, we consider it our duty solemnly to declare that this war was undertaken solely as a defensive measure to safeguard the threatened independence of the South African Republic, and is only continued in order to secure and safeguard the incontestable independence of both Republics as Sovereign International States, and to obtain the assurance that those of Her Majesty's subjects who have taken part with us in this war shall suffer no harm whatsoever in person or property.

On these conditions, but on these conditions alone, are we now, as in the past, desirous of seeing peace reestablished in South Africa, and of putting an end to the evils now reigning over South Africa; while, if Her Majesty's Government is determined to destroy the independence of the Republics, there is nothing left to us and to our people but to persevere to the end in the course already begun, in spite of the overwhelming preeminence of the British Empire, confident that that God who lighted the unextinguishable fire of the love of freedom in the hearts of ourselves and of our fathers will not forsake us, but will accomplish His work in us and in our descendants.

We hesitated to make this declaration earlier to Your Excellency, as we feared that as long as the advantage was always on our side, and as long as our forces held defensive positions far in Her Majesty's colonies, such a declaration might hurt the feelings of honour of the British people; but now that the prestige of the British Empire may be considered to be assured by the capture of one of our forces by Her Majesty's troops, and that we are thereby forced to evacuate other positions which our forces had occupied, that difficulty is over, and we can no longer hesitate clearly to inform your Government and people in the sight of the whole civilised world why we are fighting, and on what conditions we are ready to restore peace.

Salisbury's Reply

Foreign Office: March 11, 1900.

I have the honour to acknowledge Your Honours' telegram dated the 5th of March from Bloemfontein, of which the purport is principally to demand that Her Majesty's Government shall recognise the "incontestable independence" of the South African Republic and Orange Free State "as Sovereign International States," and to offer, on those terms, to bring the war to a conclusion.

In the beginning of October last peace existed between Her Majesty and the two Republics under the conventions which then were in existence. A discussion had been proceeding for some months between Her Majesty's Government and the South African Republic, of which the object was to obtain redress for certain very serious grievances under which British residents in the South African Republic were suffering.

In the course of those negotiations the South African Republic had, to the knowledge of Her Majesty's Government, made considerable armaments, and the latter had, consequently, taken steps to provide corresponding reinforcements to the British garrisons of Cape Town and Natal. No infringement of the rights guaranteed by the Conventions had up to that point taken place on the British side.

Suddenly, at two days' notice, the South African Republic, after issuing an insulting ultimatum, declared war upon Her Majesty, and the Orange Free State, with whom there had not even been any discussion, took a similar step.

Her Majesty's dominions were immediately invaded by the two Republics, siege was laid to three towns within the British frontier, a large portion of the two colonies was overrun, with great destruction to property and life, and the Republics claimed to treat the inhabitants of extensive portions of Her Majesty's dominions as if those dominions had been annexed to one or other of them.

In anticipation of these operations, the South African Republic had been accumulating for many years past military stores on an enormous scale, which by their character could only have been intended for use against Great Britain.

Your Honours make some observations of a negative character upon the object with which these preparations were made. I do not think it necessary to discuss the question you have raised. But the result of these preparations, carried on with great secrecy, has been that the British Empire has been compelled to confront an invasion which has entailed upon the Empire a costly war and the loss of thousands of precious lives.

This great calamity has been the penalty which Great Britain has suffered for having in recent years acquiesced in the existence of the two Republics.

[PF: A close reading of this text in comparison to the one reproduced above will reveal telling differences in the language used. Also Dr. Doyle's conclusions, despite the histrionic introduction, and summary are a central thesis of this work and his commentary continues below.]

Resume Conan Doyle

Is there any sane man of any nation who can contend that a British statesman could possibly have taken any other view? From the firing of the first shot the irresistible logic of events showed that either the Republics must dominate Africa or they must cease to exist.

For the sparing of the Orange Free State there might, I think, be a fair argument, but they had put themselves out of court by annexing every foot of British territory which they could lay their hands upon. For the sparing of the Transvaal there could be no possible reason. Had that State been reconstituted we should instantly have been faced once more with the franchise question, the Uitlander question, the corrupt oligarchy, the anti-British conspiracy, and everything which we had spent so much blood and money to set right. The desperate situation from which the British power was only just emerging was so fresh in our minds that we could not feel justified in leaving the possibility—indeed the certainty—of its recurrence to our children.

Remember, you who judge us, that we had done all this before. Once before within our own memories we had patched up an inconclusive peace and left these people the power to hurt us. And what had come of it? Eternal trouble ending in a great war which strained the resources of the Empire.

Could we be asked to do the same again? Would any nation on earth have done the same again? From the day of the signing of peace we should know that we had an implacable and formidable foe to the north of us, nursing his wrath and preparing his strength for the day when he might strike us at an advantage. Our colonies would lie ever, in the shadow of its menace. Who can blame us for deciding that the job should be done now in such a way that it should never, so far as we could help it, need to be done once more?

Such was the end of the first negotiations for peace. The war was resumed, and in time the second capital of the Boers was taken and President Kruger withdrew to Europe, leaving South Africa in the welter to which he had reduced it.

Then, for the second time, negotiations for peace were opened on the initiative of General Botha, which led to a meeting upon February 28, 1901, between Kitchener and Botha. Kitchener had already explained that for the reasons given above the restoration of independence was impossible, and the negotiations were carried through on that understanding. Here is Lord Kitchener's own account of the interview and of the points at issue:

Kitchener's Report

{*Telegram.*}

'Pretoria: March 1, 1901, 2:20 p. m.

28th February.—I have had a long interview with Botha, who showed very good feeling and seemed anxious to bring about peace. He asked for information on a number of subjects which he said that he should submit to his Government and people, and if they agreed he should visit Orange River Colony and get them to agree.

They should all then hand in their arms and finish the war. He told me that they could go on for some time, and that he was not sure of being able to bring about peace without independence. He tried very hard for some kind of independence, but I declined to discuss such a point and said that a modified form of independence would be most dangerous and likely to lead to war in the future. Subject was then dropped, and—

'Firstly.—The nature of future government of Colonies asked about. He wanted more details than were given by Colonial Secretary, and I said that, subject to correction from home, I understood that when hostilities ceased military guard would be replaced by Crown Colony administration, consisting of nominated Executive, with elected assembly to advise administration, to be followed after a period by representative government. He would have liked representative government at once but seemed satisfied with above.

'Secondly.—Whether a Boer would be able to have a rifle to protect him from native? I said I thought he would be by a licence and on registration.

'Thirdly.—He asked whether Dutch language would be allowed? I said that English and Dutch would, I thought, have equal rights. He expressed hope that officials dealing with farmers would know Dutch.

'Fourthly.—The Kaffir question. This turned at once on franchise of Kaffirs, and a solution seemed to be that franchise should not be given to Kaffirs until after representative government was granted to Colonies. Orange Free State laws for Kaffirs were considered good.

'Fifthly.—That Dutch Church property should remain untouched.

'Sixthly.—Public trusts and orphan funds to be left intact. He asked whether British Government, in taking over the assets of Republics, would also take over legal debts. This he made rather a strong point of, and he intended it to include debts legally contracted since the war began. He referred to notes issued amounting to less than a million.

'Seventhly.—He asked if any war tax would be imposed on farmers? I said I thought not.

'Eighthly.—When would prisoners of war return?

'Ninthly.—He referred to pecuniary assistance to repair burnt farms and enable farmers to start afresh. I said I thought some assistance would be given.

'Tenthly.—Amnesty to all at end of war. We spoke of Colonials who joined Republics, and he seemed not adverse to their being disfranchised.

'I arranged with him that I should write and let him know the view of the Government on these points. All I said during the interview was qualified by being subject to confirmation from home. He was anxious to get an answer soon.'

There followed some correspondence between Lord Kitchener, Sir Alfred Milner, and Mr. Chamberlain upon the exact terms which could be given to Botha. They ended in the following offer, which was submitted to him upon March 7. That, in consideration of a complete military surrender,

'1. There should be a complete amnesty for all *bona fide* acts of war for all burghers of the Republics. In the case of Colonial rebels, if they returned to their Colonies some inquiry must be held on their conduct.

'2. All prisoners to be at once sent back.

'3. Crown Colony government to be given as soon as possible; this in turn to change to representative government, as in all other free British possessions. The courts of law to be independent of the government.

'4. The Dutch and English languages to be put upon an equality.

'5. That the Government should help to replace the farmers on their farms, to restore their buildings, should pledge itself not to specially tax them, and should pay as an act of grace one million pounds to meet the debt incurred by the Republican governments to their own people during the war.

'6. That the burghers be allowed sporting fire-arms.

'7. That the Kaffirs should have the protection of the law but should not have the vote.

'In conclusion, says Lord Kitchener, 'I must inform Your Honour that if the terms are not accepted after a reasonable delay for consideration, they must be regarded as cancelled'.

But the wise and chivalrous Botha was overruled by the men around him, many of whom had little to lose by a continuance of the struggle. It was evident that he did not himself consider independence vital, since he had gravely discussed terms which were based upon loss of independence. But other influences had been brought to bear upon him, and this was his reply—a reply which has already cost the lives of so many of each side:

Botha's First Reply

See Botha's reply to Kitchener declining his terms supra.

De Wet and SAR Letter to OFS

De Wet had said in reference to Kitchener's terms of peace,

'What is the use of examining all the points, as the only object for which we are fighting is our independence and our national existence?' It is evident, however, that Botha did not consider this an absolute bar to renewing the negotiations, for upon May 10, two months later, he wrote the following letter to Lord Kitchener:

SAR Letter

Government Offices, In the Field, District Ermelo, South African Republic,[556]

To the Government Secretary, O.F.S.

May 10th, 1901

Sir,—

I have the honour to report to you that to-day the following officers met the Government, namely, the Commandant-General, General B. Viljoen, General J.C. Smuts (Staats-Procureur), the last-named representing the western districts. Our situation was seriously discussed, and, among others, the following facts were pointed out:—

[556] This letter from Chapter VIII of De Wet's Three Years' War.

1. That small parties of burghers are still continually laying down their arms, and that the danger arising from this is becoming every day more threatening, namely, that we are exposed to the risk of our campaign ending in disgrace, as the consequence of these surrenders may be that the Government and the officers will be left in the field without any burghers, and that, therefore, heavy responsibility rests upon the Government and War Officers, as they represent the nation and not themselves only.

2. That our ammunition is so exhausted that no battle of any importance can be fought, and that this lack of ammunition will soon bring us to the necessity of flying helplessly before the enemy. And that through this same lack it has become impossible for us to afford adequate protection to our people and their cattle, with the result that the general population is being reduced to poverty and despair, and that even the troops will soon be unable to be supplied with provisions.

3. That through the above-mentioned conditions the authority of the Government is becoming more and more weakened, and that thus the danger arises of the people losing all respect and reverence for lawful authority, and falling into a condition of lawlessness. And that to prolong the war can only lead to hastening the ruin of the people, and making it clear to them that the only authority in the country is that of the enemy.

4. That not only is our nation becoming disorganized in the manner above referred to, but that it will also most certainly happen that the leaders of the nation, whose personal influence has hitherto kept it together, will fall into utter contempt, and lose that influence which is our only hope for reviving the national spirit in the future.

5. That the people are constantly demanding to be told what hope still exists of successfully prosecuting the war, and that they have the right to expect to be informed in an honest and straightforward manner that their cause is hopeless, whenever this has become evident to the Government and the Leaders.

Up to the present time the Government and the nation have been expecting that, with the co-operation of their Deputation and by the aid of European complications, there would be some hope for the success of their cause, and the Government feels strongly that before taking any decisive step, an attempt should again be made to arrive with certainty at the results of the Deputation and the political situation in Europe.

Having taken all the facts into consideration, the Government, acting in conjunction with the above-mentioned officers, have arrived at the following decision:

Firstly, that a request should be addressed this very day to Lord Kitchener, asking that through the intervention of ambassadors sent by us to Europe, the condition of our country may be allowed to be placed before President Kruger, which ambassadors are to return with all possible speed.

Secondly, that should this request be refused, or lead to no results, an armistice should be asked for, by which the opportunity should be given us of finally deciding in consultation with your Government, and the people of the two States, what we must do.

This second proposal is, however, subject to any solution which your Government, taking into consideration the above-mentioned grievances, may be able to suggest.

The Government feels very keenly that it would no longer be right to allow things to go on as they have been going on, and that the time has arrived for taking some definite steps; it will, therefore, be glad to receive an answer from your Government as soon as possible.

I have the honour to be,

Yours, etc., F.W. Reitz,

Secretary of State. [of the Transvaal]

The answer which the President [Steyn] sent to this letter was formerly in my possession, but has been lost with many of my documents. I am able, however, to give an extract, which I received from the Rev. J.D. Kestell. It was to the following effect:—

The President was much disappointed with the letter of the Transvaal Government; he said that although there had been in the past some surrenders in the Free State, this difficulty had now been overcome. Moreover, although the ammunition had for a long time been scarce, nevertheless, after every fight, there had been enough to begin the next with.[557]

[557] 3/26/1901 Victory by General Babington over Delarey at Ventersdorp. Nine Boer guns captured.

To the question, What probability was there of their being able to continue the struggle? he would reply by asking another question—What hope had the two little Republics, at the beginning of the war, of winning the fight against the might of England? If they had trusted in God at the beginning, why did they not continue to trust in Him?

He also pointed out that if the Boer cause was really quite hopeless, the Deputation would have been sure to send word to that effect. Further, he assured the Transvaal Government that if an armistice were to be obtained, and if during it the people of the Free State were to be asked for their opinion, the decision of the burghers who were still in the field would be to continue the war.

He could not approve of the decision of the Transvaal Government to ask Lord Kitchener to allow ambassadors to be sent to Europe, for, by so doing, the Government would be showing its hand to the enemy; he added that he was very sorry that such a decision had been taken without first consulting the Free State.[558]

As to the fear expressed by the Transvaal Government, that the Authorities and the Officers in the field would be left without burghers, the President said, that even if the Government and the Officers of the Free State were to surrender, the nation would not do so.

It would be a great misfortune, he added, if the Orange Free State, which had not only lost its property and the lives of many of its burghers but also even its very independence, in the defence of the sister Republic, should now be abandoned by that Republic; that then all confidence in one another and all co-operation between Afrikanders would come to an end for ever: and that, under such circumstances, it would be too much to expect that the African nation should ever be able to rise again. If then the Boers wished to remain a nation, it was absolutely necessary to continue the war.

After having quoted various appropriate passages from the newspapers, the President went on as follows:—"All these considerations combine to make me believe that we should be committing a National murder if we were to give in now. Brethren! Hold out a little longer. Let not our sufferings and our struggles be in vain; let not our faith in the God of our fathers become a byword. Do all that you can to encourage one another."

The President concluded this very remarkable and powerful letter with the question:—

"Are we again to leave the Colonial burghers in the lurch? God forbid."

We decided to set out for the Transvaal in order to discuss the matter with the Government; and on the evening of the 5th of June we marched four or five miles from Liebenbergsvlei, to a place opposite Verkijkersdorp. We were, all told, between sixty and seventy men, including the staff and part of the bodyguard of President Steyn, the staff of General De la Rey, and eight of my staff officers.

Botha's Reply

'Commandant-Generals Camp, May 10, 1901.

'Excellency,—As I have already assured Your Excellency I am very desirous of terminating this war, and its sad consequences. It is, however, necessary, in order to comply with the "Grondwet" of this Republic and otherwise, that, before any steps are taken in that direction, the condition of our country and our cause be brought to the notice of His Honour, State President Kruger, in Europe; and I therefore wish to send two persons to him in order to acquaint him fully with that condition.

'As speed in this matter is of great consequence to both contending parties, and as such despatch without Your Excellency's assistance would take a considerable time, I should like to hear from Your Excellency whether

4/6/1901 General French, in his sweeping operations in the Eastern Transvaal, captured all the enemy's guns in that district.
4/8/1901 Colonel Plumer captured Pietersburg, the terminus of the railway running due north from Pretoria.
4/10/1901 Civil administration resumed in the Transvaal.
4/15/1901 Smuts' commando defeated near Klerksdorp. Two guns captured.
4/19/1901 Generals Plumer and Walter Kitchener co-operated with General French in clearing the Eastern Transvaal and Lydenburg district.
4/30/1901 General Blood discovered documents and banknotes of Transvaal (Government at Roosenekal, from which place Mr. Schalk Burger fled.

[558] The reply to the enquiry, facilitated by Kitchener, had not yet been received. 7/5/1901 In reply to Botha's inquires about ending the war, Kruger telegraphed to Botha to continue fighting.

Your Excellency is prepared to assist me in expediting this matter by allowing such person or persons to journey there and back unhindered, if necessary by the traffic medium within Your Excellency's control.—I have, &c., Louis Botha, Commandant-General.'

To this Kitchener answered:

'Army Headquarters, South Africa, Pretoria, May 16, 1901.

'Your Honour,—I have the honour to acknowledge the receipt of Your Honor's letter of 10th instant, and, in reply, beg to state that I can only deal with you and your superior officers in the field in regard to the cessation of hostilities, and that I do not recognise the official status of any other persons in the late Republics of the Orange River and Transvaal.

'If, however, Your Honour desires, with the object of bringing hostilities to a close, to consult with any person in Europe, I will forward any telegram Your Honour desires on the subject, and let you have the reply. Should, however, Your Honour still desire to send messengers, and will inform me of their names and status, I will refer the matter to His Majesty's Government for decision.—I have, &c.,

Kitchener, General, Commanding-in-Chief, British Troops, South Africa.'

At this period, the second week of May, the Boer cause was in very low water, as on the same date we have Botha reopening negotiations which he had declared to be definitely closed, and Reitz writing a despairing letter to Steyn to the effect that the game was up and that it was time to take the final step.

A reply was received from Kruger encouraging the Boers to continue their hopeless and fatal resistance. His reply was to the effect that there were still great hopes of a successful issue of the war, and that he had taken steps to make proper provision for the Boer prisoners and for the refugee women. ....

...............It is only necessary to refer briefly to the unofficial Boer attempts at peace. A considerable body of the Boers, including many men of influence and of intelligence, were disposed to accept the British flag and to settle down in peace. The leaders of this party were the brave Piet de Wet, brother of Christian, Paul Botha of Kroonstad, Fraser of Bloemfontein, and others. Piet de Wet, who had fought against us as hard as any man, wrote to his brother:

Piet de Wet

'Which is better, for the Republics to continue the struggle and run the risk of total ruin as a nation, or to submit? Could we for a moment think of taking back the country, if it were offered to us, with thousands of people to be supported by a Government which has not a farthing. Put passionate feeling aside for a moment and use common-sense, and you will then agree with me that the best thing for the people and the country is to give in, to be loyal to the new Government, and to get responsible government.'

Such were the sentiments of many of the best of the burghers, and they endeavoured to persuade their fellows. Both in the Transvaal and in the Free State, Peace Committees were formed among the burghers, who sent deputies to lay the facts of the situation before their brethren on commando.

The results were tragic. Two of the envoys, Morgendaal and de Koch, were shot in cold blood, the former having been first beaten. Several of the others were beaten, and all were ill-used.

This severity did not, however, stop the movement, but gave it a fiercer turn. The burghers who were in favour of peace, finding it useless to argue with their fellow-countrymen and knowing that their country was being hopelessly ruined by the insensate resistance, took the extreme course at last of bearing arms against them. There are at present three strong commandos of burghers fighting upon the British side, commanded by three Boer Generals—Marais, Celliers, and the younger Cronje, all of whom had made their names in fighting against us. ....

VI. The Farm-Burning

.........It must be admitted that the results have not justified it, [farm burning] and that, putting all moral questions apart, a burned-out family is the last which is likely to settle down, as we hope that the Boers may eventually settle down, as contented British citizens.

On the other hand, when a nation adopts guerilla tactics it deliberately courts those sufferings to the whole country which such tactics invariably entail. .... The army which is stung by guerillas strikes round it furiously and occasionally indiscriminately. An army which is continually sniped and harassed becomes embittered, and .... feels called upon to take those harsher measures which precedent and experience suggest.

That such measures have not been pushed to an extreme by the British authorities is shown by the fact that the captured guerilla has been made a prisoner of war—unlike his prototype, the *franc-tireur*..............

The first protest from the Boer side is dated February 3, 1900. In it the two Presidents accuse the British troops of burning and blowing up with dynamite the farmhouses, and of the devastation of farms. The document also includes an accusation of having used armed natives against the Boers.

Lord Roberts replied upon February 5 to the effect that stringent instructions had been given to the British troops to respect private property. 'All wanton destruction or injury to peaceful inhabitants is contrary to British practice and tradition, and will, if necessary, be rigorously repressed by me.' He added that it was an untrue statement that natives had ever been encouraged by British officers to commit depredations. ....

Why should the State which refused the aid of its own highly trained Indian army of 150,000 men, avail itself of that of savages? ....

He adds: 'I beg to call Your Honour's attention to the wanton destruction of property by the Boer forces in Natal. They not only have helped themselves freely to the cattle and other property of farmers without payment, but they have utterly wrecked the contents of many farmhouses. As an instance I would specify Mr. Theodore Woods farm "Longwood" near Springfield. I point out how very different is the conduct of the British troops. It is reported to me from Modder River that farms within the actual area of the British Camp have never even been entered, the occupants are unmolested, and their houses, gardens, and crops remain absolutely untouched.'

Roberts' 3/26 1900 Proclamation

On March 26 Lord Roberts' Proclamation spoke with no uncertain voice upon the subject of private property. It says:

'The following Proclamation, issued by me in the name of Her Majesty's Government on the 26th March, begins: Notice is hereby given that all persons who within the territories of the South African Republic or Orange Free State shall authorise or be guilty of the wanton destruction or damage or the counselling, aiding, or assisting in the wanton destruction or damage of public or private property, such destruction or damage not being justified by the usages and customs of civilised warfare, will be held responsible in their persons and property for all such wanton destruction and damage.'

...........A most striking example of British discipline and forbearance was furnished at this period, while the war could still be called regular upon the Boer side, by Rundles Division, christened the 'Hungry Eighth' by the Army. This Division had the misfortune to be stationed for several months some distance from the railway line, and in consequence had great difficulty in getting supplies. They were on half-rations for a considerable period, and the men were so reduced in strength that their military efficiency was much impaired.

Yet they lived in a land of plenty—a land of large farms well stocked with every sort of food. Why it was impossible to get this food for the men I do not know, but I do know that the prices for bread, eggs, milk, and other such things were kept very high by the wives of the farmers who were away upon commando; and that the hungry soldiers were quite unable to buy, and were not permitted to take, the nourishment which was essential.

On May 19, while Lord Roberts' force was advancing on Pretoria. De Wet sent in a despatch to complain of the destruction of two farms, Paarde Kraal and Leeuw Kop. Lord Roberts replied that these two farms were destroyed because, while a white flag was flying from the houses, the troops were fired upon from the farmsteads. 'I have had two farms near Kroonstad,' he adds,' destroyed for similar reasons, and shall continue to punish all such cases of treachery by the destruction of the farms where they occur.' ....

The next representations from the Boer Commander were more definite in their nature.

'Complaints are repeatedly reaching me,' he writes, 'that private dwellings are plundered, and in some cases totally destroyed, and all provisions taken from women and children, so that they are compelled to wander about without food or covering.'

To quote several instances: It has just been brought to my notice by way of sworn affidavit that the house of Field-Cornet S. Buys on the farm, Leeuwspruit district, Middelburg, was set on fire and destroyed on 20th June last. His wife, who was at home, was given five minutes time to remove her bedding and clothing, and even what she took out was again taken from her. Her food, sugar, &c., was all taken, so that for herself and her children she had neither covering nor food for the following night. She was asked for the key of the safe, and after it was given up by her she was threatened with a sword, and money was demanded. All the money that was in the house was taken away, all the papers in the safe were torn up, and everything at the homestead that could not be taken away was destroyed. The house of Field-Comet Buys' son was also destroyed, the doors and windows broken, &c.

'It has also been reported to me that my own buildings, on the farm Varkenspruit, district Standerton, as well as the house of Field-Cornet Badenhorst, on the adjoining farm, have been totally destroyed, and such of the stock as was not removed was shot dead on the farm.

'Further, there is the sworn declaration of Mrs. Hendrik Badenhorst, which speaks for itself.

'I cannot believe that such godless barbarities take place with Your Excellency's consent, and thus I deem it my solemn duty to protest most strongly against such destruction and vindictiveness as being entirely contrary to civilised warfare.'

The greater part of these alleged outrages had occurred on General Buller's side of the Transvaal, so the matter was referred to him. He acknowledged that he had ordered six farmhouses to be destroyed:

The following circumstances induced me to give the order. On entering the Transvaal I caused the attached Proclamation (A)[559] to be widely distributed along my line of route. We marched from Volksrust to Standerton practically unopposed. Shortly after our arrival at Standerton our telegraph line was cut on several nights following, and attempts were made to damage the military line by placing dynamite cartridges with detonators attached upon it. These attempts were all made on or in close vicinity to the estates above named.

A watch was kept and it was found that the attempts were made not by any formed force of the enemy, but by a few scattered banditti who were given shelter during the night in the houses I afterwards had destroyed, and who thence, when they could, tried to murder our patrols, and sallied out at night to damage the line. It was further ascertained that these men came and usually returned through Varkenspruit.

I directed that copies of Proclamation (A) should be personally left at each house, and the inmates of each should be warned that these depredations could not be permitted, and that if people living under our protection allowed this sort of men to resort to their houses without informing us, they must take the consequences, and their houses would be destroyed.

This warning had some effect for a day or two, but on 1st and 2nd of July the nuisance recommenced, and on the 7th July, having acquired full proof that the houses were being regularly used as shelters for men who were hostile to us, and who were not under any proper command, in fact, who were only acting as banditti, I had the houses destroyed.

'The women and children occupying the farms were removed elsewhere with as little inconvenience to themselves as we could arrange.'

Here again it is impossible to doubt that the British commanders were well within their rights.

It is true that Article XXIII of the Hague Conventions makes it illegal to destroy the enemy's property, but it adds: 'Unless such destruction be imperatively demanded by the necessities of war.' Now nothing can be more imperative in war than the preservation of the communications of the army.

A previous clause of the same Article makes it illegal to 'kill or wound treacherously individuals belonging to the hostile army.' It is incontestable that to take the cover of a farmhouse which flies the white flag in order to make attacks is to 'kill or wound treacherously,' and so on a double count the action of the British becomes legal, and even inevitable.

[559] This may be Buller's proclamation issued as he neared Langs Nek in May of 1900.

Lord Roberts' message to De Wet upon August 3, 1900, restates both his intentions and his reasons for it:

'Latterly, many of my soldiers have been shot from farmhouses over which the white flag has been flying, the railway and telegraph lines have been cut, and trains wrecked. I have therefore found it necessary, after warning Your Honour, to take such steps as are sanctioned by the customs of war to put an end to these and similar acts and have burned down the farmhouses at or near which such deeds have been perpetrated. This I shall continue to do whenever I consider the occasion demands it.

'The remedy lies in Your Honour's own hands. The destruction of property is most distasteful to me, and I shall be greatly pleased when Your Honour's co-operation in the matter renders it no longer necessary.'

This raises the question of the legality of the burning of farmhouses in the vicinity of the place where the railway is cut.

The question presented itself forcibly to my mind when I saw with my own eyes the tall plumes of smoke rising from six farmhouses, De Wets among them, in the neighbourhood of Roodeval. There is no doubt whatever that in the war of 1870—the classic type of modern war—the villages and populations near the scene of a cut railway were severely punished.

But The Hague Conventions had not then been signed.[560] On the one hand, it may be urged that it is impossible without such disciplinary measures to preserve a line of 1,000 miles running all the way through a hostile or semi-hostile country. Also that it is 'imperatively demanded by the necessities of war.'

On the other hand, there is Article L., which says, 'No general penalty can be inflicted on the population on account of the acts of individuals, for which it cannot be regarded as collectively responsible.' An argument might be advanced for either side, but what will actually determine is the strongest argument of all—that of self-preservation.

An army situated as the British Army was, and dependent for its supplies upon its communications, *must* keep them open even if it strains the Conventions in doing so. As a matter of fact, farm-burning had no effect in checking the railway-cutting and had a considerable effect in embittering the population.

Yet a General who was cut off from his base thirty times m a month was bound to leave the argument of legality to the jurists, and to adopt the means which seemed most likely to stop the nuisance. The punishment fell with cruel injustice upon some individuals. Others may have been among the actual raiders.

Roberts to Botha

On September 2 Lord Roberts communicated his intentions to General Botha:

Sir,—I have the honour to address Your Honour regarding the operations of those comparatively small bands of armed Boers who conceal themselves on farms in the neighbourhood of our lines of communication and thence endeavour to damage the railway, thus endangering the lives of passengers travelling by train who may or may not be combatants.

2. My reason for again referring to this subject is that, except in the districts occupied by the Army under the personal command of Your Honour, there is now no formed body of Boer troops in the Transvaal or Orange River Colony, and that the war is degenerating into operations carried on by irregular and irresponsible guerillas. This would be so ruinous to the country and so deplorable from every point of view, that I feel bound to do everything in my power to prevent it.

3. The orders I have at present issued, to give effect to these views, are that the farm nearest the scene of any attempt to injure the line or wreck a train is to be burnt, and that all farms within a radius of 10 miles are to be completely cleared of all their stock, supplies, &c. Granting that the penalty is legal at all, it must be allowed that it is put in a minimum form, since only one farm in each case is to be destroyed; and the further clearing of stock is undoubtedly justified, since it would tend to cripple the mobility of Boer raiders approaching the line. Yet one farm for each attack becomes a formidable total when the attacks are on an average of one per day.

[560] The First Hague Conference came from a proposal on 24 August 1898 by Russian Tsar Nicholas II. Nicholas and Count Mikhail Nikolayevich Muravyov, his foreign minister, were instrumental in initiating the conference. The conference opened on 18 May 1899, the Tsar's birthday. The treaties, declarations, and final act of the conference were signed on 29 July of that year, and they entered into force on 4 September 1900. Hague Conventions of 1899 and 1907 - Wikipedia

We have treated two causes for which farms were burned: (1) For being used as cover for snipers; (2) as a punishment for the cutting of railways. A third cause now comes to the front. A large number of burghers had taken the oath of neutrality and had been allowed to return to their farms by the British. These men were persuaded or terrorised by the fighting commandos into breaking their parole and abandoning those farms on which they had sworn to remain. The farmhouses were their bail, and Lord Roberts decreed that it was forfeited.

On August 23 he announced his decision to General Botha:

Your Honour represents that well-disposed families living on their farms have been driven from their houses, and that their property has been taken away or destroyed. This no doubt is true, but not in the sense which your letter would imply. Burghers who are well-disposed towards the British Government, and anxious to submit to my authority, have had their property seized by the Boer commandos, and have been threatened with death if they refused to take up arms against the British forces. Your Honour's contention that a solemn oath of neutrality which the burghers have voluntarily taken in order to remain in unmolested occupation of their farms is null and void, because you have not consented to it, is hardly open to discussion. I shall punish those who violate their oath and confiscate their property, no burgher having been forced to take the oath against his will.

It is quite certain that the Boer Government committed a very clear breach of the Conventions of the Hague in compelling, or even in permitting, these men to rejoin the ranks. In such, cases, says Article X., 'their own government shall not require of, nor accept from, them any service incompatible with the parole given.' This is clear as regards the government.

But in the case of the men it is different. Their promise was in a sense conditional upon effective protection from our troops. We had no right to place a man in so terrible a position that he had to choose between breaking his parole and death at the hands of his own countrymen. If we were not sure that we could protect them, we could have retained them in guarded camps, as we eventually did.

If we chose to turn them loose upon the wide veldt, then it was our fault more than theirs that they were forced into the ranks of the enemy. To their credit be it said that even under such pressure many of them were true to their oath.

But if their guilt is indeed no greater than our own, then how are we justified in burning down their houses? It seems to me that these cases are very different from those in the two other categories, and that the question of compensation to these men should be at least considered. I take it that the numerous cases where 'on commando' is marked against a burned farm on the official list, means that he had returned to commando after giving his parole.

The destruction of his house under those circumstances is, in the peculiar conditions of the case, a harsh measure, but if 'on commando' means simply that the man was away doing his duty to his country, without any question of parole, then our conscience can never permit that man to go without compensation.

We can trace in this account of the communications between the leaders the growth of those harsher measures which have been so generally deplored in this country. So long as the war was regular it is certain that nothing could be more regular than the British conduct. When, however, the war became irregular upon the part of the Boers, and their army dissolved into small bands which harried the lines of communications, the small posts, and the convoys, there was a corresponding change upon the part of the troops.

Towards the end of the year 1900 that change was pushed to considerable lengths. Certain districts which had been Boer centres, where they habitually collected time after time, were devastated and destroyed. Such districts were those of Kroonstad, Heilbron, Ventersburg, and Winburg. In these four districts about one hundred and seventy houses were destroyed.

The village of Bothaville, which was a depot of the enemy, was also destroyed. It consisted of forty-three houses.

In the Transvaal the number of houses actually destroyed for Strategic purposes seems to have been very much smaller. In the official returns only about twelve houses are so mentioned. Altogether the houses which have been burned for reasons which are open to dispute, including those of the men upon commando, do not appear to exceed two hundred and fifty.

It must be confessed that the case of these houses is entirely different from the others which have been destroyed, because they were used for active warlike operations. Of the 630 buildings which we know to have been destroyed, more than half have been used by snipers, or in some other direct fashion have brought themselves within the laws of warfare. But it cannot be said that these others have done so.

The cost of the average farmhouse is a mere trifle. A hundred pounds would build a small one, and 300*l.* a large. If we take the intermediate figure, then the expenditure of 50,000*l.* would compensate for those cases where military policy and international law may have been at variance with each other.

The burning of houses ceased in the year 1900 and, save in very special instances, where there was an overwhelming military necessity, it has not been resorted to since.

In the sweeping of the country carried out by French in the Eastern Transvaal and by Blood to the north of the Delagoa Railway, no buildings appear to have been destroyed, although it was a military necessity to clear the farms of every sort of supply in order to hamper the movements of the commandos.

The destruction of the crops and herds of the Boers, distasteful as such work must be, is exactly analogous to the destruction by them of our supply trains on which the army depended for their food. Guerilla warfare cannot enjoy all its own advantages and feel none of its own defects. It is a two-edged weapon, and the responsibility for the consequences rests upon the combatant who first employs it.

Botha's Reply to Roberts' Letter

On September 2, [1900]Lord Roberts addressed a communication to General Botha, in which he denied the existence of organized resistance except by the army commanded by Botha, declared his intention to destroy farms and confiscate stock in districts where any act of aggression was made, and threatened to transport from Pretoria and Johannesburg all women, including Mrs. Kruger, and Mrs. Botha, to the Republican lines, because as he alleged, the women were transmitting information to their people. Four days later. General Botha sent the following reply, which is reprinted *verbatim*, and the dignity of which speaks for itself..[561]

Botha's Letter

Commandant-General's Camp,

September 6, 1900.

To Lord Roberts,

Field Marshal, Commander-in-Chief, of the British troops in South Africa:

Your Excellency—In reply to your Excellency's letter of the 2nd inst., I have the honor to state the following:

Inasmuch as our entire armed force is only a small one in comparison with that of your Excellency, it cannot, of course be expected that strong commandos should be in the field everywhere, and it naturally follows that now, as during the war, what is incumbent upon us must be done by small forces. Moreover we have been compelled to still further scatter our commandos in order to be able to check the looting patrols under your Excellency's chief command, who scour the country to carry off cattle and provisions from the different farms.

2. As regards your contention that, with exception of the burgher forces under my command, no other Boer forces should be in existence, I most strongly deny this, since our armed forces are still disposed and directed in the same manner as in the beginning of the war, and in accordance with the country's laws.

3. In paragraph 3 of your letter, with which I am now dealing, it is already known to me that barbarous actions of this kind are committed by your troops under your command, not only alongside or near the railway, but also in places far removed from railways. Wherever your troops move, not only are houses burned down or blown up with dynamite, but defenseless women and children are ejected, robbed of all food and cover, and all this without any just cause existing for such proceedings.

4. With regard to paragraph 4 of your Excellency's letter, I extremely regret to learn that my burghers' and my own determination to persevere in the struggle for our independence, is to be visited on our wives and children, and this is the first instance of this kind known to me, in the history of civilized warfare. I can only protest against your proposed measures as being in opposition to all principles of civilized warfare, and excessively cruel toward the women and children, cruel especially toward elderly women, and above all toward the wife of his Honor, the President of the state, who as you must be well aware, is not able to travel without risk to her life, so that it would be simply murder to compel her to take such a journey. The pretext alleged by you, viz.: that by so doing your Excellency desires to protect yourself, against transmission of information to us, lacks all substance, since such proceedings were not considered necessary at a time when our troops were encamped in the immediate neighborhood of Pretoria. It is needless to state that we have never, by means of women and children, received information regarding operations of war.

5. If your Excellency still intends to persevere in carrying out your Excellency's plans, which I hope will not be the case, I request your Excellency to give me timely notice of the period and particulars of the expulsion, as I wish to arrange for the direct transport of the families to Europe. With regard to your Excellency's remark about proper accommodation, I am prepared to send proper carriages to a place to be indicated, and also, if required, a Cog-wheel engine, for the track between Waterval Boven and Waterval Onder, provided that your Excellency guarantees the safe return of such carriages and engine.

6. In conclusion, I desire to give you the assurance that nothing you may do to our women and children, will deter us in continuing the struggle for our independence.

I have the honor to be, etc. Louis Botha, *Commandant-General.*

[561] Alan R. I. Hiley and John Arthur. Hassell The Mobile Boer Being the Record of the Observations of Two Burgher Officers. By Alan R. I. Hiley and John Arthur. Hassell, Captains of Scouts, In the Boer Army. Grafton Press, New York. (c 1902)
Cite as: Hiley and Hassell, The Mobile Boer, Grafton Press, New York, (c. 1902) Cornell Copy: pages 224-226
https://archive.org/details/cu31924028616682

VII. The Concentration Camps

When considerable districts of the country were cleared of food in order to hamper the movements of the commandos, and when large numbers of farmhouses were destroyed under the circumstances already mentioned, it became evident that it was the duty of the British, as a civilised people, to form camps of refuge for the women and children where, out of reach, as we hoped, of all harm, they could await the return of peace.

There were three courses open. The first was to send the Boer women and children into the Boer lines—a course which became impossible when the Boer army broke into scattered bands and had no longer any definite lines; the second was to leave them where they were; the third was to gather them together and care for them as best we could.

It is curious to observe that the very people who are most critical of the line of policy actually adopted, were also most severe when it appeared that the alternative might be chosen. The British nation would have indeed remained under an ineffaceable stain had they left women and children without shelter upon the veldt in the presence of a large Kaffir population. ....

Then, again, we had learned our lesson as regards the men who had given their parole. They should not again be offered the alternative of breaking their oaths or being punished by their own people. The case for the formation of the camps must be admitted to be complete and overwhelming. They were formed, therefore, by the Government at convenient centres, chiefly at Pretoria, Johannesburg, Krugersdorp, Middelburg, Potchefstroom, Rustenburg, Heidelburg, Standerton, Pietersburg, Klerksdorp, and Volksrust in the Transvaal; Bloemfontein, Kroonstad, Bethulie, and Edenburg in the Orange Free State. ....

Having determined to form the camps, the authorities carried out the plan with great thoroughness. The sites seem to have been well chosen, and the arrangements in most cases all that could be wished. They were formed, however, at an unfortunate moment. Great strain had been placed upon our Commissariat by the large army, over 200,000 men, who had to be supplied by three tiny railways, which were continually cut.

In January 1901 De Wet made his invasion of Cape Colony, and the demand upon the lines was excessive. The extraordinary spectacle was presented at that time of the British straining every nerve to feed the women and children of the enemy, while that enemy was sniping the engineers and derailing the trains which were bringing up the food.

The numbers of the inmates of the refugee camps increased rapidly from 20,000 at the end of the year 1900, up to more than 100,000 at the end of 1901. Great efforts were made by the military authorities to accommodate the swelling tide of refugees, and no money was spared for that purpose.

Early in the year 1901 a painful impression was created in England by the report of Miss Hobhouse, an English lady, who had visited the camps and criticised them unfavourably. The value of her report was discounted, however, by the fact that her political prejudices were known to be against the Government. Mr. Charles Hobhouse, a relation of hers, and a Radical member of Parliament, has since then admitted that some of her statements will not bear examination. ....

Her main contentions were that the diet was not sufficient, that there was little bedding, that the water-supply was short, that the sanitation was bad, that there was overcrowding, and that there was an excessive death-rate, especially among the children.

As to diet the list which she gives agrees roughly with that which is officially quoted as the daily allowance at Irene Camp, near Pretoria, in July. It is as follows:

Meat ½ lb.

Coffee 2 oz.

Flour ¾ lb.

Sugar 2 oz.

Salt ½ oz.

To every child under six, a bottle of milk.

It must be confessed that the diet is a spare one, and that as supplies become more plentiful it might well be increased. The allowance may, however, be supplemented by purchase, and there is a considerable outside fund, largely subscribed by British people, which is used to make the scale more liberal.

A slight difference was made at first between the diet of a family which had surrendered and of that the head of which was still in arms against us. A logical distinction may certainly be made, but in practice it was felt to be unchivalrous and harsh, so it was speedily abandoned.

As to the shortness of the water-supply, it is the curse of all South Africa, which alternately suffers from having too much water and too little. With artesian wells and better arrangements this difficulty is being overcome, but it has applied as strongly to our own camps as to those of the Boer refugees.

There seems to be a consensus of opinion from all the camps that the defects in sanitation are due to the habits of the inmates, against which commandants and doctors are perpetually fighting. Camp life without cleanliness must become unhygienic. ....

On the question, of overcrowding, the demand for tents in South Africa has been excessive, and it may well have taxed all the power of the authorities to find accommodation for the crowds of women and children. The evil has been remedied since the time of Miss Hobhouse's report. ....

As to the suggestion that this enormous crowd of women and children should be quartered upon their kinsmen in the Colony, it is beyond all argument. There has been no offer of such wholesale hospitality nor have we any means for enforcing it.

But then we come to the great and piteous tragedy of the refugee camps, the mortality, and especially the mortality among the children. That is deplorable—more deplorable even than the infant mortality in Mafeking, Ladysmith, and Kimberley. But is it avoidable? Or is it one of those misfortunes, like that enteric outbreak which swept away so many British soldiers, which is beyond our present sanitary science and can only be endured with sad resignation?

The nature of the disease which is mainly responsible for the high mortality shows that it has no direct connection with the sanitary conditions of the camps, or with anything which it was in our power to alter. Had the deaths come from some filth-disease, such as typhus fever, or even from enteric or diphtheria, the sanitation of the camps might be held responsible. But it is to a severe form of measles that the high mortality is due. Apart from that the record of the camps would have been a very fair one.

Now measles when once introduced among children runs through a community without any regard to diet or conditions of life. The only possible hope is the segregation of the sufferer. To obtain this early quarantine the cooperation of the parent is needed: but in the case in point the Boer mothers, with a natural instinct, preferred to cling to the children and to make it difficult for the medical men to remove them in the first stages of the disease. The result was a rapid spread of the epidemic, which was the more fatal as many of the sufferers were in low health owing to the privations unavoidably endured in the journey from their own homes to the camps.

Not only was the spread of the disease assisted by the mother, but in her mistaken zeal she frequently used remedies which were as fatal as the disease. Children died of arsenical-poisoning, having been covered from head to foot with green paint; and others of opium-poisoning, having quack drugs which contained laudanum administered to them.

'In Potchefstroom as at Irene,' says Dr. Kendal Franks, 'the death- rate is attributable not so much to the severity of the epidemic as to the ignorance, perverseness, and dirty habits of the parents themselves.'

But whatever the immediate cause the death of these numerous children lies heavy, not upon the conscience, but upon the heart of our nation. It is some mitigation to know that the death rate among children is normally quite remarkably high in South Africa, and that the rate in the camps was frequently not higher than that of the towns near which the camp was situated.

Be this as it may, we cannot deny that the cause of the outbreak of measles was the collection of the women and children by us into the camps. But why were they collected into camps? Because they could not be left on the veldt. And why could they not be left on the veldt? Because we had destroyed the means of subsistence. And why had we destroyed the means of subsistence? To limit the operations of the mobile bands of guerillas. At the end of every tragedy we are forced back to the common origin of all of them, and made to understand that the nation which obstinately perseveres in a useless guerilla war prepares much trouble for its enemy, but absolute ruin for itself.

We have pushed our humanity in this matter of the refugees so far that we have looked after our enemies far better than our friends. I recognise that the two cases are not on all fours, since the Boers are compelled to be in camps and the loyalist refugees are not. But the fact remains that the loyalists are in camps, through no fault of their own, and that their condition is a worse one than that of our enemies.

At East London, for example, there are two refugee camps, Boer and British. The former has 350, the latter 420 inhabitants. The former are by far the better fed, clad, and housed, with a hospital, a school, and a washhouse, all of which are wanting in the British camp. ....

PF: What follows are several pages of testimonials and approving anecdotes. There is space for a few and they are included. .

Mr. Seaton, of Johannesburg (Secretary of the Congregational Church and of the burgher camp), says: 'The reports you send make our blood boil. They are frightfully exaggerated, and in many instances not only misleading but untrue. ... A more healthy spot it would be difficult to find. . . . There is no over-crowding.

Some weeks ago there was an epidemic of measles in camp of a very severe type, and naturally there were many deaths among the children. The doctor and nurses worked to the very utmost, and I am pleased to say the epidemic is stamped out. No doubt this is what caused the talk by the pro-Boers in the House of Commons and elsewhere, but it is one of those epidemics which could not be prevented among the class of people we have here. They had absolutely no regard for sanitary conveniences, and the officials had the greatest difficulty in enforcing the most ordinary rules of cleanliness.

Another difficulty we had was to get them to bring their children when sick into the hospital, where there is every convenience. They prefer to disobey the doctor and try the old women's remedies, which, as you know, are very plentiful among such people. The doctor has had a most trying position, and has worked like a slave. Nearly all the deaths have been from measles.

We are having a fairly mild winter. About three months ago it was bitterly cold, but they are used to outdoor life, and this is no worse than they have always been used to. The tents are all military tents, and there is no sign of leakage. I know they all want tents when they come here, if it is possible to get them. On the whole, the inmates are contented, and the children are particularly happy. They skip and play about from morn till eve.'

Mr. Scholtz, Inspector of Camps for the Transvaal, reports:

Many of the children, when they first arrived at the camp, were little better than skin and bone, and being in so emaciated a condition, it was not surprising that, when they did catch measles, they could not cope with the disease. Many of the women would not open their tents to admit fresh air, and, instead of giving the children the proper medicines supplied by the military, preferred to give them home remedies. The mothers would not sponge the children, and the greatest difficulty was experienced in inducing them to send the patients to hospital. The cause of the high death-rate among children from measles is due to the fact that the women let their children out as soon as the measles rash has subsided.

Pneumonia and bronchitis naturally supervene. Another cause is that the mothers persist in giving their children meat and other indigestible foods, even when the doctors strictly prohibit it, dysentery resulting as a matter of course. In other respects the health of the camp is good, there being only one case of typhoid out of 5,000 residents in camp.'

Here is light on the Krugersdorp Camp:

Johannesburg, July 31st.—(Renters Special Service.)—Commandant Alberts, commanding the Boers near Krugersdorp, has sent a letter to the officer commanding the British forces at Krugersdorp, stating that as he has with him on commando several families whose male relatives have recently surrendered, he wishes to know if he will receive these families, as they would like to go to Krugersdorp. The officer replied that he would be pleased to receive them, and they are expected to arrive to-day. ....

Under date November 1, an officer of the Kroonstad Camp writes:

'We have cricket, tennis, and croquet for them and they are all jolly well treated. Besides other amusements, they have a band twice a week, and the other day they got up a concert.'

It is worthy of record that the portrait of an emaciated child has been circulated upon the Continent and in America as a proof positive of the horrors of the concentration system. It is only too probable that there are many emaciated children in the camps, for they usually arrive in that condition. This particular portrait however was, as I am credibly informed, taken by the British authorities on the occasion of the criminal trial of the mother for the ill-usage of the child. The incident is characteristic of the unscrupulous tactics which have been used from the beginning to poison the mind of the world against Great Britain.

VIII. The British Soldier in South Africa

This chapter contains some interesting anecdotes but is again journalism rather than history. All vignettes, are certainly true but relate only interesting incidents of war and honourable British conduct.

IX. Further Charges Against British Troops

Expansive and Explosive Bullets

When Mr. Stead indulges in vague rhetoric it is difficult to corner him, but when he commits himself to a definite statement he is more open to attack. Thus, in his 'Methods of Barbarism'[562] he roundly asserts that 'England sent several million rounds of expanding bullets to South Africa, and in the North of the Transvaal and at Mafeking for the first three months of the war no other bullets were used.'

Mr. Methuen, on the authority of a letter of Lieutenant de Montmorency, R.A., states also that from October 12, 1899, up to January 15, 1900, the British forces north of Mafeking used nothing but Mark IV. ammunition, which is not a dum-dum but is an expansive bullet.[563] ....

At the end of the spring of 1899 some hundreds of thousands of hollow-headed bullets, made in England, were condemned as unsatisfactory, not being true to gauge, &c., and were sent to South Africa for target practice only. A quantity of this ammunition, known as 'Metford Mark IV.,' was sent up to Dundee by order of General Symons for practice in field firing. ....

By some blundering in the packing at home, however, some of this Mark IV. must have got mixed up with the ordinary, or Mark H., ammunition, and was found on our men by the Boers on October 30. Accordingly a very careful inspection was ordered, and a few Mark IV. bullets were found in our men's pouches, and at once removed. ....

What is usually known as the dum-dum bullet is a 'soft-nosed' one: but the regulation Mark II. is also made at the dum-dum factory, and the Boers, seeing the dum-dum label on boxes containing the latter, naturally thought the contents were the soft-nosed, which they were not.

It must be admitted that there was some carelessness in permitting sporting ammunition ever to get to the front at all. When the Derbyshire Militia were taken by De Wet at Roodeval, a number of cases of sporting cartridges were captured by the Boers (the officers had used them for shooting springbok). My friend, Mr. Langman, who was present, saw the Boers, in some instances, filling their bandoliers from these cases on the plausible excuse that they were only using our own ammunition. ....

Conduct to Prisoners on the Field

On this count, also, the British soldiers have been exposed to attacks, both at home and abroad, which are as unfounded and as shameful as most of those which have been already treated.

The first occasion upon which Boer prisoners fell into our hands was at the Battle of Elandslaagte, on October 21, 1899. That night was spent by the victorious troops in a pouring rain, round such fires as they were able to

[562] Unable to locate this particular publication.

[563] The design of the Mk IV hollow-point bullet shifted bullet weight rearwards, improving stability and accuracy over the regular round-nose bullet. These soft-nosed and hollow-point bullets, while effective against human targets, had a tendency to shed the outer metal jacket upon firing; the latter occasionally stuck in the bore, causing a dangerous obstruction. This was addressed by the introduction of a revised Mk V loading later in October (controversially so, as by August the Hague Convention had already made the military implementation of such expanding bullets illegal) identical to the Mark IV round apart from the addition of 2% antimony to the lead core and an additional 1.3 mm in length The concern about expanding bullets was brought up at the Hague Convention of 1899 by Swiss and Dutch representatives. The Swiss were concerned about small arms ammunition that "increased suffering", and the Dutch focused on the British Mark III .303 loading in response to their treatment of Boer settlers in South Africa. The British and American defence was that they should not focus on specific bullet designs, like hollow-points, but instead on rounds that caused "superfluous injury". The parties in the end agreed to abstain from using expanding bullets. With the use of expanding bullets against signatories of the convention deemed inhumane, the Mk III, Mk IV, and Mk V were withdrawn from active service. The remaining stocks (over 45 million rounds) were used for target practice. The Mark III and other expanding versions of the .303 were not issued during the Second Boer War (1899–1902). Boer guerrillas allegedly used expanding hunting ammunition against the British during the war, and New Zealand Commonwealth troops may have brought Mark III rounds with them privately after the Hague Convention without authorization. See: .303 British - Wikipedia

light. It has been recorded by several witnesses that the warmest corner by the fire was reserved for the Boer prisoners.

It has been asserted, and is again asserted, that when the Lancers charged a small body of the enemy after the action, they gave no quarter— too well substantiated and too familiar, says one critic of this assertion.

I believe, as a matter of fact, that the myth arose from a sensational picture in an illustrated paper. The charge was delivered late in the evening, in uncertain light. Under such circumstances it is always possible, amid so wild and confused a scene, that a man who would have surrendered has been cut down or ridden over. But the cavalry brought back twenty prisoners, and the number whom they killed or wounded has not been placed higher than that, so that it is certain there was no indiscriminate slaying.

I have read a letter from the officer who commanded the cavalry and who directed the charge, in which he tells the whole story confidentially to a brother officer. He speaks of his prisoners, but there is no reference to any brutality upon the part of the troopers.

But if this holds good of an organised force defending a position, how about the solitary sniper? The position of such a man has never been defined by the Conventions of The Hague, and no rules are laid down for his treatment. ....

The very first article of the Conventions of The Hague states that a belligerent must (I) Be commanded by some responsible person; (2) Have a distinctive emblem visible at a distance; (3) Carry arms openly. Now it is evident that the Boer sniper who draws his Mauser from its hiding-place in order to have a shot at the Rooineks from a safe kopje does not comply with any one of these conditions. In the letter of the law, then, he is undoubtedly outside the rules of warfare.

In the spirit he is even more so. Prowling among the rocks and shooting those who cannot tell whence the bullet comes, there is no wide gap between him and the assassin. His victims never see him, and in the ordinary course he incurs no personal danger. I believe such cases to have been very rare, but if the soldiers have occasionally shot such a man without reference to the officers, can it be said that it was an inexcusable action, or even that it was outside the strict rules of warfare? ....

I find in the 'Gazette dt Lausanne' a returned Swiss soldier named Pache, who had fought for the Boers, expresses his amazement at the way in which the British troops after their losses in the storming of a position gave quarter to those who had inflicted those losses upon them.

'Only once, he says, at the fight at Tabaksberg, have I seen the Boers hold on to their position to the very end. At the last rush of the enemy they opened a fruitless magazine fire, and then threw down their rifles and lifted their hands, imploring quarter from those whom they had been firing at short range. I was astounded at the clemency of the soldiers, who allowed them to live. For my part I should have put them to death.' ....

An outcry was raised when Ahmednager in India was chosen for a prison station, and it was asserted, with that recklessness with which so many other charges have been hurled against the authorities, that it was a hot-bed of disease. Experience has shown that there was no grain of truth in these statements, and the camp has been a very healthy one. As it remains the only one which has ever been subjected to harsh criticism, it may be of use to append the conclusions of Mr. Jesse Collings during a visit to it last month:

'The Boer officers said, speaking for ourselves and men, we have nothing at all to complain of. As prisoners of war we could not be better treated, and Major Dickenson (this they wished specially to be inserted), is as kind and considerate as it is possible to be.' ....

Executions

The number of executions of Boers as distinguished from the execution of Cape rebels, has been remarkably few in a war which has already lasted twenty-six months. So far as I have been able to follow them, they have been limited to the execution of Cordua for broken parole and conspiracy upon August 24, 1900, at Pretoria, the shooting of one or two horse-poisoners in Natal, and the shooting of three men after the action of October 27, 1900, near Fredericstad.

These men, after throwing down their arms and receiving quarter, picked them up again and fired at the soldiers from behind. No doubt there have been other cases, scattered up and down the vast scene of warfare, but I can find no record of them, and if they exist at all they must be few in number. Since the beginning of 1901 four men have been shot in the Transvaal, three in Pretoria as spies and breakers of parole, one in Johannesburg as an aggravated case of breaking neutrality by inciting Boers to resist.

At the beginning of the war 90 per cent of the farmers in the northern district of Cape Colony joined the invaders. Upon the expulsion of the Boers these men for the most part surrendered. The British Government, recognising that pressure had been put upon them and that their position had been a difficult one, inflicted no penalty upon the rank-and-file beyond depriving them of the franchise for a few years.

A few who, like the Douglas rebels, were taken red-handed upon the field of battle, were condemned to periods of imprisonment which varied from one to five years.

This was in the year 1900. In 1901 there was an invasion of the Colony by Boers which differed very much from the former one. In the first case the country had actually been occupied by the Boer forces, who were able to exert real pressure upon the inhabitants. In the second the invaders were merely raiding bands who traversed many places but occupied none. A British subject who joined on the first occasion might plead compulsion, on the second it was undoubtedly of his own free will.

These Boer bands being very mobile and never fighting save when they were at an overwhelming advantage, penetrated all parts of the Colony and seduced a number of British subjects from their allegiance. The attacking of small posts and the derailing of trains, military or civilian, were their chief employment. To cover their tracks they continually murdered natives whose information might betray them. Their presence kept the Colony in confusion and threatened the communications of the Army. ....

Many hundreds of these rebels passed into their hands, and most of them escaped with fine and imprisonment. The ringleaders, and those who were convicted of capital penal offences, were put to death. I have been at some pains to make a list of the executions in 1901, including those already mentioned. It is at least approximately correct:

Number	Place	Date	Reason
		1901	
2	De Aar	March 19	Train wrecking.
2	Pretoria	June 11	Boers breaking oath of neutrality.
1	Middelburg	July 10	Fighting.
1	Cape Town........	" 13	"
1	Cradock...	" 13	"
2	Middelburg.......	" 24	"
2	Kenhardt	" 25	"
1	Pretoria	Aug. 22	Boer spy.
3	Colesburg.	Sept. 4	Fighting.
1	Middelburg.	Oct. 10	"
1	Middelburg.	" 11	"
1	Vryburg (hanged).	" 12	"
Several	Tarkastad.........	" 12	"
1	Tarkastad.........	" 14	"
1	Middelburg	" 15	"
2	Cradock (1 hanged, 1 shot)..........	" 17	Train-wrecking and murdering native.
2	Vryburg	" 29	Fighting.
1	Mafeking..........	Nov. 11	Shooting a native.
1	Colesburg	" 12	Fighting, marauding, and assaulting, etc.
1	Johannesburg	" 23	Persuading surrendered burghers to break oath.
1	Aliwal North.....	" 26	Cape Police deserter.
1	Krugersdorp......	Dec. 26	Shooting wounded.
2	Mafeking.........	" 27	Kaffir murder.

Page 115 of the tract.

Allowing 3 for the several; at Tarkastad on October 12, that makes a total of 34. Many will undoubtedly be added in the future, for the continual murder of inoffensive natives, some of them children, calls for stern justice. In this list 4 were train-wreckers (aggravated cases by rebels), 1 was a spy, 4 were murderers of natives, 1 a deserter who took twenty horses from the Cape Police, and the remaining 23 were British subjects taken fighting and bearing arms against their own country.

Hostages upon Railway Trains

Here the military authorities are open, as it seems to me, to a serious charge, not of inhumanity to the enemy but of neglecting those steps which it was their duty to take in order to safeguard their own troops. If all the victims of derailings and railway cuttings were added together it is not an exaggeration to say that it would furnish as many killed and wounded as a considerable battle. On at least five occasions between twenty and thirty men were incapacitated, and there are very numerous cases where smaller numbers were badly hurt.

Let it be said at once that we have no grievance in this. To derail a train is legitimate warfare, with many precedents to support it. But to checkmate it by putting hostages upon the trains is likewise legitimate warfare, with many precedents to support it also.

The Germans habitually did it in France, and the result justified them as the result has justified us. From the time (October 1901) that it was adopted in South Africa we have not heard of a single case of derailing, and there can be no doubt that the lives of many soldiers, and possibly of some civilians, have been saved by the measure. ....

X. The Other Side of the Question

Writing in November, 1900, after hearing an expression of opinion from many officers from various parts of the seat of war, I stated in 'The Great Boer War':

The Boers have been the victims of a great deal of cheap slander in the press. The men who have seen most of the Boers in the field are the most generous in estimating their character. That the white flag was hoisted by the Boers as a cold-blooded device for luring our men into the open, is an absolute calumny. To discredit their valour is to discredit our victory. My own opinion would have been worthless, but this was, as I say, the result of considerable inquiry.

General Porter said: 'On a few occasions the white flag was abused, but in what large community would you not find a few miscreants?'

General Lyttelton said: 'The Boers are brave men and I do not think that the atrocities which have been reported are the acts of the regular Dutch burghers, but of the riff-raff who get into all armies.'

It is a painful fact, but the words could not possibly be written today. Had the war only ended when it should have ended, the combatants might have separated each with a chivalrous feeling of respect for a knightly antagonist. But the Boers having appealed to the God of battles and heard the judgment, appealed once more against it. Hence came the long, bitter, and fruitless struggle which has cost so many lives, so much suffering, and a lowering of the whole character of the war.

It is true that during the first year there were many things to exasperate the troops. The Boers were a nation of hunters and they used many a ruse which seemed to the straightforward soldier to be cowardly and unfair. Individuals undoubtedly played the white-flag trick, and individuals were guilty of holding up their hands in order to lure the soldiers from their cover. There are many instances of this—indeed, in one case Lord Roberts was himself a witness of it.

Appended is his official protest: 'Another instance having occurred of a gross abuse of the white flag and of the signal of holding up the hands in token of surrender, it is my duty to inform Your Honour that if such abuse occurs again I shall most reluctantly be compelled to order any troops to disregard the white flag entirely.

The instance occurred on the kopje east of Driefontein Farm yesterday evening and was witnessed by several of my own staff officers, as well as by myself, and resulted in the wounding of several of my officers and men.

A large quantity of explosive bullets of three different kinds was found in Cronjes laager, and after every engagement with Your Honour's troops.

Such breaches of the recognised usages of war and of the Geneva Convention are a disgrace to any civilised power. ....

[A] coward may hoist an unauthorised white flag and his braver companions may refuse to recognise it, as our own people might on more than one occasion have done with advantage. ....

From the first the position of the Boers was entirely irregular as regards the recognised rules of warfare. The first article of the Conventions of The Hague insists that an army in order to claim belligerent rights must first wear some emblem which is visible at a distance. ....It is true that .... a population which has no time to organise themselves and who are defending themselves may be excused from this rule; but the Boers were the invaders at the outset of the war, and it is absurd to say that they could not have furnished burghers on commando with some distinctive badge.

When they made a change it was for the worse, for they finally dressed themselves in the khaki uniforms of our own soldiers, and by this means effected several surprises. ....In this, as in the case of the train hostages, we have gone too far in the direction of clemency. Had the first six khaki-clad burghers been shot, the lives of many of our soldiers would have been saved.[564]

At this latter period of the war began that systematic murdering of the Kaffirs by the Boers which has been the most savage and terrible feature in the whole business. On both sides Kaffirs have been used as teamsters, servants, and scouts, but on neither side as soldiers. The British could with the greatest ease have swamped the whole Boer resistance at the beginning of the war by letting loose the Basutos, the Zulus, and the Swazis, all of whom have blood-feuds with the Boers. ....

As teamsters, servants, guides, and scouts the Kaffirs were, however, essential to us, and realising this the Boers, when the war began to go against them, tried to terrorise them into deserting us by killing them without mercy whenever they could in any way connect them with the British. How many hundred were done to death in this fashion it is impossible to compute.

After a British defeat no mercy was shown to the drivers of the wagons and the native servants. Boer commandos covered their tracks by putting to death every Kaffir who might give information. Sometimes they killed even the children. Thus Lord Kitchener, in his report, narrates a case where a British column hard upon the track of a Boer commando found four little Kaffir boys with their brains dashed out in the kraal which the Boers had just evacuated.

A case which particularly touched the feelings of the British people was that of Esau, the coloured blacksmith, who was a man of intelligence and education, living as a loyal British subject in the British town of Calvinia. There was no possible case of 'spying' here, since the man had not left his own town. The appended documents will show why the nation will not have done its duty until justice has been done upon the murderers. A touching letter has been published from Esau to the governor of the district in which he says that, come what may, he would be loyal to the flag under which he was born.

Next news of him was of his brutal murder:

'Abraham Esau, a loyal coloured blacksmith, was mercilessly flogged for refusing to give information as to where arms were buried. Inflammation of the kidneys set in; nevertheless he was again beaten through the village with sjamboks until he was unable to walk, and was then shot dead.'—Calvinia, February 8 ('Times,' February 16, 1901, p. 7 [3]).

'The district surgeon at Calvinia, writing to the Colonial: Secretary, has fully confirmed the flogging and shooting of Esau by a Boer named Strydom, who stated that he acted in accordance with orders. No trial was held, and no reason is alleged for the deed.—Cape Town, February 19 ('Times,' February 20, 1901, p. 5 [3])

'The authority for the statement of the flogging by the Boers of a coloured man named Esau at Calvinia was a Renters telegram, confirmed subsequently by the report made to Cape Town by the district surgeon of Calvinia.—From Mr. Brodrick's reply to Mr. Labouchere in House of Commons, February 21 ("Times,' February 22, 1901). ....

The original rule of the British Service was that the black scouts should be unarmed, so as to avoid all accusations of arming natives. When it was found that they were systematically shot they were given rifles, as it was inhuman to expose them to death without any means of defence. I believe that some armed Kaffirs who watch the railway line have also been employed in later phases of the war, the weapons to be used in self defence. Considering how pressed the British were at one time, and considering that by a word they could have thrown a large and highly disciplined Indian army into the scales, I think that their refusal to do so is one of the most remarkable examples of moderation in history.

[564] The commandos were so isolated they did not know about this change in policy or the deaths of their captured comrades, even when taken after active combat and surrender. See Deneys Reitz's 'Commando.'

The French had no hesitation in using Turcos against the Germans, nor did the Americans refrain from using Negro regiments against the Spaniards. We made it a white man's war, however, and I think that we did wisely and well. ....

So far did the Boers carry their murderous tactics against the natives, that British prisoners with dark complexions were in imminent danger. Thus at a skirmish at Doom River on July 27, 1901, the seven Kaffir scouts taken with the British were shot in cold blood, and an Englishman named Finch was shot with them in the alleged belief that he had Kaffir blood. Here is the evidence of the latter murder:

No. 28284 Trooper Charles Catton, 22nd Imperial Yeomanry, being duly sworn, states:

'At Doom River on 27th July 1901, I was one of the patrol captured by the Boers, and after we had surrendered I saw a man lying on the ground, wounded, between two natives. I saw a Boer go up to him and shoot him through the chest. I noticed the man, Trooper Finch, was alive. I do not know the name of the Boer who shot him, but I could recognise him again.'

No. 33966 Trooper F. W. Madams, having been duly sworn, states:

'I was one of the patrol captured by the Boers on 27th July, 1901, near Doom River. After we had surrendered I went to look for my hat, and after finding it I was passing the wounded man, Trooper Finch, when I saw a Boer, whose name I do not know, shoot Trooper Finch through the chest with a revolver. I could identify the man who shot him.'

This scandal of the murder of the Kaffirs, a scandal against which no protest seems to have been raised by the pro-Boer press in England or the Continent, has reached terrible proportions. I append some of the evidence from recent official reports from the front:

Case at Magaliesberg.—About October or November 1900, the bodies of nine natives were found lying together on the top of the Magaliesberg. Of these five were intelligence natives, the remainder being boys employed by the Boers, but suspected of giving information. The witnesses in this case are now difficult to find, as they are all natives; but it appears that the natives were tried by an informal court, of which B. A. Klopper, ex-President of the Volksraad, was president, and condemned to death. Hendrik Schoeman, son of the late general, and Piet Joubert are reported to have acted as escort.

Case of five natives murdered near Wilge River.—On capturing a train near Wilge River, Transvaal, on March 11, 1901, the Boers took five unarmed natives on one side and shot them, throwing their bodies into a ditch. Corporal Sutton, of the Hampshire Regiment, saw, after the surrender, a Boer put five shots into a native who was lying down. Other soldiers on the train vouch to seeing one man deliberately shoot five boys in cold blood.

Case of eight Kafiir boys.—On or about July 17, 1901, eight Kaffir boys, between the ages of twelve and fourteen, went out from Uitkijk near Edenburg, to get oranges. None were armed. Boers opened fire, shot one, captured six; one escaped, and is now with Major Damant. Corporal Willett, Damant's Horse, afterwards saw boys bodies near farm, but so disfigured that they could not be recognised. Some Kaffirs were then sent out from Edenburg and recognised them. One boy is supposed to have been spared by Boers, body not found. Lieutenant Kentish, Royal Irish Fusiliers, saw bodies, and substantially confirms murder, and states Boers were under Field-Cornet Dutoit.

PF: What follows are several pages documenting ~ 25 additional specific instances of this sort of inhumane treatment to noncombatants.

I do not mean by this to assert that the Boer guerillas behaved as did the Spanish guerillas in 1810, or the Mexican in 1866. Such an assertion would be absurd. The Boers gave quarter and they received it.

But several isolated instances, and several general cases have shown the demoralisation of their ranks. ....

Of the general demoralisation here is the evidence of a witness in that very action at Graspan on June 6, which has been made so much of by the slanderers of our Army:

No. 4703 Lance-Corporal James Hanshaw, 2nd Batt. Bedfordshire Regiment, being duly sworn, states:

'At Graspan on June 6, 1901, I was present when we were attacked by the Boers, having previously captured a convoy from them. On going towards the wagons I found the Boers already there; finding we were outnumbered and resistance hopeless, we threw down our arms and held our hands up. Private Blunt, who was with me, shouted, "Dont shoot me, I have thrown down my rifle." The Boers then shot Private Blunt dead. He was holding his hands above his head at the time. Lieutenant Mair then shouted, "Have mercy, you cowards." The Boers then deliberately shot Lieutenant Mair dead as he was standing with his hands above his head. They then shot at Privates Pearse and Harvey, who were both standing with their hands up, the same bullet hitting Private Pearse in the nose and killing Private Harvey. Two Boers then rushed from the wagons and threatened to shoot me, kicked me, and told me to lie down.'

No. 3253 Private E. Sewell, 2nd Batt. Bedfordshire Regiment, being duly sworn, states:

'I was at the fight at Graspan on June 6, 1901. About noon on that date the Boers attacked the convoy. I retired to Lieutenant Mairs party, when, finding we were outnumbered and surrounded, we put our hands up. The Boers took our arms from us and retired round some kraals; shortly afterwards they came back, and two men shouted, "Hands up." We said we were already prisoners, and that our arms had been collected. Private Blunt held up his hands, and at the same time said, "Dont shoot me, I am already hands up." The Boers then said, "Take that," and shot him through the stomach. Lieutenant Mair then stepped out from the wagons, and said, "Have mercy, you cowards." The Boer then shot him dead from his horse. The Boer was sitting on his horse almost touching Lieutenant Mair at the time. The Boer then shot at Lance-Corporal Harvey and Private Pearse who were standing together with their hands up above their heads, the shot wounding Private Pearse and killing Lance-Corporal Harvey.' ....

PF: Following are an additional ~30 additional documented tragic incidents of war.

XI. Conclusions

I have now dealt with the varied vexed questions of the war, and have, I hope, said enough to show that we have no reason to blush for our soldiers, ... But there are a number of opponents of the war who have never descended to such baseness, and who honestly hold that the war might have been avoided, and also that we might, after it broke out, have found some terms which the Boers could accept.

The revolt of the Boer States against the British suzerainty is much more like the revolt of the Southern States against the Government of Washington. The situation here after Colenso was that of the North after Bull Run. Mr. Methuen has much to say of Boer bitterness, but was it greater than Southern bitterness? That war was fought to a finish and we see what has come of it.

Mr. Methuen is severe upon Lord Salisbury for the uncompromising nature of his reply to the Presidents' overtures for peace in March 1900. But what other practical course could he suggest? Is it not evident that if independence were left to the Boers the war would have been without result, since all the causes which led to it would be still open and unsolved?

On the morrow of such a peace we should be faced by the Franchise question, the Uitlander question, and every other question for the settling of which we have made such sacrifices. Is that a sane policy? .... When the work was more than half done it would have been madness to hold our hand.

It has occurred to me—a suggestion which I put forward with all diffidence—that it would be a wise and practicable step to form a Boer Reservation in the northern districts of the Transvaal (Watersberg and Zoutpansberg). Let them live there as Basutos live in Basutoland or Indians in Indian territory, or the inhabitants of, a protected state in India. Guarantee them, as long as they remain peaceable under the British flag, complete protection from the invasion of the miner or the prospector. Let them live their own lives in their own way, with some simple form of home rule of their own.

The irreconcilable men who could never rub shoulders with the British, could find a home there, and the British colonies would be all the stronger for the placing in quarantine of those who might infect their neighbours with their own bitterness. Such a State could not be a serious source of danger, since we could control all the avenues by which arms could reach it.

I am aware that the Watersberg and the Zoutpansberg are not very desirable places of residence, but the thing is voluntary and no man would need to go there unless he wished. Without such a plan the Empire will have no safety valve in South Africa. I cannot conclude this short review of the South African question without some allusion to the attitude of continental nations during the struggle. This has been in all cases correct upon the part of the governments, and in nearly all cases incorrect upon the part of the people. ....

Appendix A

A curious light upon both the Concentration Camps and the question of farm burning is thrown by a letter from Tobias Smuts to General Botha which was intercepted by the British. He says:

Already several months ago General Chris Botha burned houses in Sambaansland, which is not neutral territory . . . the farm of Mr. Bernardus Johnstone was burned, or partly burned, by Chris Botha, and also the house of Frank Johnstone . . . .

When we were at Pietretief the house of Von Brandis was burned, and I was told that this was by "high order." It is in my opinion not the number of houses that breaks the principle.

'Also in connection with the transport of women .... I got the order from you to send the women away against their wish, and when I asked what to do if the English refused to take the women your answer was in that case I had to load them off within the lines of the enemy.'

Does that look as if the Boer General had any doubts of our humanity?

In answer to a complaint from Schalk Burger as to the treatment of the women General Kitchener put his good faith to a simple test. 'I have the honour,' said he, 'to inform you that all women and children at present in our camps who are willing to leave will be sent to the care of your Honour, and I shall be happy to be informed where you desire that they be handed over to you.' The offer was not accepted.

On December 6 General Kitchener gives an account of how the Concentration Camps came to be formed, which shows how entirely it sprang from the action of the Boer leaders. His statement is as follows:

'Numerous complaints were made to me in the early part of this year by surrendered burghers, who stated that after they had laid down their arms their families were ill-treated and their stock and property confiscated by order of the Commandants-General of the Transvaal and Orange Free State.

These acts appear to have been taken in consequence of the circular dated Roo; Senekal, November 6, 1900, in which the Commandant-General [Botha] says: "Do everything in your power to prevent the burghers laying down their arms. I will be complied, if they do not listen to this, to confiscate everything movable or immovable, and also to burn their houses."

"I took occasion at my interview with Commandant-General Louis Botha to bring this matter before him, and I told him that if he continued such acts I should be forced to bring in all women and children, and as much property as possible, to protect them from the acts of his burghers.[565]

"I further inquired if he would agree to spare the farms and families of neutral or surrendered burghers, in which case I expressed my willingness to leave undisturbed the farms and families of burghers who were on commando, provided they did not actively assist their relatives. The Commandant-General emphatically refused even to consider any such arrangement. He said: "I am entitled by law to force every man to join, and if they do not do so, to confiscate their property and leave their families on the veldt."

I asked him what course I could pursue to protect surrendered burghers and their families, and he then said, "The only thing you can do is to send them out of the country, as if I catch them they must suffer." After this there was nothing more to be said, and as military operations do not permit of the protection of individuals, I had practically no choice but to continue my system of sweeping inhabitants of certain areas into the protection of our lines.

My decision was conveyed to the Commandant-General in my official letter dated Pretoria, April 16, 1901, from which the following is an extract:

"As I informed your Honour at Middelburg, owing to the irregular manner in which you have conducted and continue to conduct hostilities, by forcing unwilling and peaceful inhabitants to join your commandos, a proceeding totally unauthorized by the recognized customs of war, I have no other course open to me, and am forced to take the very unpleasant and repugnant steps of bringing in the women and children."

"I have the greatest sympathy for the sufferings of these poor people, which I have done my best to alleviate, and it is a matter of surprise to me, and to the whole civilized world, that your Honour considers yourself justified in still causing so much suffering to the people of the Transvaal, by carrying on a hopeless and useless struggle."

[565] This must have been in Feb, 1901 at the Middleburg Conference.

PF: I have included a sketch of Tobias and the letter in full.

Tobias Smuts Letter

Letter From Assistant-General Tobias Smuts To Commandant-General L. P. Botha. [Letter Found Among Papers Recently Captured, And Sent Home By The Field Intelligence Department, South Africa.] (Translation.)[566]

Tobias Smuts was made an assistant commander of the Ermelo Commando, and after the Battle of Colenso was promoted to fighting general (Afrikaans: veggeneraal) on the Upper Tugela.

When the Transvaal Commando's transferred from Natal to the Orange Free State, Smuts led them as Assistant Commander General and joined in the fighting near Brandfort. Afterwards he returned to Pretoria to take part in the last session of the Volksraad. In the army officer's meeting of 2 June 1900 in Pretoria Smuts agreed with the proposal of Danie Theron to fight on. Presidents Kruger and Steyn, who first considered peace negotiations with the British, concurred.

Tobias Smuts fought in the lost Battle of Donkerhoek (Diamond Hill, 11–12 June 1900), and afterwards was sent to the Wakkerstroom area. Under the command of general Chris Botha. Smuts led the remaining Ermelo, Carolina, Standerton, and Swaziland Commandos.

General Tobias Smuts with his Krag rifle.[567] For text box quote see.[568] Tobias Smuts.[569] [570]

District Ermelo, September 2, 1901

[To:] His Honour Louis Botha, Commandant-General.

Your Honour,

To-day I received your letter, dated August 31st, 1901, in which you inform me that my suspension has been confirmed, and that Your Honour discharges me as Assistant Commandant-General.

As it was my wish to be dismissed from the responsibility, I wish to thank you for the discharge. I hope, however, that you will allow me, in the name of the sincere friendship which I hope we have had for each other, a friendship which has, at least on my side, strongly increased, to address a few lines to you in connection with my dismissal. I wish to speak open-heartedly and frankly to you, knowing that you will accept my letter in the same spirit in which it has been written.

566 Proclamations Issued In South Africa Tobias Smuts to L. Botha: https://babel.hathitrust.org/cgi/pt?id=hvd.32044089026009&seq=619&view=1up and https://babel.hathitrust.org/cgi/pt?id=hvd.32044089026009&seq=621&view=1up

567 Anglo Boer War - Small Arms and Ammunition - Page 10 - Boer War Forum Credit: Neville Constantine

568 Breytenbach II (1971), III (1973), V (1983), and VI (1996).

569 General Tobias Smuts, born 25 November 1861 in Krugerspost, in the district of Lijdenburg, was educated in Stellenbos, K. Colony. During the Houtbosberg expedition he served as Voldkornet, and with the war against Magato as Kommandiint of Ermelo. At the beginning of 1899 he was elected to the First Volksraad (First People's Council). represent. When the last war broke out, Smuts went out with the department that went to Natal, was present at the battle of Modderspruit, made the reconnaissance to Estcourt and fought on the Tugela as a civilian. Subsequently, he was appointed as assistant Commandant of the Ermelo kommando, and, after the battle of Colenso, acted as Fighter General on the Upper Tugela, in which capacity he was present in the battle of Spioenkop. Some time thereafter he was appointed with the authority of assistant Commandant General of the Transvaal Kommando's, who went from Natal to the Free State and took part in the fighting at Brandfort, whereupon he went to Pretoria returned to be present at the last meeting of the People's Council held there. was held. He fought in Donkerhoek, then went to the Wakkerstroomse and remained in the Eastern districts until the end of the war. Our [Transvaal] Military Officers: Dutch: Onze krijgs-officieren: album van portretten met levens-schetsen der. by Gustav Schoeman Preller, Frans Vredenrijk Engelenburg 1904 Catalogue Record: https://archive.org/search?query=title%3A%28Onze%20Krijgs-Officieren%29

570 Tobias Smuts (nickname Toop, November 25, 1861–August 10, 1916) was a Second Boer War Boer general and member of the Eerste Volksraad for the South African Republic. Tobias Smuts - Wikipedia

You can read it in some spare moment. I do not wish to cause you the trouble to send me a reply, which it will hardly be worth.

I therefore begin to tell you that, in my opinion, you have done me great wrong and injustice, and I shall try to explain the reasons for that opinion to you.

My suspension and subsequent discharge were according to your letter of August 18th, 1901, necessary because I have caused Bremersdorp[571] [572] to be burned down. You asked me for "satisfactory reasons." These reasons I have given you, but they appear to have been insufficient.

According to your letter, the burning of houses is against our "principles."

This I admit, where these houses are within our borders, and I would be the first to disapprove of it. But where houses are situated outside our borders and are being used by the enemy to promote his plans of operation, leaving their violating neutral territory out of the question, the burning of such houses cannot be considered to be against our principles, and such was the case with Bremersdorp.

I am convinced that you would not have acted differently yourself if you had been there. Any belligerent power would have done the same with Bremersdorp, without thinking for a moment that thereby a principle could be broken. And as to that, I think that on many occasions already that" principle" was broken.

Already several months ago General Chris Botha burned houses in Sambaansland, which is not neutral territory. About the same time Bremersdorp was burned, the farm of Mr. Bernardus Johnstone, District Wakkerstroom, was burned, or partly burned, by General Chris. (Botha), and also the house of Franck Johnstone, and I have not heard yet that His Honour has been suspended or dismissed for it.

When we were at Pietretief the house of Von Brandis was burned, and I was told that this happened by "High Order." It is, in my opinion, not the number of houses that breaks the "principle."

Also in connection with the transport of women, we took up the same standpoint as a principle, but still I got the order from you to send the women away against their wish, and when I asked you what to do if the English refused to take the women, your answer was that in that case I had to load them off within the lines of the enemy.

The burning of the house of Von Brandis and the farms of the Johnstones could do no harm whatever to our cause, but this is decidedly the case with Bremersdorp, for the reasons already stated in my previous letter, and also mentioned above.

Another reason, not mentioned by me yet, was to show the kaffirs that we will shrink from nothing if they do not remain quiet, or who cause us any difficulty.

At the most an officer who had to judge what was to be done, and who was not in a position to ask for instructions, should be punished with a reprimand and a warning not to do such a thing again.

But suppose, for the sake of argument, that the burning of Bremersdorp could do us harm, or is really in conflict with our principles, even then, in my opinion, such an action cannot be a reason to suspend or dismiss a Commanding Officer.

When an officer, through negligence or with intention, makes a mistake, bringing the Army or our cause into danger, for instance, by causing the loss of a position, or by leaving a position, or by refusing to obey orders, &c., then it is the duty of the Commandant-General to dismiss or suspend such an officer, but in a case standing entirely outside the war operations, where an officer thinks he is doing the right thing and acting in favour of our cause, and he makes a mistake or is wrong in his judgment, then, in my opinion, he cannot be punished with a punishment equal to that which he would receive in a case of neglect of duty or other offence through which the operations failed or could fail.

In the case of Bremersdorp it is an absolute question of opinion, and it has nothing to do with our war operations.

[571] Manzini (formerly known as Bremersdorp) is a large city in Eswatini (Swaziland), which is also the capital of Eswatini's Manzini Region. With a population of 110,000 (2008). It is known as "The Hub" of Eswatini. Manzini - Wikipedia

[572] The autonomy of the Swazi nation was influenced by British and Dutch rule of southern Africa in the 19th and early 20th centuries. In 1881, the British government signed a convention recognising Swazi independence, despite the Scramble for Africa that was taking place at the time. This independence was also recognised in the London Convention of 1884. Eswatini - Wikipedia

If officers must be suspended for difference of opinion with the Commandant General or the Government, then suspensions will take place daily. I have carefully considered the case, and I can come to no other conclusion than that I have acted in our favour, which was and is still my firm conviction.

All or nearly all burghers thought the same, and urged me to burn Bremersdorp. If I consider what serious mistakes have been made by head officers and others during this war, without a cock crowing over it, and if I think of what has generally been said about the evacuation of our positions on the Tugela, at Biggarsberg and other places, and if I consider what became of the officers concerned and what offices some of them hold now, then the reason of my dismissal appears so trifling to me that it borders on ridiculousness.

You know better than anybody else that I am speaking the truth. So trifling the reason of my discharge appears to me, that I absolutely refuse to accept it as the true reason, and I believe that there is something else behind it.

After eighteen months of faithful service, however weak then, and after having suffered and toiled for our cause, I had thought that I had deserved the right to be heard before I was chased away like a criminal.

Possibly our cause has enough faithful supporters, so that some person or other, who is undesirable to some commanders, can be sent away without even a single word of thanks for nearly two years of sacrifice and bitter insults.

I hope that this is the case; I have never expected thanks for my work. I know only too well that ingratitude is the reward of the world.

I hope that those who think that they can slander and supplant their fellow burghers and then make it right again at night with a prayer of three yards long, will now be happy that they have ultimately succeeded in having me chased away. I know that certain persons, through jealousy and in the hope of coming into my place, have complained to the Government, and that thereon you have received a letter from the Government. Up to now I do not even know the opinion of the Government about this case.

When I told the President, he did not give any sign of either approval or disapproval, and therefore he has not given me a chance to state my reasons. I thought it necessary to write you about this case, because it worries me that I must think that you have done me such injustice, and, as I believe, against your wish . You will now be able to better judge whether I have reasons for complaining yes or no.

Before I close, I wish to again give you the assurance that I never lost sight of the success of our came, and I always served this cause in all sincerity, and I hope to do so in the future also as a private burgher. Wishing you all success in your career,

I call myself, Your obedient servant and friend,

Tobias Smuts

Appendix B.

Count Hubner is an Austrian General, the son of the late Baron Hubner, who was an Austro-Hungarian Ambassador. On his return from South Africa he communicated his impressions to a representative of the 'Daily Telegraph.'

What follows is another flattering description of how well the camps were run.

Queen Victoria's 1858 Proclamation

It is difficult to underestimate the moral sway which Queen Victoria held over her subjects and the devotion which they brought to their admittedly Imperial goals in the latter part of the 1800s.

It was more than just the national pastime to go too far flung places in order to spread the good news of British Rule. Not only with missionary work but with military force as well. As we have seen in previous volumes, when practically the whole Churchill family goes to South Africa to assist in carrying forward Milner's 'Forward Policy', it takes on the character of a national duty to participate in what the Queen and her government is asking of its citizens. The moral basis for this was established with the Queen's Proclamation of 1858.

After the suppression of the Indian Mutiny of 1857-58 the punishment for any rebel or Indian soldier in British service who had previously sworn allegiance to the Queen included "Blowing From the Gun" This was not random terror. In the UK, subjects who revolted were subjected to humiliating punishments throughout its military history. That said, this particular form of punishment was not repeated. Contrasting the more realistic with the romanticized.

Blowing from the Gun.[77]

Suppression of the Indian Revolt by the English.[78]

After this undoubtedly barbaric exhibition of retribution came the Queen's proclamation of 1858 which recognized all people in British Dominions as right holders and stakeholders in the Empire with civil rights. Queen Victoria's Proclamation and amnesty applied to those who had laid down their arms and not committed murder, as opposed to military engagement, which was not murder, during the rebellion.[573]

At the conclusion of most of the hostilities, in November of 1858, the British government revoked the British East India Company charter and made India a Crown Colony of the empire under the direct control of the sovereign, Queen Victoria. The document that effectuated part of this change granted an amnesty to the rebels and also signalled a major shift in British policy towards its peoples.

There are many foundational documents that have shaped the British constitutional monarchy, Magna Carta, being the most notable. There are also significant documents and policies that extended aspects of this system across the British Empire, such as the Balfour declaration regarding a Jewish homeland; with respect to India it is Queen Victoria's proclamation by which the British Crown imposed direct sovereignty and in effect nationalized the Indian possessions of the British East India company and reads in part:

[573] Se Ramanlal Kakalbhai Dharaiya (1970). Gujarat in 1857. Gujarat University. p. 120. And: (https://en.wikipedia.org/wiki/Indian_Rebellion_of_1857)

Proclamation by the Queen in Council to the princes, Chiefs, and People of India (published by the Governor-General at Allahabad, November 1st, 1858).[574]

> VICTORIA, by the Grace; of God of the United Kingdom of Great Britain and Ireland, and of the. Colonies and Dependencies thereof in Europe, Asia, Africa, America, and Australasia, Queen, Defender of the Faith.
>
> Whereas, for divers weighty reasons, We have resolved, …………….. to take upon Ourselves the Government of the Territories in India heretofore administered in trust for Us by the Honorable East India Company:
>
> We desire no extension of Our present territorial Possessions; …………… We shall respect the Rights, Dignity, and Honour of Native Princes as Our own; and We desire, that they, as well as Our own Subjects, should enjoy that Prosperity and that social Advancement which can only be secured by internal Peace and good Government.
>
> We hold Ourselves bound to the Natives of Our Indian Territories by the same obligations of Duty which bind Us to all Our other Subjects; and those Obligations, by the Blessing of Almighty God, We shall faithfully and conscientiously fulfil.
>
> Firmly relying Ourselves on the truth of Christianity, and acknowledging with gratitude the solace of Religion, We disclaim alike the Right and the Desire to impose our Convictions on any of Our Subjects. We declare it to be Our Royal Will and Pleasure that none be in any wise favored, none molested or disquieted by reason of their Religious Faith or Observances; but that all shall alike enjoy the equal and impartial protection of the Law: and We do strictly charge and enjoin all those who may be in authority under Us, that they abstain from all interference with the Religious Belief or Worship of any of Our Subjects, on pain of Our highest Displeasure.
>
> And it is Our further Will that, so far and may be, Our Subjects, of whatever Race or Creed, be freely and impartially admitted to Offices in Our Service, the Duties of which they may be qualified, by their education, ability, and integrity, duly to discharge…………

This Proclamation … laid the foundation for Indian [and later, Empire wide] secularism and established the semi-legal framework that would govern the politics of religion in colonial India for the next century. ... It promised civil equality for Indians regardless of their religious affiliation, and state non-interference in Indians' religious affairs. Although the Proclamation lacked the legal authority of a constitution, generations of Indians cited the Queen's proclamation in order to claim, and to defend, their right to religious freedom," [575]

"When the governance of India was transferred from the East India Company to the Crown in 1858, she (Queen Victoria) and Prince Albert intervened in an unprecedented fashion to turn the proclamation of the transfer of power into a document of tolerance and clemency. ... they ... insisted on the clause that stated that the people of India would enjoy the same protection as all subjects of Britain. Over time, this led to the Proclamation of 1858 becoming known in the Indian subcontinent as 'the Magna Carta of Indian liberties', a phrase which Indian nationalists such as Mohandas Gandhi later took up as they sought to test equality under imperial law" [576]

These inherent natural rights of equality, social advancement, peace, good government, religious freedom, equal protection of the law and admission to civil service were actualized most effectively in India itself over the course of the next 89 years, before India gained independence on August 15th, 1947; an event that Mohandas Gandhi saw to fruition, if only for five months, before his assassination on January 30th 1948.

While most of the British Uitlanders, were gold rush prospectors, far more concerned with Transvaal wealth than political enfranchisement, there were a substantial minority who wanted to stay and put down roots in the

[574] 1858 Proclamation obtained from: www.csas.ed.ac.uk/mutiny/confpapers/Queen%27sProclamation.pdf (Retrieved 9/19)

[575] Adcock, C.S. (2013), The Limits of Tolerance: Indian Secularism and the Politics of Religious Freedom, Oxford University Press, pp. 23–25, ISBN 978-0-19-999543-1.

[576] (pages 38–39) Taylor, Miles (2016), "The British royal family and the colonial empire from the Georgians to Prince George", in Aldrish, Robert; McCreery, Cindy (eds.), Crowns and Colonies: European Monarchies and Overseas Empires, Manchester University Press, pp. 38–39, ISBN 978-1-5261-0088-7.

country. The racial discrimination practiced against the Indians and other 'asiatics' was second only to the legal position of native Africans, who enjoyed even fewer rights and freedoms under the Boer government(s).

It is important to note that in 1897 Queen Victoria celebrated the Diamond Jubilee marking her 60 year reign. The celebrations were enormous and conducted throughout the Empire. It was quite a cohesive event for the entire Empire to enjoy together. One might compare it to the Bicentennial celebrations for the United States in 1976. Looking back over the accomplishments of the various commonwealths and colonies during her reign with the accolades accorded to the Empire directed towards the Empress and Queen. It solidified the devotion to Queen and Country which by this point in her successful reign was hero worship conjoined with a policy of expanding the Empire under her aegis. The Forward Policy of the British in South Africa subsequent to these celebrations was a byproduct of this collective sense of manifest destiny and unfortunate for the Republics.

Bibliography

Many works have been footnoted in the text, enthusiastically if also somewhat idiosyncratically as to form. Restating those references again here would extend this work unnecessarily.

The full and equally idiomatic bibliography for this series is over sixty pages long and will be included in an Appendix volume to be published at the end of the series. For this volume an abbreviated bibliography is as follows. Note that works are cited by topic rather than alphabetically and listed in order of importance to the work.

A Century of Injustice

At the advent of the South African War (Second Anglo-Boer War), F.W. Reitz, in his capacity of State Secretary of the South African Republic, published an overview of Anglo-Boer relations in the nineteenth century. Francis William Reitz, A century of wrong. Issued by F. W. Reitz, state secretary of the South African Republic. With pref. by W. T. Stead. 1900. Jan Smuts co-author. And: https://babel.hathitrust.org/cgi/pt?id=coo1.ark:/13960/t2d79wr7w&view=1up&seq=1&skin=2021

#1 - A century of wrong. Issued by F. W. Reitz, state secretary of ... - Full View | HathiTrust Digital Library

And: https://babel.hathitrust.org/cgi/pt?id=coo1.ark:/13960/t2d79wr7w&view=1up&seq=1&skin=2021

Catalog Advanced Search Results | HathiTrust Digital Library And: A Century of Wrong by Jan Christiaan Smuts - Free Ebook (gutenberg.org) Identifier: https://www.gutenberg.org/1/5/1/7/15175/ Produced by Jonathan Ingram, Garrett Alley, and the PG Online.

Originally composed in English it was translated into Dutch by Francis' second wife Cornelia Maria Theresa Mulder as Eene eeuw van onrecht, (A Century of Injustice).

The second Dutch edition of the book carried the text 'Op last van den staatssekretaris der Z.A.R., F.W. Reitz' ('By order of the State Secretary of the S.A.R., F.W. Reitz'), without mentioning the author's name.

This English text is was published by: "Review Of Reviews"[577] London, Mowbray House, Norfolk Street, W.C.

The English translation, reproduced here, only carried the name of Reitz, and has a preface by W.T. Stead dated January 1st, 1900. The English edition contained more material than the original Dutch edition. A Century of Wrong - Wikisource, the free online library J.C. Smuts is indicated as author, but probably only edited the introduction and the end of the book, in collaboration with the historian E.J.P. Jorissen. The rest of the text was probably prepared by J. de Villiers Roos.

See Also:

Reitz, F.W., [J. de Villiers Roos, J.C. Smuts, E.J.P. Jorissen,] Eene eeuw van onrecht (Pretoria [1899]), 49p.

Reitz, F.W., [J. de Villiers Roos, J.C. Smuts, E.J.P. Jorissen,] Ein Jahrhundert voller Unrecht: ein Rückblick auf die süd-afrikanische Politik Englands: autorisierte Uebersetzung aus dem Holländischen, veröffentlicht auf Veranlassung und unter Mitwirkung von F.W. Reitz (Berlin: Walther 1900), 96p.

A Century of Injustice

Cornelius W. Van der Hoogt, A century of injustice; synopsis of a message to the people of South-Africa, sent by the government of the South-African republic. Baltimore Md. November 1899. University of Wisconsin Copy: https://babel.hathitrust.org/cgi/pt?id=wu.89100085885&seq=5 Author: Smuts, Jan Christiaan, 1870-1950. Author: Cornelius W. Van der Hoogt, Joubert, P. J. (Petrus Jacobus), 1831-1900. Orange Free State (South Africa). President, 1896-1900 (Steijn). Published Baltimore, Md., 1899. Catalog Record: A century of injustice; synopsis of a message... | HathiTrust Digital Library

Author: Smuts, Jan Christiaan, 1870-1950. Author: Cornelius W. Van der Hoogt, Joubert, P. J. (Petrus Jacobus), 1831-1900. Orange Free State (South Africa). President, 1896-1900 (Steijn). Published Baltimore, Md., 1899.

See Also: Een eeuw van onrecht. Med een inleidend woord door H. J. Kiewiet de Jonge.

[577] The Review of Reviews was a noted family of monthly journals founded in 1890–1893 by British reform journalist William Thomas Stead (1849–1912). Established across three continents in London (1891), New York (1892) and Melbourne (1893), the Review of Reviews, American Review of Reviews and Australasian Review represented W.T. Stead's dream of a global publishing empire. Review of Reviews - Wikipedia

The authorship has been ascribed to J.C. Smuts, to F.W. Reitz and to J. de V. Roos. General Smuts is considered responsible for the greater part of the text. First published at Cape town. Issued also in English with title: A century of wrong, and in German as: Ein Jahrhundert voller Unrecht.

Translation of A century of wrong. Catalog Record: Een eeuw van onrecht | HathiTrust Digital Library

NY Public Library: #1 - Een eeuw van onrecht. Med een inleidend woord door H. J. Kiewiet ... - Full View | HathiTrust Digital Library

The Story of the Boers

The Story of the Boers By Cornelius W. Van der Hoogt, Baltimore, MD., March, 1900.

Catalog Search: https://archive.org/search?query=creator%3A%28Cornelius%20Van%20der%20Hoogt%29

U. Cal Copy, Bradley Co.: https://archive.org/details/storyofboersnarr00vand/page/n9/mode/2up

NYPL Copy Harper Edition: https://archive.org/details/storyboersnarra00whitgoog

War with the Boers, H. Brown, London
Harold Brown, War with the Boers: an account of the past and present troubles with the South African republics London: H. Virtue, [1902?] Catalog Record: War with the Boers : an account of the past... | HathiTrust Digital Library
Five scans, all of University of Wisconsin–Madison origin.
Vol 1: #1 - War with the Boers : an account of the past and present ... 1. - Full View | HathiTrust Digital Library
Vol 2: #9 - War with the Boers : an account of the past and present ... 2. - Full View | HathiTrust Digital Library
Vol 3: #9 - War with the Boers : an account of the past and present ... 3. - Full View | HathiTrust Digital Library
Vol 4: #9 - War with the Boers : an account of the past and present ... 4. - Full View | HathiTrust Digital Library
Vol. 5 coauthored by E. Sharpe Grew. #11 - War with the Boers : an account of the past and present ... 5. - Full View | HathiTrust Digital Library

Boer Politics, By Yves Guyot Translated from the French John Murray, Albemarle Street London 1900. Boer Politics by Yves Guyot - Free Ebook (gutenberg.org) https://gutenberg.org/ebooks/17968 p. 108

James Anthony Froude[578] Oceana: or, England and her colonies. Longmans, Green, 1912 Edition. First Printed in January 1896. Catalog Search: https://archive.org/search?query=title%3A%28Oceana%29%20AND%20creator%3A%28Froude%2C%20James%20Anthony%29 U. Cal Copy: https://archive.org/details/oceanaenglandcol00frouiala

Outspan.com Copy:

The Story of the Boers By Cornelius W. Van der Hoogt, Baltimore, MD., March, 1900.
http://mailto:rjwilson@outspan.com/?subject=The%20Story%20of%20the%20Boers
https://web.archive.org/web/*/http://mailto:rjwilson@outspan.com/*

Preface: http://www.outspan.com/books/boers/boers01.htm
https://web.archive.org/web/20010307023321/http://www.outspan.com/books/boers/boers01.htm
Policy of Mediation: http://www.outspan.com/books/boers/boers02.htm

578 James Anthony Froude FRSE (23 April 1818–20 October 1894) was an English historian, novelist, biographer, and editor of Fraser's Magazine. From his upbringing amidst the Anglo-Catholic Oxford Movement, Froude intended to become a clergyman, but doubts about the doctrines of the Anglican church, published in his scandalous 1849 novel The Nemesis of Faith, drove him to abandon his religious career. Froude turned to writing history, becoming one of the best-known historians of his time for his History of England from the Fall of Wolsey to the Defeat of the Spanish Armada. James Anthony Froude - Wikipedia

Struggles of the Boers: http://www.outspan.com/books/boers/boers03.htm
https://web.archive.org/web/20010419201029/http://www.outspan.com/books/boers/boers03.htm
A Century of Injustice: http://www.outspan.com/books/boers/boers04.htm
An Earnest Representation, Joubert: http://www.outspan.com/books/boers/boers05.htm
A Proclamation, Steijn: http://www.outspan.com/books/boers/boers06.htm
Official Despatches: http://www.outspan.com/books/boers/boers07.htm
Reply to Mr. Chamberlain: http://www.outspan.com/books/boers/boers08.htm
The Sand River Convention: http://www.outspan.com/books/boers/boers09.htm
The Pretoria Convention: http://www.outspan.com/books/boers/boers10.htm
The London Convention: http://www.outspan.com/books/boers/boers11.htm
Het Volkslied: http://www.outspan.com/books/boers/boers12.htm

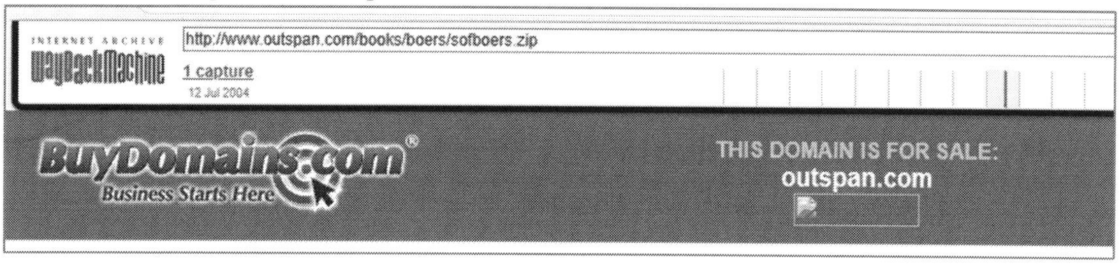

Moritz, Garrett B. - From the Jameson Raid to Bloemfontein: Debating the Origins of the Boer War. 1998 https://web.archive.org/web/20061029192730/http:/www.gtexts.com/college/papers/s1.html Retrieved 1/22/25.

Byron Farwell, The Great Anglo-Boer War. New York: Harper & Row, 1976.

Arthur Keppel-Jones, South Africa: A Short History, 3rd revised edition. London: Hutchinson and Co., 1961.

Wolfgang J. Mommsen, Theories of Imperialism. Trans. P.S. Falla. Chicago: University of Chicago Press, 1982.

Hobson, John Atkinson. Catalog Search. Internet Archive: https://archive.org/search?query=creator%3A%28John%20Atkinson%20Hobson%29

Hathi Trust: Catalog Advanced Search Results | HathiTrust Digital Library

J. A. Hobson, The War in South Africa, Its Causes and Effects, 2nd ed. London: James Nisbet and Co., 1900. The war in South Africa; its causes and effects: Hobson, J. A. (John Atkinson), 1858-1940 : Free Download, Borrow, and Streaming : Internet Archive [579]

Capitalism and imperialism in South Africa New York: Tucker Pub. Co. 39p.

Princeton Scan: Capitalism and imperialism in South Africa : Hobson, J. A. (John Atkinson), 1858-1940 : Free Download, Borrow, and Streaming : Internet Archive

Hathi Trust Catalog Record: Catalog Record: Capitalism and Imperialism in South Africa | HathiTrust Digital Library

J.A. Hobson, The Psychology of Jingoism. London: G. Richards, 1901.

The psychology of jingoism : Hobson, J. A. (John Atkinson), 1858-1940 : Free Download, Borrow, and Streaming : Internet Archive

Harvard Scan: Page by Page only: #7 - The psychology of jingoism, by J. A. Hobson - Full View | HathiTrust Digital Library

Jean van der Poel, The Jameson Raid. Cape Town: Oxford University Press, 1951. (pages 259-260).

R.C.K Ensor, England 1870-1914, Vol. XIV of The Oxford History of England, ed. G.N. Clark. Oxford: Clarendon Press, 1936.

Ethel Drus, "The Question of Imperial Complicity in the Jameson Raid," English Historical Review, LXVIII, 1953.

[579] John Atkinson Hobson (6 July 1858–1 April 1940) was an English economist and social scientist. Hobson is best known for his writing on imperialism, which influenced Vladimir Lenin, and his theory of underconsumption. J. A. Hobson - Wikipedia

Bernard Porter, "The Pro-Boers in Britain." The South African War: The Anglo-Boer War 1899-1902. Ed. Peter Warwick et al. London: Longman, 1980.

Ronald Robinson and John Gallagher, "The Partition of Africa." Imperialism: The Robinson and Gallagher Controversy. Ed. William Roger Louis. New York: Franklin Watts, 1976.

License Links

Google Earth License Links

Copyright Discussion

[580] Creative Commons License: Creative Commons license - Wikipedia and About CC Licenses - Creative Commons

[581] If the work was commercially published within 75 years of the end of the calendar year in which it was made, Crown copyright will last for 50 years from the end of the calendar year in which it was published. https://copyrightservice.co.uk/copyright/p01_uk_copyright_law Flow Chart: Crown copyright flowchart 2015

Future creators should continue to follow the permissions, guidelines and requirements from the original source and author/uploader who is cited. Links to Creative Commons, Google Earth and other licenses are noted in the license links section.

So far as can be determined, as of 2025, the text and images used to illustrate the first person accounts included in this volume reside in the public domain in the United States having all been first published prior to January 1st, 1930 as well as in all other jurisdictions which employ any of the following copyright regimens:

1. A copyright regimen that grants an author's works subsisting copyright for seventy (70) years pma[582] or less.
2. A copyright term subsisting for 120 years from the date of creation or first publication.
3. And such jurisdictions that apply the Rule of the Shorter term to an author's pma date or publication date.

This work will not be marketed or deliberately sold in any jurisdiction with a longer copyright term. See Also: 2025 in public domain - Wikipedia

Copyright for the assembled compilation of this material, or substantial portions thereof that would comprise separate articles or works unto themselves is retained. This work and the series in sum comprise a derivative work. Literary, dramatic, and adaptation rights of the saga demonstrated and explicated by this series is retained.

Otherwise, with respect to the underlying texts and images recast in a more permanently accessible form I choose to pay forward my creative energy to the people who lived through these experiences and it has been a pleasure to find and assemble their collective words and images in a new synoptic and synergistic arrangement.

Except where noted otherwise, every effort has been made to ensure that no material has been used without an attributed source. However, if any non-attributed source, incorrect source, or copyrighted material used without permission or justification, has been included then I would be grateful for information that would enable any errors or inappropriate inclusions to be corrected or omitted in subsequent impressions.

Starting from creation, to publication, through to purchase, archiving, and digitizing, this annotated, illustrated and expanded edition is the sixth step in the journey of these works. My thanks go to all who have helped preserve and perpetuate these important historical records.

[582] post mortem auctoris or "pma" [post mortem author]

Endnotes

[1] Heroes of the Boer War. Review of Reviews, 1903. and File:FWReitz VA0947.jpg - Wikimedia Commons

[2] Times History War in S.A Vol 5 (1907) Photo by Duffus Bros., Cape Town

[3] South African Railway System circa 1900: File:SouthernAfricaRailwayMap 1901.png - Wikipedia

[4] Cover of Cornell University Edition scanned by HathiTrust and title page from the same volume.

[5] General Botha, the Career and the Man, By Harold Spender, 1916 Google Books, UCAL-Davis: https://books.google.com/books?id=dxw1AQAAIAAJ

[6] Adapted from an original appearing in Hiley and Hassell's, The Mobile Boer, Grafton Press, New York, (c. 1902) "The above map, comparing South Africa with Europe was published by "C.I." as long ago as Jan 6th, 1900."

[7] General Botha, the Career and the Man, By Harold Spender, 1916 Google Books, UCAL-Davis: https://books.google.com/books?id=dxw1AQAAIAAJ

[8] General Botha, the Career and the Man, By Harold Spender, 1916 Google Books, UCAL-Davis: https://books.google.com/books?id=dxw1AQAAIAAJ

[9] Extent of British Empire Over Time. Mandates and protected states are shown in a lighter shade. https://commons.wikimedia.org/wiki/File:The_British_Empire_5.png Author: RedStorm1368

[10] Victoria Image Credit: Wikimedia Commons. And https://www.thehighlandersmuseum.com/?p=29363

[11] File:Queen Victoria -Golden Jubilee: https://commons.wikimedia.org/wiki/File:Queen_Victoria_-Golden_Jubilee_-3a_cropped.JPG Author: Alexander Bassano

[12] File:FWReitz VA0947.jpg - Wikimedia Commons

[13] Jan Smuts photographed in Stellenbosch when he obtained his B.A. degree from the old Victoria College, predecessor of Stellenbosch University. The degree was in both literature and science. He won a scholarship of £100 a year to study at Cambridge University where obtained his law degree. Smuts Graduation Picture: Lêer:Smuts 1891.jpg - Wikipedia

[14] After Pretoria: The Guerilla War Vol 3 Feb., 1901

[15] Repository: Library of Congress Prints and Photographs Division Washington, D.C. 20540 USA
http://hdl.loc.gov/loc.pnp/pp.print
https://www.loc.gov/pictures/resource/fsa.8e00860/

[16] General Smuts Vol 1 by Millin Sarah Gertrude (1936) p.159 File:Smuts Boereoorlog.jpg - Wikimedia Commons And Genl Jan Smuts en sy staf te Concordia, Mei 1902 - Deneys Reitz - Wikipedia

[17] Davitt, Boer Fight for Freedom, 3rd ed. 1902. (Duke Scan)

[18] Heroes of the Boer War. Review of Reviews, 1903.

[19] Heroes of the Boer War. Rompel, Frederik, Introd. by Albert Pfister; preface by W.T. Stead. London: Review of Reviews, 1903. Chapter XX. Pages 168-171

[20] Times History Vol 1

[21] File:W.T. Stead by Mills, 1905.png - Wikimedia Commons

[22] Richard Harding Davis, With Both Armies in South Africa. Charles Scribner's Sons, New York 1900

[23] With the flag to Pretoria Vol 2 This is in May 23. This is only 125kb Larger one is available.

[24] Davitt, Boer Fight for Freedom, 3rd ed. 1902. (Duke Scan)

[25] Great Trek map full - Great Trek - Wikipedia Author: Disco.

[26] File:BoerGriquaRepublics.svg - Wikimedia Commons Author: Seb az86556

[27] Davitt, Boer Fight for Freedom, 1902 (U. Cal. Scan)

[28] Slow and Sure - JM Staniforth - Uitlander - Wikipedia

[29] Elliott & Fry Portrait: File:Robert-Gascoyne-Cecil-3rd-Marquess-of-Salisbury (cropped).jpg - Wikimedia Commons

[30] File:Boer Legation VA0949.jpg - Wikimedia Commons Author Atelier Straugh, formerly Kameke, The Netherlands

[31] SA National Archives: http://www.nationalarchives.gov.za/node/1236

[32] War with the Boers, H. Brown, London [1902?] Vol 1

[33] Heroes of the Boer War. Review of Reviews, 1903.

[34] Heroes of the Boer War. Review of Reviews, 1903.

[35] Langsnek Tunnel, July 1900. Damaged northern portal after being blown up. - Atom site for DRISA
P1628_01.jpg (1400×814) (drisa.co.za)

[36] South Africa; its History, Heroes and Wars. [1899]

[37] Creswicke, Louis South Africa and the Transvaal War, Vol. 2 1900 Photo by Knight, Aldershot.
[38] The Biograph in battle: its story in the South African War related with personal experiences. by William Kennedy Laurie Dickson, London: T. Fisher Unwin, 1901. Catalog Search: https://archive.org/search?query=title%3A%28The+Biograph+in+Battle%29
[39] The Biograph in battle: its story in the South African War related with personal experiences. by William Kennedy Laurie Dickson, London: T. Fisher Unwin, 1901. Catalog Search: https://archive.org/search?query=title%3A%28The+Biograph+in+Battle%29
[40] The Biograph in battle: its story in the South African War related with personal experiences. by William Kennedy Laurie Dickson, London: T. Fisher Unwin, 1901. Catalog Search: https://archive.org/search?query=title%3A%28The+Biograph+in+Battle%29
[41] Proclamations in SA, https://babel.hathitrust.org/cgi/pt?id=hvd.32044089026009&seq=301&view=1up
[42] Proclamations in SA, https://babel.hathitrust.org/cgi/pt?id=hvd.32044089026009&seq=301&view=1up
[43] Proclamations in SA, https://babel.hathitrust.org/cgi/pt?id=hvd.32044089026009&seq=302&view=1up
[44] Black & White Weekly Vol 1-2 1899-1900
[45] Original Source: Edwin Sharpe Grew: Field-Marshal Lord Kitchener. His Life and Work for the Empire. London 1916. Volume 2. File:Kitchener at the Peace Conference that ended the Second Boer War.png - Wikimedia Commons On 28 February 1901 British commander Lord Kitchener met Boer commander Louis Botha at Middelburg, Transvaal. The talks failed to bring peace and Kitchener commenced the barbed wire and block house campaign to thwart attacks by Boer guerilla fighters. Category:Middelburg Peace Conference - Wikimedia Commons Also: File:The Second Boer War, 1899-1902 Q68497.jpg - Wikimedia Commons
[46] File:Kitchener at the Peace Conference that ended the Second Boer War.png - Wikimedia Commons
[47] Image: Hillegas, With the Boer forces, 1901 (Photograph by Leo Weinthal, Pretoria.) and quote: With the Flag, After Pretoria: The Guerilla War Vol 3 p. 91 1900.
[48] Page 13 https://www.britishnewspaperarchive.co.uk/viewer/bl/0001684/19010309/091/0013
[49] Southport Guardian - Saturday 23 March 1901 page 5. Col 7 https://www.britishnewspaperarchive.co.uk/viewer/bl/0001783/19010323/121/0005
[50] Southport Guardian - Saturday 23 March 1901 page 5. Col 7 https://www.britishnewspaperarchive.co.uk/viewer/bl/0001783/19010323/121/0005
[51] Southport Guardian - Saturday 23 March 1901 page 5. Col 7 https://www.britishnewspaperarchive.co.uk/viewer/bl/0001783/19010323/121/0005
[52] Southport Guardian - Saturday 23 March 1901 page 5. Col 7. https://www.britishnewspaperarchive.co.uk/viewer/bl/0001783/19010323/121/0005
[53] File:Philip Rudolph Botha (1851-1901), Boer War general.jpg - Wikimedia Commons
[54] Navy & Army Vol 14 p. 309 June 14th, 1902 Photo Copyright by 'Kodak"
[55] File:ABO Holkransmonument, wesfaset, Vryheid.jpg - Wikimedia Commons Author: JMK And: Memorial Holkrans Massacre - Vryheid - TracesOfWar.com Author: JMK. The monument commerating the massacre at Holkrans by Zulus, near the end of the Second Boer War, on 6 May 1902. In the massacre, 56 people were murdered.
[56] Black & White Weekly Vol 3 1900.
[57] Philadelphis Press. "Ten Thousand Miles from Tip to Tip" meaning the extension of United States domination from Puerto Rico to the Philippines. Contrast with a map of the United States of 100 years earlier in 1798. File:10kMiles.JPG - Wikimedia Commons
[58] Hillegas, Boers in War, 1900.
[59] Hillegas, Boers in War, 1900.
[60] 0258.pdf
[61] With the Flag to Pretoria Vol 1 p. 250
[62] Webster Davis, John Bull's crime; or, Assaults on Republics. 1901 New York The Abbey Press
[63] Image: File:Webster-davis.jpg - Wikipedia
[64] Webster Davis, John Bull's crime; or, Assaults on Republics. 1901 New York The Abbey Press
[65] Webster Davis, John Bull's crime; or, Assaults on Republics. 1901 New York The Abbey Press
[66] Webster Davis, John Bull's crime; or, Assaults on Republics. 1901 New York The Abbey Press
[67] Webster Davis, John Bull's crime; or, Assaults on Republics. 1901 New York The Abbey Press

[68] Webster Davis, John Bull's crime; or, Assaults on Republics. 1901 New York The Abbey Press

[69] https://commons.wikimedia.org/wiki/File:Mapa_Cor-de-Rosa.svg Rose Colored Map. Author: Lokal_Profil

[70] File:Fashoda Incident map - en.svg - Wikimedia Commons Creator: Mozzan

[71] No Fight A Political cartoon by JM Staniforth: A French poodle begs for scraps from a British bulldog, commentary on the Fashoda Incident. 26 October 1898 File:No Fight - JM Staniforth.png - Wikimedia Commons

[72] With the Flag to Pretoria, H. W. Wilson Vol 2 Dec., 1899.

[73] History of War SA, Birch, 1899

[74] File:UndershawCirca1900.jpg - Wikimedia Commons

[75] Sir Arthur Ignatius Conan Doyle by the English photographer Herbert Rose Barraud. File:Arthur Conan Doyle by Herbert Rose Barraud 1893.jpg - Wikimedia Commons

[76] Arthur Conan Doyle in 1914 File:Arthur Conan Doyle by Walter Benington, 1914.png - Wikimedia Commons

[77] https://commons.wikimedia.org/wiki/File:Blowing_Mutinous_Sepoys_From_the_Guns,_September_8,_1857_-_steel_engraving.jpg
https://en.wikipedia.org/wiki/Blowing_from_a_gun

[78] Suppression of the Indian Revolt by the English, which depicts the execution of mutineers by blowing from a gun by the British, a painting by Vasily Vereshchagin c. 1884. Note: This painting was allegedly bought by the British crown and possibly destroyed (current whereabouts unknown). It anachronistically depicts the events of 1857 with soldiers wearing (then current) uniforms of the late 19th century.
https://en.wikipedia.org/wiki/Suppression_of_the_Indian_Revolt_by_the_English

Made in United States
Orlando, FL
05 November 2026

90230220R00201